Mindprint

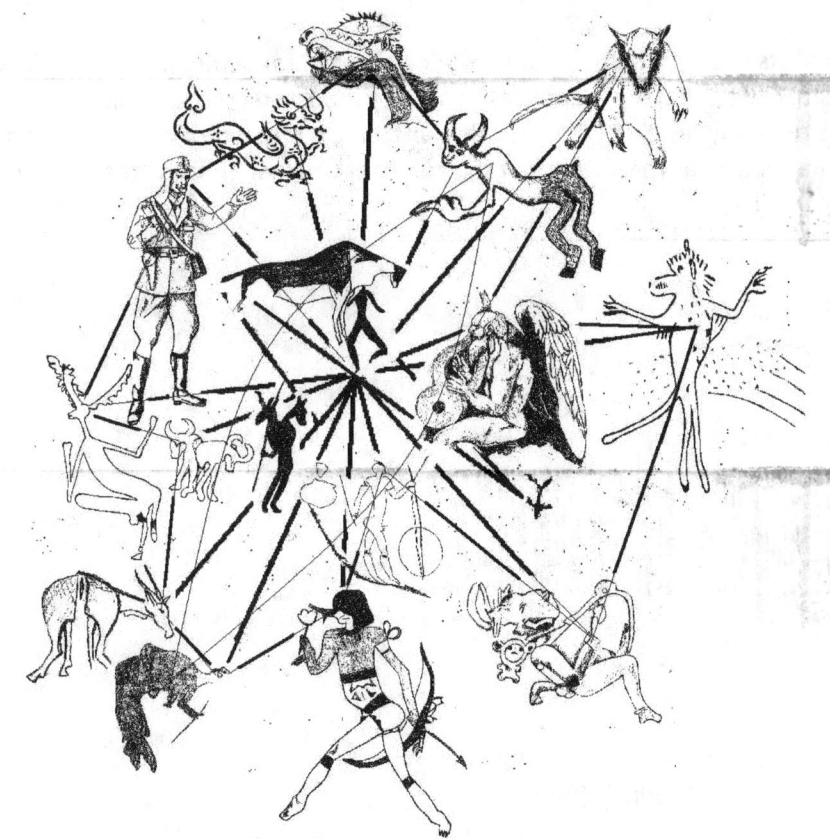

The subconscious art code
Edmond Furter

Edmond Furter
Mindprint
The subconscious art code

2014
Four Equators Media [<(^)>] Johannesburg
Lulu.com

Black and white edition
ISBN 978-0-620-59685-5

ISBN 978-0-620-59685-5
90000

9 780620 596855

Font type Calibri 11.4 point
Design by Four Equators Media [<(^)>]

Cover image from a mural by Raffaello Sanzio (Raphael); The school of Athens, Vatican. The philosophers are modelled on Italian artists.

Back cover from an Arabian rock engraving of bee people at Bir Hima (Lars Bjursom /Saudi Aramco World /SAWDIA) and from Gobekli Tepe.

Website: www.edmondfurter.wordpress.com

Dedicated to Doreen and Denise Lee.

'Who has put wisdom in the innermost being, or given understanding to the mind? Who can count the clouds by wisdom, or tip the water jars of the heavens, when the dust hardens into a mass, and the clods stick together?' (Job 38;36)

'Experience befalls, strikes, overwhelms and transforms us. We undergo experience.' (Heidegger)

"Research is to see what everyone has seen, and think what no-one has thought.' (Albert Szent-Gyorgi)

'If we knew what it was we were doing, it would not be called research.' (Albert Einstein)

Index

Summary

The introduction explains how to read the illustration labels, and outlines the sequence of types that are supported by the structural grid in inspired art. It also notes some aspects of their disguise.

Chapter A illustrates six examples of the typological sequence, and explains structural sets in nature, myth, grammar and our subconscious.

Chapter B illustrates the structure in our iris and bodies, and explains our structural perception, inspiration, consciousness, psychology and disguise.

Chapter C illustrates the structure in our hands, and explains the co-incidence of structure in our bodies, culture, events and literature.

Chapter D illustrates cosmic structure, and explains structural cosmology, astronomy and astrology.

Chapter E illustrates cosmic polar structure, and explains structural time, Ages, archaeo astronomy, planets and spherical doubling.

Chapter F demonstrates artistic structure in a famous painting by Pierro de Cosimo, and explains structural symbolism, artistic functions, initiation and esoterica.

Chapter G demonstrates a rock art painting process, and explains structural inspiration and compulsive expression.

Chapter H tests illustrates mindprint in two Egyptian decanal sets (Narmer and Dendera), explains conscious aspects of expression, and the Tarot trump sequence.

Chapter J lists the attributes and concepts of the sixteen types and reduces these to tables. It formulates a statistical test, applies the test to 170 artworks, and explains the results.
This chapter also demonstrates how to identify visual types and archetypal structure in art, speculates on the possibility of prior discovery, and lists the few inherent ambiguities among some types.

Chapter K compares scientific and esoteric paradigms, illustrates natural 'art', and speculates on the implications of the discovery of mindprint for some sciences and crafts.

Chapter L demonstrates mindprint in 200 artworks, grouped by their dominant themes, and compares rock art against schooled art. Some notable details are explained in captions.

The postscript explains how the visual types and structure were found.

How to read the illustration labels

Readers inclined to scan the illustrations before reading the text, will find that a standard set of labels and axes mark individual figures in a peripheral (outer edge) sequence of sixteen types. The labels use familiar astronomical designations as shorthand for equivalent myths, emblems, icons and concepts. Artistic figures are not constellations or zodiac signs, but visual equivalents of the mythic and cosmic structure that nature and culture express in various media, such as species or body reflexology.

Type Aries, Taurus, Gemini, Cancer (ar, ta, ge, cn) and so on, are more recognisable than type 3, type 2, type 15, type 14. Their dual level identifications are type Aries t3 t18, type Taurus Pleiades t2 t17 and/or type Taurus Auriga t1 t16, type Gemini t15 t0, type Cancer t14, and so on. The illustration labels abbreviate these as ar3, ta2, ta1, ge15, cn14 and so on.

Four adjacent pairs each relate to the same myth and constellation group (such as type Taurus t1 t16 and type Taurus t2 t17, labelled as ta1 and/or ta2). Type Aquarius t5 t20 and type Aquarius t5 t21 are unique for sharing the same lower number. Seven figures carry a second layer of identifications, such as type Aries t3 t18 or type Pisces t4 t19, but are labelled by the lowest of their two type numbers (such as ar3, pi4). Tables start with the type numbers for ease of comparison.

The annual zodiac sequence and the number sequence counter-rotate, just as hours reverse the seasonal order (see the Decans section).

The twelve zodiac signs only partially express archetype, while sixteen constellations allow variant configurations and optional decans (adjacent myths or concepts). Each figure usually expresses one or two of the range of about four to six typical attributes (see the Tables and Statistical test). Attributes such as a posture, size, gender, status or implements allow an apparently wide range of expression, yet each remain related to basic sets of concepts.

Artistic types are interspaced by four structural features, which are also cosmic and astronomical; the galactic gate (labelled Gate), opposite the galactic centre (labelled Gal), and the galactic pole (labelled pG), opposite the galactic south pole (labelled pGs or Axis, that should be read as polar Axle). The standard sequence of figures and the four structural points in all inspired artworks thus appear as pairs of opposites, such as type Aries opposite type Libra (ar3 opposite li10), type Taurus Pleiades opposite type Scorpius Claws (ta2 opposite sc9), type Taurus Auriga Orion opposite type Scorpius Ophiuchus (ta1 opposite sc8), the north and south galactic gates, the pairs of poles, and so on.

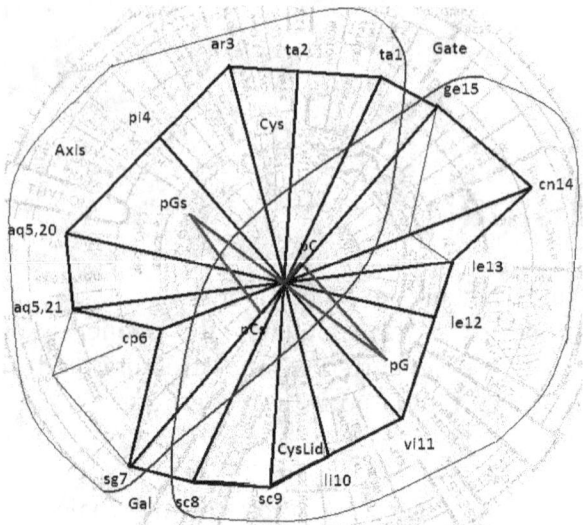

Chart [a]. The standard mindprint typology labels and axial structure in art, here applied to iris reflexology points.

To visualise the spherical sequence in an artwork, focus on the outer edge of figures, connected by point-to-point lines between their eyes, forming a starburst shape. Viewing and comparing artworks figure by figure, axis by axis, and in their polar context, offers glimpses into the holographic genius of subconscious inspiration and expression.

Artists are not aware of the sequence of types, nor of the axes. The geometric centre is a function of the process of inspiration and expression, analogous to the ecliptic pole, or earth's yearly rotation around the sun, invisible in the sky. No viewer could see the sky in this projection, and very few star maps project the cosmos in the way that art expresses conceptual structure.

The 200 illustrations are grouped by dominant or notable themes or types, however each work contains the full cycle of types, some with their adjacent doubles. The captions explain some aspects of art, archaeology, archetype and mindprint.

Double imprints contain two spheres, some with interlocking figures like two gear wheels, perhaps as perceived by two contra-rotated brain spheres.

Readers who get to know the structure of visual expression will make many of their own discoveries about art, culture, perception, our subconscious, archetype, and ultimately about nature.

Readers who want to identify mindprint in artworks that are not illustrated, may follow the steps in the Identification method section in Chapter J.

Our subconscious artefact

Introduction

The core content of art, myth and culture around the world is identical. Beneath thin layers of flamboyant styling and learning lies a surprisingly standard structure, which is beyond the conscious control of artists, mystery schools or secret societies. All inspired artworks containing more than ten figures express a standard, involuntary sequence of types. Each type is characterised by one or two of its optional attributes and by its relative position. The types are spaced as paired opposites around an irregular ellipse, and precisely anchored to a standard axial structure, hinged on a geometric centre with tri-polar elements.

The structure emerging in the illustrations and statistical analysis, is a visual grammar or art code, never before described in esoterica, art history, archaeology, psychology or popular crafts.

Archetypes could be labelled in mythical, seasonal or astrological terms, yet none of these sets are origins of archetype. All are equally partial and imperfect expressions of pre-existent structure. The structure of nature, culture and perception is largely subconscious, not fully verbalised by artists or viewers. These subconscious meanings are rendered partially conscious by identifying relevant features and thus types, and comparing them to a list of averages. The axial geometric structure in the positioning of the eyes of the sequence of figures is made visible by drawing a set of lines that cross in one point. This structure is visually disguised by some radial distortion (a kind of starburst shape similar to the refraction of light), variety of subject and style, and the two standard deviations; to a heart as a spiritual eye, and to a womb as an unborn eye.

Visual expression arises from nature and our collective subconscious. It involves all forms of figurative arts and crafts, including engravings, murals, frescoes; spiritual, religious, political and portable artefacts; professional and amateur art. The 'readable' elements in visual expression indicate a similar structure in myth, literature, cosmology, calendric cycles and nature, confirming the role of what philosophy and psychology describe as archetype. Myth likewise uses characters differentiated by stock attributes, actions, motivations and episodes, and expresses natural, social and cultural structure. Art is less constrained by conscious cognitive processes than myth, which is bound by verbal, acoustic and dramatic grammar. Narrative arts unfold in a broken linear sequence, requiring of hearers or readers to visualise relationships and patch elements into a cumulative temporal sequence. Visual art is more direct, more impulsive, more compulsive to artists and viewers, more layered, and closer to inspiration.

Mindprint requires re-alignment of a range of assumptions, ultimately our entire paradigm of what art, design, inspiration, culture and humanity are.

The archetypal imprint, referred to as mindprint, tupos (imprint), art code, human subtext, Furter grid or archetypal art code, is predictive and testable.

Practical proof of the persistence and prevalence of mindprint in art is illustrated in 200 of the 400 artworks and rock art works listed in the Index.

Some of the testable attributes, and average occurrences of the standard sequence of types that are marked by the standard axial grid, are;

t1 t2 Taurus   48% twisting
t1 t2 Taurus   19% bovine
t3 Aries   42% neck long or bent
t4 Pisces   26% rectangular
t4 Pisces   25% squatting
t5 t20 t21 Aqu 44% varicoloured
t5 t20 t21 Aqu 31% action
t5 t20 t21 Aqu 30% horizontal
t5 t20 t21 Aqu 24% large
t6 Capricornus 48% ingress or egress
t7 Sagittarius 25% bag
t8 t9 Scorpius 34% bent forward
t8 t9 Scorpius 31% strength feat
t10 Libra   53% arms in V or W posture
t10 Libra   34% with a staff
t11 Virgo   87% on her womb
t12 t13 Leo   85% on his heart
t12 t13 Leo   14% feline
t12 t13 Leo   11% inverted
t14 Cancer   45% ingress or egress
t15 t0 Gemini 33% rope
t15 t0 Gemini 21% bag
t15 t0 Gemini 16% smiting.

Polar markers also follow average occurrences;
Ecliptic pole   49% (26% limb joint)
Galactic pole   81% (68% limb joint)
Celestial pole   60% (50% limb joint)
Galactic south pole 65% (50% limb joint)
Celestial south pole 55% (37% limb joint).

Based on overwhelming statistical and geometric evidence of the collective, universal, subconscious sequence of optional attributes in inspired art, and conceptual relationships between the optional elements of each type; the tables of myths, icons, constellations and concepts in this study are proven. They describe the standard content and structure of visual expression, as an involuntary art code arising from subconscious inspiration.

Additional variant expressions of each type should also be considered, for example type Gemini t15 as a rope (33%), and/or bag (21%), and/or creator (such as Ptah), and/or smiting (16%), and/or twinned as in the concept of Gemini (8%), and/or canine, and/or with a hip wound, and/or in a boat shrine (of minor percentages).

Identification of types rises above 90% if these variants (discussed in the Attributes section, Tables and captions) are considered together. These optional attributes all express components of their coherent concepts, with a minimum of ambiguity (see the few ambiguous elements identified at the end of Chapter J).

The typological concepts (detailed in the Lists and Tables) could be summarised as;

Type t1 t16 Taurus Auriga and Orion as rain diviner
Type t2 t17 Taurus Perseus as rainmaker
Type t3 t18 Aries Cetus as dragons or moon queen
Type t4 t19 Pisces Pegasus as sun twins
Type t5 t20 Aquarius Pegasus as world baptist
Type t5 t21 Aquarius as world spirit
Type t6 Capricornus as Pan
Type t7 Sagittarius as manifestation
Type t8 Scorpius Ophiuchus as giant strongman
Type t9 Scorpius as giant healer
Type t10 Libra Bootes as nature spirit
Type t11 Virgo as womb
Type t12 Leo as king inverted
Type t13 Leo as king's heart
Type t14 Cancer Ursa Minor as time calibrator
Type t15 t0 Gemini as creator
Ecliptic pole as hinge of annual, seasonal time
Galactic poles as hinges of equators of limb joints
Celestial poles as hinges of daily time and hours.

Every mindprint is unique and never copied except in mechanical reproduction (see variants of Poussin's Arcadian shepherds at theme t5 t20). Like different offspring of the same parents, or fingerprints, each version is a new combination of chromosomal halves, perhaps as re-combinations of inspiration and expression, spirit and body, eye and hand.

Mindprint is an all-or-nothing event. There are no half done or entirely scrambled sequences or geometric structures, provided that a bare minimum and variety of figures or geometric shapes are present. There is no perfect mindprint, yet the quality of imprints show surprisingly little variation, even between masters and novices. In quality it also resembles DNA, geared to produce near identical but variant members of a species.

The orientation, perspective plane, angular allocation, figures and number of figures all change, yet averages and core iconic content remain constant.

The subconscious disguise

The subtext in all myth and art follow the same rules, yet the diction and grammar of our visual language has never been described. Some components are hidden by simplicity, some by complexity, and all by layers of colourful, emotional, localised, historicised, appealing and supposedly cultural distractions.

There are also barriers to the enormity of the idea that each of us carries the potential to express all our cultural resources, and that any small group of us could re-draft myth, legend, art and civilisation from inspiration.

The involuntary, subconscious, sequential and geometric imprint has gone unrecognised in art and science, with the possible exception of conscious modifications in some palettes (see Egyptian palettes at theme t3, African palettes at theme t8, and a Bolivian disc at theme t12), or among arrays of hourly decans (see theme t12), or by some classical masters such as Nicholas Poussin (see his work in several theme sections).

Among the reasons for the novelty of mindprint in the global era are the divisions between various sciences, such as archaeology, anthropology, art history and psychology, as well as the divide between science, religion and crafts such as iconography, amulets, ritual, astrology, alchemy, emblems, kabbalah and prediction. Another level of disguise lies in the layered nature of archetypal holograms, defeating fixed paradigms and explorers who enter the subconscious without the proverbial Ariadnian thread of Theseus.

Subconscious crafts

Holistic inspiration contains simplistic attributes and geometry, yet the resulting whole is of iconographic complexity beyond the conscious scope of any artist (see the Commission Impossible section). Artists are as unaware of holographic visual logic as the Italian committee that confirmed traditional constellation names by choosing among time-honoured and new figures and labels in the astronomical mapping frenzy of the late 1700s and early 1800s. Conscious and subconscious elements both seem necessary to express spiritual inspiration. Likewise in myth and literature, conscious poetic themes are 'steaks' to distract the 'watchdog' of conscious thought, while inspiration applies poetic elements to its own ends. Poems and pictures have to make some conscious sense, but conscious concepts are less rigorous and thus more 'creative', as modern artists acknowledge. Many hints of the underlying archetypal structure in nature and perception went unexplored in science and unresolved in esoterica. Researchers have to remove the conscious splints from our scientific eye to see the beams in our minds' eyes.

Archaeo astronomers who find supposed 'astronomical knowledge' in artefacts, totems, site plans and initiation (such as Gary A David in Orion zone) read conscious scientific practice into subconscious archetypal expression. Some artefacts contain archetypal as well as astronomical elements (see the Decans section, and a Bolivian disc at theme t12).

However, when zodiacs, planets or constellations are included in art they usually do not correspond to the subconscious structure, and merely add to the layers of conscious camouflage (see a kabbalistic or Rosicrucian cave at t6. See Poussin's Helios and Phaeton at t2 t17). Art does not derive from astronomy or any science. Astronomy does not care for myth except as handy labels. Astrology as a craft cares little for myth or art, using one particular abstract application of the celestial sphere cradled (and rocking) in the ecliptic sphere.

Astrological structure demonstrates only part of the larger archetypal structure.

Structural archaeology

Artistic structure is a practical philosophy, expressing our human hologram in endless apparent variety. One of the implications of our subconscious visual standard is that we need only a limited visual diction and grammar to access the hologram of universal structure. It is not the preserve of sages alone.

Language and myth also allow subconscious access, via the subtext of parable, drama and grammatical structure, but they need a much larger vocabulary and opera (work), dominated by conscious manipulation, and with no guarantee of subconscious genius (as the mass of novels and movies demonstrate). Art is a more reliable guide to archetype. Admired works of art without mindprint or with serious structural defects could not be found, but such works may yet be found.

The archetypal sequence and geometric imprint does not appear in art that is highly commercialised, overly conceptualised, made by mostly mechanical means, of isolated components, or lacking public recognition.

Some isolated figures in artworks express only individual types, and rely more on cultural context than intrinsic elements in the work (see the end of theme t1 t16).

Demonstration of a fixed subconscious sequence and geometry in most figurative and even fully abstracted scenes, pose a range of implications for several crafts and sciences.

This multi-disciplinary study demonstrates the primary function of art and culture as extending our individual conscious access to elements of subconscious, archetypal structure. The persistence and prevalence of mindprint in art indicate that culture is universal, and localised or appropriated only by a thin veneer of styling. The core content or art remains unseen (unless identified as revealed in this study), and operates at several levels beyond conscious manipulation. It is sufficiently complex to be untouchable and meddle-proof.

Subconscious iconographic complexity applies equally to rock art, schooled art and amateur art worldwide. No systematic research or interpretation has ever comprehensively or consistently identified or described the archetypal structure or its context in art or culture. Archetypal iconography was misinterpreted as random or incidental totems, cultural diffusion, or historic 'development'. This study revives an entirely different cultural paradigm. The new kind of art analysis demonstrated here reveals more about all of us than any artist ever imagined.

Some alternative titles to this study illustrate the theme, and the field of interdisciplinary research that could be labelled structural archaeology;

Our visual grammar
Many cultures, one story
Subconscious brush
The human hologram
The whole picture
Our structural instinct
Instant culture
In our own image
Indelible imprint
Ropes of the sky
Born artists
Grand parade
The archetypal, collective, subconscious typology and geometry in compulsive visual expression.

Keywords; mindprint, art code, visual archetypes, axial imprint, Furter grid, cognitive archaeology, structural archaeology, subconscious.

The typological sequence in our art

Each of these six rows of figures, row (a), (b), (c), (d), (e) and (f), is taken in a circular sequence from the outer edge of a famous artwork. The works are of different cultures and eras. Each figure expresses one of the four or five typical, optional attributes of the archetype it represents. Some figures directly compare visually, or in concept (see similarities in each column, and compare the mindprint Attributes, Tables and Statistics sections). Each artwork thus expresses our global but subconscious visual grammar. Each artwork also confirms its sequence of types by the standard axial grid (see the full works in the illustration section).

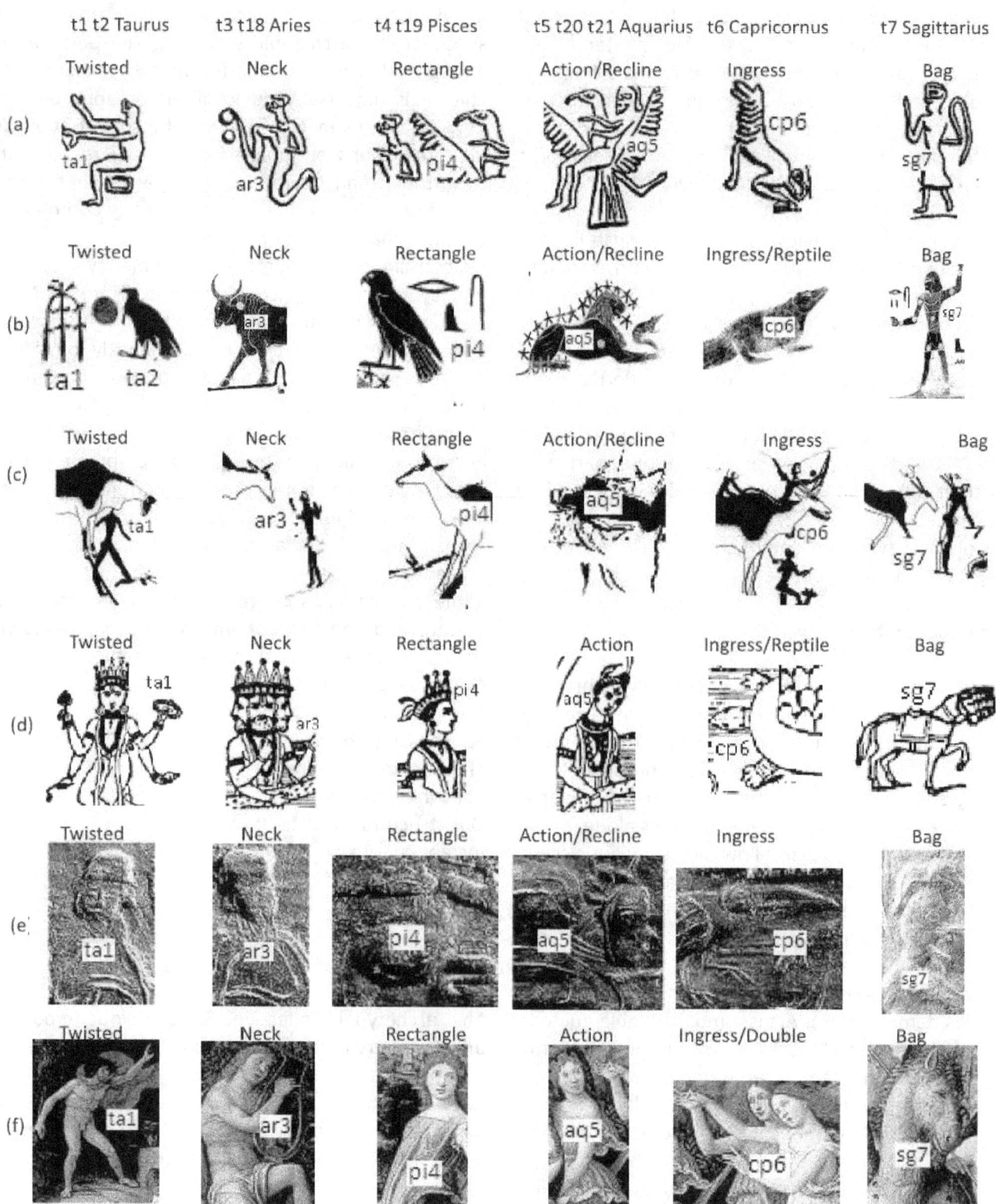

(a) From a Babylonian cylinder seal with Etana on an eagle (Sitchen. See theme t2 t17 on p114).
(b) From an Egyptian duat decans group on the Seti 1 tomb ceiling (see theme t8 on p175).
(c) From an African shelter at Maclear, Linton panel (Iziko Museum. See theme t5 t21 on p149).
(d) From an Indian Vishnu pillar in the Mahabharata (De Santillana. See theme t15 on p236).
(e) From a Chinese funeral tile print of the Queen of the west (El Shaughnessy. See theme t11 on p197).
(f) From a European Renaissance painting of Parnassus, by Mantegna (see theme t11 on p191).

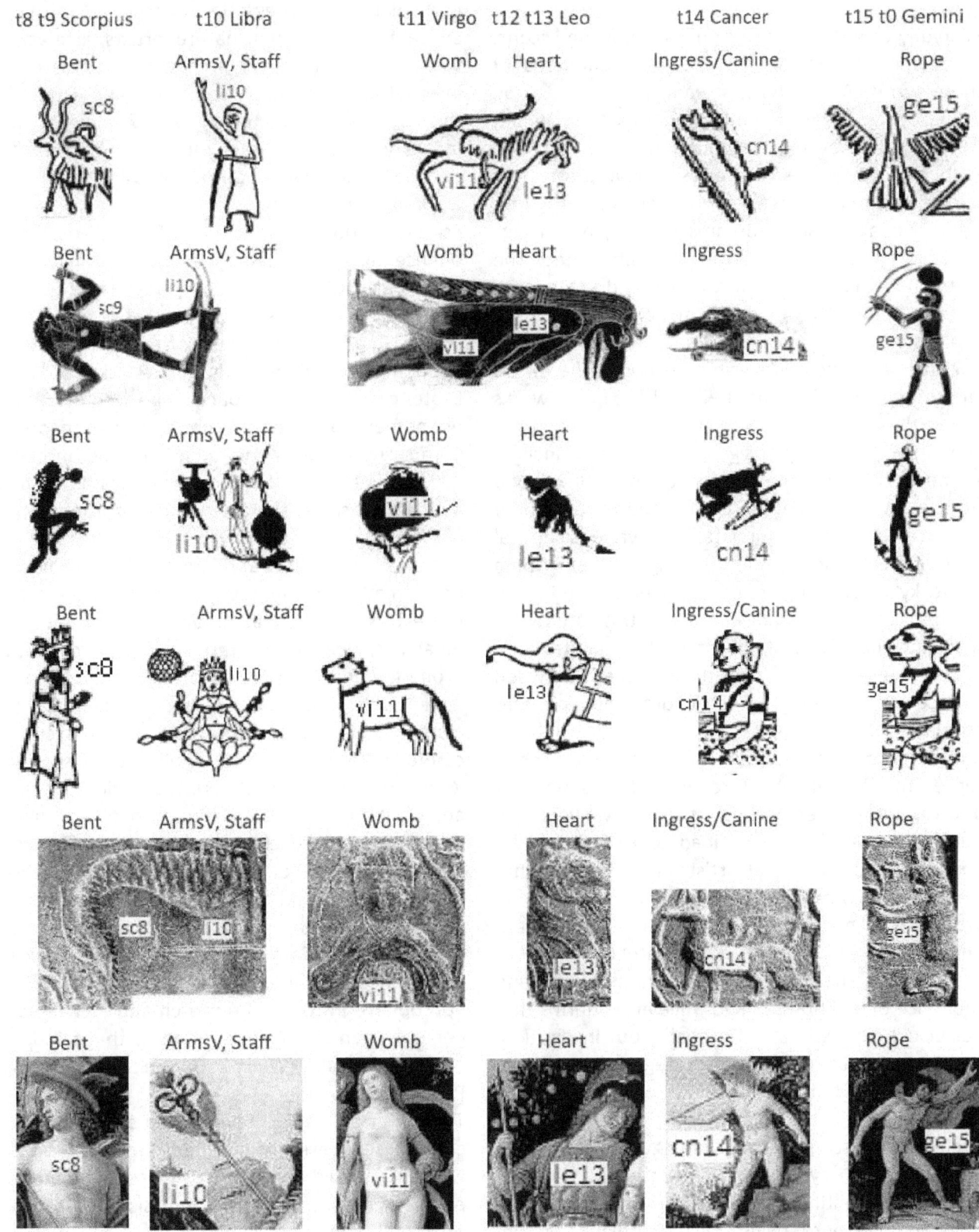

Comparing our semi-conscious sets

Chapter A

Everyday objects are also signs, symbols and icons, functioning across and beyond the definitions of these terms. A bag, bow, stream, tree or antelope each participate in several categories (skin, plant, water, individual and so on) and the attributes of each add yet more categories (hairy, protection, female, mother, large, horizontal and so on). Figurative art, just as dreams and myths, strings together groups of categories and attributes. The extent to which artists or viewers understand the intended and the inherent structure of artistic expression, is immaterial. As a Nobel laureate scientist said when asked about a horseshoe on his laboratory door, "I do not believe in it, but it works anyway!"

Semiology, the study of signs, "has come to include elements of structuralism, which had developed from a branch of linguistics attempting to identify universal and meaningful patterns in various cultural expressions." (Adams; Art through time). Noam Chomsky's work on grammatical structure laid some of the general groundwork for this study by revealing the universal, inborn syntactical structure in all languages. He also distinguished between surface or conventional structure and inherent grammatical structure.

Structuralism teaches that art does not merely represent elements of nature, and that the meaning of art is not dictated only by artists and viewers. The mimetic (copyist) view ascribed to Plato could be misread as implying that artists should paint what they see. However, as in myth and literature, an artwork does not represent only what it shows. Plato implied that artists must not violate the inherent meanings in their subjects. The standard set and sequence of attributes in figurative art confirms that our visual expression, and probably our inspiration, speaks a language of essences, categories, attributes and types (Levi-Strauss; The raw and the cooked, 1969).

Even a simple scene of about ten figures could evoke an entire myth cycle, much like different versions, operas and paintings of scenes from the Nibelungen cycle, or the hero twins, or the Trojan War do.

Inspired art always expresses sufficient and often superfluous meaning and coherence. The minimum of required complexity is difficult to define.

Mindprint identifications in 400 artworks reveal that one of the sixteen types usually dominates in an artwork, with some of its attributes attached to its opposite and to some other figures, or to the setting or orientation of the work. The illustrations are grouped by these dominant themes, demonstrating how some structural elements and themes support particular icons. Integration of content, format and concepts confirms that nature, artists, artefacts and viewers are tools of archetypal expression. As internet architect Vince Cerf said when asked about the Architect character in Matrix movies; "What makes you think you are outside the matrix?!" Art outside archetypal structure is not art, and a people without art is not a culture.

Esoterica, our archetypal craft, and mechanistic science agree on categorising items, events and processes, but disagree on what categories, items, events and processes are. Science confines and divides itself into the study of ever smaller sets of phenomena and ever larger chucks of theory. Esoterica instead, roams between sets of phenomena, accepting nature as its own theorem.

Comparing the elements of sets to one another (or tacking) is the staple diet of esoterica; body nodes, animals, kinships, slaughter portions, runes, letters, planets, signs, icons, days, months, years, totems, chemical elements and more. Its problem (or problematisation, in terms of formulating its own theses) is in unequal totals and partly unequal meanings, leaving esoteric analysts (or tackers) prone to combining or subverting some elements of larger sets, and elaborating or diluting some elements of smaller sets. Archaeology is currently carefully probing tacking applications (see Alison Wylie, Bernstein and others). Theoretical disunity, or application of evidence based on different theories, hypotheses, approaches or assumptions, "intertwine different strands of mutually supportive evidence and use one strand to cover a gap in another... the cumulative weight of disparate, multidimensional evidence and data can be rationally decisive... intertwined cable-like arguments are more appropriate in rock art research and archaeology in general, than chain-like arguments that fall down if one link is weak." (Wylie 2002, in Lewis-Williams and Pearce, 2012).

Tacking at best could reveal blind spots in a chosen cultural set, research problem, or conclusions. At worst it could assume conscious meanings in essentially subconscious expressions, through no error of 'theoretical disunity' itself.

Mindprint offers a standard typological sequence and structure to test cultural expressions against, including ritual, myth, pantheons and art. The risk of introducing an artificial structure as mediator between self-identified expressions, such as an Old Kingdom Egyptian set of gods and an Aztec myth cycle, are outweighed by the advantages.

For example, Australian song lines offer a range of motifs in a fixed sequence that could compare to the myth cycles and sub-cycles that Homer wove into legendary episodes in verse epic. Partial identification in one set, such as song lyrics, could clarify and complete other sets of the culture, and of other cultures, such as South American plateau rock art or grail romance ritual.

Archaeology and anthropology should be as integrative in the study of culture, as culture is integrative in appropriating elements of the right shape, sound or meaning to express the unwritten and subconscious structure of nature and archetype. If inspired art were random, there would be little point in tacking (comparing and labelling) art to themes in myth. But "rock art is not an open-ended record of anything and everything that occurred to the image-makers" and there is "selectivity of subject matter."

(Lewis-Williams and Pierce, 2012). Decades of rock art research, mainly in the 1970s by Vinnicombe, Maggs, Pager and Lewis-Williams, saw rock art as part of "a specific ritualised practice." Yet attempts to identify its components were sporadic, and erased by the pervasive paradigm of cultures as being separate, each with its own supposed rituals, development and partial diffusion (see the categorically negative, dismissive and derisive academic view of archetypes in rock art in the Science and Esoterica section).

Mythological and ethnological sets such as pantheons, rituals and amulets, offer self-defined classes and categories to test visual sets against. The approach of comparing rock art to mythology by tacking (Alison Wylie, 1989, and 2002, after Richard Bernstein, and after Clifford Geertz) recognises our impulse to visualise inspiration. Art, particularly nationalist and spiritual art, thus helps to sustain myth, but neither is the origin of the other.

Bernstein wrote that rock art researchers could resort to "concepts that are not necessarily familiar to the people being studied, [to] make intelligible the symbolic forms." (cited in Wyllie, 1989). The present study follows Bernstein's lead in that respect, and applies all accessible concepts and cultural contexts, therefore a universal human cultural context, to each culture. Overwhelming commonalities are revealed below the thin differentiating layer of material, style, politics, fads, programmes and labels.

Perpetual elements in myth and art indicate that supposed mythical innovation, acculturation, diffusion and historisation are all mere mutations, 'running to stand still', just as genetic mutation is essential in keeping a species ahead of competitors and environmental cycles. The resulting transformations therefore should not be seen as constant improvement or unilateral evolution, but as constant diversification to fill our niche, which itself is structured and part of natural structure. There is every indication in archaeology that the core content of human culture and spirituality remains constant, with physical and stylistic changes mainly in response to population density and thus to practical specialisation.

For example, rainmakers and rain animals appear worldwide in similar forms and rituals, and as "diverse depictions" in each seemingly distinctive culture. San groups, though genetically related, speak several mutually unintelligible languages. There is every reason to identify rain animals in diverse forms among all San paintings as distinct from other figures, icons or archetypes. There is also evidence of rain animals and other archetypal icons worldwide in rock art, religious art, folk art, amulets, alchemical emblems and pantheons.

Each artwork, when analysed as an iconographic set, expresses only some attributes of each type. For example, type Libra t10 may be scales, a wheel of fortune, a man with a staff, or a pair of claws attached to a Scorpius figure.

Type Taurus t2 Orion or Auriga may be a hunter, charioteer, surveyor, tree or tower. Pisces or Aquarius Pegasus may be a field, garden, pool or horse, sometimes sharing their mutual attribute of a rectangular shape and the abstract concept of bounded and contained life or paradise. All these options never appear in one artwork or myth.

If 'tacking and disunity' (comparison to other kinds of artefacts) could serve the interpretation of San rock art, then it could serve all art and myth, adding more strands to the rope of characters, sequence and geometric structure inherent in culture and perception. Since archetype is incidental with nature, art and science, and by definition pervades all our expressions, its forms could be consciously identified and isolated in every self-defined set, such as zoology, totems, calendars, hour decans, lunar mansions, pantheons, myth cycles, Hercules' labours, zodiacs, geomancy, divination, I Ching verses, alchemy, chemistry, physiology, palms and iris reflexology. An artwork is likewise a self-defined set.

Most species inherit complex eyes, described in physiology as an organ too complex for animal or human brains to fully use. Our eyes see more than we could know, yet we have not fully studied even that which we do see and could understand. Brains are described in archaeology as having grown from the use of hands and thumbs, yet we have not fully studied what we re-create and perceive. Mindprint offers a toolkit for these studies.

The subconscious content of a large number of engravings, tiles, pots, palettes and canvases in every known culture and era, enabled the cracking of the art code. Once reduced to archetypal elements, the 'transmission gear' of mindprint could test any visual set (artwork), and test averaged components of any number of sets (artworks) against one another, aided by the standard geometric structure as a kind of visual scaffolding.

Animal sets

The animal kingdom offers the most immediate analogy of natural structure, just as localised ecosystems offer immediate diagnosis of social prospects for prosperity. Divination is therefore closely aligned with the animal kingdom (Robert Temple; Netherworld). Our experience of nature also relies on conceptual 'elements' and cosmic directions. The Watkins dictionary of symbols explains the primal natural analogy; "Animals have always been the most immediate, powerful and important foundation for symbolism. No other source in the natural world has provided such a richly varied range of iconography.

Most human qualities are personified from close observation of animal forms, habits and characteristics. Psychology has followed religion in attaching to animals the essential symbolism of instinctual, unconscious, libido emotions... they are more in touch with unseen cosmic forces than humans. Their frequently superior physical and sensory abilities led to the general belief that they have magical or spiritual powers. For shamans they are a means of access to these powers... Most Egyptian gods were personified by animals, and elsewhere too, the most prestigious symbolised not brute passions, but spiritual qualities." (Jack Tresidder, 1999).

Greek culture is seen as ruled by a human pantheon, but Greek gods including Zeus often assume animal qualities (bull, snake, swan, eagle, goat, hart, scorpion, lion, hydra, fox, dog and so on), just as some Asian gods transform into various incarnations. Tresidder summarises our conceptual

and structural use of animal types; "Medieval bestiaries assumed that animal symbolism could be strictly classified, an idea supported by a surprising degree of cross-cultural uniformity in the concepts embodied by different animals."

Artists would agree. This study recognises categorisation, classification and analogy itself as our universal impulse.

Mythic sets

Myth and art enable spiritual meanings by analogy, or by invoking and comparing concepts that are intrinsic to nature and culture. Joseph Campbell wrote; "Myth functions to harmonise persons with society, the cosmos, and themselves. It serves to link them with everything outside and within themselves."

This study is based on visual sequence and geometric context, just as grammar uses sequence and context to enable layers of meaning. Some of the basic elements of art and grammar do not carry inherent meaning, but an artwork, like and essay or story, enables its meaning by invoking structural elements and structure itself.

All artworks require some initial effort to decode or strip away superficial style before the work stands suitably dressed to the conscious mind. Yet it is always naked to the subconscious. Jung used context, forms, leitmotifs, events, rationales, persons, moods, situations, phenomena, attributes and symbols to highlight parallels and similarities between myths and experience. So do clairvoyants, healers, artists and critics.

Rank and Jung note that myth is the "collective dream of a whole people." Healing power, named hermeneutics after the spiritual healer type, Hermes, "has a beneficial effect on the psyche by consciously linking the distant past, ancestral heritage, which is still alive in the unconscious, with the present, thus establishing a vitally important connection with consciousness... As the most conservative product of the human mind, religions are bridges to the ever-living past, which they make alive and present. A religion that can no longer assimilate myths is forgetting its proper functions. Its spiritual vitality depends on the continuity of myth, preserved only if each age translates the myth into its own language and makes it an essential content of its view of the world." (Jung 1963).

Healing and religious practice invariably access and express archetypal applications. These functions equally apply to art, and are more testable in art. If myth is cohesive, and operates by clusters or haloes of meaning, and is "form-in-itself, of fundamental coherence, enabling something to manifest in form," (Bierenbaum), then myth and art are formative and coherent. This study reveals the hierarchy of forms in art, never made explicit before. Myth could be an archetypal only if it were collective and coherent. Myth must gather, unify and organise every experience in a primordial ('of prior order') conceptual structure and illustrate the primordial gathering in its own implicit structure.

Thus the 'signature' of myth is structure itself. The poet WB Yeats wrote that myth is the primal collector, and such a network of inter-collections that "one cannot tell one thing without telling a hundred others... Mythemic units may be combined, correlated, clustered, condensed, and mythographic analyses have to concentrate on interconnections among them to bring into view the whole network."

Philosophy and science also collect, order and describe nature, and therefore is also self-descriptive and mythic. Thus myth is the "origin of philosophy." (Hyland, 1973). Yet our conscious mind and the conscious layers in myth and art remain at arm's length from archetype. Our collective ego could assimilate only fragments of our contradictory inner and collective selves.

Some philosophers rely on subconscious 'truth' or form; "The ultimate criterion for interpretation is the satisfaction of the person to whom it pertains. If it rings true for him, it has value." (Cohen, 1974). Yet there is no way to measure 'the ring of truth', and the 'concerned person' in art could be anyone.

Myth remains a partial expression of outer and inner experience, including cultural 'feedback' experience such as mythemic elements in ritual, myth, songs and art. Legendary landscapes, the mythic sky and conventions likewise tack to myth, always with partial overlap. A constant stream of 'revelations' from esoteric 'traditions' (see the attributed Gospel of Judas) indicate that myth is esoteric, yet readily ritualised, personified and legendised, remaining inherently structured, therefore prone to formulism, institutionalisation and exoteric assumptions. Thus archetype masquerades as history, or in crafts such as prediction or science.

Living traditions support networks of healers, painters and oracles, as in the former Mediterranean world, or the Matobo region of Zimbabwe before the political and military disruptions since the 1970s. Without such constant renewal, traditions tend to fossilise and theologise, even in the inspired words of bards such as Zarathustra, Homer, Moses, the Vedic poets, Snorri Sturlasson, Wagner, Picasso or Dali.

To view culture as a product of incremental development, or artefacts as limited by stages of cultural development, is to aggrandise humanity with expanding our consciousness and culture from a clean slate of primate motivations. We did neither. Myth is perceived as the result of history and politics, but the reverse applies.

Archaeologists find the illustrations of myth in art to be "apparently fragmentary" (Lewis-Williams, 2012). The same comment applies to any mythology, with their variant versions and facility for re-interpretation, yet they all maintain the universal set of meanings, with some support from religious or political conventions.

There is every reason to compare all cultural expressions, including literised (consciously organised and recorded) mythology, folklore, esoteric and iconographic fragments. There is little gain in the study of one culture, or one particular myth cycle in isolation, or 'untacked'. Divided and isolated, they reveal only fragments.

Iconic sets

Icons as building blocks of art are identified by their repetition. Birenbaum (1988) writes; "A motif can be identified for practical purposes simply as any detail that recurs: a kind [type] of character, place, structure, animal or plant, or any feature of the narrative process as it unfolds." Mindprint supports and expands this view in identifying recurrent types of characters, mostly people, animals and semi-geometric figures, in a particular sequence and symmetrical structure of pairs of opposite, in every relatively complex artwork.

On comparing icons, Jung wrote; 'To draw a valid parallel, it is necessary to know the functional meaning of the individual symbols, and whether they have a similar context.' (Jung, 1936, 1959). Mindprint demonstrates this functional and contextual identification process. Individual symbols acquire function by their attributes and by their relative positions in the archetypal visual structure. Their function is confirmed in parallel myths, symbols or artworks worldwide. Knowledge of any myths, symbols, signs, customs and cultures thus helps to identify types and reveal their subconscious functions.

Grammatical sets

Artists follow visual grammar without thinking, as we need little prompting to acquire language, and do not need to explain grammar to use language.

The skill is inbuilt; culture just adds the style (or diction and current quirks) from endless mutations. Artistic grammar is thus a tool for studying cultural, natural and perceptional meanings and archetypal structure itself, just as anthropology uses myth and ritual to study culture.

Grammar does not demystify language, rhetoric, literature or perception, nor does mindprint demystify art.

Most people are not fluent in the visual language of their own or other cultures, but could learn it just as they could learn mathematics, geometry, medicine, chemistry, architecture or engineering. Our subconscious speaks one mythic and visual language, from before the Ice Age to today in all cultures, changing only in the orientation of one of the three celestial polar axles (see the Polar chapter).

Alphabets function at a more optional and conventional level of expression. Sounds and letters, like angles and sections of outlines, are the bare bones of a set that could codify meaning. We use structure at various levels simultaneously. This faculty is not incremental, although its application is practiced and refined.

Grammatical assumptions like proto-Sanskrit and proto-Semitic that imply development from a human mind capable only of using directly representational grunts and clicks, or art and writing developed gradually from pictograms, misrepresent our massive capacity for sets and structures. Without hundreds of sciences and a billion books, we expressed humanity as well in hunting mammoths, as in dissecting mammoth DNA. Human vocal chords may have developed in hominids, but grammar, including its penchant for group differentiation and social bonding, also operates in grunts and clicks, as it does in Bushman languages, Basque and French. Likewise, the domain of art extends into geometry (see semi-figurative blobs at t3 and t12). Archetype informs an infinity of languages, a gallery full of artistic styles, and instant cultural ensembles.

Art history tracks superfluous stylistic elements at the cost of exploring the core language of art, perhaps in subconscious recognition that visual language is untouchable and unchanging while only style is 'creative' and individual.

Graphic art is more exacting and more instantly expressive of archetype than verbal, literary or performing arts. People have to apply gestalt (seeing wholes in parts, or filling in holes between parts) more rigorously to hearing stories or music, reading, watching opera, ballet or dance, than to glancing at artworks. Yet while the full sequence and structure is in front of our eyes, it remains subconscious, like vivid waking dreams. Art invites and tolerates more revisit, contemplation and review than re-reading a book or re-viewing an opera.

Visual artists have to work harder at reflecting nature (in the broad sense), and could not fudge (swop, omit, contract or add elements) as writers, composers or even birds do. Many artists struggle to break from this compulsion and to divorce themselves from what has been labelled symbolism, as in artistic and verbal statements by Salvador Dali and others. Artists rebel against carrying this additional subconscious burden of proof of the spiritual truth of their work, in envy of performing arts that could rely on the audience to do half the work, and the greater opportunity for performing artists to display their individual styles, faces and pet subjects. Visual art, supposedly the freest form of expression and creation, is now revealed to be as rule-bound as music or grammar, and more innately structured than alphabets, diction, myth, spirituality or religion. Visual aesthetic rules are therefore more capable of formulation than other cultural media.

Science erects its theoretical scaffolding around bits of 'reality', partly in similar frustration at nature's habit of explaining itself, partly in imitation of natural revelation by its 'signatures', and partly in frustration that nature reveals her structure in ways beyond the grasp of neat conscious logic (see an alchemical allegory of nature and science in a hill and cave at t6).

Academic art hinges on conscious concepts, traceable logic and definable culture, thus acknowledging that personality, creativity, symbols, culture and expression itself are definable. Yet conceptual artists also express the collective subconscious cultural imprint that we did not expect to be definable (see Pippa Skotnes' donkey in the Sanlam Collection).

Art could be seen as our impulse to transform instinctual energy by inspiration and technique into aesthetic form (Adams; Art through time). Yet analyses of our artistic impulse, inspiration and instinct are usually subservient to our academic obsession with technique and texture. Art history seldom probes or reveals any elements of our collective subconscious (compare academic analyses of any famous artwork with its mindprint analysis, such as Leonard French's The Bridge at theme t5 t20).

Mindprint is a useful departure for art criticism and appreciation, since it reveals how themes, artists, cultures and humanity express aspects of the standard holographic framework of inspiration in a wide range of contexts, and how visual grammar enables visual 'rhetoric'.

Glimpses of subconscious structure

The sequence of archetypal attributes and geometric structure that is consciously traceable in inspired art is directly comparable to similar structures in the human eye, body, hand, myth, cosmos, ritual and healing experience of all cultures in all eras. Artists and the cultures they serve are impelled and compelled to express inspiration in the standard mould, camouflaged by apparently episodic scenes, incidental detail and unique styles.

Analogies between seemingly separate sets confirm natural and cultural holism (a term coined by South African Union Prime Minister Jan Smuts). The apocryphal Gospel of Thomas, 22 advises; "Make two into one, inner like outer and vice versa, upper like lower, male and female single... eyes in place of an eye, hand in place of hand, foot, image, then you will enter [the kingdom]."

This esoteric kingdom is as integral to us as dreams or thoughts. The Hypnerotomachia Poliphili by the anonymous 'Franciscus Colonna' evokes holism in these terms; "From whichever way one enters it, one is caught in the same bewildering circular complexity as in a labyrinth, for it has no deductive order in the abstract sense, but instead resembles an organism tightly closed in itself, or a monumental Art of the Fugue."

Sleep and dreaming confirm that our practical and spiritual realities are equal needs. Access to our subconscious is therefore not confined to special people, cultures, places, substances or rituals, but as close and frequent as dreams or daydreams. Artistic structure equates and equalises cultures, and demonstrates that art was never invented or lost.

Healing and art are thus among the first and eternal professions, not idle pursuits, but a theatre of our minds and lives, our eternal virtual reality.

Art is not noted for inducing trance, as a range of other practices such as music, dance, dehydration and fatigue are, but inspired art may support dreams and inform dreamers by a kind of roadmap. Trance may be termed ritualised or dramatised dreaming, but even trance is not necessarily a visible or notable event. In charismatic churches some members would speak in tongues, while visions in a more or less waking state could be less visible, and perhaps a sustained or incremental process. Most artists could not pinpoint a moment of inspiration for a work. Artists are inspired by waking dreams, or alcheringa as the Australian Aranda tribe label it. Bushman myths often mention dreams rather than trance, although they regularly participate in, and their artists often depict ritualised trance. Scenes of

dancers with herms, Pan, Bacchus and other sylvan characters do the same in classical art, while the modern equivalents are concerts, drumming circles, carnivals, games and gymnasiums.

Jung postulated a process of active imagination (in which the artist is passive), allowing 'active' images to surface into awareness as if objectively present (Alex Duffey; Dreaming with open eyes, the mind as sixth organ of perception in San rock art. 2001c. He cites D Price-Williams; The waking dream, 1987).

The persistent or collective content in art emerges in this study as attributional, sequential and geometric, therefore structural and not stylistic. Likewise 'eidetic' imagery (U Neisser; Memory observed, 1982) is described as not specific and perhaps not even visual, but rather impressions of qualities that artists project in visual terms, and that poets project in narrative terms. Many people fleetingly recall dreams as a specific mood, linked to a vaguely familiar place, person or action. Psychologist Finke wrote of "mental images, physical objects and events as functionally equivalent, as revealed by their perceptual and behavioural effects, [which] stimulate visual processing mechanisms." (RA Finke; Levels of equivalents in imagery and perception, 1980).

Many societies cultivate mental imagery skills, just as academia does today. The intricacies of social heritage and kinship are as good for structural training as the sets of ecology, theology or any science are. The ultimate aim seems to be entering "various levels filled with specifically organised cultural meanings." (Alex Duffey, after Finke). Perception involves "abstractions, making the mind a sixth organ of perception... a window onto different levels of reality... [consciously] regarded as independent of the dream-images."

Duffey sees dream visions (perhaps more properly termed visualised concepts) as sustaining mythical beliefs and cultural material. "Retention of this information depends on how well the material is organised." Thus religion is also a structural pursuit.

Duffey's concept of "culture-patterned waking dreams" raises culture to the role of archetype, yet culture by definition is not capable of patterning the same dreams worldwide.

Healers tend to instruct apprentices or artists to seek particular kinds of vision. Assimilation of some subconscious elements and thus archetypal inspiration into consciousness, favour prepared minds (see the Anthropology section). Many philosophers and academics, including Lincoln, Duffey, Biesele and Lewis-Williams derive the idea of cultural "framing" from this typical social transaction, yet others, including Duffey, note that these inner experiences are also "unsolicited", as in the Greek and German formulation of 'befindlickheid' (susceptibility or subjection).

All people could express and recognise subconscious structure, but only artists (in the broad sense, including writers, actors and prophets) make a career of raising elements of our common subconscious domain within reach of our conscious domain.

Dreams straddle our consciously known and subconsciously sensed worlds, and bridge our supposedly individual and collective realities. Inspired art has a similar function to our daily need for sleep and dreams, since art expresses and sustains therapy, re-induces similar experiences, and multiply the healing effect. We need reminders of our other halves, or collective other half, in waking hours, as much as we need optional waking cycles during sleep, where dreams also play the reverse of their usual role by edging us back to consciousness. We dream to access physical, mental and spiritual healing, yet dreams also prompt our conscious slapsticks, such as threats, to keep us awake and alive.

A preliminary figure of 2% of people capable of recalling trance visions is cited by Graham Hancock in Supernature, from a study of natural DMT levels in the brain. He also notes that the measure of temporary removal of the equally natural suppressant of DMT, by some ingredients of ayahuasca, is more definitive of trance experience. Other studies found that 15% of all populations are prone to suggestion under hypnosis, demonstrating the social functions of our collective subconscious. Researchers who lived with Bushmen say everyone participate in healing dances, and ritual healers could be as many as one in five (P Myburgh; Bushman culture. Theosophy Johannesburg presentation, 2013). Stage hypnotists demonstrate that nearly all people are capable of acting out suggestion, particularly in a social context involving group instigation and expectations. We are natural actors and artists. Our allegories rehearse practical functions such as hunt, war, quest, cultivation, herding, cooking and healing, identical with spiritual functions.

Inspired art in its surface appearance also straddles our conscious and subconscious, physical and spiritual, visual and conceptual worlds, using real, surreal and fantastic elements. Art, including rock art, favours themes with social and ethical elements, invoking stock episodes and therefore collective concepts, even in small and simplistic artworks.

One of the main functions of art appears to be expression of structure itself. Totem or token animals in ritual, such as the snakes that Moses raised on staffs, could be no more than inducers of access to structure, as an end in itself.

The function of myths, gurus and motivational speakers in more or less coherent groups, and the function of political statues on civic squares, hint at the same effect; it does not take much prompting to activate a social compact or polity. Culture enables healing by raising social trust.

If art functions as a spiritual nudge, it is demonstrated in this study to be much more exacting, and as nuanced as myth, legend, history, literature, politics or medicine. Each work of art is a little opera, highly structured, with some standard and some creative options, some room for viewers to ignore or elaborate some elements, and leaving much to rehearse and to return for. Some artworks remain popular for centuries.

Our collective consciousness is recognised as structured, and so narrowly ritualised that it is formulated in national and international laws and conventions. Our dream world, for all its occasionally surreal and supposed free-ranging creativity, now appears to be equally structured and thus capable of description.

Our subconscious layers

Consciousness keeps a lid on the trials, horrors and treasures of self-expression and self-realisation below. The contradictory function of the Shadow and perhaps most of the psyche as both inhibitor and guide is spelled out by Jung and many of his reviewers.

Wikipedia summarises Jung's description of our subtext as well as any academic source does; "The collective unconscious shows no tendency to become conscious under normal conditions, nor can it be brought back to recollection by any analytical technique, since it was never repressed or forgotten. The collective unconscious is not to be thought of as a self-subsistent entity; it is no more than a potentiality, handed down from primordial time as mnemonic images or inherited in the anatomical structure of the brain. There are no inborn ideas, but there are inborn possibilities of ideas that set bound to even the boldest fantasy, and keep our fantasy activity within certain categories: 'a priori' ideas, the existence of which cannot be ascertained except from their effects.

"They appear only in the shaped material of art [or myth, or nature] as the regulative principles that shape it; only by inferences drawn from the finished work [or nature] can we reconstruct the age-old original of the primordial image."

These parameters and principles are now described in the analytical technique of mindprint with its set of attributes and axial grid. Jung never imagined just how exacting the role of archetype in art is, nor how much we could infer of archetype from art alone. Artistic subjects range apparently freely inside and outside the physical realm, as the surreality or idealism of many artworks (including rock art) testify, yet like cartoon strips or soap operas they repeat certain themes and structures, using a narrow range of specific visual and conceptual elements.

Mindprint reveals the subconscious visual structure in art and confirms that our mind is "not a collective layer of individual minds, but a universal field inextricably connected to nature," as in Jung's view. Mindprint incidentally clarifies damaged or contested components in artworks, enabling them to speak volumes from our collective subconscious, despite the limited conscious intentions of the artist.

Visual types are semi-conscious

It takes a lifetime of study to master calendric, symbolic, iconic, alchemical and esoteric processes at the conscious level, and these crafts remain prone to conscious individual and cultural errors. Artists instead access our collective subconscious vision that is free of error by definition.

Archetypal repertoire in myth, legend, artefacts, crafts and inspired art, is more detailed than basic broad categories recognised in literature and in analytical psychology. All archetypes appear in context with other archetypes, each as a parcel or halo of meaning, traceable in all cultures (see the Index, listed by continent and country). Our repertoire of characters and episodes is constant (see the Attributes and Tables sections), confirming regular access to our collective subconscious. Our spirituality, perception and even experience is enabled and constrained or 'framed' by the same archetypal repertoire that we imprint on our artefacts.

We have every reason to expect cosmic logic to pervade our thoughts and deeds, yet we imagine ourselves as free thinkers. Art is our ultimate self-portrait, including delusions of grandeur in our conscious Ego layer.

Recognition of archetypes in iconography, by the conventional definition, requires experience of the relevant culture. However highly co-incident figures or episodes in different cultures should be considered archetypal elements, irrespective of their claims to either diffusion or independent development. Large pantheons or broad, general concepts such as father, mother, hero, enemy, victim, hunter, healer, leader, monster, teacher, initiate, thunder god, fertility agent and so on, include as much conscious elaboration as core structural features. Lack of a generally agreed finite list of visual archetypes and their minima of elements is surprising.

The structure in our eyes and bodies

Nerve endings or lymph nodes in our eyes follow a sequence related to the structure of our bodies, perception and artistic expression (homeopathic reflexology map by Dr Bernard Jensen. Mindprint labels and geometry by Edmond Furter). We see with our eyes, brains and nervous system.

The geometric centre of opposing nerve links, or symmetrical pole of nodes, is not in the centre of the iris, but offset by about 20 degrees (taking the median ring of the iris, about where the lung, the back and other organs are marked, as a hemisphere (of 180 degrees, and the outer iris as folding out a third of the 'underside', adding up to about 240 degrees). Right and left eyes are near identical, but contra-rotating and 'geared' or mirrored between the heart and bronchial axes.

Markers for the conceptual celestial poles are uncertain. The horizontal plane of the body, on the Leo-Aquarius axis, tags the orientation of the human iris and body to Age Taurus1 -Taurus2, which is also the orientation and era tag of many rock art works, and of alchemical art in all Ages. However the centre of the human iris, perpendicular (90 degrees) off the galactic polar axle, tags the iris to Age Pisces-Aquarius, our current era. These two transitional era tags may imply that our physical features are oriented outside the history of expressional time (see the Archetypes section). They do not imply that we acquired consciousness in any particular Age or era.

Ages are named after the position of the spring equinox, the season of highest biological activity. Taurus retains some attributes of spring, despite having lost the equinox about BC 1500.

Sequence loops

Many categories of natural expression, such as elements, species, atoms, DNA and other structures, could be listed or mapped by their intrinsic attributes. Variant configurations or 'periodic tables' of atomic elements, for example, demonstrate that natural structure is accessible to human consciousness. Some physics tables require doubling and loops. Haemoglobin has a similar structure, with apparently random points of contact and overlay, nevertheless following bio-chemical structural logic. Mindprint demonstrates a similar looped structure in the splitting of some types, doubled overlay of a section of the sequence, and additional optional or 'recessive' attributes of each type (see the Tables). Salvador Dali used limb joints to express structural concepts (see the Polar chapter.)

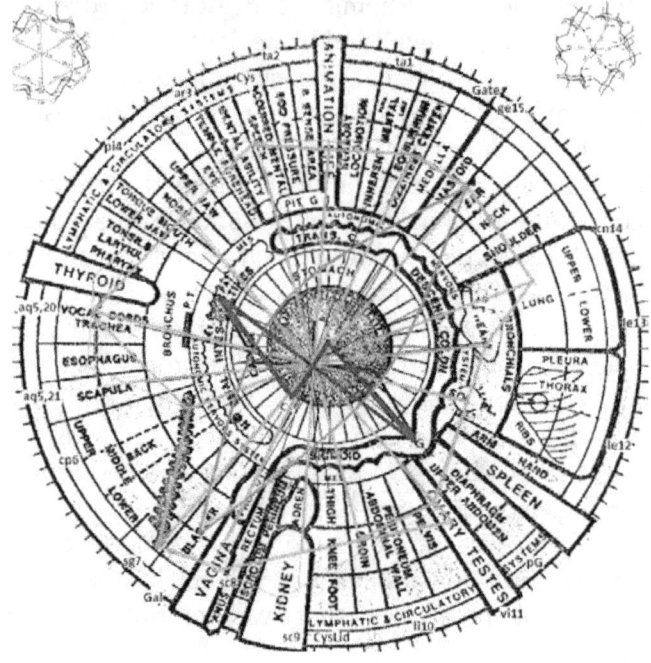

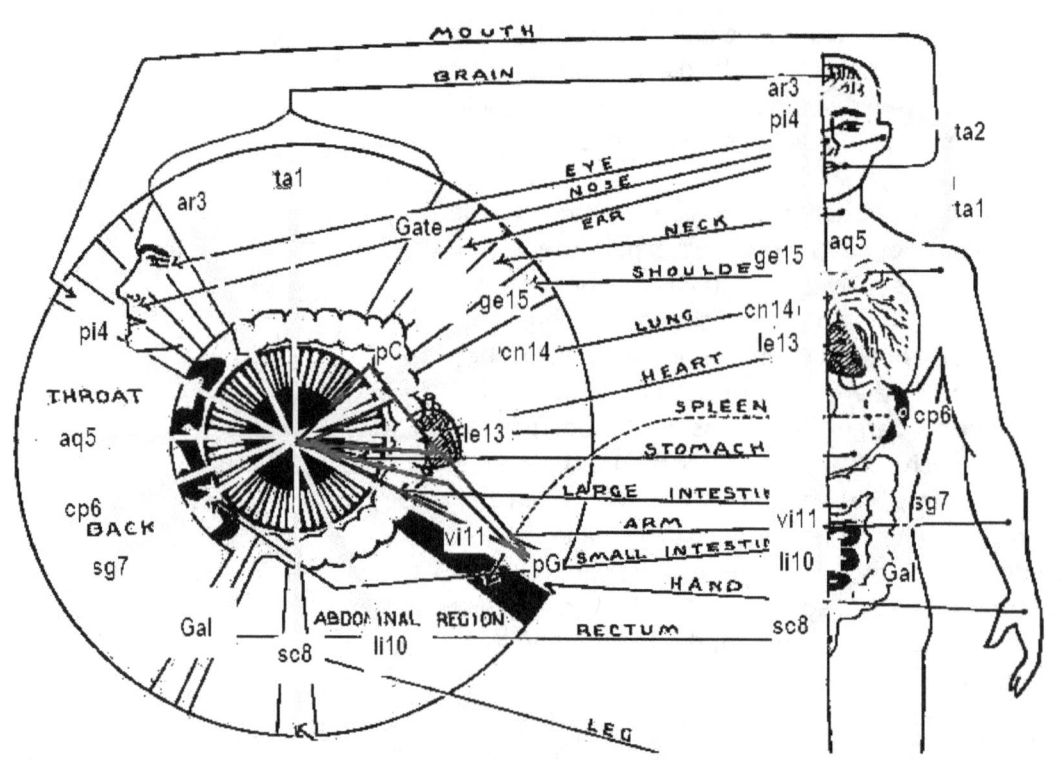

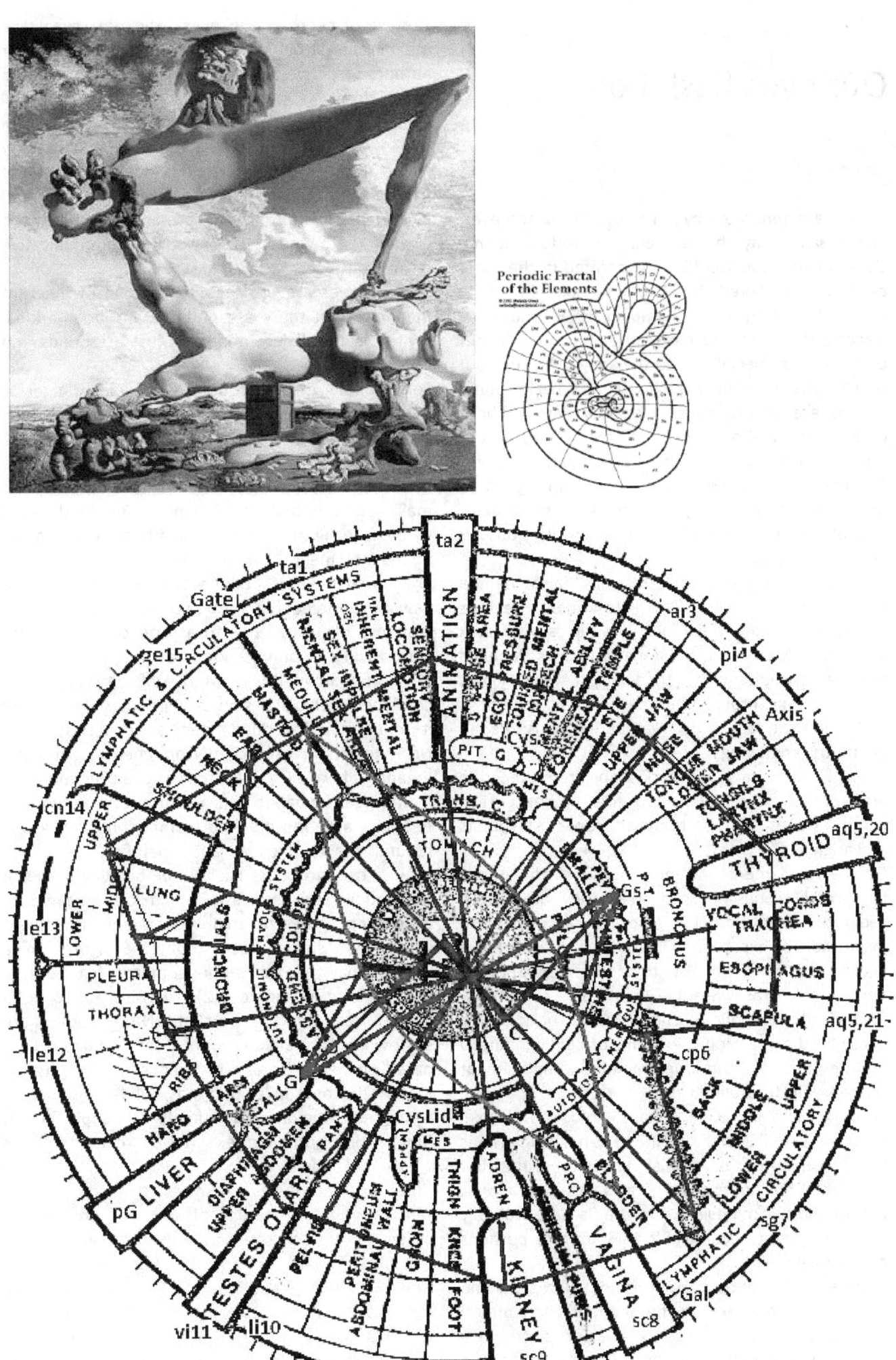

Periodic Fractal of the Elements

Our eyes flash Boo

Chapter B

Images are generated by our visual cortex and eyes, in the same way that our ears re-produce sound. Oto-acoustic emission (OAE) generated in the inner ear was predicted by Thomas Gold in 1948, demonstrated by David Kemp in 1978, and since traced to cellular and mechanical functions in our ears. Hearing specialists cite the adage 'If you shout Boo to the ear, the ear shouts Boo back'. Some sounds are spontaneous in healthy ears, without external stimulation, accounting for 'roaring water, thunder and voices' that accompany visions. Prophets and healers attest to learning of a microcosm from spirit guides, in the guise of bees, animals, voices of thunder, winged angels, gods, or an eye in a triangle.

The wide repertoire of entoptics (also named phosphene shapes) as an oto-visual effect is extensively recorded in rock art, typically in rock engravings, but also in some paintings labelled 'geometric tradition' in archaeology (Lewis-Williams and Dowson; Through the veil: San rock paintings and the rock face. Also Marguerite Prins; Redan geometric engravings).

Entoptics are a range of stock shapes reproduced in art, such as sets and nested sets of dots, grids, curves, waves, circles, triangles, ropes, starbursts and angles.

Geometric elements in representational art, usually in surreal scenes, indicate that they are not a separate 'tradition', but aspects or phases in inspiration or expression. The net effect resembles expressionism, which aims to render inspiration as approximate as possible, instead of neatly formalised symbolic scenes. Most rock art is considered expressionist in terms of being generally un-intentional, un-programmed and not conceptually formulated art.

Entoptics appear to be a hard-wired neurological function, enabling sight itself and generating visions that artists do not consciously understand, but that feel right. Thus our eyes and brains flash Boo back at nature and our minds see only the flashes, probably since our physical state could tolerate only portions of inner light.

Geometric elements in art, present in all regions and eras, and prevalent in herder and agricultural societies, were classified by shape and placed in a table by Lewis-Williams and Dowson, but the context of geometric 'likeness' did not reveal any meanings or structure. Misguided attempts by other authors to derive alphabetic writing from entoptics came closer to revealing how culture uses visual elements in the service of structural expression. Still they were misled by the general evolutionary expectation to find conscious 'development' of particular alphabets from certain entoptics and pictograms, as if prehistoric, pre-literate artists were groping towards conscious communicative refinement.

Some shapes are attached to a range of inherent meanings, but these are mutable and open-ended, inviting cultural determination, just as sounds and letters do.

For example, a spiral could mean snake, danger or growth. Even very young primates recoil from spirals, but not all spirals represent snakes or danger.

Abstracted shapes, colours and sounds also depend mainly on context for meaning. Rounded could mean sexually mature, such as a healthy woman of abundant means. South African self-professed archetypal novelist Etienne Leroux makes literate play of this archetypal form in an episode linking the response of a prize bull to a prize cow, to a prize wife driving a bouncy sports car past the paddock. Yet rounded could have a range of meanings. Once combined with other shapes, particular elements of its inherent and ascribed meanings are activated.

No entoptics are sufficiently attached to particular meanings to allow a grammar, or even rudiments of a universal alphabet. Since entoptics are typically fleeting, and morph into components of living, natural images such as antelope, fish, trees, and snakes, they are more likely to be building blocks of perception and expression, and not capable of expressing figures or archetypes except in context with other shapes (see geometric figures in a Scottish palette, and semi-geometric figures in a Bolivian disc at theme t12). Likewise amino acids code for life only as part of DNA. Entoptics are somewhat like electrons, protons, neutrons and other elemental forces in chemistry and physics, meaningful only in compounds, while compounds, analogous to individual animals or people in art, function in a group context. This context emerges as a flattened sphere.

When art historian Ernst Gombrich was accused of "an attempt to embrace history with theories of psychology and biology", he replied; "I claim that the formal characteristics of most human products, from tools to buildings and from clothing to ornaments, can be seen as manifestations of that sense of order which is deeply rooted in man's biological heritage. Organic life is governed by hierarchical structures which secure the interaction of internal functions, such as heartbeat and breathing, but also assist our adjustment to the environment. Here the role of the 'sense of order' is complementary to the perception of meaning, because the detection of food, mates or danger, first requires orientation in space and anticipation in time."

Since impulses to all our senses are replicated in our sensory organs and mind, even the raw material of experience is indirect. Our senses repeat their exposure to nature, and our brains hear only the reproduction or imprint. We therefore could only see and replicate at certain frequencies, particularly a range of pre-programmed shapes and meanings that are distinctive at those frequencies and patterns.

Archetype is likewise not directly present in nature or in the figures re-created in art, but 'translated' via what philosophy terms physis and dighe (see the Philosophy section).

We have an appetite for order within our range of sights, sounds, numbers and hypotheses.

Inspiration seems to work with what comes to the eye and hand, framing scenes with sufficient potential, shuffling or manoeuvring figures into the best possible position. Art thus emerges as a dialogue between inspiration and conscious considerations, just as finches weave slightly different nests to the same pattern, compromised to the best available material and location.

Structure in shapes

As in grammar, some underlying structural elements appear as 'punctuation marks' in art. The role of geometry extends beyond stylistic design or 'visual strength' to the core content of art and perception. Geometry also underlies concepts of direction and time as a continuum of structure at all levels of consciousness.

Figures, particularly their limb joints, are essentially angles. Artists habitually use limb joint angles to redirect the wandering eyes of viewers back to the conscious focal points of design, but are not aware of their subconscious structural roles. Limb joints such as hips (rumps in animals), shoulders, knees, elbows and feet, are revealed in mindprint as marking the conceptual galactic equators (see the Christian theme of the flight into Egypt at theme t12, and many other examples).

These formative or generative equators in art lie along two interlinked ovals of limb joints.

Some were traced incorrectly via feet in this study, before the role of all limb joints emerged.

Some were traced by angular point-to-point lines before their ovoid nature emerged while preparing the illustrations.

Plants, ropes and paths in rock art sometimes trace part of these secondary equators, hinting that artistic inspiration or expression hinge on these interlocking circles.

Nature uses a similar set of properties and shapes to express physics, chemistry and biology, including our organs of perception themselves. Nest shapes, named formlings in archaeology, are among the constant features of rock art, expressionism, cubism and some other styles, hovering between abstract geometrics and representation (or re-presentation, since natural features already express archetype, and natural images in art selectively re-express nature). Formlings could re-present physical items such as termite eggs, termite nest interiors (see theme t13), caves (see themes t6 and t15), beehives, honey cakes, coats (see themes t9 and t12), bags (see theme t15), clouds, fungi, intestines, huts, doors, domes, windows or tympanums (arches above lintels, see theme t11), or concept clusters related to these items, such as Taurus t1 t16 as a hanging tower of swallows' nests. Visual archetypes thus resemble grammar in requiring layers of constituent sounds, words and phrases to follow a combination of innate and conventional rules.

Formlings relate mainly to the background or canvas of perception. They invoke themes of a shelter, cave, boat or ark holding a range of species, including fish and giraffe. Formlings are not securely identified as an attribute of any particular archetype. They seem to appear in, around, or from the four structural points dividing the mindprint sequence, incidental with galactic features, thus in our conceptual framework rather than its figures. In cosmology, these four points are the two opposing galactic gates, where the galactic equator (Milky Way) crosses the ecliptic equator (sun's apparent orbit); and their two cardinals (squared points) at the galactic poles near the ecliptic between types Leo t12 and Virgo t11, and between types Aquarius t5 and Pisces t4.

These four structural points now co-incide with the current equinoxes and solstices. Our era is subconsciously celebrated as axial in some artworks in this study, notably by Pablo Amaringo (see theme t5 t21). Geometry also plays more localised roles among figurative types.

For example, anthropomorphic (half-human) artistic figures include swift people (see theme t1 t16), bee people, mantis people (t9), moth people, X people (t1 t16) and Y people (t14). Geomorphic (half shape, half figurative) rock art figures have a similar repertoire, such as cone people, H people (t15), V people, palette people, coat people, bell people and tree people. These kinds of figures are not types, and most of them could figure several types, while some tend to figure particular types.

Unrealistic features, such as forms, sky ropes, flight and deformities, are reminders that art is not realism, and that realism is not the function or measure of art. Individual, cultural and collective reality (more properly named perception) extends beyond conscious comprehension to geometric and conceptual projection and gestalt.

Different levels of perception and expression are subject to natural laws not yet fully studied, partly due to our ego-driven obsession with logic, causation, demonstrable laws, 'development' and supposed cultural evolution. Science studies mainly the acquired, conventionalised and learned elements of attributes, in a paradigm of cultural diffusion that seeks 'real' (consciously understood), quotable meaning in art and myth, and downplays eternal 'unreal' (subconsciously understood) or unsaid (but retrievable) meanings. Yet we have an entire set of attributes and geometry, or visual diction and grammar, reserved for expressing subconscious meaning.

No conspiracy, but no coincidence

Identification of the axial structure in art requires elimination of other possible explanations, such as coincidence, globally conscious convention, or after-images of manmade structures such as basket weaving spokes, wheels or hut lattices. After-images or retinal imprints could result from staring at any features in high contrast lighting, but these last briefly, and are typically overlain by different stares. Many cultures do not use latticed huts, and exposure of infants to axial artefacts, such as lampshades, is inconsistent.

Consistence, persistence and precision of the mindprint sequence and axial structure in all cultures, places and ages, rule out coincidence.

Artistic inspiration does not display its axial grid. Mindprint is not taught at art school. Perspective grids and radial grids are not axial, are instantly obvious, and not linked to a sequence of figures. No archaeology or art tradition hints at axial chalk lines, snap lines or ruled lines connecting eyes in rock art or formal art.

Astronomy as instigator of an axial grid is a red herring, since artists seldom paint scenes as a wheel (see an exception in dharma wheels). When they do, the mindprint geometric pole does not co-incide with the design centre. Mindprint axes converge on a point analogous to the ecliptic pole, which appears to daily rotate around the celestial pole, and is revealed only by the annual solar path.

The only viable explanation for mindprint is that it is inherent in our perception, inspiration and expressions, and that we have a spiritual compulsion for visual grammar.

The vortex of visual inspiration

Maurice Cotterell demonstrated that some artworks when duplicated and rotated over themselves, are picture generators (see the Mexican Palenque lid at t4). Boer prophet, Siener (Seer) van Rensburg spoke of a pain at the back of his head, perhaps involving the visual cortex, and "churning images... that stabilise, and figures emerge." (Prof AWG Raath and N van Zyl).

Nostradamus wrote of a vortex in his brass bowl of water, perhaps stirred to induce visions. Surreal artists such as Bosch and Dali emphasise limb joints, typically in translucent, coral (flesh-coloured) hues that some esoteric traditions label as a phase of incarnation or evolution of a spiritual 'prior race'.

Inspiration may well dictate only an oblique circle of limb joints, interlinked with its own inverse view, and bridged by a circle of eyes emerging from the limbs, forming a tri-circle ([)(]).

Visual inspiration seems to be initially free of groundlines or orientation planes before expression fixes inspiration to a canvas (see a Russian rock pavement engraving of four mindprint spheres at theme t12).

Adjacent spheres are usually linked two by two, hinting that spheres, like figures, also emerge from, or split into two vortices, each a potential double mindprint pair. If spherical vortices generate pictures, then artworks should retain some of the structure of their generation, as they seem to do by leaving many limb joints arranged along two ovoids crossing at two very specific points (labelled 'Gates'). Vortices in art are usually shown as bags at type Sagittarius t7 or the adjacent type Scorpius t8, both types flanking the galactic centre, identified in this study as perhaps an anchor point for initial artistic inspiration.

The other position in the sequence related to vortices, particularly bags and ropes, is directly opposite the galactic centre, at the galactic gate between types Gemini t15 and Taurus t1 Auriga, where the doubled galactic equators in artworks cross again (see ropes in the Seti 1 ceiling at theme t8, and ropes or energy lines in several images at theme t15).

One of the two overlapping galactic equators (marked out by limb joints) is usually nearly circular, while the equator of eyes is distorted into a starburst shape by apparent jostling to fit, as if they were secondary considerations. The doubled pair of galactic equators frames the central overlap area. Remnant vortex or 'churn' groups at the four galactic, structural corners of mindprint express the concept of becoming, or incarnation and excarnation.

Churn pillars appear in art at the two galactic gates, and on the two galactic polar axle points 90 degrees away (see Indian and other churn groups positioned at types Leo t12 and Aquarius t5 t20). Artists, and therefore all people, may perceive strings of objects in the shape of a pre-existent and inherent galactic concept, as if viewed from both sides of a sphere projected around the annual ecliptic axis, which is also an inherent concept. All shapes are pre-existent, as Plato wrote. A sphere crossed or formed by armilla (bands at various angles) is perhaps the primal archetypal structure.

Gestalt and Occam in parts, wholes and categories

People, animals and insects perceive parts of typical forms or events as complete but obscured or unfolding. Dynamic interplay of parts and wholes, or background and foreground, is noted in the Tao Te Ching in China about BC 155; 'A wheel is made of 30 spokes, but the space between the spokes determines the form of the wheel'.

Art is a function of gestalt at several figurative and structural levels. Visual memory grows rapidly in infants, and comes to play major roles in conscious perception. Yet visual memory populated by experience (including viewing of artworks), of necessity remains rooted in perception and thus in archetype, since nature, culture and art all express or use archetypal structure. Thus the foundation, building blocks and 'wallpaper' of perception are informed by archetypal elements, never by entirely random elements. Artists could express only archetype, despite conscious attempts by Salvador Dali and others to break the bonds of symbolism and thus of subconscious structuralism (the 'shirt is only a shirt' parade was well publicised).

Each figure in inspired art expresses part of a sequence and structure that is also partially recognised in nature and in the sky. Yet attempts to trace constellation outlines in an artwork soon dissolve in a maze of rotations, inversions, retrospects, contractions, extensions, hemispheric intrusions, blank spaces and extras.

Conceptual as well as geometric structure is at work in both expressions, but they speak different languages, requiring mutual translation. Artistic, mythical, cosmic and astronomical structures overlap but are not identical, and neither expression of archetype is perfect. If a perfect expression could be concocted, then only one myth cycle, one set of attributes, one history, one painting, one symphony and one star map would be required, all translatable into a stereotypical table of attributes. Archetype clothes its expressions in variety.

Gestalt is a function of our practical need to normalise or standardise variety into classes, and to separate apparent categories and levels of figures.

Structural anthropologist Levi-Strauss found "underlying patterns of thought in human activity", and perception to be based on "binary opposites". His opposites are extended in this study beyond isolated pairs of "goods to think". Pairs of opposites on a conscious or even symbolic level remain superficial. Geometric diagrams, images, contexts and rituals expressing sets of related binaries are more complex than fragmentary one-on-one lists, as even the familiar format of kinship diagrams prove.

Sets of opposites extend into the realm of 'woolly logic' and intuition, which is as rigorous, but quicker than conscious computation. Intuition applies conceptual gestalt to sets and between sets. If this process were conscious, it would be a full-time occupation. We do not have the luxury of plumbing the subconscious depths of characterisation and ensemble in every scene or image.

Occam's razor (cutting away unnecessary detail) is the flip side and necessary companion of gestalt. Too much assumption based on too much detail lead to overload and some erroneous deductions. Gestalt and Occam both, as multiplier and divider, adder and subtractor of conscious detail, assume underlying order, largely a load of meaning not instantly relevant, and with some superficial imperfection. Without our access to prior order, wholes and parts would be chaotic constructs on a trial and error basis. There is more practical and scientific gain in assuming holistic order, partially expressed in self-defined sets such as art, than in wilfully assuming arbitrary scenes or man-made, cultural order.

It is essentially human and cultural to imprint meaning by sequences and constellations of categories to express a subtext. However it is a function of nature and archetype that certain shapes, textures, sounds and numbers are disposed to certain meanings, as several hieroglyphic sets demonstrate.

Inspiration works in wondrous ways with any sets that come to hand.

Structural disguise

All recognisable attributes are potentially iconic in terms of gender, age, posture, texture, context, proximity, alignment or grouping. Four or five predictable attributes attached to each of twelve figures, in sequence, as opposing pairs on six axes, could be taken as the minima of a structure that raises attributes to character types. It clears the boundaries of chance, but also introduces some camouflage.

In high-similarity camouflage, labelled 'blending', visual, auditory or textual objects and their surroundings are made nearly indistinguishable. (Behrens; Art, design and Gestalt theory, 1998). This kind of camouflage is at work in natural and artistic scenes. Types are as invisible as a person or a dress in a crowd, unless some of their features are unique, familiar or pointed out.

Experiments with patterns of dots and lines found certain gestalts to be enhanced by our innate tendencies to constellate (group) elements by similarity, proximity and continuation, thus seeking structural economy (Max Wertheimer; Theory of Form, 1923). Such tendencies are inborn, not learned, yet complex. "Interplay of grouping tendencies is far from simple... judgments about similarity or proximity are comparative, in intricate compositions. Parts may connect by one grouping tendency (colour, proximity or continuation) but disconnect by others (shape, size or direction)". (Behrens, 1998).

Artists embraced gestalt theory in that it seemed to offer scientific validation of principles of composition. A French byname for gestalt theory is 'la psychologie de la forme'. Due to its emphasis on flat abstract patterns, structural economy and implicit nature, gestalt theory became associated with our eternal tendency towards 'aestheticism', the assumption that, like music and architecture, art is essentially abstract design.

Ellen Lupton and J Abbott Miller write in Design Writing Research, 1996; "Design is, at bottom, an abstract, formal activity" in which the "text [subject matter] is secondary, added only after the mastery of form". Aestheticism as a conscious programme was anticipated in 1851 by John Ruskin in his book Stones of Venice, initiating the arts and crafts movement; "Arrangement of colours and lines is an art analogous to the composition of music, and messages or rhetoric.

The strongest layer of structural camouflage in art and even in icons and emblems (which strive to be blatantly obvious) is the human habit of viewing art and cultural expressions as man-made, and its

entirely independent of the representation of facts." (Behrens 1998).

Abstract expressionism followed this concept. The aesthetic movement emphasised differences between representation and design. "As music is the poetry of sound, so is painting the poetry of sight, and the subject matter has nothing to do with harmony of sound or of colour." (James Whistler; The gentle art of making enemies, 1878. The movie 'Mr Bean goes to America' makes subtle pay of the title of this book by casting the owner of Whistler's painting of his mother, as a military general aiming to make friends in the conformist art world).

The conscious principles of design are now revealed as limited to vague spatial balance. These programmes and principles pale in comparison with the elegant complexity of the universal structure and archetypal 'programme' of artistic inspiration. For all the intellectualisation of the last two centuries, art continues its various functions in impulse, compulsion, visual stimulation, healing, social comment, iconic conversation and structural expression, changing merely in stylistic texture. The core functions and content of art remain blissfully unaffected by stylistic and conceptualised elaboration. Artists are unaware of the standard structure of inspiration, and the very few who may be, do not draw attention to it. Their focus is on society, politics and other functions. Cognitive elements like styling develop, diverge and recede, much like genetic traits, but subconscious elements remain constant in all ages and cultures, much like DNA structure.

Figurative and design similarities worldwide are ascribed in archaeology and art history to natural constants, such as hunting and ritualised experience, but the repertoire of design and iconography has never been sufficiently studied to reveal the subconscious standard and its priority over practical considerations.

In the preface to the 2000 edition of Art and Illusion, Ernst Gombrich argues that the concept of mimesis, or natural verisimilitude, is a misunderstanding; no image resembles nature, and all operate on visual conventions. What Gombrich calls 'Töpfer's Law' dictates that each image of a face has an expressivity and individuality, no matter how badly drawn.

Lichtenberg and Rorscharch used our capacity for projection in various ways. Gombrich tellingly points out that reaction, comprehension and expression are not the same as communication. Art is myth, not structure as developed from accumulated 'knowledge', independent of nature, and diffused by cultural transfer. This historicised and developmental paradigm is subtly but consistently misleading. Spiritual inspiration and experience is structural, not accumulated as technology is, and retrieved from an incorruptible source.

Psychological structure

Mindprint expands the context of the mind mirrors of Freud and Jung, in laying bare the content and structure of our highest spiritual expressions in art. Culture is as much subject to conscious dissection as chemistry or physiology is, but requires a non-mechanistic paradigm.

Czech psychiatrist Stanislav Grof developed transpersonal psychology after the psychoanalytic tradition of Freud, Jung, Alfred Adler, Otto Rank, Wilhelm Reich and others. Yet Grof cast his view of ailments and treatment in causal, mechanistic and fundamental terms, writing that people could access "memories of historical [?], collective, cross-cultural, karmic, phylo-genetic, and evolutionary [?] events [?]" [question marks added in this study].

Did history shape, and continue to shape archetypal content? Could history be read as the result of the supposed evolution of our consciousness? Or do we access archetype, pre-existent and embedded in the structure of creation, as in the Greek, Vedic and esoteric paradigm? Grof found that memories were organised archetypally and thematically, supporting the premise of this study that history, characterisations, figures and attributes are not cumulative. Yet Grof devalues archetype to a social agreement in his assertion that "traumatic experiences are connected to qualitatively and archetypally similar experiences from our collective past". He thus discounts the function of structure prior to human experience, and implies that early man had fewer archetypes, based on a smaller pool of experience; that archetypes became more standardised and elaborated by learning; and that the human subtext remains subject to further experience. These assumptions are not supported in this study.

Instead, expressions of archetype are probably static, yet as varied as genetics, incalculably older than humanity and slowly mutating through its inherent varieties, prompted by conditions and mutations in other life forms.

We always express our visual structure and content by artefacts, figurines, body paint, jewels, tools, art and ritualised behaviour. We have not lost or gained any media of expression, merely multiplied their applications.

Archetypal principles, described by various labels in various cultures, are defined by Grof and Richard Tarnas as "not, as the modern mind had assumed, wholly nominalistic, intra-psychic factors. They are not just categories of the human psyche, unconsciously projected onto a separate external reality... rather, as in Jung's later formulation of the psychoid character of archetype, they are creative powers inherent in reality, or metaphysical and cosmological principles, ordering factors and archetypal images in the psyche." This paradigm also informs the present study.

Hillman hoped to restore "a more aesthetic and mythic mode of being", using psycho-analysis and 're-sacralisation'. "You can't open your mouth without a god speaking," he wrote (see Pan or Kokopelli as a flautist and a discussion of Ian Anderson at t6). Relevant to art, Hillman may as well have written, 'you can't draw a picture without archetype appearing.'

The structure in our hands

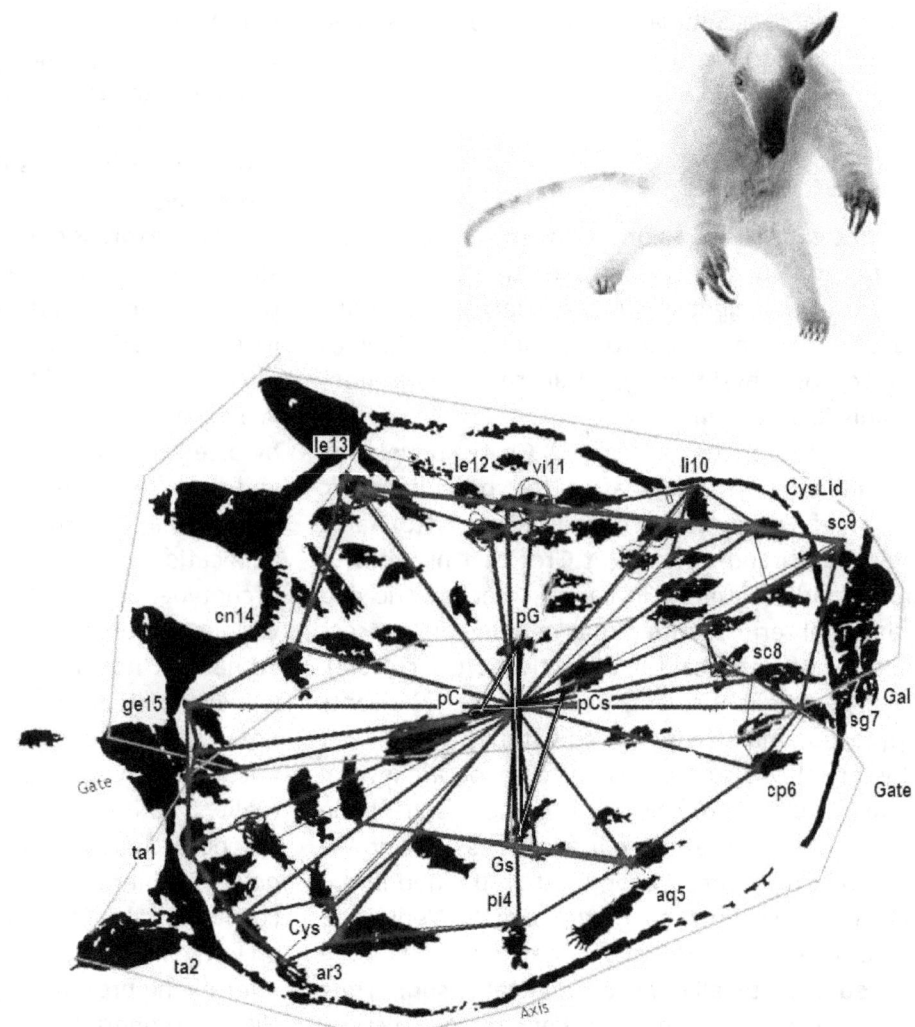

Nerve endings or lymph nodes in our palms follow a circular sequence related to the structure of our bodies, perception and artistic expression (palm reflexology areas by Nete Burnford, Theosophical Society SA. Mindprint analysis by Edmond Furter). We experience reality and make artefacts in our own image.

Polar markers are uncertain, but the horizontal plane of an extended hand (here vertical) seems to tag the orientation of human hands to Age Aries, which is also the orientation of astrology. This does not imply that our hands, or the craft of astrology had developed at any particular time. Some conceptual and structural aspects of cosmology co-incide with the orientation of some aspects of human hands, and with the era when the spring equinox had precessed (moved backwards) to the middle or the start of seasonal Aries, about BC 850 or BC 150. Astrology recognised the primacy of Aries even when spring was still in Taurus, and after it had left Aries.

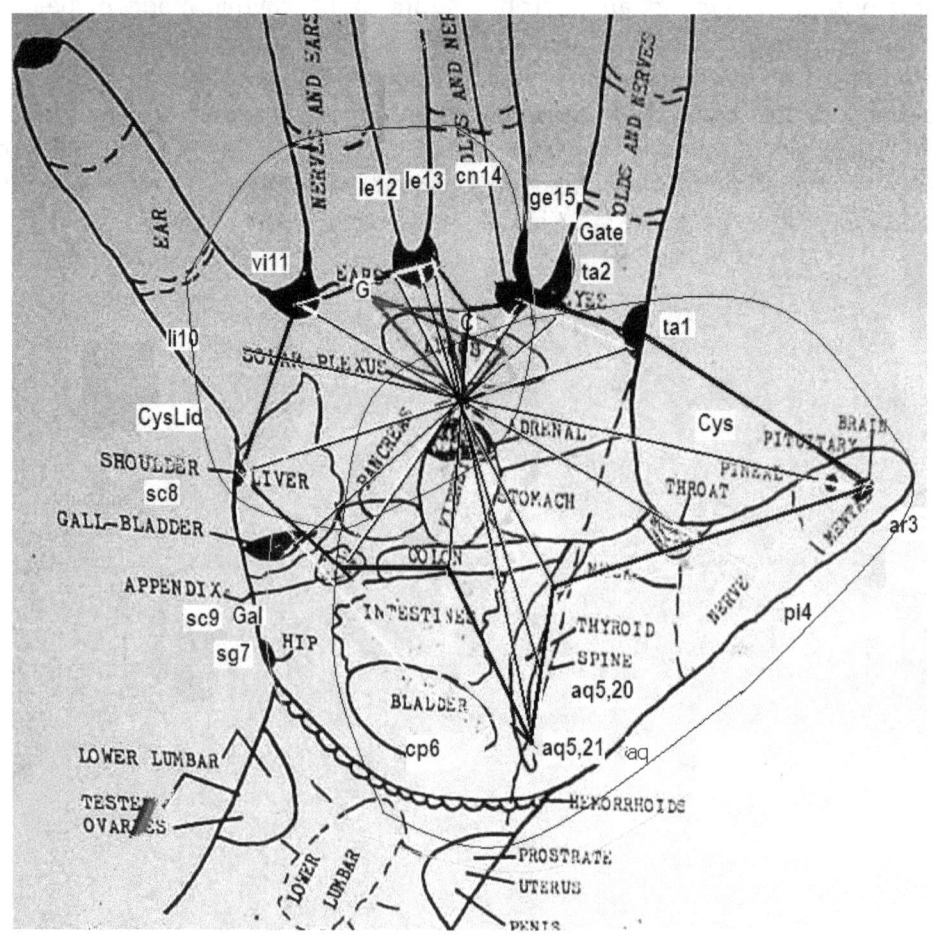

Footprints of time

Type Scorpius t9 as an antbear (aardvark porcine) behind its track as a fish pool, a kind of palette or cartouche (Lesotho, Botshabelo fish pool track. SA Archaeological Bulletin. Mindprint analysis by Edmond Furter). It resembles the Egyptian Seth animal, opponent of Horus in the marshes, who also sometimes appears in this position in the sequence, but more often at t15 or t7, on which axis this figure and its footprint stand.

Type Scorpius t9 in myth could appear as a lawgiver (an attribute shared with the adjacent type Libra t10), and in some myth and astrology is linked to Scorpius as its claws.

Palettes and painted pebbles also express the concept of an environmental footprint (see type Libra t10 as a lord of nature in Egyptian art at theme t10. See African pebble palettes with fish at theme t8). Inspired artworks are moulded on a spherical concept, with integrated northern and southern features.

Celestial polar markers on a fish tail and fish mouth, on the probable horizontal plane of the work, lie between type Gemini t15 and type Taurus t1, on the gate. This is also the position of the current midsummer sun, thus tagging the inspiration as Age Pisces-Aquarius, our current era.

A cosmic palm

Type Aries t3 and type Taurus t2 as the two 'eyes' of a finger or mountain peak, holding a model of a ritual scene (Peruvian Moche jug in a hand shape. Mindprint analysis by Edmond Furter). Handprint and footprint myth is global, expressed in tales of yeti, the hand of fate, and the Bible's 'mene tekel, weighed and found too light'. The corresponding point in astrology is the Scorpius claw star Graffias, opposite the Taurus Pleiades and also on the ecliptic, a better calibrator than the head star. The Graffias concept and its place in the stellar myth map marks the Arabic moon station Iklil, Crown of the Forehead, in India named Mitra, Friend, one of the Adityas, figured as a ridge or row (RH Allen) as it is here, half a world away in Peru. Type Scorpius t9 and Libra t10 Lupus (Wolf), here figured as a wolf, are often one figure. Between Taurus and Aries lies the Mystic Basket (see a Roman sarcophagus at theme t11) opposite the Basket Lid between Scorpius and Libra in Lupus, wolf.

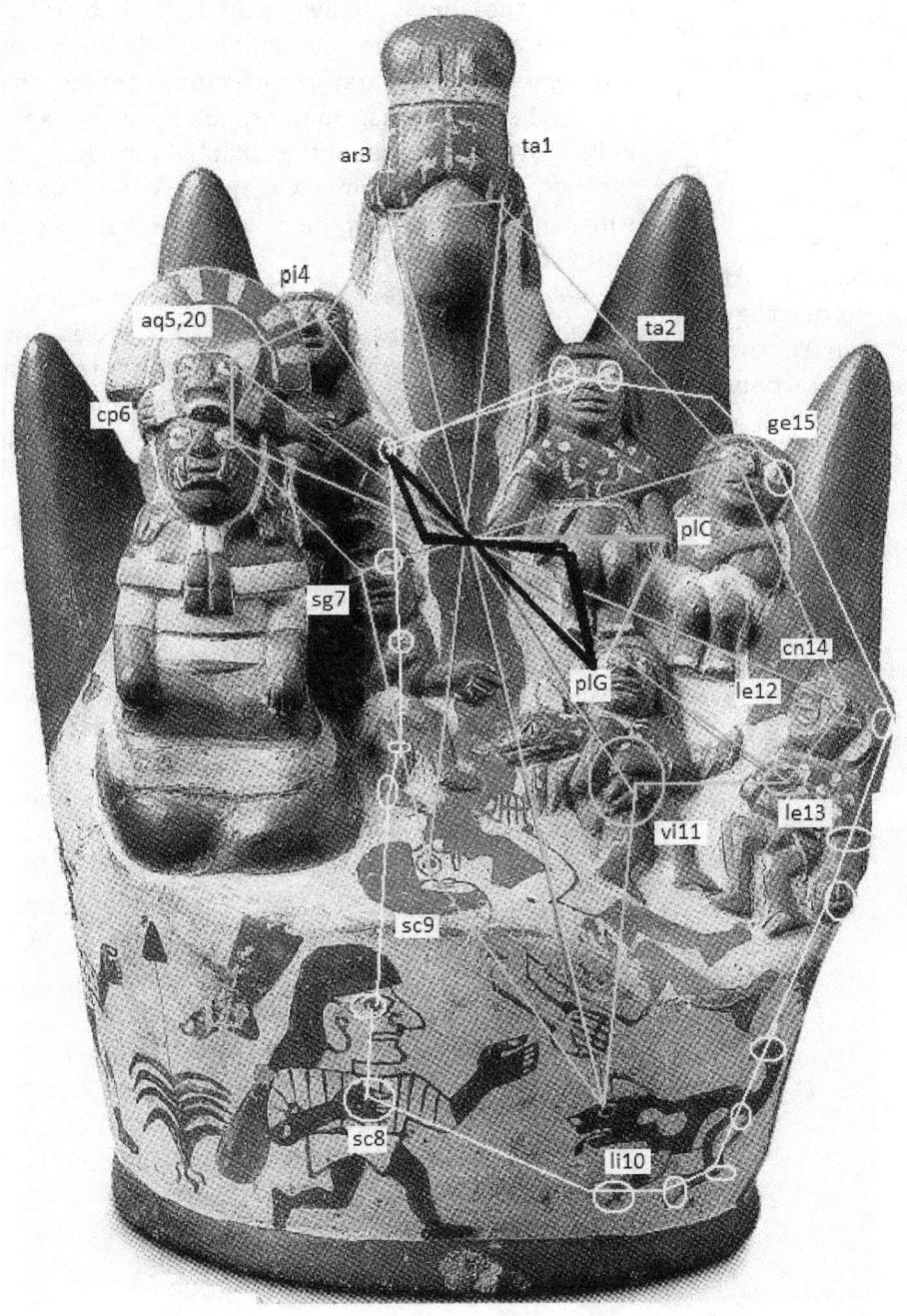

Our inner and outer structures converge

Chapter C

Since we see with our eyes and brains, and shape artworks by eye-hand co-ordination, it is worth tracing the structure in our iris and palm reflexology points. Esoterica label this approach of seeking the nature and application of a resource as inherent in the resource itself, as 'signatures'.

We think with our bodies as much as our brains, including temperature homeostasis, stomach glands and a range of involuntary impulses. Comparing the artistic axial arrangement to the iris, and to the sequence of organs and limb joints in the palm, reveal about eight commonalities; (types Aries t3 Brain-Brain, Taurus t2 Ear-Sinus, Taurus t1 Neck-Nerves, Gemini t15 Lung-Lung, Leo t13 Heart- Heart, Virgo t11 Womb-Womb, Scorpius t9 t8 intestinal, Sagittarius t7 and Capricornus t6 intestinal, and Sagittarius t7 Hip-Hip). The four 'galactic' structural points may relate to limb joints in reflexology, as they do in art (see the Statistics section). Yet there is some projectional or 'canvas' disjuncture between each set, since irises are flat and symmetrical, while palms are flat and asymmetrical.

TYPE EYE PALMRIGHT ART

TYPE	EYE	PALMRIGHT	ART
t3 ar	Brain	PituiPineal	Neck
t2 ta	Ear	Sinus	Twisted
t1 ta	Neck	Nerve/Eye	Twisted
gate	shouldr	struct	SHOULDR
t15 ge	Lung	Lung	Bag, rope
t14 cn	Kidny	_____	Ingress
t13 le	Heart	Sol/Heart	Heart
t12 le	Spleen	Intest	Inverted
poleG	hand?	structure	ELBOW?
t11 vi	Abdom	Womb	Womb
t10 li	Leg ?	____	Arms
t9 sc	Testes	Liver	Bent
t8 sc	Rectm	Gall	Strong
galax	back	structure	HIP
t7 sg	Livr?	ApndxPancr	Bag
t6 cp	Spine	KidnyAdren	Tree/Ingress
t5 aq	Mouth	Colon	Supine
t 5aq	Nose	Thyroid	ManLarge
axis	skull	structure	JAW
t4 pi	Eye/Brain	Nerve	Squat.

The spatial arrangement of organs in the body could also be listed, but since bodies are rounded and symmetrical, the sequence involves several planes. Apparent disjuncture of links between two-dimensional (linear) sequences of iris nerve endings and body nerve endings, follow a set of two jumps and inversions, forming an analemma (figure of eight or infinity curve). Nature also traces such a curve by a spot of sunlight through a pinhole, or shadow from a cliff or pillar at the same hour during a year. The Tuthmose 3 tomb plan's sequence of Duat hours and directions likewise follow two jumps in a cardinal (crosswise) adjustment (see theme t12). His tomb orientations reveal an ideal rectangle as in Sed festival courts. Likewise mathematical fractions could be traced in human neuro physiology, just as a standard set of fractions is consciously mapped by the Horus eye sigil, and consciously used in Albrecht Durer's body proportions.

Among the medical evidence that healing is transmitted by pure sympathetic vibration or attunement to holographic structure, are healing songs, chants, dances, rhythms, colours and shape-imbued water (homeopathy). Kabbalists label this function 'identification'. No man is an island, sufficient unto himself, nor an individual unique unto himself.

Bio-feedback devices developed from radiology, synthesised our impulse to heal by frequencies. The health applications of micro-electronics are relevant to this study of a standard visual structure imprinted in art, for demonstrating that a standard physical vibrational structure is imprinted on and by every person. Bio-feedback operates on the principles that particular conditions of ill health co-incide with specific deviations from the pattern; that deviations are identifiable with known diseases; and that a nudge from the collective healthy pattern coaxes the body into rectifying the malady. The developer, William Nelson, has a circuitous explanation involving subatomic particle vibrations. Thousands of Scio, Rife and other operators worldwide know that the patient does not have to be hooked up for analysis and therapy, a hundred times more comprehensive, faster and accurate than conventional medical diagnosis. All the device operator needs is a patient's birth date, time and place, name, and a few biographical details.

Biofeedback therefore includes automated astrological analysis. The device also reads the standard pattern derived from a database of thousands of healthy people, and nudges the identified patient's pattern towards the standard.

This study should consider only two of these contested issues; there is a standard suite of human frequencies, identifying each organ and system; and every person is a variant expression of this standard, like a fingerprint, iris, face, DNA or hair colour. All human hair is a combination of the same materials, yet every colour is sufficiently different for a spectroscopic scanner to identify an individual in a crowd from a sample. By extension, healing could therefore operate on an individual, social or global level.

A work of art could have no therapeutic value if either the archetypal sequence or structure, or the querent, were not represented and compared. Random images, random spacing, or galleries without viewers, have no value to people or to a culture. We have to 'plug in' and visual art is ideal to initiate this intimate engagement.

Archetype dressed as culture

Concepts such as the Egyptian tep zepi (before time, or outside time) indicate that archetype is not a Greek invention, nor a figment of philosophical or psychological imagination, but a consistent recognition that we glimpse an encompassing cause in the effects of nature and culture. The duat, or underworld populated by figures, formulae and routes, is an intermediate consciousness, perhaps our nearest approach to the unknowable structure of time, space and energy.

Archetype does not directly translate into nature, but does so via a function that could loosely be termed structure, shape, or physis. "Physis enables nature to speak on behalf of being. Physis is simultaneously the potentiality and manifestation of nature, logos and dighe (ruler and organ). As physis, archetypes are the potenti that rule and organise the manifestation of rules and organisations. Archetypes employ nature, gods, heaven and earth to bring the essence of man to the fore. The essence of these phenomena is united and organised in rules and patterns, as an ensemble of things. Archetypes thus organise man and nature, earth and gods, man and gods, heaven and earth, into an ensemble so that they mirror each other's essence." (GW van Eeden; A phenomenological analysis of archetypes, 1993).

The processes of Original Power or Being transforming concepts into a rule and pattern that underlies our essence, is named the human subtext in this study. Direct rational access to our essence is not possible. Our conception of timeless essence is tied to time-bound experience, yet our essence "manifests in its entirety in every experience, hidden from us, bound to imagination (a combination of intuition and sensing). Essence comprises its own logic, rules and recurring patterns. Man is constantly becoming what he already was." (GW Van Eeden, 1993).

The Egyptian term 'coming forth by day', as in the title of the so-called Book of the Dead, applies in this context. In the simplest possible terms, according to Wikipedia, archetype is "a pattern of behaviour, a prototype on which others are patterned or emulated, a Platonic philosophical idea of pure forms which embody the fundamental characteristics of a thing... patterns of thought or image, universally present in individual psyches. Archetypes are constantly recurring symbols or motifs in literature, art or mythology." These motifs have never been listed in a comprehensive context. First used in English in the 1540s, the word archetype derives from Latin archetypum, Latinisation of Greek archetupon and adjective archetupos, first-moulded, a compound of arche, beginning or origin; and tupos, pattern, model or type. Archetypal hypotheses include Plato's 'ideas' as pure mental forms, imprinted in the soul prior to its role in the physical world. In the seventeenth century Francis Bacon used the word. Sir Thomas Browne listed archetypes by symbolic names, demonstrating the double life of concepts on conscious and subconscious levels. Archetypes are collective in the sense that they embody fundamental characteristics rather than specific peculiarities, as Jung found. This study demonstrates that archetypal characteristics contain specific but optional 'peculiarities', explaining their variations.

The concept of psychological archetypes was advanced by Jung about 1919 to interpret observations, as it is used in this study. A group of memories and interpretations associated with an archetype is labelled a complex, in this study labelled a type, abbreviated by a zodiac equivalent and a 't' number (such as Pisces t4), or with a decanal 'determinant' added (such as type Pisces t4 Pegasus, or Cetus, or Andromeda).

Jung treated archetypes as psychological organs, analogous to physical organs in that both are morphological (shaped) constructs of nature. He initially saw psychic 'organs' as products of natural evolution, contradicting Plato's identification of archetypes as pre-existent to the world. This study finds no evolution in the expression of archetypes in the art of any known region or age. Evolution is therefore not relevant to art or culture, and confined to macro bio-physical cycles much longer than the brief history of culture or mankind. Changes in material culture are more firmly linked to mutation, population growth and specialisation than physical evolution. 'Development' is prevalent among the assumptions of every aspect of every science, revealing evolution itself as a paradigmatic archetype.

Archetypal events

In instances of synchronicity, the usual division of mind and matter is notably transcended, revealing the underlying unity of our inner and outer worlds. Psyche and cosmos then appear to be two aspects of a cosmic psyche, or undivided reality. Man is the "unwitting instrument of unconscious impulses and complexes... [from] a seething cauldron of instincts, whose sublimated expression lie behind humanity's most elevated cultural aspirations and achievements."

The collective subconscious is a framework for the assignment of meaning. (Jung, 1955; Mysterium Coniunctionis). Archetype manifests via 'formative principles of behaviour patterns, dispositions that continually influence our thoughts, feelings, and actions.'

Mindprint demonstrates this framework of meaning and manifestation in our visual and mythic recreations. Artists express the basic cycle and structure in almost every work and incidentally demonstrate synchronicity by clothing types in related conscious meanings.

Myth lends names and attributes to people and events, as in the universal practice of naming children for heroes, kings, prophets, apostles, gods and places.

Attempts to 'tie them down' to initial, original characters or events follow a false trail. Eliade wrote in The sacred and the Profane; "Myth is an example of primordial time, since it seldom has a beginning or end." (See supposed 'predictions' of the 2001 9/11 terror attacks on New York in art by Valentine, Mutwa and Morgan-Lefay at theme t1 t16).

Events could never explain mythical events, wrote De Santillana and Von Deschend. Yet some events, such as the New York terror attacks, rehearse legendary events such as the Tower of Babel, and express eternal, spiritual, emblematic episodes such as a city struck by fire and discord. Archetype manifests in events as much as it does in famous or infamous personalities, myth and art.

De Santillana cites many philosophers on the irrational logic of mythic expression; "mythical figures invade history under counterfeit presentments, and subtly shape it to their own ends... if one tried to pinpoint them as persons and things, they would melt before his eyes. They reveal their nature as functions of the general order of things."

Myth also demonstrates a 'vast complex of variables, yet containing recurrence, thus eternity and infinity, one of the preoccupations of philosophy and art.' (Umberto Eco; Infinity of lists). There is no original myth, and no school, book, club or secret society that teaches ultimate truth, only variant manifestations of eternal structure. "Myth is not a text whose original version, unaltered and true, must be determined.

Myth may be transmitted in ways other than the spoken word... masks, statues, architecture, music, choreography, body markings, are all related to a coherent system of signs." (Yves Bonnefoy; American, African and Old European Mythologies). Apparently infinite variety in expression is reducible to an ideal formula, though no artwork could be a perfect or prime example.

Our emotional constitution

For all its philosophical complexity, interpretation of myth is a passive or receptive activity. Jung (1945) wrote that emotion is not instigated by our activity, but by events that happen to us. Heidegger wrote of experience as something that "befalls, strikes, overwhelms and transforms us. We undergo experience."

Art and myth have similar functions; to express structure that invokes individuation or self-identification and attunement of our body, mind and emotion to our roles in nature and culture.

Individuation, the ultimate human task, is to more fully express who, what, where, when and how we are, individually, socially and collectively. Myth and thus art have a "formative or formatting function." This study confirms that structure enables meaning. The communication scientists who coined the motto 'the medium is the message' never imagined the extent of its application in art, nor the extent of structural codes in art and media in the broad sense.

Archetype may well be pure structure, devoid of content, a kind of macrocosmic set of mannequins of shapes and types, a stage marked by axes, populated by endless combinations of its repertoire in multiple layers of scale. Likewise energy, chemistry, biology, kingdoms and histories express macro and micro levels of structure in waves and particles, usually in both, attracting and releasing energy in what physics and esoterica both label as light. The wonder of human consciousness is that we could consciously contemplate part of our ordered cosmos and our place in it, with the aid of flashes of archetypal light.

This study offers ample evidence that the conscious part of our consciousness is capable of describing substantial parts our collective subconscious expressions of archetype in various media, and equally capable of turning a blind eye to natural order. We like to paint ourselves as imposers of logical order, despite our emotional and sub-ordinate constitution.

Literate structure

Literature science recognises archetypes in recurrent images, symbols or patterns. Symbols are more effective than direct statements, as politicians, artists, journalists and advertisers know. Mottoes dress up their motives in typology, such as soap opera characters, to activate the power of structure and emotion. Allegory, figures of speech, parables and extended metaphors are the essence of wit and motivation. Writers sell the sizzle, not the steak, as the advertising adage goes. Myth and legend appeal to our range of emotions and our sense of identity, not to our 'knowledge'.

Literature formulises myth, casting fragments of realism and plausible surreality in the mould of suggestive structure. Gestalt operates in myth as the 'of course' factor in archetypal motifs of apparently infinite variety. Stories by Rider Haggard (She who must be obeyed), Arthur Conan Doyle (Lost world), and Hollywood scriptwriters trade in episodic gestalt by dishing up riddles that invite easy solutions. Doyle's and Haggard's novels, written from the hip (on hearsay and wishful thinking) are "exciting narrative apparently devoid of conscious psychological intentions, [which] interest psychologists most of all," wrote Hubert.

"Such a tale is constructed against a background of unspoken psychological assumptions, and the more unconscious the author is of them, the more this background reveals itself in unalloyed purity to the discerning eye."

Without archetypal elements or implicit sequences, stories, dramas and movies would be bland, quirky, not therapeutic and unpopular, like a genetic mutation without collective advantage. If icons arose from arbitrary correspondences and diffusion, they should have developed ever larger cultural differences. Yet this study finds only superficial stylistic elements to be divergent and localised. Core content and structure are more consistent than archaeology or art history have ever acknowledged.

Structure in verses, hours and stars

A Mishnah (Verse) of Jewish wisdom literature by Rabbi Judah HaNasi (Prince, thus a descendant of David) demonstrates the allusive power of a deceptively simplistic list of attributes. Mishnah 5;6 is a microcosm, or universe in a verse;

"Ten things were created on the eve of Sabbath at twilight;
Earth mouth
Well mouth
She-ass mouth
Rainbow
Manna
Rod (of Moses)
Shamir [dragon insect fluid]
Text [scroll]
Writing [core content]
Tables [of law or creation]
And the sepulchre of Moses
And the ram of Abraham
And the destroying (spirits)
And tongs made with tongs."

The set probably refers to hourly asterisms (star markers or hourly decans), recited from east to west. Six are seen in the first watch, and up to ten during a winter's night, with two or three added from memory of other seasons. Some of these are wilfully cryptic and cultural in a tribal sense. Some common explanations are added in brackets, and some esoteric explanations in square brackets.

Emblematic lists are typical of wisdom literature, as in Zoroastrian Persia ('three things are good to think, and four gladden the heart of philosophers'). Ten things require two to make the lowest mathematically pliable hour sequence of twelve, but here three or four are added instead, hinting that more than stars or hours are at stake. Wisdom literature typically sanitises and disguises esoteric structure in decorative turns of phrase, poetic flourish, and dramatic punchline delay, all in aid of memory and sustained repetition. The point is not in 'knowledge' but in structure.

Obvious answers to riddles usually invoke small contradictions that lure hearers or readers to better answers. Decans offer the initial answer, here listed by their better known zodiac anchors, by retrograde (reverse) recital;

**Mishnah 5:6, astrological identification
(Edmond Furter; Archaeo astronomy lecture
to the SA Astronomical Society, 2009);**

Ten things were created on the eve of Sabbath at twilight,
Pisces Pegasus rectangle as square mouth /spring
Aquarius and Cetus spout as round well mouth
Capricornus sea-goat as she-ass mouth
Sagittarius galactic equator as rainbow
Scorpius galactic centre as manna
Scorpius with Libra as rod (of Moses)
Libra Serpens /Virgo Bootes shamir [spirits]
Virgo as a rolled scroll of text
Leo or Cancer as writing
Cancer or Gemini as tables (of law or creation)
Gemini as sepulchre of Moses
Taurus or Aries Perseus as ram of Abraham
Aries Cetus and Triangulum as tongs with tongs.
? as destroying (spirits) [move to shamir at centre].

The fourteenth item could be a polar or galactic feature, or a Rabbinical explanation of the enigmatic shamir, more invitations to look beyond night hours or the calendar and deeper into the relevant Biblical texts with their own mild contradictions, as Witztum and Rips demonstrated in statistical analysis of an interspaced subtext (M Drosnin; Bible Code).
Re-numbered to mindprint types, the little list reveals the affinitive power of simplistic attributes. Each "thing" is ambiguous to two adjacent zodiac constellations, thus describing decanal asterisms bridging the familiar constellations. Some Babylonian, Indian, Arabic, Egyptian and Greek decans, or lunar mansions, are explicitly identified as border markers dividing constellations (RH Allen; Star names and their meanings). Night hours offer an entire 'lunar' (celestial) astrology, as in the Chinese horary (hourly) system. Decanal identification should suffice to illustrate that fourteen things in a circular sequence require as many dividing borders;

Mishnah 5:6 with decanal borders and visual attributes;

t4 t19 Pisces and t5 Aquarius Pegasus; earth
(see paradise gardens at t4 t19)
t5 t20 Aquarius Pegasus and Cetus spout; well
(see ocean churns at t5)
t5 t21 Aquarius and t6 Capricornus; zebra
(see equines and painted skin at t5)
t6 Capricornus and t7 Sagittarius; Cygnus?
[ingressed to the poles?]
t7 Sagittarius and t8 Scorpius Galactic equator;
rainbow (see spheres at t7)
t8 Scorpius and t9 Scorpius Galactic centre; manna
(see dots at t8)
t9 Scorpius claws and t10 Libra Serpens; staff
(see staffs at t9 and t10)
t10 Libra Serpens and t11 Virgo Bootes; claws
(see V and W postures at t10)
t11 Virgo and t12 Leo Ursa; text scroll
(see wombs at t11)
t13 Leo heart and t14 Cancer Ursa Minor; writing
(celestial pole as unrolling scroll)
t14 Cancer and t15 Gemini; tables of cosmic law
(see time at t14 and creators at t15)
t15 Gemini and t1 Taurus Orion; sepulchre
(see underworld churns and towers at t15 and t16)
t2 Taurus and t3 Aries Perseus; ram
(see spring sacrifices at t2)
t3 Aries Triangulum and t4 Pisces; tongs
(see caduceus necks at t3 t18)
[t3; destroying (spirits), moved to t10 -t11 as claws].

These bridging decans are readily reduced to twelve conceptual attributes.

Mishnah 5:6 with concepts, listed from t1;

t1 t2 Taurus sacrifice
t3 t18 Aries twined caduceus
t4 t19 Pisces rectangle or cross
t5 t20 Aquarius water
t5 t21 Aquarius equine (horse)
t6 Capricornus ? [ingressed]
t7 Sagittarius rainbow, galaxy, flood
t8 t9 Scorpius healer
t10 Libra staff
t11 Virgo rolled
t12 t13 Leo core, unrolling or inversion
t14 Cancer unrolled (time)
t15 Gemini tomb or ark.

Since hours go round in circles, contrasting each with its opposite reveals another layer of the holographic Mishnah riddle;

t2 Taurus v t9 Scorpius, sacrifice v healer
t3 Aries v t10 Libra, caduceus v staff
t4 Pisces v t11 Virgo, cross v circle
   (paradise v womb)
t5 Aquarius v t13 Leo, horse v heart (flow v roll)
t6 Capricornus v t14 Cancer, ?[ingress] v time
t7 Sagittarius v t15 Gemini, flood v ark.

Axial opposites in art likewise counterbalance twelve, fourteen or sixteen figures' eyes (with one heart and one womb instead) with the eyes of opposing and complementary figures. Any sequence of attributes, particularly closed circular sequences, is a reminder that archetype expresses the one and the many, in each figure and in the whole. Each artwork or myth compensates for lack of inclusion of all the optional attributes of each type, by completion of the cycle and its geometry.

Alchemical writers demonstrate their reliance on emblems as a kind of visual opera. Myth, literature and music use a similar range of semi-conscious tools in composition (repetition, inversion, extension, condensation, phrasing, harmony, counterpoint, modulation, transposition, intrusion, citation, and so on). Art uses similar tools on conscious, semiconscious (symbolic) and subconscious levels. Artistic design inversions extend from direct visual balance, to invisible but implied inversion of parts of the conceptual sphere. Art does not tolerate a row of figures, however well rendered or styled. Visual art has to be composed at a conscious 'story' level, with some visible geometric rigour, and a very particular sequential, attributional, axial, planar (horizontal) and polar structure at subconscious level (see De Cosimo's Discovery of honey, in the Artistic structure section).

Our visual set and structure is an involuntary hologram, beyond the conscious ability of artists to learn or teach. Art as a concept map is analogous to myth, cards, cosmology and star maps, but does not duplicate any of these cultural expressions, even when ostensibly illustrating a myth, story, emblem or zodiac.

Mindprint dictates some extensions of the Jungian paradigm of the collective subconscious. It is more densely populated, more exacting, and more persistently present in our eyes, bodies, hands, minds, thoughts, behaviour, stories and artefacts, than even psychology imagined.

The structure in our cosmos

A star map in northern hemispheric ecliptic projection and grid (Skychart version 3.0.1.6, here precessed to 2016. Mythic constellation variants, division meridians and mindprint labels by Edmond Furter). No observer could see this view of the sky, yet it reflects the structure of cosmic concepts as expressed in most artworks, of all cultures and Ages. Ecliptic projection is the most holistic translation of the concepts of time and season to a flat surface, to which we instinctively add analogous natural and cultural attributes, thus expressing archetype on the stellar canvas.

Astronomy is not the origin of archetype, just as classes of natural order among species, human tabulation, opera and artworks are all imperfect expressions of aspects of archetype, and none are 'original'. Since myth and astrology are generally known, this study uses mythic and zodiac (ecliptic equator) labels to demonstrate archetypal structure in art.

Constellations are here divided by the galactic cardinal (cross) structure, and by unequal angles aligned to our subconscious visual structure of sixteen types as revealed in this study.

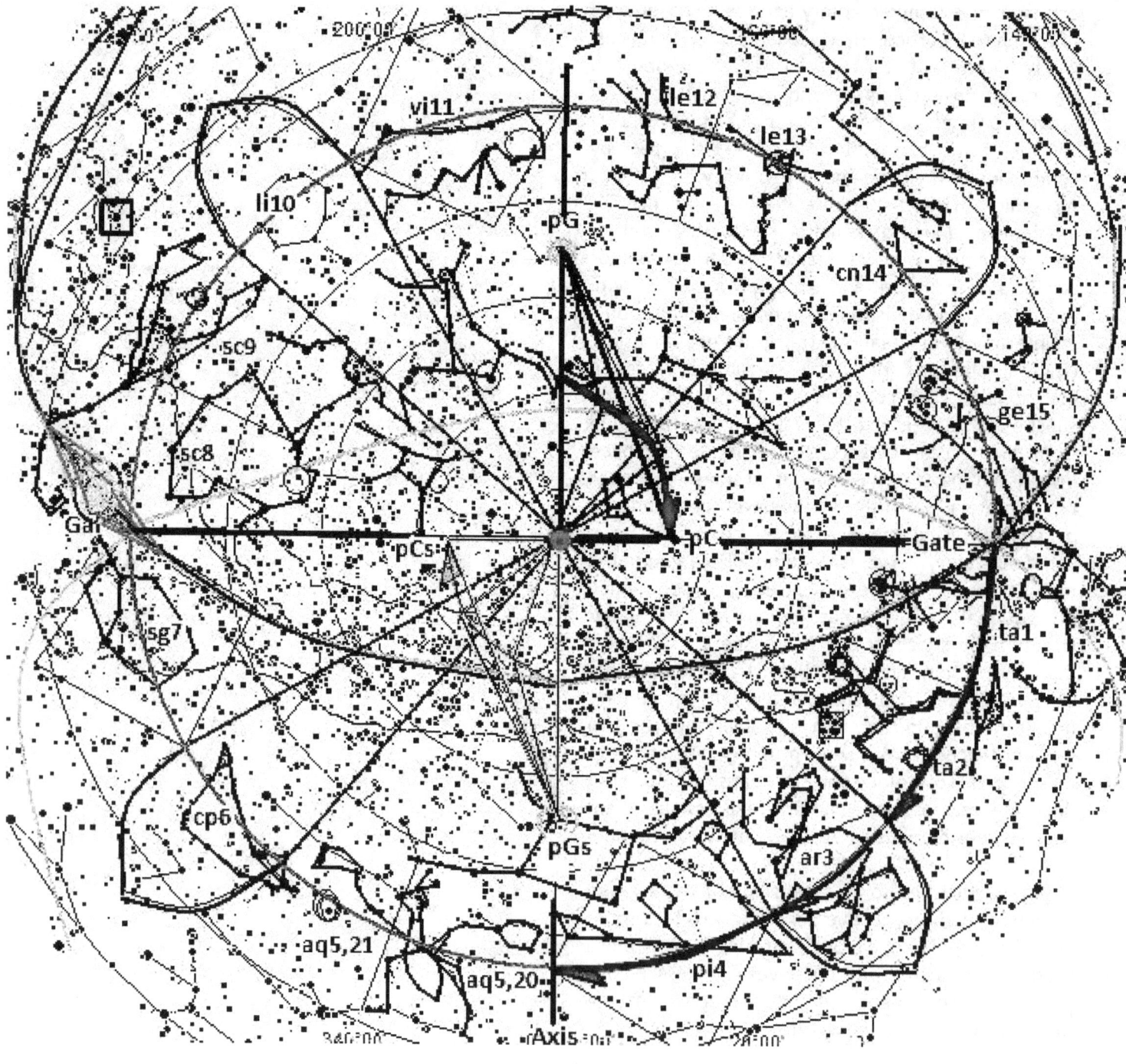

The band of figures around the ecliptic favours pairs of opposing and complementary figures of near equal extent, supported by two, three or four adjacent constellations (decans) each. Constellation figures follow gestalt rules (perceptive wholes among parts) by connecting nearest and largest stars in stick figure form, favouring lucida (brightest stars as visual anchors).

Most available star maps are projected differently, around the celestial (daily rotation) polar axis (pC and pCs), with a celestial reference grid which is continually updated to keep track of the slow migration of earth's rotational poles and equator against the stellar backdrop.

Pole E is the ecliptic pole, an imaginary axle for earth's yearly orbit around the sun (which appears to us as the sun's orbit passing through zodiac constellations). Pole E south (pEs) is always directly behind pE in inspired art. These poles are static, and could move only if the earth's orbit around the sun, or the plane of the whole solar system changed. Meteorite impacts or solar rotation wobble may have caused an ecliptic offset of about one degree in the human era.

Poles C and Cs are the celestial poles. The northern is currently at the hoof of the loose foreleg or jaw, over the galactic gate between Gemini and Taurus. The southern is currently nearing Hercules, over the galactic centre (which is between Sagittarius and Scorpius). Both are 23.4 degrees from pole E. These poles are visible in the sky due to earth's daily rotation, appearing to us as stellar rotation. Most sky maps and grids centre on one of these two celestial poles. Here both are shown, as if the sphere were transparent, just as artistic inspiration expresses our mindprint. The celestial poles slowly swing around the constant ecliptic pole, the path of their former positions here marked out by arrow tracks. Most cultures divide the celestial equator (not shown here) by 18, 24 or 36 bright stars or asterisms (small open clusters or groups of stars) as hourly markers, named decans.

Poles G and Gs are the static galactic poles between and north of Virgo and Leo (above), and between and south of Pisces and Aquarius (appearing also 'north' if seen on a transparent sphere). The galactic equator is visible as a concentrated band of stars in the sky (shown here by northern and southern oblique circles, offset above and below). The galaxy around us is angled against the plane of the solar system by about 63 degrees. The imaginary axle through the plane of frozen rotation of the galaxy is an invisible concept.

Astronomers cite star and planet positions on a celestial grid, using the current spring equinox (here at the bottom) as a zero point, and either the north or south celestial pole as the highest point (here right or left of the centre). The celestial poles (and thus midsummer) have moved in the last 7000 years or more, since about BC 6300 or earlier, from between the two other poles (when the three poles lay in line, and the southern polar trio likewise). Earth may have had higher obliquity (tilt) then, perhaps 26 degrees, so the celestial 'swing' is ever tightening due to some righting (earth's spin is moving more upright to its orbital plain). Precession moves counter-seasonal, against the direction of the yearly sun cycle, and also moves the equinoxes (spring and autumn ecliptic crossings) at the same rate in the same direction. The summer meridian (north-south line) by definition follows 90 degrees after spring.

Dates, angles and rates of movement in distant millennia are uncertain, despite scientific assumptions applied in astronomy automation. Science assumes obliquity to remain within small margins, in a predictable cycle of its own, yet there is some evidence of prehistoric high obliquity. The rate of precession is also known to change, yet assumed in science to remain nearly even. This study does not use astronomical dating older than about BC 3000, but uses relative dating instead, such as 'Age Taurus 1'. Only one artwork hinting at Age Gemini was found (see a Niaux Ice Age bison herd at theme t15) and none tagged to a supposed Age Cancer, Age Leo or earlier. Celestial polar markers were found only on or near the Leo axis (Age Taurus), Cancer axis (Age Aries), or Gemini axis (Age Pisces). These tags mean only that some aspects of each artistic inspiration is framed by a particular Age or era, just as we tell time by an approximate number of minutes after an hour. Many polar markers are between two of these axes, taken to imply 'some time before the next transition', just as we tell time by an approximate number of minutes before an hour. Captions in this study note these in-between markers as Age Taurus-Aries, Age Aries-Pisces, or Age Pisces-Aquarius, implying sometime during the last two centuries before and during an Age transition.

Since Age Aquarius has not yet started at the time of writing, the inspiration of works tagged as Age Pisces-Aquarius refers to the current era. Where a series of celestial polar markers appear in art, like a calibrated gauge, the concept of Ages is usually part of the general theme of a work, yet it could not be read off as a scale, partly since the angles of mindprint in art are not regular, and since inspirational time is outside historic time.

Our astronomical sets

Chapter D

Animal species, extinct, alive and probably also future mutations, express aspects of archetype, just as artistic types do. Animal shapes, habits and family trees, like all natural sets, are quirky, involving some gaps and duplications.

The sky is also a canvas for some aspects of archetypal structure. Astronomical and astrological concepts are a function partly of spherical, planar and dynamic elements in the cosmos, and partly of perception bias, down to incidental gestalt detail in constellation lines.

The shape of our eyes, hands, brains and minds dictate how we map the world and the sky. Gestalt functions like a filing cabinet for hundreds of adjacent figurative options to edge one another towards distinction into clusters, and towards analogy with similar sets in nature, such as ecosystems and kinship. Some astronomical quirks have become part of myth, and some zoological quirks are imprinted on the sky, yet within our apparently quirky star lore lies an equally rigorous structure. Trade-offs between archetypal structure and natural categories are endless. Rigour could be sought only in trimmed-down correspondences between sets. Chunks of species, behaviours, dots or events have to be cut away as incidental, interpolated or superfluous. Few of the 300 odd visible stars (a rough average from the Flamsteed catalogue, but other catalogues could differ by up to 100 stars per constellation), in each of the 80-odd constellations actively figure the constellation, even if stick figures are fleshed out into near 3D images (which some could). Some constellations are instantly recognisable by as few as seven stars, or less, down to five, four or even two if the context of adjacent constellations is shown.

Occam's razor also applies to myth; a mere suggestion of each is sufficient. Wolf, snake, dragon, horse, goat, bear and the rest come with ready-made reputations, with some surreal griffins added to cover current vacancies in the species tree and to express optional variants of the types.

Despite many obvious similarities between the elements and structures of myth, art and astronomy, the analogy is incomplete, as each answer to archetype within the dictates of its own medium, and each reveal and hide parts of its expression from our conscious and communicable perception. Art is particularly valuable for its ability to raise semiconscious and subconscious expression within the reach of consciousness, and thus to support individual enlightenment. This function of art is not cumulative in the way that technology is, despite our impulse to hoard celebrated art in museums. More swallows do not make a warmer summer.

The popular impulse to seek scientific and technological records in art dwell on geometric engravings, artefacts, totems and site layouts claimed to be 'astronomical' as if they were remnants of a systematic enquiry or geodetic survey (Gary A David; Orion zone. Andis Kaulins; Stars, stones and scholars. Wayne Herschel; Hidden Records). "All is astronomy," said Eusebius. Like Orion correlation theorists, he understood astronomy as a repository of 'knowledge'.

The animal kingdom and many other sets lay better claims to reflecting conscious and practical knowledge, while the sky expresses mainly structure. This study responds to Eusebius with evidence that all is structure. To prove its priority over astrology, myth could call on constellations and stars to merely state their names. Stars are named for myths, myths are not named for stars.

Some totems and attributes adopted by Hopi kachinas (ritual troupes) do co-incide with star lore, but the correlation is limited to a handful of constellations and asterisms, not comprehensive astronomy or astrology. Totem identity has several other functions instead.

Artefacts in many cultures are supposed by loose consensus in popular culture to contain star maps, while their common cause is archetypal and symbolic expression instead. The Hermetic dictum of 'As above so below' has misled the popular archaeology paradigm to the myth of a former super-culture that had supposedly developed and taught astronomy, sustained by secret societies. Cultures and their 'knowledge' then degraded or transformed into myth.

Since the sky is synchronous with nature, and recognition of its parts is a global impulse, our cultural motto is rather 'As below, so above'. There are few scientific or grand-scaled historic records in art, while countless cues indicate the contrary; there is art in our crafts and sciences.

Even some philosophical studies fail to recognise the pervasive functions of archetype. Kuhn writes that the correlation between our experience and the sky "draws on method, interpretive principles and the cosmological perspective provided by astrology." (Kuhn; Archetypal cosmology). The craft is seen as a formative power itself.

This persistent correlation theory is replayed in many books on the relative position of some pyramids and temples built to map Orion's belt or the Pleiades. This view of correlation reduces major religious projects to secret astronomy theme parks, and reduces natural structure to a function of human logic, as if order emanated from our conscious minds, and as if culture imposed order on nature. Secret astronomy is a contradiction in terms, since no aspect of the craft could be hidden from enquiry. Orion, the Pleiades and some other asterisms are part of the conscious programme of cultures, but merely as a handy myth map.

Some supposedly astronomical figures and concepts have multiple circulations as mythic, artistic, astronomical and historical figures, such as king Perseus (type Taurus t2 Perseus), queen Berenice (type Virgo t11 Galactic pole at Coma Berenices) or Hercules (type Scorpius t8 Ophiuchus Hercules, and elsewhere in the sky).

Artists borrow from myth, history and the sky, but seldom the whole sky, sometimes just the zodiac with its stereotypes. When art illustrates zodiacs, it usually does so in decanal (celestial) allegory, and independent of the involuntary, subconscious mindprint (see a kabbalist astronomical mountain at t6, and Poussin's zodiac hoop at theme t2 t17, and decanal sets at theme t12). Our subconscious does not recognise celestial zodiacs or decans as sufficiently archetypal for the purposes of art. Among the 400 works examined in this study, a minority are limited to twelve types, and very few figures resemble zodiac stereotypes. The zodiac is a limited application of the archetypal set in an annual, celestial paradigm. Few artists claim astrological inspiration or astronomical expertise.

Artists rather use mythical, legendary, literary, historic, realistic, characteristic, emblematic images to express a more encompassing structure. Artists casually queried had no conscious idea of a structure or sequence resembling mindprint, and only vague ideas about archetypes. They consider astrology a craft that could be learned, and have no intention to illustrate astronomy. Why paint star maps when our outer and inner worlds of conscious and subconscious inspiration and experience beg for expression?

Confirmation bias versus open minds

Archetype informs nature, which in turn co-informs perception and consciousness, a continuum of expression including us and our culture. The process does not function in reverse. Culture does not inform perception or nature, although we sometimes consider some of our impulses to be products of our conscious conventions. We label mythic elements by legendary names, as if history had formed our subconscious. This error arises from confirmation bias and may be labelled our collective Narcissus complex. Its resolution lies in pantheism, that may be labelled the Perseus complex, a paradigm involving all the layers of consciousness.

Nature and culture teach only prepared minds, as the Dogon elders say. Despite Jung's eloquent explanation of the layers of personality and soul, and of UFOs as techno myths, the 'ancient astronomy, ancient alien, or ancient alien astronomy' authors harp on the supposedly scientific rhetoric of 'millions of other suns and planets, statistical probability of intelligent life, and unlimited evolutionary and technological advances of higher forms of life'.

Many scientists did not get Jung's message either, and harp on rhetoric of oral traditions, cultural diffusions, traders, escaped slaves and shipwrecks. It would take hundreds of lucky travelling artists or poets (like Camoens), and a global art tradition surviving 4000 years, to sustain the Perseus myth cycle and two lion-dog dragons with entwined necks from Babylonia to Mexico, and a dying bull with a bleeding nose as rain, fertility and dream ritual, from Persia to thousands of rock artists in the deserts, mountains and plains of the world. If spiritual icons were sustained by communication and convention, then an eland bull in a death posture, bleeding from the nose (see theme t2 t17) should be labelled 'Persian religious icon brought to Africa by early traders'. If popular astronomy authors are right, the bull could be labelled 'Image of Taurus constellation, celebrated in art, and inspiring the Perseus myth.' Such labels would be equally false.

Academia is almost obsessed with ignoring correspondences between artefacts or behaviour in different cultures, unless they are linked by cultural contact as well as theoretical constructs of 'development'. When De Santillana and Von Deschend write of the supposed "enormous effort" of early people in "gaining understanding of astronomy" and "constructing" language, they mistake nature as science, and instinctive behaviour as theory. What seems to archaeo astronomers to be records of 'developed' sets of constellations, gods or heroes, are parallels between imprints of archetype.

So-called 'correspondence theory', as Bauval and Hancock label it, is one of the main layers of camouflage that keep our archetypal expressions hidden from conscious view.

Constellations and sky maps are usually unmistakeable, but they are absent in most rock art and art, despite consistent efforts by many authors to spot them. Ironically, correspondence theories have not identified the standard artistic set, geometry or subconscious context, despite and probably due to its close resemblance to star maps.

The best canvas for archetypal structure is astronomy, and its most complete analogy is astrology, for combining place, time, identity and relationships relative to three equators and three polar axles. Yet there is no primary or finite expression of archetype, and astronomy could not claim any natural priority among the other expressions of structure.

Art sometimes illustrates conventionalised archetypal sets such as pantheons, zoos, battles, icons or zodiacs, and all art thus appears to be second-hand expression. Instead, these 'given' sets are grafted onto the standard subconscious visual sequence of attributes and geometric structure, and less reliably on fragmented conventions.

A study of 9000 doodles (spontaneous drawings) showed that 60% contained ornamental elaboration of a stereotyped kind, indicating an inborn, collective tendency to make certain patterns, especially in a state of inattention.

The galactic cross arm

A tree on a horizon is a ready natural analogy for a cross, the concept of vertical and horizontal intersection. A tree imagined from above is also an analogy for an axial or radial structure. Trees are stock themes in myth and art, including rock art (see a Zimbabwean tree at theme t2 t17), sacred art (see the Mayan Palenque lid at theme t4), and secular art (see an Afro-Portuguese couple under a tree at theme t3). The close fit between mythical and artistic cruciforms, such as world trees or paradise trees, confirm that myth and art are sometimes consciously aligned, and always structurally aligned. The Nordic, Mexican or Australian mythical tree (see the Djullirri double imprint at theme t15) is part of the framework of stock concepts. Mindprint reveals this framework as four cardinal points dividing the sixteen standard types, usually marked by non-figurative features such as limb joints, plants, paths, streams, trees or pillars. The four galactic corners of the conceptual cross are often expressed as churn groups including a reign, rope, snake or post and its operators or handlers.

The polar cross arm

Even insect eyes are guided by the galactic equator, a navigational aid since it maintains its general direction for some hours, sometimes lasting the course of a night. It switches orientation in the visible hemisphere during the year from (|) to (/) to (-) and back to (/) and (|), thanks to its position as a kind of curved crosspiece or crossbow to the ecliptic equator (planetary path).

Beetles use the galactic equator's orientation to maintain their chosen direction while rolling dung balls away from a source, and from competing beetle eggs (Marcus Byrne; Dancing with the stars).

The polar axle between the two galactic poles is squared to the galactic equator and its gates, forming the invisible arrow of a crossbow. The conceptual galactic north pole is invisible in the sky, but usually marked in art near and between Leo and Virgo. The galactic south pole is likewise a spatial concept, near and between Aquarius and Pisces. Southern features are on the 'underside' of the conceptual sphere, but 'visible' by conceptual flattening and 'transparency'. Thus an ecliptic meridian (north-south line) across the galactic poles, is 90 degrees from the two gates where the galactic equator crosses the ecliptic. This meridian extends the arrow, trunk, stem or obelisk of the cosmic cross. The cross is hard to imagine on a sky rotating around a point which is not on its (ecliptic) centre, but on the offset (celestial) pole. The cross is thus distorted into curves by projection on celestial-centred maps, but remains a clear cruciform concept in myth, iconography and art.

The concept of the infant Achilles being held by his heel over a cauldron, is one example of how we use myth and constellations to express the conceptual galactic pole at Coma (Hair), over Crater (Grail), flanked by his parents as type Virgo t11 and type Leo t12 retro.

These figures and episodes would not be in any myth or legend, nor on any star map, if there were no archetype, collective subconscious, or visual expression of universal structure. Concept and myth remain prior to legend and astronomy.

Ernst Gombrich's discussion of the cross as a universal symbol uses the concept of an archetype, even though he rejects the term. He does not accept Jung's idea of a 'collective subconscious', despite his own experience of seeing a mandala as a hypnagogic image. However Gombrich does accept that part of our psychological make-up is 'a disposition to accept degrees of order as potential metaphors of inner states'.

Art history, like archaeology, clings to the paradigm that we impose order on nature. The title of this study, Mindprint, should therefore be clarified as implying a natural or oto-conceptual imprint on and by our minds, not developed by or emanating from our conscious conventions.

Galactic equators

Myth and art express several structural components, in addition to the usual characterised types. Some of the limb joints of typological figures participate in two interlocking equators, termed galactic equators in this study. Paths and rivers in myth play the same role. In the sky, the galactic river crosses 'under' the figures equator in two opposing places, named gates or bridges. Several myths include characters and episodes off the seasonal path, in a river, sea, or sky instead. These may well be conceptually galactic and not fully typological.

Galactic types, perhaps transformative or transitional rather than typological in nature, have their own sequence. In this list the label 'tg' means galactic type, derived from their incidental or nearest ecliptic (zodiac) type;

tg15 Gemini Monoceros (Unicorn)
tg14 Cancer Argo Vela (Ship Sail)
tg13 Leo Argo Carina (Ship Keel) Heart
tg12 Leo Argo Puppis or Caput (Ship Bust)
tg11 Virgo Crux (Cross)
tg10 Libra Centaurus
tg9 Scorpius Centaurus hoof, Lupus (Wolf)
tg8 Scorpius Ophiuchus, Galactic centre
tg7 Sagittarius Cygnus (Swan)
tg7 Sagittarius south; Scutum (Shield)
tg6 Capricornus Cygnus?
tg5 g21 Aquarius Vulpecula (Fox)
tg5 g20 Aquarius Lacerta (Lizard)
tg4 Pisces Cepheus (Sea monster)
tg3 Aries Cepheus
tg2 Taurus Perseus
tg1 Taurus Auriga.

Limb joints naturally outnumber figures by about one to nine (potentially thirteen, but most figures are usually in profile), spread inside and outside the equator of eyes (together forming three interlocking rings). Limb joints tend to avoid the figures equator, except for occasional hip or rump wounds, which are usually on or near the two gates.

One of the pair of galactic equators along limb joints in art is often nearly circular. Doubled galactic equators (see the Cosmic map) raise the possibility that inspiration could arise in the visual cortex of one or both brain spheres, as a stereo or holographic vision.

On double-sided artefacts such as palettes, they are doubled again, forming a pair to anchor each main equator of figures. The two galactic equators often fill the available rock canvas, or allocated part of a canvas or artefact, confirming other hints that inspiration may start as a vortex of limbs (see buck bags in rock art), or that artists may be inspired by a banded (armillary) sphere unfolding into a near symmetrical set of three interlocking circles on a cruciform framework.

Inspiration thus includes a holistic vision, involving features that require a lifetime of observation or years of study to appreciate in the conscious mind, yet expressed by artists, including novices worldwide.

Visual intuition is thus revealed as standardised, collective, subconscious and compulsive, as it is in myth, spirituality, social order and other cultural domains. Artists need not know astronomy, for it is not the origin or aim or art. Astronomers could not learn much from art. Esotericists study all expressions of cosmic order, and so should anthropologists, archaeologists, psychologists, historians, writers and theologians.

Celestial updates

The celestial pole is often on a jaw or other limb joint. Since the Egyptian concept of a mouth opener, Wippet, is a decan of type Cancer t14 Ursa Minor, Small Bear, jackal, or small bull foreleg, the distinctive shape of the mouth opening device may thus be solved (with the added complication of the former summer in Leo Ursa as a large foreleg, when spring was at the Taurus jaw, then moved to a small jaw opener shape at the Pleiades in front of the Taurus jaw). This is the jawbone that Samson used to 'kill a lion' when the celestial pole moved summer from Leo Ursa Major to Cancer Ursa Minor in the Age Taurus-Aries transition. The jaw is the only singular limb joint (shoulders, elbows, wrists, hips, knees and ankles are all doubled), the only joint capable of limited movement, and in only one direction.

Explaining a hologram and its moving parts in words could be tortuous, but necessary, since two-dimensional (flat) images are not fully up to the task either. The overall structure expresses a sphere with three equators, and thus three sets of poles on three axles. Two of the equators are inevitably doubled in projection around any of the three polar axles. Art compacts two hemispheres into one, squashing the conceptional sphere flat along the main (ecliptic) axle, leaving the main equator of conceptual figures (and constellations) relatively unchanged (just narrower towards the centre and wider towards the outer edge), and folding out the peripheral features (edges) to complete the top hemisphere's images. Some of the remaining southern polar features (on the bottom) are made visible through the 'top'. The visual similarity of art and the sky globe does not extend much further, however their cosmic conceptual constructs do. Mindprint art is an excellent mind map, but only a vague and general sky map.

Astrological structure

Zodiac signs (not the same as constellations) are merely mechanically divided strips of sky (Louis MacNeice; Astrology) ever moving backward as if the first point of Aries were pinned to the spring equinox.

Constellations carry more meaning than these twelve slices of stereotype. Constellations are static and host a range of optional expressions of archetype, down to the ascribed qualities of individual stars in the so-called Ptolemaic system.

Zodiac signs move backwards by one degree in 72 years, across a sequence of twelve sharply bordered concepts, their attributes determined mainly by planets passing through their territories, likewise calculated from the slowly moving spring equinox. People with their 'sun in Aries' are born while the sun is in the constellation Pisces (soon to change to Aquarius). 'Sun in Pisces' natives were born while the sun is in Aquarius, and so on.

Astrologers and astronomers work on an abstract clock face of twelve areas, currently pinned 30 degrees (1/12) or two hours (2/24) prior to the constellations and planets. Planetary positions are calibrated, published, and read off on the false clock face. The current separation of almost 30 degrees does not invalidate astrology, which in turn does not invalidate the Ptolemaic paradigm. The sky thus mirrors two unfolding sequences, hinged on two poles and grids; ecliptic and celestial.

Astrology and astronomy both remain only mirrors. "Heaven's motions provide [conceptual] coordinates for time and place on earth," wrote De Santillana and Von Deschend in Hamlet's mill. "Earthly concepts have been transferred to [concepts of] heaven, and inversely. Geographical features cited [in myth] may imply either domain, or both... True events, even in an official epic like the Persian Shahnama, are not earth-directed, they tend to move upwards. This is the original form of astrology [bottom-up]... cosmography is made up of inextricably intertwined data. To say that events on earth reflect those in heaven is a misleading simplification. Form and matter go together. Myth has no historical basis, however tempting the reduction, the euhemerist trend, from Euhemeros, the first debunker [of myth in favour of history]. Myth is essentially cosmological, yet studies have not cleared up the decisive points of the cosmological system ruling the Enuma Elish, Gilgamesh Epic, Era Epic and other alleged poems," writes De Santillana.

Mindprint confirms the above version of the somewhat contradictory views of De Santillana and Von Deschend, here of the precedence and presence of archetype in myth, sky, art, culture and history. Poems, however, are only poems. Mindprint offers the detailed cosmological system of 'decisive points' in myth that they sought.

Jung followed astrology to its philosophical and esoteric conclusion. He at first sought physical, causal connections between patterns in personality traits or actions, and patterns in astrology, but could not rely on flimsy veils such as solar magnetic storms and tides [the modern equivalent is entanglement at sub-atomic particle level], and opted instead for a "holographic view of total interconnection" without physical links.

KE Kraft likewise gave up on seeking physical and statistical proof of personality patterns, and reverted to traditional, stereotyped meanings to draft a symbolical system named typo-cosmy. Stereotypes are useful, and for good reason. Archetypal expression in myth, literature and art is complex, yet functions on surprisingly simplistic traits.

People respond to recognition of archetypes in their own character, behaviour and events with shocks of recognition, and recoil from unpalatable traits, which are softened by defence mechanisms. A mirror is only as clear as the mind of the viewer. Allegories or other people's faces therefore make better mirrors, delaying self-recognition and allowing viewers of prepared mind to buy into the story. Stories, like mirrors, hinge on stereotypes to unpack their complex meanings.

Time is a great equaliser, since seasons, hours and the course of lives and cultures are essentially the same everywhere. Apparent cycles of 'qualities' in the sky offer a mirror of individual and collective fortunes, or rather tendencies, a book of a thousand shapes, creatures, characters and events, ready to record and re-tell endless stories, yet reducible, as all the best human artefacts are, to an accessible set of mnemonics (memory aiders) grafted on a natural base. This set requires sixteen types, each with a range of optional attributes, and several structural features. Twelve monolithic stereotypes seem to apply more directly to the qualities of time, not character.

Furze Morrish writes; "It seems time is a concrete continuum containing qualities of basic conditions, manifesting simultaneously in various places." (Louis MacNeice; Astrology).

Mindprint identifies the components of holographic space and time, mapping these 'qualities of basic conditions' by their attributes, sequence and geometric relationships.

Jung spelled out the implication of synchronicity for science, which is equally relevant to art; "If there are non-causal combinations of events, we should have drastically to revise our view of things." Yet we did not, and are not likely to. Non-causal connections melt into the 'background' of nature and perception. Our mind blots out its own structure and thus has a blind spot for artistic and cultural structure.

Some sets borrow images, symbols and names from one another, as alchemy borrows from astronomy, astronomy from myth, alphabets from numerology, trump emblems from seasonal poem cycles, and mindprint from the Tarot trumps. None of these are motivated only by imitation. Crafts and categories do not arise from, or develop from one another. Astronomy and mythology did not await one another, nor track the supposed development of one another.

Astronomy does not need myth to teach it parts of the spherical concept, it just resorts to more or less appropriate and popular figures and mythic labels. Art never needed permission from mythology, astrology, religion or Tarot cards to express archetype, it just does.

The three poles of time

Type Aries t3 t18 as entwined dragons, with its opposite type Libra t10 as a rampant eagle (Babylonian cylinder seal impression. Identification by Edmond Furter). See identical dragons on the Egyptian Narmer palette at theme t3 t18. See a Mishnah verse citing "tongs made with tongs" in the Literature section. Poles, perception, physics and astronomical time literally hinge on equal but opposite or cardinal action, as XX-shaped tongs do (see the Cosmic map). There are persistent links in myth and art between polar and precessional iconography, and Aries-Libra t3-t10 axis, and its cardinal, the Cancer-Capricornus t14-t6 axis. The frequent attributes of Aries t3 t18 are 'long neck' and 'entwined', allocated before the universe was formed, expressed in nature, ritual, myth and art as crocodiles, ostriches, giraffes, dragons, a U-shaped gate, and constellation Aries, with its necks framing a blank centre or 'egg' on the ecliptic.

The moon braids its way around us, and across the sun's path, 'stitching' eclipses in cycles of between eighteen and nineteen years. The lunar number is expressed at Aries t18, and the solar number at Pisces t19, entwining concepts of seasons, calendars, eggs, dragons, equators and poles. The eagle expresses Libra t10 Bootes or Horus with raised arms holding the polar circle, or Draco around the ecliptic pole, or Ursa Minor at the celestial pole.

The 'Mideastern' and 'Egyptian' polar pair is equalled in eastern art by a dragon and phoenix pair, the best-known celestial (daily earth rotation) symbols. They clutch a slippery ball that expresses the celestial pole over Leo Ursa, near the coils of Draco in Age Taurus, now between Cancer Lynx and Ursa Minor.

The southern counterpart of Leo t12 Ursa Major's tail, hoof, or retro head, is Aquarius t5 Phoenix, former clutcher of the celestial south pole, expressed in Chinese, Arabic and other mythology. Phoenix lost the southern celestial pole to Tucana (Bird of Paradise), and more recently to Octans (a small obelisk shape), which is antipodal (hemispheric opposite) to Ursa Minor. A crop circle showing Phoenix in its ignited nest expresses resurrection and the Age Pisces-Aquarius polar configuration (England 2009, June 12. See another iconic crop circle at t14). The three poles form an L or |\ shape, with a mirrored foot expressing its lower hemisphere, forming a /JL\ shape, as if seen on a transparent sphere (see the Cosmic map).

Type Aries t3 t18 as a dragon pair clutching at a polar pearl (Australian Christmas Island Territory contribution to the worldwide postage stamp design series of 2000). The island is near the international dateline. The nominal millennium was the nearest century number to the forthcoming Age Pisces-Aquarius transition.

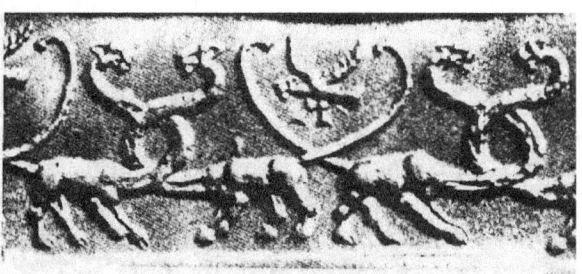

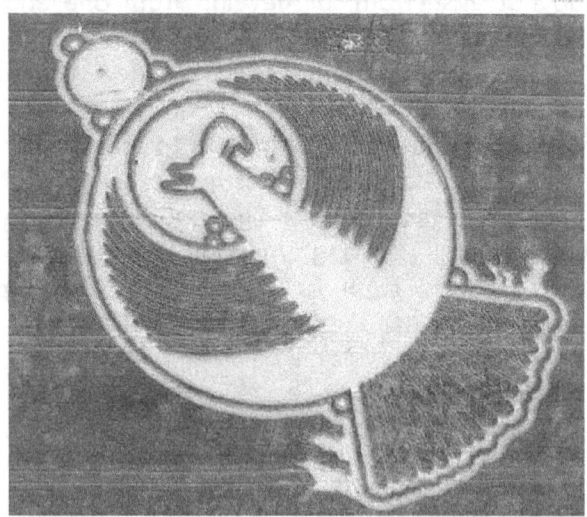

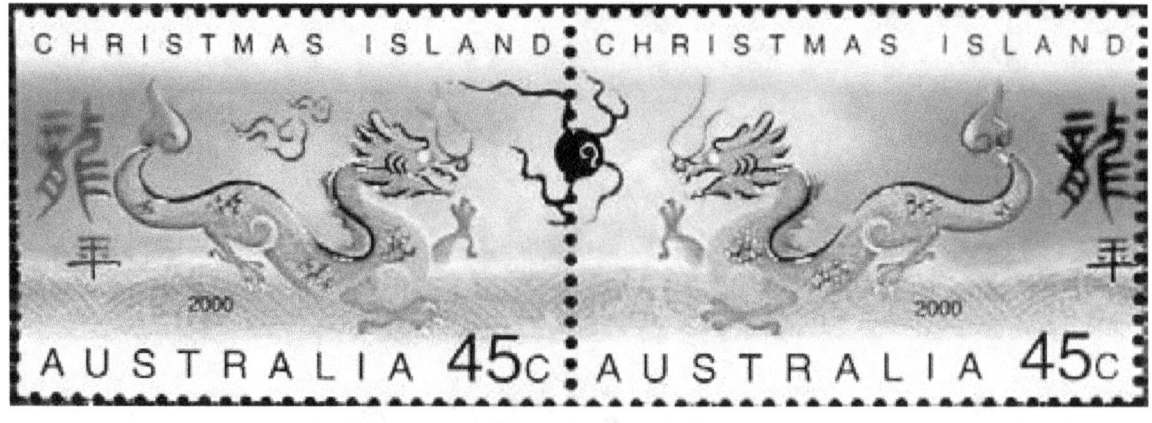

A mix and match mock-up

A typical mindprint sequence and structure composed of figures sampled from different cultures and eras, to illustrate a typical Age Pisces-Aquarius configuration. Manipulation here accounts for a good number of limb joints on the galactic equators, about 15+14=29, or 11+14=25 in the adjacent rotated example. Most real artworks score even better. This seemingly frivolous tally is subject to chance, but confirms the many other indicators of inspirational and expressive quality.

A mock update

A typical mindprint sequence and structure composed of figures sampled from different cultures and eras. Polar and galactic features, as well as the horizontal plane, illustrate how an Age Aquarius inspiration structure may soon differ from art framed in the current era. Most inspired artworks express the artist's prior or current Age, but some anticipate their forthcoming eras (see Peruvian art by Pablo Amaringo at theme t5 and elsewhere). Only these two images and the cover design in this study imitate art, the other images are real artworks.

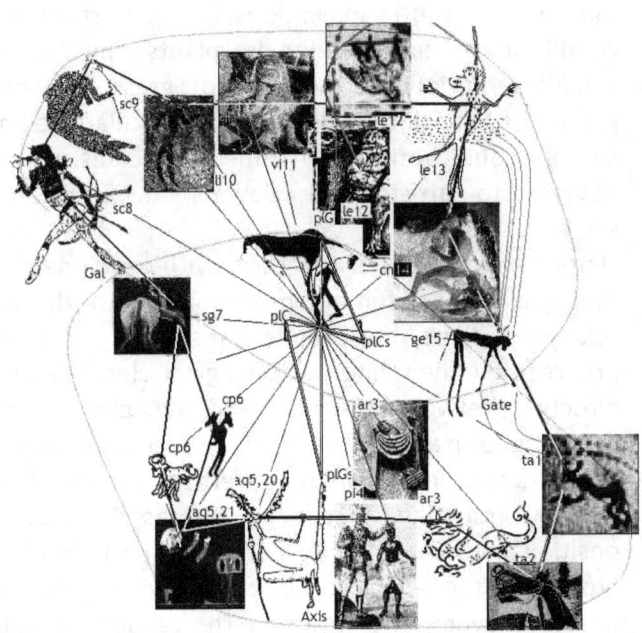

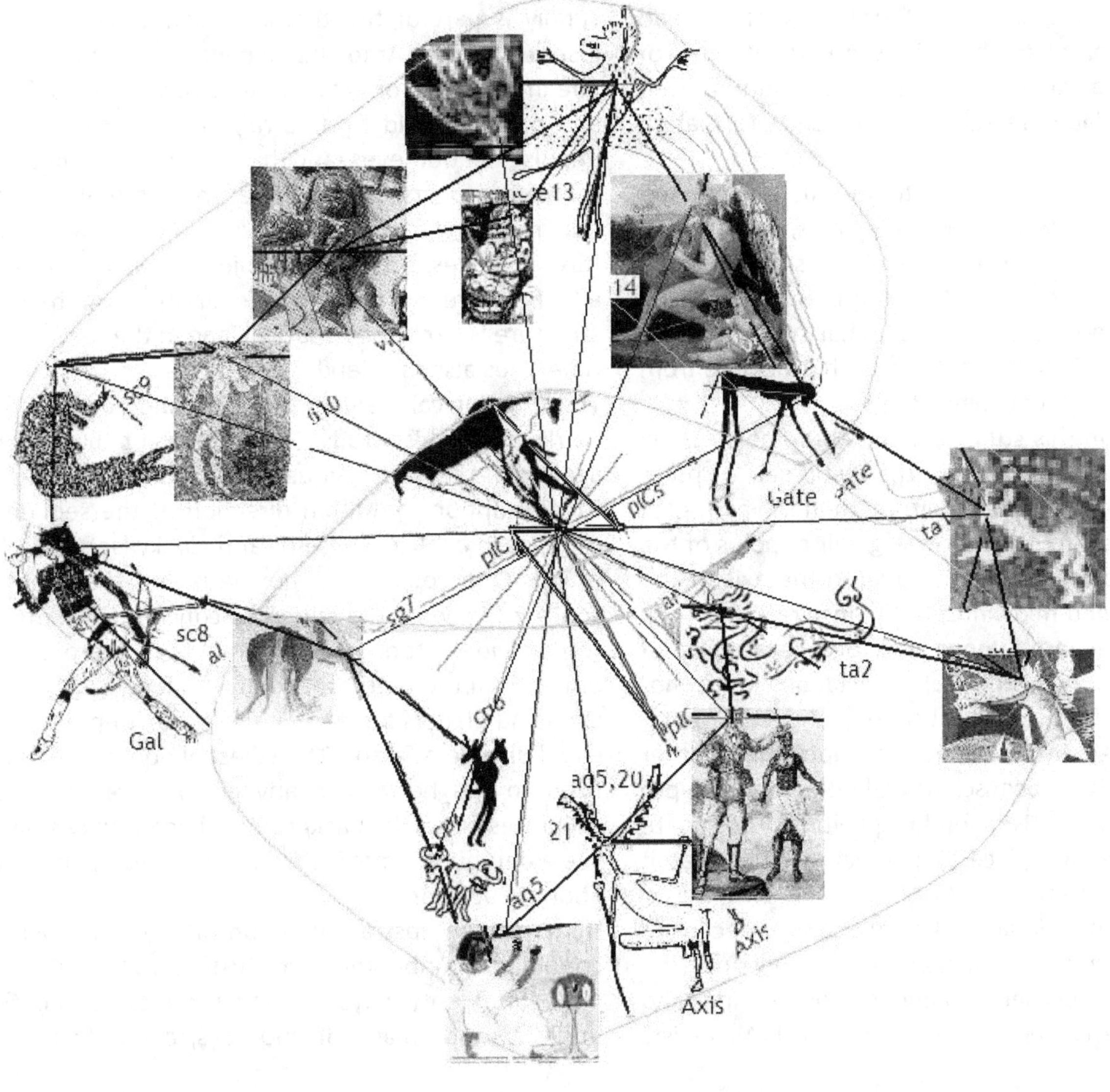

Our calendric sets

Chapter E

Canvas or rock orientation, and even changes in posture and groundline during the work, does not affect the quality of artistic structure. Visual inspiration may thus include an axial grid that could be rotated, with figures affixed to it by their eyes. Each figure may be free to rotate as the eventual canvas orientation requires, like merry-go-round big wheel carriages fixed by universal joints to the spokes of a wheel. Carriages remain balanced by gravity, but their attachment points remain relative to the hub at the ecliptic pole.

Sparse figuration in a work could hint that the inspiration or expression is mainly polar and related to Ages, incidental with the theme of ancestors and a former era (see Poussin's Arcadian shepherds at theme t5 t20, and Morgan-Lefay's Masks at theme t5t t21). Sparse works also necessitate the use of some feet, ankles, knees or other limb joints instead of eyes to complete the axial sequence (typical of Poussin and a minority of artists), thus hinting that limbs and galactic features may precede formation of the figures.

The tri-polar structure in mindprint is usually marked by limb joints. Jaws, shoulders, elbows, wrists, hips, knees and ankles are good analogues for rotation anchors, or see-saw points of equal and opposing reaction. No pole in the cosmos, solar system, galaxy or universe is absolute or static. Each articulate from the other, just as limb joints do.

Every image in this study contains three polar axles; the static geometric centre; the static pair of poles of two oblique galactic equators, themselves traced by limb joints; and the precessing pair of poles of the implied set of celestial equators (on the axis of the midsummer and midwinter of the inspirational Age). Polar markers are among the best examples of synchronicity, or meaningful co-incidence in art, not traceable by physical causation. Celestial polar dating is used in this study to supplement other evidence of the subconscious and holographic depth of inspiration. Temporal qualities permeate character, events, place and direction in art, as it does in esoteric crafts.

Calendric themes in art and esoterica (see decans at theme t12 and elsewhere) go far beyond the paradigm of 'peasant calendars for sowing and reaping' (see calendric icons at theme t14). Artists express inspiration not merely in terms of characters, characteristics, postures, relative positions and geometry, but our conscious, semi-conscious and subconscious visual ensemble includes several layers of temporal frameworks. Half of the conscious temporal meaning in rock art is lost on city dwellers, since most of us can no longer tell a month from subtle indications in the posture and condition of various animals, plants and human activities. Variety in the type of grass that one gender of a species would eat at a particular age and season, could be inferred from many clues, plainly obvious to artists and viewers in subsistence societies.

Nature endows all her creatures with positional and timing skills. Bees remember the position of the sun relative to the horizontal plane, and trace its progress by their internal biological clock to map direction between the hive and a nectar source, adjusting for passing time as they dance their code. They transfer direction to a vertical beehive cake face by assuming directly upward as the current position of the sun, then dancing a pattern while buzzing a frequency, continuously allowing for the unseen movement of the sun. The capacity of bees to tell and communicate direction, time and food supply is part of the theme of some rock art and inspired art (see Arabian bee people at theme t8).

The implication for art is that no surface, no subject and no day could be neutral, or mere clay to the impulse of our eyes and hands. We are wired to recreate aspects of the same process that formed our planet, life, consciousness and culture. Like Russian boxes, art, artist, subject, object, time and all of nature nestle into one another. Archetypal structure is expressed spatially and in the textures of time, thus also in calendars.

The typological sequence is numbered by hour markers in this study, retrograde or backwards against the seasonal sequence. No conclusive reason for the optional rotation direction of the sequence of types in art (clockwise or anti-clockwise) could be found. One could be a northern and the other a southern view of the spherical concept. One of the retrograde factors could be an hour 'zero point' effect from the natural tendency to face east, where stars and planets appear. The direction of precession could also be a factor. The celestial equator remains fixed to the horizon in any given place and thus calibrates hours. Its background changes very slowly, like a belt buckle moving from the hip to the navel in about 7000 years.

Hours are an abstract function of days. The Mayan continuous, unbroken, unadjusted, rolling 'month' cycle of twenty days, in larger cycles of thirteen 'months' and 'years' of 260 days, correlate to 260 personality types. Character diagnosis by Mayan birthday is surprisingly accurate. Days are one of the calibration points of time due to calendric slippage. For that reason, astronomy maintains a day count (name Julian Days).

The Chinese continuous cycle of twelve years, in a larger cycle of five 'elemental' eras, render 60 year-types that have gained some recognition for supplementing the more universal month personality types.

No astronomical cycles correspond precisely, and their current values may have been subject to many factors, such as obliquity, asteroid hits on the moon, acquisition and loss of satellites (moons), and orbital diameter variation (earth orbiting nearer to, or further from the sun), perhaps accounting for Ice Ages and tropical ages, such as our current era.

Artificial time marked by multiples of short crystalline pulses or 'atomic clocks' does not keep time with any natural cycle either. Time is a sea of clocks ticking by different pendulums, and indicator hands waving on different dials. Biological processes and thus our bodies are intimately connected to some of these large and small cycles. So is culture.

Ages follow archetypal sequence

Artworks show a full round of hours and seasons in the framework of a precessional Age, which may be up to about 3000 years prior to the work, or recent, or about a century ahead of the work. The main element of 'mutation' found in the structure of artistic expression (and probably intrinsic to inspiration) is the Age update. Age Gemini-Taurus, Taurus 1, Taurus 2, Taurus-Aries, Aries, Aries-Pisces, Pisces, or Pisces-Aquarius is noted as the inspirational Age at the end of every caption in the illustration section. This tag affects only some structural markers, orientation to the horizontal plane, and attributes of the current and former spring equinox position among the types (see a Taurus Pleiades sigil in the Aries position in a Babylonian seal impression at theme t2 t17).

Timeless archetypal structure acquires a modest history of expression in nature, named Being or Epoch in philosophy, a formative veil between pure structure populated by timeless concepts, and figures clothed in shapes, attributes and dynamics. Van Eeden cites Heidegger's use of the Greek word Physis as Being, with two meanings; Logos or original union, and Dighe or original organisation, a kind of essence of manifestation. Physis as transcendence is timeless and eternal, while Being is representation or manifestation in the form of an empirical concept, specific to an epoch. These concepts offer an analogy for how formless and timeless structure

manifests in forms and time, and for how conceptual inspiration manifests in visual and mythic expression.

Heidegger uses epoch to refer to the history of being, or "revelation of being in which being itself remains concealed." He also referred to "principles that manifest in an era."

Johnson (1974) wrote; "When a new era begins in history, a myth for that era springs up. Myth is primordial time (arche tupos), and representation of archetype in historical time." Our art suggests that we are in the habit of shutting out part of the plainly visible picture, thus we may well have temporal blind spots too. Science does not recognise mythic eras.

Epochs of archetypal expression in culture are named Ages in esoterica, and defined by various supposed creations, races or cultures of increasing or decreasing value, aligned to astronomical precession.

Structural anthropologist Levi-Strauss found "underlying patterns of thought in human activity" including "long cycles of mythic patterns" in which some themes dominate in turn. Yet these themes are explained as a function of 'thought and history', thus collective consciousness, which does not account for mindprint or its calibration to inspirational Ages. The 'long cycles' of structural anthropology seem to coincide with astrological Ages, a constant feature of esoteric thought in all cultures. Ages are linked on an a-causal, synchronistic basis to slow precession of the daily celestial poles and equator, against the direction of the annual orbital equator.

Mindprint demonstrates semi-conscious access to the subconscious structure of visual and mythic expression, partly by geometry. Ages are likewise in the semi-conscious realm, and require geometry to read. It could not yield to cognitive archaeology (the study of what we think), but yields to what could be termed structural archaeology (the study of what we express).

Ages in art

In Art and Illusion, Ernst Gombrich cites Wolfflin's principle that "not everything is possible in every period." Zerner writes of "cultural pressure that channels individual efforts."

Inspirational Ages in art, tagged by markers as well as polar and planar (horizontal and vertical) features, are not sufficiently calibrated to resolve dating issues. Art is essentially outside time, and only refers in passing to expressional history, a kind of history of time itself as it literally changes the angle of its connection to place. Inspired art dates itself by this correspondence angle, tacking angle, or planar angle between time and place.

Jung's overstated concept of art is worth repeating; "The social significance of art is being constantly at work, educating the spirit of the age, conjuring up forms in which the age is most lacking. Unsatisfied yearning of the artist reaches back to a primordial image in the unconscious which is best fitted to compensate the inadequacy and one-sidedness of the present. The artist seizes on this image, raises it from deepest unconsciousness, brings it into relation with conscious values, transforming it until it can be accepted by the minds of his contemporaries... so art represents a process of self-regulation in the life of nations and epochs." (Carl Jung; Readings in the History of Æsthetics; Art as Archetypal Form). Jung overstates the individual, social and national roles of art, but glimpses its global role as expressing a calendric framework. This view reduces art to a commentator on largely man-made events, or a confluence of circumstances, what history now labels a panarchical discourse (LH Gunderson and CS Hollling; Panarchy, transformation in human and natural systems). Mindprint and its inspirational Ages now prove to be larger than national cycles and more primordial than history.

Tarnas finds in Cosmos and Psyche; "Cyclical patterning [of planetary transits] radically enhances our understanding of cultural evolution [?] as a vast historical development that is shaped by dynamic archetypal forces, powers that move within a collective psyche, that is in turn rooted in, and expressive of a cosmic ground." However, mindprint implies that there is no 'evolution' or 'development' in human spirituality or culture, merely a modest history of expression that philosophy recognises as Being or Epoch, wherein consciousness is passive.

Any discussion of astronomical Ages aggravates scientists and astronomers, and challenges esotericists. In this study it requires more than its fair share of discussion to overcome the usual easy assumptions of causes and effects, and to inform the apparent contradiction between timeless archetype and its time-bound expressions.

The Age tagged in artistic inspiration often co-incides with the precessional and thus polar framework of the Age just prior, or the Age that inspired the cultural or religious reference of the work. Cultures or religions emerging about the same time, though very distant in place and styling, seem to be framed by the same polar dating configuration. Christian, Olmec and Mayan cultures demonstrate myth consonance keyed to Age Aries elements, in recent centuries updated to Age Pisces elements (see polar and spring markers in the Tello obelisk at t8).

Hindu, Buddhist and Egyptian New Kingdom religions and traditions were consonant in Age Aries, typically updating Age Taurus icons to Aries by swopping and migrating some attributes of the types bearing the spring point.

Mesopotamian, Naqada and Egyptian Old Kingdom myth and art were consonant in Age Taurus.

Iconographic calibration is readable in informal art, folk art (see an early Egyptian mural at theme t12), religious art (see palettes at theme t3 t18, and a Bolivian disc at theme t12) and political art (see a formal Egyptian battle mural at theme t7). Art thus confirms and clarifies esoteric traditions, and hint that inspiration rather than oral or literate traditions sustain crafts such as astrology. Art itself emerges in this study as a subconscious craft.

Five Ages

Where in the sky, and when in history Ages begin and end, is contested among esoteric schools and religions. Mindprint demonstrates the validity of a semi-regular demarcation of types among Ptolemaic (constellation-based) concepts. Whether the Age Taurus-Aries transition followed these archetypal constellation rules and allowed Aries only 20 degrees from about Delta Arietis, or followed astrological rules and allowed Aries 30 degrees starting from Taurus Pleiades, and when these 'Perseus' transitions could be dated to, requires a separate study. The question may reduce to fixing the where and when of either the archetypal first point of Aries (being the last point of Age Aries by precession), or the middle of Age Aries, or the last point of Aries (being the first point of Age Aries). Answers also hinge on the rate of precession at these various times, perhaps linked to obliquity.

Ancient 'peg' dates are few and far between. Two records of the celestial longitude (angular distance from the spring equinox) of the star Leo Regulus (type Leo t13 heart) are candidates for midsummer markers, but the position of the spring equinox at the time is not secure, and the angle may have to be translated (reduced in this case) into ecliptic grid terms. The data is probably celestial, while myth, art, calendars and Ages function in an ecliptic framework.

Taurus Pleiades held the spring equinox nominally about BC 2200, perhaps earlier since the rate of precession may have been slower then. The supposedly catastrophic sky tilt that De Santillana and Von Deschend trace in Icelandic myth may be largely archetypal. If its only natural counterpart is the very gradual wobble, it is still sufficient to render archaeology, astronomy and history at odds over Greek, Egyptian and Babylonian dating (David Rohl;

Lords of Avaris). While dating errors of about 150 years mean little in the slog of Ages, they make a lot of difference in Mediterranean and Mideast history, and could make apparent nonsense of the supposed match between Ages, eras and Egyptian dynasties. There are some indicators that Egyptian rulers were named for astronomical configurations, as the Egyptian nomes (districts) were. However their names and titles may well refer to inspirational dates, just as Popes are renamed for the spiritual ancestors of their rule, and as artworks are auto-dated to approximate eras.

In mindprint demarcation, the 30 degrees of Age Pisces lasted about 2100 years, following Age Aries of only about 1400 years, which followed Age Taurus 2 and Age Taurus 1 of about 2800 years jointly. In those centuries, the value of time, years and even days should not be assumed from current values.

Some astronomers and geologists recognise that "earth [rotational] obliquity may have been greater than 54° [almost lying on its 'side' relative to earth orbit] during most of its [geological] history. High obliquity may also provide a natural explanation for the present inclination of the lunar orbit with respect to the ecliptic at 5°, which is otherwise difficult to explain." (DM Williams, in Nature 1998 Dec 3; Low-latitude glaciation and rapid changes in the Earth's obliquity explained by obliquity-oblateness feedback. Co-authors James F Kasting and Lawrence A Frakes).

Numbering Ages by archetypes is near incidental with the Mayan myth of five Ages. Only five Ages of a potential of sixteen (or four of a potential twelve) could be traced in this study, including the immanent Age Aquarius. No artwork securely keyed to an Age Gemini inspirational framework was found, but could still be found. Type t15 t0 Gemini incidentally carries the zero and the highest number (15, or implied 16 if the doubled 5 is taken as 6) in the decoded Tarot sequence. Typology, with its inherent numerology, starts with type Taurus t1.

Ages in archaeo astronomy

Archaeo astronomers date cultural sites based on horizon azimuths (angles of rising, setting, and maximum deviations of sun, moon or planets from celestial east and west). This method had initially concluded some dates at great odds with archaeology, as in Alexander Thom's survey of Stonehenge and some other surveys of barrows and shafts. Ironically, archaeologists now accept the dating of Thom and other astronomers, and have adjusted their definitions of Late Stone Age and Bronze Age monuments and sites accordingly. The major cause of this variance in dating is the

assumption of a nearly static earth obliquity, dilating a little smaller, then a little larger (the Newcombe curve). Variant archaeological datings of Sumerian, Egyptian and Greek eras add to the scramble (David Rohl; Lords of Avaris). There are several loosely defined schools of archaeo astronomy. The azimuth (horizon angles) dating school was formalised and popularised by Prof Alexander Thom. It is prone to several problems of assumption, interpretation, as well as faulted historical and archaeological data.

The 'ethnography as astronomy' school was popularised by Prof Giorgio de Santillana and Prof Hertha von Deschend in Hamlet's Mill, a review of a specific theme in Icelandic myth that they ascribe to a major shift of one of the poles. Their paradigm of myth as proto astronomy, though not clearly formulated, is not supported in this study. They included a few images at the back of their book, briefly captioned, and not directly related to the text, including a Guinea calabash carving (see theme t12) implying 'primitive astronomy'. The present study found several other calabashes in the carving tradition in West Africa containing mindprint, but only vague rumours of a supporting astronomy or astrology tradition. Islamic scientific documents preserved at Timbuktu in Mali contain very little astronomy (Thebu Medupe; Cosmic Africa project. Also a movie documentary on his work).

There is more substantial Arabic astronomy in the Middle East, but lacking myth and art, as usual in astronomy. Some Mali treatises deal with determining great circle directions to Mecca, measuring time by the sun to determine noon, and little else. A vesica piscis (fish section) in the outline of saureans (lizards or crocodiles) on Guinea calabashes, appears in an Arabic treatise in Mali, derived from noon shadow pattern geometry. There are some astronomical icons in the primitive (informally schooled) calabash, yet one icon is misplaced by conscious interference, and it functions on all levels as myth, not science.

Dogon culture contains the usual allegories and myths of fish people, shooting stars, spherical concepts and culture heroes, but little astronomy (see the Anthropology section). The calabash carving remained a provocative curiosum, a rhetorical prompt that seems typical of archaeo astronomy literature.

This study takes ethnography and archaeo astronomy to their more logical conclusion; Icelandic poets (however long-winded the vowel combinations and cycles of Snorri Sturlasson) and artists work in an encompassing archetypal, subconscious cycle and geometry of types, parts of which incidentally resemble the myth that is also used in astronomical labels.

The lunatic fringe of the 'conscious, literal, historic origins' paradigm seeks extraterrestrial super-cultural origins for everything from myth to buildings to DNA. These fringe ideas are sustained by an archetype that could be labelled founder effect, or culture heroes (perhaps an attribute of type Gemini t15 t0 and Type Taurus t1 t16 Auriga-Orion, flanking the galactic gate where souls allegorically churn in and out of the physical and conscious realms).

Paradigms of the same kind also pervade science. Science is the un-confessed sponsor of the lunatic fringe by its 'invention, development and culture' paradigm. If an invention or development seems super-human or outside its designated cultural context, popular imagination will populate history with travelling super-humans, instead of accepting that any people anywhere could heal, carve, move rock, make telescopes (Robert Temple; Crystal sun), compose epics, move mountains (by juggling co-ordinates) and express archetypal sets for their own sake.

The mindprint sequence of stereotypical attributes forming holographic types, with its earthbound cycles and its analogy to earthbound sets such as the physiology of eyes, hands, the animal kingdom, and our particularly oblique and wobbling view of seasons and Ages, piles on evidence that no supposed aliens could be involved in art, or in any of our cultural structures such as grammar and gods. Life in a different mixture of gases, gravity, radiation and time cycles would express archetype differently. Aliens do not make finches, humans, pyramids, crop circles or art. There are simpler explanations in our complex consciousness.

The perpetually expected collective 'transformation' (all too easily equated with evolution) is an archetype itself. The only effect on history would be another set of subtle iconographic changes which myth expresses as somehow catastrophic, as in the recent '2012 calendric zero' hype. Neither Age Aries nor Age Pisces changed human behaviour or art, nor would Age Aquarius, hinging on a further slight change in the position of the celestial poles.

Age Aries

Occasional eclipses in Aries activate its attributes of zero point, double dragon, twined necks, orbital tracks, egg, shield, calendar reform, synchronisation, spiritual and temporal covenants. Aries forms a snaky ladder, or extended hinging tongs. Its seasonal end (or precessional start) divides its quarter of the sky in half (45 degrees from the gate, and 45 degrees from the polar axle). Even now, with spring near the 'first point' of Pisces, where the stereotypical 'first point of Aries' has been dragged by astronomy (like

turning the face of a clock to reset the time instead of adjusting the clock hands), Aries constellation remains the conceptual zero point. Times are not created equal, nor are events as a function of time. Just as artistic types carry clusters of related attributes taken from a continuum of shapes and concepts, so relative times are defined by a sequence. However time is read from a moving zero point, not on a static dial. Tacking sets of space against time, labours against seasons, or characters against hours, requires only a mutual zero point and respective rotational directions. No two sets in concept, nature or culture tack perfectly, likewise types and time remain somewhat out of synch. Types are centred on a concept analogous to the ecliptic pole, and time is centred on a concept analogous to the celestial pole. Their equators cross at the two equinox points, a moving node that enforces iconographic updates.

Arian elements such as Amun came into their own in Age Aries, but like all of the sixteen types, were ever present before and since.

Alexander the Great had become the pivotal emperor of the Western world in the latter half of Age Aries, about BC 332. He is shown with ram's horns on some medallions. His family coat of arms was a goat skin aegis, two skins tied together with the wool on the inside, icon of a divine parenthood in Jupiter by the goat Amalthea. Classical art shows Alexander in battle with two moon faces on his armour, confirming the lunar and calendric aspects of Aries.

Age Aries ended about BC 150, with various sources giving a variety of dates. Julius Caesar was a Roman Agnus Dei, Lamb of God; 'Constant as the northern star, of whose true-fixed and resting quality there is no fellow in the firmament', wrote Shakespeare in Julius Caesar. The tragedy tracks the emperor's brutal death or subconscious suicide by instigated senatorial conspiracy, and a step change in the decline of empire.

Knowingly or subconsciously, the dramatist ironically relates the Arian ruler to the mobile celestial pole in Cancer at Ursa Minor, nearing Polaris. Though it was not quite polar yet, as it nearly is now, the Aries celestial meridian lay across Polaris for some 4000 years, thanks to the direction of polar precession along a celestial cord (flattened edge of the polar circle, aligned between Aries and Virgo). Caesar remains even today, 2100 years after his assassination and four centuries after Shakespeare's verse drama, a constant icon of military, political and esoteric prowess, and of sacrificial death, nominally for the freedom of the Arian empire. Rome's chaotic legacy after the death of its most iconic leader is a typical set tragedy for an Age transition.

Cosmic punctuation at the end of the Roman era is confirmed by messianic expectations in many Roman colonies, as in Judea, where John Baptist, Christ and Judas Iscariot became sacrificial characters. Egypt produced similar figures at the time, including Cleopatra and her sister Arsinoe who died in exile as a priestess at the temple of Artemis in Ephesus, Turkey.

Countries outside the Roman sphere had still more characters to personify the transition.

Julius Caesar, high priest and titular calendar reformer, understood precession. His advisors also exchanged calculations with their new Egyptian subjects.

Shakespeare had good material to work with, in history already bent to archetypal types and times.

Spring sacrifice assumes cosmic significance at the cusp of Ages. The ides of March was a remnant of a belated calendric reform that had moved spring into nominal March. The spring date was changed by calendar reform in Caesar's name.

Christ in several respects is also an Aries-Pisces transition character. After Rome had adopted Christianity, royals sought and found family ties with wandering Jews to declare themselves descendants of the newly legendised mediator (Baigent, Lee, and Lincoln; Holy blood, holy grail).

Several elements in the lives and legends of Julius Caesar and Christ run parallel; kingship (emperor and designated dictator versus ceremonial 'king of Jews'), priesthood (high priest versus teacher), disputed books (Sibylline extortion for oracular books versus temple scrolls removed to Qumran, or to the rival temple at Mount Hermon, with a rival priesthood still at Svat), calendric dispute (calendar reform versus a prophecy and birthdate disputed between Pharisees and Sadducees), Egyptian visits (conquest, calendar reform and conspiracy with Cleopatra versus a flight into Egypt), oration (senatorial and funeral speeches versus Judaic sectoral debates, sermons, and apostolic letters), death for a doomed cause (pileus of Roman freedom versus Judaic self-government), death instead of a criminal (prisoners set free versus the 'Caiaphas or Jesus' vote), betrayal by a protégé (Brutus versus Judas), torn cloth or hat (pileus, versus vera icona or 'veronica', true image, temple veil and shroud), wreath crown (laurel wreath and refused imperial crown versus crown of thorns), public opinion divided (civil war versus the Caiaphas vote, the Sanhedrin's split loyalty, and Pharisee-Sadducee factions), alleged arrogance (dictator versus 'king of Jews' and 'son of God'), and birth from a virgin (reputed Caesarean section versus unmarried mother).

Brutus betrays his friend, mentor and king who is destined for political sacrifice, mints dagger coins (Triangulum) for his rebel troops (see t3 t18), and fall on his own sword. Judas betrays his prophet and perhaps family relation (Benjamin and Judah were related), who is destined for sacrifice, receives silver coins, hangs himself or is disembowelled. Judas Iscariot's second name might mean 'assassin', based on a word for 'dagger'. Judas dies on the Field of Blood or Potter's field, near where Abraham was once directed to sacrifice his son, Canaanite style, when his dagger (Triangulum) was stayed to substitute an Arian 'ram in a thicket'. In the Gospel of Judas, the Apostles see a vision of Jerusalem priests sacrificing and slaughtering animals, and Judas writes of "sacrifices brought to completion." Caesar dies by the plot and daggers of fellow senators, Christ in a plot by fellow spiritual teachers including the Sanhedrin, Jewish elders acting as Roman vassals. His precursor, John Baptist, is beheaded, a Taurus t1 Auriga and Aquarius t5 t20 type, both 45 degrees either side of Triangulum, both at one of the four galactic corners, both reputed for clutching heads (see Auriga Artemis types clutching goats, and healers wearing a skin tailcoat with the head still attached behind at theme t5 t20).

In the Gospel of Judas (57), Jesus says to Judas; "Look up... stars around a cloud... the star that leads the way is your star [Aries Triangulum?]." The victim is inciting his would-be assassin to a coup, like Caesar incited the plotters in a series of irreversible steps.

Brutus adopts the pileus emblem after assassinating the legal protector of the freedom that the cap symbolises. The Roman pileus of liberty, a conical cap, appears on Brutus and the conspirators' field campaign coins flanked by two daggers, incidentally expressing t3 t18 Aries Triangulum, a dagger shape, knife of double-dealing Perseus, who carries a head in a bag.

Analogies between archetypal icons, constellations and historic images that happen to find their way onto coins, buildings, tombs, stamps and art, do not imply that artists and engravers keep one eye fixed on the heavens, one on heraldry, and their minds bent towards a continuous iconographic story. Rather, our collective imagination tends to select, sometimes to engineer and to record archetypally relevant events and icons. Gestalt is a function of selective experience and memory grafted on archetypal structure.

Propaganda is a particularly rife area for archetypes, since propagandists invoke archetypes, but usually fail to bend them to their ends. Archetypes instead tend to bend politics to their own ends. Comedy and tragedy by definition are partly pre-ordained.

While Caesar is styled in a mixture of history, propaganda and synchretic (combined) Roman myth, the Gospel is styled in Levantine wisdom literature, eschatological Egypto -Assyro -Judaic motifs, colonial politics and textbook Greek myths, syncretised in some years of correspondence, travels and visits between Hellenised multicultural scribes, and rehearsed in the slums and catacombs of Rome and her colonies, including servant quarters of elite resorts such as Baia (Pozzuoli, near Rome). These two sets of codes are recognisably different, yet the archetypal content in both consistently centres on Aries Agnus types, processes, characters and icons. Caesar and Christ stand for two sides of the same coin, mirrored by the movement of spring from Aries to Pisces.

Julius Caesar had extended the Arian administration of Rome to far-flung parts, but Arian or any other archetypes need no diffusion to be universal. The same administration, under a succession of cultures, soon extended Piscean administration to the world, including its new church and its colonial Agnus Dei.

Age Pisces

Pisces appears in some star maps as two fish on ribbons, thus 'crossed fish', like the XP chi-rho symbol of the Christian church, or a V framing the Pegasus square as a pond, field, square-bodied horse or elephant.

Icons of Ages are popularised in retrospect, as Age Aries was. Sacrificed lambs with bent necks, or as skinned quarries, or speared Aries-Cetus dragons, appeared only after the end of Age Aries, since about BC 150. For that reason Age Pisces icons are rare among the welter of Age Aries and Age Taurus-inspired artworks, but would yet come to dominate iconography.

Age Pisces may be legendised as the Cetus Whale being harpooned (on a larger scale than Moby Dick) or horses or elephants massacred. The next Age may be dominated by icons marking the demise of Age Pisces, perhaps a dying horse (see a horse smiter in rock art at theme t15), divided or united field such as the Berlin Wall, inverted fish, speared whale, or the last Bushman (see Mandela's San and Aquarian features at theme t5 t20).

Popular millennial expectations ran high, especially in the former Mayan region, of which the world expected calendric fireworks in 2012 that fizzed out into speculations on the Arab spring and regime changes, as such expectations regularly do. Eternally sporadic new age fever, well recorded for the last 2000 years, spurred by hype about the years 2000,

2012 and the Scandinavian Ragnarok of February 2014, may have prompted some artists to anticipate Age Aquarius before its imminent date in 2016 (derived in this study from the date the spring equinox would be 90 degrees from the Gemini-Taurus gate, which is now our midsummer marker).

The celestial pole now clings to the hoof or panhandle tip of Ursa Minor, between the Gemini-Taurus gate and the ecliptic pole. The mobile pole will gradually slip away over Taurus Auriga towards Camelopardalis (Giraffe), while the southern celestial pole gradually leaves Octans to head for Crux (Southern Cross), figured as a giraffe in some African star lore (see a Bushman hunter's 'giraffe' hand-signal in a paradise scene at theme t3 t18. See giraffe forequarters as a polar gauge in rock art with X-shaped giraffe people at theme t1). Since a giraffe resembles an equine, it echoes the Pegasus (Horse) theme shared between type Pisces t4 and Aquarius t5 t20. Since it has a long neck suitable to the Agnus (Lamb) theme of a spring sacrifice (see Picasso's Guernica at theme t1 t16, and several horses in the type Aries t3 position), the current transition may already be figured in some illustrations in this study.

Age Aquarius

Whether a new universal zero point would arise in Age Aquarius, or whether the signs (not constellations) would just keep on precessing, slipping backwards against the seasonal round by about one degree per 72 years (currently slightly speeding up), could not be resolved in this study. Age Aquarius may enforce the first major inconographic shift in the last 90 degrees, partly since the first point of the sign (celestial zodiac concept) of Aries would venture more than 30 degrees from where it left Aries constellation territory (by mindprint allocation of the sky, keyed to galactic and polar corners). Astronomy tables would become awkward, citing the sun or a planet or a star's position as '1 degree Aries' while the planet or star is at 30 degrees Aquarius, or 40 degrees Aquarius if the uneven constellation angular widths of mindprint are followed.

Aquarius is variously figured as a healer, angel, bull (see the Narmer palette at theme t3 t18), lion (see the Seti 1 decans at theme t8), horse (Pegasus), elephant (see Bernini's fountain in Rome and in the Hypnerotomachia Poliphili, and eastern elephants on Cetus turtles), pond, or monkey (Aquarius retro, facing backward).

The calendric and iconic logic that pictured mobile, archetypal spring as a hunter or bull in Age Taurus 1, as a bull or monstrous hero in Age Taurus 2, a ram or dragon in Age Aries, and a fish or horse in Age

Pisces, may resort to a bull again, or an angel, perhaps with Pegasus wings or a Whale spout. There are still too few Age Aquarius myths and artworks to tell.

Planets may animate attributes

Planetary positions may calibrate epochs within Ages, particularly the slow-moving Jupiter and Saturn and their trigon of major conjunctions that moves in slow steps around the ecliptic, somewhat like a twisted triangular turbine piston in a rotary engine. Most major typological attributes are so prevalent that planetary parallels are ruled out: type Leo t13 is marked on his heart in 85% of works, Virgo t11 on her pregnant womb in 87% of works, Taurus t1 or t2 is a bovine in 19% of artworks. No planet could be in Leo, Virgo, Taurus or any other sign or constellation more than 6% to 8% of the time (depending on which division is used) on average over about a century. Planetary mirrors should therefore be sought among the minor (rare) attributes, such as feline, canine, double-headed, or functions not yet identified.

Planetary icons may be as easy to identify as the sixteen stationary types, four galactic corners and three sets of poles are, partly since there are only seven visible luminaries or 'moving stars' (Uranus perhaps an eighth), with polarising attributes in their complementary pairing of Sun and Moon, Jupiter and Saturn, Mars and Venus, Mercury and the asteroid belt or Uranus. They are figured in all cultures, including early Islamic art. Yet the prospect of untangling planetary attributes from tupos (place or constellation types), both claiming ecliptic space, is daunting due to the high apparent orbital frequency of the inner planets (Venus, Mars, and Mercury's loops around the sun).

Planets may be 'switches' activating decanal (optional) aspects of each of the sixteen types, or the general theme of an artwork. Future studies may well divide each type into five or six planetary components or decanal elements, and test whether the slower planets could be isolated as reflecting these. For example, type Scorpius t9 may well consist of typological elements such as Chelae (Claws), bent forward, Serpens Caput (Head), Bootes Corona (Crown) lamp, Lupus (Wolf), fire torch, and so on, with typically one or two activated by the presence of planetary concepts, in inspirational time as usual, not necessarily reflecting planetary positions at the time of the work.

Nostradamus in his Centuries noted planets in various positions in times past and future as a permutation exercise, revealing events likely to co-incide with the activation of certain types. Part of the wide variety of interpretations of his verses may well lie in reading his astronomical or astrological terms as either ecliptic or celestial positions, while the other is subconsciously intended, or either positional or planetary attributes, while the other is intended (Mars could mean Aries, Aries could mean Mars). The broad historic scope of his verses adds the question of precessional Ages; which Aries does he refer to if it were celestial, since the celestial positions move with precession? A set of emblems reputed to be painted by Nostradamus, or by an inspired illustrator, may resolve aspects of his enigmatic verses. Both sets require translation into archetypal terminology first.

Most apparent predictions hinge on archetypal elements or on individual types and not the full structure. Nostradamus did not predict, he expressed patterns in events, down to minute details keyed to archetypal icons, personalities and places. There will always be a city, tower, king, goddess and war to act out the repertoire.

Nostradamus was a healer, prophet and astronomer, but astronomy is no requisite for prophecy, as Siener van Rensburg, Credo Mutwa and countless other prophets prove. Enoch recorded prophecy with apparent astronomical detail that he either did not understand, or could not clearly express.

We should study their iconography, not their astronomy, culture or politics. If Nostradamus were a painter, he may have made emblematic art. His verses express archetypal inspiration in iconographic doggerel, a mixture of folk phrases and learned terms, or academic slang. The greatest seer resorted to alchemical language to express patterns in what we perceive as history.

As in the work of Jung, planetary astrology in its classical or scientific versions proved too broad and too dynamic to reveal the structure of myth and art. Planetary types on a stereotypical astrological 'board' are insufficient to the task, just as astrology requires a formidable bank of data and processes to translate its celestial clockwork into history.

The mindprint spiral chart clockwise

Chart [b1]. The subconscious sequence and structure of visual archetypes forms a semi-spiral clasp.

Below is an example of the typological sequence and geometric structure in seasonal, clockwise direction, in formal art (Egyptian afterlife on payprus. Mindprint analysis by Edmond Furter). The galactic centre between types Sagittarius t7 and Scorpius t8, both as hieroglyphic figures, is a canal vortex (see hieroglyphs as figures also in Babylonia and Mexico). A sand mound formed by water expresses the idea of becoming in Egyptian theology. Giza waterworks, including the Sphinx reservoir (Robert Temple) and lower shafts (Edward Malkowski) incidentally express the concept of the galactic centre and four galactic corners. The galactic poles are both on the edges or 'elbow' banks of akhet horizon hieroglyphs, representing desert hills in a cross-section of the Nile valley. A celestial polar marker on the elbow of an extra, polar Gemini t15, tags the inspiration as Age Aries-Pisces, but his hand tags the earlier Age Aries, and the foot of a benben bird on an obelisk provides for the future Age Aquarius. Artists are not conscious of most of the aspects of the iconographic hologram that they express.

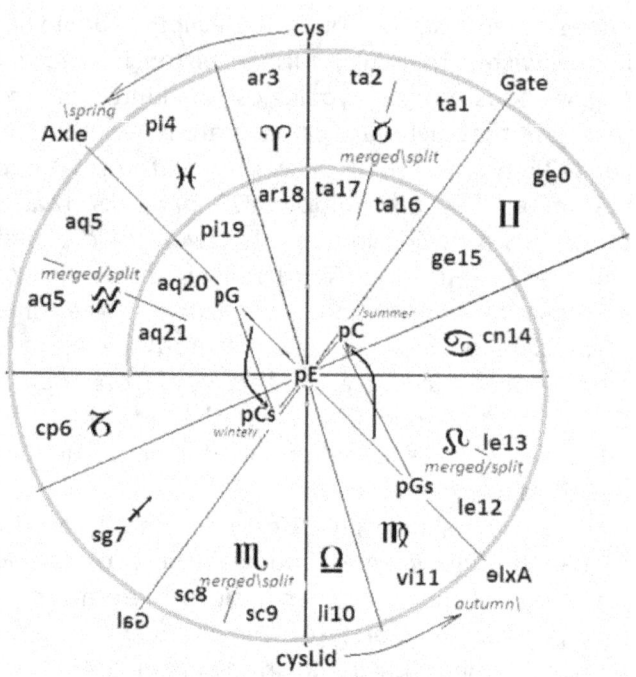

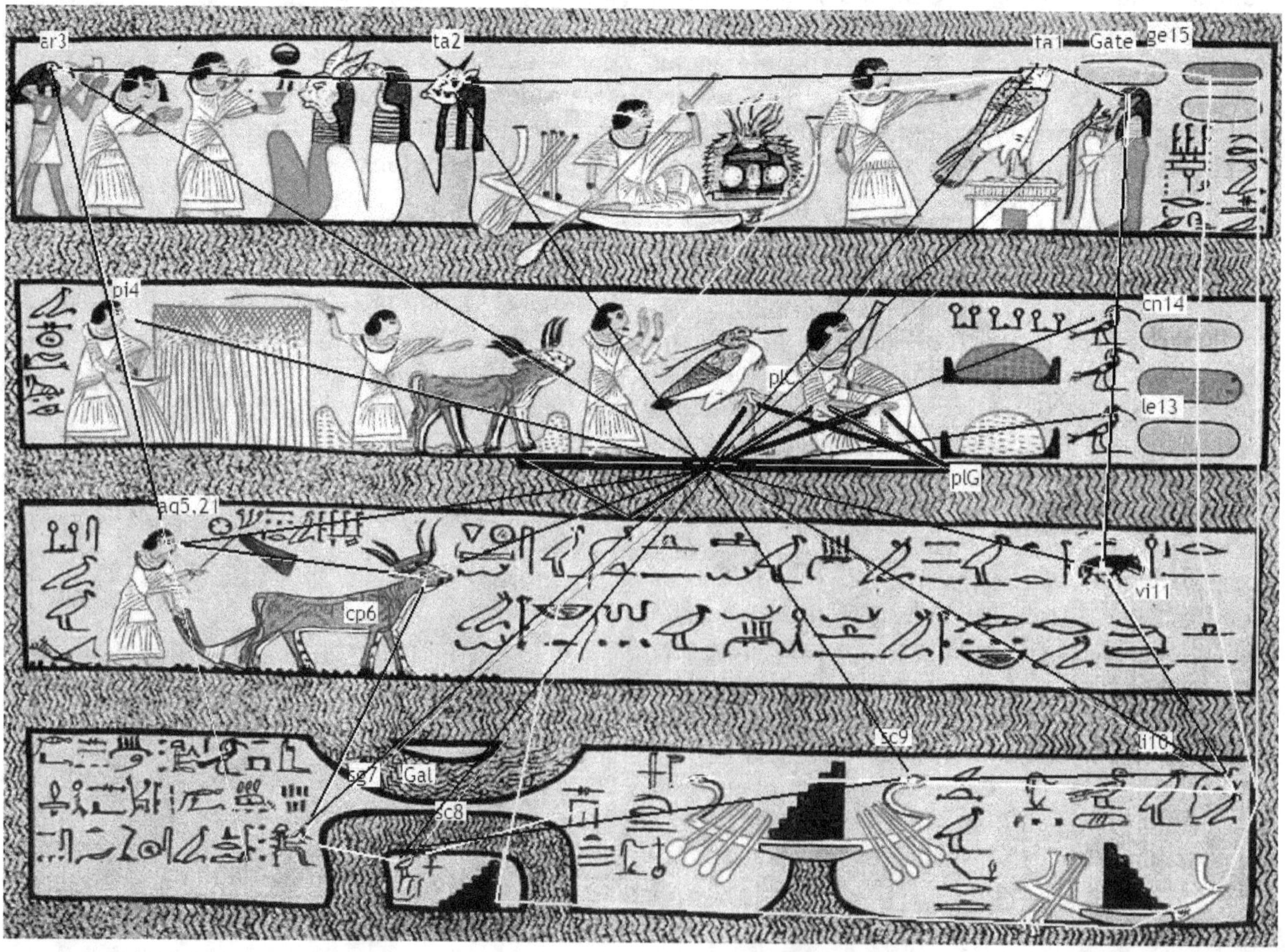

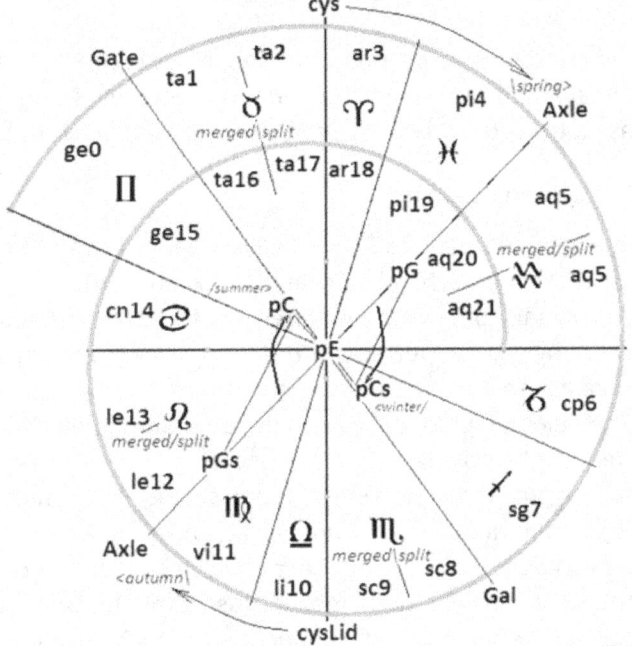

The mindprint spiral chart anticlox

Chart [b2]. The subconscious sequence and structure of visual archetypes forms a semi-spiral clasp.

The graph applies to art, emblems, icons, cosmology, astronomical decans and Tarot trumps (see the Decans section, and the Tarot section).

The graph may also apply to some core sections of the periodic table of elements, often tabulated as a spiral or cone with tangential loops or layers involving fractal geometry. Nature herself and crop circles also express conical projections.

Below is an example of the typological sequence and geometric structure in Australian rock art (Kimberley Foundation. Mindprint analysis by Edmond Furter).

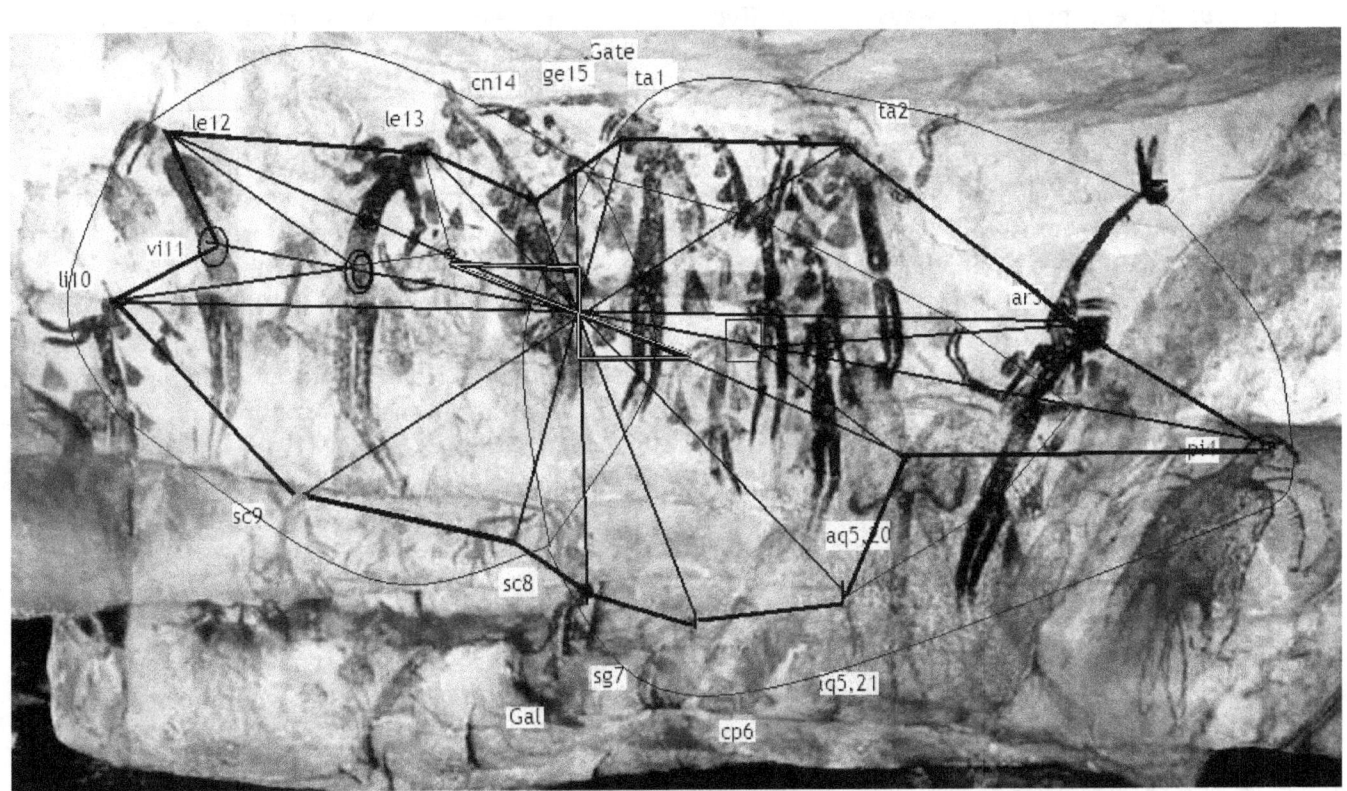

The structure in our art

Type Scorpius t8 t9 Ophiuchus as a giant tree-stump face holding a bee colony, with satyrs and people collecting honey and preparing mead (Pierro De Cosimo; Discovery of honey. Mindprint analysis by Edmond Furter).

Ecliptic equator figures are each identified by some of the attributes (gender, posture, function or implements) of their type, as well as by the position of their eyes in the circular sequence, and axes to the eyes of their opposite types.

Type Taurus t1 Auriga as a satyr kid below an adult hand, recalls the goat kids of Artemis. Type Taurus t2 Pleiades Perseus as the crouching leader with a mirror or ladle, recalls the rainmaker posture. Type Aries t3 Triangulum as a wielder of bellows or a hammer, recalls the instruments of sacrifice. Type Pisces t4 Pegasus is male, with an implement of two rectangles. Type Aquarius t5 is a prominent priest, here with a tuning fork. His more human appearance, and position between satyrs and women with human technology, inverts his usual attributes of being the half human among regular people or animals (see men with painted legs and antelope with human hind legs at theme t5). Type Capricornus t6 is a boy with only the lower legs of a goat, as in Pan and sea-goat myth. Type Sagittarius t7 is more animal than human, as in centaur myth. Type Scorpius t8 t9 Ophiuchus in the mouth of the trunk over a spring or pool, expresses the galactic centre. Type Libra t10 has one arm in a V-shaped position as usual, his regular staff here figured by some herbs. Type Virgo t11 is always a womb. Type Leo 12 t13 is always a heart, often linked on a bare chest or back, here both. Type Cancer t14 is often the eye of the Leo or Virgo type, here of both. Type Gemini t15 as Bacchus expresses his usual function as a large creator churning bodies or souls, and his doubled nature is expressed by a passenger. The Geminian axis continues to another doubled figure, a satyr carrying a companion on his back (see a jackal abducting a sheep in a paradise parody at theme t3).

Every expression of mindprint contains choices among optional attributes, and some imperfections. Here type Sagittarius t7 has his back turned, an attribute more usual of the adjacent type Scorpius t8 Ophiuchus (which here is combined with type Scorpius t9). Type Aries t3 is not figured by its eye, but by a hand operating a bellows or hammer, which is a kind of buck bag more typical of the eight types flanking the four galactic corners. The overall sequence and structure remains clear.

Artistic equators

Ecliptic equator points follow a sectioned, angular outline, with economy of line in some sections, as here between the eyes of type Taurus t1, Type Gemini t15 and type Cancer t14, which are connected by a continuous line.

Galactic equators (thin oblique semi-ovals) always cross the figures equator (ecliptic) between types Taurus t1 and Gemini t15, and between Scorpius t8 and Sagittarius t7, overlapping in the interior and continuing in two exterior lobes. These two equators usually divide compositional groups, here culture and nature.

Subconscious inspiration and conscious composition always overlap, yet artists are not aware of using attributes, postures, sequence or standard structure.

Polar triangles in art

The galactic pole (pG) is always near the equator, between type Leo t12 Crater (Grail) and type Virgo t11, usually on a limb joint, here on the shoulder of a crawling figure, perhaps drunk with mead and thus relevant to grail and elixir concepts.

The celestial pole (pC) is usually on a limb joint near the ecliptic pole (axial focus), and on or near the axis of the current or recent summer solstice, thus near type Gemini t15, type Cancer t14, or in older works near type Leo t13 or t12. Here the celestial pole is on the shoulder of a satyr mother just after the Gemini t15 axis, where the celestial pole was just before Age Pisces. Her elbow marks a preceding Age. Her jaw marks Cosimo's forthcoming (now current) Age Pisces-Aquarius.

The galactic south pole (pGs) is always between types Aquarius t5 and Pisces t4, but not always marked. Here it is on the jaw of an extra figure (marked on an eye in error before the role of limb joints was statistically confirmed).

The celestial south pole on the hip of type Aries t3 tags the inspiration as Age Pisces, or just prior to Age Pisces, although De Cosimo worked in late Age Pisces. The retro inspiration confirms the theme of a long gone paradise.

Inspirational dating is a subtle geometric, mythical, conceptual and iconographic aspect of archetypal expression, demonstrating the depth of holographic structure in artistic inspiration or expression. Even gifted nature spirits such as De Cosimo, on par with the best artists and rock artists in the world by any definition, did not consciously know mindprint, and could not fake it.

Both sides of a flat sphere

Mindprint structure compares to a sphere, imagined from above the sun and simultaneously from above the earth. Armillary spheres, the basis of time and navigation instruments such as astrolabes, also express concepts of earthbound space and time, from a merger of these two apparently contradictory perspectives. In addition to the dual angelic perspective from infinitely far above, which is north by convention, the mirrored and almost equal perspective from the south is included in art.

A model of perception requires parts of two armillary spheres, the northern one flared out and cut generously around its equator to retain complete zodiac and decans figures (see the iris image), as well as the complete southern galactic equator (see the Cosmic map). The southern hemisphere is cut stingily to avoid zodiac duplication, but its mirrored view of the galaxy is retained inside the squashed centre, as well as outside on the flared rim. Thus mindprint contains two armillary sets, of three poles and five equators each. The ecliptic pole appears as one since they are viewed or 'squashed' along their own axle. Celestial equators are not shown for the sake of simplicity.

The resulting myth map differs from astronomical maps in reducing the celestial pole (of daily rotation) to a minor role, focussing on the ecliptic pole (of yearly orbit), and assigning the celestial equator or equators to a minor role, focussing on the ecliptic equator instead. There are no degrees of difficulty among the miracles of perception and expression.

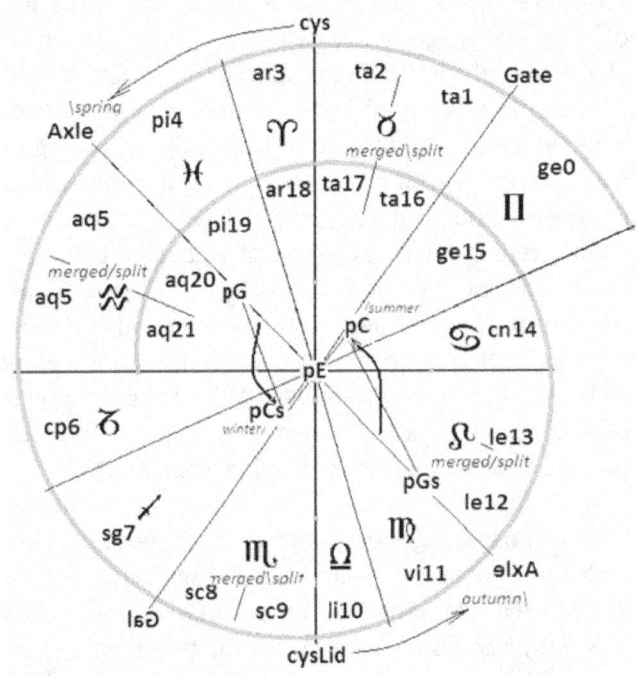

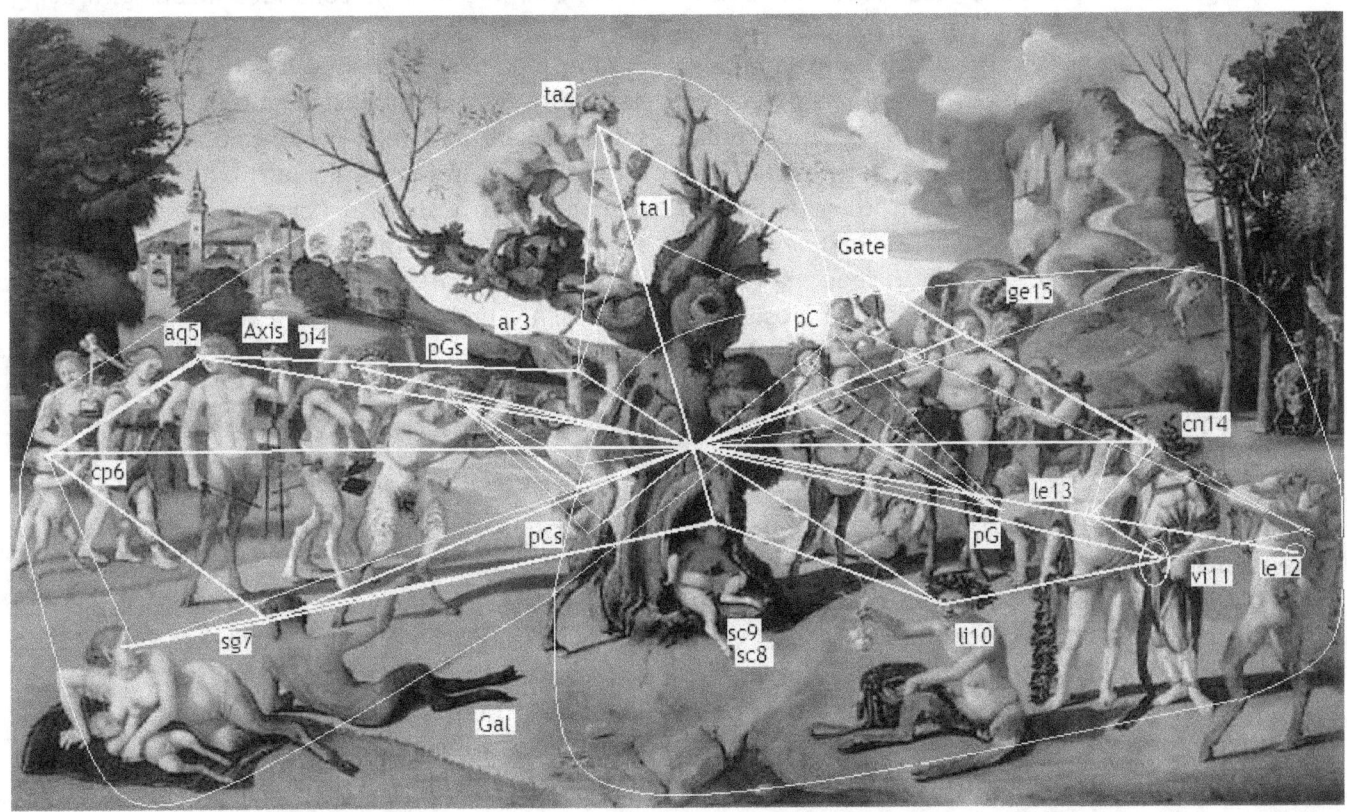

Conscious and subconscious meaning in art

Chapter F

Recurrent attributes and the geometry of their sequence reveal sixteen types in art. The periphery of their eyes is generally oval, but radially distorted, like a wheel with sixteen spokes of varied length. Occasional equatorial line economy along the 'rim' (the eyes of three, four or even five figures being on the same peripheral line) strengthens visual coherence, but ironically adds disguise to the oval, like flattening out one quarter of an oval net shape.

Even convex or warped surfaces accommodate mindprint art. Warped surfaces may induce more equatorial line economy (see Bulgarian goat people at theme t15, or the Namibian 'White Lady' panel at theme t5 t21, with a near rectangular equator formed by four sections of outline economy).

Types identify themselves by figurative attributes, such as posture, gender, objects (in the way that the Eight Immortals of China are recognised by their signature implements), and their relative positions in the peripheral sequence. Some of these categories are recognised as symbolic by the artist and culture members, such as a healer's bandolier strap or arms-back posture, a hunter or warrior's weapon, a dominant bull, a pregnant ewe, mother, newborn, species, age, season, enemy, threat, family relationship, and so on. Most attributes are recognised as having more than their apparent meanings by viewers everywhere. Real, everyday categories also bear semi-conscious symbolic meaning, as well as subconscious and positional meaning. Art speaks a language of familiar words, but with a grammar of its own.

For example, people grasp some of the meanings of the Tower of Babel legend, the New York terror attacks, and Bruce Springsteen's lyrics about the event (or rather about Western reaction to the event, related to the opposite type at Scorpius t8, including the attribute of a feat of strength), at various conscious and subconscious levels. Most people could explain that the Bible uses the legend to teach lessons based on the ideas of pride, blasphemy, cross purposes and retribution. Iconographers could add concepts related to the

four bee 'races' or tribes, different meanings attached to slightly different buzzing frequencies, beehive raids, regicide, and competing religious and economic blocks. Mindprint adds the archetypal label type Taurus t1 t16 Auriga and Orion, allowing direct comparisons with this type in any other artwork. Some of the arguably 'real' meanings related to pride, exploitation, trade, states, colonies, mud towers, swifts, lightning and gates are certainly symbolic, arguably semi-conscious or subconscious, and thus 'unreal', not generally understood, yet still effective on emotional, aesthetic and spiritual levels. This study therefore does not draw a sharp distinction between conscious and subconscious levels, or inherent, iconic, symbolic and archetypal meanings. The study is itself enabled by overlap of the levels of consciousness and kinds of meaning.

Members and non-members of the culture of an artist, such as Zulu artist Credo Mutwa (see two of his reputed 9/11 prediction works at theme t1 t16), understand his paintings at various levels at different times (such as before and after the infamous terror attacks), and could verbalise some of their understanding. Many are misguided by ready and popular assumptions of 'prediction' and 'history', particularly after the iconic events.

Members of the globalised Western culture express and understand some archetypes in the story and movies of the Wizard of Oz, but may not consciously or verbally link the Oz tower to Babel or the world tree, or to any symbol at all, or may simply not care to verbalise meanings with no apparent practicality and of apparently foreign cultural styling.

As an example of semi-conscious meaning, a dying horse under a rain of bombs is understood as the collateral damage and suffering of war, yet its bent neck, as a type of sacrificial lamb, is understood by some viewers, its Trojan Horse aspect understood by others, while some of its attributes as inverted rainmaker, its posture as Perseus holding Medusa's severed head or as the head itself, and its role as a former spring marker updated to Age Pisces Pegasus (Horse), are understood by the artist and viewers at a subconscious level.

Picasso painted a billowing white face as a kind of scream in Guernica (see theme t1 t16), perhaps without intending to visually cite Dali's billowing white face titled 'It just popped up', and both without intending to express an attribute of type Gemini t15 t0. Salvador Dali painted elephants on spindly legs without recognising (or being recognised for expressing) some of the attributes of the type now identified as type Pisces t4 Pegasus.

Zulu healer Credo Mutwa painted several scenes of what he describes as tribal history, creators, gods, ancestors, judgement of kings and supposed aliens, unaware of rare structural icons such as a squatting baboon at the spring equinox (see Mutwa's Rain tree trio at theme t1 t16, and a Babylonian cone at theme t11). Mutwa painted a multi-headed and long-necked dragon resembling the Apocalypse Angers tapestry of 1375 in Paris, which he may have seen in a book, but he had no conscious way of knowing where to place the dragon, which he termed an ancestral monster mother figure in the context of his Afro-Christian myth. Yet she stands in her usual place in the subconscious sequence as the type now identified as type Aries t3 t18, a long-necked dragon. In the rain panel, Mutwa placed a long-necked bird in the type Aries t3 t18 position instead.

Dali, Picasso and Mutwa are among many inspired artists who implicitly answer the question of conscious and subconscious categories; they see their work in cultural terms, as learned, idealised, didactic experience, unaware that every culture and creed (the Latin word that gave Credo Mutwa his first name) is a thorough mixture of renewed and borrowed expressions, and unaware of much of the meanings even in the plainly visible attributes they paint. Rock art and schooled art in all ages are no different.

Attributes, internal context and cultural context in art operate simultaneously at several cognitive and cultural levels.

In these examples the subconscious itself is revealed as an integral part of consciousness, partly accessible, layered, universal and therefore collective, yet with some seemingly hidden components. Most of the meaning and function in art, including rock art, should therefore be understood as 'unreal', meaning that it did not (and does not) consciously represent its meanings to the artist or to most viewers.

Some contemplation and effort is always rewarded by layers of meaning, approaching the underlying archetypal structure. Some meaning remains subconscious, yet not wasted, nor beyond logic.

Even conscious meaning requires some effort to understand and assimilate into various contexts. 'Real' categories in rock art, such as bags, hunt, dancing, animals and half humans, partly understood in their cultures and in all cultures, are just as much subconscious. Prophets struggle to relate their visions in sermons or in writing, gurus resort to parables, artists resort to mythical scenes. Mindprint confirms that every artwork is a continuum of meaning. Symbolic figures and attributes by definition are both real and unreal, yet there are firm universal links between their meanings on variant levels of consciousness, irrespective of cultural emphasis.

Mindprint is a lens that raises subconscious visual meanings to conscious appreciation. A residue remains subconscious, and yet another residue in each work remains imperfect or less accessible, compared perhaps to relatively more 'true' images or more rehearsed myths such as the Trojan War or Eternal Battle.

The mindprint equator, axial pattern and polar features are entirely subconscious to artists and viewers, yet anyone could memorise the sequence and some of the attributes of types, and test their identifications by drawing axial lines.

Mundane interpretations of art, for example 'a bombing raid, stag hunt, ritual, bullfight, or lion stalk incident' are valid on a conscious level to the artist and any culture familiar with war, bovines and felines. However conscious or cultural logic seldom contradicts, overrides, distorts or invalidates the collective subconscious types, seldom interferes with the sequence, and does not seem to affect the geometric structure at all.

Thigh and rump wounds or arrow shots offer examples of partly conscious archetypal meaning in art. Poisoned arrows in a rump could slow down the quarry during the initial chase, and minimise contamination and spoilage of the meat. Even such apparently practical considerations in art usually mirror universal, enduring and spiritual themes. Hunting finesse does not account for the prevalence of rump wounds in many icons in all cultures and Ages, often placed at type Gemini t15 t0 (see the Tables of types).

The New Testament motif of a Roman soldier spearing Christ in the thigh is a popular theme in religious art, based on more than one Bible verse. Tarot trump 0, Jester, is bitten on his thigh by a dog, and his other level of expression, trump 15, Devil or worldly creator, is linked by chains from his thighs to Adam and Eve type figures, forming a churn group with ropes.

This mythic and artistic icon is not necessarily learned from prior cultures, but even where it is acquired, only its place in eternal archetypal structure could sustain it.

There is no reason for any culture to borrow its mythology or art from prior or richer cultures, while its own poets and artists have the same on offer. The same 'partly conscious' status applies to all the features of archetypal inspiration, 'tradition' and style.

Art's core content and function

Mindprint in art demonstrates that there is no original experience or creativity, yet we sing hallelujah. Nature and all spiritual traditions embrace repetition. Whether we need to understand the structure of the song is an academic question. This study demonstrates that large parts of artistic inspiration, expression and their uses go unstudied. By the same token, schooling, academia and conceptualisation do not affect the core content, function or quality of visual art. Other arts and crafts are more dependent on academic and technological advances. Art is among the Stone Age crafts updated merely by materials and superficial styling, just as language still uses sounds, diction and grammar, and music still uses frequencies, texture, timing, phrasing and ensemble. An inborn neurological function is visibly at work in art.

There are few limits to the tales that expression could tell, and few limits to what people could know, but many limits to what we could formulate, and yet more limits to what we could learn and teach. Pictures and emblems are good at revealing structure, as esoteric traditions such as alchemy and kabbalah demonstrate. Yet most pictures only enable knowledge, and rarely carry knowledge itself (as technical diagrams or flow charts do).

This study sought differences in spiritual inspiration between cultures, ages, eras and individual artists, but found only persistent core content and structural quality. We tell the same stories and trace the same pictures untaught. Rock art, perceived as a mixture of spiritual and mundane inspiration, is as cultural and political as formally schooled art. Recent analyses of some contact period (post European migration) rock art in southern Africa as 'protest art', or 'desperate spiritual rituals for protection against a superior force', are moving towards equating rock art with art, yet still seek literal explanations for every figure, attire and posture. Iconic logic dictates that each figure need only be itself, not requiring logical permission for its presence or posture, and not requiring conscious explanation from the artist. Art historian Alex Duffey confirms "the fact that there seems to be no progressive increase in visual sophistication" in San rock art over several thousand years (Alex Duffey; Dreaming with open eyes, 2001c).

Standardised quality is true of all artistic traditions, and of other cultural expressions such as myth and ritual. Artistic quality applies particularly to geometric structure and typological attributes. Both are now testable (see the Statistics section).

If art in the making transforms experience into structure, then in the viewing it could transform structure into experience. Jung saw artists as activating archetypes, and art thus as a hermeneutic (magical) process; "The creative process, as far as we are able to follow it at all, consists in unconscious activation of an archetypal image, elaborating and shaping it into a finished work". This "activation" is now confirmed by the apparent compulsion of inspiration for completion of the standard sequence and pattern. Jung continues; "By giving it shape, the artist translates it into the language of the present, and so makes it possible to find a way back to the deepest springs of life." (Readings in the History of Æsthetics).

Hermeneutics, for all its learned ring, has wide and varied meanings. Eliade understood it as more than interpretation. He used speculation to awaken archaic heritage, and to re-member myth. Interpretations become myth to be interpreted in turn.

In this view, the present study is itself mythical and transformative. "Creative hermeneutics changes man; it is more than instruction, it is also a spiritual technique susceptible of modifying the quality of [individual] existence... it ought to produce in the reader an awakening" (Strenski, 1987).

Eliade found that consciousness could bring to light only that which was and is always there. He regarded interpretation as experience endowing the canvas or outlines of myth with content and meaning. Eliade also regarded interpretation as re-discovery of timeless meaning, that does not require us to understand the experience or its context. These views seem to contradict the currently dominant art interpretation and training model. Art is not a progressive movement, as Leonard Cohen said he had come to realise of music and poetry; 'It's still just music and lyric.' Art history thus is a contradiction in terms, or a term to describe itself as an academic pursuit, not its subject.

"There is no art, only artists", Ernst Gombrich posed as an opening statement in The story of art. This study finds the inverse; all people are potential artists in the narrow and the broad sense of the term, and we all paint or see variations of the same picture. Artists do not shape art, but art shapes artists. There are no artists, only art.

As archetype is camouflaged in natural expression, so it is in culture. Van Eeden explains human expression thus; "What man says or thinks is the product of articulation in which he has no conscious part save to articulate it. In most cases man is not even conscious of what he is actually articulating, as is evident in certain poetry [and art]. Archetypes move themselves into existence and form the ground for bodily experience, physical expression, overt and covert behaviour. Man's body is the vehicle of this movement towards an expression of his essence."

Art infuses structure with structured scenes. The resulting holograms (or parts of the hologram, by definition) give new meaning to the stock phrase 'art for art's sake'. In this perspective, all communication is framed by archetype, which by definition is largely subconscious.

As an example of the opposite, academic paradigm of "cultural patterning", Alex Duffey sites David Lewis-Williams on the "well-known meandering red line with white dots which is found over so wide a geographical area that it seems impossible that it could have been independently conceived by different artists." (See examples in the Linton panel at theme t5 t21, where a 'rope of the sky' links the polar figure and type Libra t10; and in the Egyptian Seti 1 tomb ceiling at theme t8; and ropes, reigns and ribbons in Eskimo and Nordic art). Academia ascribes "standardised forms of the majority of the figures in San rock art" to cultural patterning and to "single painters who moved around". This study indicates the opposite, that artists and cultures all express "standardised forms" or rather standard concepts, often in similar forms.

Ouzman notes that "repeated patterns suggest that individual artistic inspiration was subject to some more widespread cognitive system." (Sven Ouzman; Towards a mindscape of landscape; rock art as expression of world understanding, 1998). Yet science seems incapable of formulating our mindscape or cognitive system. Esoterica is forever chipping away at our mindscape in stories, games and naming of parts, but seems as far from a synthesis of consciousness as the physics unified field theory is from explaining 'dark matter'. Travelling artists do not explain culture, and big bangs do not explain creation.

Mystery and initiation

Mindprint has been invisible for as long as any tradition and records could recall, yet rumours of secrets encoded in art are a constant source of various mystery theories.

Nicholas Poussin revealed something to his patron Louis Fouquet, who wrote to his brother, the finance minister, of a secret "which kings would have great trouble extracting from him... [which] perhaps no one in the world will rediscover in the centuries to come... this could even be turned to profit... these things are so hard to discover that nothing on earth

could have greater value or be their equal." Poussin's use of the classical pentagonal design grid is taken by some authors as a map of southern France leading to the tomb of Christ or a Cathar treasure. His Arcadian secret may rather relate to the archetypal art code, perhaps applied to validating masterpieces or copies of masterpieces.

Isaac Newton had discovered evidence of a Bible code that he thought to encrypt aspects of cultural history, not realising that a literary code implied that the text was inspired, expressed in archetypal grammar, therefore subconscious and not at the service of crypto historians. The inspired writers may nevertheless have introduced conscious markers in the conscious level of the story to tag their revision of mythical fragments such as the Flood. They had to suppress their Egyptian heritage while in Babylonia. Artists are also no strangers to diplomacy and propaganda. Ironically, text and code in myth, as in art, remain largely independent, just as DNA and non-coding DNA co-exist in every living cell. Inspiration is the master cryptologist that accommodates human juggling.

Tribal initiation also carries a mixture of history, politics, legend, myth and spiritual content, in which history is of minor importance.

Griaule's expedition in Mali on the Upper Volta River from 1931 to 1947 waited sixteen years for Dogon sages to explain their symbols (Marcel Griaule; Conversations with Ogotemelli, 1965, introduction by Germaine Dieterlen). The secrets were "open to all who show a will to understand, and by social position and moral conduct is judged worthy, patient, and in a required state of mind." Answers and questions unfolded cumulatively through the years. In 1931 some Dogon started explaining at a simple level at Ogol, a double village. Sanga region totemic priests were involved in the somewhat counter-missionary ritual. Ogotemelli explained for 30 days, stretching into years, and a successor followed up (Griaule; Dieu d'Eau). The subject of water gods alone required several days of a meandering flow of information (Griaule; Le Renard Pale [Pale fox], 1960s).

Their conscious expression of spiritual visions may have been adapted to political and diplomatic strategies, as shamans habitually do. The supposed 'knowledge' is not in rational form, but coded in myth and art, some as sand drawings. Disguise seems to be part and parcel of inspiration and expression, understood as secrecy, but evidently implying non-rationality. Those of 'ready mind' are encouraged to see the vision themselves, and days of explanation may merely serve to prompt the eventual inspiration, which is again disguised by its own format and by perceptions of tribal or 'secret society' formulae. Such traditions briefly feed on renewed expressions by initiates. The anthropologists took the spiritual tales as ancestral oral tradition, just as popular culture understands sacred books. They paid insufficient attention to Dogon art, assuming the meaning to be encoded primarily in stories motivated by events and cultural missions, and carried in memory.

Prevalence of the identical imprint in all rock art and art traditions and epochs, indicate that there is no secret tradition, merely a blind spot in our perception of art and human nature. There is no conscious or unbroken astronomical, astrological, iconographic, alchemical or artistic tradition via Africa, Europe, Sumer, Babylonia, Egypt, Assyria, India, China, Greece, Persia, Australia, Rome and the Americas. No committee instructed or oversaw the carver of the Narmer palette. Petrarch and the Tarot trump designers never saw Egyptian murals, could not read hieroglyphs, were not astronomers, and knew no Babylonian cosmology to imitate. They may well have compared emblems, games and mythical figures, including glimpses of Chinese art, and matched up (tacked) star lore with 'Spartan' (stick figure) constellations to arrive at a set similar to mindprint art, but it remained wrapped in symbols, never consciously found and thus never lost. Esoterica, 'logical' philosophy and 'high' art are mutually repellent. To look for sustained organisations or conspiracies of silence in art would be as misleading as labelling south Pacific men's long house societies, or tribal kraals with men's social enclosures in Africa, or female initiation sites worldwide, as branches of one or other stem of Freemasonry. Some Masons did visit them, and some 'primitive' societies did integrate more or less Masonic elements, but that does not imply diffusion or unbroken oral tradition from any particular meeting or compact made in France, Scotland, Germany, Jerusalem, Babylonia or Egypt. Initiation is a spontaneous, universal practice that could only derive from global and repeated access to the collective subconscious.

Secret societies were formed, and will continue to be formed everywhere, as one of the ritualised expressions of archetype and the impulse to dramatise and share spiritual structure. Art, like myth, ritual and religion, offers conscious prompts to invoke subconscious experience, inspiration and expression, thus activating cycles of virtual and ritual experience. Art is perpetual revelation.

Cultures appropriate art, but assume its content and even its comprehension to be learned and taught (as Gombrich initially did in opposing the idea of 'innocent eyes').

Poussin may have stumbled on aspects of an art code, perhaps in his own work, probably believing it to be subliminally taught by prior masters. Ogotemelli believed insight to be revealed by ancestors named Nommo, in half human fish forms, shown in many rock art and Babylonian images as Oannes (see the Babylonian Pazuzu plaque at theme t5 t20).

Art has a more rigorous structure and content than dramatic poetry or literature, allowing more secure identification of its elements, yet archaeology, like shamanism resorts almost exclusively to ethnography (folk tales) to interpret 'ethnic' art in rationalised form, partly for not expecting art to explain itself. This study demonstrates that art does explain its own structure and subconscious content. Visual inspiration may even be a larger source of inspiration to narrative myth, than ritual and events are. Yet visual myth is hidden in plain sight under the causal, common sense and theoretical assumptions of artists, viewers and scientists.

Ironically, complexity and simplicity are both at work in the eternal disguise. Who would expect initiation and spirituality to hinge on concepts and images as simple and varied as grids, ropes, nests, bowers, blobs, tails and dots, and as obvious as animals, hunting, dancing, history or legends?

Archetypal expression attaches itself to natural shapes and images, thus initiating the first layer of its own disguise. Some tribal teachers and initiates understand this simplicity. It takes time to unlearn common sense, and initiates require some assurance or permission to graduate. It could take years of rambling by a healer, or years of unlearning supposedly logical assumptions, to see the pattern implicit in shapes and everyday attributes. To follow its implications against the dictates of cultural assumptions is harder still. Culture and race is a state of mind, as American and South African activists taught

Dogon and Amerindian sand drawings, typically cruciform and axial, get across to some teachers and initiates in the right frame of mind after all.

Instant culture

Culture is dispensable, since it is infinitely recoverable. No culture has ever monopolised archetype, and no artistic tradition could monopolise the spherical structure of inspired art. Instead of supposed 'framed idiosyncrasy', or cultural and individual development (Lewis-Williams and Pearce, 2012), all the attributes and structural components of inspired art are in the collective, global, conscious and subconscious domain.

Only some superficial stylistic elements are 'framed' (culturally determined and understood) by culture members, and idiosyncratic (unique to the artist). Culture is widely integrative, since its content is standard.

There is no original or pure culture, just as there is no original or pure language, set of genes, DNA, chemical component or reaction. Some cultures and languages briefly standardise stylistic elements and thus stagnate some of their formal elements and perhaps compromise some content, but stylistic mutation inevitably continues.

Confirmation bias tends to hide conscious evidence of this integration and mutation. Class systems and class mobility offer several stock mechanisms for integrating and normalising cultural migration, such as wealth, titles, jobs and initiation. Cultures integrate motifs from many others without effort, as Rome did, partly since each could be readily assimilated into other expressions of archetypes. Eclectic (selective) and synergist (integrative) cultures offer historic records of conscious acculturation (see an Achilles shield of Megiddo at the end of theme t15). Cultures harking back to high (forceful, exploitative or rich) cultures, do so not just in imitation and aspiration, but for the marvels of archetypal expression in the timeless content already there. The modern obsession with 'brands' demonstrates our tendency to uncritically assimilate cultural currency.

Some authors are puzzled by apparently fully formed and self-assured Egyptian or Central American iconography and mythology, ascribing it to 'mature' immigrant, adopted or disrupted cultures. Revealing icons as archetypal, and thus of inherent logic, retrievable by any people anywhere, at any time, corruptible only by distorted ritualisation, resolves the question of emergent cultures. Visual archetypes shed light on the genesis of all cultures, whether 'transplanted' or mainly of independent 'development'. Both these paradigmatic terms could be replaced by the term perpetuation. Only some stylistic elements are culturally unique, and usually briefly so. Labelling any set of core motifs 'Mayan' or 'African' is misleading if it implies cultural invention, or that only members or students of the identified culture could understand or express them. Artists or healers of foreign cultures often understand some artworks or rituals better than culture members. For example, African healers could explain why skulls and forelegs were buried separately at an archaeological site in the Netherlands, and could demonstrate the relevant rituals.

Several mixed race pirate tribes offer examples of instant culture, hinting at kinds of culture, or rather mutation and maturity levels, just as toddler, childhood, adolescent and adult sub-cultures transform.

The iconography of pirate art worldwide is near identical. Naqada art is the legacy of a raider tribe. In South Africa, Khoe, Griekwa, Korana and Amatola are the main raider cultures of the late 1700s, 1800s and early 1900s. Their appearance and visions are recorded in many rock art works (hundreds in the case of Amatola; see maces, herbs and horses in rock art at themes t5, t12, t13 and elsewhere). The iconography of outcasts, raiders and pirates, despite their wilful 'clean slate', initially emphasise the repertoire of misrule and argot (rogues' code), overlain onto the standard artistic sequence of types and structure. Soon ethics and respectability rear up. Culture matures and mutates, as it did in Egyptian art.

The smiting mace, animal tail and a range of pirate icons remained in Egyptian rituals for millennia, from splitting skulls to moulding minds.

Style and some design elements may be instantly recognisable as Babylonian, Egyptian, Nordic, Khoe, Amatola or Mexican, yet the sequence of types, and even dominant themes, when stripped of superficial style, is identical in all cultures. A Mexican tree with birds, hero and a dragon (see a crocodile composite at theme t3 t18), is near identical to a Nordic runic work (see Odin's dragon at theme t3 t18), and similar to some Chinese and Egyptian dragons (see a T-shaped silk drape at theme t5 t21). Even elaborate emblems, icons and heraldic groups involving caved hills, dogs, palettes, lion tamers, birthing, bulls, churn groups and so on, know no cultural boundaries.

Inspiration comes through the musician, not from the musician, as stylist Richie Havens of the hit tune 'Freedom' said in his regular stage banter.

All artists design potential masterpieces without learning mindprint grammar, many lacking only coordination or stylistic skills. To study the structure as an academic visual grammar would probably not improve art, and may detract from the stylistic variety that seems to be as necessary to culture and to our egos as the core content is.

Most icons do not appear in isolation, but are linked like rhapsodic melodies, each representing more motifs than are visibly present on the canvas, each shedding or activating attributes to form a new whole in each work. Visual structures are more layered than even artists recognise.

Some Mayan artists have developed a style that allowed their sets of iconic images to auto-express further layers by duplication and partial overlay, thus picture generators and animation (Maurice Cotterell; The amazing lid of Palenque). Some gifted or methodical artists may visualise images as animated, and some viewers may be able to do the same. No visual or mathematic feat is beyond occasional prodigies, born in every population and active in every culture. Some figures and features in Nordic and Siberian drums (see theme t5 t21 and theme t12) and rock gongs worldwide confirm that myth, ritual and craft traditions sustain multimedia or operatic type functions of art, as it does in temples and church decoration.

Coincidence of shamanic drum designs with medieval T-O or ((t))-shaped maps are archetypal. Every artist and culture conceives of this shape to express cosmic ideas. Borrowed features or styles, perhaps from medieval T-O world maps, merely camouflage the ever-present conceptual context (see the inverted (T)-shape or /JL\-shape in the Polar chapter).

Incorporation of Christian and other Western motifs into Nordic drum repertoires, such as church buildings, towns and Biblical labels, confirm that living myth is integrative. Political or highly ritualised cultures divorced from living inspiration tend to become exclusive, territorial and formulaic, restricting and interfering in the functions of healers, as church histories demonstrate. However the roles and value of art in culture remain largely unaffected. Science and popular science agree that culture is largely a function of gradual development and diffusion, contrary to the philosophy and psychology of archetype. Archaeo astronomy is entirely sold on the conscious and material paradigm of culture, spelled out in this scholarly summary; "Coincidence of details in cumulative thought have led to the conclusion that it all had its origin in the Near East. It is evident that this indicates a diffusion of ideas to an extent hardly countenanced by current anthropology." (De Santillana and Von Deschend; Hamlet's mill). The two professors, and gurus of ethnographic archaeo astronomy, discount archetypal pre-eternity in this equation, in the same book that presents Amlethus and his mill as something similar to archetypes.

Well-formulated archetypal expression is easy to mistake as borrowed content. Homer and Shakespeare re-worked a range of prior sources, but they use very little duplication. Artists have even fewer primary sources than storytellers.

This study could not find artistic elements of "cumulative thought". The paradigm of 'tribal memory' is discounted in several studies that found oral history to be compelling but instantly compiled fiction (Amanda Esterhuyzen; Mokopane disaster, presentation to Archaeological Society, 2011). Of

cultural and scientific records, De Santillana and Von Deschend wrote: "Original themes could flash out again, preserved almost intact, in the later thought of the Pythagoreans and of Plato... tantalising fragments of a lost whole." Their premise is that a traumatic astronomical event or episode was recorded, theologised into myth, and gradually lost or scrambled. However, all culture is made up of fragments ("These rags have I shored against my ruin", as TS Eliot wrote). Art has to weave the whole cloth in every work, a greater stretch to our minds than the rags of myth.

Conscious paradigms

Primitive thought as supposedly different from modern thought is a baseless fiction of colonially sponsored history, archaeology and anthropology, that some sciences and popular culture seem ever incapable of shaking off. De Santillana and Von Deschend raise few eyebrows even today with this perspective; "We cannot expect to gauge the thought of our remote ancestors, wrapped as it is in its symbols." However some of their other perspectives grope towards the universality of supposed primitive thought; "We think we have now broken part of that code... There are seeds which propagate themselves along the jetstream of time. Universality is in itself a test when coupled with a firm design... one way of checking signals thus scattered in early data, lore, fables and sacred texts is comparative morphology. The reservoir of myth and fable is great, but there are morphological markers for what is not mere storytelling of the kind that comes naturally."

The present study agrees with the ideas of a code, sequence and morphological (structural) markers, all similar to the terminology of archetype, however these do come naturally.

An art analysis trial run

While developing structural art analysis, this study tested its application on an exhibition by Vanessa Von Mollendorf (see Man-eater mantis at theme t7) and in an informal opening address. In hindsight it reveals insufficient distinction between archetype and astronomy; "This is a deceptively simple work revealing subconscious inspiration than could not be faked... The southern polar precessional circle is expressed as a round table on a tripod. In the consonant place in the myth map of the sky, is a southern circumpolar constellation named Mensa (Table) near a roundish nebula named the Large Magellanic Cloud.

"The expressionist Bushman art backdrop on a wall, rendered in a triptych shape by incidental perspective, corresponds to the northern polar region at Draco, Hercules, and Ursa Minor, which are archetypal elements in southern hemisphere art as much as northern hemisphere art.

"The theme echoes religious sacrifice scenes once popular in Persian art and Roman murals, as a type of assurance of 'all protocol observed'. It also evokes an archetypal set keyed to type Scorpius t8 tail and Ara (Altar), yet another southern circumpolar element at the current midwinter meridian, but midsummer to our hemisphere. At a deep and highly camouflaged, yet rigorous and geometrically provable level, these paintings date their inspiration by astrological eras.

"The wall backdrop as a wide perspective cubic room continues the time and place conversation in the other works. The chequered floor is a stock alchemical theme, appropriate here. This work allows its inspiration to speak in many tongues. At its core it is expressionist, unembellished by texture, and suffers only from lack of texture.

"Another work includes expressionist geometric entoptics, typical of some Bushman and Khoe styles or phases of expression. 'Flight' is a therianthrope with a half-human phoenix on the southern polar axis, and a galactic equator as an interrupted row of golliwog dolls. The phoenix continues the southern and polar mythical elements in the exhibition."

Since that initial trial run, mindprint was incidentally found in the work of three other amateur artists, confirming that inspiration and expression does not await figurative skills, technique, working time, experience or stylistic maturity. Neither does it await cultural development.

Doubled spheres

Inspired art sometimes expresses two spheres adjacent to one another, appearing at first glance to be hemispheres, like a sphere cut in half, the lower half turned outward, and both laid down with 'skin' sides up, as Solomon threatened to do with a baby claimed by two mothers. Yet each mindprint sphere, including both adjacent spheres, labelled 'doubles' in this study, has its own 'overflow' to complete its equatorial images, and each has two sets of polar triangles and equators. Doubled mindprints resemble biological osmosis (cell division) or DNA growth, since both parts are wholes, just as acids in

chromosome strands acquire their opposite numbers to complete their spiral strands. Double imprints contra-rotate in their sequential direction, implying that one sphere may be south side up, with its northern polar features 'showing through' from below instead.

In doubled imprints, a disruption in the rock, or added linear image such as a rope, tree or design feature, usually separates the two spheres (see Chauvet cave at theme t5; Trois Frere cave at theme t5 t21; Australian trees at theme t15; a densely packed USA engraving at theme t5 t20; and an Egyptian battle and votive scene with a column of hieroglyphs intruding at theme t7).

Doubles link up imperfectly, as if there were some 'gear slippage'. Only one axis could continue across both halves, but usually the engagement is skewed, hinting that artists first 'site' or place their expression for one sphere on an available canvas, adjusted to the horizontal or vertical plane of the inspiration, and complete the imprint or at least the initial large anchor images (see the Layers illustration and chapter). The artist could then focus on the other half, perhaps adjusted to a slightly delayed inspiration, or the other brain sphere, or to the dictates of the remaining canvas, view, or working posture.

Groundlines, or horizontal orientations, seem to be set with the artist's initial glance and periodic reassessment of a rock or canvas, perhaps accounting for the likely reach of his or her arm.

The layers in our expression

Painting phase 1

Reconstruction of painting phases based on overlap as well as mindprint geometry, reveal that this artist first painted a vertical and horizontal pair or pairs (one or two on top and below, and one or two left and right, at A and/or B). The first two potential axes may cross anywhere, thus the first four figures, and even the fifth may be approximately spaced. From the sixth figure and thus the third axis onward (including two of these eight figures and one of these four axes), every eye (one heart and one womb in their specific places instead) must be on its axis to form the standard mindprint grid.

This first phase established the four large or doubled types (Taurus t1 t16 and Taurus t2 t17, opposite Scorpius t8 and Scorpius t9; Leo t12 and Leo t13 opposite Aquarius t5 t20 and Aquarius t5 t21). Two or four of these initial or prior figures (perhaps by a different artist) were probably entirely overpainted in phase 2 or 3.

Painting phase 2

The artist painted a third cardinal (crosswise) set of four figures, on the near-vertical and near-horizontal axes C, with their eyes (womb for type Virgo t11) aligned across the established point. Type Gemini t15 has an extra polar counterpart, its eye position inferred by ears. Already the artist had to be instinctively precise in placing seven figures on four axes. This phase added the median-sized figures; types Gemini t15, Virgo t11, Sagittarius t7, and Pisces t4 (its eye position also indicated by its ears).

Three polar axles emerged in this phase; the central (pE) on an implied jaw (its southern counterpart is always underneath it); (pGs) on type Pisces t4's jaw; (pC) on an inferred eye, and (pCs) on a knee or genitals. The pG axle is confirmed by the horizontal plane, and the pC axle is confirmed by the vertical plane of this phase.

Painting phase 3

The artist painted a fourth cardinal set of four figures on the diagonal axes D, with their eyes on axes crossing at the established point. The artist had to be instinctively precise in placing eleven figures on six axes, which together with the initial five figures appear as sixteen figures (minus two or four overpainted) on six or seven precise (but unmarked) axes. This last phase added the small (thin angular wedge) cardinals; Cancer t14, Libra t11, Capricornus t6 and Aries t3.

Layers of paint

Dense overpainting reveals some aspects of expression that are probably independent of inspirational processes (South Africa, Giants Castle Park Main Caves North I. RARI. Mindprint analysis by Edmond Furter). The painting order could be reconstructed if each figure was a distinct episode, a technique named stratigraphy (Thembi Russel; Nobody said it would be easy; Ordering San paintings using the Harris matrix, SA Archaeological Bulletin 67, 2012).

Archetypal analysis reveals that the artist worked in pairs of opposites. Each opposing pair has diminishing leeway as it is confined by adjacent axes. However, another stratigraphy example contradicts the assumption that each figure is completed as a separate episode (see the 'Three magi' rock art herders at theme t13).

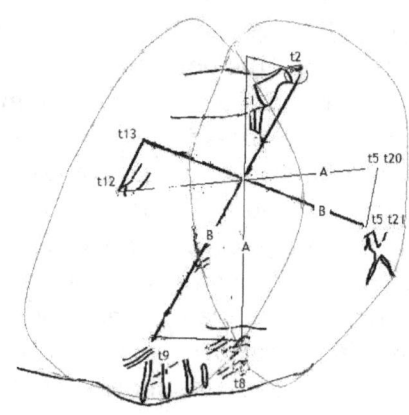

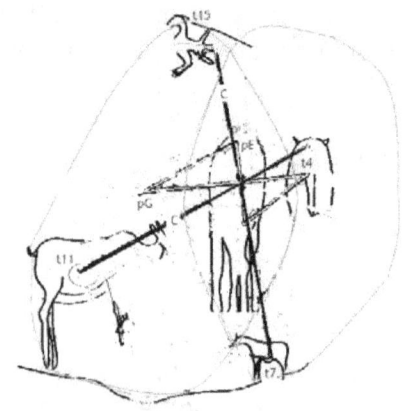

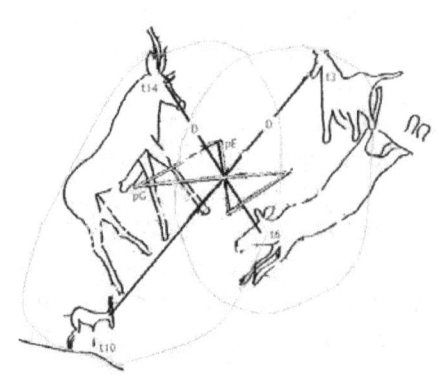

Layers of time

Archetypal, pre-creational structure is inherent in all energy, matter, life and spirit, including time cycles. The slow wobble of earth's celestial pole (see the Cosmic map) is the only notably non-cyclic element of cosmic time. The polar configuration in art tags the inspiration to a precessional Age or transition era.

In this example, celestial polar markers (the ends of the short polar axle, on the vertical plane) lie just before (precessionally just after) the types Gemini-Sagittarius t15-t7 Gemini-Sagittarius, near our current midsummer and midwinter. Indicators of 'just after Gemini t15' are interpreted in this study as late Age Pisces, about AD 1000 to 1850. 'Between types Gemini t15 and Taurus t1' (also possible here, since type Taurus t1 is overpainted) is interpreted as Age Pisces-Aquarius, in the last two centuries before the forthcoming transition. Most works are inspired by their preceding or current eras.

Layers of mind

The usual radial distortion (irregular starburst-shaped equator) of the sequence of eyes indicates that each image may radiate (slide somewhat in or out) at the artist's subconscious will, partly due to spacing compromises. Some half-formed figures (see a vortex in rock art at theme t7) indicate that inspiration may initially literally hinge on limb joints along two intersecting circles, from where individual figures may then rotate to place their eyes on different axes, where they may then acquire relevant attributes.

Partial symmetry, and the hemispheric split and overlap of some peripheral limb joints (marked by thin oval curves in this study), seem to mirror the partial neurological split and overlap of functions in the visual cortex and other parts of the partially split and duplicated brain, with 'polar' links via glands such as the pituitary. Half our brains and bodies may be dedicated to subconscious and autonomous functions, as we spend half our time in sleep. Rdegular conscious overlap of different levels of consciousness is the province of dream experience and inspiration. Artists express holographic structure similar to nature and perception itself, using natural and cultural sets such as physiology, chemistry, physics, mythology, ritual and crafts, which likewise are based on nature.

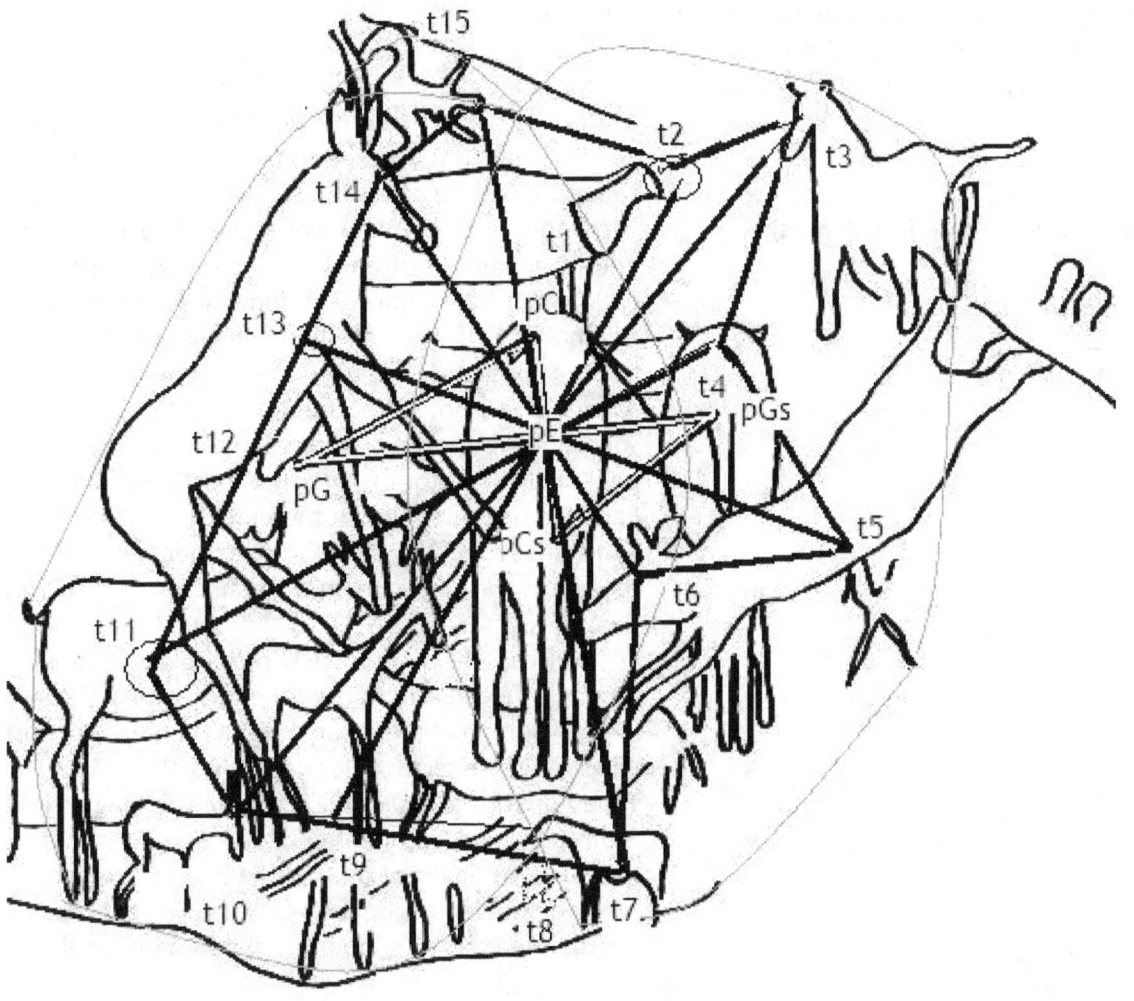

Digging through paint layers

Chapter G

A San (Bushman) painting in the South African Drakensberg containing the usual mindprint, also contains some dense overpainting that drew academic analysis of its paint layering. Comparison of the two very different kinds of analyses reveals that the artist painted cardinal (cross-spaced) sets of four, and perhaps pairs of opposite figures together. Figures in a small, distinct part of a large rock canvas in Giants Castle park Main Caves North I, were arbitrarily numbered 48 to 70 (Thembi Russel; No one said it would be easy. Ordering San paintings using the Harris matrix. SA Archaeological Bulletin 67, 2012). Russell identifies four episodes, plus figure [55] as a fifth episode, but does not note opposing or cardinal spacing, nor any potential peripheral sequence or geometric order. The paint layers now reveal four cardinal (cross) groups, first four plus four, then another four, then another four. It seems as if the peripheral sequence was embedded in inspiration, expressed as four sets of crosses, composed of eight sets of opposing pairs of types. Readers bored by tabulation could merely note the regular pattern that emerges (ignoring the initial arbitrary recording numbers), and return to the text.

SA KZN Main Caves North I
(arbitrary figure numbers, episodic columns);

```
EpiA EpiB EpiC EpiD
[49] ____ ____ ____
____ [??] ____ ____
____ ____ [54] ____
____ ____ ____ [48]
[68] ____ ____ ____
____ [67] ____ ____
=[69]== [66]==[50]=
____ ____ [53] ____
_57? ____ ____ [60]
[58] ____ ____ ____
____ [59] ____ ____
=[71b]==[70a]=====
____ ____ [52] ____
____ ____ ____ [56]
[99] ____ ____ ____
____ [65] ____ ____
____ ____ [51] ____
____ ____ ____ [55]
```

SA KZN Main Caves North I (arbitrary figure numbers, type and zodiac columns added, structural cross completed by blank lines ==;

```
Type Zod EpiA EpiB EpiC EpiD ZODIAC

t2 t17 [49] ____ ____ ____ Taurus
t1 t16 ____ [??] ____ ____ Taurus
Gate  ==== ==== ==== ==== GATE
t15 t0 ____ ____ [54] ____ Gemini
t14    ____ ____ ____ [48] Cancer
t13  [68]_ ____ ____ ____ Leo
t12  ____ [67]_ ____ ____ Leo
PIG   ==69 ==66 ==50 ==== GALACTIC POLE
t11  ____ ____ [53] ____ Virgo
t10  _57? ____ ____ [60]_ Libra
t9   [58] ____ ____ ____ Scorpius
t8   ____ [59] ____ ____ Scorpius
Gal  =71b ==== ==== ==== GALACTIC CENTRE
t7   ____ ____ [52] ____ Sagittarius
t6   ____ ____ ____ [56] Capricornus
t5 t21 [99] ____ ____ ____ Aquarius
t5 t20 ____ [65] ____ ____ Aquarius
Axis  ==== ==== ==== ==== AXIS
t4 t19 ____ ____ [51] ____ Pisces
t3 t18 ____ ____ ____ _[55] Aries
```

The missing figure [??] is inferred in this study, as probably obliterated by [50] and [51]. It is numbered [x1] below.

Archetypal analysis using mindprint attributes (see the Tables section) and typological statistics (see the Results section), reveals the usual peripheral sequence of types.

Type Taurus t2 (19% bovine) is on the eye of an antelope, which is often in the top central position in rock art and alchemical emblems. It is often near a rainmaker, hunter or underworld visitor (48% twisted posture) analogous with type Taurus t1 Auriga or Orion, here probably overpainted. It is sometimes between the twisted rainmaker and the benedicting creator of type Gemini t15 (see an early Egyptian Nekhen mural at theme t13).

Type Aries t3 (42% with a long or bent neck) is on the eye of a horse, as in several examples in this study.

Type Pisces t4 Pegasus (26% rectangular-bodied) is on the inferred eye of an antelope with unusually long legs, or the eye of an overpainted antelope of which only the rectangular flank is visible.

Type Aquarius t5 t20 or t21 (31% overbearing action) is on the eye of a strident person. The mark behind it may be a remnant of another figure, since this type is often doubled. Its opposite at type Leo t12 may be overpainted. Type Aquarius t5 sometimes lends some of its attributes to its opposite or to its adjacent type Capricornus t6, as it does here (types Aquarius t5 are on average 30% horizontal, 31% overbearing action).

Type Capricornus t6 (on average 48% far towards or away from the centre) is on the eye of a figure that significantly breaks the outline of the irregular equator with its ingress. It adopts some of the attributes of type Aquarius t5 that it overlays.

Type Sagittarius t7 (26% bag) is on the womb of a small antelope, more usually the eye of a newborn or minor animal.

Type Scorpius t8 t9 is or are damaged. T8's opposite (at type Taurus t1) is overpainted, and its eye position is not confirmed.

Type Libra t10 is on the eye of a small antelope with straight horns, as it sometimes is (see an early Egyptian mural at theme t13).

Type Virgo t11 (88% on a womb) is one of the most consistently expressed features of mindprint.

Type Leo t12 (11% inverted) is omitted or overpainted, but its attribute of up-ending extends to the highly rotated groundline of the composite figure that overlays its position. This type sometimes exchanges some of its attributes with its opposite at type Aquarius t5 t20, as it does here. Type Leo t12 Ursa is sometimes a tall, strident, angular figure linked to the polar region).

Type Leo t13 (85% on a heart) is one of the most consistently expressed features of mindprint. Its initial figure may be overpainted, but the visible figure retains the geometric attribute.

Type Cancer t14 is on the eye of an animal that also expresses type Leo t13, as it often is in compact scenes.

Type Gemini t15 (33% with a rope) is on the eye of the top human figure between horns and a linear shape. It is often a creator or ordering principle (16% smiting), sometimes wounded on the thigh, and in recent centuries sometimes a polar figure such as a bird (a concept it shares with type Cancer t14 Ursa Minor).

The ecliptic pole (49% marked, 26% on a limb joint) is on the inferred jaw of the central antelope.

The galactic pole (81% marked, 68% on a limb joint) is on a knee (common) or genitals (rare).

The galactic south pole (65% marked) is on the inferred jaw of t4.

The celestial pole (63% marked, 50% on a limb joint, 13% on a mark or eye) is on the inferred eye of the polar figure.

The celestial south pole (55% marked) is on a hip (common) or genitals (rare).

The precise axial grid and the identities of each adjacent and opposing type, multiply the confirmations of the equatorial sequence to the level of certainty, despite the damaged type Scorpius t9, extensive overpainting, and an unusual attribute at type Sagittarius t7.

Galactic equators could be traced along many of the limb joints (the thin oval lines are here slightly misplaced to avoid confusion with the equator of eyes), totalling nineteen on the left (galactic north equator and extension) and eleven on the right (galactic south equator and extension). The total of 30 limb joints is about average for a sparse scene (however this study does not base any key data or conclusions on the position or features of the conceptual galactic equators). Four episodes of cardinal sets emerge from the sequence (here in columns), starting with a doubled set.

**SA KZN Main Caves North I
with typological numbering;**

EpiA	EpiB	EpiC	EpiD	MYTH
[t2]	____	____	____	Taurus
____	[x1]	____	____	Taurus
====	====	====	====	GATE
____	____	[t15]	____	Gemini
____	____	____	[t14]	Cancer
[t13]	____	____	____	Leo
____	[t12]	____	____	Leo
pG ==	pG ==	pG ==	==	POLE G
____	____	[t11]	____	Virgo
__?_	____	____	[t10]	Libra
[t9]	____	____	____	Scorpius
____	[t8]	____	____	Scorpius
Gal ====	====	====	====	GALAXY
____	____	[t7]	____	Sagittarius
____	____	____	[t6]	Capricornus
[t5a]	____	____	____	Aquarius
____	[t5b]	____	____	Aquarius
====	====	====	====	AXIS
____	____	[t4]_	____	Pisces
____	____	____	[t3]_	Aries

The order of cardinal (cross) sets is clear, perhaps painted in opposing pairs (the layers do not indicate, but do not contradict a paired sequence). The sequence of attributes related to types in the equator is equally clear (compared to about 400 listed artworks, of which about 200 are illustrated, and 170 statistically tested). Switching tabulation from columns to rows, it could be concluded that the artist started with;

**Four figures, forming the cross
[t2] [t13] [t9] [t5a]; and their adjacent cross
[t1] [t12] [t8] [t5b]; then the flanking cross
[t15] [t11] [t7] [t4]; then structure, and then cross
[t14] [t10] [t6] [t3].**

The archetypal numbers emerge in the usual strict sequence, read in columns from bottom right to top left, or the other way by following seasonal (zodiac) labels. The order of painting within each cardinal (cruciform set of four figures), however, is unclear, since the four members of each set are far apart and few of them share an overlay or underlay of paint. Thus top layer figures may 'rise' by one or two phases (for example t10 [academic number 60] could be in phase two, three or four), and some of the eight bottom layer figures may 'lower' by one level to an initial phase. Figure t9 [58] and t7 [52] could move one level down, since they were placed in phase B based only on an underlying smudge [71b] that is not attested by any outline or by any mindprint geometry, and that may already have been a smudge, or smudged out on purpose before the artist started painting. Figure t5a was not numbered, nor accounted for in the matrix, and seems to underlie t10 [57].

With these options accounted for, still no number-for-number sequence could be confirmed, and some assumptions on which bottom layer figures belong prior, and which top layer figures belong later in the order, are required. Conservative dropping and raising of some of the initial and final figures by only one level, without contradicting the strata, indicates this painting order;

[t2] opposite [t9], cross to [t13] opposite [t5a]
[t1] cross to [t12] opposite [t5b], cross to [t8]
[t15] opposite [t7], cross to [t11] opposite [t4]
[t10], cross to [t14] opposite [t6], cross to [t3]

This table, converted to zodiac equivalents for readers familiar with its oppositions (180 degrees apart) and squares (90 degrees apart), and for ease of following characters instead of numbers, reveals an axial logic in an alternating axial and swastika-shaped pattern of painting;

Taurus t2 and its opposite Scorpius t9, cross to
Leo t13 and its opposite Aquarius t21,
add Taurus t1, cross to;
Leo t12 and its opposite Aquarius t20, cross to
Scorpius t8. Diagonal to
Gemini t15 and its opposite Sagittarius t7, cross to
Virgo t11 and her opposite Pisces t4, diagonal to
Libra t10, cross to
Cancer t14 and its opposite Capricornus t6,
cross to Aries t3.

The few assumptions added to the initial and final phases of the compacted Harris matrix (of which some points are contested between Russell and Pierce), thus confirm one another. Our subconscious eyes, hands and brain halves (each functioning as a near complete sphere) are accurate at placing axial pairs. However the artist could return to any figure and add or adjust its opposites' eye position at any stage, or more likely, elaborate a body part over another figure. The neatly progressively symmetrical sequence of cardinal sets and opposites revealed in this artwork, is broken in other artworks by a more haphazard sequence (see the 'Three Magi' rock art work at theme t13). All nevertheless elegantly complete the typological sequence and artistic structure.

The portion of the densely painted rock art shelter discussed here is clearly of a single inspiration.

Assumptions of overpainting by accumulation over years, or by different artists, or use of supposed stylistic features to fill stratigraphy gaps, are therefore not borne out. Painting was not haphazard or chance.

Many rock art panels are considered cumulative, painted by several contributors in different episodes, and the artist's supposed "intentions" changed or subverted by additions. However mindprint geometry, usually with little redundancy, indicates that either a single artist expressed visual inspiration, or a collaborator or different artist may have been induced to a similar inspiration and was impelled to elaborate a work. Changing brushes, paint or styles is expected in inspired art, since rock artists are typically not focussed on style, but on expressing, sustaining or re-inducing experience. Variety of techniques and style have misled some researchers into assigning different artists, eras or cultures to some works now revealed as single, phased inspiration or expression. Science studied the layers and the order of painting in art, but did not see the types, sequence, or geometric structure that it did not expect to see. Science thus emerges as culturally framed, and imposing its own paradigm on its subject.

The structure of inspiration, expression or both, is hardy. Artists have a subconscious but persistent compulsion for what attributes to figure where, and exactly where to space their eyes and probably some of their limb joints. Errors or false starts in expression, extremely rare in all ages and continents, seem to involve axial pairs. An artist's error in Zimbabwe's Murhwa cave (see theme t5 t21) indicates that either type Libra t10 or type Aries t3 were painted by subconsciously mistaking the position of the head of the opposite figure. Artists have a built-in eye alignment skill, which on rare occasions is misled by gestalt, seeing wholes in misleading parts. Some complex works with up to 100 figures, including 32 eyes on 16 axes (see Russian Sayan Zaba at theme t15), stretch intuitive eye alignment to the limit and invokes the possibility that some axes may be due to chance. Where the usual ten to 22 figures, and thus five to eleven axes are involved, chance is not a factor.

The double life of decans

Another kind of layering in art is the co-existence of the sixteen types with larger calendric sets. Decanal cycles in Persia (Bundehesh), China (sieu or houses), India (nakshatras or Brahmanas), Arabia (stars of entering, roadside inns, manzils, mansions, resting places of the moon, jufur), Egypt, Greece, Chaldea and Coptic Egypt (RH Allen, 1899), equate with lunar cycles. Both demarcate the celestial equator by stars or clusters into 28 or 32 or 36 portions to mark hours. Hourly decans rise at dusk about ten days apart, thus a new first hour of the night is chosen every ten or eleven days.

The Koran notes decans in Sura 10; "God had appointed her stations, that you may know the number of years and computation of time." Since the moon and planets do not keep constant time with the stars, and are usually not directly on those portions of the celestial equator within their reach (the moon hugs the ecliptic equator within five degrees north or south), lunar mansions at rising or setting (horizon permitting) or culmination (highest point) are hour markers, and seasonal calibrators in steps of about four minutes per day, an hour every 15 days, or a 1/36 decan every ten days. Supposed 'peasant time reckoning' offers more than a means of dividing night watches among sentries, but less than archetype. The celestial equator is not fixed. Precession of the equinoxes (the two points where it crosses the ecliptic) by one degree in 72 years (at the current rate) moves the celestial equator in a motion similar to a hula hoop swung around two hips. The celestial equator of about BC 15 000 (by scientific estimate) was about 25 degrees or more north or south of its current track and about 90 degrees ahead of current seasons. The net effect is that lunar mansions remain prone to updating, and thus could not be primary bearers of timeless archetype. Egyptian decanal sets could remain unintelligible despite intensive study, even to most of the ancient and modern Egyptians.

Decanal sets are personified, imbued with attributes that are not directly related to their asterisms, used in addition to zodiacs (see decans in the margin of the Dendera zodiac), in addition to pantheons, and are endlessly shuffled into variant sequences, such as the Ramses 1 and other decanal 'families' (O Neugebauer and R Parker; Egyptian astronomical texts 3, 1969). If decans were merely astronomical, the sequence would have been standard, at least in Egypt, or at least in the Old Kingdom, but it was not.

Decans swop attributes, change names and appear in different episodes, like soap opera characters. Typical of consciously conceptualised, personalised and politicised icons, they swop attributes with other lists, and thus personify listing itself. Decans are now hours, then gods, directions, words, servants; typically expressed in rows, confirming that they are not ecliptic (solar) types, nor limited to a stable typological number like twelve or sixteen. Decans are acknowledged in China and Egypt to derive from a horary (hourly) sequence, and to carry limited iconic value. They resemble chemical compounds. Yet decans also express variations on their parent constellations and thus live double lives. Their attributes may be alternatively reflected by nearby planets, in the synchronistic sense.

Academic and popular researchers alike cannot agree on any single pairing of Egyptian gods or decans with asterisms. Ancient Egypt's three competing theologies demonstrates that decans or pseudo-types are not limited to art, but extend to myth and legend.

An entire system of horary astrology had developed in China, but it did not seem to find mythological counterparts, apart from loose parallels with the more universal ecliptic zodiac and twelve animals allocated for their hours of activity (also adopted as sigils of the twelve-year or 60-year cycle). 'Lunar' mansions are too indirect, mutable (changeable) and complex for ethnography, mythology, rock art, murals, and therefore archetypes to accrue or 'tack' to.

Some decanal sets resort to simple zodiacal attributes, while some zodiacs use celestial and therefore decanal terms. These hybrid sequences are archetypal as well as conventional, and therefore candidates for conscious expressions of archetype, but probably perceived as just zodiacs or hours.

Decans remain a grey area between archetype and symbols, conscious and subconscious, natural and cultural, calendric and conventionalised expression. In contrast, zodiacs are stable in sequence and number, but too few to express archetype. Between the zodiac twelve and decanal 36 lies archetypal territory; the rule of sixteen. Some minimalist art contain only twelve types, particularly Indian emblematic art, but most mindprint art, including Indian art, contain sixteen types.

The cosmic division of constellations and myth demonstrate a sufficiently complex yet sufficiently finite application of twelve with four doubles, thus sixteen, interspaced by structural and polar features.

Mindprint and decans
on the Narmer palette

Illustration H1

The Narmer palette front demonstrates the archetypal art code in a decanal set, in stock Egyptian pre-dynastic style (mindprint analysis by Edmond Furter).

TYPE, ZODIAC as FIGURE (ATTRIBUTE)

t3 Aries as a spouted pot (neck backward)
t2 Taurus Pleiades as a large star
t1 Taurus Orion as a sandal-bearer (twisted)
t15 Gemini as Hathor cow (frontal face)
t14 Cancer as chisel and hammer (furthest egress)
   (Y-shaped)
t13 Leo as Horus falcon
t11 Virgo as Horus womb
   and eye of an Asiatic or marsh enemy
t10 Libra as King's brother's genitals and hand
   (neck twisted, opposite t3)
t9 Scorpius as defeated
   (twisted, opposite t2)
t8 Scorpius as ribbon (tails)
t7 Sagittarius as prisoners' hands
t6 Capricornus as prisoner (nearest ingress)
t5 Aquarius Pegasus as a pond
t4 Pisces as the king's heel

Galactic pole on Horus' hand
Galactic south pole on the twin's heel
Celestial pole on the king's genitals or shoulder,
   and on the vertical plane
The inspiration is of Age Aries or just prior.

The palette carries the same figures and nearly the same sequence of attributes on both sides. Here the figures are in a court or festival context, centred on type Gemini t15 as a smiting, ordering pharaoh. Several optional links flip the sequence between the two sides, in the 'transparent' method of some Egyptian murals.

On the palette's reverse side (see theme t3 t18), type Leo t13 is the heart of a catfish (spelling part of 'Narmer'). Type Virgo t11 is the womb of a dwarf, on a symbolic level representing a client culture paying homage by its wise men and women.

The dwarf resembles a figure in Queen Hatshepsut's Punt colonnade, perhaps a Khoe Queen of Sheba (Alex Duffey; Hatshepsut's expeditions to southern Africa, AENES presentation, 2009. Brenda Sullivan; Africa through the mists of time). Her function and conceptual role is more important than her particular tribe. On the subconscious level, the royal fish and the subject queen are foreign vassal healers from the interior that feeds the Nile. Thus the nominal lion of Ethiopia is subjugated.

The same event in Ethiopian eyes is politically different (see an Ethiopian Sheba visiting Solomon at theme t15).

Some dwarfs are identified with rainmakers (Jack Tressider; Watkins Dictionary of symbols). Empire needs flattery by tribes with apparently semi-human features or languages, considered more in touch with animals and nature, and thus rainmakers, herbalists and fertility or defensive spell casters.

Bushmen and Khoe or Nama (born of occasional pre-Bantu and pre-colonial admixtures) fulfilled these functions to migrating Iron Age African Bantu tribes and to emergent mixed Korana, Griekwa and Amatola bands in South Africa. They served settlers even during the systematic genocide and cultural extinction of Bushmen by regional masters such as the Zulu, Dutch, British and Boer. Even now the mixed South African culture requires Bushmen, spiritual owners of the land, to bless the nation (see Bushmen figures and language in the coat of arms at theme t5 t21).

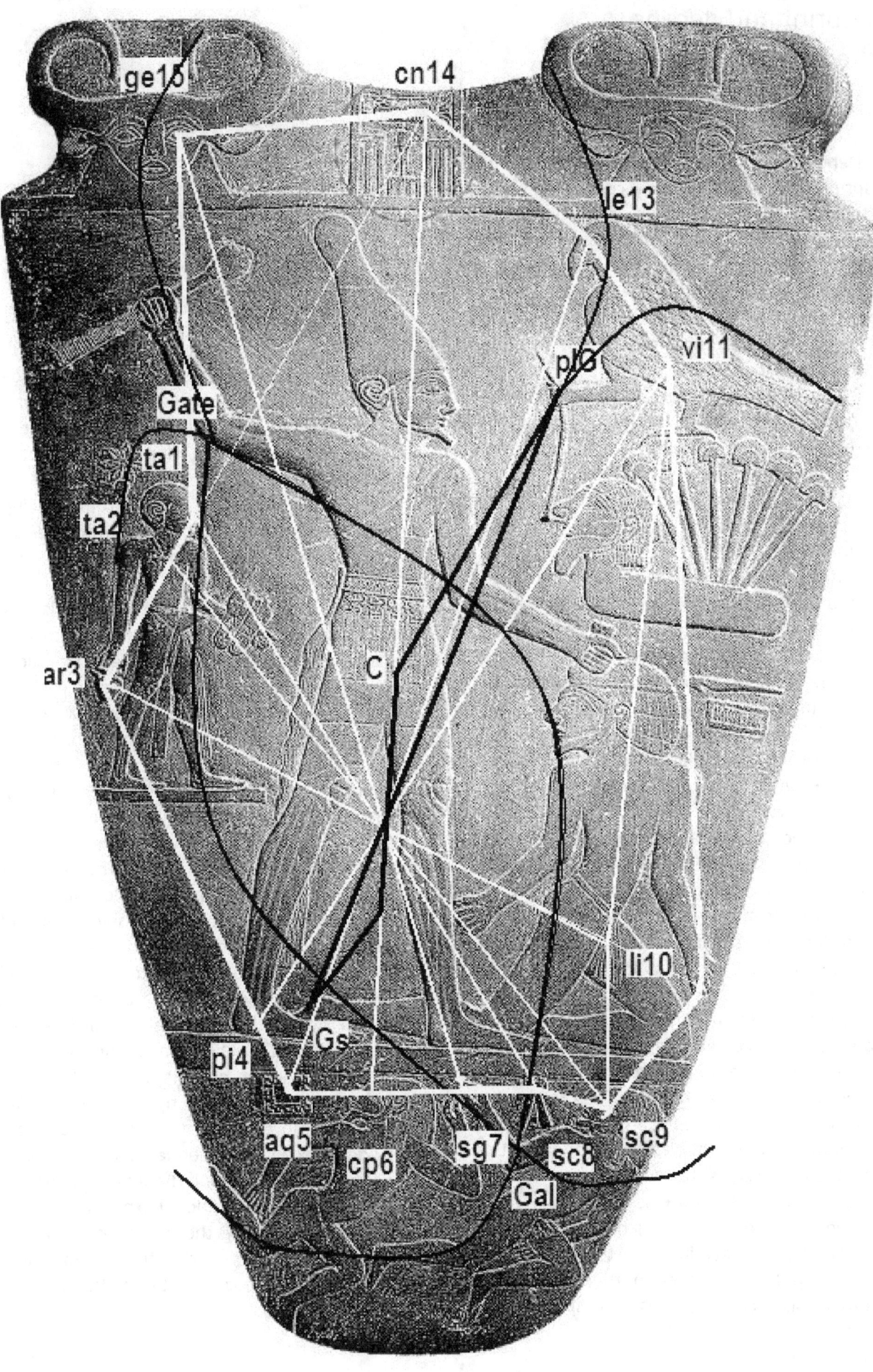

Mindprint and decans
in the Dendera zodiac

Illustration H2

The Dendera round zodiac ceiling demonstrates mindprint in a quadruple concentric set of constellations, signs, decans and determinants (Louvre, or a plaster cast replacement at Dendera. Mindprint analysis by Edmond Furter. Spring and polar section inset for clarity).

A spring equinox baboon marker sits back to back with type Aries t3 t18 Triangulum as a slaughtered quarry or buck bag. Their tails or entrails together reach down to the Aries ram tail, which in turn hangs down to the Pisces ribbons (where the Cetus Whale tail is figured). A baboon is a moveable concept, not a constellation.

It marks the equinoxes, and relates to one of Thoth's manifestations, resolving some of his historic ambiguities.

The spring sun or moon is under the baboon, displaced from Aries to just on the Pisces side of the tails, which also extend the Pisces latter ribbon, or forms a third ribbon (see the Cosmic map). The spring sun or moon determinant (pictorial sign) is repeated in Pisces, as a figure holding a spring sacrifice. The opposite sun or moon or lunar node is on the Scorpius constellation axis, but pictured in Libra, confirming ambiguity among the other precession markers.

The four major constellations are doubled, and all sixteen ecliptic axes are uniquely vortexed in order to link northern decanal eyes, through zodiac eyes, to southern decanal eyes, to their determinants in the border (see similar but linearly regimented decans in the Dendera crypt lotus bulb carving at theme t2 t17).

Stereotypical zodiacs usually do not contain the mindprint sequence and axial structure. The implied vortex and iconic elegance here indicate inspiration beyond the needs of astrology or astronomy (see a vortex in rock art at theme t7). This ceiling is useless to astronomical observation or calibration, but good to access subconscious structure.

Some authors read the work as having been partially re-carved to add Babylonian -Greek -Roman constellations to Egyptian constellations, and to update the poles to precession, thus accounting for 'generally misplaced' features. The spacing is now revealed as evenly vortexed.

The solution here indicates a single, inspired design, matched to nearly all the constellations, with only the type Leo t13 Ursa bull foreleg misplaced or re-assigned, and the Draco Hercules Taweret hippo uncertain.

Spherical grid distortion arises from moving the perspective or projection point from the centre of a radial grid to another point, without moving the equator calibration.

However projectional distortion is never symmetrical, nor uniformly rotated, as this grid is. There is no astronomical vortex grid tradition. The stroke of genius to express precession by dragging either the peripheral sequence backward, or the polar sequence forward, is probably subconscious.

The ecliptic pole is on the jaw of the Wippet jackal on a plough, itself on a bull foreleg here figuring part of Draco (which more usually figures the celestial pole).

The galactic pole is on a staff foot. The galactic south pole is on an extra fish mouth or 'jaw', figuring Pisces Prior on the conscious iconic level, but the Cetus (Whale) spout on the subconscious level.

The celestial pole is on type Gemini t15 Ursa Minor, as the jaw of a tiny rear-facing canine, reclining on the other side of the bull foreleg, which is a slightly misplaced type Leo t13 Ursa Major (continuing its earlier career as the celestial polar calibrator). The celestial south pole is on the jaw of the Taweret hippo (who more usually figures the ecliptic pole). Her womb (extra to the sequence of types) is on the type Libra t10 axis, among the inherent precessional ambiguities in this transitional expression.

The celestial poles tag the inspiration to Age Aries-Pisces, confirming the spring sun or moon entering Pisces, and archaeological dating as Ptolemaic, in the early centuries AD.

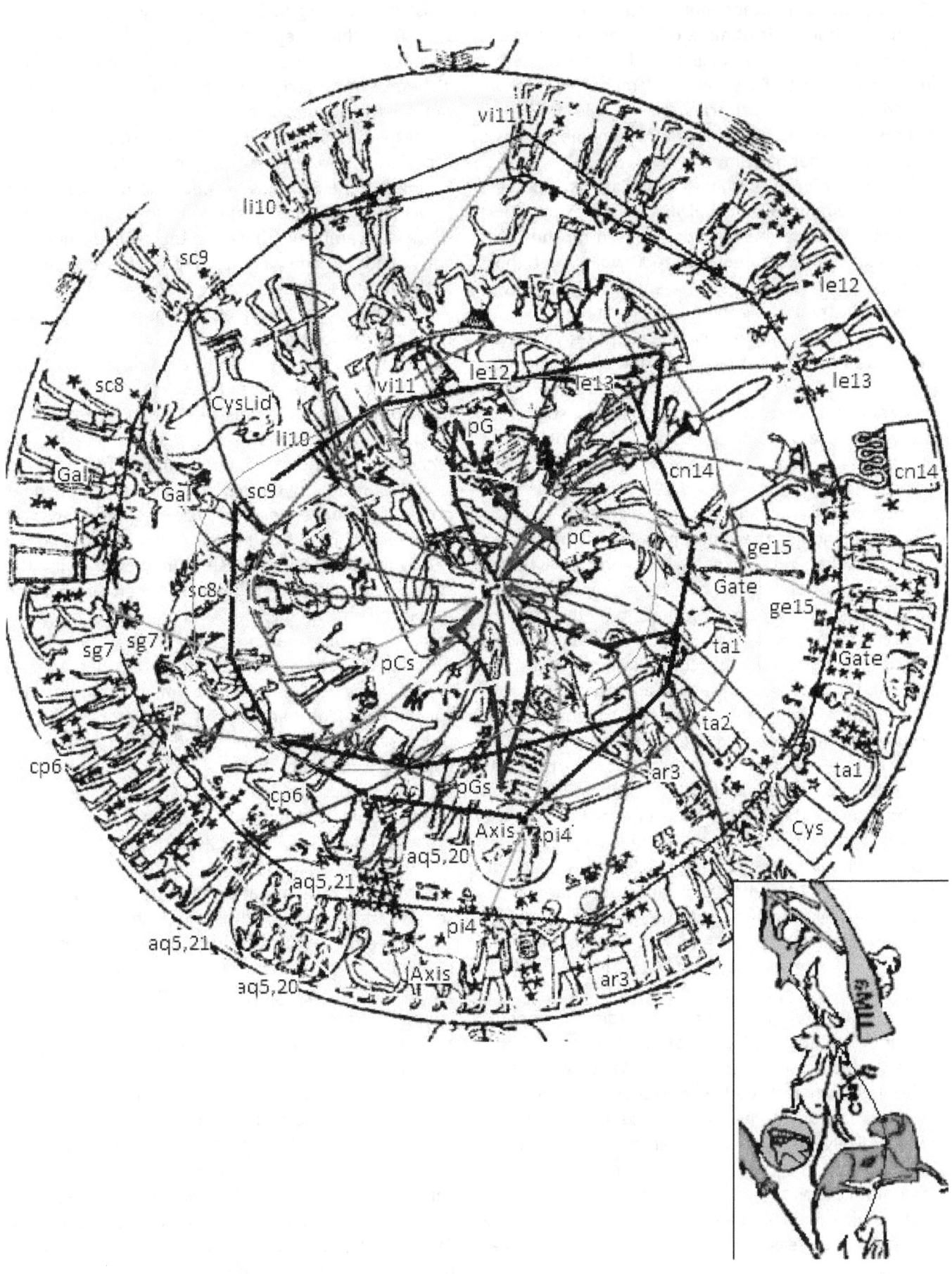

The Tarot trump sequence

Tarot cards and other emblematic sets, of which there are hundreds of more or less popular versions showing trades, animals, birds, gods, chaps (characters), letters, spheres, elements and so on, continue the eternal tradition of talismans. Full decks are typically 56 or 60 or 72 in number, plus a smaller number of trumps.

Emblems reference icons, constellations, numbers and combinations as equal archetypal expressions. Books and esoteric applications based on the Tarot deck have proliferated over 600 years, yet most artists, iconographers, scientists and even psychologist Carl Jung shied away from this deck.

Academic assumptions of the supposed arbitrary and wishful nature of talismans and all of esoterica, and the necessary admixture of charlatanism in esoteric crafts, add to the conscious stigma of talismans. Yet art, notably rock art, spiritual and religious art, contain and even hinge on talismanic elements (F Thackeray, 2012). The Tarot deck contains seasonal and decanal elements, like the 'books of hours' that once popularised myth as a kind of archetypal alphabet, a function now assumed by fables, cartoons and movies. The numbered cards and court suites are decanal, but the trumps (triumphs, or exaltations, similar to planets while transiting their 'home' constellations) seem to anchor the deck in mythical and archetypal terms.

Esotericists continue to graft Tarot trump emblems onto other sets of archetype, and onto zodiac signs and sometimes on constellations. Surprisingly, astrologers have variously misidentified and misallocated the twelve constellations in the 22 trumps, due in part to the doubled types (types Taurus t1 and t2, Leo t12 and t13, Scorpius t9 and t8, Aquarius t5 t20 and t5 t21), and repetition of the label number t5 (contracting the doubling of type Aquarius t20 and t21), and the overlap of seven types by a second layer (t0/t15, t1/t16, t2/t17, t3/t18, t4/t19, t5/t20, t5/t21).

Camouflage of the identity of Tarot trumps is intrinsic and formidable. Tarot numbering may have been a lucky conscious or subconscious guess that 'felt right', or may derive from a spiral layout that proved its worth to psychics or artists. Numbering is more likely to have been simply recognised as implicit in the designs, or extracted from a panoramic artwork that contained the 22 figures.

The initial problem that led to this study was to identify the designer of the Tarot trumps. That question is answered in the finding that all artists express the standard sequence and spatial structure. The question could now be rephrased as who numbered or reconstructed the numbering of the Tarot trumps. It could be a poet like Petrarch, an artist like Mantegna (who probably did not design the Tarocchini deck that bears his name. See Parnassus at theme t11), a printer in Basel, or any alchemist or esotericist in the iconographic hothouse of the early Renaissance.

No set would be complete without some error. In the Tarot 'Marseilles' sequence, trump 8 as Strength (type Scorpius t8) and trump 11 as Justice (type Virgo t11) are swopped in some decks. Since there is no ambiguity between these types, myths or constellations, the variant is probably due to an authoritative error.

The overlapped section of trumps co-incides with the known positions of the spring equinox; Age Gemini t15 t0, Age Taurus t1 t16, Age Taurus t2 t17, Age Aries t3 t18, Age Pisces t4 t19, plus the forthcoming Age Aquarius t5 t20 and Age Aquarius t5 t21. Earlier Ages are not reflected in the archetypal chart overlap, nor in mindprint art, nor in iconography or mythology. Visual inspiration does not confirm precession as a cycle, despite our gestalt assumptions based on symmetry and perpetuation. Our wobbling soli-lunar system may even swing the spring point like a pendulum between Gemini and Aquarius, centred on Aries, and precession may turn to progression some time (20 degrees?) from today, or about 60 degrees from about BC 850. Age Aries as an astrological zero point may support this speculation. Plato, among the speculators who take precession as a cycle, presented it as a second-rate hypothesis or assumption.

Natural structures such as atomic layers and haemoglobin, and natural sets such as the periodic table of elements, are reflected in subconscious artistic expression. Both are rooted in archetype. The myth of the embrace of the primordial couple, so tight that a hero child had to push them apart to allow creation, applies as much to the two entwined strands of DNA in our chromosomes, as to the set of 21 or 22 chromosomal pairs, types, the 22 Tarot trumps, our eyes, hands, conscious and subconscious, where the conceptual half-spiral binding sixteen concepts is hard-wired.

The mindprint table is a quirky list, or snark, a word coined by James Joyce and adopted by the composer Mike Batt in The hunting of the snark, which is a motto or anthem for this study. The cycle of types is somewhat like that which nuclear physics describes as chiral, a directional set of atomic particles or forces having several elements of asymmetry, as in biology, elements of time and chemistry (notably 'transition' elements and isotopes). Archetypal sequence follows laws of energy that are different from the neatly directional, sequential and cyclic world that our conscious minds believe us to live in.

Compulsive inspiration

Subconscious expression in the service of spiritual inspiration is unerring, despite ardent search in this study for defective, contradictory or absent types, or misplaced geometric elements. We are hard-wired to see and express scenes in this way, and equally disposed to deny that we do so and to fancy ourselves thinkers of original thoughts and painters of original scenes. Art is our intimate hologram of infinitely varied scenes, populated by myths and legends, hidden in plain sight in galleries, museums and books, locked behind our equally hard-wired conscious paradigms of what history, myth, astronomy, archetypes and art should be.

An artwork is not done until all the figures of the inspiration are positioned in their allotted spaces, in addition to, or perhaps despite the less exacting function of making some immediate conscious sense to the artist and likely viewers. In the context of archetypal expression, the perpetual dictum of 'art for art's sake' acquires new meaning. Whether other people would see it, or understand it, or use it in initiation, seems of lesser importance than its completion. Apparent chaotic overwork in some rock art and abstract art around the world indicates a predominant inspiration and expressive impulse, at the cost of recording or communication on a conscious level.

Inspirational dating may extend beyond polar markers and orientation, perhaps to the subconscious choice of which attributes of each type are activated. The usual tri-polar and triple equatorial features are too holistic, detailed, precise and 'tacked' to nature, to be planned, measured out, taught or consciously designed. Polar and structural features, intimately related to equatorial features, add further layers of complexity beyond conscious artistry. Only compulsion could be this consistent.

In Art and Illusion, Ernst Gombrich at first found that innocent eyes do not exist. We have to "learn to look and to see", we cannot make sense of what we perceive if it is totally novel to us, and we require schemas or visual pre-conceptions to gradually become attuned to reality (see a parody involving these ideas in a colonisation scene at t3 t18). Yet later, in The Sense of Order, Gombrich finds that order is not imposed on the external world by conscious will. We instinctively and thus compulsively order experience spatially and temporarily.

Layers of expression

Spiritual art is understood in academia to be based on hallucinations that are "construed in trance", recalled and "no doubt formalised as they were painted." (Lewis-Williams and Pearce, 2012). However 'formalisation' of buck bags, sky ropes, flying people, falling buck, half humans, saurian antelope and such surreal features need not imply that the artists and their clients or society understood these forms, or even that the forms represented the implied hallucinations, which may rather be termed lucid dreams, and may not be primarily visual.

Archaeologists acknowledge that sacred art is ritualised, but persist, in the words of M Biesele, in explaining art and ritual in terms of "communally held beliefs" being "operationalised... adding to the store of people's knowledge", while some motifs in art "do not become the source of many more paintings."

This study could not find cumulative nor dead-end motifs. Mindprint implies the very opposite of these conclusions of random, incidental and vetoed expression. Our collective subconscious and nature are the dual sources of the sets of attributes, their sequence and geometry in art. It is not individual or cultural, nor trial and error, nor bounded by a "set of beliefs" built on a supposed store of spiritual "knowledge". Artistic and mythic structure is not a function of knowledge.

Lewis-Williams and Pierce see iconography as "the significance of images for their makers... impossible to study without an iconographic baseline and social context of the imagery." They call for adducing ethnographic (mythic) and lexical (conscious) meanings, from neuro-psychological and other evidence to guide a theoretical and methodological framework to explain San rock art. Mindprint offers these meanings, frameworks and methods in sixteen limited sets of attributes, and a simplistic, standard geometric structure, with endless close affinities to nature and culture, and endless examples.

A dictionary of artistic and iconographic typology and structure is overdue, but no faith or set of "beliefs" are required.

This study is enabled by conceptual unity, as well as the principle of partial and imperfect expression. Where one sequence of icons, symbols, myths or gods may omit, underplay or overplay a type, others fill in. Culture itself functions by disunity, traceable by 'tacks' among its artefacts.

The main ingredients of the most elusive aspects of culture; being aesthetics, beauty and inspiration, were thought to be indefinable, infinitely mutable, independently created, supported only by high culture, transfused, learned and fragile. They now appear to be highly standardised by subconscious impulse, unlearned, robust, and accessible to any prodigy or peasant anywhere. All it requires is a ready eye, mind and hand, a canvas and a piece of charcoal.

Cognitive archaeology denies archetypes in rock art, and does not gather or apply visual iconographic data, apart from conscious symbols provided by the available myths of the culture of the painters.

Presuming that artists enter trance in expectation of certain experiences, and record largely culturally expected visions, cognitive archaeology expects healers to find what they consciously expect to find, and the science itself does not find what it believes the artists do not expect to find. "San religious beliefs and experience was constrained, or framed, by the individual image-maker's intellectual and social milieu," writes cognitive archaeologist David Lewis-Williams (SA Archaeological Bulletin, 2012, p78).

Science denies that people and cultures participate in a collective or universal subconscious. Yet conscious contact with the symbolic and collective subconscious realm is one of the causes, effects and aims of ritual, and particularly of art.

Popular culture consumes spiritual experience as a type of adventure tourism or escapism. Most popular anthropology or 'ancient mystery' writers trade in archetypes, without addressing or even mentioning archetypes. Some popular writers start off on the premise of an ancient super race (EF Malkowski; Ancient Egypt 39 000 BC, Civilisation X. 2010). Some start on the super race or space 'contact' premise (Robert Temple; Sirius mystery), then migrate to an academic view. Most academics start from the opposite premise, of an ancient primitive race blessed by evolution. Some academics migrate to an appreciation of the complexity of primitive cultures (Francis Thackeray; The principle of sympathetic magic in the context of hunting, trance and southern African rock art, 2013. The Institute for Human Evolution, Wits University). The middle ground where these mutable paradigms should meet remains elusive.

The premise of this study is that we are the same super race we have been for at least 100 000 years, with great variety in individual aptitude. Population spikes and advantaged prodigies, such as Poussin, Mozart, Einstein, Bernard Banneker, Freud, Werner von Braun and Jimi Hendrix, are sufficient to account for works of genius such as the Narmer Palette, world wonders and space flight. We are equally capable of cultural erasure and genocide (Nineveh library, Alexandra library, Mexican codex bonfires, Italian bonfires of vanities, extermination of Bushmen, gypsies, Jews, Palestinians and Rwandans). Healing and transformation seems to apply only to individuals, not to cultures or humanity at large.

Layers of meaning

Jung noted the formulaic nature of art in his approach of circumscription (finding relevant meanings or 'signatures' in dreams) to diagnose and prescribe appropriate myths, on the assumption that outer and inner experience and health determine their own spheres of meaning. Jung scoured peripheral meanings to reveal core meanings, confirmed in this study by the finding that each type includes a halo of related meanings.

Heidegger wrote that "a poet or thinker with his moral legein grants a world for a nation to live... by responding to the logos of earth, sky and gods... The framing-in of a world is a work of the founding physis, carried by mythos and spelled out by poetry... If we think we are interpreters, we steal from ourselves. Interpretations remain translations in different words, not revelations of truth and meaning." This view applies to the meanings conventionally readable in Camoens, Picasso, Brink, Coetzee and all moralising (in the broad sense of the word) artists. This view is also relevant to the conventional meanings of spiritual texts. The arts translate the universe into a microcosm of the human subtext. The grammar of art, however, may well extend beyond interpretation, and thus reveal truth and ultimate meaning. The fault of occlusion is not in our art, books or eyes, but in our minds that we cannot understand the full meaning of what is in front of our eyes.

Holistic types t1 to t15

Chapter J

Some of the attributes of the sixteen types identified in this study are discussed here in their astrological context, which is convenient for combining personification and spatial relationships. These concepts are then reduced to lists of different kinds (categories) of concepts and attributes in the Tables. The most visually distinctive and apparently most frequent attributes are then statistically tested in art and rock art.

Type Taurus t1 t16 Auriga, Orion and Hyades

Type Taurus t1 t16 Auriga expresses swift people, half-human swallows often mistaken as mermaids, linked to water, mud, nests, skyscrapers and cities. The star Rohini (Little Deer) corresponds to Artemis clutching a pair of antelope or goats.

Type Taurus t1 t16 Orion has no clearly defined head, or only a separated head nearer the ecliptic. He was god of the dead in Age Taurus 1, a function moved to Taurus Perseus and Algol (the severed Medusa head), in Age Taurus 2, identified with John Baptist, who was also beheaded.

Type Taurus t1 Hyades is the bull head. See a V-shaped lotus bulb in the Dendera crypt at theme t2 t17 for a rare example of visual 'Spartan' (stick figure) correspondence feedback (conscious elaboration) in art.

These three concepts and constellations relate to rain divination; Auriga and her swifts as spiritual heralds of rain, Orion as her underworld counterpart, and the bull head as rain in the natural world.

Type Taurus t2 t17 Perseus and Pleiades

Type Taurus t2 t17 Perseus has a mirrored shield, sword, twisted posture, a bag with the Medusa head, or sometimes himself has a monstrous head. Shields usually record and signify the owner's deeds, battle honours and sacred gifts, a kind of book. Perseus has one foot on the Pleiades, one arm reaching to type Aries t3 where he holds the Medusa head, another arm on the galactic equator that curves over him from the gate and his rear foot on type Taurus t1 Auriga or the gate.

Sometimes he faces and flanks type Gemini t15 to form a churn pair. One way of harmonising his concept, calendric position, myth and stellar Spartan (stick) figure in visual logic, is to see Algol as a mirror, reflecting Perseus' own face, or reflecting the missing heads of Auriga and Orion.

Algol is also the cysta mystica with a snake (mystic basket, see a marble sarcophagus at theme t11), or a bag containing a monster head with snake hair, held by Perseus, who cut it off by aiming a blow from a glance in his mirrored shield. In some Achilles shield designs, the cysta is a turtle, whose plastron (belly plate) is used as a divination device in China. Between types Taurus t2 and Aries t3, an unidentified figure, artefact, or wound sometimes appears in inspired art. Algol is about 23 degrees north of the ecliptic, equal to earth's current obliquity, its position antipodal (spherical opposite) to Scorpius t9 Lupus, sometimes expressed as a basket lid. Astronomy does not hold the answer to mysteries, but by holographic effect it points out the myths that do.

Type Taurus t2 t17 Pleiades is the initial severed bull leg (O Neugebauer and RA Parker; Egyptian astronomical texts, III). It is also a rain bag, buck bag, bones bag, snake bag or ophiotaurus (cow-snake), particularly in its role as approximate spring marker for Age Taurus 2. The first severed bull leg was Ursa Major over Leo, torn from a former spring at Taurus Hyades, a jaw shape. Pleiades and Ursa Major assumed the same arrangement, but with the jaw pictured in profile. Its attributes include fertility, rain, seven sisters or brothers, and calibration, partly since it is just short of 90 degrees ecliptic (and was just over 90 degrees celestial) from type Leo t13 Regulus, the heart on the ecliptic equator and the prime calibrator in all astronomies.

The Age Taurus 2 concepts and constellations relate to rainmakers, in contact with the spiritual and natural ecology of the adjacent type Taurus t1 t16, but active in the real world.

Type Aries t3 t18, Cetus and Triangulum

Type Aries t3 t18 favours U-shaped outlines such as palettes, pockets or portals. Aries was always considered a primary marker, even before Age Aries, when the spring equinox was still in Taurus. Dragons under queens or knives appear in religious iconography in the Common Era, replacing the spring bull sacrifice marker.

Type Aries t3 Triangulum (Dagger) is the instrument of sacrifice and the mark of assassins such as

Benjamin, Brutus and Judas. Benjamin tribesmen were reputed left-handed assassins, expelled in legend to become the first lost tribe of Israel. The Indian Upanishads, Mudaka 7 -112, links the number 18 to sacrifice; "Ritual sacrificial forms are unsafe boats, the 18 in which is expressed the lower work."

Above Triangulum is Andromeda, a horizontally flying princess, sometimes figured as a skinned goat or buck bag (see the Dendera zodiac in the Decans section).

Not all decans of all types are neatly figured in myth and less so in the sky.

Aries Agnus Dei (Lamb of God) icons are stamped into Passover candle wax remnants by the Pope in the Vatican on certain festive and elective occasions. Agnus Dei signifies the Church militant in the human world, despite carrying the 'wound' of mortality. Its standard post signifies a 'triumph' or spring relay marker of the Arian Age, starting about BC 1500. The Agnus staff also signifies an impaling spear, crucifixion or speared dragon.

Postage stamps issued worldwide in 2000, themed on the Year of the Dragon, demonstrate our innate tendency to link cosmic cycles with curved-necked dragons. Agnus asserts itself in most of these designs. Committees, commissions, commemorations and icons offer the ideal canvas for archetypes. Agnus was invoked by the mere terms of that project; 'calendric stamp' (see the Polar chapter illustrations). Some dragon stamp designs said more than the philatelic committees or artists intended, involving eclipses, antitheticals, the international dateline, celestial versus ecliptic co-ordinates, long necks or bodies, and Cetus, the scaly decan of Aries currently just above the celestial equator, or just emerging from 'water' in mythical terms.

Cetus, composed of two parts, is expressed in two ways in art. The larger part under Pisces is the Whale body, with a long tail stretching rearward and up to its pentagonal tail-fin under Aries; or the tail is rendered as its retro (rear-facing) head, with a long neck stretching down to the body. Concepts or figures rendered rear-facing tend to be monstrous. They do not face the western horizon they daily move towards, nor face the oncoming annual sun that moves west-east, but face the slow precessional migration of the four seasons. Jonah, probably personifying a planet, could not enter the Cetus main body below Pisces, since it is out of reach even to wide-ranging Mercury. Yet Mercury or the moon could be 'swallowed' in the Aries ram head north of the ecliptic, and literally pass up or down the Aries necks in incremental transits, down to the Cetus tail, to return north and be 'spat out'. A planet in temporary retrograde (apparent orbital reversal, due

to our view from an orbiting earth) could trace a loop between the two Aries Agnus necks, as Mercury sometimes does.

The moon on occasion crosses the centre 'bowl' of Aries where it could eclipse the sun, or be eclipsed by the earth's shadow if the sun is in Libra. Both main luminaries are half a degree in apparent diameter, and so is the earth's apparent shadow core at the lunar orbit distance, a kind of dark dagger that earth swings around the orbital plane, slashing across our moon in cycles of 18 to 19 years.

Type Pisces t4 t19 Cetus and Pegasus

Type Pisces t4 t19 Pegasus (Horse) expresses a horse, elephant, or antelope in profile.

Type Pisces t4 t19 the latter fish, as a pileus, cap or helmet of woven or matted wool (felt), symbolises initiation or freedom. It is also a precessing spring symbol, and was thus attached to various attributes in turn through the Ages. The latter fish divides Aries from Pisces. A pileus with stars above represents the Dioskouroi or Castor and Pollux twins, as remnants of the shell of the egg from which they hatched. Underworld god Nergal wears a multi-layered cap, resembling a torn veil. As clutcher of a pair of goats or kid dragons, he is associated in turn with Gemini Monoceros, Taurus Auriga, Aries Agnus and Pisces.

The hero twins are also spring icons (see twins clutching the type Gemini t15 and Taurus t1 Auriga rope at the galactic gate, while vaulting to type Pisces t4, on an Olmec obelisk at theme t8).

Type Aquarius t5 t20 retro, Cetus spout and Pegasus head

Type Aquarius t5 t20 Pegasus as a horse, elephant, tomb or pond, is shared with type Pisces t4 t19. These two types also flank and share the polar axis (a meridian line over the two ecliptic and two galactic poles) across Pegasus and across the galactic south pole at the Whale spout). The type itself sometimes expresses its adjacent 'corner churn' as a blast, trumpet, Pentecost, font or fountain, over a trio of figures.

Type Aquarius t5 t20's primary attributes include high priest, half fish, half antelope, double skin, tailcoat head, Oannes, John Baptist, active posture (reinforced by Pegasus), mantis (ambiguous with type Scorpius t9, but here the flamboyant and colourful types), body paint, multicoloured legs, Anopheles mosquito or retro ambling monkey.

Type Aquarius t5 t21 and Southern Fish

Type Aquarius t5 t21 often expresses a world spirit, complementary to its opposite type Leo t13 as a cosmic ruler, and sometimes a lord of animals (ambiguous with type Libra t10). Slight intrusion by the knotted tail of Capricornus is incidental with type Aquarius t21's occasional crossed legs, itself somewhat ambiguous with type Pisces t4.

Type Capricornus t6, Delphinus and Cygnus

Type Capricornus t6 expresses images of Pan, Krishna, didgeridoo players in Australia or Kokopelli in America. These characters are all forest guardians and fertility agents, linked to a one-legged posture, flute music and frivolity. Ian Anderson of Jethro Tull, in his early blues performances is the very picture of a trance dancer, featuring repetitive riffs, a buzz of harmonica and bass, hairy body and earthy, surreal lyrics, a kind of rural and hippie ideal. He chose the flute and developed the stance by impulse, taking his a cue from a local news report about his own apparent gimmick. Many years and albums later, he discovered in a press conference in India that he resembled Krishna (Ian Anderson; Jethro Tull, Living with the past, DVD, Eagle Vision). Anderson campaigns for forest conservation around the world, including the UK and South Africa's Wild Coast, thus acting as Pan. The flute attribute sometimes appears as amphibious breathing, perhaps trance induced by near asphyxiation. Didgeridoo resonators, reticulative breathing and elephants express the same theme. Type Capricornus t6 is sometimes horned, or a reptilian with scaly skin.

Type Sagittarius t7, Corona Australis and Scutum

Type Sagittarius t7 often expresses a figure of minor status in the context of the work, such as young, or being carried. It may figure as a bag, or emergent life, opposite the type Gemini t15 creator, or with a bag or rope.
Type Sagittarius t7 Corona Australis is an erect and curved tail, sometimes figured in art (not the L-shaped tail of type Leo t12 Galactic pole).

Type Scorpius t8 tail, Galactic centre and Ophiuchus

Type Scorpius t8 Ophiuchus is often expressed as a giant, or a figure performing a feat of strength, such as taming monsters.

Type Scorpius t9 head, Lupus, Serpens and Centaur

Type Scorpius t9 head or Serpens Caput (Snake head) expresses a hand, handprint, palette or cartouche. The hand of God or fate, as in the Babylonian and Biblical 'mene tekel', weighed and found too light, appears among star names as Scorpius Graffias, Writing Finger. See a Judaic and an African hand of God in Mutwa's Soweto Culture Village rain hut mural at theme t1 t16. See painted palette pebbles that could be expressions of the concept of footprints, similar to the modern buzzword of environmental or carbon footprint, in an African palette at type t14.
Types Scorpius t9 and Libra t10 as lawgivers are linked in some myth and asterisms. The types are often linked as one constellation (see the Augustus gem at theme t10). In art the type is often figured as a healer on two staffs, or with antlers, or with a lamp.

Type Libra t10, Bootes, Centaurus and Hydra tail

Type Libra t10 Bootes expresses balance, law, Justice, (shared with type Virgo t11), fate, duplication, printing, tupos, the ISO 14001 environmental impact management standard, lord of animals, and Noah adjacent to type Virgo t11's ark. Bootes constellation lies ecliptic north of Virgo, his staff over Libra.
Cognitive archaeologist Prof David Lewis-Williams chose a rock art image of a young man body-painted white, holding staffs and a shield for the renovated South African coat of arms (see the Maclear Linton panel at theme t5 t21). He duplicated and mirrored it to make an identical antithetical (facing) companion, removed the shield that already appears in the given frame, and the staff and spear that already appear as crossed 'arms' above the shield (incidentally expressing the opposite, type Aries t3 Triangulum, Knife). Mindprint analysis of the Maclear Linton panel reveals that the coat of arms expresses type Libra t10, wheel turner, lawgiver, calibrator, environmental balancer, Ka soul or instructor, as he is in the Namibian White Lady painting (see theme t5 t21).
Type Libra t10 sometimes continues the twined caduceus of his opposite, type Aries t3 t18, the primal shield, necks, arms or axe shape (see U-shaped gates at theme t3 and t3 t18). Type Libra t10 and its opposite are also the archetypal seats of the lunar nodes (dragon's head and tail in astrology) and their eclipse cycle of 18 to 19 years.

Type Libra t10 Hydra's tail and Lupus are antipodal (spherical opposite) to the mystic basket (see type Taurus t2 Algol), sometimes expressed as a basket lid or 'flying saucer' with looped hinges (see Buddha's death at theme t8). He bears related meanings of microcosmic and spiritual power concentration. Situated in the sequence between pregnancy and wisdom, he figures life cycles, rise and fall of status, a stock theme in emblematic and iconographic art (see Wheel of Fortune insets at theme t10).

He is present in all cultures, in Egyptian art as a polar balancer (see the Seti 1 ceiling at theme t8), in nearly identical arms-up posture as in the Linton panel at the other end of the continent. Any limited contact there may have been between envoys of Queen Hatshepsut and the Maclear district, devoid of gold or diamonds, and devoid of other signs of contact with Egypt, probably did not include the tomb ceiling motif.

Type Libra t10 Bootes in the Egyptian tomb ceiling is identified in Egyptology and archaeo astronomy as Dinwiddie, spearman of a bull foreleg. This name perhaps approaches Dahudi, equivalent to David, a shepherd king. Since Egyptian was written without vowels, and many words contained glottal stops or non-sounds, it was mangled in Greek and English, so a little further mangling to give the figure personality could not hurt. This David bears the shape and posture of type Libra t10 Bootes (its constellation label refers to a shepherd, as David was). The conceptual spear from its front hand also figures the tail or retro neck of type Leo t12 Ursa, its head on the polar axis. David therefore is a celestial polar marker or turner, its spear or catapult ever extending and moving upward to keep track of the wandering pole. His rear arm is formed by Corona Borealis, a good catapult or spear-thrower shape (see migrants with catapult slings at theme t8). His rear hand and staff stands over type Scorpius t9, opposite type Taurus t2 Pleiades, ecliptic anchor of the bull foreleg, thus this type is doubly aligned to bull legs.

The Maclear figure stands on a rope of the sky, or power line, and is linked to bovine limbs (the famed bull foreleg, bull bag, foetus, or extended Ophiotaurus from the galactic gate), holding a staff and spear over a shield below (see type Libra t10's opposite at type Aries t3, as an empress with a shield), and a staff in his rear hand on the type Scorpius t9 side. Adjacent types Libra t10 and Scorpius t9 share the attribute of trance rituals and holding staffs. Most type Libra t10 figures around the world express some, or at least one of these attributes.

Type Virgo t11 womb, Corvus and Galactic pole

Type Virgo t11 always figures a pregnant womb, sometimes linked to the galactic pole as her prior child. The type is sometimes linked with an ark, crow, shower from a grail, or Hydra (Water snake). These images demonstrate the enduring presence of archetype in subconscious inspiration, expressed in myth, icons and art.

Type Leo t12 retro, Crater and Ursa Major

Type Leo t12 expresses framing, inversion, doors, gravity, rotation, pendulums and precession. Type Leo t12 Ursa and the Draco tail marked off the movement of the celestial pole in the distant Age Taurus 1. Ursa's retro version (head pictured on the east, towards Virgo) looks more like a horse, as does Leo retro, incidental with mythical horses such as Odin's multi-legged Sleipnir. Extra legs could express frozen motion, incidental with the pendulum theme. Multi-bodied figures appear in all cultures, rooted in visionary experience. They usually appear at type Leo t13 or t12.

Type Leo t13 heart, Hydra, Sextans and Ursa Major

Type Leo t13 Regulus pictures the heart of a lion or horse, below Ursa Major, a large bear. Both are often pictured retro (with a head on the other side), or double-headed, or multi-limbed.

Type Leo t13 Hydra (Water snake) is a long inverted (south side up) Sphinx extending below types Cancer, Leo and Virgo, its paws just below Cancer, its chest and head below and mirroring Leo Regulus (royal heart), its body as Sextans under Leo, its belly at Leo Crater under the polar axis, its rump at Virgo Corvus or pecked by the Crow (see rump wounds at theme t13), and its tail below Libra (see the mystic basket lid in a scene of Buddha's death at theme t8). Hydra as a macro Sphinx spans a quarter of the sky, as some Chinese macro-constellations do, containing smaller animal figures within (a trait also of type Aquarius t5). Hydra lies south of the ecliptic and mostly south of the celestial equator, thus in celestial 'water', from which it had slowly emerged in the last 90 degrees of time (four Ages by the archetypal division into sixteen types). Its reputed treasure hall includes time, which type Cancer t14 controls.

Type Cancer t14, Lynx, Ursa Minor, Hydra head and Ascellus (Beehive)

Type Cancer t14 Ursa Minor as a bull foreleg, jawbone and midsummer is discussed with type Taurus t1 t17 Pleiades above. It is sometimes a small canine such as a jackal, or a scarab (see theme t14).

Type Gemini t15 t0, Monoceros, Canis Minor, Lynx, Ursa Minor and Gate

Type Gemini t15 stands with his or their prior foot on the galactic gate or bridge, and an arm or arms reaching up to Ursa Minor, where the celestial pole have been for the last two Ages. Either or both of these concepts, and the double-bodied nature of Gemini as creator or hero twins, are figured as a rope, thong, thread, chain, bridge or footprints, persistent themes in visions, art and mythology in all cultures (see type Gemini t15 holding ropes in the Seti 1 ceiling at theme t8, and various ropes of the sky at theme t15). This rope is also a spring icon, and thus moves with precession (see Taurus Perseus type figures controlling Aries dragons by ropes in the Narmer palette at theme t3 t18).

The pole is also a type of eagle's nest, and Horus as a smiter like an egret killing its sibling, as royals often do.

Type Gemini t15 Canis Minor is expressed as a small dog or a rump wound, a theme that deserves more study.

Typological tables

The most practical tabulation of archetypes in art is by using the twelve familiar zodiac constellations as an analogy and mnemonic, but retrograde (as decans do), allocating two numbers each to the four large constellations (thus sixteen, as the Tarot trumps do), and doubling the quarter of the cycle with a spring equinox history by a second layer of types.

The total of sixteen appears to be fifteen; the doubled type Aquarius t5 t20 and t5 t21 share the same lower number.

The four structural points (two galactic crossings and two polar axial points) remain unnumbered, since they do not account for time or space.

Types by constellations and myth equivalents;

t3 Aries as Triangulum Knife, Andromeda Sword
t2 Taurus as Perseus Rainmaker or diviner hero
t1 Taurus as Orion Hunter, Auriga Charioteer
t15 Gemini as Canis Major Dog, Anubis, or as Lynx
t14 Cancer as Hydra head, catfish, or Ursa Minor
t13 Leo as Ursa Bear Pole bearer, Hydra body
t12 Leo latter as Crater Grail, or Ursa Major Bear
t11 Virgo as womb, or Corvus Crow
t10 Libra as Bootes Herdsman
t9 Scorpius as Serpens or Lupus Wolf
t8 Scorpius latter as Ophiuchus Giant or Ara Altar
t7 Sagittarius as galactic centre, Cygnus, Scutum
t6 Capricornus as Foal, Delphinus, Southern Fish
t5 Aquarius as Pegasus Horse legs, South Fish
t5 Aquarius latter as Pegasus fore, Cetus spout
t4 Pisces as Pegasus square Pond, Cetus body.

Types by trumps, constellations, and functions;

TYPE TAROT CONSTELLATION, FUNCTION
t1 Juggler Taurus Orion, rain diviner quester
t1 t16 Tower Taurus Auriga, gate, shepherd
t2 Priestess Taurus Pleiades, as rainmaker
t2 t17 Star rain Taurus Perseus, as rain hero
t3 Empress Aries Andromeda, as queen
t3 t18 Moondog Aries Cetus, as Agnus dragons
t4 Emperor Pisces Pegasus Cepheus, throne
t4 t19 Sun twins Pisces, spring children, paradise
t5 Pope Aquarius Pegasus, as priest
t5 t20 Judge Aquarius Pegasus, as blessing
t5 t21 World Aquarius legs, as healer
t6 Choice Capricornus, as trio, merman
t7 Chariot Sagittarius, as horse team, centaur
t8 Strength Scorpius Galactic centre, as opener
t9 Hermit Scorpius Ophiuchus, Lepus, snake, wolf
t10 Wheel Libra Serpens Cauda, as claws, tails
t11 Justice Virgo Bootes, as Maat principle

t12 Hanged Leo retro, Crater, Pole galactic, trial
t13 Death Leo, as reaper on horse, multi-bodied
t14 Time Cancer Hydra, as former summer
t15 Daemon Gemini, Monoceros, gate, creator
t15 t0 Jester Gemini, as nature spirit, Icarus.

Types by constellations, decans, myths, attributes;

TYPE CONST MYTH ATTRIBUTE
t1 t16 Taurus Orion Hunter weapon, pointing
t2 t17 Taurus Perseus Hero twisting
t3 t18 Aries Cetus Dragon neck, craning
t4 t19 Pisces Androm King crossed, ruling
AXIS TREE ALIGNED
t5 t20 Aquarius Pegas Priest lurch, blessing
t5 t21 Aquarius leg Healer legs, painted
t6 Capricornus Choice reptile, inward
t7 Sagittarius Chariot young, manifesting
GALXY POOL POT
t8 Scorpius Lupus Wolf tail, taming
t9 Scorpius Ophiuc Gaint bent, trance
t10 Libra Serpens Maat arms, staff
t11 Virgo Bootes Maid womb
plG Virgo Coma POST LIMB JOINT
t12 Leo Crater Horse invert
t13 Leo Ursa Lion heart
t14 Cancer Ursa Opener time, twining
t15 t0 Gemini Canis Ptah rope, creating
GATE SNAKE PATH
t15 to t21 overlap t0 to t5 b,
Galactic types tg22 to tg34, overlap t0, t1, t7, t8.
Polar types tp35 to tp59, overlap some tg types.

Types by their shared decanal borders;

t15 t0 Gemini and t14 Cancer
share Lynx, Ursa Minor
t14 Cancer and t13 Leo
share Hydra, and Ursa Major
t13 Leo and t12 Leo share Ursa Major
t12 Leo and t11 Virgo
share Crater (Grail), Galactic pole
t11 Virgo and t10 Libra share Bootes
t10 Libra and t9 Scorpius share Serpens
t8 Scorpius and t7 Sagittarius
share Galactic centre, rift
t7 Sagittarius and t6 Capricornus
share Cygnus (Swan)
t6 Capricornus and t5 t21 Aquarius
share South Fish
t5 t20 Aquarius and t4 t19 Pisces share Pegasus
t4 t19 Pisces and t3 t18 Aries share Andromeda
t3 t18 Aries and t2 t17 Taurus Perseus share Algol
t2 t17 Taurus and t1 t16 Taurus
share Hyades (Bull)
t1 t16 Taurus and t15 t0 Gemini share the Gate.

Types by Constellations and Trumps;

TYPE CONSTELL   TAROT TRUMP
t1 t16 Taurus Orion   juggler /Tower struck
t2 t17 Taurus Pleiad Priestess /Star woman
t3 t18 Aries Cetus   Empress /Moon dogs
t4 t19 Pisces Andrm   Emperor /Sun twins
AXIS BETWEEN POLES
t5 t20 Aquarius Peg   Pope /Judgement
t5 t21 Aquarius leg   Pope /World spirit
t6 Capricornus   Choice of Paris
t7 Sagittarius   Chariot
GALACTIC CENTRE
t8 Scorp Lupus   Strength virtue
t9 Scorp Ophi   Hermit in trance
t10 Libra Serp   Wheel of fortune
t11 Virgo Bootes   Justice virtue
GALACTIC POLAR AXLE
t12 Leo Crater   Hanged man
t13 Leo Ursa   Death, unnamed
t14 Cancer Hydr   Time angel virtue
t0 t15 Gemini Canis Fool, unnumbered
GALACTIC GATE   [Querent?].

Types by function;

t1 Taurus hunter or diviner
t2 Taurus rainmaker
t3 Aries braider
t4 Pisces multiplier
t5 20 Aquarius ritualiser
t5 21 Aquarius globaliser
t6 Capricornus ascender
t7 Sagittarius manifestor, diffuser
t8 Scorpius opener, mover
t9 Scorpius bent healer
t10 Libra animator
t11 Virgo generator
t12 Leo inverter
t13 Leo reaper
t14 Cancer calibrator
t15 Gemini roper, churner.

Types by optional artistic attributes;

t1 t16 Taurus Auriga as Rain queen
t1 Taurus Orion as Rain king diviner
t2 t17 Taurus Hyades as Rain animal
t2 t17 Taurus Pleiades as Rain
t2 Taurus Pleiades Perseus as Rainmaker
t3 Aries Andromeda as Moon queen
t3 t18 Aries as Moon dragons
t3 t18 Cetus tail as Moon monster
t4 Pisces Pegasus as King's throne
t4 t19 Pisces axial group as King's rule
t4 t19 Pisces Cetus as King's domain
t5 Aquarius Pegasus as World healer
t5 t20 Aquarius Phoenix as World emblem
t5 t20 Aquarius Equuleus (Foal) as World travel
t5 t21 Aquarius Piscis Austrinus as World spirit
t6 Capricornus as Pan or a reptile
t6 Capricornus Delphinus, Dolphin, as Pan's fish
t6 Capricornus Microscopium as Pan's flute
t7 Sagittarius and Corona Australis as Chariot
t7 Sagittarius Aquila Eagle as Chariot mover
t7 Sagittarius Scutum (Shield) as Chariot horse
t8 Scorpius Ara (Altar) as Strength's sacrifice
t8 Scorpius Galactic centre as pool
t8 Scorpius Serpens cauda (Snake tail) as net
t8 Scorpius tail as Strength's tail
t9 Ophiuchus (Giant) as Sage's spirit
t9 Scorpius head as Sage in trance
t9 Scorpius Lupus (Wolf) as Sage's guide
t9 Scorpius Serpens (Snake) as Sage's staff
t10 Libra (Scales) as Lord's balance
t10 Libra Bootes, Herdsman as Lord of nature
t10 Libra Serpens Caput (Snake head) as staff
t11 Virgo as Womb
t11 Virgo Bootes (Herdsman) as Womb guardian
t11 Virgo Coma (Hair, galactic pole), as newborn
t11 Virgo Corvus (Crow) as Womb's spirit
t12 Leo retro as King's horse
t12 Leo retro Coma at pole Galactic, as King's son
t12 Leo retro Crater (Grail) as King inverted
t13 Leo and Leo minor as King's heart
t13 Leo Sextans (Sextant) as King's instruments
t13 Leo Ursa Major (Bear) as King's guard
t14 Cancer and Ascellus (Beehive);
    Time angel, canine
t14 Cancer Hydra head as Time dragon
t14 Cancer Ursa Minor as Time polar angel
t15 Gemini as Creator
t15 Gemini Lynx as Creator's birds
t15 Gemini Monoceros (Unicorn) as Creator's couple
t15 t0 Gemini Canis Minor as Creator's animals.

A statistical test for artistic types
in the geometric sequence and grid

Initial geometric testing of about 400 artworks (see 200 illustrated) representing all regions and eras, chosen for a minimum of eight peripheral figures, revealed ten or more axial points on eyes (two on a womb and a heart instead), positioned on five or more axes crossing at the same point. Most examples have twelve, fourteen or sixteen figures in an irregular ovoid, thus on six, seven or eight axes. Each figure represents a different cluster of structural optional attributes, in a constant sequence, clockwise or anticlockwise.

Scenes with fewer than eight figures may be considered sequentially and geometrically inconclusive, and also happen to be a minority in most cultures. Scenes with more than 50 figures may also be considered inconclusive, unless they cluster into type groups, or unless the scene divides into two or more spheres (see a USA Rochester Creek double imprint at theme t5).

Figures with an eye (heart for type Leo t13 and womb for type Virgo t11) on an axis with an opposite figure, were allocated type numbers in sequence, allowing merging or interchange between the adjacent doubled types (Taurus t2 and/or t1, Leo t13 and/or t12, Scorpius t9 and/or t8, Aquarius t5 t21 and/or t5 t20). Types Leo t13 and t12 in particular often merge or exchange their attributes.

Two polar axles form two triangles as a kind of clockwork, variable in a narrow range, on or between the axes of four or five particular types. The relationship of the polar triangles to the horizontal plane has six variations.

A test was devised to determine the average frequency of the apparently most common and least ambiguous optional features in inspired art.

Types Taurus t1 t16 or t2 t17 may be a bovine [1b] or hunter [1h] or bovine and hunter [1bh] or in a twisted or kneeling posture [1t].

Type Aries t3 t13 may have a long or craned neck [3n] or be a composite dragon [3d].

Type Pisces t4 t19 may be squatting or have crossed legs [4x] or a rectangular body [4r].

Types Aquarius t5 t20 or t5 t21 may be horizontal [5h] or varicoloured [5v] or highly active [5a] or have a cloak [5c] or be notably large [5L].

Type Capricornus t6 may be horned [6h], double-headed [6d] or far ingressed or egressed towards or away from the centre [6i] or a reptile [6r].

Type Sagittarius t7 may be manifesting from a bag or have a bag [7b] or be of minor size or status [7m].

Type Scorpius t8 t9 may be among the four large figures [8L] or perform a feat of strength such as taming a beast [8s] or be bent forward [8b].

Type Libra t10 may have an arm or arms in V or W position [10v] or a staff [10s].

Type Virgo t11 may be marked on her pregnant womb [11w].

Types Leo t12 or t13 may be marked on his heart [12h] or inverted [12i] or be a feline [12f].

Type Cancer t14 may be far ingressed or egressed towards or away from the centre [14i] or be a small canine or feral [t14c].

Type Gemini t15 t0 may be doubled [15d] or a group [15g] or with a rope [15r] or bag [15b] or smiting [15s].

Type Ecliptic Equator (eqE) may be a radially angular (starburst) [eqEa], and roughly elliptical [eqEe], and notably ingressed or egressed at two opposing points [eqEii], being types Cancer t14 and/or type Capricornus t6.

Type Galactic Pole (pG) may be a limb joint or marker between types Leo t12 and Virgo t11 [pGj], or horizontal or vertical to the plane of the work from the Ecliptic Pole (geometric focal point) [pGhv], or have a spherical counterpart on its axis [pGs].

Type Celestial Pole (pC) may be a limb joint (including a jaw) [pCj] over type Leo t13 or Cancer t14 or Gemini t15, or a marker [pCm] near the centre [Cii], or horizontal or vertical to the plane of the work from pG or pE, or have a counterpart on its axis [pCs].

Type Galactic Equator (eqG) and Galactic Equator South (eqGs), may be slightly irregular ellipses

[eqGe] and cross a large number of limb joints (hips, knees, feet, shoulders, elbows, hands) [eqGj].

In artworks where more than a third of the figures are large, small, bovine, bent, arms up, inverted, or of any listed attribute, such attributes are not recognised as statistical data. Thus an artwork may be tested for these attributes in the sequence of figures that are marked by axes to their eyes (with two standard exceptions);

t1/2b/h/t. t3n/d. t4x/r. t5h/v/a/c/b.
t6h/d/i. t7b/m. t8/9L/s/b. t10v/s.
t11w. t12/13/i/f. t14i/c. t15d/g/r/b/s.
eqEa/e/ii. pGj/m/h/s. pCj/ii/hv/s. eqGe/j.

Many additional distinctive attributes of figures on the axial grid may be identified in further studies, such as;

t1 t2 Taurus in a rain ritual
t3 Aries under a weapon
t5 Aquarius with an equine
t6 Capricornus as a reptile
t7 Sagittarius with a large circle
t12 t13 Leo as a feline
t12 t13 Leo as multi-limbed
t14 Cancer as canine or with a small feline
t15 Gemini with a canine
t15 Gemini with a coil or snake.

The frequencies of any of these attributes in their relative positions could be expressed as percentages, in turn defining each type if there is a low variance among different samples. The optional attributes of each could also be reduced to related concepts, such as type Gemini t15 as creator, or type Sagittarius t7 as physical manifestation.

For example type Scorpius t8 or t9 Ophiuchus may be large, tame a lion or snake or beast, carry a pillar or club, cross a river, or combinations of these, but never all of these together. If type Scorpius t8 Ophiuchus (near Hercules) is large in most art works, or often a tamer, or sometimes has a pillar or club, and if no other type stakes a similar profile, then type Scorpius t8 is defined as the universal, subconscious artistic version of Hercules, including in cultures that do not know his Greek name. The validity of the test rises if Hellenised or any other culturally styled art does not show a significantly higher profile of Herculean attributes in the type Scorpius t8 or t9 or their circumpolar positions.

For example type Gemini t15 could be identified either by a rope, bag, mace or other ordering tool, or a smiting posture, or being doubled, wounded on the thigh, as a small canine or a small feline. However usually only one or two of the frequent attributes are expressed in an artwork. Only two of these attributes are tested in the sample. Alternate (either /or) percentages should also be considered; if type Scorpius t8 or t9 is either big, or a tamer, or has a pillar, in more than half of artworks, that should be more conclusive than a significant percentage of one of its regular attributes.

Collective attribute percentages should also be considered; if type Scorpius t8 or t9 has any one of its designated attributes, in a work where most of the sixteen types in the sequence and some other features (such as polar markers) each have any one of their designated attributes, and their eyes on their axes, then the identity of all the figures as well as the archetypal geometry in the work is conclusive.

Mindprint art statistical test results

A total of 170 artworks were tested for their apparently most prevalent typological attributes in the standard sequence, and marked by the standard geometry. Variations ranging from 2% to 11% were found between random batches of 50 each. Since variations are of the same order as the percentage of damaged, overpainted, indecipherable or idiosyncratic figures, the variations are not individually cited, and the results are considered as consistent in large (170) and small (50) samples. Samples of 20 invoke significant variations on the order of 50%, and may display some cultural bias. Selection of damaged or geometric (as opposed to figurative) works, could introduce additional variations on the order of 10%. Minor frequency attributes such as birds, tails, snakes and social status show generally larger variations in small samples, but these features were not statistically tested in the total sample, although they are discussed in the text and illustration captions. Some damaged and low resolution artworks are illustrated to demonstrate the diagnostic value of mindprint, but not used in statistical analysis. Purely geometric figures are not included in statistics, however some semi-geometric or silhouette figures, such as two Bolivian discs and two Scottish palettes (see one of each at theme t12) are included in the statistical test.

Artistic attributes test results (sample 170);
t1 t2 Taurus 48% twisting
t1 t2 Taurus 19% bovine
t3 Aries   42% neck long or bent
t4 Pisces   26% rectangular
t4 Pisces   25% squatting
t5 t20 t21 Aqu 44% varicoloured
t5 t20 t21 Aqu 31% action
t5 t20 t21 Aqu 30% horizontal
t5 t20 t21 Aqu 24% large
t6 Capricornus 48% ingress or egress
t7 Sagittarius 25% bag
t8 t9 Scorpius 34% bent forward
t8 t9 Scorpius 31% strength feat
t10 Libra   53% arms V or W
t10 Libra   34% with a staff
t11 Virgo   87% on her womb
t12 t13 Leo   85% on his heart
t12 t13 Leo   14% feline
t12 t13 Leo   11% inverted
t14 Cancer   45% ingress or egress
t15 t0 Gemini 33% rope
t15 t0 Gemini 21% bag
t15 t0 Gemini 16% smiting
t15 t0 Gemini 08% doubled.

Polar markers found in the expected positions are;
Ecliptic pole 49% (26% limb joint)
Galactic pole 81% (68% limb joint)
Celestial pole 60% (50% limb joint)
Galactic south 65% (50% limb joint)
Celestial south 55% (37% limb joint).

Statistical test results discussion

Results are overwhelming for;
t10 Libra 53% arms V or W
t11 Virgo 87% on the womb
t12 t13 Leo 85% on the heart
Galactic pole 81% (68% limb joint)
Celestial pole 60% (50% limb joint)
Galactic south 65% (52% limb joint).

Results are conclusive for;
t1 t2 Taurus 48% twisting
t3 Aries   42% neck long or bent
t5 t20 t21 Aqu 44% varicoloured
t6 Capricornus 48% ingress or egress
t8 t9 Scorpius 34% bent forward
t8 t9 Scorpius 31% feat of strength
t10 Libra   34% with a staff
t14 Cancer   45% ingress or egress
t15 Gemini 33% with a rope
Ecliptic pole 49% marked (26% limb joint).

Results are significant for;
t1 t2 Taurus 19% bovine
t4 Pisces   26% rectangular
t4 Pisces   25% squatting
t5 t20 t21 Aqu 30% horizontal
t5 t20 t21 Aqu 31% action
t5 t20 t21 Aqu 24% large
t7 Sagittarius 26% with a bag (of manifestation)
t15 Gemini   21% with a bag (of creation).

Results are notable for;
T8 t9 Scorpius 10% with a bent tail
t12 t13 Leo   11% inverted
t12 t13 Leo   14% feline
t15 Gemini 16% smiting
t5 Gemini   08% doubled.

Type Virgo t11 is usually marked on her visibly pregnant womb (87%), and/or appears with a pregnant figure (4%), or is figured by another womb-like feature such as a jug (2%). Thus the image and concept of a womb, or unborn eye, is always expressed in this position in the artistic sequence (94%).

Type Leo t13 is usually marked on his heart (85%), sometimes on type Leo t12 in works containing all sixteen types instead of just fourteen or twelve combined types. Where the eye instead of the heart is on this type's axis, his chest may be marked in another unique way (2%). The heart is sometimes expressed at the opposite type, Aquarius t5 instead (3%). Thus the image and concept of a heart, or inner spiritual eye, is always expressed in this position in the artistic sequence (90%).

Type Capricornus t6 and/or its opposite type Cancer t14 is usually notably far towards or away from the poles (48% and 45% respectively). Either is sufficient to identify their mutual axis as notably indenting the ragged equator (their combined frequency was not tested). See a discussion of the celestial polar roles of these two types in the Astronomy text, and among the captions.

The galactic north pole is usually on a limb joint (68%), sometimes on an artefact, rarely on an extra eye (5%), often confirmed by an opposing galactic south pole marker (65%), thus always marked (81%).

Celestial polar markers confirm the conceptual northern perspective preference, also indicated by the relative positioning of variant attributes inside or outside the sphere. However some artists, irrespective of their position on earth, sometimes conceive of the artistic sphere from the south.

The northern or conceptual 'topside' galactic pole is always marked (81%). The southern or conceptual spherical 'underside' galactic pole is usually marked by a limb joint (65%).

The celestial pole is often marked by a limb joint (50%), rarely by another feature (13%) or an eye (7%), thus chance may play a role. However, conclusive and consistent results for the other two kinds of poles on limb joints, indicate optionality (63%).

The conceptual celestial equator, probably doubled into northern and southern versions, may be inherent in the ecliptic equator (round of figures marked by eyes), perhaps as a triple, alternating equator, that may account for their radial distortion of the figures, like atomic orbital shells. However no test could be devised to account for the potential role of the celestial equator or pair of equators.

The celestial south pole is often marked by a limb joint (37%), rarely by another feature (18%), almost never by an eye (3%), thus a total of 55%, confirming optionality. Larger variations in this feature were found among small samples. Only one celestial polar marker usually appears (their combined frequency was not tested), consistent with the inspirational Age or theme of each artwork, diminishing the role of chance.

The ecliptic pole is often on a limb joint (26%), sometimes on other notable features such as a heart, face, head, genitals, or wound (23%), and rarely on an eye (5%). Chance may play a role in some of these markers, but conclusive and consistent results for the other two kinds of poles on limb joints, and consistent minor results for poles on markers or eyes, indicate optionality. The axial centre is either marked in a consistent variety of ways (49%), or not marked (51%).

Overwhelming results for polar markers on limb joints (as visual and conceptual proxies for inter-dependent poles in the cosmic 'body'), as well as consistent indications of two galactic equators along limb joints, and the low but consistent level of polar markers on eyes (5%), indicate that poles are a kind of counterpoint to types, somewhat like verbs or tenses anchor sentences, or like vowels and the aleph (non-sound or punctuation) anchor consonants in words. Most elements of mindprint are clearly visible (womb, arms up, staff), some at semi-conscious symbolic level (heart, limb joints, orientation), and some are geometrically inferred and traceable (equators, gates, polar triangles).

Results confirm the geometric Attributes and Tables. Validity of the test could improve with refinement of the correlation between concepts and attributes, separation of types into decanal elements, and more examples. Southern African rock art and European schooled art are over-represented in the sample of 170, however examples from all known cultures indicate that mindprint is universal, down to the range and magnitude of the optional attributes of each type.

Conceptual and arguable traits were identified, but not statistically tested.

Statistical test conclusion

Based on conclusive and some overwhelming statistical and geometric evidence of the collective, universal subconscious sequence of optional attributes in inspired art, and on the conceptual and esoteric relationships between the optional elements of each type, the tables of myths, icons, constellations, decans and concepts should be considered proven as describing the collective, subconscious standard artistic expression of archetypes.

If variant expressions of each are considered, such as type Gemini t15 as a rope (33%), and/or bag (21%), and/or creator (such as Ptah), smiting (16%), twinned (8%), canine, hip wound, lynx, boat shrine, unicorn (all of minor percentages), then identification of all types rise to around 90%, in addition to the usual exact geometric proof of the sequence.

Some minor elements of uncertainty remain, due to;

[] Damage, gaps, flakes (about 0.6% average)
[] Overpainting (see the Layers section, that may also apply to some schooled art, about 0.2% average)
[] Low resolution reproduction (about 1.5%)
[] Misidentification for lack of cultural or natural knowledge, or bias (1%).
[] Misidentification for lack of spiritual experience or bias, such as geometrics, vortices, hieroglyphs, or half-human kinds (1%?).

Elements of uncertainty may total to between 4% and 5% on average. Most works are undamaged, clear, sufficiently figurative, and testable for simplistic attributes, leaving mainly universal spiritual expressions as unknown unknowns.
Negligible levels of uncertainty, and the persistent presence of untested attributes, such as type Scorpius t9 or t8 as a snake or scorpion, confirm that artistic inspiration and expression are compulsively meaningful and complete.
Very few individual conscious artistic quirks seem to interfere with the artistic process in sufficiently complex scenes, with notable exceptions such as Egyptian decanal proliferation, use of some feet as figures (as by Poussin), or contraction of attributes in sparse scenes (as by Blake).
Stylistic elements do not interfere with the artistic process at all, even the extreme puzzled tiling of Mexican and Pacific carvings, or hieroglyphic integration of Egyptian, Olmec and Mayan carvings, overwork in Ice Age engraving, geometric or abstract elements worldwide and in expressionist works (such as Picasso), or surreal transparent layers of Dali.
Geometric and semi-geometric figures (see a Scottish palette and a Bolivian disc at theme t12) are probably proto-figures from an intermediary stage of inspiration or expression.
It is very difficult to find rock art or artworks of some complexity (eight to 30 figures) that do not conform to the axial structure, or that contradict the typology, and these are typically heavily damaged or inadequately recorded.

How to identify types and structure in art

Finding mindprint in a work of art is as simple as finding correspondences to any archetypally complete set or sets of about sixteen (twelve to twenty) items, such as pantheons (lists of gods), myth cycles, epics, emblems, lunar mansions, trumps, historic or fictional characters, constellations, heraldic devices, lyrics or animals. Researchers should tack art to sets that they are familiar with, and use the Furter grid and tables for confirmation. Here is a shortcut method to finding the archetypal art code;

[] Identify a likely periphery of figures in a roughly elliptical arrangement.
[] List the figures in circular sequence by any distinctive attribute, such as a posture, season, function, species or device.
[] Provisionally tag the list or the artwork with likely type numbers, such as type Libra10 for a figure with a staff, Aries3 for a long neck, Leo12 or Leo13 for a feline, Taurus1 or Taurus2 for a twisting hero or a bovine, Aquarius5-20 or Aquarius5-21 for skin paint or a lurching posture.
[] Tag figures ingressed or egressed towards or away from the centre, as Capricornus6 or Cancer14.
[] Tag a pregnant figure as Virgo11, an adjacent major figure as Leo12 or Leo13, and the adjacent figure on the other side as Libra10.
[] Infer a clockwise or anticlox sequence, and provisionally complete the numbering.
[] Count the number of eyes (one per figure in the periphery, for example 17), assume the lower even number (for example 16), subtract two (for example 14), skip half of this number (for example 7) between eyes, working in both directions to find pairs of likely opposing eyes. Draw tentative axes between these.
[] If three or more axes cross at the same point, find the likely Virgo11 womb, and Leo12 or Leo13 heart, and tentatively redraw errant axes by not using their eyes, unless their eyes also find counterparts across the geometric centre.
[] If three or more peripheral figures remain unaccounted for, assume a higher equal number (for example 18), and repeat the test with higher numbers.
[] Complete all the possible axes.
[] Resolve the sequence by splitting up or combining the major doubles (Taurus1/2, Aquarius5-t20/5-21, Scorpius8/9, Leo12/13).

[] Connect the equator from eye to eye (with the two exceptions).

[] Draw an oblique circle, half across the sphere, and half around the outside, crossing the equator between Gemini15 and Taurus1, and between Sagittarius7 and Scorpius8, along the route of most limb joints, such as hips, knees, feet, shoulders, elbows, hands.

[] Draw an opposing oblique circle along limb joints, crossing the equator at the same two points, but reversing interior and exterior halves.

[] Find one or two polar markers for the two oblique circles, between Leo12 and Virgo11, or between Aquarius5-20 and Pisces4, near the equator. These poles are often on limb joints.

[] Find a polar marker nearer the axial pole, on or near the Gemini15, Cancer14 or Leo13 axis, which is often a limb joint, perhaps a jaw, vertical or horizontal from the axial centre or from one of the galactic poles. Connect this marker to one of the galactic poles to form a polar triangle.

[] Mirror the polar triangle on the other side of the ecliptic pole, if exactly mirroring markers are found. Infer the inspirational date (spring) from the type that precedes the polar axle (midsummer) by an ideal 90 degrees (approximate, not measured out on the distorted grid).

[] Apply the set of labels to each figure and the four structural points in sequence, or two labels each (and/or, marked =/ below) to the four major types if they are represented by one figure (which is typical if the total is only twelve or fourteen);

[ta1]=/[ta2] [ar3] [pi4i] pGs
[aq5-20]=/[aq5-21] [cp6] [sg7] Galaxy
[sc8]=/[sc9] [li10] [vi11] pG
[le12]=/[le13] [cn14] [ge15] Gate.
poleC. poleCs. The geometric centre is pE.

[] On a separate page, list these type numbers, with basic distinctive attributes or character names found in the artwork, to compare to other artworks, mindprint statistics, stories, myths or typological sets.

Commission impossible

As a somewhat frivolous test of whether artists are part of a conspiracy to perpetuate supposed secret or 'ancient lost knowledge', or plagiarise master artists and cover their tracks with stylistic changes, consider a 'commission to express the archetypal art code'. A mindprint, archetypal tupos, or Furter grid commission would have to include these terms;

[] Express about twenty figures, with about sixteen peripheral, on an irregular oval,

[] in typological sequence,

[] based on an episode or scene in any myth or history or fantasy cycle of any culture or style,

[] aligned by their eyes on an irregular axial grid, · with the exception of type Leo t13 and type Virgo t11 having their heart and womb respectively on the grid.

[] Displace types Capricornus t6 and Cancer t14 closer or further than other figures from the geometric centre.

[] The sequence may be clockwise or anticlockwise.

[] Apply some economy of line in the periphery.

[] Apply artistic compositional strength independent of the axial grid.

[] Mark the axial pole by a limb joint, or leave it unmarked.

[] Mark a secondary pole over either type Pisces t4, Aries t3, Taurus t2 or Taurus t1, by a limb joint.

[] Mark an eccentric pole just inside and between types Leo t12 and Virgo t11 by a limb joint.

[] Overlay an eccentric periphery around the eccentric pole, marked by many limb joints, to interlock the periphery between types Gemini t15 and Taurus t1, and between types Sagittarius t7 and Scorpius t8.

[] Include the concepts of hero, bovine, dragon, man, field, large, horn, animal, pool, arms, crutch, staff, womb, child, heart, small, couple, hazard, and others in their appropriate places.

[] It may be practical to design opposing pairs together.

[] The figures have to express a probable scene, ambiguous with history and myth, identifiable to a particular culture.

[] The work has to be original, compelling, pleasing and elegant.

[] Elements of plagiarism from known works, or more than three contorted features for the sake of geometry are penalised.

[] Astrological stereotypes are penalised.

[] Hallmarks of spiritual inspiration or social ritual are awarded additional points.

Such a commission is of course possible, but difficult and pointless. Faking inspiration would take more shuffling and re-design than inspiration and paint. This study had no need to commission any artist to consciously work the miracle that all artists habitually work subconsciously (see two clumsy mix-and-match mindprint mock-ups in the Polar section to illustrate an Age transition, where the grid is based on iris reflexology points).

There are thousands of excellent complex artworks in galleries, museums, collections, foundations, rock shelters, and on the Internet, particularly on tourism sites.

Finding mindprint in nearly every artwork featuring Notre Dame Cathedral, for example, is no more remarkable than finding mindprint in nearly every rock art panel, distinct grouping, or painting in the world. It is more difficult to find relatively skilled and recognised artworks that do not contain mindprint, apart from portraits, landscapes, still-lifes and commercial decoration.

Duplications and conventions

Archetypal sets and individual types favour images intended for mechanical duplication, such as cylinder seals that replicate themselves in cyclical sequence (see a Babylonian seal at theme t2 t17), tile moulds (see a Chinese tile at theme t11), print block carvings (see an Italian garden scene at theme t2 t17), cards (see Tarot trumps insets), coin dies (see coins at theme t3 t18), and stamps (see the Polar chapter). Duplication usually involves a commission, thus the artist has to express a collective impulse.

The Greek word tupos means "a struck blow, impress of a seal, coin mint, print, mark, track, footstep, figure, image, statue, outline, sketch, draught, original pattern, model, mould, type, system, form or doctrine" (Liddell and Scott, 1984). A type resembles a previous occurrence and predicts further expressions.

Greek philosophy of BC 600 revived the quest of sages as the problem of the One and the Many, describing nature's duplication as the deduction of Many from One, or seeing Many as unsubstantial variations on One. Umberto Eco explores the theme of hoarding, listing, collecting and museum curation in his book, Infinity of lists, illustrated by several works in the Louvre which are now revealed to contain mindprint. To the Louvre, and to this study, a few examples could not be enough.

Handmade copies of inspired art retain some of the original inspiration, but transform, 'translate' or incorporate it into a new mindprint in the eye and hands of the copyist. For example, Poussin's Adoration of the golden calf (see theme t2 t17 and theme t5 t20) was translated into an etching with a similar composition, and a similar but different mindprint. A stock Egyptian theme of a tree of life with birds, regularly copied for the tourist market on papyrus, typically shows five axes (the lowest number accepted as constituting mindprint in this study, requiring only ten features in exact positions), most with different species and different positions.

Like offspring of the same parents, each version is a new combination of chromosomal halves, perhaps as re-combinations of inspiration and expression, spirit and body, eye and hand. Each result is as unique yet as standardised as a fingerprint.

Only personal subconscious compulsion could enforce this kind of quality control. Even hasty tomb murals of stock scenes by apparently junior craftsmen, such as the Ramses 6 rendition (see t8) of the Seti 1 decans, express their own mindprint themes and therefore their own inspiration, like a poet writing a sonnet or a composer re-interpreting the gloria with a new melody and lyrics.

Mindprints in artistic copies (except mechanical copies) are all of different angular shape (degrees between axes), equatorial outline, orientation, polar markers, and galactic features, yet allocate some traits from the standard set of attributes to each type in its standard position, while some remain unsaid, or implied by the context. As soon as an artist chooses to express some attributes, others crowd in to complete the picture by archetypal rules. Remarkably few iconographic ambiguities appear in conventionalised images, despite multiple 'copies' over thousands of years, and ambiguation in the conscious meanings of individual figures. The same applies to melodies and myths.

Mindprint is an all or nothing event. There are no half done or entirely scrambled sequences or patterns, provided that a minimum of figures and features are used. There is no perfect mindprint, yet the quality of imprints show surprisingly little variation, even between novices and masters. The orientation, perspective plane, angular allocation, figures and number of figures all change, yet averages and core iconic content remain constant and timeless, while the polar triangles track the limited framework of spiritual time.

Extensive works contain up to four adjacent mindprints (interlocking in pairs), each with similar but different features.

At a larger scale, clusters or oeuvres of mindprints in the work of an artist, group, region or culture may express localised options of the visual myth cycle, or at least a signature style, such as Homer's legends or Nordic boundary stones (see theme t13). This study could not detect layers of inherent meaning in the core content of art beyond individual works.

Some regions contain repetition of themes and styles, incidental with the impulse of artists to group their works into exhibitions, periods and cultures, and the compulsion of academics and some artists to form movements. This 'schooling effect' hints that the collective subconscious, like chemistry and physics, may well have further layers, scales or shells of expression, probably confined to styling.

Artists in every culture innovate and often radically change elements of styling, yet inspiration and impulse (not mere politics and convention) direct the deeper levels of art, in the way that DNA expresses only some potential, optional traits such as hair colour in the body, while its mutations invisibly tick over to express recessive variations on the theme of the species in tandem with environmental changes, without adding to or detracting from the structure of the DNA. Slower mutation among some isolated groups, such as Bushmen, may be ascribed to slower environmental and social changes, accounting for their supposedly 'older' DNA that should not be seen as less 'developed' or more 'original'. Rapid mutators elsewhere (including Africa and the Pacific islands), typically owning highly multiplied material cultures, should not be seen as more evolved people, nor as having evolved their own cultures. The same kind of mutation applies to inspiration, expression and even conscious styling. It is running to stand still.

Archetype eludes consciousness

No evidence of learning or teaching mindprint could be found in this study. Where expressions could become formulaic, as of decans in Egyptian afterlife scenes, the figures and attributes become more layered and scrambled, as languages on the allegorical tower of Babel construction site did.

Cognitive (knowing) manipulation of some mindprint elements by some artists, or even minor schools, is not ruled out, just as poets and cultures manipulate archetypal themes and mythology by adding layers of convention, and citations of former notable 'classic' expressions. In some double imprints on palettes or discs (see a Bolivian disc at theme t12) there is cause to suspect that the artist or school recognised archetypal inspiration for what it is, and knowingly combined two inspired works. It is equally possible that some artist, cult or culture had used a verbal or other intervening pattern, such as legend, theology, astrology or calendric images, to express that insight. Some palettes, plaques, murals and ceilings express astronomical as well as spiritual concepts. Using Occam's proverbial razor to cut away unnecessary assumptions, leaves the inevitable conclusion that most artists engaged on work containing astronomy, myth or both, thought either to be the 'original' motivation for stock attributes, sequences and geometric patterns, and enquired no further. Some artists did, and do understand archetype as prior form, and characters as expressing aspects of natural order, but such

insights, like those of Jung, tend to remain bogged in the paradigm of culture as a human construct, and an 'incomplete work in cumulative progress', as individual experience seems to be.

Likewise, most poets and dramatists inspired to use mythical motifs, probably think of them as mainly or at least partly historic, legendary and didactic. Also in literature, hints of astrology tend to be taken as handed down by inventors and cultures, not as windows into archetype. Few artists are bold enough to consider themselves as original conduits of universal inspiration, least of all without their conscious knowledge. Yet mindprint implies that all artists are re-creators of pre-original inspiration, their eyes and hands as tools in the hands of archetype and nature.

Many artists strive to reflect natural and cultural order in their work, and endlessly manipulate their subjects and some of their objects to serve their views of that order. Yet no work, artist or school examined in this study offers incontestable evidence of conscious manipulation of mindprint or any other types, sequence or geometry.

Archetype could be read by numbers, but not painted by numbers. Alchemical art such as Egyptian medical and cosmetic palettes, Chinese cauldron scenes and European transmutation emblems, offer an artistic category to search for occasional conscious appreciation of mindprint expression, but not by many of its practitioners. Mindprint describes the structure of expression, extending the toolbox of art criticism, art history, archaeology, anthropology, psychology, and other humanities, but not of artists.

Ambiguous types

Ambiguity is no stranger to mythology, nor to astrology and astronomical labels, mostly due to random errors with sporadic conventional careers. Some ambiguities are 'honest' iconographic mistakes and have surprising literary careers, just as translation errors among star names tend to take on a life of their own, probably due to the authority of some anthology authors (RH Allen; Star names and their meanings). A few are due to inherent ambiguity, as noted in some illustration captions, and in the sections below.

Visual types in art are less ambiguous and highly distinctive if their optional nature is revealed. Some attributes of some types are ambiguous, not all attributes of all types. Artistic structure is robust enough to accommodate partial ambiguities. Minor interchange and ambiguation of some attributes in iconography is attested in many traditions, such as Renaissance emblems (see a Wheel of Fortune at theme t10). For example, a wolf attaches to type Scorpius t9 head or to the adjacent type Libra t10, but not to any of the other ten clusters of meaning. Bear or pole-bearer attaches to type Leo t12 t13 Ursa, and was historically transferred to type Cancer t14 Ursa Minor in Age Aries, but is not attached to any of the other types (except the southern counterparts of the two). Knife attaches to type Aries t3 t18 Triangulum, and to adjacent type Taurus t2 Pleiades if wielded by Perseus, and not to any of the other types.

Three types of sevens

Seven stars in a ladder type cluster are unmistakeably type Taurus t2 t17 Pleiades, although only six are generally visible. However, seven stars in a row, or in two rows, also indicate type Leo t12 t13 Ursa, a larger ladder shape. This ambiguity has led to endless confusion about the Egyptian Dinwiddie, Bull leg spearman, based on eternal confusion between Taurus Bull, Taurus Pleiades bull leg or Wippet mouth opener (jaw), and Ursa Minor as host to the daily celestial pole (the daily, visible pole), speared (or 'poled') by the up-in-arms Bootes. The ambiguity remains since Taurus was a bovine forequarter in concept and picture, its rear obscured by Auriga and Orion as vaulters. While Taurus hosted the spring equinox, the celestial pole was its usual 90 degrees away in Ursa Major over Leo. As the spring marker precessed to the Taurus Pleiades cluster (its iconic position), the celestial pole was still over the seven stars of the Bear, a large foreleg shape, but approaching Ursa Minor, a small foreleg shape.

Two ambiguous corners

Type Aquarius t5 as a Pope, with its upper layer type Aquarius t5 t20 as an axial blast and natural judgement, is ambiguous with type Taurus t2 Pleiades as a rain priestess or rain animal, and its upper layer type Taurus t2 t17 Perseus as rainmaker. Their ambiguity extends to misidentification of Tarot trump 17 (Star) as 'Aquarius', on account of her water jugs, and Tarot trump 5 (Pope) as 'Taurus', for vague reasons, and Tarot trump t5 t20 (Judgement) as 'Taurus Orion', on account of its trio of figures and southern underworld position.

Opposite numbers and their cardinals (90 degrees apart) occasionally swop attributes, just as some opposites do. The type Leo t12 to type Aquarius t5 t20 axis, and its cardinal type Taurus t1 to type Scorpius t8 axis, share meanings of martyrdom; a dying lion opposite a world spirit, and a dying bovine opposite a dreaming healer. Some artworks express the type Leo-Aquarius axis as a lion-dragon steed or hanged man, opposite an emergent man, and the type Taurus t1 to Scorpius t8 axis as a hunt quarry opposite a sacrificial altar. Some show a grail opposite a baptist, and a calamity opposite a beast tamer. These trials and feats should not be confused with type Aries t3 t18 Agnus (lamb), the unblemished sacrifice of spring, or type Capricornus t6 as scapegoat.

Three horses

Horses attach to types Aquarius t5 Pegasus and the adjacent Pisces t4 Pegasus and to the ecliptic (solar) pole on the polar axle between these two constellations, and across to Leo t12 retro (whose stick figure makes a better horse than a lion), and to Aries t3 for its long and bendable neck, a trait of equines such as okapi, zebra, and pseudo-equines such as giraffe. However horses are rare in art in other positions, even where astrology labels indicate equine elements, such as Taurus t1 Auriga (Charioteer), Capricornus t6 Equuleus (Foal), Sagittarius t7 as a centaur, or Libra t10 Centaurus. Even in this relative ambiguity, twelve of the sixteen types and three of the galactic corners are almost never expressed as a horse (except in single-species works).

Age-bound seasonal ambiguities

Type Aquarius t5 t20 opposite type Leo t12 (and their cardinals) are due for yet another layer of calendric ambiguity when they assume spring and autumn equinox positions. They are already laden with remnants of attributes from three prior ages. Thus type Leo t12 Crater (Grail) as a hanged man, galactic pole and polar axis, may inherit some attributes of type Virgo t11 Corvus (Crow), Spica (the womb star) as corn and bodily grail (already in evidence in the popularity of 'sacred bloodlines' myths revived by Baigent, Leigh and Lincoln in Holy blood, holy grail, which is novelised by Dan Brown in The Da Vinci code), a search for second comings and sacred births, or its inverse as slaughter, flanked by types Libra t10 and Scorpius t9 Lupus (Wolf). Which set of attributes eventually stick (or tack) to the revised type Leo t12, would be determined by iconisation gestalt, including closest analogy to the relevant archetype, highest distinction, least ambiguity, extent of demise of Age Aries icons, and rise of immanent Aquarian spring themes.

Type Aquarius t5 t20 could acquire aspects of type Pisces t19 Cetus Whale extinction, or Pegasus field, pond or horse division, relevant to marine defence and resources borders. Age Aquarius polar adjustments may include the cutting loose of the smaller bull foreleg (see the Seti 1 tomb ceiling at theme t8), its spring elements as sacred lakes, its summer elements as falling towers (see theme t1 t16, and Buddha's death at theme t8), and its autumn elements as inversion. However it is presumptuous to predict which aspects of stock events would graft themselves onto epochal themes in inspired art. The core sequence and pattern would remain the same, at least in the ecliptic framework of visual expression. Only modest polar and celestial seasonal elements would subtly change.

Sheep and goat ambiguities

Type Aries t3 t18 Agnus ambiguates with type Capricornus t6. The Gospel theme of baptism is connected with the Capricornus scapegoat, while the crucifixion is linked to Aries, the sacrificial lamb. In African mythology likewise there is some overlap of sheep and goat symbolism, but the scapegoat element of the goat is clear, for example in Credo Mutwa's poem on goats. The goat is a 'questioning animal', as opposed to the 'questing beast' in adventure and romance. The similarity serves to camouflage both types, but context always clarifies conscious assumptions. One of the elements of conflation is that Capricornus is a cardinal point of Aries, being 90 degrees before Aries in the seasonal round, having carried the midwinter solstice while Aries hosted spring. Midwinter has as much calendric significance as the spring position. Many ancient calendars take midwinter as new year, as Julius Caesar reverted to in his Egyptian-inspired calendar reform.

Confirmed identities

The necessary detour into iconographic and mythic ambiguation in the sections above, should not obscure the observation that archetypal attributes, whether imprinted in myth, art or the sky, remain sufficiently distinct from one another, as well as sustained by their sequence, geometric structure and attributes. About ten positive and negative considerations confirm the identity of each type in any artwork.

Compared to other symbolic iconic systems, such as phonemes or alphabets, visual iconography is more distinct and more resistant to conventional meddling.

For example, languages mutate and do not attach to sounds or letter shapes except by convention that has to be laboriously learned. Languages, without consideration of their meanings, thus resemble visual styles and conscious elements in art.

Consciously arranged elements in art, as in myth, ritual and literature, often confuse some attributes, as in various attributions of Tarot trumps to letters, runes, seasons and the zodiac. Only when two systems are both reduced (or elevated) to their archetypal constituents, sequence and structure, could they be compared, and raise their subconscious structure into consciousness. Each set of categories tends to camouflage its structure differently.

Archetype's habitual media of myth, art, ritual and constellations are much less arbitrary than popular culture or academia imagined. Taurus, Leo, Virgo, Scorpius, Aquarius, Orion, Ursa Major, Ursa Minor and many of the other 80-odd constellations and astronomical structures, down to individual stars, have maintained identical or similar names, identities, attributes and concepts in all cultures (RH Allen, 1899), while also allowing variants and macro figures.

Scientific and esoteric paradigms

Chapter K

An academic sceptic of archetypes in rock art explained the status quo view thus; "Whether archetypes are the ultimate origins of spiritual experience, structured thought and imagery, is a supposition that enjoys diminishing support. To accept this supposition there would need to be strong universal evidence for the existence of such archetypes. The fact that only a small selection of individuals, all of whom have read Jung, hold to such a belief or consider that there is sufficient universal evidence, is cause for concern. The patterns, if real, should be immediately obvious to all, yet they are not.

"They are closer to the realm of faith. You have to believe in order to see them. For me this is overwhelming evidence that Jungians see what they want or expect to see, rather than there being any real archetypal patterns in the material evidence. It does not surprise me then, that San rock art has eluded independent [scholarly] searches for archetypes. No rock art researcher has produced independent [scholarly] statistical evidence which demonstrates their presence. Those who want to find archetypes will twist the evidence in rather tortuous ways so as to 'reveal' them. I can think of no rock art images in southern Africa with such characteristics. To find suitable imagery would require considerable stretching of the definition. If one is flexible enough with one's definition one can end up finding supporting evidence for even the craziest of explanations."

These views are admirably clear, but no longer valid, following the overwhelming and cumulative evidence reported above and demonstrated in the illustrations, amounting to proof of diametrically opposite views. However, these academic scepticisms do apply to tortuous scientific diffusionist illogic, as in Asian dragons supposedly deriving from sharks; "The cultural drift from West to East, along the south coast of India... was effected mainly by sailors who were searching for pearls. Sharks constituted the special dangers the divers had to incur in exploiting pearl beds to obtain the 'giver of life'... people dwelling in the neighbourhood of the chief pearl beds regarded the sea as the great source of life, and the god who exercised these powers was incarnated in a fish, ancestor of Dagon. The sharks therefore had to be brought into this scheme, and they were rationalised as the guardians of the storehouse of life-giving pearls at the bottom of the sea... Out of these crude materials the imaginations of the early pearl fishers created the picture of wonderful submarine palaces of Naga [snake] kings with vast wealth of pearls and gold, precious stones and beautiful maidens, under the protection of shark dragons." (Bullfinche's Mythology, citing Dr GE Smith).

This scientific and popular science paradigm could be replaced by a simpler, diametrically opposite, archetypal explanation that applies to sea bounty and sea monsters in all cultures (see Korean and Russian whaling images at theme t12).

Confirmation bias is not just an individual psychological effect, but a major social function and cultural mechanism sustaining supposed common sense, collective consciousness and ego. It is valuable to society, but useless to science by its own definition of its quest to remove emotional bias from data and interpretation. Cognitive research has identified our automatic, subconscious tendency to seek out and reinforce information that confirms our preconceptions, and to ignore, distort or discount information that contradicts these. Human 'creativity, free-ranging thought, and cumulative knowledge' are among those preconceptions. We suppress and reinterpret experiences that contradict these. "Preferred and rewarded beliefs are established in our collective minds and behaviour, and we consider them common sense, obviously true. Yet peer pressure is often wrong." (Bert Slagmolen; Apollo 13 presentation on incident root causes, Saacosh, 2013). Peer pressure errs on the side of least resistance, easy gains, respectability and popularity. Unpopular and unpatriotic science does not attract funding. Many ideas of cultural evolution are pretensions to progress, rational self-determination and autonomy. Scientific views of crafts as pseudo-science reveal science as a pseudo craft.

Kuhn described how our psychological energy is invested in maintaining and promoting our dominant paradigms, even in the face of anomalies and contradictory evidence. Yet he found that our usual resistance to radical ideas and anomalous data is also an essential element in the dialectic of change (Thomas Kuhn; The structure of scientific revolutions, 1996). There could be no agreement and therefore no transformation in our self-image or culture without scepticism and trials of viability.

Our conscious code is remarkably successful at sustaining the species and physical life quality by exploitation, but not very good at the self-analysis that Plato and other sages recommend. Science prides itself on data and technological advances apparently gained from some of our cumulative, collective efforts, yet scientific advances "sometimes come from the most unexpected quarters, proclaiming the most unlikely messages, often to a sceptical or even hostile audience." (Thomas Kuhn).

Mindprint seems set for this kind of reception, since there is scant academic or esoteric literature in general support of its data, applications or conclusions, outside structural linguistics, anthropology and psychology, all currently minor trends.

Split into specialisations, science loses most of its capacity to transfer its gains to society. Literature, drama, art, psychology, anthropology and archaeology take scant notice of each other, and all reject the conceptual paradigm of integrative crafts such as alchemy and esoterica.

Movements and counter-movements distort conscious thought, as all conformism does. Plato wrote in his Seventh Letter that names and sentences (onomata and remata), and thus our conscious codes, do not enable essential insight. Likewise theories, conscious logic and paradigms could be helpful, or could actively prevent practical insight and spiritual gains.

Given the dominance of rational thought in studying irrational human functions, such as art, spirituality and ritual, tellingly named cognitive archaeology, mindprint may well be met by a range of rationalisations.

Science is always at risk of departing from nature and pursuing its own logic, as it did under the followers of Aristotle, and in polemical reaction against alchemy in the spirit of the supposed 'classical revival' and rationality in the Renaissance. Some art movements demonstrate the same reactionary tendency, and misinterpret Greek culture as the 'rise of rationality'.

Ironically, one of the figureheads of physical science and technology spent much time tracing a code in the Bible, which statisticians confirmed 350 years later.

Newton "looked on the whole universe and all that is in it as a riddle, a secret which could be read by applying pure thought to certain evidence, certain mystic clues which God had laid about the world to allow a sort of philosopher's treasure hunt to the esoteric brotherhood. He believed that these clues were to be found partly in the evidence of the heavens and in the constitution of elements (and that is what gives the false suggestion of his being an experimental natural philosopher), but also partly in certain papers and traditions handed down by the brethren [?] in an unbroken [?] chain back to the

original [?] cryptic revelation in Babylonia... he himself wrapt the discovery of the calculus in a cryptogram when he communicated with Leibniz. By pure thought, by concentration of mind, the riddle, he believed, would be revealed to the initiate." (Keynes; Newton the Man, 1947. Question marks added in the present study).

Invoking 'original cryptic revelation' in a specific place or culture implies that Newton, or perhaps his biographer, was subject to the common illusion that the spiritual realm opened to mortals only once, or very rarely, and the rest of us are cultic imitators. Mindprint demonstrates that the spiritual realm is within our daily reach, and its codes lie within natural and spiritual logic, habitually 'written' by artists.

Cryptology is inherent in the divide between our subconscious and conscious minds and institutions. Science prefers artificial categories and rules to describe supposedly artificial culture. Natural structure serves physical science well in manipulating matter and energy by universal laws and constants, but there is not much room for archetypal structure in human studies.

Quantity versus evolution

Science by definition makes no assumptions, but scientists, institutions and funders of technology do. The imperial paradigm ingrained in science lingers in recurrent cultural concepts such as 'develop, evolve and transmit'. Only a paradigm shift to the apparently opposing assumption of human culture constants, with a fixed range of mutation, could consciously describe our utter embedding in natural and thus archetypal structure.

Evolutionary assumptions are themselves archetypal, and long predate Darwin. Democritus of Abdera wrote; "Men's progress was the work not of the mind but of the hand," implying that thumbs allowed us manipulation, which exercised our brains. However, that episode had closed before the era of Homo Sapiens and art, since there is no evidence of short-thumbed or long-thumbed artists, or of half-formed mindprints, in the art of any age. Ensembles apparently without complex art, such as Blombos shelter near Mossel Bay on the African south coast (published by Henshilwood and others), have complex crafts, including textiles, needles, hafting, glues, composite tools and cosmetics at the BP 100 000 level.

An abalone shell containing a mixture of ochre powder and seal fat, with a small stirring or application stick, all propped up by two pebbles, was a cosmetics palette, ritual tool kit and grail, a Leo t12 Crater type probably linked to the same rituals and myths expressed in the Arthurian romances. Many ochre trade pieces with geometric marking resemble branded cosmetics at the BP 70 000 level. There are similar ensembles of the same age in Europe (F D'Errico; Stone Age ensembles in Europe. Bordeaux University presentation to Origins Centre, 2010). The 'out of Africa' and the 'out of Europe' schools make equal claims.

Von Deschend, whose paradigm in Hamlet's Mill is challenged in this study, wrote that most philosophers tend to forget "the enormous intellectual effort involved [in cultural 'evolution'], from metallurgy to the arts, especially in astronomy. The effort of identifying the only presences which totally eluded the action of our hands, led to pure objects of contemplation, the stars in their courses... from which all arts look their meaning." Yet the application of human eyes and brains to crafts, arts, astronomy and cosmology does not require a collective, cumulative, or enormous effort today, nor does it seem to have been particularly difficult to thousands of Iron Age, Bronze Age, Stone Age and Ice Age artists, some of whom are represented in the illustrations and statistics here. Metallurgy required major physical efforts before the likewise major slog of mass production, gas and industrial technology, but it was a work of structural devotion to smelters, as it was to alchemists, the act more important than the product. Armillary spheres are likewise intellectual and spiritual tools, but they are equally effective at low-tech levels, such as basketry, as in grand bronze models with exact calibration. They require as much effort to master today as they did thousands of years ago. Stone Age pebble bundles and elaborate 'dice' pieces found in Scotland served prepared minds as well in raising some subconscious structure into conscious thought, as astronomy parks and the enormous intellectual effort of research, backed by the enormous physical effort of industry, do today. Our current concept of the heavens is advanced over that of supposedly primitive cultures, but only by better instruments and data, not better perception, brain power, wisdom or scope of applications. Our technology awes us with apparently evolutionary advances, yet all the applications of the last century follow from only three innovations in using two particular energy sources; fire and electricity.

Culture change or supposed cultural evolution, a pervasive concept applied in categories where it has no place (as Von Deschend said in a television interview), implies that artistic expression, including design, conscious and subconscious meaning, structure, applications and inspiration, should have improved over the last 6000 odd years, or at least since the Ice Age. Yet only the numbers of artists and works have increased, apace with exponential population growth. The supposed "enormous effort" of evolution looks more like a function of quantity than quality. Our myth, art, music and dance, among our highest spiritual expressions, remain as varied in theme and effort as ever (see dancers at theme t15). Popular fallacies rooted in concepts of evolution include perpetual New Age expectations of collective spiritual evolution, usually linked to religious eschatology (end times, or general cultural erasure), as if to explain why we have not yet ascended to a race of sages. Evolution alone is not a sustainable concept, since a series of evolutions require a series of calamities. Of these we likewise have no shortage in real and mythical floods, twilights of the gods, Armageddons and final battles. Our resurgence was remarkable.

Our religions and sciences are not entirely to blame for these notions, since evolution, endings, beginnings and golden ages are archetypal ideas that we are prone to think, see, concretise and acculturate.

Scientific habit of forcing its subjects into a historical, developmental perspective, ironically appears even in studies of archetype (Keiron Le Grice, 2009; Birth of a New Discipline, Archetypal Cosmology in Historical Perspective). Le Girce writes of 'emergence of archetypal cosmology from the confluence of ancient Greek thought, depth psychology, and astrology,' as if archetype, cosmology and psychoanalysis were new, or improved.

'Science history' implies that science had always improved, and would further improve. It does not take much prompting of popular imagination by science to lose account of the roles of population density and material technology, to label most changes as 'advances' with some 'setbacks', and to ascribe these to supposedly ever improving human 'knowledge' and cognitive skills (as opposed to data) that could be gained or lost.

Mindprint supports a diametrically opposing paradigm; arts, crafts and sciences are static or cyclic rationalisation, and history is the study of our rationalisations in the human epoch. Cosmology likewise has a history only of temporal mutation in Ages, not an evolutionary, technological, conceptual or cognitive history.

Nature is also an artist

Illustration K
Some crop circles express shapes and axes related to orbits, time, solar wind, pendulums, biology and eyes, in combinations of natural and conceptual (artificial) lines, curves and angles (Eye or dragon

head at Picked Hill, Woodborough near Alton Barnes, August 2012. Eye among circles at Milk Hill. Keyhole at Wiltshire's Yarnbury Castle. Sources; Cropcircleconnector. Jim Peyton). Sundials demonstrate that nature and culture also overlap in arts and crafts. Crop circles indicate a kind of natural 'culture' (see a crop circle of type Cancer t14 as a time scarab at theme t14, and a crop circle phoenix in the Polar section). Nature is the primary expression of archetype, making and sustaining galaxies, solar systems, bio-chemistry, kingdoms, genii, species, souls and layers of consciousness. It should be no surprise that nature, infinitely structured, sustaining creatures who in turn express minute aspects of ecology and archetype, is itself capable of visually representing aspects of archetypal, holographic structure on a natural surface. If nature can make planets, DNA and eyes, it can make pictures or imprints of orbits, sequences and eyes.

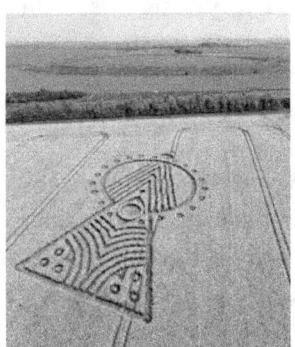
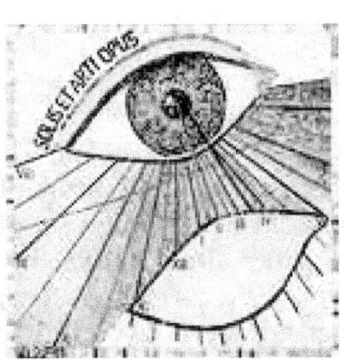

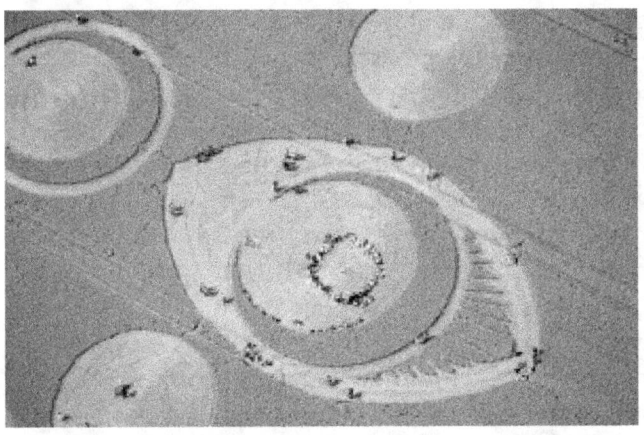

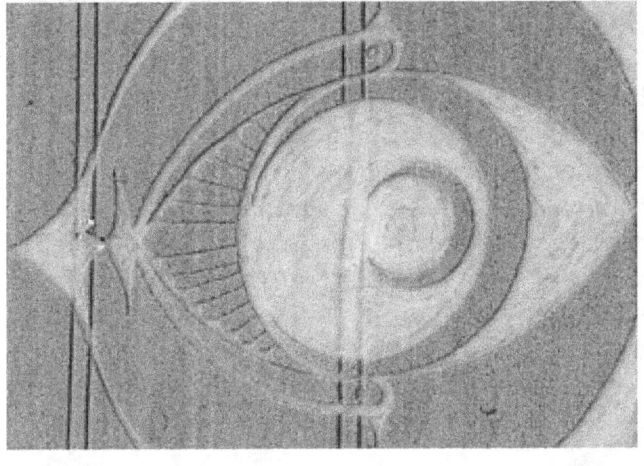

Our blind spots

The crop circle repression saga offers evidence of some of our conscious blind spots. Repression, as Freud demonstrated, is a strong motivator. Motivation is possible only within our emotional repertoire (see the Psychology section). There is not much ego confirmation value in the idea of the collective subconscious. We understand that nature sustains insects, dolphins, falcons, spiral shells and DNA, and that we are the pinnacle of creation. We are uncomfortable with the idea that nature could imprint images of her creatures on herself, and more uncomfortable yet that the imprints are made on stems of 'our' cultivated crops. Art is understood as the province of culture, not nature.

Crop circles are among the subtle yet persistent signs that defence mechanisms and the peer pressure of conscious, logical respectability, is a silent conspiracy of egos. We are programmed to elaborate our individual and collective egos, and to remain blind to many aspects of our real nature.

Healers, artists and entertainers function as our mediators, crossing our Shadow land to negotiate with our Anima and Animus (archetypal Female and Male counterparts), hopefully to activate self-realisation by raising our inner Self into our Ego. This process is of necessity individual, while humanity at large remains schizophrenic (split-brained) and apparently individual on this side of life.

Healers are born in several guises, as saints, prophets, priests and psychologists, but most enduring as poets (Homer, Shakespeare or Camoens), architects (of the Seven Wonders and other marvels) and artists. Seeing some great visual works or monuments even once could have long-lasting healing effects in many viewers, despite the usual layers of politics and distorted history in the conscious minds of artists and viewers. Life without art is incomplete and unhealthy.

Artists and viewers celebrate the marvel of variety, and do not see or marvel at the collective standard sequence or structure. However artistic expression of natural structure now appears to be a law of perception, and a natural and cultural wonder.

Distilled myth is compelling to scholars and historicisers. Expeditions to Ararat and speculations about Babylonian origins (as by Newton), bloodlines, secret societies and aliens confirm that many people suffer from historitis, confusing spiritual and physical reality at the cost of experiencing and expressing both realities in the present. Newton did not realise that his own inspiration and revelations were as important as those of Babylonia, Issac or Moses.

Esoteric structure

Esoterica, which means intrinsic meaning (as opposed to exoteric, assigned meaning), operate on correspondences. It thus follows the fuzzy logic by which culture uses and occasionally updates meaning (such as trains taking the place of horses). Whether tacking chakras, numerology, astrology, letters, planets, gods, principles, kinship, hunting or military orders, esoterica is a structural craft.

Some authors combine esoteric and academic follies by assuming that modern astrology is superior to medieval or ancient astrology, as if ever more subconscious 'knowledge' were rising into our supposedly expanded consciousness, at least in occasional revelations. A recent book blurb (the only text that authors could blame on publishers) for Tarnas summarises; "Correlations between planetary cycles and the major patterns of world history by philosopher and cultural historian Richard Tarnas has given to the discipline a new, unexpected credibility... this ancient symbolic system, following decades of reformulation through its encounter with depth psychology, humanistic and transpersonal psychology, is once again worthy of serious consideration."

As if classical symbolic systems and astrology were at a disadvantage? Californian researchers have merely regained the status of Delphi.

Tarnas continues; "As a unifying, integrating principle of universal unconscious, the self or something like it appears to underlie and orchestrate the correspondence between planetary movements and the archetypal dynamics of human experience, impelling the evolution of human consciousness [?] through the medium of the cosmological archetypes, much as on a personal level the self serves as an integrating and transforming teleological principle within the individual psyche." Tarnas sees humanity maturing just as an individual matures, a 'common sense' idea that applies to some phases of tribal or empiric history, but not to humanity. Population explosions, rampant exploitation and subjugation seem profitable form the inside, but from every other view they are bubbles. How or why consciousness could evolve, and why it should await Delphi, depth psychology or improved astrology, is not clear. Access to our collective subconscious is as intermittent as it ever was, and 'transformation' is merely a series of individual glimpses of our place in the cosmos. Science and esoterica should identify and remove the blind spots of confirmation bias such as 'evolution of consciousness' from their respective eyes and theoretical glasses to enable more people to take conscious glimpses in our subconscious mirror. Waiting for evolution does not cultivate the 'prepared mind' required for individual transformation. The only evolution allocated to us on earth is the number of people subjecting our Egos to our inner Selves, and the number of years we live after individuation. Any cultural benefits are just an occasional bonus. In spirituality, there is no sign of evolution. Earth remains Grade 12, new learners start at Grade 0, all share the same set of hard-wired skills, some are gifted in particular skills, most have to learn to apply their capacities, and most die un-individuated.

Some spiritual teachings hold that souls are not individual, but collective, and each portion of soul represents the soul pool while in the illusion of individuality in the flesh. This hypothesis raises the possibility that karma, also a hypothesis, applies equally to the drops of soul apparently divided among people, and that each person is working away at aspects of our collective karma, just as artists express apparently different images, populated by the same set of attributes, in the same sequence, fixed to the same axial pattern, with only a slight precessional update to incidental polar markers every few centuries. In this view, earth remains a school and a society. Schools, institutes, societies and humanity never graduate.

Archetype offers a bridge to scientists and artists to integrate the study of conscious and subconscious cultural expression. Some former cultures did so and their art raised large tracts of subconscious territory within conscious access, serving viewers of a prepared mind. Popular culture is still drawn to the remnants of Babylonian, Bushman, Egyptian, Chinese and some American cultures, partly for being poorly served by Western scientific and technological culture. Our material multiplication and its intellectual institutions have raced ahead of our spiritual and physical needs. Integrated consciousness offers individual, collective, scientific and esoteric rewards. Science and esoterica should both serve us in our lifelong struggle to overcome our vast capacity for suppressing our collective inner identity below our Shadow.

Schizophrenic sciences and arts increase the difficulty of harmonising partners and colleagues with the inner Animus or Anima, and the task of expressing the inner Self in the conscious Ego. Some culture and religions, distinctive only in their theological elaboration, view this achievement as a second or spiritual birth.

Mindprint concerns our self-image, constantly expressed in all art and cultures, but repressed and requiring holographic health to emerge into individual consciousness. Art demonstrates subconscious access as a prerequisite of individual transformation.

Archetype is the male element providing the formula, while art is the female element providing substantial elements to express the formula. Once demonstrated visually, their union in any craft or science cannot remain 'unseen'.

Mindprint implications for human sciences

Mindprint holds several implications for a range of sciences and crafts.

Artists, archaeologists, anthropologists, mythologists, psychologists and sociologists could learn more from one another, and from cultural artefacts worldwide, than the current parameters of each science allow.

Scientists could follow the example of esoterica in comparing apparently unrelated sets, or 'tacking form disunity'. Some of our ancient ancestors put us to shame for having practiced more holographic culture and science than we do, even with the aid of our automated data and analytics bordering on artificial intelligence.

Historians and art historians could accept archetype as an implicit, collective, subconscious 'programme' in all cultures. Calendric features on macro and micro level could reveal a limited history of archetypal expression, which is either cyclic or pendulous, but probably not evolutionary. Adaptation and mutation could resolve supposed evolutionary evidence in the material record and in cultural goods such as myth.

Artists could take pride that they express archetypal structure from spiritual inspiration as their core craft, not as embellishment or design. This study has several implications for art history and thus for artistic training, but few for practical art.

Psychologists and sociologists could investigate personal and social healing techniques by exposing patients to relevant, standard elements of form and identity, in the way that the allegorical Asclepius or Moses raised allegorical serpents on staffs to heal the people and the land, the legendary Arthur raised a grail, and Jung diagnosed and prescribed myths to patients. Patients need not necessarily consciously understand the ailment or treatment.

Archaeo astronomers could recognise the human capacity for imposing a standard universal conceptual set and structure on material culture.

Our range of conscious and subconscious symbolic, social, health and political applications is perpetually original, and untaught.

Astrology could re-incorporate sidereal (stellar and constellational) horoscopes into tropical horoscopes, or use ecliptic calibration and notation, or combine the two systems.

Of new discoveries, Humboldt wrote; "First, people will deny a thing, then belittle it, then decide that it had been known long ago." This study takes the opposite premise that everything was long known, remains accessible, and is selectively shut out by our conscious preoccupations and assumptions.

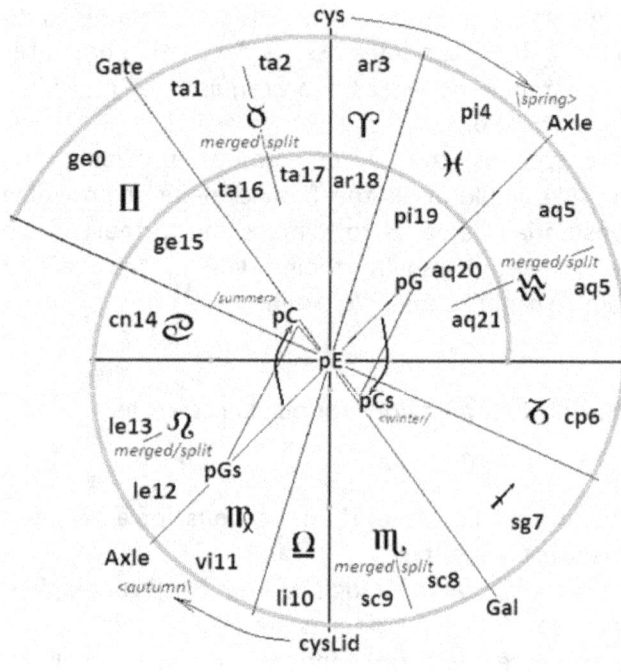

Myth map, mindprint, eyeprint, handprint, and icon table

[] t1 t2 Taurus, twist/kneel, bovine, bird, seven, large
[] t3 Aries, neck, bent, dragon, impaled, multi-head
[] t4 Pisces, rectangle, squat, male
[] t5 t20 t21 Aquarius, action, horizontal,
            large, colour, tailcoat
[] t6 Capricornus, near/far, Pan, reptile, double-head
[] t7 Sagittarius, bag, junior, bow, travel
[] t8 t9 Scorpius, bent, trance, strong, male, large
[] t10 Libra, arms V/ W, staff, balance, wheel, shield
[] t11 Virgo, womb
[] t12 t13 Leo, heart, chest, feline, invert, male, large
[] t14 Cancer, nearer or further, canine, calibrating
[] t15 t0 Gemini, rope, smite, create, wound, double

[] Ecliptic pole, central, singular
[] Galactic pole, limb joint, between Leo and Virgo
[] Galactic south pole, limb joint, between aq5-pi4
[] Celestial pole, limb /marker, over le13 /cn14 /ge15
[] Celestial south pole, limb/mark, over aq5, cp6 /sg7
[] Polar triangle, mirrored 'north' and 'south',
      one triangle side on horizontal or vertical plane.

More variant and optional attributes of the sixteen types are discussed in the Attributes section and listed in the Tables.

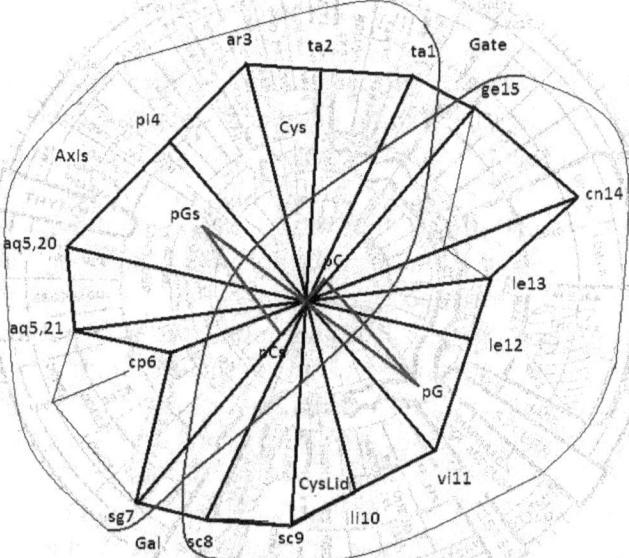

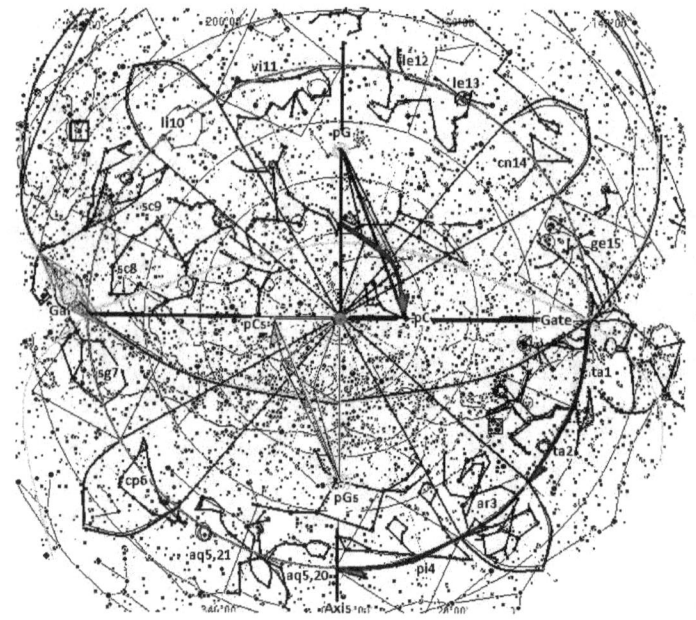

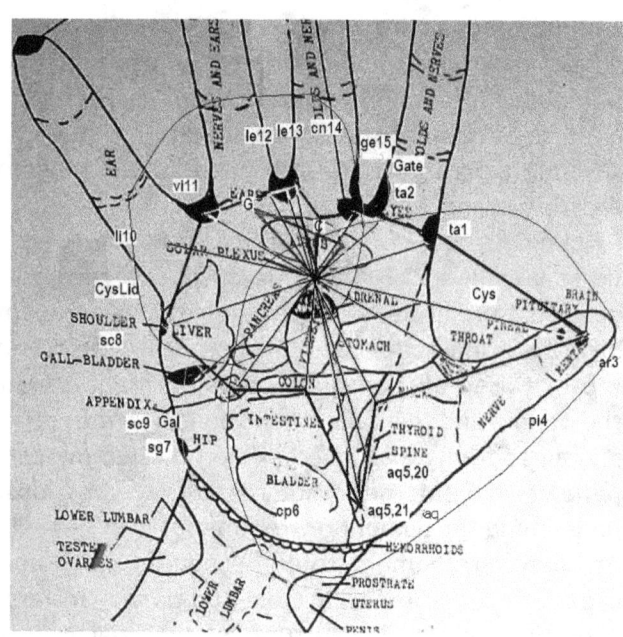

Mindprint art and
sixteen themes illustrated

Type Taurus t1 t16 Auriga and Orion; Rainmaker and hunter

Perseus in a dance circle

Type Taurus t1 Auriga Orion and/or Taurus t2 Perseus as a rainmaking healer (South Africa, Free State, dance and eland bags. Vinnicombe 1976. RARI. Mindrpint analysis by Edmond Furter). These two adjacent types are often conflated. Perseus, in myth a twisted figure glancing rearward by his polished shield as a mirror to strike at Medusa's head, is one of the most constant characters in mythology and art. He twists or kneels on Taurus t2 t17 Pleiades, often as a rain bull rider, holding the severed head of Medusa (that tops the latter side of Aries t3 t18) in a bag. His other foot is rearward at Taurus t1 Auriga. His own face is often monstrous. Every figure in the periphery expresses a type, in the standard sequence (see the Tables), and is on an axis (a straight line across a common point) with its opposite type. Aries t3 t18 is a buck bag person with a long neck. Aquarius t5 t21 has painted legs and is partly horizontal. Capricornus t6 is a trio, and ingressed towards the centre. Sagittarius t7 is an emergent vortex bag person. Libra t10 has an arm up and a staff. Virgo t11 is pregnant, but here, unusually, also male (not unique in rock art or art). Her companion is a pregnant bee person (see bee people at theme t8). Leo t13 are two figures marked on their hearts, confirmed by economy of line in the figures equator from Leo t12 to Cancer t14. The implied southern galactic equator (thin oval on the right) centred on the galactic south pole, is nearly circular, confirming the possibility raised in many mindprint works, that inspiration or expression involves the concept of a bright oblique circle, visualised from two sides simultaneously and resolving into limb joints. The eyes of figures form the seasonal round, analogous to the ecliptic equator, or conceptual course of the sun.

Artistic inspiration, like myth, expresses a pre-existent archetypal sequence and standard axial grid, which is also expressed in physiology, perception, sophistry (as opposed to academic philosophy) and esoteric crafts, by a process of gestalt (seeing wholes and patterns among apparently random shapes, dots or movement). Symmetry of opposing types, and of polar markers (demonstrated by two triangles), confirms holistic inspiration and iconographic complexity beyond the conscious scope of artists, who express spiritual impulses in terms of real or idealised figures, events, issues, protocols, politics, techniques and perhaps criticism.

The geometric centre, named ecliptic pole for convenience, is marked in about half of the art works tested. The galactic pole is on a foot, the celestial pole on the hand of a bent figure on the Cancer t14 axis, and the celestial south pole (in the triangle on the right) on a raised hand or club. These poles are on limb joints as usual. The two celestial markers on the Cancer-Capricornus axis, tag midsummer and midwinter as they were in Age Aries, which is the inspirational framework of many works made during Age Pisces.

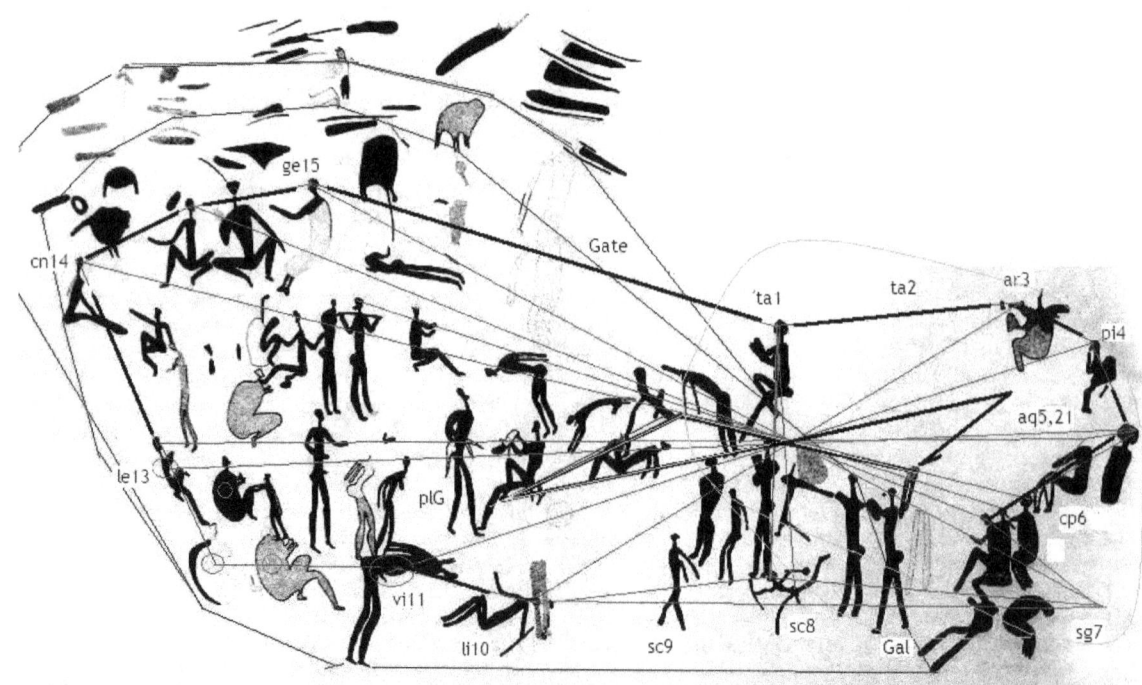

A healer in archetypal heaven

Type Taurus t1 Auriga and t2 Perseus as an ascended healer (Spain, church dome with the ascended Christ. Mindprint analysis by Edmond Furter). Every figure expressing a type, in the standard sequence, is on an axis with its opposite type. The angled view of the domed surface introduces slight loss of axial focus.

Virgo t11 is on a womb as usual, opposite Pisces t4 as Mary or Magdalene with a child, an Age Pisces spring marker. Her flanking position in the design is balanced by Cancer t14, summer marker of the preceding Age Aries. Cancer t14 could be John Baptist as an Ages transition figure, or Joseph as earthly father.

Aquarius t5 t21 is a churn pillar top (see churn groups at theme t5 and t15). Libra t10 has one arm up and a staff. Leo t13 is marked on the heart of the Virgo t11 figure, as usual in small groups. The sequence is divided by a vertical line from which the angels seem to emerge, incidental with the galactic gates axis and with soul gate myths (see theme t8 and theme t15). Iconographic and mythical complexity forces this study to resort to astronomical terms. Various crafts, such as myth, art, astrology, decans, calendars, pantheons, emblems, alphabets, cards and alchemy, express archetypal structure in their own way. Some borrow

images, symbols and names from one another, as alchemy borrows from astronomy, astronomy from myth, and alphabets from numerology.

Terminology should not be read as diffusion of a system, paradigm or philosophy arising from or developed from another. Astronomy and mythology did not await one another, nor trace the supposed development of one another. Astronomy does not need myth to teach it parts of the sky; it just resorts to more or less appropriate and popular figures, and uses handy labels agreed by universal democracy. Art never needed permission from mythology, astrology, religion or Tarot cards to express the archetypal sequence or pattern, it just does.

Iconographic complexity is well developed in the religious art of every culture, but remains rooted in holistic inspiration. The only detectable manipulation in this work is swopping of the usual Scorpius t8 or Sagittarius t7 galactic centre post (half pillar), with the occasional Aquarius t5 t20 trumpet. This type of variance does not instantly divorce an artistic programme (convention) from archetypal structure, it just loses some iconic focus and gains some camouflage.

Core attributes, such as clusters of concepts, shapes, characteristics, characters and mythical events are more consistent than archaeology or art history acknowledge.

The ecliptic pole (axial centre) is marked by Christ's lower hand and hip (see hip wounds at theme t5 and theme t15). The galactic north and south poles (triangle points left and right, visible on the conceptual sphere, as if transparent), are limb joints as usual, here angelic elbows.

Celestial north and south poles are tagged by Christ's heart (more usually figured as Leo t13) and by his knee, just prior to the Gemini t15 and Sagittarius t7 axis, therefore just after the Age Pisces solstices by precession (since Ages move backward against the seasons), incidental with the Age of the work. The polar clockwork is a standard subconscious feature in inspired art.

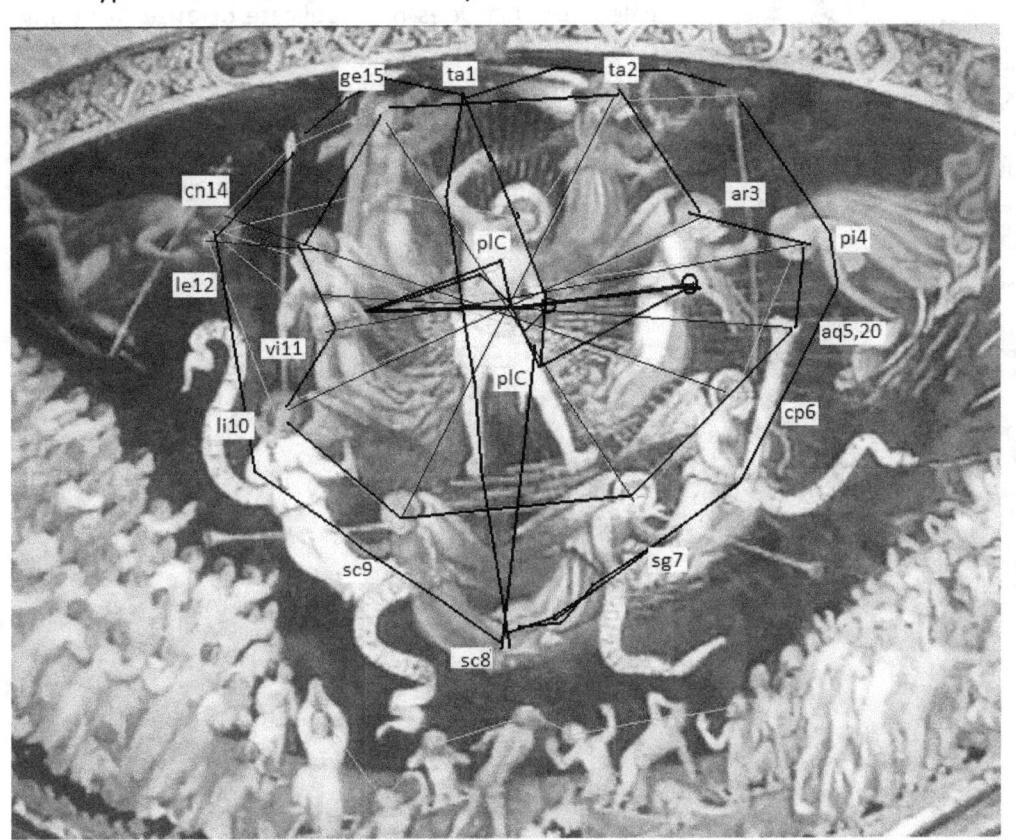

A shrine to healers, inspiration and structure

Type Taurus t1 t16 Auriga or Perseus as the central figure of a hunter trio, over a giraffe bag (South Africa, Barkley, Wodehouse 2. SA Archaeological Bulletin. Mindprint analysis by Edmond Furter). Attributes of Taurus t1 t16 Auriga and Orion include a clutch of three arrows or spears, and lightning (the polar group is duplicated and inset without axes on the right, with just two thin lines added to mark the revealed ecliptic pole).

Taurus t2 t17 Pleiades Perseus, sometimes at the other foot of the hero, here is a giraffe X person, controlling a rampant Aries t3 t18 animal combined with the concept of a Medusa head (see giraffe dragon controllers in the Narmer palette at theme t3 t18). The three giraffe X people with their spears, flanking the Taurean trio, also form a cosmic churn group (see Indian and other churn images at themes t15, t11, t8 and t5).

Leo t13 as a feline man is defined by his exposed chest, and expresses some attributes of his opposite type (Aquarius t5 t21 as a large man in active posture with dappled or painted skin), here also extended to the Leo t13 companion, perhaps a hyena, which is characterised as canine and feline in myth. Their opposite at Aquarius t5 is a dappled lion instead.

Polar markers on the giraffe bag's hoofs, and on arrow flights, tag the inspiration to Age Pisces-Aquarius. A range of markers from the giraffe knees to its infolded rear hoofs, provide for earlier Age Aries, and future Age Aquarius. The giraffe forequarter is a kind of buck bag. Since its eye is on the Leo t13 axis, and it is an equine, it is also a kind of horse of death and life (see Tarot trump 13 as death on a horse). Camelopardalis (Giraffe) is constellation north of Taurus t1 Auriga, reaching almost to the current celestial pole, by the kind of coincidence that arises from conflating one inspired expression of archetypal structure with another. Camelopardalis is a belated addition to the astronomy map, and now stands ready to receive the celestial pole when it leaves the hoof of Cancer t14 Ursa Minor (pictured as a smaller bull foreleg in Egypt) in the coming centuries. The inspired rock artist was as unaware of these iconographic subtleties as the committee that confirmed traditional constellation names and chose among newly inspired labels and gestalt 'Spartan' stick figures in the scientific mapping spree of the 1700s. The southern antipodal (hemispheric opposite) counterpart of Camelopardalis is Scorpius t9 Lupus Wolf, extending to the celestial south pole if it borrows the two bright front hoofs of Centaurus, perhaps roped on as Samson roped torches to fox's tails (see a Chinese tile at theme t11).

The artist pictured spiritual reality, not Babylonian, Greek, Indian, Roman or Arabic mythologies as astronomy does. There is no need to re-invent or to borrow the cosmic wheel.

Iconographic games of snakes, ladders, and flipping the game board around, is necessary to follow the depth of holographic meaning inherent in inspiration and expression, and to illustrate how art expresses concepts analogous to myths, cards and calendars. Art does not duplicate or arise from any other system. Every medium is an independent, perpetual (never original) expression of the underlying structure of meaning that underpins matter and mind.

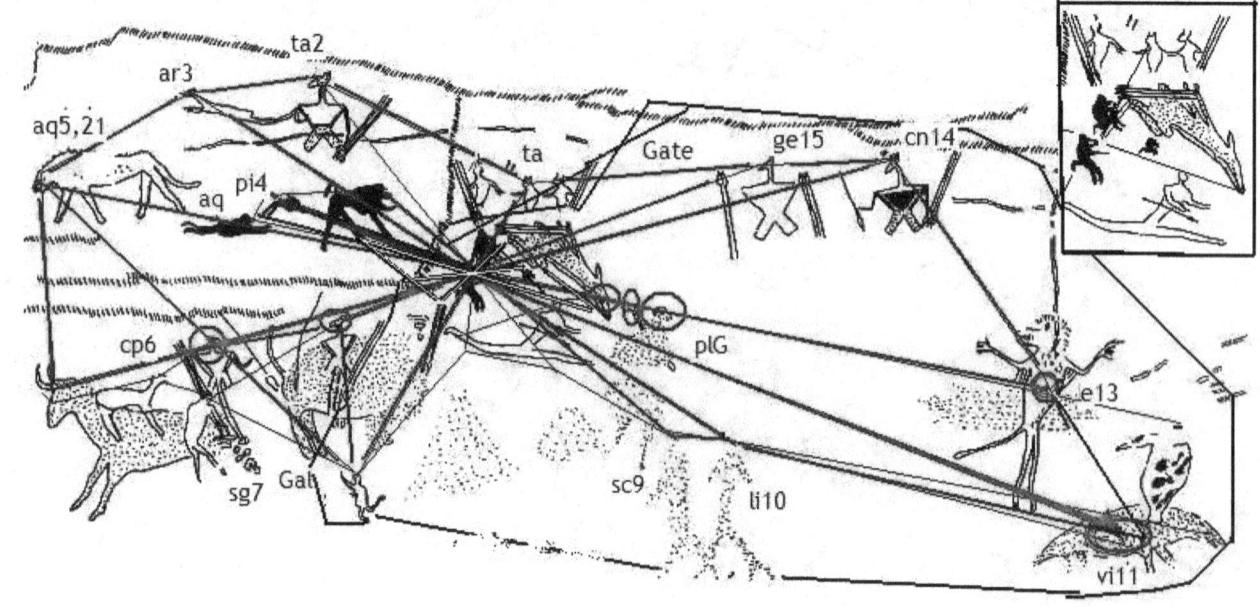

A parody of birth

Type Taurus t1 t16 Perseus as a dying horse in a falling city under bomb blasts (Picasso; Guernica, Spanish civil war. Prado. Mindprint analysis by Edmond Furter). Taurus t16 is often expressed by battle, the desperate but standard solution to opposing vested interests of masters at odds, blamed on superficial differences in cultures or language. The usual Taurus t2 t17 eye and rain theme is here an intimately domestic electric eye, flanked by a bull foreleg as a lightning bag. Leo t13 is the heart of a victim, Virgo t11 a hidden womb, Libra t10 a severed foreleg (see the Seti 1 ceiling at theme t8).

Sagittarius t7 has a severed head, as in some Egyptian icons (see the Narmer palette at theme t3 t18). Gemini t15 is a billowy face. Leo t13 t12 is inverted. Aquarius t5 is a heart, as it sometimes assumes attributes of its opposite type, Leo t13. Aries t3 is a bull with craned neck, as in some Egyptian decans, more usually a smaller animal or dragon with a craned neck.

The sequence could be figured in both directions. Re-structuring is incidental with the Taurus t16 theme of a falling tower. If labelled anticlockwise, Taurus t1 is a lightning bull, Libra t10 a staff clutched in a hand, Aquarius t5 a man in active posture, and Aries t3 t18 a horse with a long curved neck.

In Picasso's prior sketches, the horse already had its victim's neck, hinting that inspiration is expressed in stages, or that archetypal attributes attach to relevant figures already assigned their positions in the sequence (see battle or slaughter scenes in Amatola rock art, and an early Egyptian mural at theme t13, and with bee people at theme t8; each with a Virgo t11 inverted and slaughtered in a parody of birth). Two counter-rotating mindprints compete for expression here, a common feature of complex works in one sphere.

Gemini t15 is near identical to a billowing white face of another inspired Spanish painter, Salvador Dali, which he titled 'It just popped up'. Its jaw on the celestial pole, and one of the optional vertical planes, tag Age Aries-Pisces, the former traumatic Ages transition. Other markers and another vertical option indicate the forthcoming Age Pisces-Aquarius transition, again incidental with the theme of seasonal and political change.

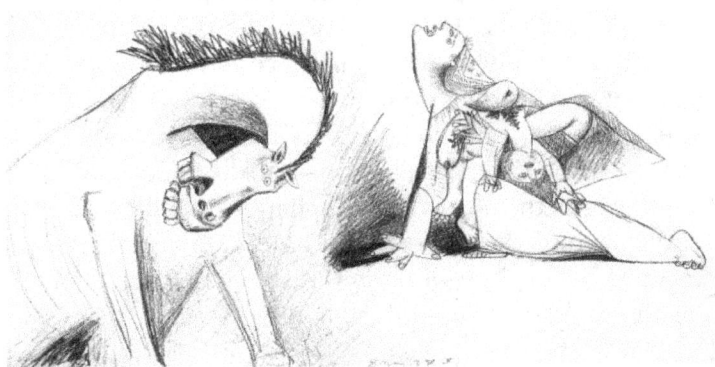
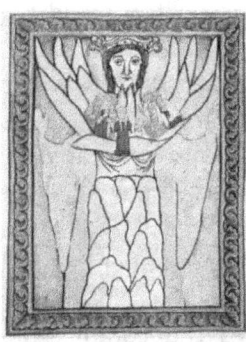
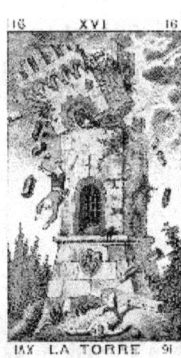

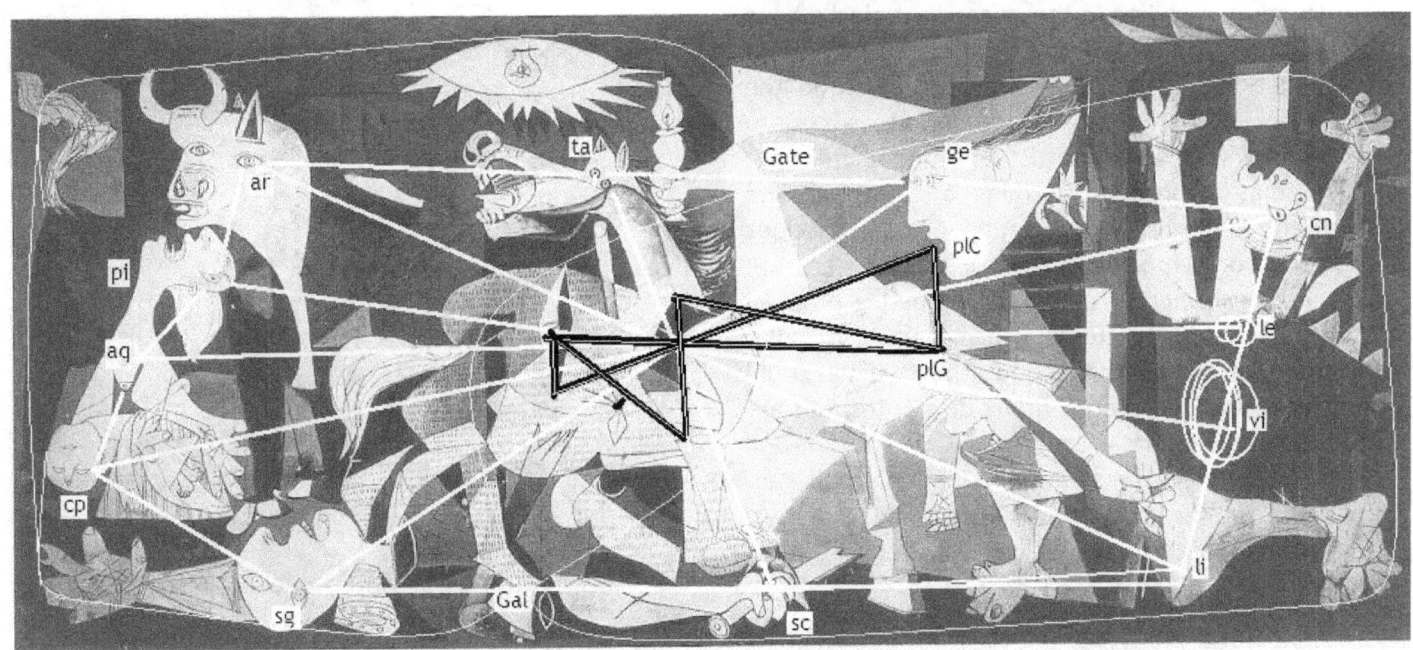

A Babylonian clock

Type Taurus t2 t17 Auriga as a bird on a forked staff and an arrow (Babylonian kudurru boundary marker cone. Rawlinson. Mindprint analysis by Edmond Furter. See a side view at theme t11. See other conical mindprints on bowls at theme t15).

Between Taurus t2 t1 and Gemini t15, in the galactic gate, is a squatting and backward shuffling dog, instead of a bull or healer, marking spring in Age Gemini-Taurus or Age Taurus 1. This spring dog, sometimes at the opposite autumn equinox, or at midsummer or midwinter, appears in some cultures as a baboon or dog-headed baboon (see the Dendera zodiac in the Decans section). Canis Minor was on the celestial equator in Age Taurus, hinting that a former spring marker was adopted from Gemini, then reverted back once spring had moved into Aries and the celestial equator lay over the eye and rump of Taurus instead.

Precessional markers usually face retro (rearward), to oncoming Ages, as all these figures do, and as hourly decans do. Retro figures are usually monstrous versions (see decans at themes t8 and t12). The boundary stone may have been a public or court clock, perhaps marking sunlight hours by the shadow line (terminator) along its conical face. Its three polar or planetary markers on top could tag orientations for spring, to one extreme for summer, back to the spring position in autumn, and to the other extreme for winter. A conical dial requires technical thought and some trials, perhaps by technocrats who, like astronomers today, do not care for artistic or mythological images. When artists have free reign, the mindprint sequence and structure overrides the conscious symbolic programme, or at least survives the commission. This work is a zodiac in the sense that clocks have divisions that could be decorated with concepts or constellations. The artist probably understood the given icons as composed by convention, as modern astronomers do. Like all artists he probably did not know that inspiration contains a sequence and geometric structure independent of conscious meanings or symbols. The major figures here are defined by shrines or altars, some bearing omphali (cones with rope patterns), each a navel or solar plexus of a place or direction. These altars could mark former Ages, places, hours or months, but are initially, and ultimately, concepts.

If updated today, the spring dog, baboon, bull, ram or horse would sit between Pisces and Aquarius, over the spout of the Pisces t4 Cetus (Whale) monster.

The elephant trunk, sleeve, knife or axe over Aries t3, expresses Andromeda and Triangulum, confirming the Hindu motif of a severed trunk or axe (see Indian churn groups at theme t15). This conceptual merger is an iconographic delight; a trunk over a long neck, a severed trunk over the knife that severed the Medusa head, a trumpeting nose over a fire-breathing dragon and ram's horn, an axe handle-shaped trunk over an axe-shaped constellation; all on a womb-shaped cone as the conceptual inverse of an axe.

Virgo t11 Bootes is a circumpolar U-shaped staff top with two heads (see a side view at theme t11). The celestial pole is on the Bootes jaw of the staff, on the head facing Leo t12, marking midsummer as freshly arrived in Leo from Virgo (by precession), confirmed by the Geminian spring dog arrived at Taurus t2 (end of Taurus in seasonal terms). This spring dog has yet to shuffle over the bird staff and arrow group, implying that the Pleiades marked the idea of spring even before it had hosted the spring equinox, unless the inspiration or the commission was conservative.

Other celestial polar markers provide for future Ages and aeons. Some are in the claws, beak, legs and tail of Leo-Cancer Ursa Minor retro as a retreating scorpion. The bears make good scorpion concepts and stick figures. In Age Taurus they may have figured the popular Babylonian Scorpion Woman, summer to a Scorpius autumn.

The polar trio adds markers to the polar gauge, confirmed by the crosspiece of an ankh-shaped club adjacent to the Aquarius t5 spear. Archaeological dating favours the earlier, Age Taurus dating, making this one of very few works in this study to speak the 'old heaven and old earth' mindprint grammar.

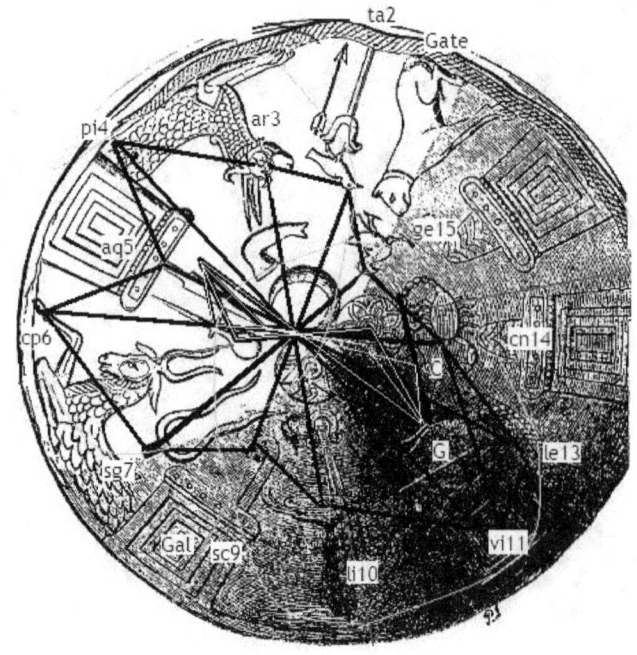

An Ice Age bauble

Taurus t2 Perseus as a twisted bird-headed stick man over a bird bauble and arrow (France, Lascaux cave, Shaft of the Dead Man). The figure is often identified as 'an astrological scene of Taurus the Bull goring Orion the Hunter', but is more likely a rain healer with his tools, before a vision of Taurus t1 Auriga as a thunder bull, all in conceptual terms. The stock episode co-incides with myth and constellations, however the scene is not a star map. The rear half of the bull is in Gemini, its intestinal wound or genital bag on the galactic gate. The long spear is Taurus Hyades (Bull face), the bird and six dots are Taurus Pleiades, and the rhino is Aries. The angle of the healer fits the position of the celestial equator in Age Taurus.

Artists do not rely on constellation concepts or figures, since they have direct access to conscious concepts, semi-conscious symbols and icons, and the subconscious hologram. Painting astrology would be as limiting as painting by numbers.

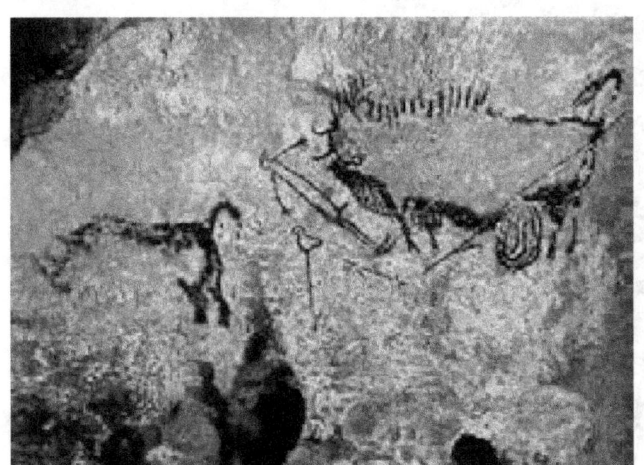

A galactic gate in a tree

Type Taurus t1 t16 as a bull man in a rain trio (South Africa, after Credo Mutwa; Soweto Culture Village rain hut mural, 1976. Gilbert Briscoe. Johannesburg Heritage. Mindprint analysis by Edmond Furter). Some types are multiplied, such as Taurus t1 Auriga and Orion as two hunters and a tree (the semi-conscious tree symbol is confirmed as related to Orion in the CSIR Hartebeeshoek Radio Astronomy observatory display, citing Thebe Medupe's Cosmic Africa project). The bull man could also figure Gemini t15, which is here elaborated into four extra figures, perhaps born of tribal education motivations while subconsciously figuring the unusual churn group. Spermiforms stand in for some figures (see spermiforms in a Bolivian disc at theme t12). He compared African, Christian and European mythology in his books and art, in visionary and prophetic style. The Rain hut murals were destroyed in the 1976 youth riot, and its belated partial reconstruction by collaborator Musa Ntanzi in about 2003 is sparse and without mindprint, but retains some of the standard sequence of types. The squatting monkey is a spring marker spanning several Ages. It reaches for spring rain in Taurus, its head is in the mystical basket position (see theme t11), its lower hand in Aries, its tail over Pisces and Aquarius. The tip of its unnaturally long tail continues to the Age Pisces midwinter axis in Sagittarius t7. The celestial pole on the rain queen's knee tags the inspiration to Age Pisces-Aquarius, our current era.

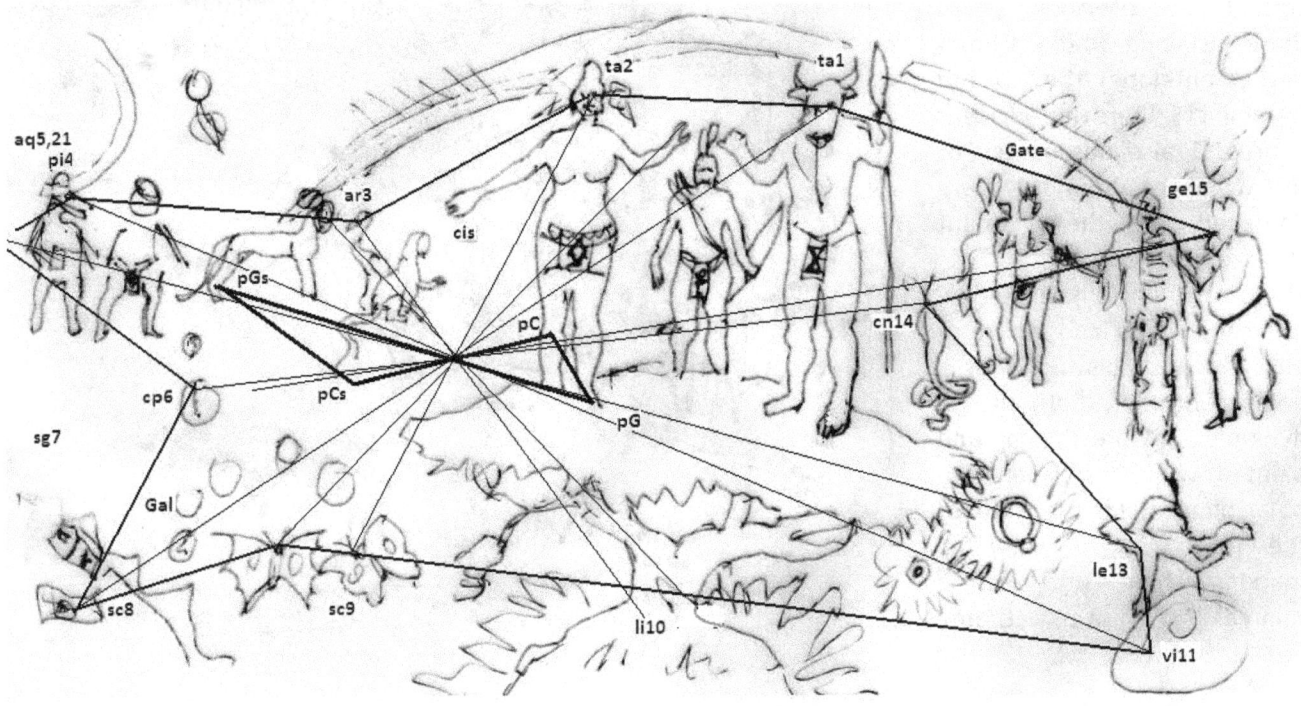

A rain tree and rainmaker

Type Taurus t2 t17 Pleiades as a rain tree in a pool or cloud (Zimbabwe, Matobo range, Domboshawa. Goodall 1958. Garlacke 1987. SA Archaeological Bulletin. Mindprint analysis by Edmond Furter). This type of tree is a shrine in most cultures (see Tarot trump 2, Priestess, in a shrine between two pillars with a veil, and Tarot trump 17, Star, a naked Pleiadean sister decanting water from two jugs with a rain tree topped by a rain bird). The two overlapping types express aspects of the same concept.

Painting of the swarming cloud could itself have induced or sustained inspiration, episodes of expression, or healing for the artist, clients and visitors. The Matobo range had several operating oracles up to political genocides in the 1900s (see other Zimbabwean oracle images at theme t8).

The galactic centre between t7 and t8 is marked near the pole by a rain hippo, shiny with mud. Scorpius t9 is a fresh water barble, an African catfish that could grow as large as a man or antelope, here expressing the idea of a long tail. In the Narmer palette, as part of the name Narmer, 'Catfish chisel', it expresses Cancer t14 Hydra (see theme t3 t18). Similar animals could express different attributes in different contexts, such as the long or craned neck of Aries t3 t18 (here just long, under a long-necked antelope), the ropes of Gemini t15 (here its adjacent Taurus t1 also has ropes), or the womb of Virgo t11 (here damaged, but the pregnant state remains clear).

The polar triangle is marked by the hand, head and elbow of an extra Aquarius t5 t20 as a polar controller, both are in dynamic postures, and one painted white as usual. The polar figure holds the trunk of the rain tree or lightning, marking him out as a rainmaker, a theme

sometimes found in Aquarius t5 t20, also expressed as Waterbearer. Slight ambiguity between Aquarius t5 as a Pope, a type of rainmaker, with its adjacent Aquarius t5 t20 as an axial blast or natural judgement, and Taurus t2 t17 as a rain priestess or rain animal, led to the usual misidentification of Tarot trump 17 (Star) as Aquarius, on account of her water jugs, of Tarot trump 5 (Pope) as Taurus, and of Tarot trump 20 (Judgement) as Orion, on account of its trio of figures and southern underworld association. These confusions are incidentally rectified in this study, confirming the Tarot sequence as highly rigorous, but more layered than previously assumed (see the Tables in the text).

The celestial south pole on the central figure's elbow, on the t6-t14 axis, tags the inspiration as Age Aries, implying that the work was done in the centuries after BC 1500, or that the inspiration is retro to the artist.

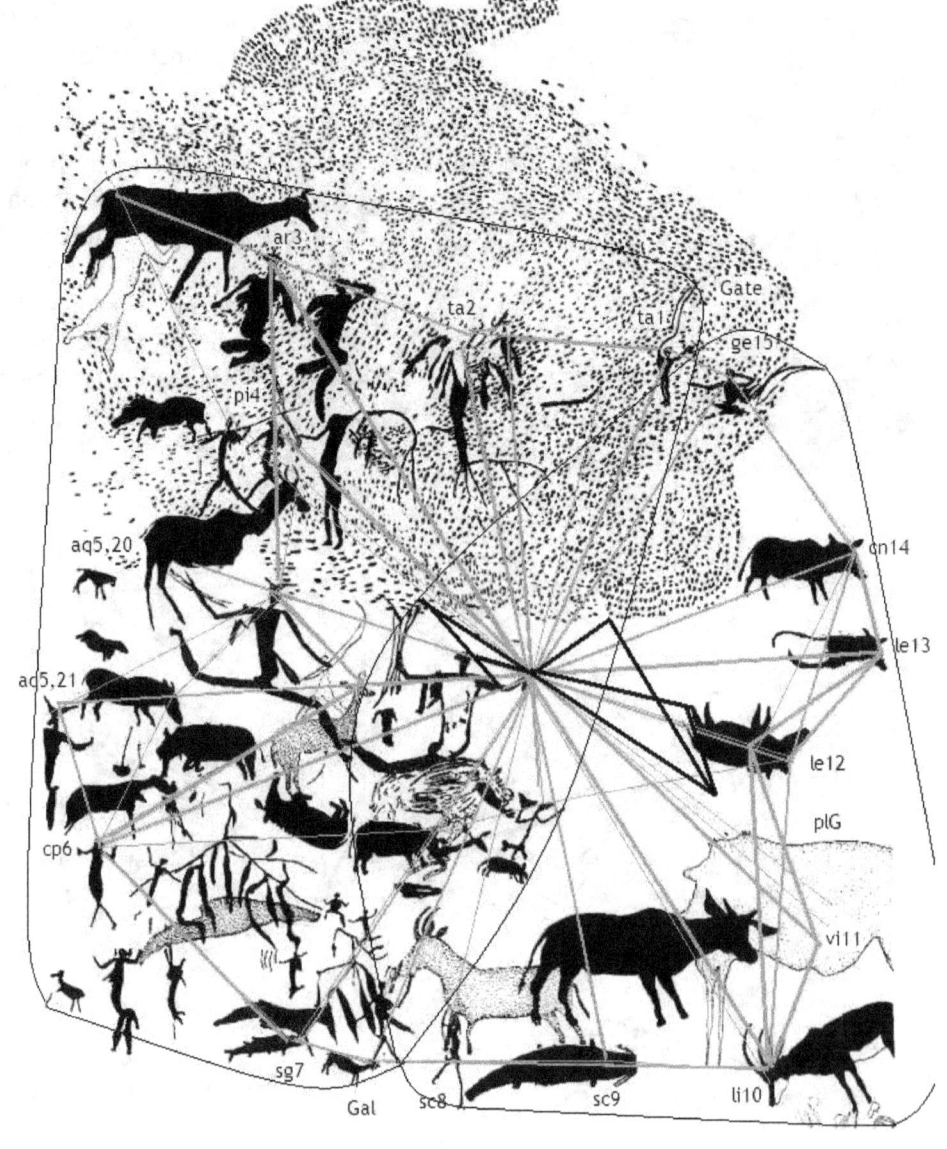

A tree speaks its heart

Type Taurus t1 t16 Auriga and Perseus as a bird on a cross tree (Mexican Palenque temple, maize god and axial tree in a textile copy of a relief engraving. Mindprint analysis by Edmond Furter). The tree figures the galactic structure of mindprint, as in some Greek art (see a Minoan jewel at theme t12), Nordic art, and other traditions. The bird's head resembles parts of Taurus Perseus, its body resembles parts of Taurus Auriga, and its tail resembles Gemini (see a combined Auriga-Gemini figure in the Lascaux shaft at theme t1). Either way, it derives from the concept of a galactic gate, and thus also resembles parts of the opposite gate at Scorpius-Sagittarius, again as concepts, not as a visual mimic. Notable trees express the concept of four directions, seasons and orientation, not astronomy. The figure sequence, marked by axes and an irregular angular equator, resembles zodiac figures or constellations only in concept,

and is named ecliptic equator in this study for convenience. Alchemical compounds are likewise named after planets. The mythical tree is an analogy and framework for a set of ideas, just as the sky is. Many cultures conflate the two, and many people, mostly not artists, assume that art derives from astronomy, but this quick and often unspoken conclusion is one of the layers of camouflage that kept mindprint camouflaged. Some artists and thinkers such as Plato understood both as analogies, expressing a deeper, pre-existent structure in nature and perception, and understood perception as born of nature and not independent.

Aries t3 is a face mask on the chest of the main human figure. Some of the faces could be flower people, as in other Mexican and Pacific trees. Leo t12 is on a tree branch, and Leo t13 on the eye of the woman on the right, as it sometimes is, instead of on the heart of a man as it usually is. These small deviations from the mindprint standard (confirmed in detailed analysis of 600 works of

rock art and art in this study), are eloquent once the polar triangles are marked, revealing the tree's heart as the ecliptic pole, and its jaw and genitals as celestial poles, as if animating the half human tree by a borrowed heart. The celestial polar markers, as if 'speaking its heart', are confirmed by the vertical plane, and tag the inspiration as Age Pisces-Aquarius, a little prophetic for the work, but in line with the axial nature of the immanent Age. For the first time since Age Gemini-Taurus, conventionally reckoned to about BC 4300 but probably earlier, equinoxes and solstices now align to galactic features. Instead of uncertain historical dating, the previous axial era could be dated relatively, as '90 degrees ago'.

Iconographic logic may seem strenuous in text, but it is instantly accessible in images, although it requires some visual grammar to 'read' its subconscious, holographic detail. Artists and most art lovers know that a picture paints a thousand words, but the few authors who have followed visual 'texts' to archetypal level, were misled by visual citations (similarities to other work and other systems) into assuming that artists borrow consciously and randomly, while they borrow with inherent iconic logic (see Picasso's Guernica citing Dali's billowing face at theme t1). Only inspired artists could express cosmic structure. Patrons, religions and monumental commissions recognise archetypal genius on a subconscious level. In the conscious realm, most art studies are misled by assuming artistic genius as individual, and artistic meaning as cultural, while both are universal.

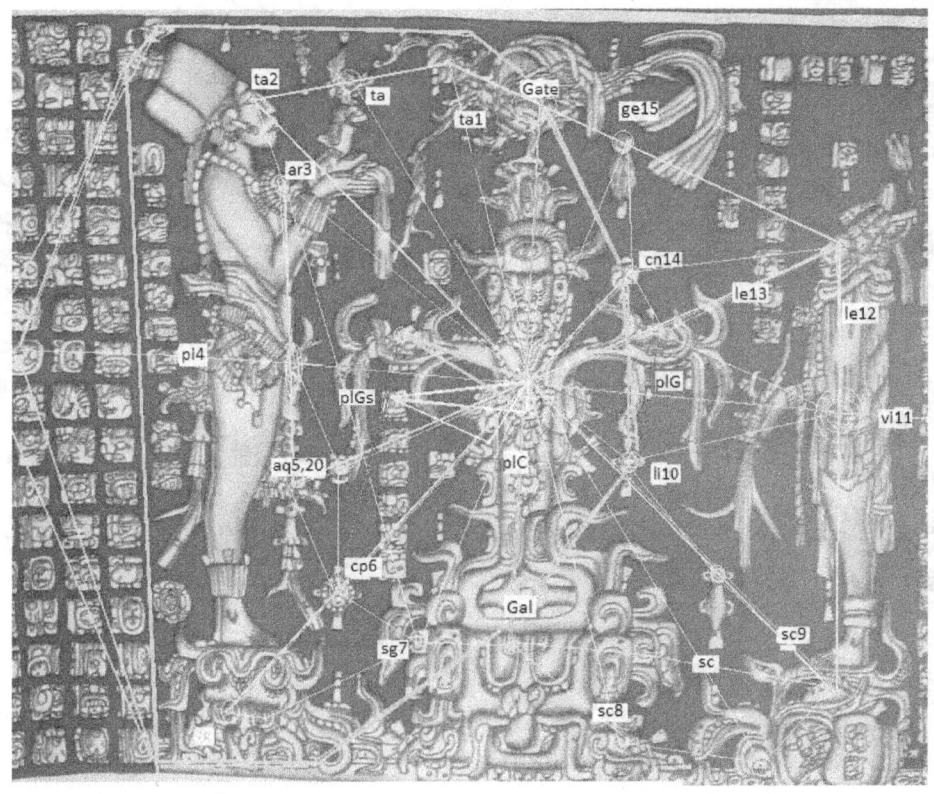

Fish people as swift people

Type Taurus t1 t16 Orion as a bird, fish or swift person (Easter Island, Hau Kota boulder engraving. Bradshaw Foundation. Mindprint analysis by Edmond Furter). For lack of figures, the artist added articulated (linked-in) fish in the tails of other fish. A figure extending below the Pisces t4 human feet is implied by a tail remnant below, hinting that the human emerged from a seal shape. The work is on a 3m boulder, but in a compact style, comparable to carved palettes (see fish people in South African beach pebble palettes at themes t8 and t14). Pisces t4 resembles Rapa Nui (Easter Island) bird people, developed in isolation from other cultures, yet these figures are recognisably swift people, some with bird beaks, figured as swallows, penguins or seals on other continents. Galactic poles are remarkable for marking an isolated human head (left) and a human hand. Celestial poles are set by the nose and forehead of the octopus person, and a probable vertical plane, to Age Aries-Pisces, typical of palettes (see theme t3) and of work of the last centuries BC, yet this work may be Age Pisces, and the inspiration thus retro. Another identification sequence is possible, also typical of palettes as double-sided, flip-over or contra-rotating expressions of the two spheres of our eyes, hands, brain and perspective.

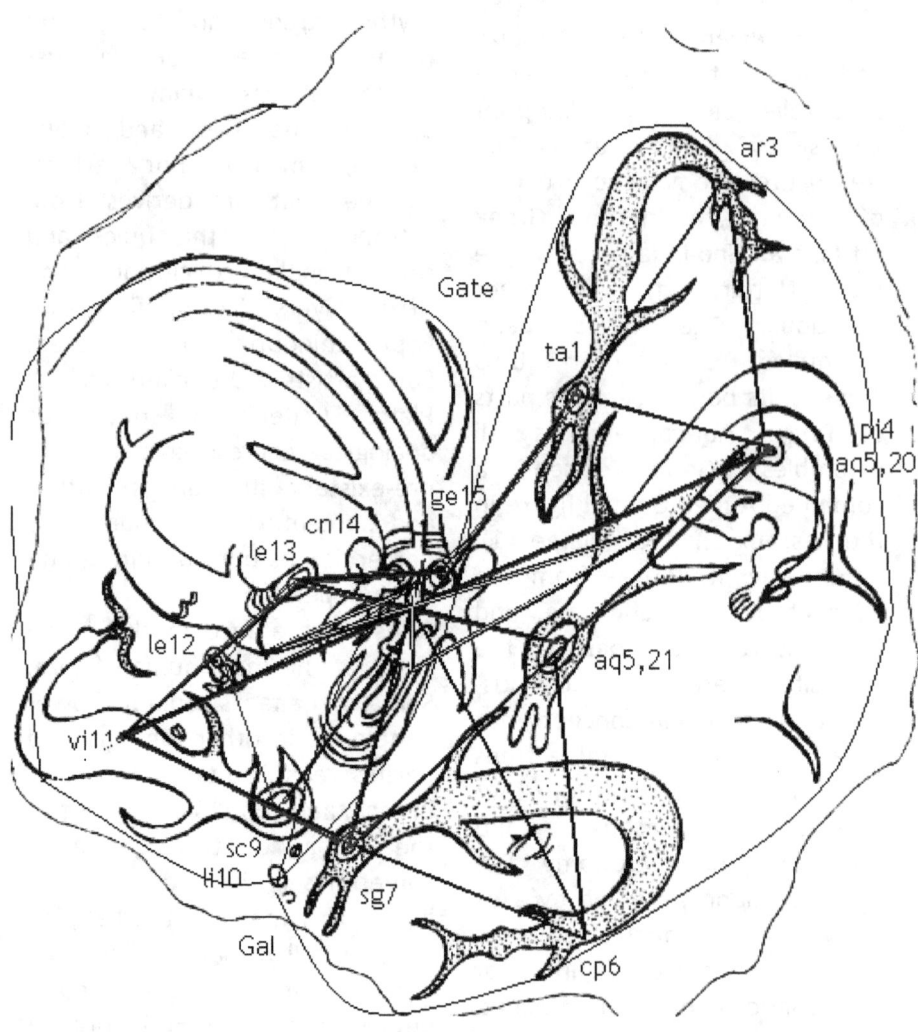

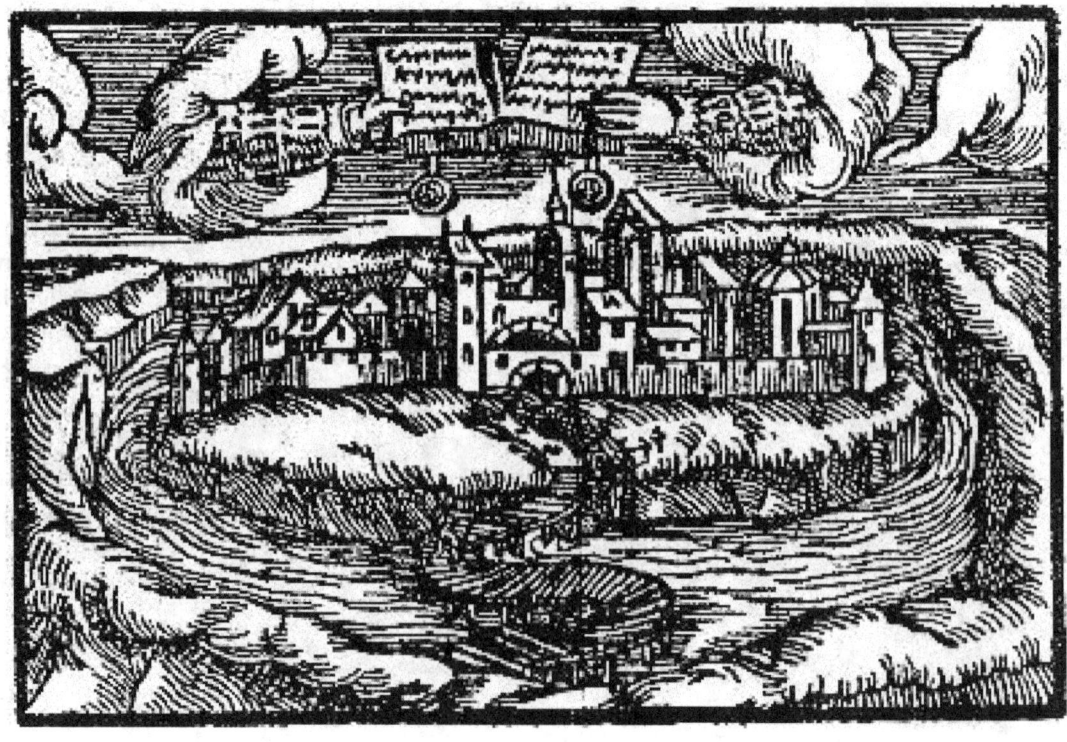

World trade and cold war

Type Taurus t1 t16 as a city state's tracts and towers subjected to trade and policy transformation (Basil Valentine; Alchemical emblem from a series. 1300s).

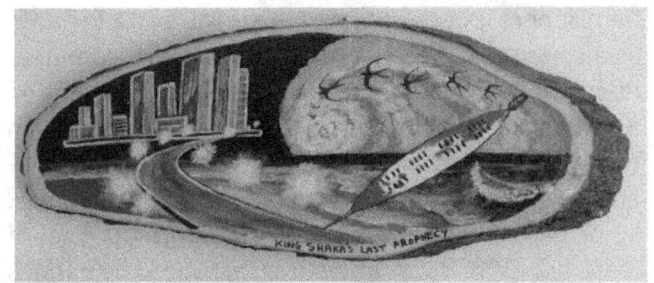

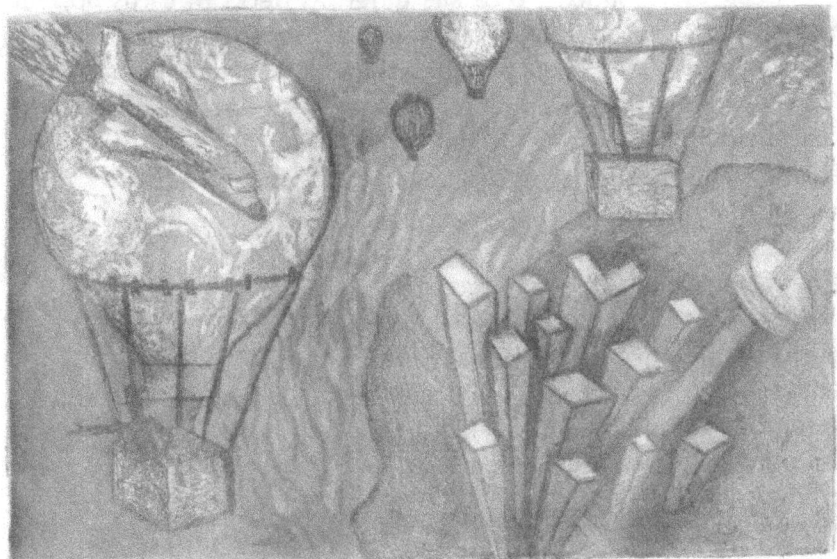

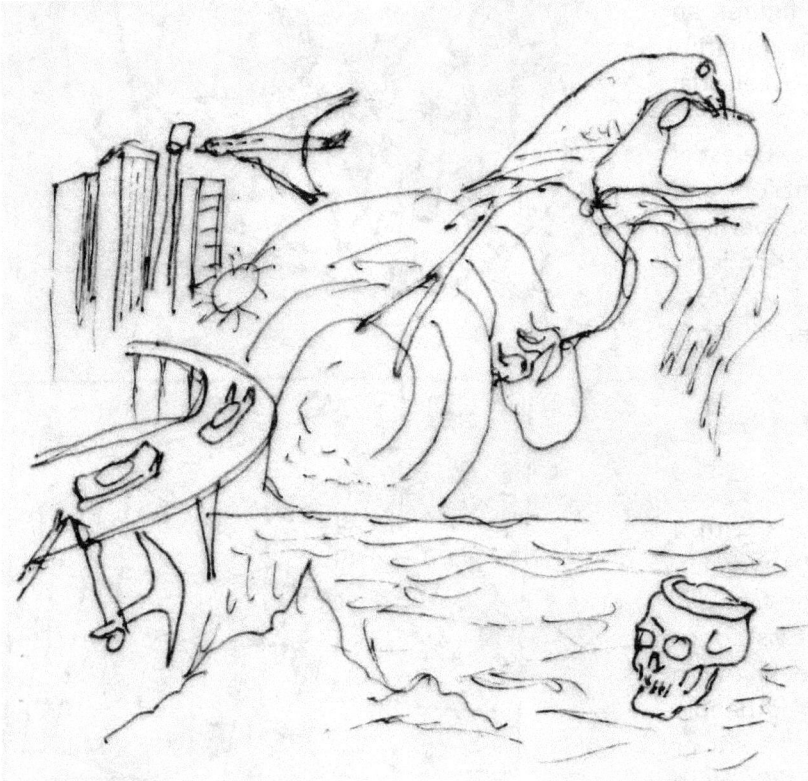

The adjacent motto reads; "Giving too much out of hand brings sorrow and want to the giver, for if it fails he shall be beaten with his own weapons... overmuch giving away had made you proud... Then shall all be torn up... But if you had considered that no one should set himself against the poor, and had also recognised your liberty to be against your neighbour, you would have abstained therefrom. But your own heart had seduced you, and your wisdom has been reckoned openly as folly." These double-sided verses could apply to any country or economic block in world trade and foreign policy, before and after the 1300s, or the city states of the Renaissance, or the USA terror attacks. The image and verse expresses the current academic concept of history as a panarchical discourse (LH Gunderson and CS Holling; Panarchy, understanding transformation in human and natural systems).

This is one of the few single types illustrated out of mindprint context in this study. Every series of alchemical emblems expresses the eternal sequence, but their numbered sequences, like the verses of Nostradamus are variously scrambled. German religious ecstatic Hildegard of Bingen embroidered the type in isolation. Zulu healer and alchemist Credo Mutwa painted many scenes of the type (see plaque and panel insets). His cultural village in Oppenheimer Park, Soweto, below the tower commemorating housing improvements by mining companies, was destroyed in the 1976 riot about oppression and the enforcement of the Dutch-based Afrikaans language in schools, extending the implicit tower of Babel theme to the 'confused languages' sub-theme. The Soweto Kliptown tower commemorating the Freedom Charter, resembles the Oppenheimer tower, but has a skewed top (see Tarot trump 16, Tower).

Jeanne Morgan-Lefay painted the theme in blazing colours as hot air balloons over Johannesburg, like Mutwa, including jet aircraft over skyscrapers (before seeing Mutwa's art). All these works were made before the New York terror attacks, but are not predictions.

Type Taurus t2 t17 Pleiades; Rain priestess

A rain bag churn and bull leg update

Type Taurus t2 t17 Pleiades as a bull bag with rain (Egyptian decans for Ramses 3. Mindprint analysis by Edmond Furter). Gemini t15 is a rope controller, Taurus t2 t17 a bird, Taurus t1 t16s a papyrus clump knot, sharing its axis with Aries t3 as a crocodile. The two Taurids are swopped (see the Seti 1 ceiling version at theme t8) and shown inside Pisces t4 Pegasus as a rain bull leg or divination bone bag, with its split hoof roped across to the galactic centre at Scorpius t8 (likewise swopped with its own t9), and roped to the galactic pole and polar axis held by Leo t12 t13 Ursa, which is combined with Draco. This is the same ophiotaurus (cow snake) that Bushmen describe as a rain animal (see theme t7, the intestinal animal with bee pirates at themes t8, and t15). Some myths and astrology express this ensemble as Perseus; one foot on the Pleiades, one arm reaching to Aries t3 or the Medusa head, another arm on the galactic equator, his rear foot on Auriga over the gate, sometimes facing and flanking Gemini as a churn pair. The bull leg is acknowledged in Egyptology (O Neugebauer and RA Parker; Egyptian astronomical texts, III) and popular culture (Robert Bauval) to arise from Taurus Pleiades. Here, its short hoof on the Gemini t15 rope figures an extra celestial pole (which is marked by the Aquarius t5 foot) on the Cancer t14 axis. The real celestial pole is likewise under the imagined hoof of Cancer t14 Ursa Minor, midsummer to Age Aries. Celestial polar markers on the Aquarius t5 t21 front foot and hip, tag the inspiration to Age Aries, perhaps incidental with the work. The re-interpretation is no less inspired than the Ramses 3 or Seti 1 versions. Each rain bag, rain dance and culture is partly conventional and perpetually original.

A rain bag with snakes

Type Taurus t1 t16 as a lightning priestess with a bird and snakes (USA, Cienega Mesa turtle woman. Mindprint analysis by Edmond Furter). The figure is a bag or carapace, but in the usual twisted or swastika posture (see Tarot trump 17 kneeling with two jugs or rain bags). Ball people or turtle people are more usual at Aquarius t5 t21, a world spirit or enclosure (see a Pazuzu altar at theme t5 t20). Here

the Kilroy-type head participates in the sequence. Taurus t1 t16 Auriga as a pair of lightning snakes is a common theme in semi-geometric engravings (as at the SA Ottosdal pyryphollite ridge female initiation site). Both pairs of snakes also trace part of the galactic equators (one equator viewed from both hemispheres) between the gates. Taurus t2 Pleiades as a spring rain bird sits on a stem sprung from near Pisces t4 as a spring sun (see a spring somersault in an Olmec obelisk at theme t8). Ritual rainmakers in many cultures carry divination bags with a kit of animal knuckles, tokens, keepsakes and symbols. Some carry bags of 'rain things'. Mindprint is a set of 'bare bones' or stock attributes, activated by various contexts. Dice kits differ, as decks of cards do, but their interpretations are subconscious standards.

A celestial pole on the head of the short snake tags the inspiration to Age Aries-Pisces, in the last centuries BC, a common inspirational dating of palettes, shells, bowls, calabashes and discs.

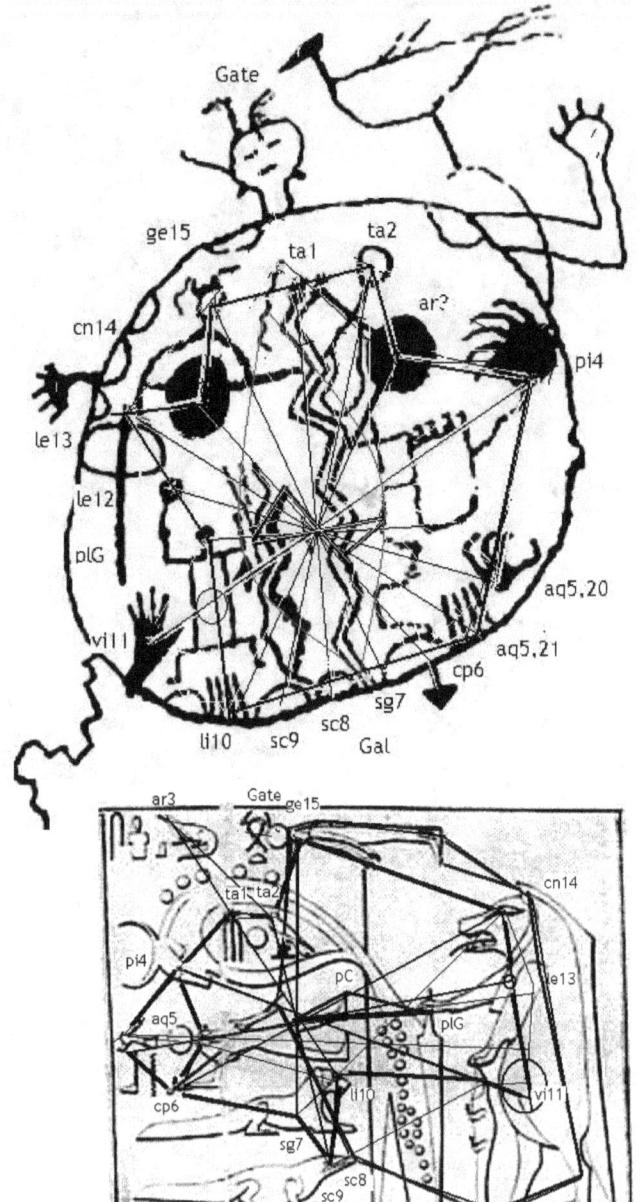

A lotus snake rain bag

Type Taurus t2 t17 Pleiades as a rain priest holding a rain flower bulb enclosing a snake, in a figurative linear set, doubled and mirrored by a heraldic linear set (Egyptian Dendera crypt north mural with lotus bulbs. E Chassinat; Dendera temple. Mindprint analysis by Edmond Furter). The kneeling posture is typical of Perseus, one arm upward to control rain and a Medusa head in a bag. Aries t3 is a hand and absent head of a djed pillar with arms raised, more typical of its opposite Libra t10, but with a long neck as usual. Taurus and Aries sometimes flank the mystical basket (see a Roman sarcophagus at theme t11), here the djed pillar, as in the Osiris, Nebuchadnezzar and Moses legends of a trunk coffin or basket.

Libra t10 is marked on the eye of his snake staff. His own head appears after Scorpius t9 t8 (neither confirmed by opposites), thus he stands in for Scorpius t8 Ophiuchus (Serpent holder). Taurus t1 as a knifeman defends Gemini t15 as a deceased soul against the Apop snake at the gate, for which the bulb snake stands in. In a rare coincidence with constellation shapes, or visual feedback (conscious recognition of a similarity between myth, icon and art), the bulb's shape and angle expresses Taurus Hyades (Bull head), from its V-shaped face, along straight horns, to the stars Taurus Auriga alpha, El Nath (Horn), nicknamed Nail of the sky (Alpha Aurigae in astronomy), and the prior tip of Orion's club. If the reclining horns are connected by a semicircle, as here, and as in buccranium solar discs, the rounded tip touches the gate. This gate is the annual crossing of the sun over the galactic river, nightly peril in mythology, and one of the four structural points of cosmology. The jaw end of Taurus Hyades extends into a stem, sometimes figured as a chin rest (see a forked staff and arrow in a Babylonian engraving at theme t2), down to Aries

Cetus tail. The lotus stem bends back around to the Aries t3 djed pillar base, tying up loose ends of the inevitable disjunction between conceptual order, decanal order and constellation order.

The bulb snakes, of which some technological assumptions such as 'ancient lasers and DNA manipulation' have been elaborated by some authors, are no more enigmatic than thousands of surreal rock art works. The bulbs are conceptual and spiritual mechanisms, ophiotauri (cow snakes. See an animal with entrails for a head with bee people at theme t8). Healers describe rain animals of varied shapes with shiny skins, lured in dreams from waterholes, led by sky ropes like zeppelins, and gently milked (Bleek, cited in G Spiller; Origins films, DVD. Wits University). These visionary shapes, though resembling hippopotami, are all named 'snakes'. Rain animals are controlled by healers in the guise of Taurus t1 or t2 Auriga (Artemis), Orion, or Perseus (see the Narmer palette at theme t3 t18). Their opposites and cardinals also sometimes appear as snakes, dragons, bags or churn groups (see Scorpius t8 Ophiuchus, Serpent holder, or Horus and Set turning the pneuma lung pump by lotus flower stems. See Indian lotus flower churns with snake ropes on lotus petals. See Mexican tree pillars. See a Fafnir ribbon-dragon and braided tree at theme t3 t18).

Aries t3 in the upper register is a cartouche under Maat ostrich feathers, usually identified with its opposite, Libra t10. The axial geometry is compacted by the linear arrangement, typical of decans with calendric, pantheonic and theological elements. Repetitive upper register emblems or hieroglyphs are place holders for emerging attributes. The Dendera crypt south mural is near identical, but with a double imprint and two antithetical rain bulbs. The artists as usual were unaware of the extent of the underlying sequence and pattern in nature and culture.

Celestial polar markers are uncertain, but the horizontal plane between the t14 and t15 axes, tags the inspiration to Age Aries-Pisces, incidental with the Ptolemaic era.

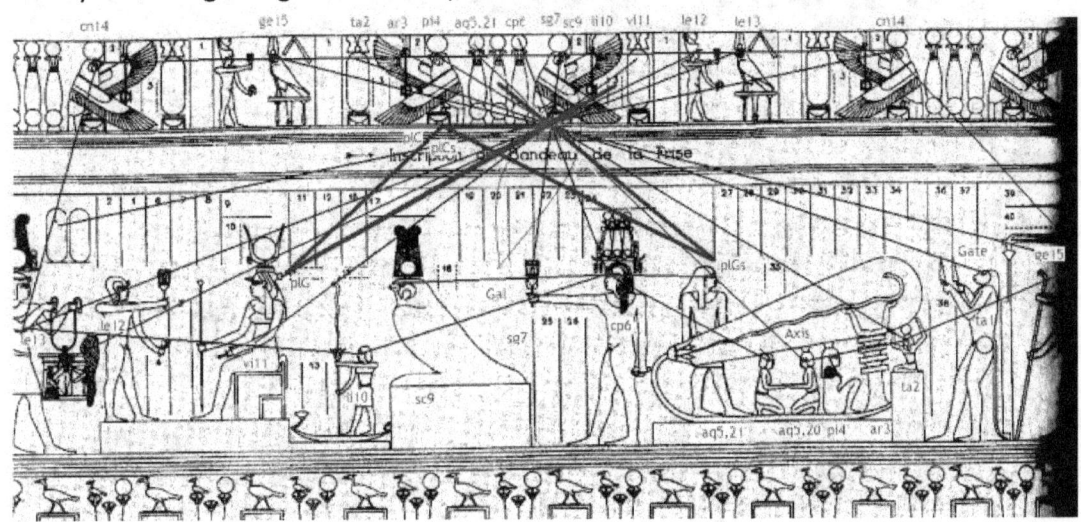

Samson with a bull and bees

Type Taurus t2 t17 Pleiades as a line of bees from a rain bull's hump (South Africa, KZN 22b rain bull. G Anderson. Mindprint analysis by Edmond Furter). The beeline forms an emerging Taurus t2 radial, without an axial counterpart at Scorpius t9. This is one of very few features found to mark a mindprint axis. The theme recalls the Biblical Samson, carcass and bees, identified by some orientalists as in the 'oldest' layer of Bible 'sources', which should rather be read as an eternal, archetypal, subconscious and perpetually renewed sources. Samson, here perhaps the large Scorpius t8 Ophiuchus (Strength), or Sagittarius t7 Galactic centre as potbellied with a feather headdress, is ever alive and well. See V-people in a USA rainbow scene at theme t14, USA Barrier Canyon at theme t3, and a Russian multitude engraving at theme t15. See bee people at theme t8. Circumcision and initiation may be part of the theme. See De Cosimo's Discovery of honey, among the initial examples in the text section, and dying lions at theme t13. Parables of honey, virility, sleep and dreams may be due in part to honey's effect of lowering blood pressure. The human heads may have been painted in white chalk (the most easily damaged colour in rock art), signifying spiritual characters or ancestors in Greece and Africa.

Pisces t4 t19 is entangled with the transforming Aries t3. Its opposite at Virgo t11 is entangled with another figure while transforming. Celestial poles on a bovine shoulder (recalling bull foreleg myths) and a hand, tag the inspiration as Age Pisces.

A rain bull victim

Type Taurus t1 and t2 as rain bulls or hunt targets (Russia, Elangash hunting scene. Mindprint analysis by Edmond Furter). T2 does not have an axial opposite, since the other three major types are not doubled, hinting at steps of elaboration (see the Layers section in the text). Aries t3 is a bow or string or arrow fight (its opposite Libra t10 is often a staff) shot from Aquarius t5 to the Taurean hump. The airborne bows form a fish section, an attribute of Taurus t2 t17 and of Aquarius t5 t21. Taurus t1 could be another hunt victim, or a hunting dog, an attribute of the adjacent Gemini t15 Canis.

Celestial poles on a large pair of hoofs or paws, and on horns, tag the inspiration to Age Pisces-Aquarius. Our midsummer sun also lies between Gemini and Taurus, at the top of the club of Taurus Orion, whose belt currently marks the lowest point of our celestial equator, where a dog, Gemini Canis major, reaches with its paw (see theme t15 t0).

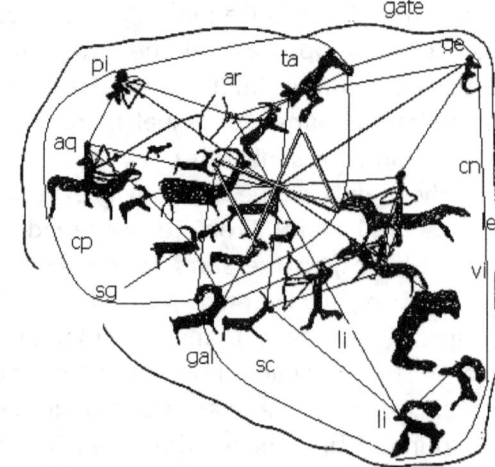

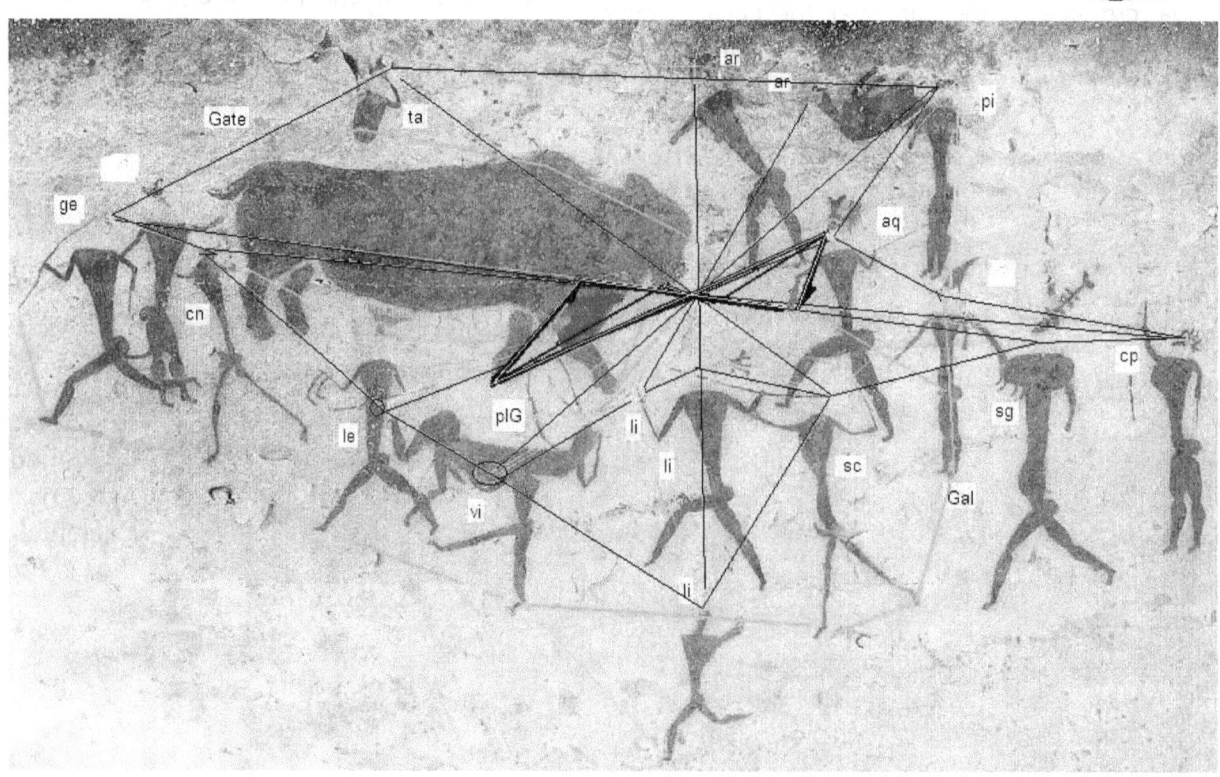

Bull priest, ram priest

Type Taurus t1 t16 as a golden calf, between Aries t3 as Moses, and Gemini t15 as Aaron in a splitting imprint (engraving after Poussin, overpainted, named San Francisco pastiche. MH de Young Museum. Mindprint analysis by Edmond Furter). The two separating spheres agree on Taurus t1 as the bull, Cancer t14 on Aaron's genitals, Leo t12 on a ram fount head, Virgo t11 on a vase, and Aquarius t5 as a midwinter priest. Galactic equators cross on the bull foreleg, and on the hip of the kneeler, who is Scorpius t9 in the right sphere (see bent figures at theme t9), but Libra t10 in the left sphere (see W-shaped arms at theme t10). Bovine sacrifices appear in rock art worldwide. A galactic pole in the left sphere on a jaw, doubles as a celestial pole to the right sphere, where a galactic pole is on a ram fount jaw.

Double imprints seem to form by phased splitting (see Buddha's death at theme t8). The spheres tag the inspiration as Age Aries or Age Aries-Pisces, both confirmed by the top central hand as Aries and Pisces.

Another bull priest

Type Taurus t2 as a golden calf, between Gemini t15 as Moses with laws, and Aries t3 as Aaron conducting ritual (Poussin; Adoration of the golden calf. Scotland National Gallery. Mindprint analysis by Edmond Furter). The Biblical story invokes Egyptian, Hyksos, Canaanite, Syrian and Babylonian myth, as well as the Ages. Here, Moses is at Age Pisces midsummer. In other versions, the two brothers swop roles. Celestial polar markers tag the inspiration as Age Pisces-Aquarius, prophetic for the Renaissance, but incidental with the theme of transition.

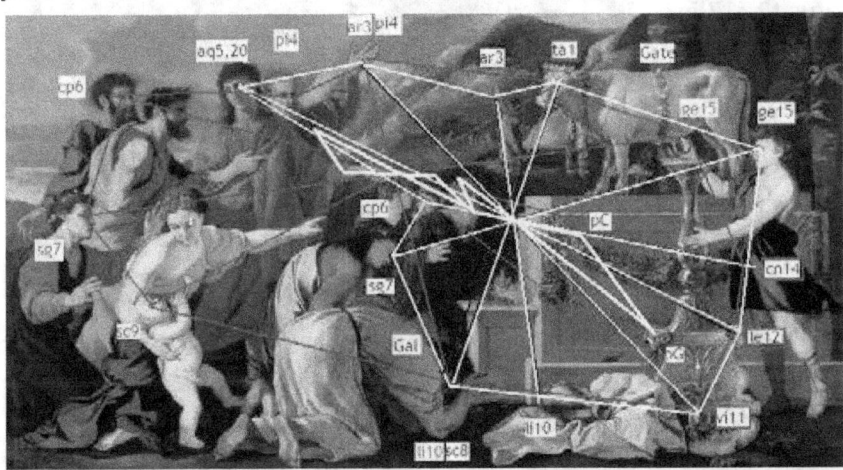

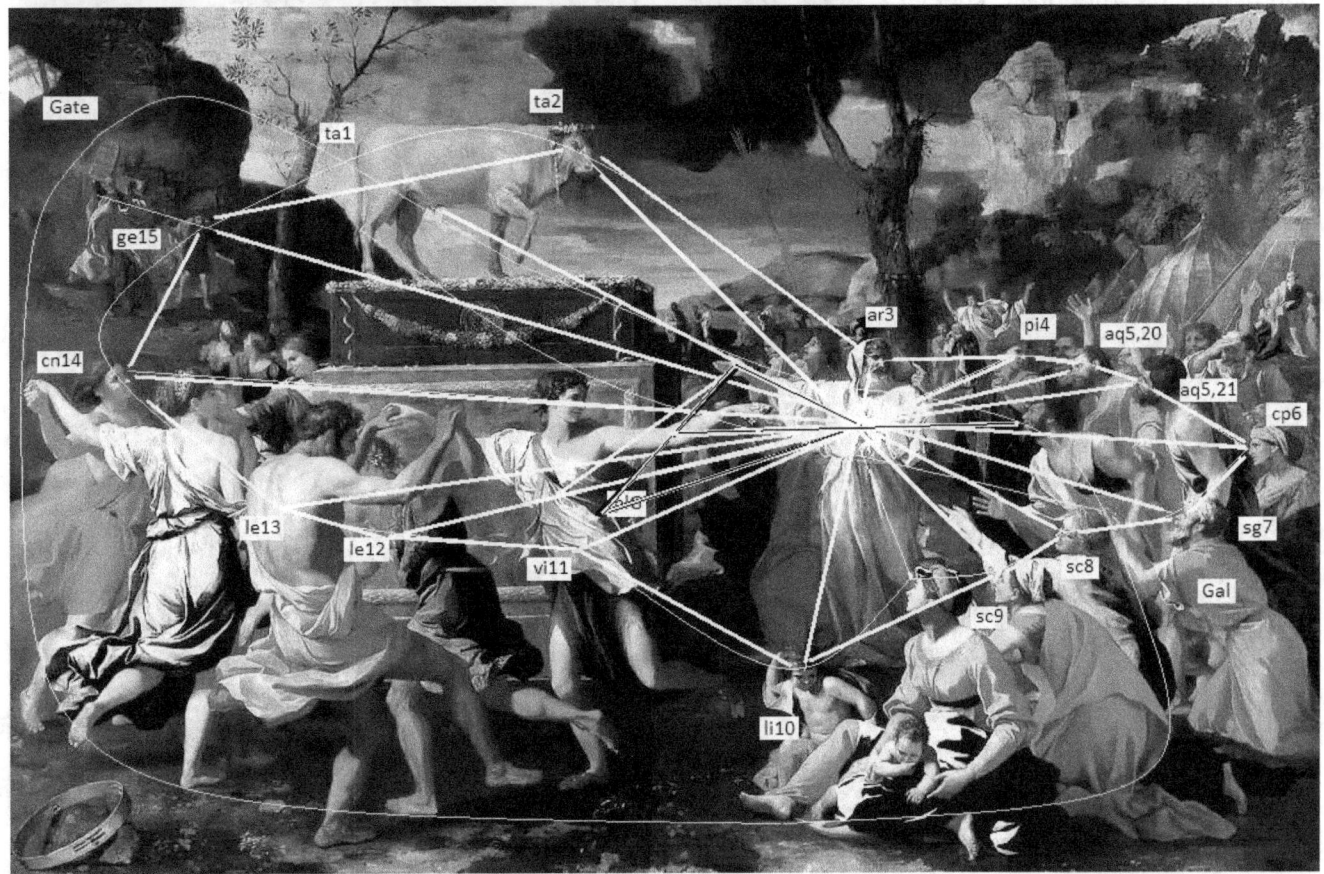

Type Taurus t2 t17 Persus; Rain diviner

Seasons dragged back

Type Taurus t2 t17 Pleiades and Perseus as a rain god (Babylonian cylinder seal of Etana on an eagle. Sitchen. Mindprint analysis by Edmond Furter). The Perseus posture is expressed in the extra figure below Taurus t2 and below the Pleiades seven stars sigil, as a kneeling hero with a bow or shield to glance and shoot backward. Taurus t2, on the Pleiadean throne, has a device on a strap, perhaps a bag or a toppling tower or city (see Taurus t2 t17 in a Guinea calabash at theme t12). The seven dots of Taurus Pleiades (here eight dots, as in Tarot trump 17), and the three stars of Taurus Orion are both dragged to Aries t3 as spring icons. Shorthand for Aries is usually one star (RH Allen; Star names). There is also a slight scramble on the solstice axes, at Leo t13 t12 and its opposite Aquarius t5 t21 t20, perhaps due to iconic adjustments from Age Taurus to Age Aries, one of the few works in this study to strain the mindprint sequence. The strain is evident in the extra lion on the Libra t10 Lupus (Wolf) axis, perhaps a herd dog. Celestial poles on Libra t10's hand, and on the polar kneeler's head, tag the inspiration as Age Taurus-Aries, some time before BC 1500 and before the equinox reached the star Aries delta (Delta Arietis in Latin). The work is probably a little later. A continuous clay rollout may add a mindprint spanning the bookends of the scene, and a galactic equator chain. Duplication attracts archetypal inspiration.

A Shrine to healing and time

Type Taurus t1 t16 Auriga and Orion as a stupa dome image on a gate to a dome (Indian stupa gate carving at Sanchi. Mindprint analysis by Edmond Furter). Celestial poles are set by a range or gauge of markers, and by the vertical plane, to Ages past and eras within Age Pisces. The centre of the doorway provides for the future Age Aquarius, when the celestial pole would reach the Scorpius-Taurus axis by precession. Galactic equators are marked by two smooth-curved intersecting circles, hinting that inspiration may hinge on two intersecting circles of limb joints, perhaps projected via two brain spheres, resulting in an irregular and angular equator of eyes.

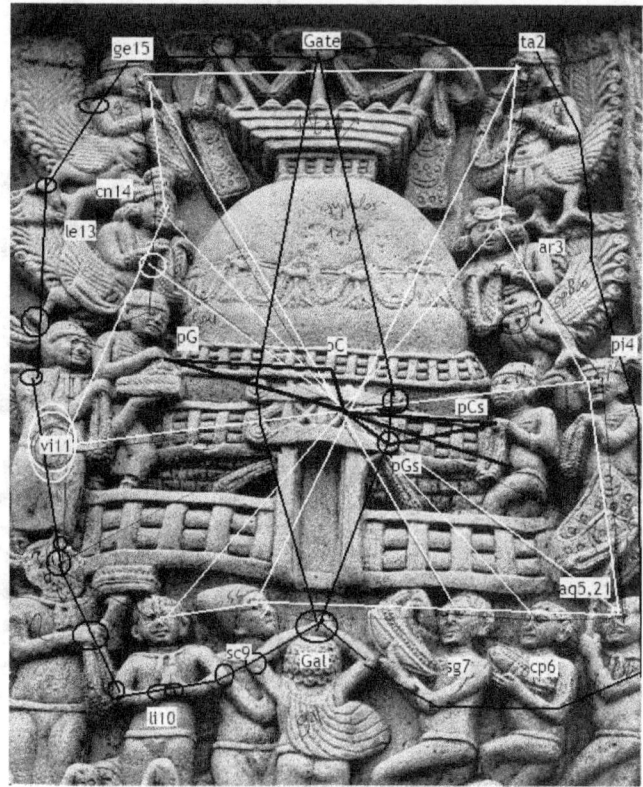

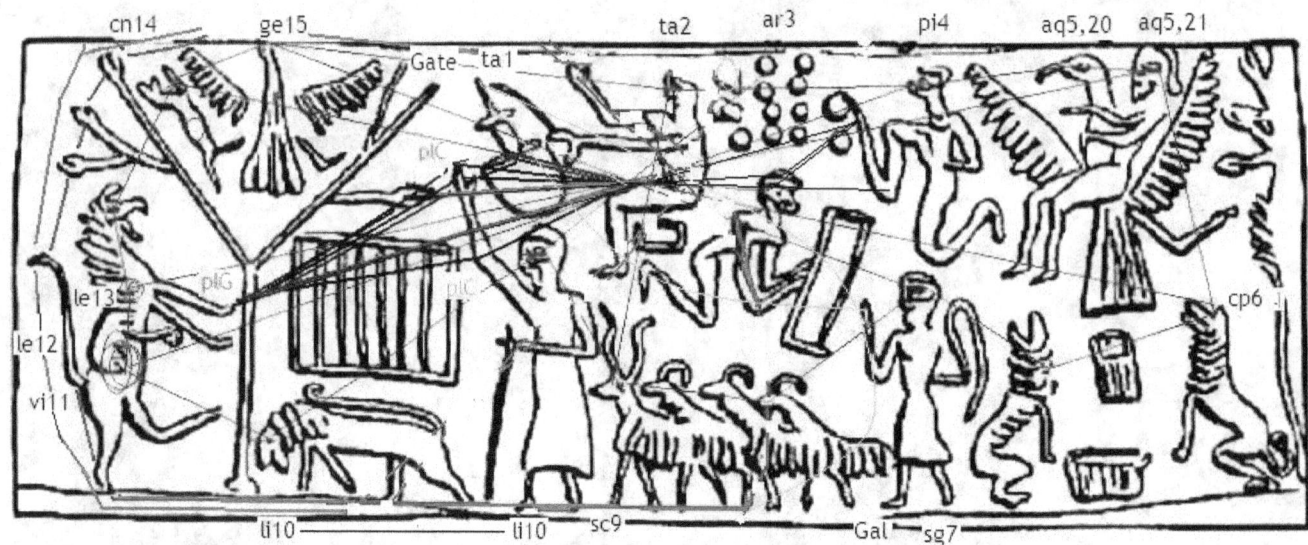

Water woman with a rain bag

Type Taurus t2 t17 Pleiades as a rain bag priestess (South Africa, water bag and trance group. Origins Centre. Mindprint analysis by Edmond Furter). Zigzag arms figure the parallax of rippling water, eels, rain or lightning. Aquarius t5 has painted arms, painted legs, or an apron or tailcoat (see John Baptist images at theme t5), as some church elders also use. The theme of dapples extends to a guineafowl without dots, and fish with guineafowl dots. The bird is noted for its trance-inducing plumage and cry, and ability to mate with chickens, celebrated in myth and in societies such as the Republic of Tarentaal (Guineafowl, also meaning 'Garbled language' in Afrikaans) at South Africa's North-West University. Turkey icons play similar roles in American cultures.

Celestial polar markers on a shoulder and a bag knot, and the main horizontal plane, tag the inspiration as Age Taurus-Aries, although an alternative horizontal plane tags Age Pisces.

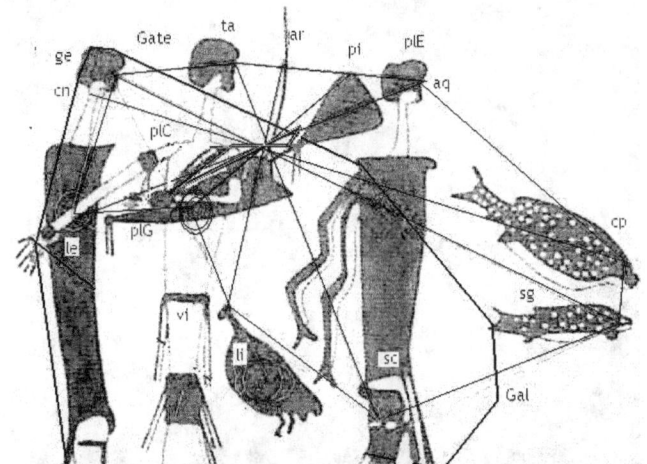

A rain and beer maker on a cup

Type Taurus t2 t17 Pleiades as rain, grain and beer (Mayan cup rollout with dogs. National Geographic. Mindprint analysis by Edmond Furter). Chewing and spitting gain to make beer for elders is still one of the symbolic functions of young girls in some tribal parts of Africa (Tswaing culture drama, 2010; Ditsong Museum).

Gemini t15 Canis is a dog, its breath of fiery ropes at the ecliptic crossing over the galactic stream, at its narrowest flow. Here the sun wades through every year, seen in Egyptian myth as a nightly hazardous crossing or diagonal skip across the southern hemisphere. Companions on the sun boat have to ward off Set and an Apop snake. Scorpius t9 Lupus is a wolf, extending the canine theme (see an Indian destroyer with canines at theme t6). Like some Mayan murals and carvings, this vase may be a picture generator, hinting at holographic depth in subconsciously inspired expressions of archetype, more complex than astronomy. Study of the sky or of any sufficiently complex part of nature or culture could induce holographic inspiration and archetypal expression.

Celestial polar markers on the vertical plane tag the inspiration to Age Pisces.

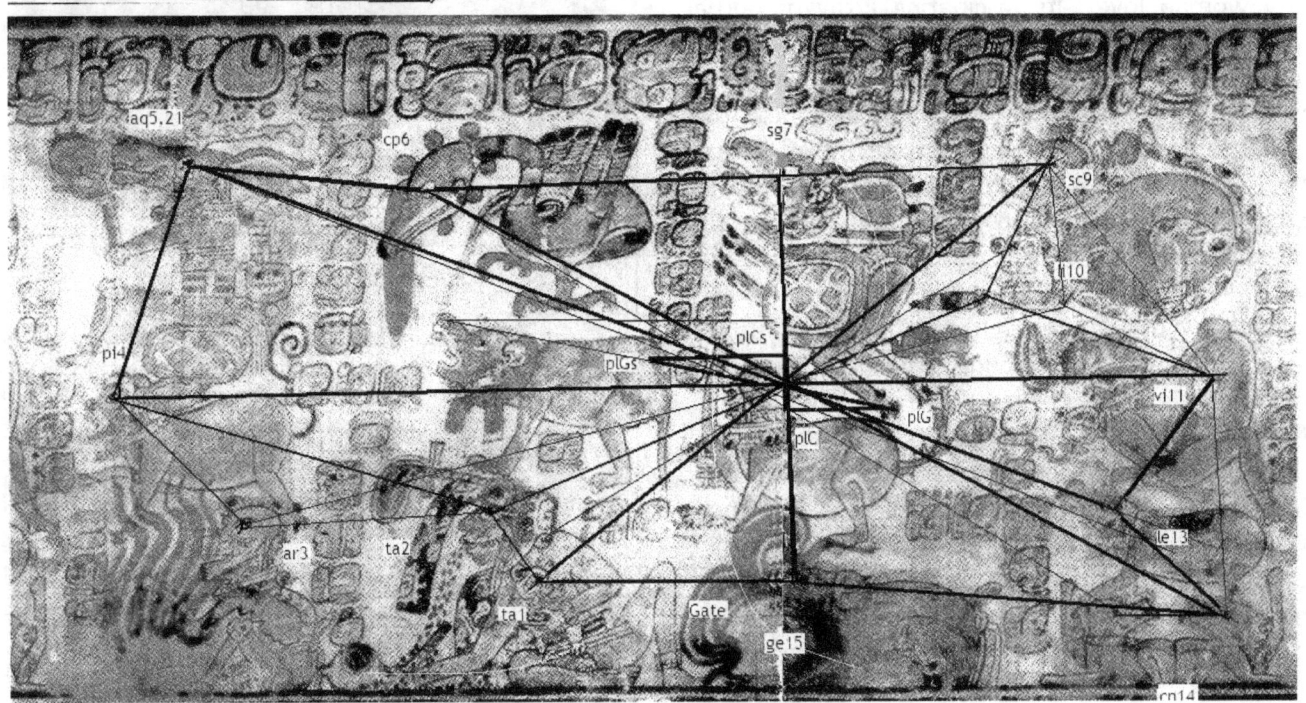

A healer on a rock

Type Taurus t2 t17 Pleiades as Buddha with disciples (Pakistan, Buddha with an antelope and mandala in rock art. Mindprint analysis by Edmond Furter). Libra t10 is a reclining antelope with a long neck, more usual of its opposite Aries t3 t18. Scorpius t8 Galactic centre as a mandala (see engravings of circles at type t8) expresses the vortex wheel of manifestation often turned by the adjacent Libra t10 (see Tarot trump 10, Wheel), flanked by Sagittarius t7 as a buck bag vortex. Mindprint contradicts the artificial division between rock art and art. The galactic poles are on Buddha's feet. The celestial pole on his elbow tags the inspiration to Age Pisces-Aquarius, our current era, incidentally dating the work. The guru and the culture are earlier.

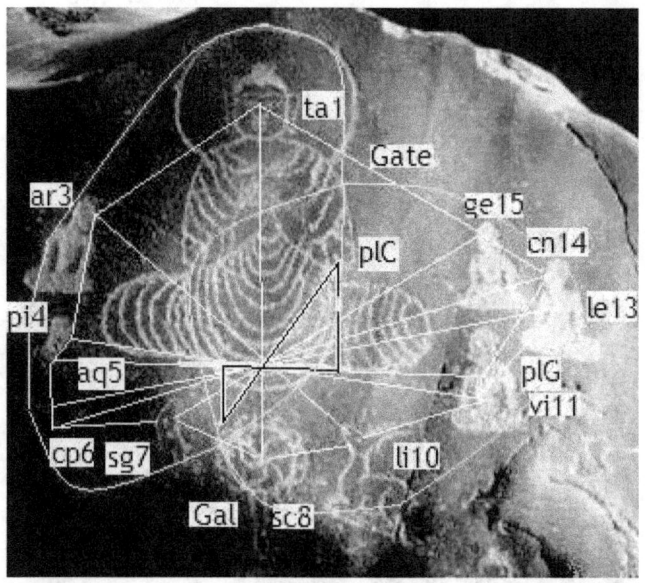

A garden healer

Type Taurus t2 t17 as a herbalist in a garden (Colonna; Hypnerotomachia Poliphili, Rome, 1500. Mindprint analysis by Edmond Furter). The book's title means Sleep Dream Strife of the All-lover, or City woman lover. Its fascinating array of herbal, floral, architectural, musical, processional, ritual, alchemical, cultural and other sets, alternate between hyper-real and surreal episodes. The Hypnerotomachia is glaringly absent from Umberto Eco's recent book, Infinity of lists. Its arrays of archetypes are illustrated with some stock printing press woodcuts, or printing block collages, some with inherent mindprints (as here), others just scrambled or isolated. Elsewhere is the Bernini elephant fountain, among the few instantly recognisable images, and a horse statue with cupids (both figuring Pisces t4 Pegasus). A series of group dance patterns resemble the process of ritual, inspiration, or visual expression. The anonymous Colonna (Pillar) was apparently capable of recalling dream visions. He may have copied some text from manuals, or strung together descriptions of picture catalogues as prompts to himself and to readers.

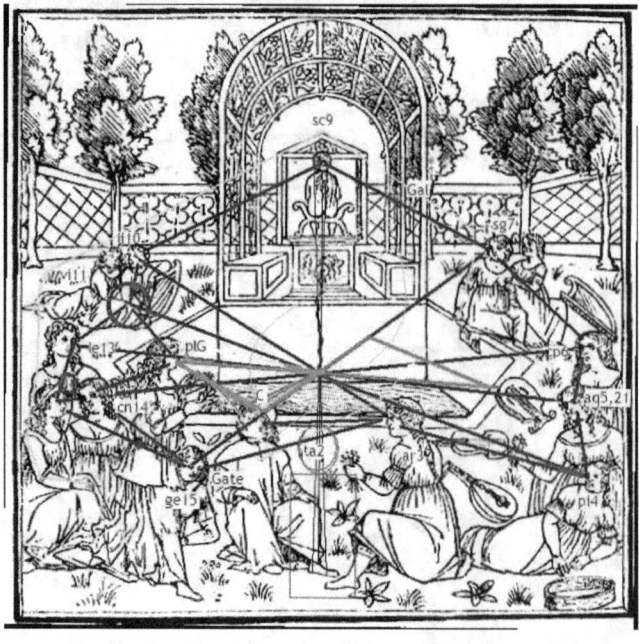

A rain shrine parody

Type Taurus t2 t17 Pleiades as a foot, opposite the hand of a rain goddess, in a subconscious structural parody (Poussin; Helios and Phaeton. Mindprint analysis by Edmond Furter). The usually leading figures of Taurus t2 and Gemini t15 are here reduced to a foot and a flower bud in a spilt cornucopia, and their usual attributes transferred to their opposites. Cancer t14, Time angel, is asleep. Leo t12 and Leo t13 are swopped, as in many other works. This is one of the most shuffled sets of archetypal attributes found in this study, on par with Poussin's Arcadian shepherds (the acclaimed version, see theme t5 t20), with limb joints and galactic equators dominating the design. Perhaps the gifted artist re-worked his designs, allowing conscious symbolism to interfere with subconscious expression, or allowing planetary themes to override the positional themes of mindprint. The goddess and her consort are under a zodiac canopy that parallels part of one of the galactic equators, but ironically not the figures equator. Zodiac Capricornus is omitted, or on a hidden fold of the canopy bend. Zodiac Taurus is behind the head of a goat that figures Leo t12, and may be a misplaced Cancer t14 expressing its opposite, Capricornus t6. Here is evidence that mindprint is more meaningful than the zodiac.

A celestial polar marker on Sagittarius t7's shoulder, and the vertical plane, tag the inspiration as Age Pisces late, incidental with the work.

A perception toolkit

Inspired art could be seen as images circling a sphere, which is cut open about 26 degrees below the equator and folded out to retain the lower parts of the main band of figures intact to a view from above. The galactic equator is perceived as remaining entire, with the 'cut' lower half flipped to the outer edge. The southern 'underside' section of the galaxy is also made visible, and its outer, further section is also folded out as an exterior loop. These two intersecting equators of densely packed stars, resolving into limb joints in art, may be the initial conceptual framework of inspiration. Artists are not aware of this holographic slicing, squeezing and splicing, and merely impose the inspired, standard conceptual template or subtext on real or unreal scenes, juggling until their eyes are in place, and the whole looks and feels right. This eternal wonder of perception is experienced by healers, expressed by artists, accessible to viewers, testable by a simple sequence and geometry, yet infinitely varied in appearance. Attributes and the structure expressed in mindprint are more constant than any supposed race or culture, since it derives from archetypal, pre-existent structure, that we also express in our shapes, motivations, actions, myths, languages, and concepts, which we mistake as 'invented and developed'.

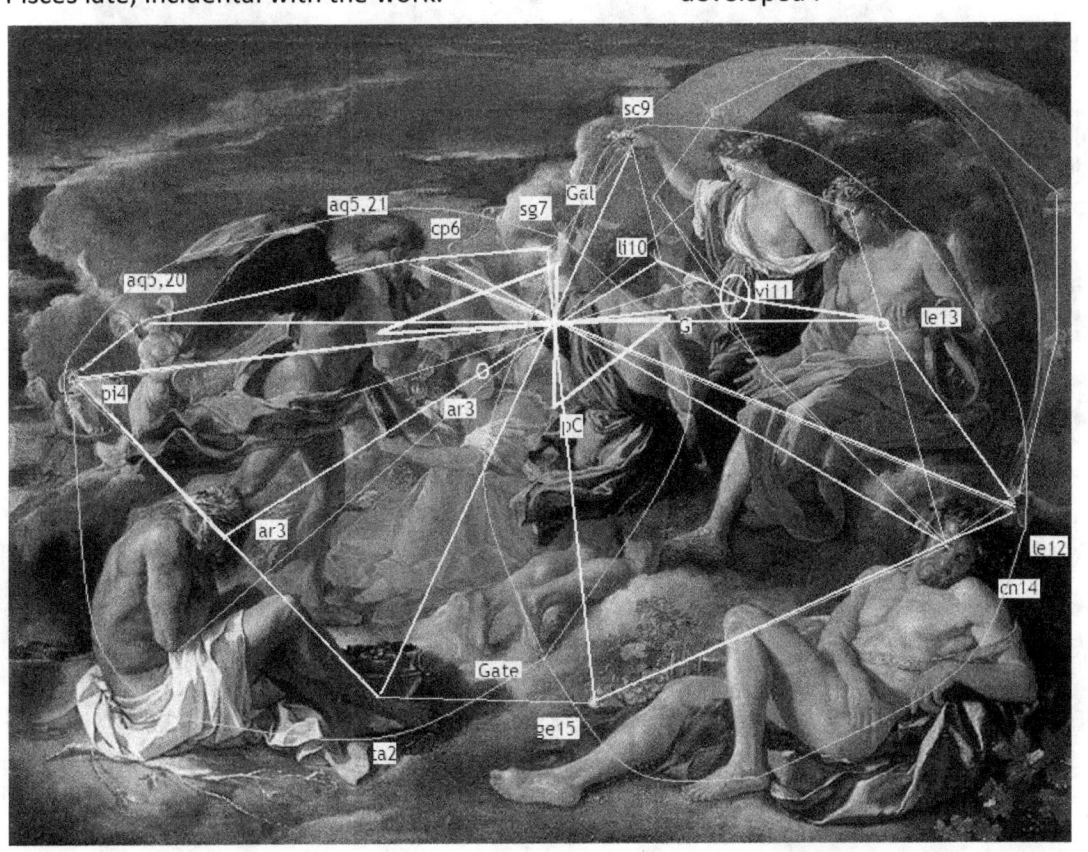

Type Aries t3 t18; Moon queen and moon dragons

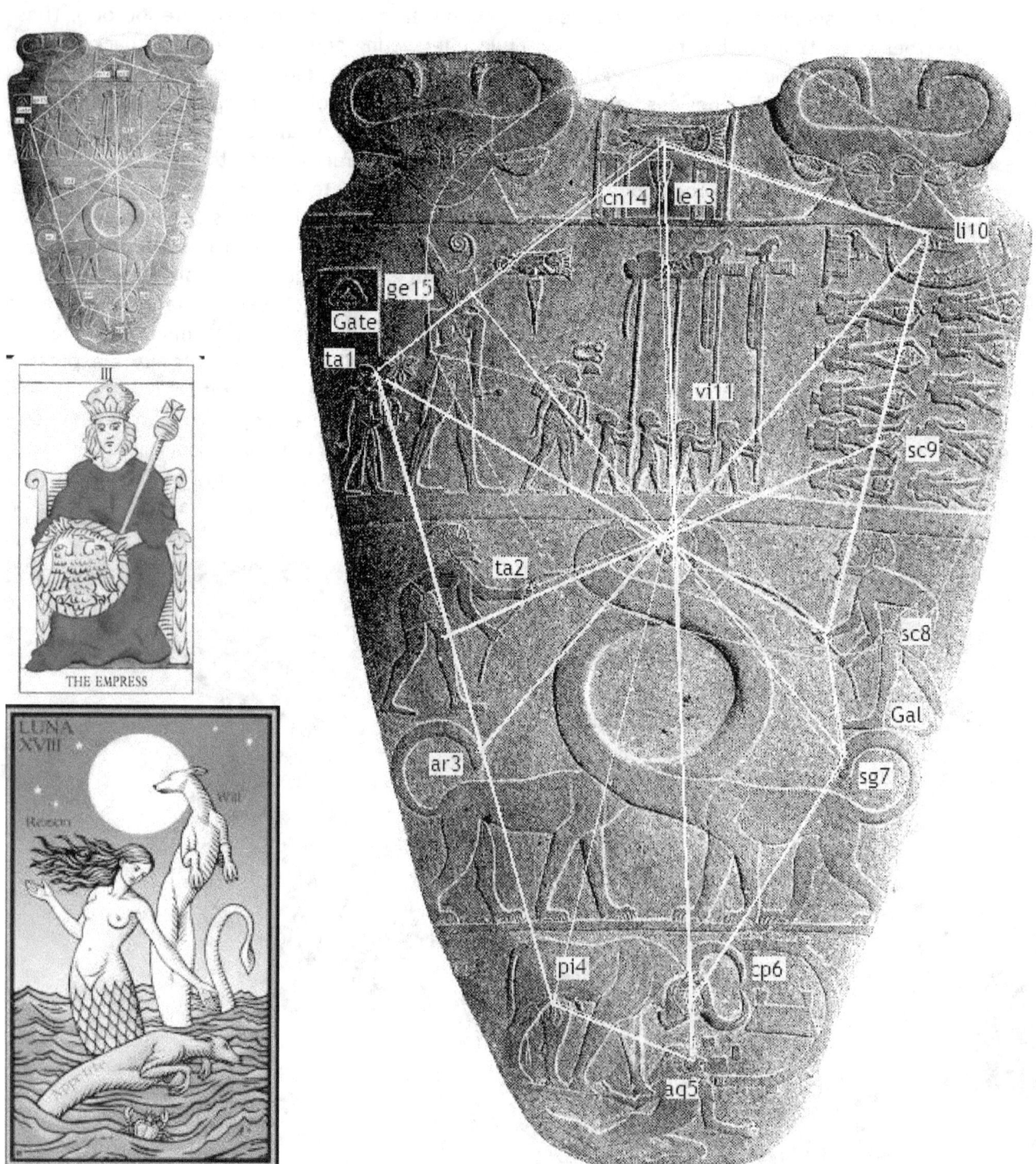

Egyptian dragons

Type Aries t3 t18 as entwined moon dog dragons (Narmer palette from Hierakonpolis. Egyptian Museum, Cairo. Mindprint analysis by Edmond Furter). The palette shape expresses the concepts of a knife or axe, hafting to an axis, caduceus, and gore (spherical section). In the sky, this meridian axis (here vertical) connects the Cetus Whale tail (dragon body below), via a vacant ecliptic (planetary) area, Aries neck, Triangulum (Knife) next to the Medusa head, to Cepheus (galactic sea monster or king), Draco, Bootes Corona (snake arm), Serpens (Snake or staff), Libra as uroburos snake, and Lupus (Wolf). Considered equatorially (here horizontal), Aries lies midway between the Gemini-Taurus gate and the Pisces-Aquarius axis. It hosted the spring equinox from about BC 1300 to BC 150. Sometime in that Age, the zero point of myth, calendars and astrology co-incided. Celestial poles on a foot, and the centre of the bowl, tag the inspiration to Age Aries. An alternative mindprint (a kind of double imprint, typical of palettes, discs and plaques) has celestial poles on the left dragon eye reigned by Perseus (monster slayer), and on the right dragon throat reigned by Ophiuchus (Snake handler). The sequence also allows optional transitions to some of the figures on the flip side, incidental with the theme of lunar nodes and eclipses (see the palette's front image in the Decans section in the text).

Mexican dragons

Type Aries t3 t18 as facing moon dog dragons framing the ecliptic pole, in a triple concentric imprint (Mexico, Aztec sigils and hieroglyphs in a squared tablet. Mindprint analysis by Edmond Furter). See a Babylonian seal with entwined dragons in the Polar section in the text. The hieroglyphs are also time sigils, thus a decanal set. Aries t3 is a queen at the crossed dragon tails, labelled by a framed shield (see Tarot trump 3, Empress). The sequence is repeated on three concentric (equatorial) registers; by determinants (hieroglyphic attributes), as well as heads, and hieroglyphs (see a concentric double imprint in a Bolivian disc at theme t12). The celestial pole is marked by a dial pointer, which is curiously dipped off the horizontal plane, tagging the inspiration as Age Aries late, incidental with the iconographic theme. Ambiguation of most of the figures with their adjacents, and the dipped plane, indicate that an Age Aries work was updated to Age Pisces and indicate some conscious recognition of calendric elements. Egyptian decans and the dates of some festivals acquired their ambiguity in the same way. Conscious calendric, semi-conscious astrological, and subconscious archetypal elements all ambiguate when mind and spirit collaborate. If updated today, the celestial polar pointer would indicate the torch at lower left.

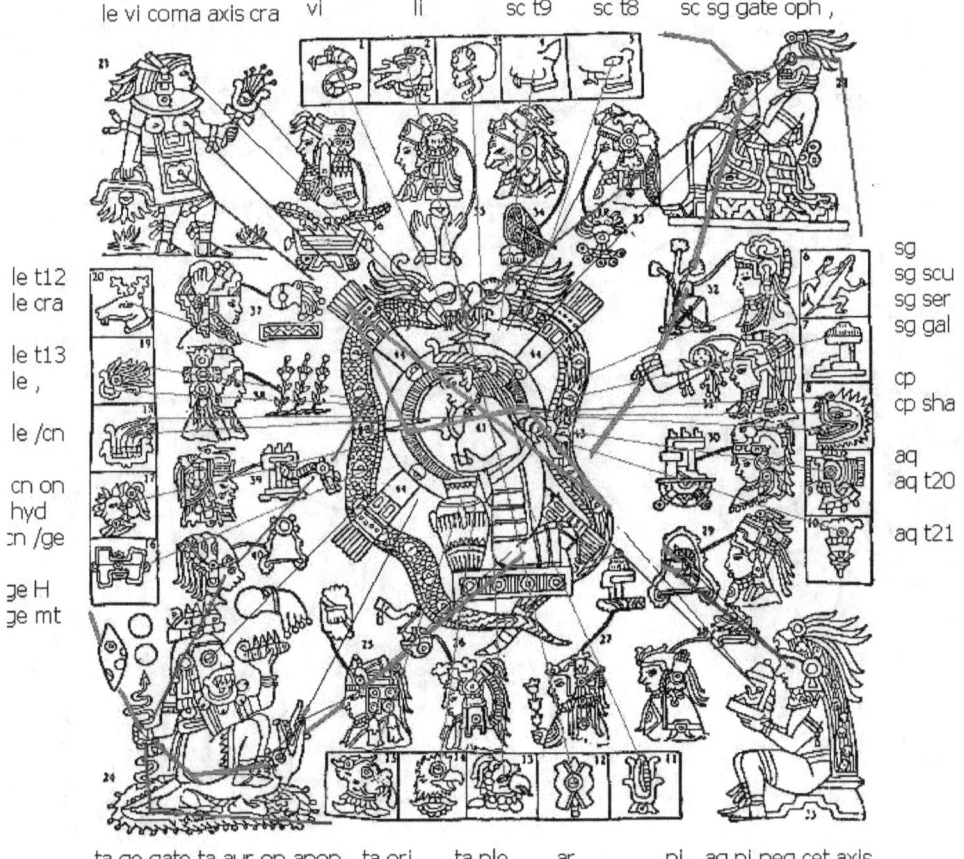

le vi coma axis cra   vi   li   sc t9   sc t8   sc sg gate oph ,

le t12
le cra

le t13
le ,

le /cn

cn on
hyd
cn /ge

ge H
ge mt

sg
sg scu
sg ser
sg gal

cp
cp sha

aq
aq t20

aq t21

ta ge gate ta aur on apop. ta ori   ta ple   ar   pi. aq pi peg cet axis

A palette person in America

Type Aries t3 Triangulum (Knife) as an axe, shield, or palette person (USA Barrier Canyon, shield person. David Lee. Mindprint analysis by Edmond Furter). Aries is nature herself, often figured with a shield (see Tarot trump 3, Empress). The type appears in a Gaulish (French) Armorican coin or medal that could also be astronomical, as a large sword between a dragon and a twisting hero (Taurus t2 t17), labelled 'weapons cult' in most sources. A sky rope skips along from Gemini t15 to the Pisces t4 tail, tracing the position of the spring equinox in the last three Ages, or four Ages if Taurus is given its due as a double type. As in all the works in this study, with a rare few possible exceptions noted, this is spiritual art, not astronomy, and incidental resemblances are due to the structure of nature and perception, the source and origin of structure in culture, including zoology, grammar, time cycles and icons. Each is perceived as a separately structured whole by our built-in capacity for gestalt, and inhibition against animism. Gestalt itself is a function of the repertoires of archetype, since we choose classification attributes, usually very simple ones such as shape, colour, movement and size, within our perception boundaries. North American rock art has a variety of bag people, ball people, V people and bell people, some with figures on or in them, as in rock art worldwide. The African equivalents include coat (karos) people. Celestial polar markers and the horizontal plane tag the inspiration as Age Taurus-Aries.

Lion dragons

Type Aries t3 t18 as lions flanking a dragon, with lion people and antelope people (Babylonian seal with Enkidu and lions. Sitchen. Mindprint analysis by Edmond Furter). Composite and antithetical (facing) animals are typical of Aries. See a lion person in South African rock art at theme t1, antelope people in many rock art images, and an antelope mask man on a Mexican shield at theme t15. A celestial pole on the Gemini t15 shoulder, and the horizontal plane, tag the inspiration to Age Taurus 1 -Taurus 2, among the few works in this study of that early inspirational pedigree. Markers for Age Aries are less distinct, but also linked here for comparison.

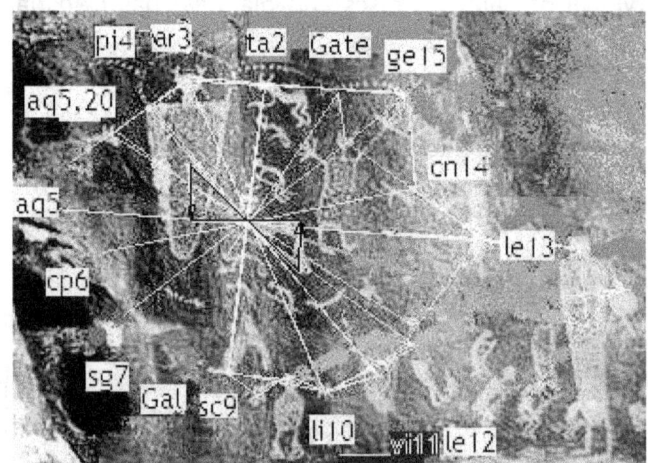

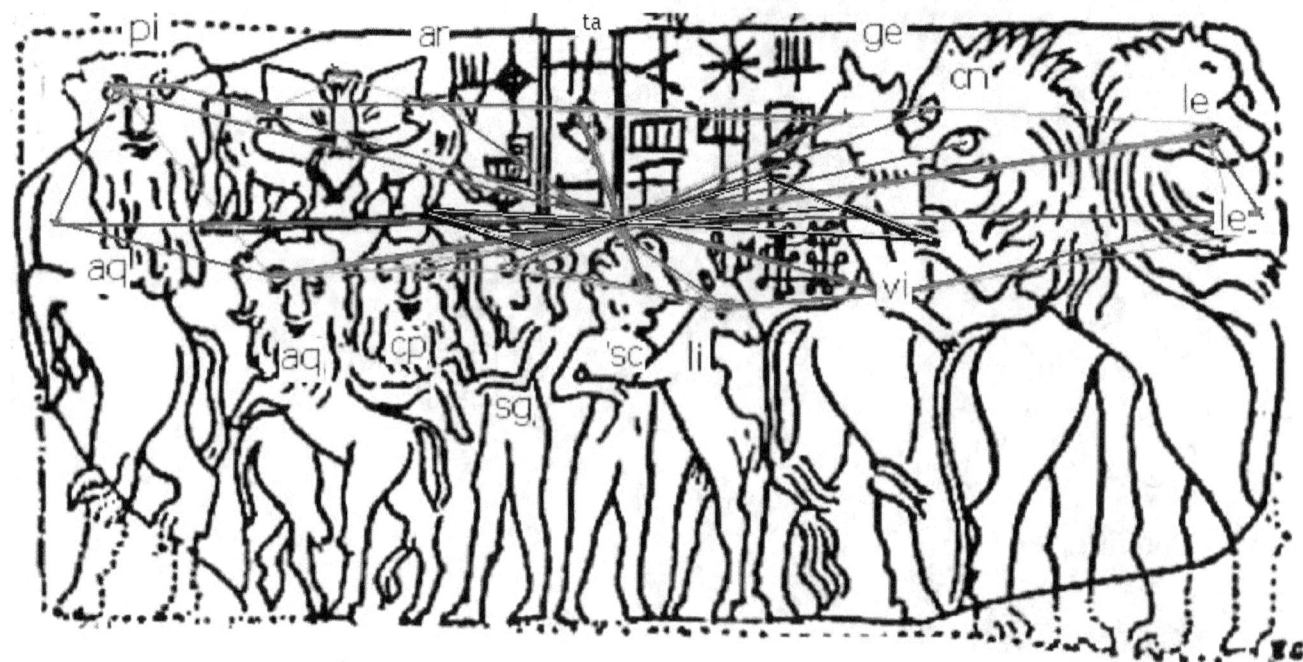

Horned animal as a seed bag apron

Type Aries t3 as a woman's apron or seed bag (African cup rollout of women with digging sticks. Ditsong Museum of cultural history. Mindprint analysis by Edmond Furter). The singular item resembles a 'horned animal' of Chinese mythology, some cast in bronze plaques (inset from a Chinese state exhibition tour, Ditsong Museum, 2009). Rituals in Ethiopia and Zimbabwe, involve women taking crop seeds to a priest to bless by inserting a phallic stone into a bag, thus a thong-shaped bag also signifies a female apron and genitals. Digging sticks weighted by bored stones were common practical, symbolic and perhaps currency items in the Iron Age. Crops do not require ploughing, merely small holes, a practice slowly reclaiming the destructive ploughing practice of commercial agriculture of the last century (Olga Lehmann; Look beyond the wind, biography of Hans Merensky. Merensky Foundation). Taurus t2 Pleiades is figured by a digging stick adjacent to the seed bag, standing for spring, rain, ploughing, planting, seeds and grain (see a Mexican cup and discussion of beer and (isi)Limela Digging Stars at theme t2).

The celestial pole is marked by an inferred jaw, tagging the inspiration to Age Pisces-Aquarius.

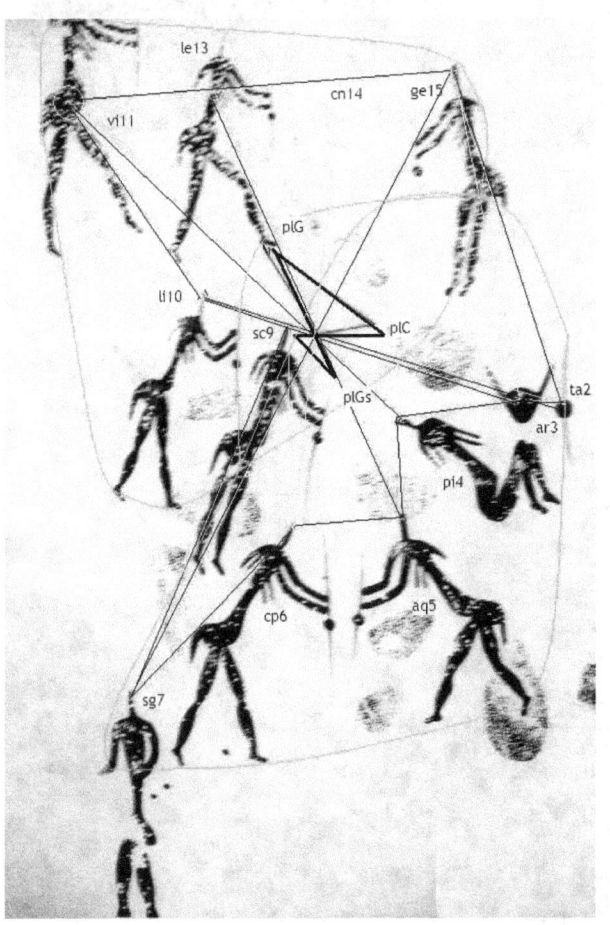

Pirates of Triangulum

Pirates and weapons cults identify with the icon of Aries t3 t18 Triangulum, incidental with a dagger-shaped asterism hovering over Aries, expressing dragons and their cure. In myth it is linked to the Taurus t2 Perseus dagger, sometimes figured as a massive sword in the place of Andromeda, required to behead the adjacent Medusa. A Gaulish Armorican tribe identified themselves with Aries, and minted coins bearing a large sword. The Roman senators who assassinated Julius Caesar minted a pileus of freedom flanked by daggers in their field coins in the ensuing civil war. See daggers and crosses of Montreal de Sos at theme t4.

Vikings, an example of arch piracy, sailed on dragon-headed ships, and their art abounds with swords (see a Swedish Fafnir dragon ribbon at theme t3 t18). Tribes of convenience adopt the attributes of pirate bands worldwide; feathers, coats, drugs, violence, hyperactivity, fluid alliances, fast transport, weapons, shock tactics, reigns of terror, hoarding, racial mixture, dictatorial leadership, rogue's codes and slang language (adapted from Neil Price; Vikings. Aberdeen University; Origins Centre guest lecture, 2012). If mountain pirates seem a far-fetched idea, consider Korana history, including their boats and cannons on the Orange River near Uppington as a seamless extension of their horse-mounted regime in the semi-desert Northern Cape.

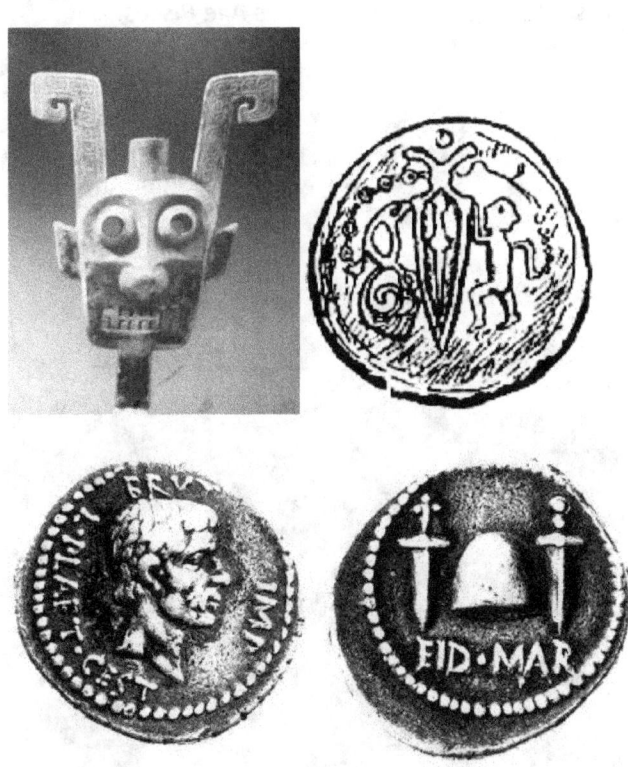

A U-shaped cattle gate calendar

Type Aries t3 as a U-shaped cattle gate ritual (Algerian Sahara, bovine ritual at Ouan Derbauen by Fulani nomads. Ankonline.com. Mindprint analysis by Edmond Furter). Two palm branches are bent to form a palette-shaped gate, a ritual recalling Moses in Midian, or Jacob 'showing coloured sticks' to his stock at a watering hole to multiply more than Laban's. See palm branch gates with notches as calendric devices at theme t14, staffs at theme t10, and scapegoats at theme t6, all cardinal (squared) to one another. Aries t3 t18 as an axe, knife, palette, throne, queen with a shield, U-shape and entwined necks, is a calendric zero point.

Desert princes time their husbandry to the best hours, months and years by cosmic structure. Chinese year cycles include Bull in the Gate, the recent one in the 60 year cycle of five twelve-year rounds being in 2009. Agriculture and archetype converge, just as astrology and alchemy (proto chemistry) are parallel expressions of the same structure. There is no esoteric or scientific error in using celestial cycles to calibrate cosmic logic, as long as the co-incidence does not extend to physical influence. Astronomy is one of many clock dials that tell archetypal time, but requiring so much data, interpretation and translation into worldly affairs that physical events often precede computed outcomes, a false triumph of craft over intuition.

A celestial pole on the hoof in the U-shaped gate threshold tags the inspiration as Age Pisces.

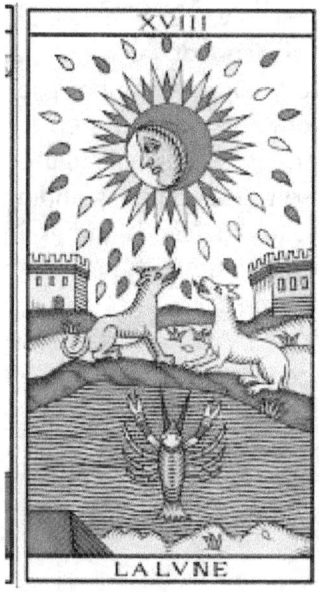
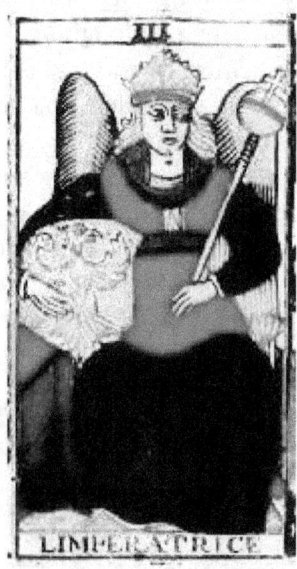

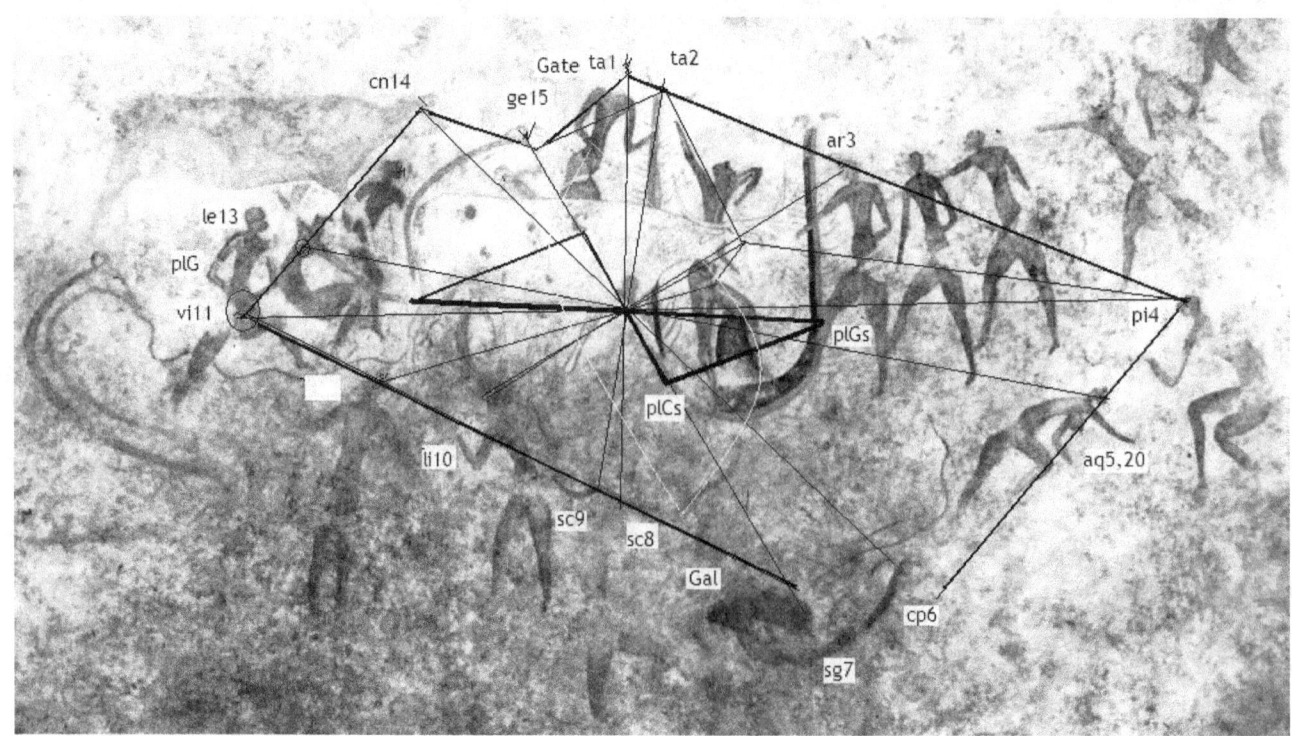

A python and apples oracle

Type Aries t3 t18 as a snake raised on a tree (Greek vase rollout with Hercules at the Hesperidian apple tree. Mindprint analysis by Edmond Furter). One of his twelve tasks take Hercules to an oracle of pythia, snake priestesses in trance on irmsul tree chairs (see the Externsteine chair at theme t4), here identified as Sagittarius t7 and the galactic centre. Scorpius t9 t8 Serpens or Sagittarius t7 Scutum (Shield) is the snake head, licking or spitting out a flint knife. All tribes and nations establish oracles; Amazons (Artemis at Ephesus in Turkey), Greeks (Zeus at Delphi, Olympus, and elsewhere), Egyptians (Amun at Siwa), Chinese, Romans (underworld at Baia near Rome), Germans, Africans (Zimbabwe Matobo shrines, see t8), South Americans (Nazca lines), Mexicans and Australians (shelters on song lines).

The celestial pole is marked by a hand and an apple of dusk on the Gemini axis, tagging the inspiration as Age Pisces, although earlier Ages are also provided for.

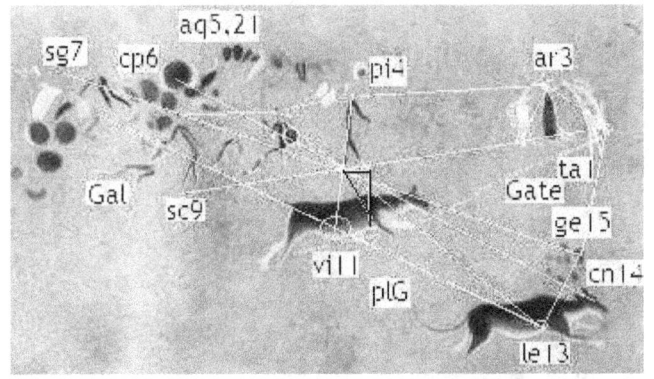

An antelope bower gate

Type Aries t3 as a bower gate, trap, or slaughter post (South Africa, KZN 179hc bower. Vinnicombe. Mindprint analysis by Edmond Furter). Two saplings are bent and tied to form the device with symbolic and subconscious structural meanings, as an inverted U gate, or wild game version of a domestic ritual (see palm branch gates with notches at Cancer t14). Scorpius t8 Galactic centre is a palette shape, continuing the general Arian theme. Leo t13 is uniquely figured as a lion with antelope head (see lion people and antelope people together in a Babylonian seal at theme t3). The neurological school in archaeology understands entoptic visions as progressing from shapes, to stick figures, to naturalistic figures (Lewis-Williams and Dowson; Through the veil: San rock paintings and the rock face. South African Archaeological Bulletin 45). Blobby shapes raise the possibility that visual inspiration could be an axial arrangement of amorphous (formless) blobs morphing into buck bags. See theme t7. See semi-geometric figures in a Bolivian disc at theme t12. See two bags held by Leo t12 Ursa, or by the facing Libra t10 Bootes, in Tarot trump 12 (Hanged man).

A sky rope from the Virgo t11 womb to the Aries t3 antelope bower could imply that they are newly born, or manifesting, but there are usually no conceptual links between these two types. A celestial pole on a foot between the Gemini and Taurus axes, tag the inspiration as Age Pisces-Aquarius.

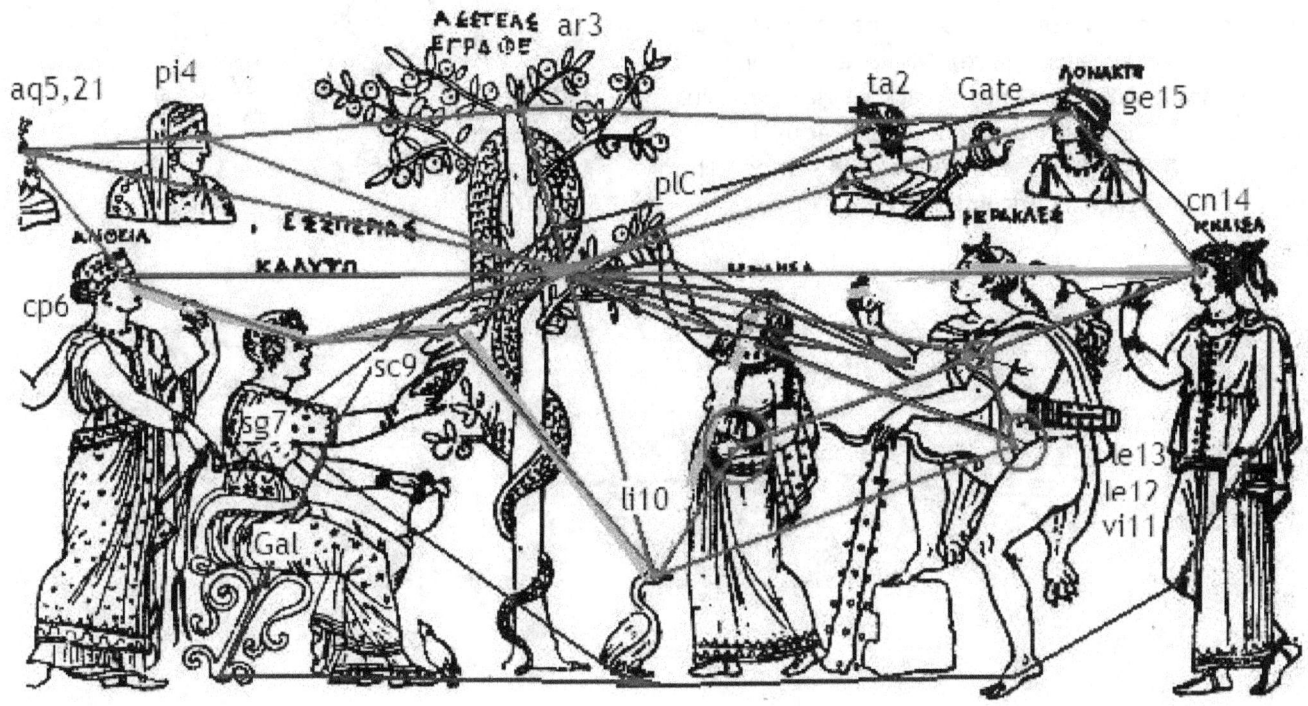

Type Aries t3 t18;
Moon dragons

A moon bag with an antelope

Type Aries t3 as a buck bag and moon (Mongolia,
Ningxia bag. Mindprint analysis by Edmond Furter).
Aries and its opposite Libra t10, also appear in moon
circles in Egypt's Dendera zodiacs (see the Decans
section). Leo t13 is a supine sperm shape (see
spermiform figures in a Bolivian disc at theme t12).
Aries t3 Triangulum is sometimes two back-to-back
skin bags (see the Dendera round zodiac in the
Decans section, where icons, hieroglyphs, Egyptian
and Greek constellations co-exist). Aries t3 t18
attributes include axe, knife, palette, shield, pool,
drum, bowl, gestation, calendar, moon, eclipse and
mirror image. Buck bags at other types express the
themes of skin, bones, spirals and manifestation.
Several crop circles express Aries t3 t18 and its
cardinals as moons and pendulums. Polar markers
and the horizontal plane tag the inspiration to Age
Pisces-Aquarius, our current era.

A cosmic python

Type Aries t3 t18 as an okapi (giraffe-zebra hybrid)
or long-necked antelope, in a triple imprint, right
sphere (Zimbabwe, Gulubabwe, Elspeth Parry,
Amabooks. Mindprint analysis by Edmond Furter).
Pisces t19 Cetus (Whale) is a python as a kind of ark
carrying animals and people, its back from Pisces t4
to Scorpius t9, its belly extended along watery
decans three quarters around the equator, via
Eridanus (River), Lepus (Hare), Monoceros (Unicorn),
and Hydra (Water snake). Its back carries Aquarius
t5 t20, t5 t21, Capricornus t6, Sagittarius t7 and
Scorpius t8, its curled tail figuring the sting. The
vertical plane tags the inspiration as Age Pisces.

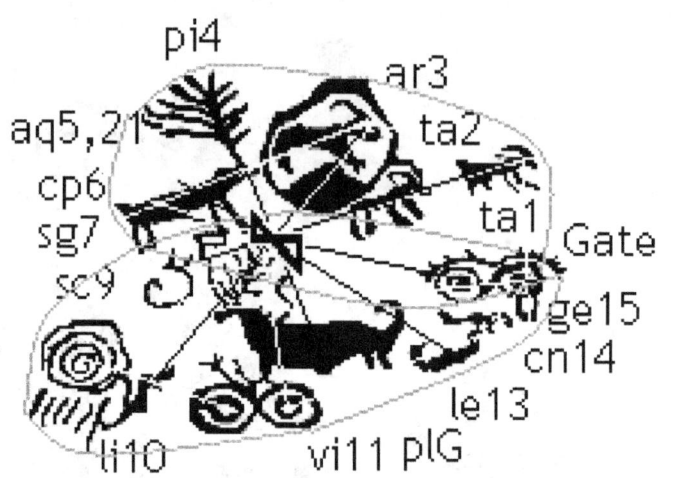

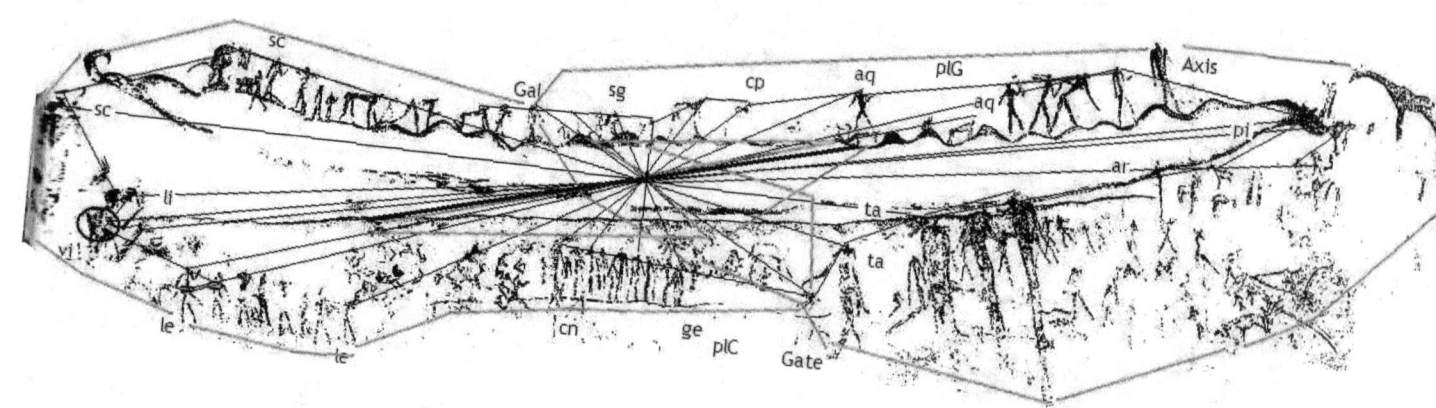

Odin's eclipse map

Type Aries t3 t18 as dragon banners (Sweden, Fafnir and dragon ribbons. Mindprint analysis by Edmond Furter). Capricornus t6 is a tail knot, as it has in astrology, and in its VS-shaped sigil. Here, the sigil on the top knot spells a lunar node, one of the two mobile points on the ecliptic equator where the moon crosses from north to south, or south to north, named dragon's head and dragon's tail in Chinese astrology. Lunar nodes set up the opportunity for eclipses, if the sun or the earth's shadow happens to be in the same place on the ecliptic. They occur in Saros cycles of between 18 and 19 years. Since the two luminaries are the same apparent size, each about half a degree in diameter, the moon could obscure the sun, or earth's shadow core could obscure the moon. Moon shadow tracks on earth (eclipse paths) occur in complex cycles of mainly latitudinal (horizontal) shallow S curves. Nordic myths, and this schooled rock art work, express calendric and eclipse themes, independent of the sequence and structure of mindprint (see the Narmer palette and Mexican dragons at theme t3 t18).

Taurus t2 is a dragon swallowing another Gemini t15 is the hero Fafnir, crossing the galaxy at the gate. Cancer t14 Ursa Minor (and thus the celestial pole and midsummer) is on the hoof of the rampant foreleg of Leo t13, usually Odin's horse of many legs, Sleipnir (see Gotland boundary stones at theme t13). The foreleg is also typical of Aries t3 as Lamb of God, clutching a standard post holding a banner above, here as a frame.

Libra t10 has an arm up and a staff as usual, here a kind of Aaron's tree and caduceus. Libra t10 as Fortune often turns a kind of wheel with life cycle emblems, here forming a subsidiary cycle (a circle is added for clarity). Scorpius t9 Lupus is a wolf, a decan it shares with Libra t10. Aquarius t5 t21 is vari-coloured as usual, and shares the Ygdrassil tree with Pisces t4. The tree expresses the concept of an axis through the ecliptic and galactic poles, on the galactic polar axle (see axial trees in Mexico, as in the Palenque temple at theme t1 t16). Pisces t4 was sometimes figured as two birds on two ribbons, notably in Persia.

It is hard to believe that the underlying structure of holographic iconography went unnoticed by the artist, or by the poet (the likes of Snorri Sturlasson), who composed (re-compiled, redacted or reviewed) the now familiar myth cycle, but harder to believe that poets and artists consciously understood their conventional tales, images and cultures as expressions of the archetypal sequence and structure. They did not have books, galleries or internet, and could hardly be expected to know that all cultures had the same dragons, moon bags, heroes and cosmic trees. Poets and artists who did tour the world, took language and stylistic differences as evidence of independent arbitrary origins and development, and their own myths and styles as superior. What they borrowed was quietly assimilated.

The celestial pole is marked by the horse's jaw, tagging the inspiration to Age Aries, incidental with the theme. A knot provides for Age Pisces, incidental with the work.

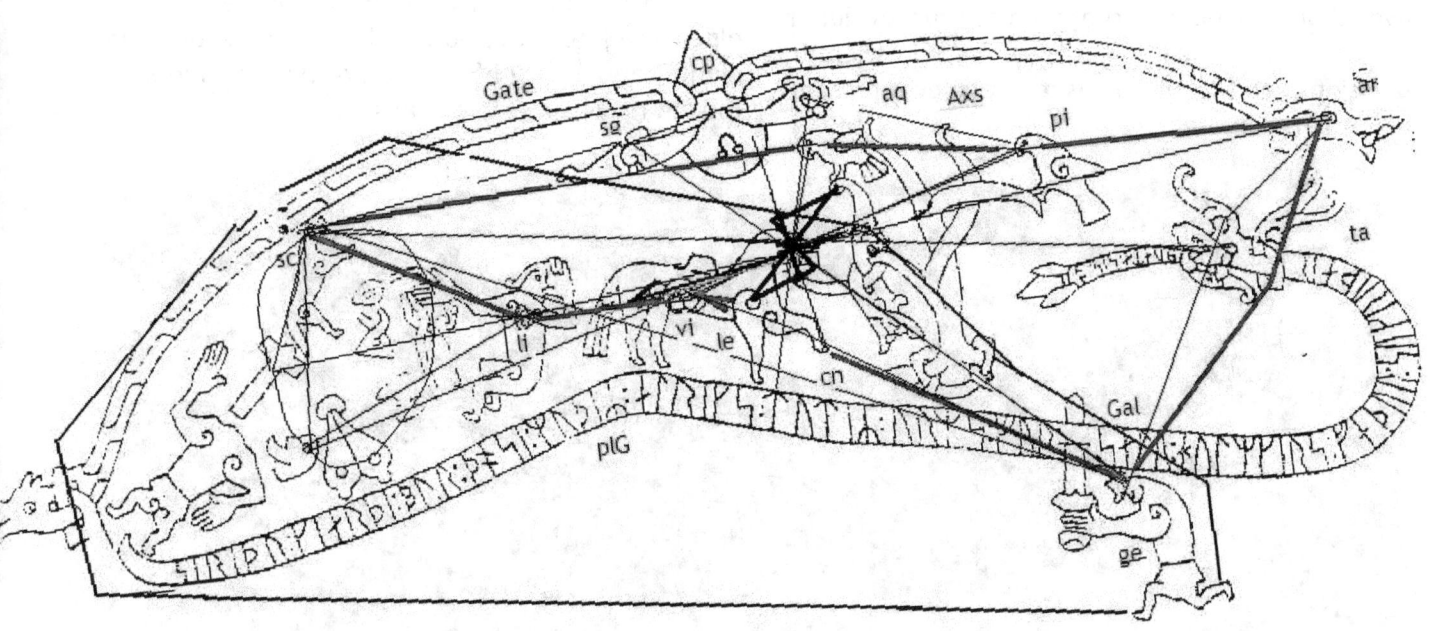

Ostriches in paradise

Type Aries t3 t18 as ostriches in Eden, in a double imprint (Egypt, Naqada pot, grave 454. Mindprint analysis by Edmond Furter). Aries is opposite Libra t10 Bootes or Serpens as a butterfly tree wheel, which links the double imprint. Ostriches are human counterparts in myth. The sigil of the Egyptian concept of balance and justice, Maat, is an ostrich feather (see a judgement scene at theme t5 t20. See ostriches at theme t12 t13). Feathers incapable of flight also signify incarnated souls. Their large eggs are linked to resurrection (Watkins Dictionary of symbols), and spring festivals such as Easter. In spiritual hierarchy, traceable in Bushman myth and elaborated in Helena Blavatsky's theosophy, the long neck of this survivor of the dinosaur age signifies a half risen state from gravity, above reptiles (which are proto-mammals of warm and cold blood), with the pineal gland as third eye (P Myburgh; Theosophy Johannesburg presentation, 2013). Theosophy, based on visionary cosmology, is cast in a quasi-evolutionary and quasi-historic mould. Bushman ethnography expresses archetypal structure in parables of the animal kingdom, including ostriches as proto-humans. They are sacrificed to allow people to rule the animal world. Myth makes no distinction between saurian, primate and human eras, but speaks of a time before time. Theosophy speaks of eras such as Lemurian, Atlantean and Fall, yet sees their creatures or souls as ever present. Some Theosophical writers obscure archetypal and spiritual perspectives by assigning quasi-historical dates to a progression of physical incarnation, tagged to scientific dating, and extended forward in ever shorter periods of supposed spiritual evolution on earth. Bushmen have fewer pseudo-scientific delusions, and their myths express ever-present, individual processes.

Ostrich had fire, spoke, and held coals under his wing. He was tricked by a promise of berries into a patch of thorns where man could barter fire for his release. In art, as in myth, practical implications such as down feathers for tinder, ostrich sinews for bowed fire churns, or arms-up, arms-back ostrich dances, are not the origin, sustenance, function or full explanation of myth. A larger complex of interrelated practical, visual and structural logic sustains myth. Aries t3 t18 involves eternal repetition, improvement, exploitation, sacrifice, balance, renewal, crossing consciousness levels, healing, and calendars. There is little logical or practical reason for Bushman myth to link ostriches to the moon, apart from their large eggs, yet they consistently do, despite speaking several different languages. Ostrich eggs are hung in Eastern Orthodox churches as resurrection symbols, and appear in Arabic and Portuguese exploration legend, owing more to archetype than to occasional eyewitnesses. In Theosophy, the Adamic soul is seen as halved, and half risen, incidental with the twined necks of Aries t3 t18 as antithetical dinosaurs (see and Babylonian dragons in the polar section). Annual flotilla excursions from river valleys into desert wadis continued until the Nile was dammed. See boat themes in Nordic and Egyptian rock art and art. See Hathor as an arms-up dancer, and as a cow head on the Narmer palette at theme t3 t18. See tree and paradise scenes at themes t6, t10 and t14. See Maat and wheel images at theme t10. See H-people dancers in Turkey and American Indian art. See mountain ranges as paradise borders in Mideast and USA art.

A celestial polar marker on the central ostrich feet on the right, tags the inspiration to Age Aries-Pisces, in the last centuries BC. Naqada culture is much older. The artefact could be a late example, or some identifications may be in error, or polar markers on the left may be invisible or absent.

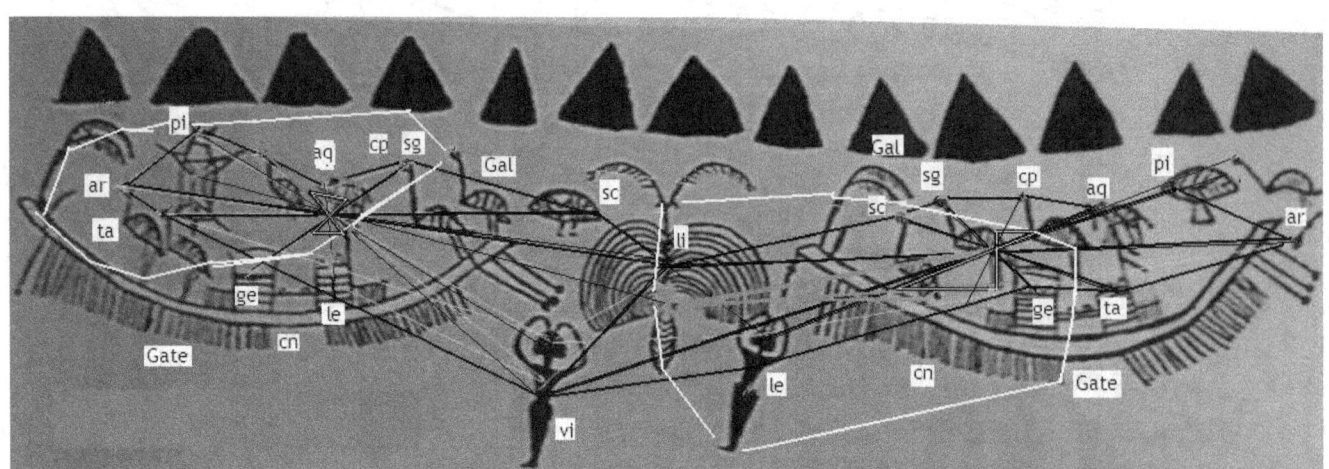

Solomon's cattle bag

Type Aries t3 t18 as the tail of a cattle bag or moon, pool, drum or gate (Algerian Tassili massif, Tissoukai cattle circle. Ankhonline.com. Mindprint analysis by Edmond Furter). See a turtle giant in USA Cienega Mesa art at theme t2 t17. The image recalls Solomon's legendary brazen vessel and altar, traceable in Grecian temples. Archaeology does not reconcile the Biblical Solomon with the temple in Jerusalem, but there are candidate sites in Sudan, Persia, Babylonia, Syria, Santorini, Crete, Egypt, and Greece. The same ensemble of a temple, pillars, vessels, altars, cattle stock, drums, ritual and calendric calculation existed in every Bronze Age city, and in temples and burials of desert princes in the Sahara.

Scorpius t9 Lupus could be a canine or feline, an attribute shared with Libra t10, where it often turns a wheel of fortune, as here (see a Renaissance Wheel emblem with a wolf at the handle). Ambiguation between Scorpius and Libra extends to their opposites at Taurus and Aries, where the V-shaped raised arm of Libra appears as an extra Taurus (see the mystical basked between Taurus and Aries on a Roman sarcophagus at theme t11). Virgo t11's womb over the horns of the circle is extended by the bag or pool. The heads of Leo t12 t13 and Virgo t11 share space, confirming that the position of both their eyes is immaterial to mindprint since their heart and womb are on their axes. Celestial poles are tagged by the horizontal plane to Age Pisces late, in recent centuries.

An Adamic paradise

Type Aries t3 t18 as two ecliptic poles, in a double imprint (Roelant Savery; Paradise, 1626. Berlin State Museum. Mindprint analysis by Edmond Furter). Aquarius t5 t20 t21 appears as an Adamic group and as a giraffe group. Celestial polar markers are uncertain, but the vertical plane in both spheres tag the inspiration to Age Aries, any time from about BC 1500 up to the last centuries BC, predating the work by about 3000 years, incidental with the theme of a past sufficiently distant to be imagined as idyllic.

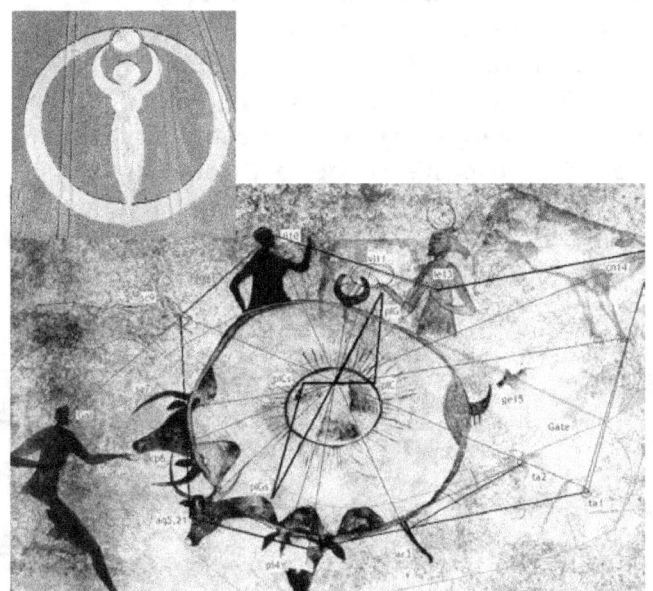

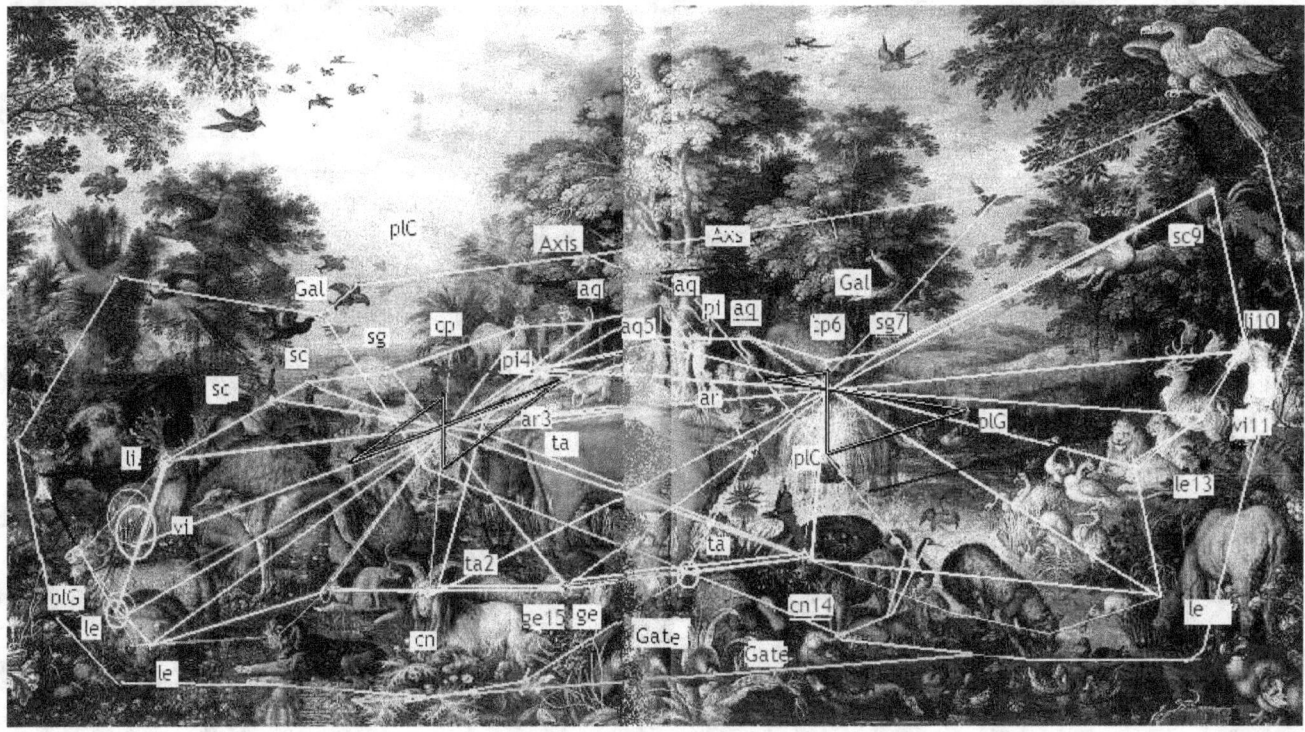

Three paradises

Type Aries t3 t18 as a turtle, and as a hunter named Ostrich, and as a crocodile, in a triple imprint (South Africa, Cyril Coetzee; T'Kama Adamastor. Wits University, 1997. Ivan Vladislavic, Wits Press 2000. Mindprint analysis by Edmond Furter). The 9m long canvas serialises events from an Andre P Brink novel, First life of Adamastor, a parody of Camoens' Os Luisidades, itself an extension of Atlas and other classical myths. Camoens invented Atlas' brother, Adamastor, with stock episodes such as a foam maiden, wooden idol, tricked monster turned to rock, repeated effort (as of the Flying Dutchman), and re-incarnation. Brink applied Camoens and myth to socio-political commentary through indigenous eyes. Coetzee serialises the novel with stock woodcut themes from early travel books by alchemical printers. He was inspired to add an Adamastor theme to two other large canvases in the skywell of the library, before finding the commission, and then the Brink novel. Coetzee is an art academic, and studied esoteric traditions, yet nothing in his writing, analysis of this work by other academics, a presentation at the Theosophical Society or a site visit, hinted at conscious knowledge of an archetypal sequence or axial grid in art.

Colonising paradise

T3 t18 Aries as a turtle, triple imprint left sphere.
T1 t16 Taurus as hunter 'Ostrich', signalling 'giraffe'
T2 t17 Taurus as Eve, mirror, Medusa (twisted)
T3 t18 Aries as a turtle female (dragon eggs)
T4 t19 Pisces Cetus as a turtle male below in parody
T5 t20 Aquarius as the healer Chameleon (colour)
T5 t21 Aquarius as the healer's blue hat (colour)
T6 Capricornus as a lamb bound for sacrifice
T7 Sagittarius as a naked maiden baptised
T8 Scorpius as a hunter, strong with wine
T9 Scorpius as a ram, craned neck [out of place]
T10 Libra as soldiers with staffs
T11 Virgo as wombs of holy mother, halo and ship
T12 Leo as the heart of swan ship
T13 Leo as the heart of swan egg boat
T14 Cancer as a coloniser, baptiser (twine and polar)
T15 Gemini as an abduction group.
Pole E as Baptist's solar plexus. Pole G as holy mother's heart. Pole G south as baptised girl's palm. Pole C as baptist's jaw. Pole C south as baptist's genitals. These markers tag the inspiration as Age Aries. The tag predates the work by about 2300 years, typical of modern designs with strong Aries themes.

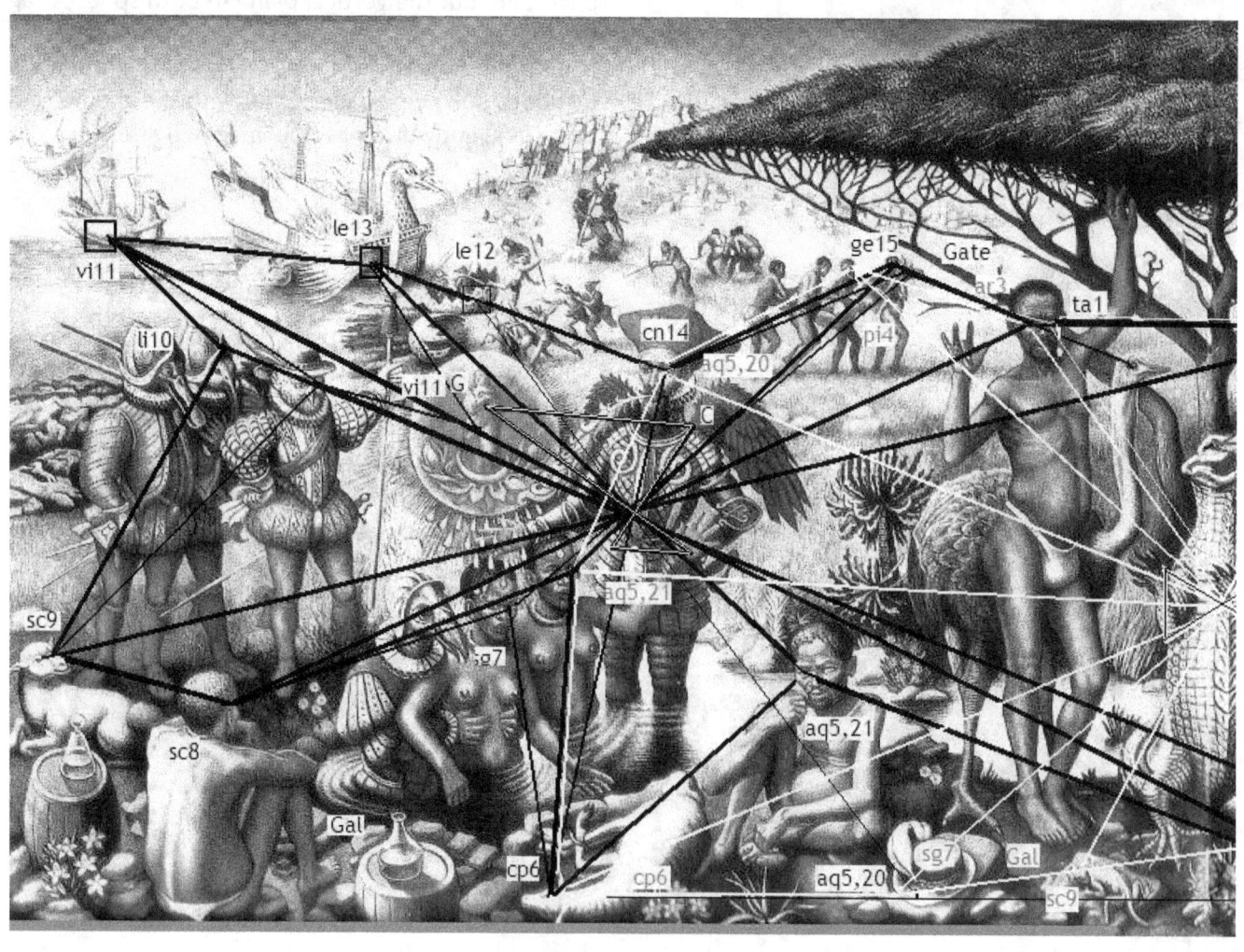

Paradise imperfect

Type Aries t3 t18 as T'Kama (Ostrich, 'Da Gama') Adamastor, in a triple imprint, central sphere. Some figures maintain their identity, others switch to their underlying attributes, here incidental with the parody theme. Triple imprints are rare, hinting that one of the spheres is splitting in two.

T2 t17 Taurus as Eve, mirror, Medusa (twisted)

T3 t18 Aries as man 'Ostrich', 'Giraffe' (necks)

T4 t19 Pisces as abduction group

T5 t20 Aquarius as baptist, uniform (colour, action)

T5 t21 Aquarius as maiden baptised (colour)

T6 Capricornus as lamb bound for sacrifice

T7 Sagittarius as healer's hat (bag)

T9 Scorpius as chameleon (long tail)

T10 Libra as turtle rearing up

T11 Virgo as turtle womb

T12 Leo as hunter captured and inverted

T13 Leo as heart of soldier with prominent chest

T14 Cancer as colonial captor with twine (time)

T15 Gemini as jackal man and re-abduction (churn).

Pole E as crocodile heart. Pole G as rabbit thigh. Pole G south as crocodile thumb. Pole C as Eve's thigh. Pole C south as crocodile elbow. The inspiration is tagged as Age Aries-Pisces.

Departure from paradise

Type Aries t3 t18 as a crocodile in a triple imprint, right sphere (Cyril Coetzee. Mindprint analysis by Edmond Furter).

T3 t18 Aries as crocodile dragon

T2 t17 Taurus as Eve, mirror, Medusa (twisted)

T15 Gemini as re-abduction group (churn)

T14 Cancer as colonial captor with twine (time)

T13 t12 Leo as mercurial homunculus in halo

T11 Virgo as swan ship womb and ship's bust

T10 Libra as oxen (horns W-shaped)

T9 t8 Scorpius as raptor trussing hunter (strong)

T7 Sagittarius as raptor trussing hunter

T6 Capricornus as captor's heel

T5 t21 Aquarius as trussed hunter (horizontal)

T4 t19 Pisces as raptor soldier.

Pole E as rope binder's hand Pole G as rope binder's shoulder. Pole G south as rope binder's lower hand. Pole C as rope roll. Pole C south as rope binder's hip. The inspiration is tagged as Age Aries-Pisces, confirmed by the theme of transition from dragon to baptism, hunter to hunted, spirit to flesh, game to domestic stock, paradise to prison, arrival to departure.

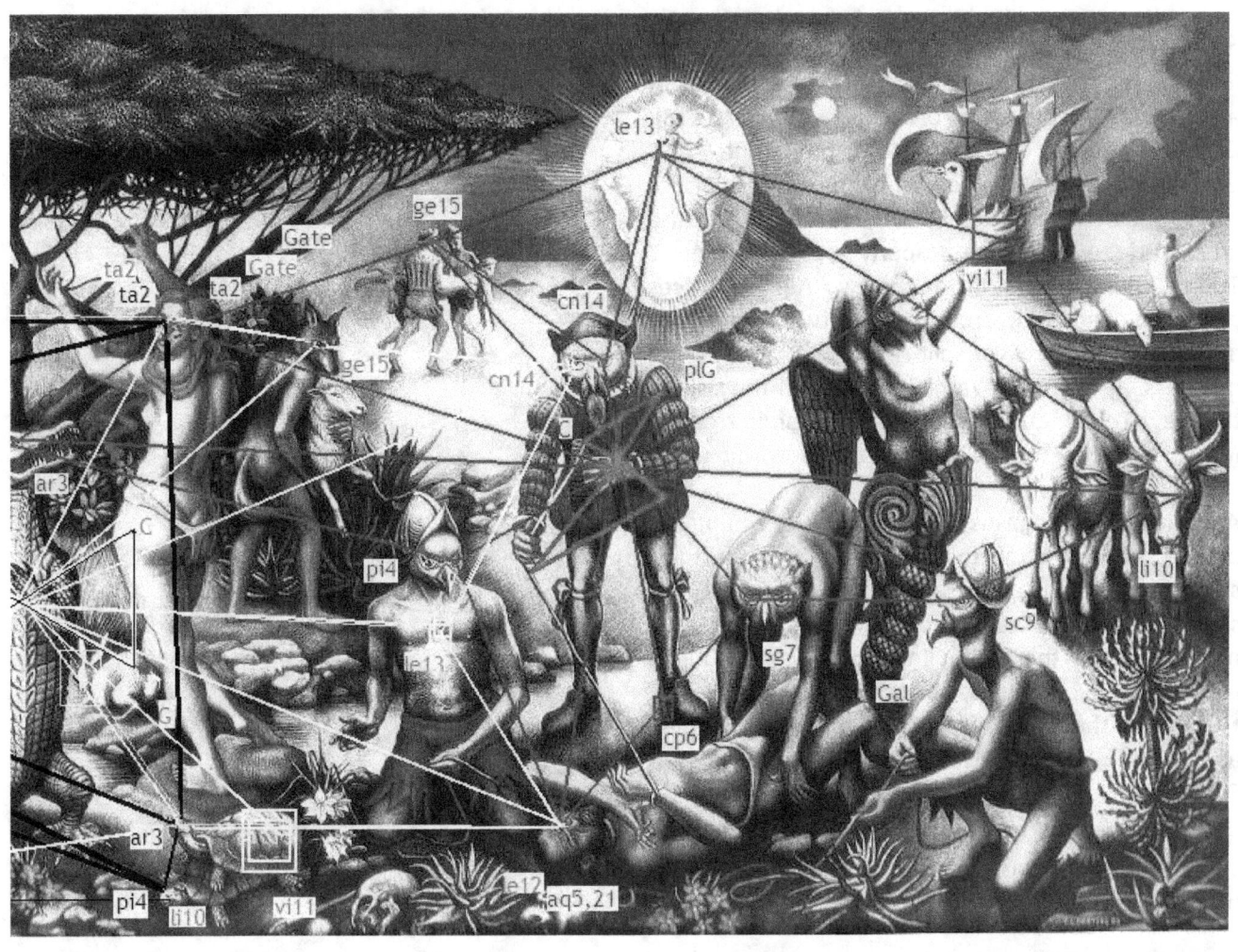

Type Pisces t4 t19; Sun king

A rent veil

Type Pisces t4 as a St John's cross >X< on an Agnus Dei (Lamb of God) post, over the vacated head of Christ as a sacrificed lamb (Germany, Externsteine deposition relief carving. Mindprint analysis by Edmond Furter). Capricornus t6, a sacrificial type, clutches the post instead. The post also figures the adjacent Aries t3 t18 Triangulum, Dagger, associated in the New Testament with Judas Iscariot and the Roman agenda. The attributed Gospel of Judas reveals the supposed betrayer as playing an archetypally ordained part in a sacrifice drama, and as chief exegete (explainer) of esoteric Christianity (R Kasser, Meyer and Wurst. National Geographic). Aries t3 Andromeda is Mary with a shield-shaped veil, its end knotted or twined, as Aries t3 t18 usually is. Gemini t15 is an apostle subduing or smiting Cancer t14, as in stock images of a king and his brother in Egypt (see the Narmer palette front in the Decans section in the text). Cancer t14 is sometimes a tree, here an Irmsul stool bent to a new purpose, incidental with the celestial pole moving from the meridians of Cancer to those of Gemini. The tripod theme also features in images of a labour of Hercules at an oracle (see theme t3 t18). Calendric themes include seasons, hours and Ages. Virgo t11 is a man marked on his hip, unless Pisces t4 is taken as the Lamb banner instead of the crossed tip, which more properly is part of Aries t3 Triangulum. Duplications at the two Aquarii, Pisces and Aries, and their opposites the two Leos, Virgo and Libra, indicate a split into two imprints in progress, as in the proverbial 'rending of the veil' in the New Testament crucifixion (see cosmic trees in Mayan art at theme t4, Pacific art, and Nordic art at theme t3).

Aquarius t5 t21 Pegasus is figured by the rectangular plaque, where the motto 'King of the Jews' (perhaps signifying a Canaanite sacrificial rite), is usually shown in religious art. Leo t13 is the heart of a monster below the groundline. Aquarius t5 t20 is in his usual active posture, opposite Leo t12 as a man trussed in the coils of a Hydra monster, a fallen angel often shown inverted (as in a carving of Shemhazai in Rosslyn chapel in Scotland).

Galactic poles are on the elbow of Virgo t11 and the vacated jaw of Christ that spoke the poetic words 'they know not what they do'. Celestial polar

markers on both hands of the ingressed Aquarius t5 t20 (the lower hand broken off, but probably touching Christ's hip), are on the Cancer-Capricornus axis, tagging the inspiration to the solstices of Age Aries, confirmed by mother Mary's eye at Aries t3, opposite Christ's and Mary Magdalene's eyes at Libra t10.

A polar axis to heaven

Type Pisces t4 as the joker god's genitals, in a double imprint (Mexico, Palenque sarcophagus lid relief carving. Mindprint analysis by Edmond Furter). See the iconographic role of genitals at funerals in Egyptian embalming scenes at theme t15 t0, and in Buddhist art at theme t8. The central figure is identified in archaeology as a deceased ruler falling into the underworld, or ascending to heaven. Mindprint confirms that he is part of two imprints. Pisces t4 t19 and its decans Pegasus (Horse) and Cetus (Whale), are figured here on a larger scale, as two rectangular underworlds or monster maws. The rectangular outer frame also repeats Pegasus (see a field, pool, manger or furnace at theme t4 t19, and a tomb, manger or horse at theme t5 t20). Inspirational dating of the lower sphere confirms the spring equinox in Pisces near Aquarius, over Cetus and under Pegasus, on the axial tree churn (see cosmic trees in Pacific art, and in Nordic art at theme t3 t18).

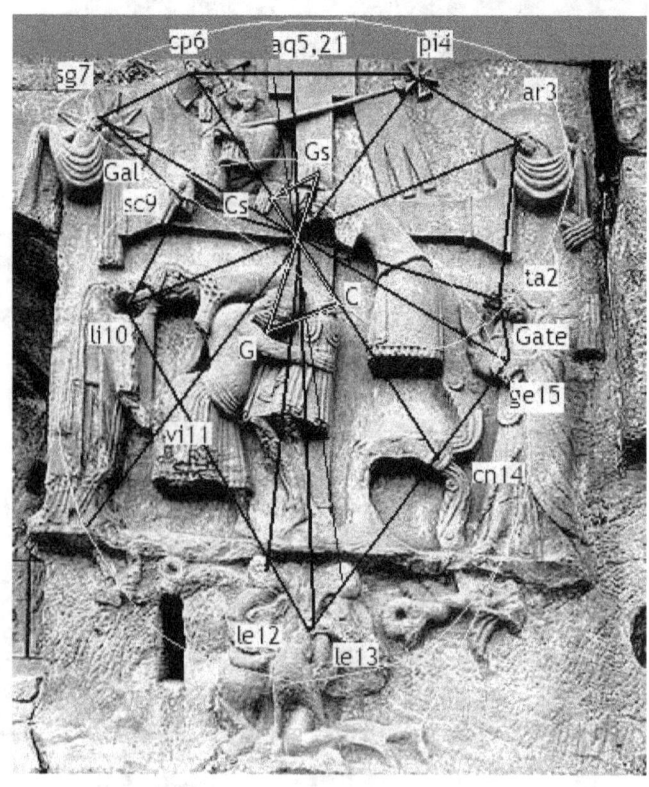

Pisces t4 is often a king with crossed legs and mace in decree posture, and its decan Pisces t19 a pair of solar twins flanking a furnace under a solar disc. The adjacent Aquarius t5 is often a high priest in blessing posture, and its decan Aquarius t20 an ancestral group at a tomb. The Palenque artist expressed all this, probably without astronomy lessons. Mayan astronomers may well have taken notes from inspired art on how best to label various parts of their sky. Floating faces at Aries and Scorpius recall ancestral visions typical of oracular experience (RF Paget; In the footsteps of Orpheus, finding and identification of the lost entrance to Hades, Oracle of the Dead).

The margin contains reference points for rotating copies or after-images of the pattern over itself, operating as a picture 'movie' generator (Maurice Cotterell; The amazing lid of Palenque).

Among the populist assumptions by one-horse theorists, is a concocted view of astronauts or space colonists and tutors with rockets and laser tools, as idle and ridiculous as ideas of Phoenician traders, spies and prospectors spreading bloodlines of demigods, or reptilian Illuminati populating and ruling the world by genetic manipulation. Conquerors did and do subjugate and inseminate distant empires, but they were, and are all human, and could never dictate the content or structure of spirituality or myth, only of ritual and religious styles. All myths include founders such as Oannes, sustained by glimpses of our collective subconscious realm, as real or unreal as sub-atomic energy shells or light particles. Science could do well to study our subconscious access to archetypal structure with equal diligence and budgets as are devoted to nuclear physics, or the official supposed Search for Extra-Terrestrial Intelligence (SETI).

Galactic equators (the three thin oblique circles) are more symmetrical than the irregularly angular ecliptic equators formed by the eyes of figures, as usual. Four galactic equators are stacked vertically, the two central ones merged in soap bubble fashion. Only double mindprints touching at or near one of the two polar axes allow this kind of linkage. Celestial polar markers in the top sphere on halved eyes and the vertical plane, tag the inspiration to Age Pisces, incidental with the identity of the main figure, and the Age of the work. Celestial polar markers in the lower sphere on the subtly tilted horizontal plane, tags the inspiration to Age Pisces-Aquarius, incidental with the base of the polar tree as current spring, somewhat prophetic for the work, but incidental with the Egyptian Duat low point between hour 4 and hour 5 (see the Seti 1 tomb decans at theme t8).

Avaris harbour

Type Pisces t4 Pegasus as a dignitary of a trade empire (Greece, Thera /Santorini Akrotiri mural. Mindprint analysis by Edmond Furter). The island was a rich Phoenician capital, a type of tower of Babel (see theme t1 t16), before its long dormant volcanic caldera, a bowl that probably included rings of land and sea, blew out. The event is linked by some authors to Plato's Atlantis fable, the Exodus, or among the preludes to the Trojan War. The name Atlantis may arise from oceanic trade. Avaris in the Egyptian delta was the seat of Hyksos and Phoenician kings, complete with pleasure gardens and exotic game, after Babylonian (Nineveh) and Persian examples (see water paradise themes in Egypt at theme t6, in China at theme t4, in Mexico and Indian colonial structures in Cambodia, expressed in civic water features, gardens and zoos). The Thera mural is on three or four lintels, and probably contains several mindprints. The same kinds of colonial themes appear on the skylight walls of the Wits University William Cullen Collections Library in Johannesburg, including Cyril Coetzee's T'Kama Adamastor (see theme t3). The architect had modelled the facade of the Petit Trianon at Versailles, and planned gold mining and international trade scenes for the skylight, over an equatorial inscription citing a Biblical verse on Phoenicians; 'They that go down to the sea to trade in ships'.

Leo t13 t12 and their opposites Aquarius t5 t21 t20 each figure five times, a unique contrivance, on a conscious level perhaps to cite all the nobles in the narrative. Celestial poles are apparently not marked, and the horizontal plane tags an impossible Age Aquarius, thus the work could be Age Taurus1, Taurus 2 (here calibrated by five axes), or Age Aries.

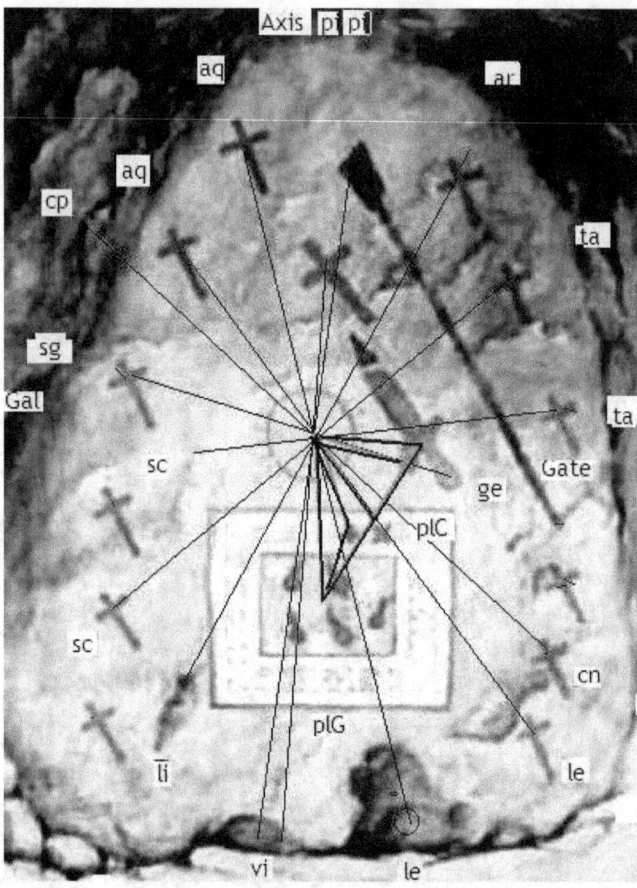

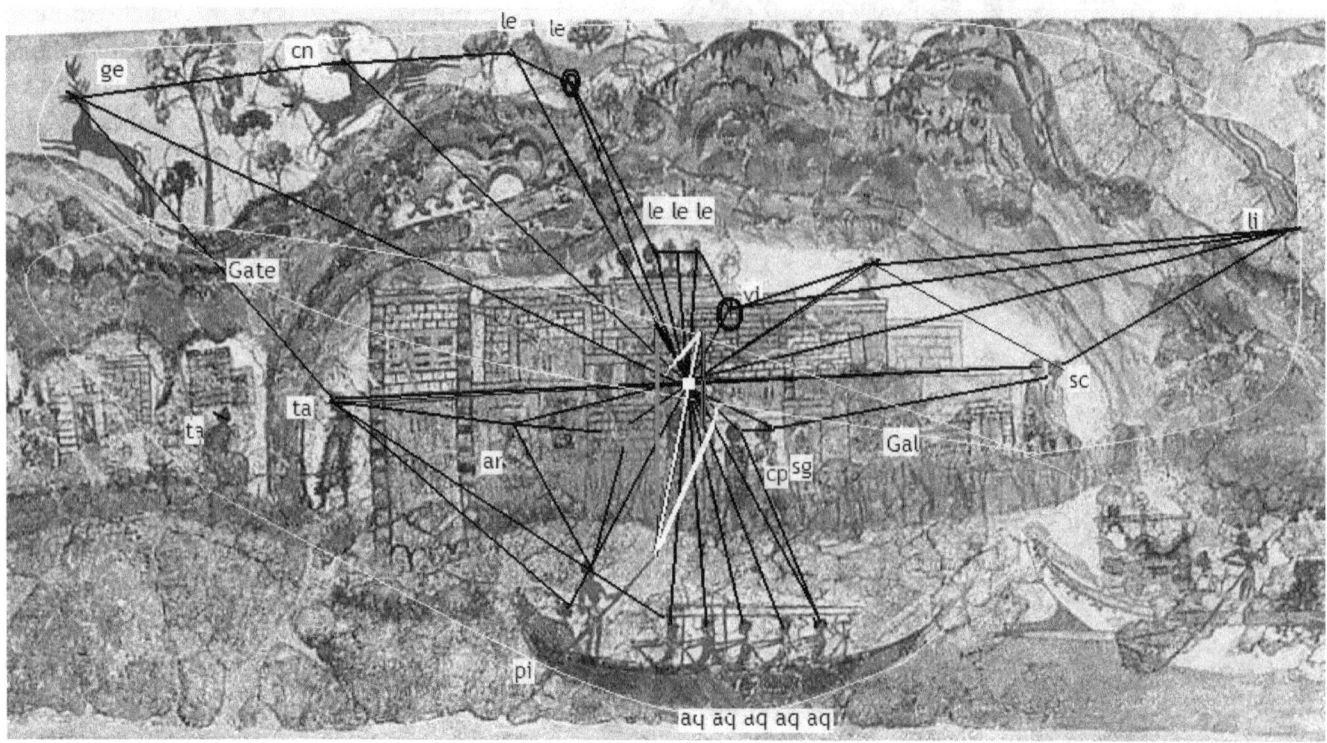

Polar axis over a camp

Type Pisces t4 Pegasus as an up-ended funerary oar over a rectangular camp or cemetery (France, Montreal de Sos grail theme painting in a cave. Perhaps an illustration to Eschenbach's Parsifal by A Gadal. Mindprint analysis by Edmond Furter).

The site is one of several linked to militant Christian initiation in the Crusades era, or pseudo-Templar revivals. Leo t13 as a reclining lion, and Virgo t11 as its quarry (hunt victim), or perhaps a lamb, flank the vertical axis from the central top ingressed cross, probably figuring the galactic south pole (see palette shapes with geometric figures in Scotland, and in Bolivian discs at theme t12).

The ecliptic pole is circled, one of very few works to prominently mark the focal point of mindprint (see a Swedish engraving of a ship under a starburst at theme t14). Five celestial polar markers along the camp margin and the sword hilt, form a kind of gauge of Ages, from Age Taurus 1, Age Taurus 2, Age Pisces, Age Pisces-Aquarius, to Age Aquarius.

The horizontal plane confirms the inspiration as Age Pisces-Aquarius, perhaps a little prophetic for the artist, or the work is a recent renovation, or freehand copy. If the oar blade is a spring marker, it confirms Age Pisces, at odds with the plane, but expected in a partly copied and partly renovated work. The oar recalls the Egyptian port and westernmost Nile mouth, Canopus (Oar) on the delta coast, which incidentally is an oar shape. In astronomical terms, Argo Carina Canopus (Ship Keel constellation, Rudder star) is a southern circumpolar star below the Gemini-Taurus gate, which is here figured by the crosspiece of the broken sword. The image links the concepts of summer at the oar blade, and spring at the sword cross, confirming the current axial era. Some figures may have a conscious function as solar and seasonal markers, typical of dagger shapes on stones exposed to small patches of seasonal sunlight, as at some sites in the Alps (so-called Iceman monoliths), USA, south America, Ireland and elsewhere, raising the possibility that the design is copied from a stone outside the cave, perhaps in a Bronze Age cemetery. Even without seasonal astronomy, the work is an iconographic delight.

A water paradise

Type Pisces t4 as a boatman and a duck (India, Buddha converts a Brahman. Mindprint analysis by Edmond Furter). See water paradise themes in an Egyptian coffin lid at theme t15 and in some Chinese tiles. Tight grouping of figures around the vertical axis is similar to the Santorini Atlantis mural at theme t4.

Celestial polar markers on the invisible oar blades tag the inspiration to Age Pisces-Aquarius.

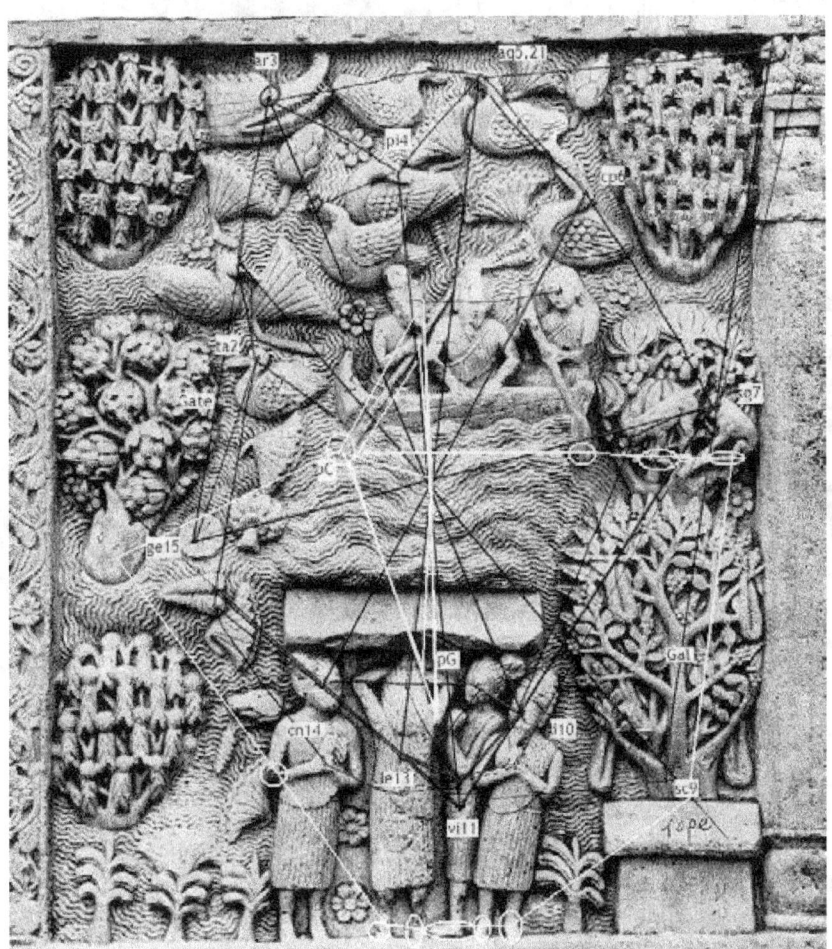

Type Aquarius t5 t20; World baptist and judge

Mandela as a composite triple type

Type Aquarius t5 t20 as Nelson Mandela (Mexico, Cuajiniciulapa Mandela Day festival mural, by South African artist Eljana van der Merwe. Sunday Times. Mindprint analysis by Edmond Furter). Aquarius often appropriates attributes of adjacent types (see a USA Piedra Pintada hand-drawn rock art copy at theme t5 t20) and lends some attributes to other figures. Mandela is a Xhosa, an eastern Bantu tribe with some admixture of Bushman genes and language. He is also the integrator of the highly diverse South African nation, with a half Portuguese wife (see a Bushman man and Portuguese woman as Adam and Eve in T'Kama Adamastor at theme t3 t18) thus Mandela is a 'painted', ordained figure, incidental with attributes of the type, and the South African rainbow flag. As herder, lawyer, chief, terrorist, prisoner, negotiator, politician, president, Nobel Peace Prize recipient, culture hero and icon, Mandela expresses Aquarius t5 t20, noted as priest, baptist, undertaker, shape-shifter and angel in the Tables and other images. Popular figurines feature Mandela with prior president FW De Klerk, who expresses the Pisces t4 t19 attribute of a twin (see Tarot trump 19, distinct from the unequal twins of Gemini t15). Here, Gemini t15 is a large mask or face, as it often is (see Salvador Dali; It just popped up). Taurus t1 t16 Orion is a tower, as it often is.

Virgo t11 is probably on Graca Machel's womb, cropped off the mural. Celestial poles on Mandela's ears, and the horizontal plane, tag the inspiration to Age Pisces late, incidental with his implied third eye and the implied sun behind him as Pisces (see Tarot trump 19, Sun), and furnace themes at the lighthouse and hut. Archetype does not respect the artist's conscious mind or agenda, but uses both to imprint itself. It also appears in commissioned works and collaborations, as this work is reported to be.

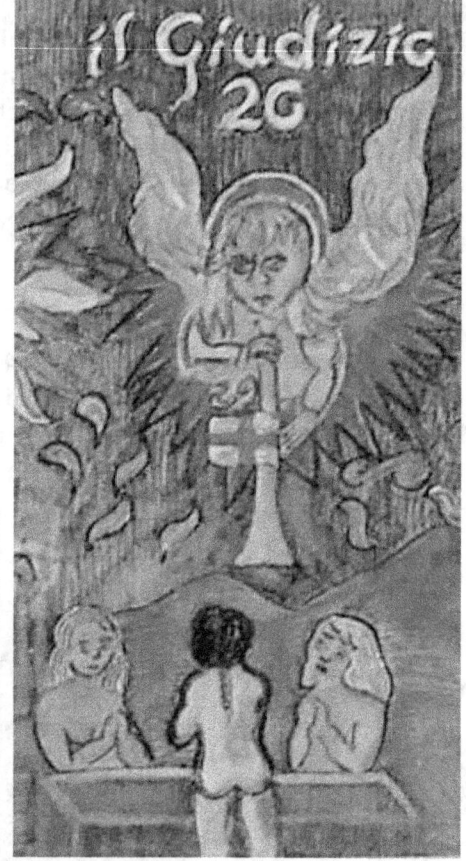

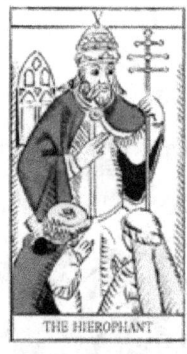

THE HIEROPHANT

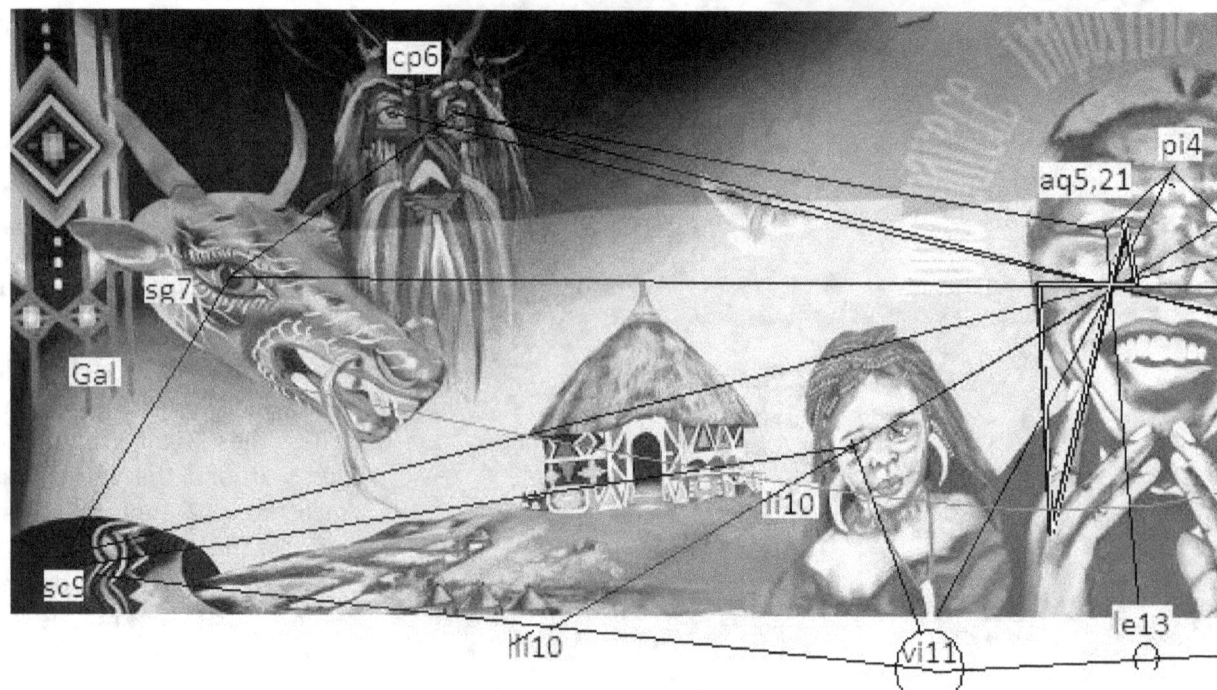

A priest blessing nature and ages

Type Aquarius t5 and Pisces t4 combined, as a priest blessing nature spirits (Egyptian papyrus, judgement hall west. Smithsonian Museum. Mindprint analysis by Edmond Furter). The lower register is an Aquarius t5 t20 judgement scene, as in Tarot trump 20. Leo t13 and Virgo t11 are figured by Osiris and Isis, who more often stand at Taurus t1 Orion and Auriga. Taurus t1 Orion here is the deceased brought before Osiris. Judgement functions are performed by the usual four Taurine cardinals; t2 bull (here an eagle griffin), t13 lion (here Osiris' heart, slightly misplaced since the axis also marks the Virgo t11 womb), t9 eagle (here a vulture or winged Horus eye), and t5 angel (here the Aquarius t5 priest).

The only doubled adjacent types in mindprint to be overlain by their own higher numbers as well, are Taurus t1 t16, Taurus t2 t17, Aquarius t5 t20 and Aquarius t5 t21.

Semi-regular doubling and overlap defeat one-on-one correspondence attempts (see the Attributes, Tables and Tarot section in the text).

Celestial polar markers on a series of about nine of the fourteen nature spirits, function as a gauge, calibrating eras in Age Aries and Age Pisces. The vertical plane confirms the inspiration as sometime during Age Pisces. The start of the gauge could be determined only if the angle of earth obliquity at the start of Age Taurus were known. Astronomy and archaeo astronomy assume only small and cyclic obliquity variations. The subconscious iconographic logic of mindprint probably does not extend to the relative lengths of the sides of polar triangles, just as the sixteen irregular and varying angular widths of the axial grid do not express any particular meaning. Even polar angles are close to the 'vanishing point' of the layers of meaning and structure that art could express, or that we could consciously read in art.

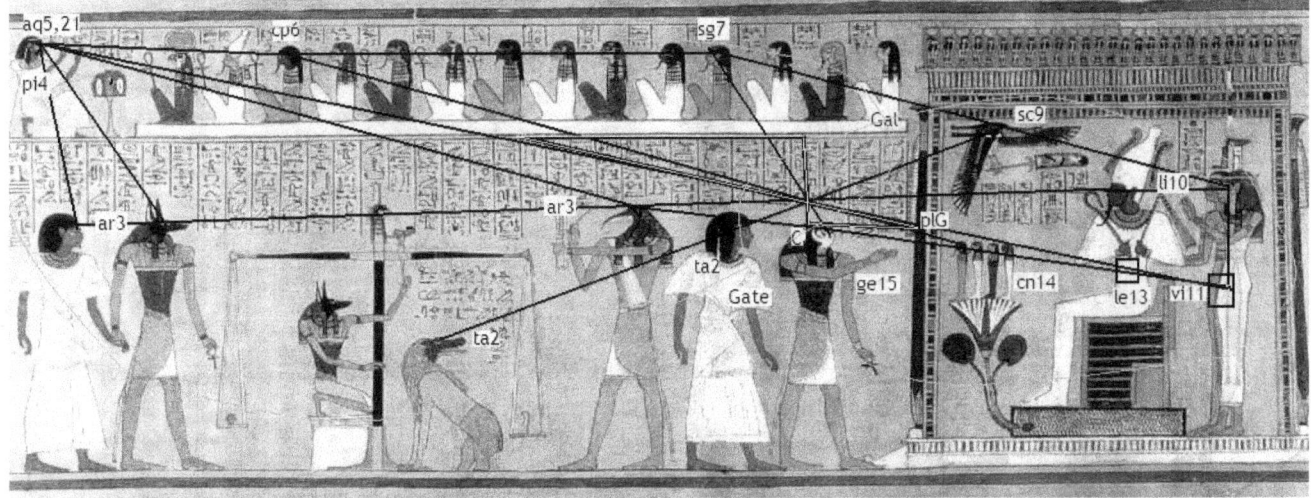

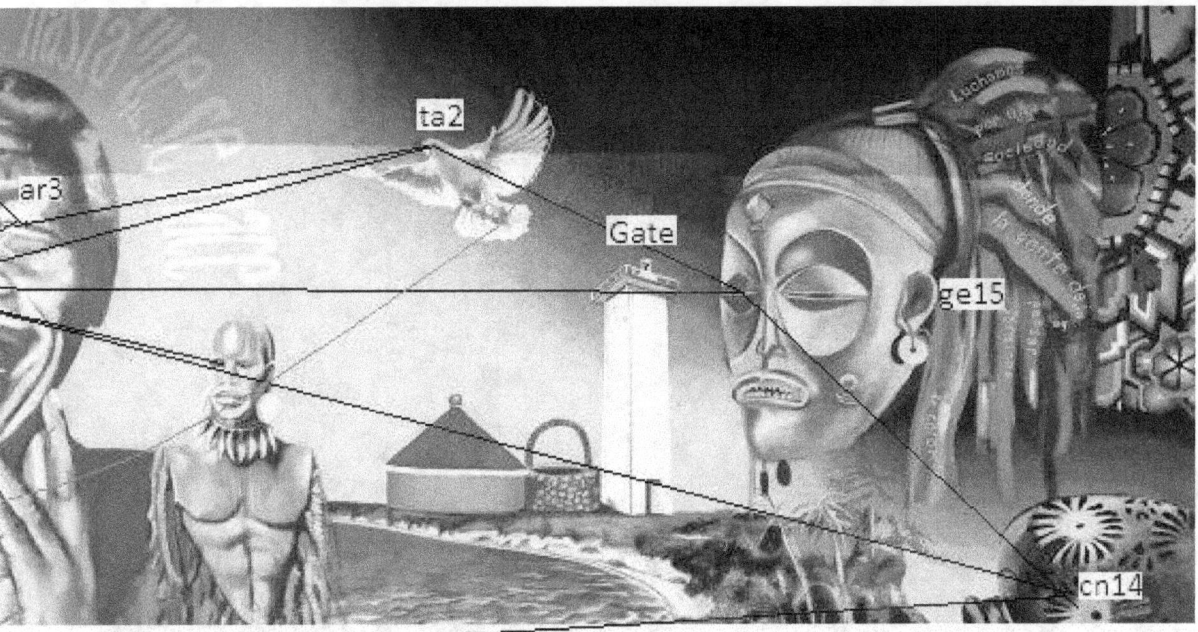

A baptist at a healing dance

Type Aquarius t5 t20 as a healer in an antelope skin tailcoat with the retro antelope head still attached (South Africa, dance with an antelope head. Gavin Anderson; Interpreting rock art. Mindprint analysis by Edmond Furter). John the Baptist, a desert hermit and visionary character, is usually figured with a camel skin coat (S Gibson; Cave of John the Baptist, 2005), sometimes with the animal's head still attached to the tails (inset; a camel-headed cloak in the Wilton diptych of Richard 2, by Bohemian artists, in the London National Gallery). Gibson takes folk rituals as 'archaeological evidence of the historical reailty of the Gospel story', against the better advice of nearly all archaeologists working in Palestine, and against the implications of this study. Several Baptists did and do exist, in every place, time and culture, a more difficult concept than the common assumption of one unusual prophet leaving a legacy and relics. When pilgrims asked a reliquary priest about the existence of another John Baptist finger in another church, also claimed to have touched the forehead of Christ, he explained that theirs was the finger of John the Baptist as a young man!

Christian art may have 'inherited' the camel-headed coat from paganism, but every culture is more likely to have re-invented, or rather re-expressed it, along with the entire myth cycle and round of figures.

This South African artist was very far in place and time from Canaan, Palestine and the rare European miniature illuminations featuring the icon.

The saint's legendary beheading is in iconic contrast with the intact head of his coat, a hint that mythic logic remains a step or two beyond conscious logic. The type is slightly ambiguous with adjacent Capricornus t6 in its double-headed guise, but the latter is usually horned, the heads identical, and on the same level (see theme t6). Aquarius t20's legs and body are painted, as they often are. Celestial polar markers on a foot and a shoulder, and the horizontal plane of most of the figures, tag the inspiration to Age Taurus-Aries, probably retro to the work. However the southern polar triangle (here the lower one, held by the dancer touched by the Aquarius priest) has a range of markers, a kind of gauge of Ages up to its hand on the Sagittarius-Gemini axis, thus an Age Pisces inspiration.

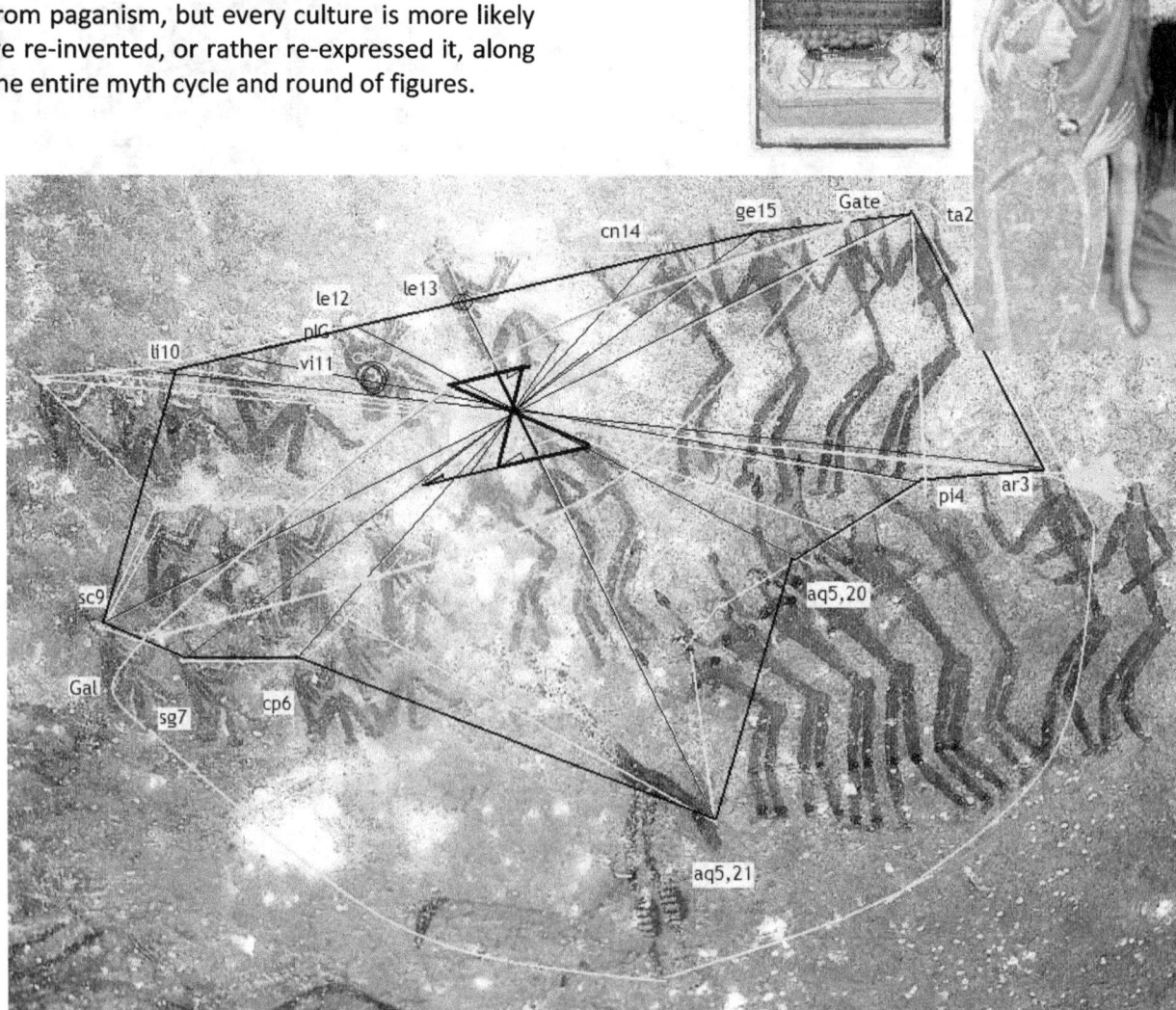

John Baptist in bronze

Type Aquarius t5 t20 as John Baptist in several episodes (Italy, Florence Baptistery door bronze panel. Mindprint analysis by Edmond Furter). The work may have informed some of Michelangelo's commissioned inspiration for the Cistine chapel. John appears at least twice (see the same narrative device in an Indian monkey offering honey at theme t5 t21, and in T'Kama Adamastor at theme t3 t18), here slightly scrambling the figure sequence, and expressing the Aquarian t20 attribute of shape-shifting. The two Johns may express Aquarius t20 and t21, or the adjacent Capricornus t6 as equal-double-headed.

Several works themed on Aquarius t20 feature nearly nondescript figures at that position itself, while the work in general carries the theme. Some identifications are uncertain and the focal point is slightly diffuse, the only generally acclaimed work in this study that could be termed 'mindprint uncertain', perhaps due to the process of transferring an inspired design from paper to plaster, then reduced by mechanical tongs to a mould, then a cast. If an exception proves the quality rule, this is the exception.

Celestial polar markers on the central figure's shoulder, and the vertical plane, tag the inspiration as Age Pisces late, incidental with the work.

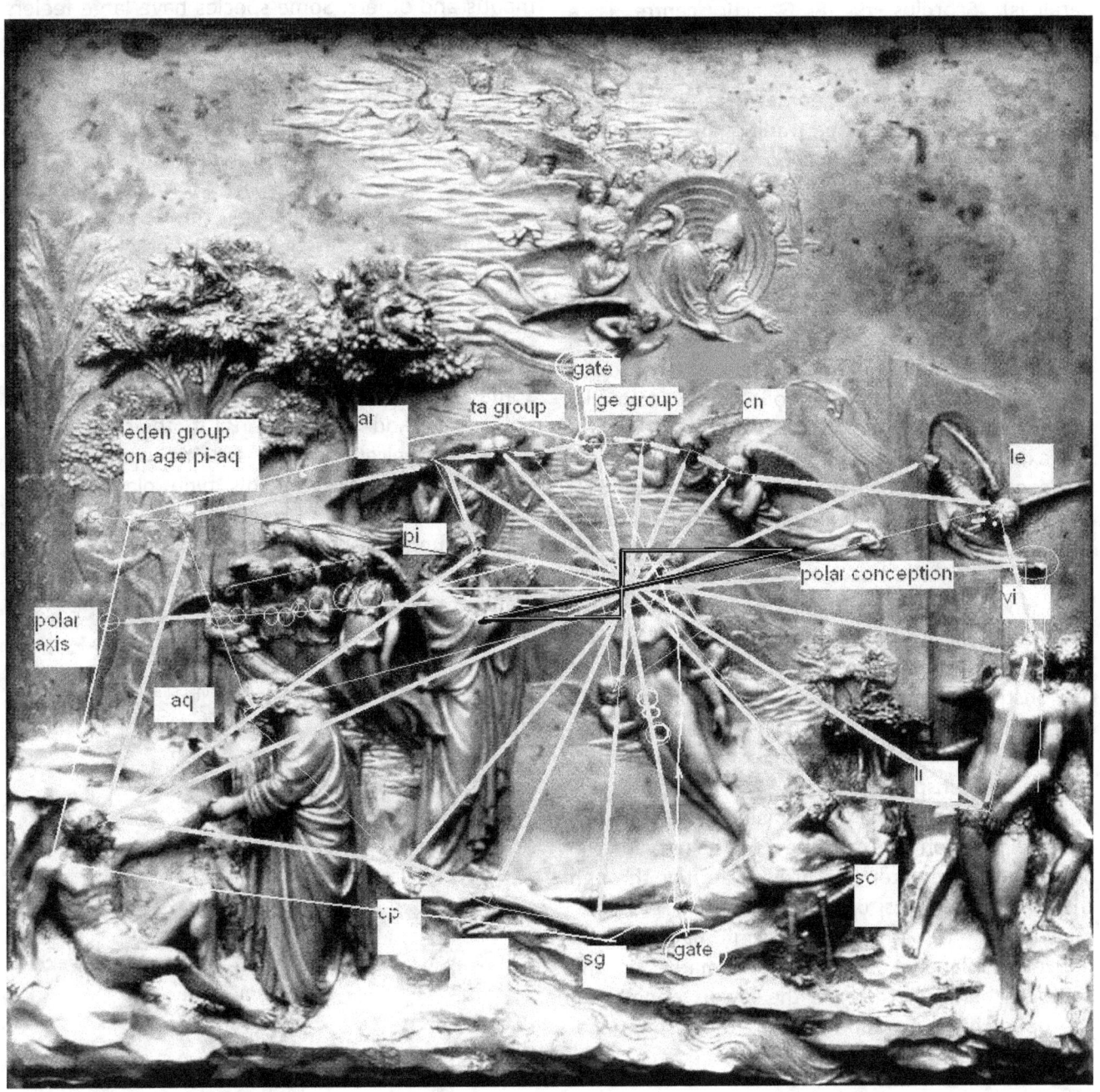

New world, same shapes

Type Aquarius t5 t20 and t5 t21 as a thunder spirit and world spirit (USA California, Piedra Pintada engraving, freehand copy. Mindprint analysis by Edmond Furter). The main figure is a large, horizontal, active, composite, dappled, benedicting healer, river baptiser, or nature spirit, as Aquarius often is, partly in his usual vesica piscis halo, here around his head, conflated with some Capricornus t6 attributes (see an African antelope man-boat with mushrooms at theme t15. See a lightning woman in another USA rock art image at theme t2).

Virgo t11 as a comb-shaped ship or multi-legged animal is an autumn marker (see the Egyptian Hierakonpolis disc at theme t12 for stylistic parallels). Scorpius t9 t8 Galactic centre is a luminary, as it often is.

The site is distinct from the Brazilian Pedra Pintada. Some features are semi-geometric, and many are assumed to be 'cultural and traditional', such as the animal skins on the left, and Libra t10 as a kachina doll, a ritual pageant mascot typical of Hopi culture (Gary A David; Orion zone). The work has some unique features, such as Leo t13 Ursa's bandy legs, perhaps localised stylistic elements. The whole gives the impression of traditions explained to initiates, with integrated mythical and ancestral stories. Mindprint remains independent of conscious meanings, with enough symbolic overlap to make the subconscious typological sequence apparent. The axial pattern is never apparent, revealed only in the sequence, itself identified only when reduced from its cryptic cultural disguise to universal attributes, such as shape, gender, posture and function.

This work is notable for its elegance (compact simplicity), and for hovering between geometry and figures, also between rock art and art. It demonstrates that provenance (time, place, source and cultural context) remain subordinate to universal and timeless structure, however seemingly conceptual in inspiration.

The ecliptic pole is on the main figure's elbow. Celestial poles on an extra elbow on the left, and the lightning bolt or water arm, provide a gauge through the preceding Ages up to the Gemini t15 axis, midsummer to Age Pisces, confirmed by the horizontal plane. A celestial polar marker in the southern hemisphere (here the lower triangle) on the upper hand or club, confirms the inspirational tag as Age Pisces.

A healer at ritual violence

Type Aquarius t5 t20 as a pirate priest (South Africa, Mount Currie Amatola raid, KZN beh1 1r. Dowson. Origins centre. Mindprint analysis by Edmond Furter). Aquarius' feathers, staff, mace and outline compare directly with pirates worldwide, including Naqada raiders or immigrants into eastern Egypt (see theme t3 and inset box) and north American raiders (see a USA Box Canyon image at theme t15). His posture is active as usual, and he may figure a painted official, sanctified for a particular role, such as Pope. Praying mantis attributes include aggressive postures (see a typical stance of Aquarius over dying lions at theme t13), ambush of bees and insects, and varicoloured camouflage, as of the Idol mantis and others. Some species have large feelers and a large frontal comb on the head, resembling feathers (dead leaf mantids, and phyllocrania paradoxa). Mantids or locusts sometimes represent Scorpius t9 as healers in trance, but aggressive healers, the church militant, and mantids fit the Aquarian bill. This priest's legs form an emergent antelope bag, reversing the more usual therianthrope mixture of antelope body with human legs (see theme t5 t21). His position behind the front recalls Moses at the battle of Rephidim against the Amalekites, having his arms lifted to signal or to influence the balance of power.

Some priests sanctify violence and exploitation as holy war, and pardon sins if their adherents overstep ethical bounds for national gain. A mundane expression of this type played out at Marikana hill near Rustenburg, where a healer applied supposed bullet-proofing potions to sanctify mine workers on strike for various causes (Philip Frankel; Between the rainbows and the rain, Marikana massacre, 2013).

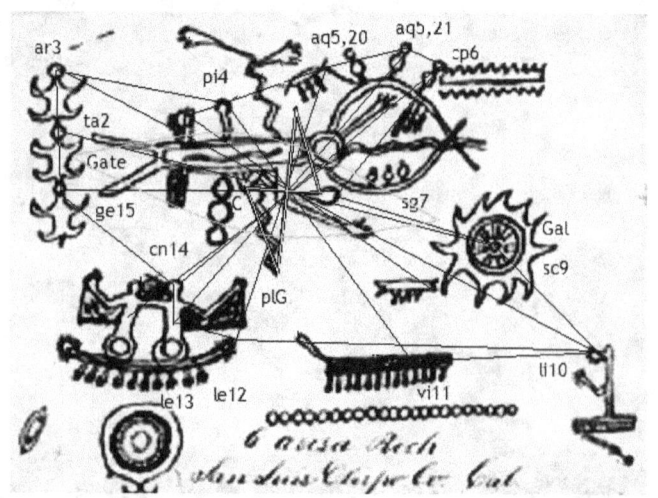

Mass sacrifice and desperate redress of natural balance in battle, as in the Trojan War, Boer trek (migration) of 1838 (see some Voortrekker monument marble frieze panels at theme t12), Hitler's initial troop sacrifice in a political scuffle, tribal revolts, South Africa's Bulhoek, Sharpeville and Soweto uprisings and suppressions, Pearl Harbour, kamikaze pilots, and the USA terror attacks of 2001, operate beyond the supposed logic of delusions of immunity or a shortcut to paradise. Suppression is a pretext for war and regime change. Blood-stained flags legitimise ownership, and the rituals of violence, such as handing over a Bible to the supreme Inca, act out unwritten archetypal texts. The large cardinals of the Taurus t1 t2 group in the foreground could be among the first painted. The small cardinals, Aries, Cancer, Libra and Capricornus, could be among the last painted, as in the Layers example in the text. Celestial polar markers are uncertain, or may tag Age Aquarius, somewhat prophetic for the 1800s.

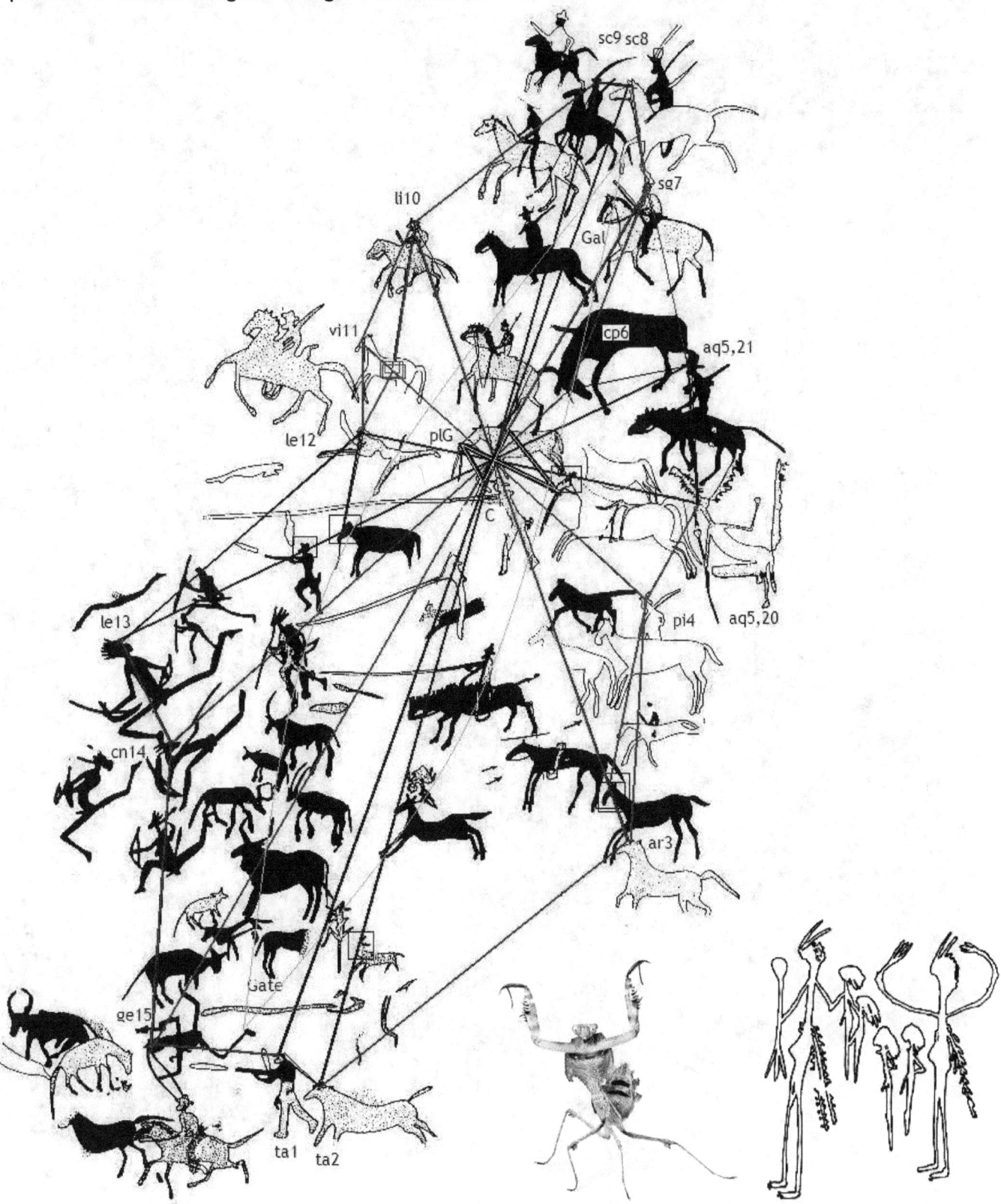

Two pages from a new world book

Types Aquarius t5 t21 as nature spirits, and Aquarius t5 t20 as a double-headed animal, in a double imprint (USA Utah Emery county, Rochester Creek. National Geographic. Mindprint analysis by Edmond Furter). Two equal heads indicate Capricornus t6,

but a tailcoat head indicates Aquarius t5, typified by John Baptist.

Pisces t4 t19 is a hippopotamus and porcine on the left, and a water dragon on the right, but the right imprint also shares in the Piscean hippo.

On the right, Virgo t11 has afterbirth, morphing into a rainbow, the left part of which partly traces the

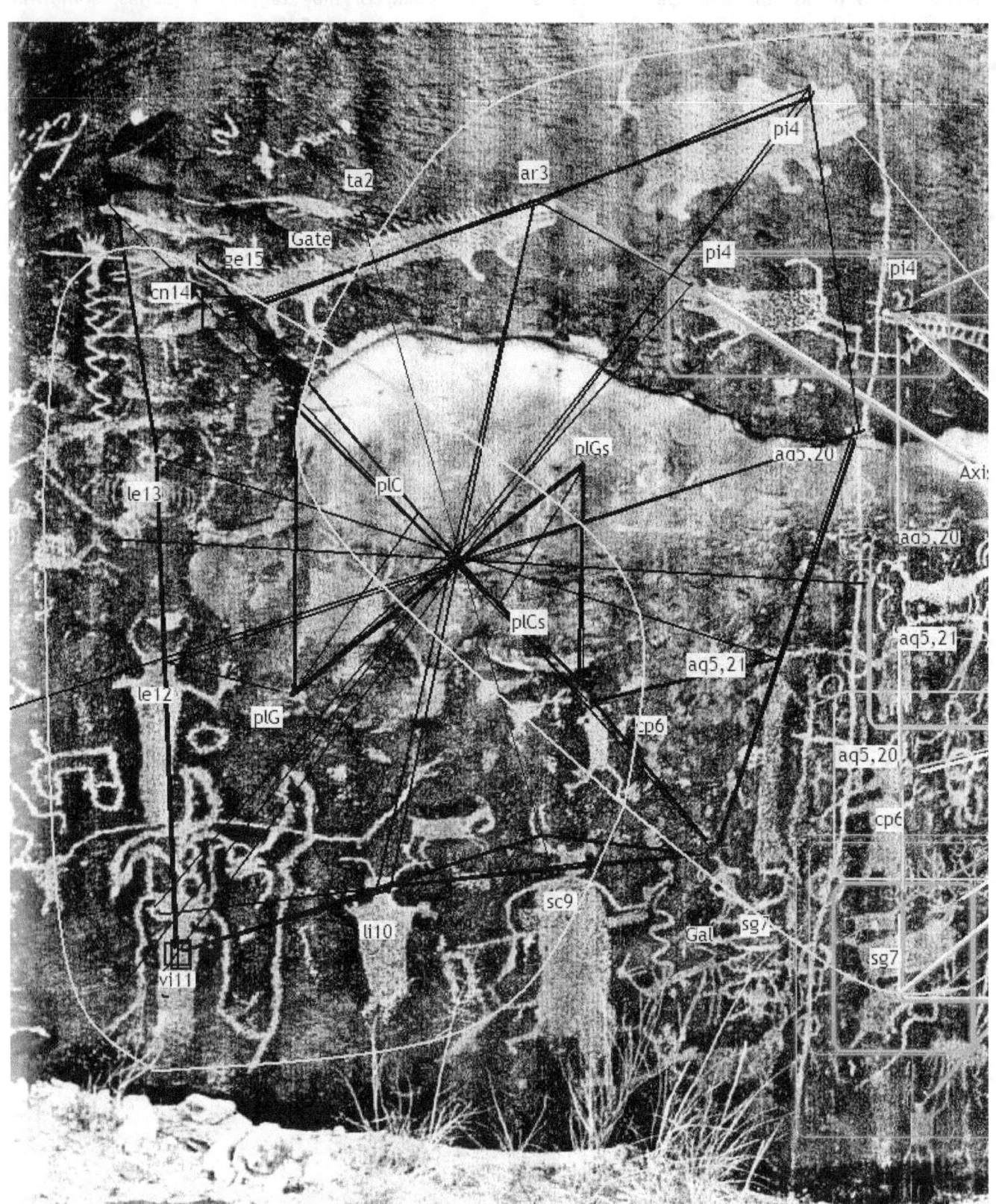

path of one of the galactic equators. Sagittarius t7 has antlers. Several types are doubled, not just the usual major four. On the left, Leo t12's polar extra as Leo t12 Ursa (Bear), is a box person. Galactic equator linkage is slightly skewed, as all mindprint features are, perhaps in translation from holographic inspiration to expression on a two-dimensional plane. They align only where two imprints are linked on or near the Pisces or Aquarius axis. Corner cardinals are of Pisces, and the division rope is an additional Pisces t4 t19 figure, perhaps expressing spring season and the equinox. Celestial polar markers tag the inspiration on the left as Age Aries or Pisces, and on the right as Age Pisces.

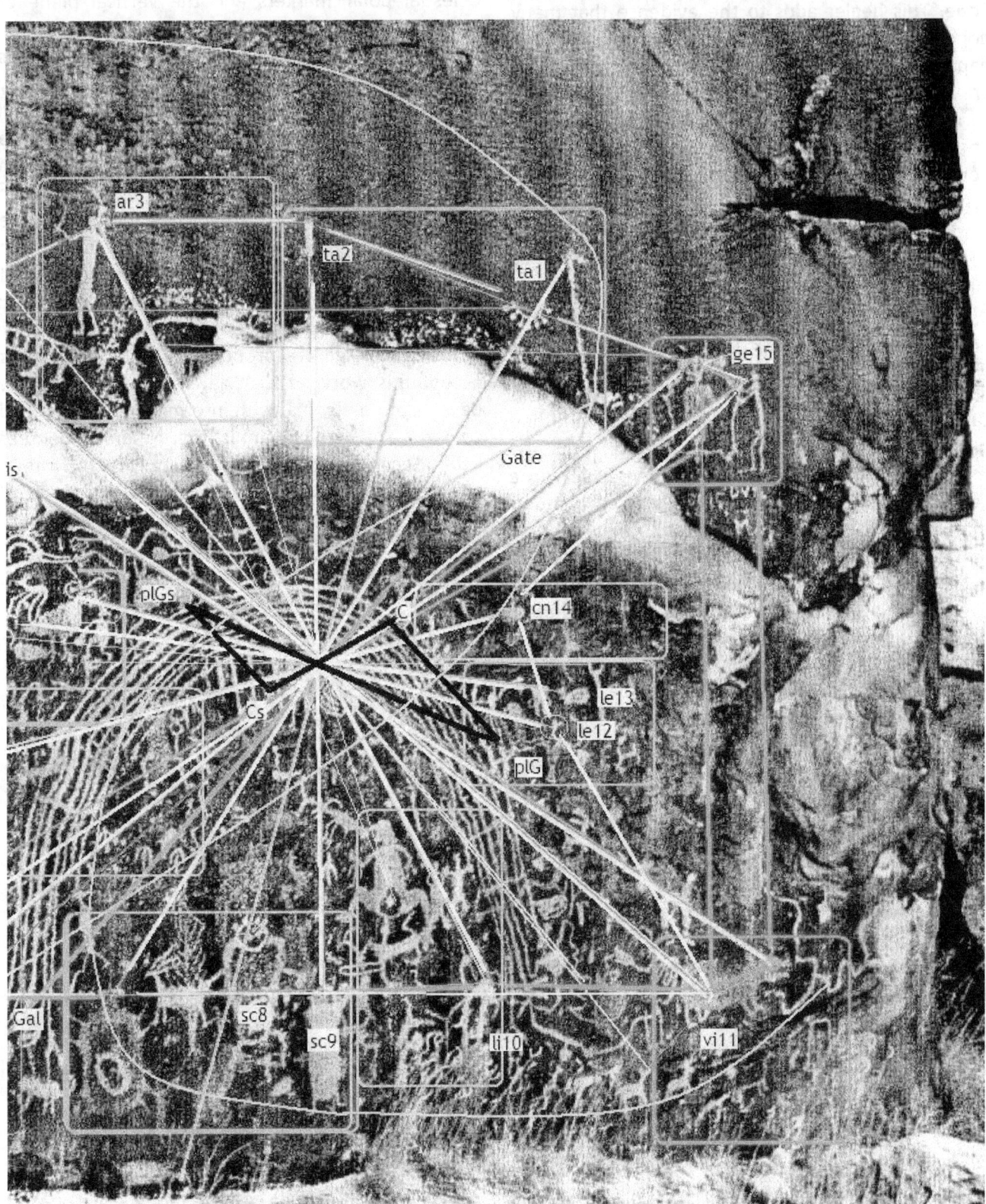

Ice Age bull men

Type Aquarius t5 t20 as a bull man, rampant (climbing) and rear-facing, in a double imprint, left half (France, Trois Frere cave [B], overworked. Breuil 1952. Mindprint analysis by Edmond Furter). The dominant themes include tomb, chasm, milling, Pentecost, stampede and trap hunting or cliff hunting. Aquarius t5 themes include chief priest or Pope. This healer adds to the evidence that many popes worldwide preceded the Roman and Avignine papacy, some with their own Cistine ceilings. In rock art and in art, Aquarius t5 t20 is one of the most varied figures, sometimes rampant, or kneeling (see an Amatola sorcerer at theme t5 t20), or retro as here (facing east instead of the usual west, sunrise instead of sunset, towards Pisces t4 instead of towards its companion Aquarius t5 t21 and adjacent Capricornus t6). A twisted posture is more usual at Taurus t2 Perseus, a quarter of the sequence later.

Aries t18 and the Taurus t17 pair are massive figures, each spanning a quarter of the imprint, hinting that the artist may have started with them and their opposing and cardinal figures (see the Layers section in the text. However, another stratigraphy test contradicts the 'swastika' sequence; see the 'Three Magi' rock art at theme t13). The artist may have elaborated an earlier work, hinting that single portraits or small groups may express particular types, or remain incomplete expressions, overworked by others. Inspired artists would rarely overwork or scramble a completed mindprint. Apparent chaotic overwork in some rock art and art, indicates a compulsive inspiration, at the cost of representation and communication. Whether other people would see it, or understand it, or use it in initiation, seems of lesser importance than its completion. Attributes are optional, but not arbitrary. However the conscious, logical meaning of art is more optional and largely arbitrary to the artist and to likely viewers.

Aries t3 t18 may have been intended as Taurus t2 initially, confirmed by the absence of its opposite Libra t10. Errors in expression, extremely rare in all Ages and continents, seem to occur in axial pairs, indicating that artists perceive or express figures in pairs.

Aquarius t5 t21, adjacent double and possible companion to the much-reproduced bull man 'sorcerer' (dreaming healer or patient), is apparently figured only by arrows and a wound, or may be figured as trampled. Ritual image wounding is meaningful down to body parts, and reconcilable with spiritual experience (Francis Thackeray; The principle of sympathetic magic in the context of hunting, trance and southern African rock art). Wounds of Christ or Odin compare directly to rock art and universal ritual.

Celestial polar markers and the vertical plane of some of the larger figures, tag the inspiration as Age Gemini, the only work in this study tagged by this early iconographic date. The celestial pole briefly lay between the ecliptic and galactic poles when all three poles were on the meridian separating Virgo t11 and Leo t12, in Age Gemini-Taurus. It then moved through the Leo Ursa (Bear) meridians, then over Cancer, and recently over Gemini (see an Age Gemini-Taurus work in Niaux cave at theme t15). In Age Gemini, as here, the celestial pole lay north of Virgo, moving through Bootes towards the galactic polar axis and Leo. Archaeologists assign very early dates to Ice Age art, around BP 25 000, and most accept this work as Ice Age, which however may have lasted millennia, with intermittent warmer and colder snaps. Age Gemini is 'more than 90 degrees ago'. Reconciliation of the dating of art history, archaeology and astrology is outside the scope of this study. Mindprints in Ice Age art, irrespective of which Ice Age and of what date, should lay to rest any lingering ideas about artistic 'development, evolution and diffusion'.

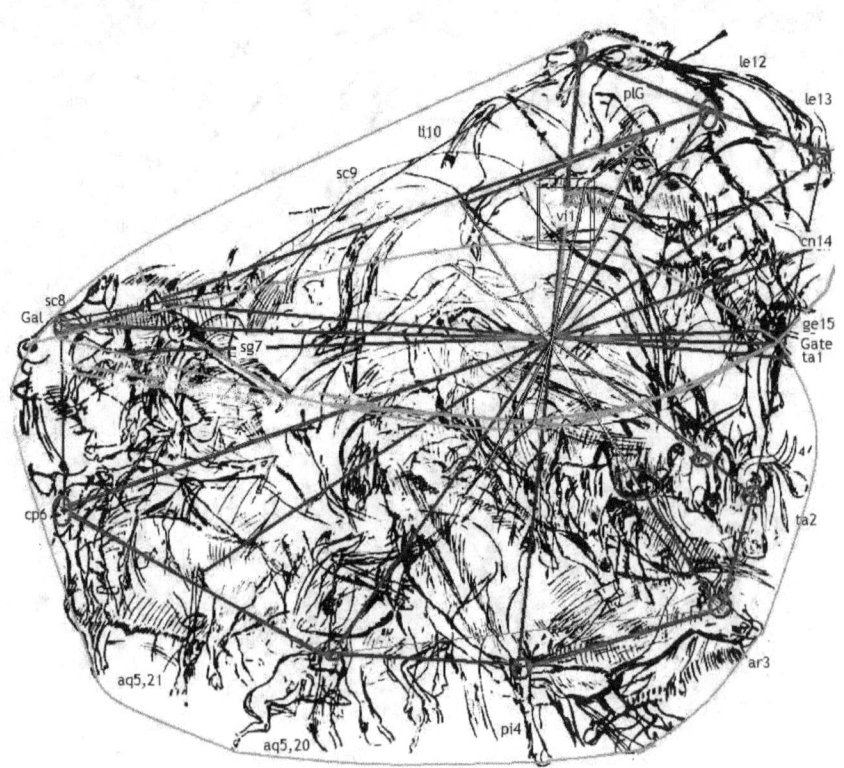

Baptist, anointer or embalmer

Type Aquarius t5 t20 as an anointer or embalmer (Egyptian jewel of Queen Ah-Hotep, Thebes. Mindprint analysis by Edmond Furter). The role of sacred oils in coronation is noted in Egyptian ritual, the New Testament, French history and grail romances. Leo t13 is a falcon eye instead of a heart in the cartouche on the left, but it carries a bowl that figures Leo t13 Crater (Grail). Virgo t11 is a pneuma (lung symbol) cross, linked by its handle or windpipe 'eye', instead of its 'womb'. Some icons are misplaced, such as an isolated Taurus t1 t2 cartouche with a knot of three reeds at far right, instead of flanking the Taurus figure as a determinative (context pictogram). This compact work has twelve eyes on six axes (see hieroglyphs as figures in Egyptian works, and in Mexico at themes t3 t18 and t4). Celestial polar markers on a shoulder and an elbow (the latter imprecise) tag the inspiration to Age Pisces, that started in the Ptolemaic era.

Before and after the flood

Type Aquarius t5 t20 as a boat bust (prow beam figure) in a double imprint (Babylonian seal with boat groups. Mindprint analysis by Edmond Furter). The scene and themes compare directly to Nordic boat scenes (see theme t15. See a ship bust as a separate figure in T'Kama Adamastor at theme t3 t18).

Here, Aries t3 t18 Andromeda is a healer with a caduceus serpent staff, forming a kind of wheel, both being attributes of his opposite at Libra t10 as wheel turner. The staff may represent a real artefact, such as a noon shadow post or pendulum, calibrated by curves to compensate for seasons, associated with Moses, Aaron and Age transition figures. Celestial polar markers on the tamer's shoulder and the healer's elbow, tag the inspiration as Age Taurus-Aries, at an obliquity of about 30 degrees. Markers in more recent works tend to tag the recent earth obliquity of about 24 degrees. These inspirational features are concepts, and any challenge to the history of obliquity and the Newcomb curve must await real (conscious level) archaeological evidence, such as solstice orientation angles and an array of new dating techniques. Most symbolic and iconic content in art are 'unreal', meaning that it did not, and does not have conscious meanings to artists or viewers. Mindprint attributes, the axial structure and polar features, are subconscious, and would remain so, except to people who memorise the sequence and its optional attributes, or test art against the standard template (see the Identification section in the text). These attributes, grids and angles, however simplistic, are like parables and dreams, resembling some aspects of nature and the cosmos due to the common, source of structure.

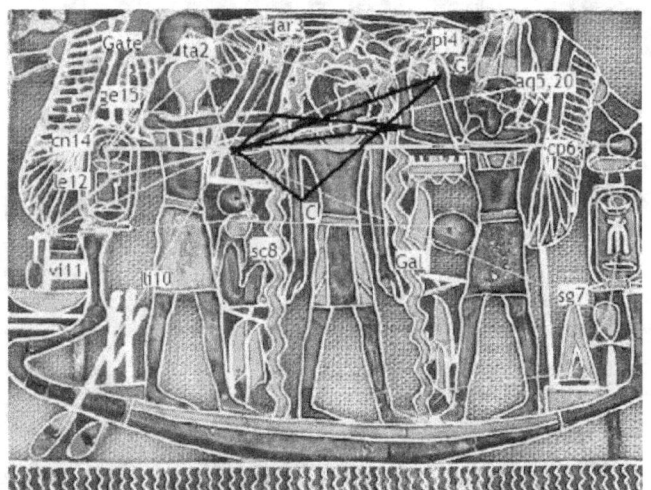

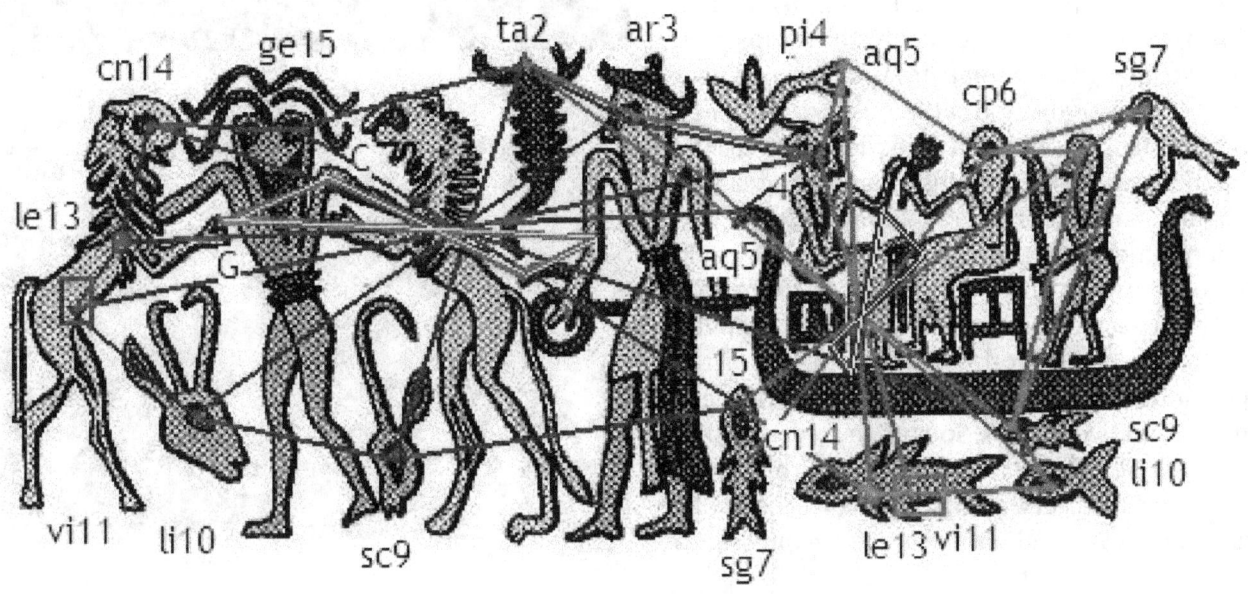

Once upon a time in Arcadia

Type Aquarius t5 t20 as water pouring from the jug of a crowned shepherd (Poussin; Et in Arcadia earlier version, 1627. Chatsworth house. Mindprint analysis by Edmond Furter). Mindprints in each of Poussin's renderings of the theme, and in copies of the theme by other artists, are all different.

Gemini t15 is sometimes a figure with a crosier (shepherd's crook, and bishopric insignia), here just a crosier by itself, typical of the use of staff ends, feet and hands to complete the axial pattern in several Poussin works. Completion of mindprint is a subconscious obsessive compulsion to inspired artists. This study likewise had to acquire sufficient examples to illustrate all the types before it could be completed.

Sparse figuring hints that the inspiration is mainly polar, therefore related to Ages, incidental with the theme of ancestors and transition. Polar markers on a hand (overpainted) and knee, and the vertical plane of the three crowding figures, tag the inspiration to Age Pisces, in the first centuries after about BC 150.

Mindprint is also in Arcadia

Type Aquarius t5 t20 as father or elder shepherd with a group at a woodland tomb (Poussin; Shepherds of Arcadia, acclaimed version. Mindprint analysis by Edmond Furter). This is one of the poorest mindprint sequences in this study, with only six figures bearing known standard attributes (Cancer, Leo, Virgo, Aquarius, Aries and Gemini). The rest are expressed as feet (typical of Poussin), a staff tip and a mountain cliff. However the galactic equators are among the most symmetrical in this study, accounting for nearly all the external limb joints of the four figures (in total three heads, two shoulders, three elbows, two hands, three hips, four knees, two feet; or nineteen from a potential but impossible 28 in profile format in this sparse scene). Art history recognises the aesthetic value of the arrangement of limbs. This study demonstrates that limb joints are the main features along two secondary, interlocking equators. Limb joints could be the initial basis of visual inspiration or expression (see the Galactic section in the text). Popular fascination with this work hinges as much on the composition (that also includes pentagonal angles), as on the intuitively mysterious theme, drawn into speculations about sacred bloodlines. This study demonstrates that each version of the theme by Poussin, imitators and other artists, expresses a

different mindprint, usually more completely than here, and even occasionally double imprints. 'Also in Arcadia' implies that even rural people have access to the structure of sacred drama, as this study demonstrates in art and rock art in all corners of the world, some made by shepherds.

Celestial polar markers on both hands of Gemini t15 tag the inspiration as Age Aries-Pisces, in the last centuries before about BC 150. The vertical plane provides for Age Pisces, incidental with the work.

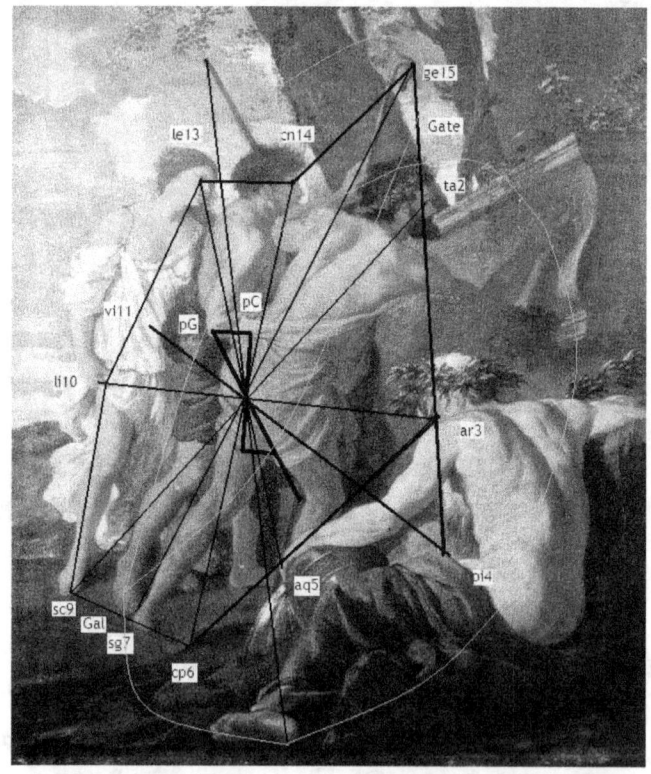

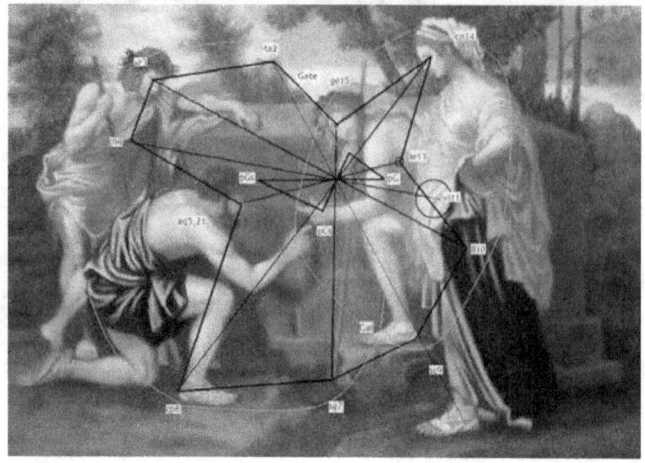

After Arcadia

Type Aquarius t5 t21 and t5 t20 as the foot and heel of two shepherds (England, Shugborough Arcadian monument plaque after Poussin, attributed to Elizabeth Yorke. Mindprint analysis by Edmond Furter). Aquarius t5 t21 is in active posture as usual, though here combined with Pisces t4 t19 and its royal ordination posture. The theme and figures in various versions and copies are near identical, but mindprint in each work is different, confirming that inspiration is never copied, incapable of copying, and an all-or-nothing event. There are no half done sequences in art, provided that a bare minimum of figures, features and skill is present. A few are slightly scrambled, but in predictable ways. Gemini t15 is a medallion in the centre of the monument, its opposite Sagittarius t7 on a crypto animal face in an unusual rock, a kind of lamb and lion, or footrest (this is the only crypto figure noted among about 10 000 figures in this study. See a real lion at the base of a similar monument in Montreal de Sos, and a real footstool in the Externsteine carving at theme t4).

If the monument and its image say, among other things, that God is also in England, or England is also Arcadia, mindprint confirms both. Artistic inspiration and access to subconscious heritage and treasure is not confined to Greeks, Phoenicians, Palestinians, French, English, Arcadians, Rennes le Chateau, painters, or rock artists.

The ecliptic pole is on a wrist. Celestial polar markers on the vertical plane, tag the inspiration to Age Aries-Pisces.

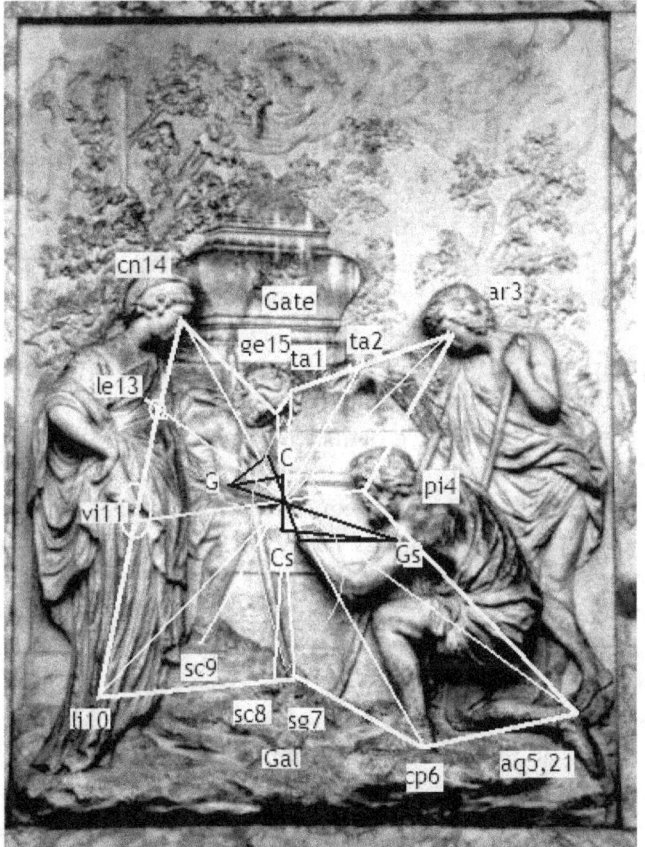

An Indian arcadia

Type Aquarius t5 t20 as a central tree at a shrine (India, Sanchi stupa north gate; a monkey offers honey to Shaka, BC 50. OnMark Productions. Mindprint analysis by Edmond Furter). The usual supplicant trio of Aquarius t20 express adjacent types, typical of its mixing and matching nature. Libra t10 and Scorpius t9 adopt their usual arms-up posture. Artists in different cultures, continents and eras, express figure sequences and even entire works that seem to have inspired one another. Poussin and this Indian artist were on the same inspirational page. Celestial polar markers on an inner eye and a topknot, and the horizontal plane, tag the inspiration to Age Pisces, are of discovery and colonisation of paradises and continents.

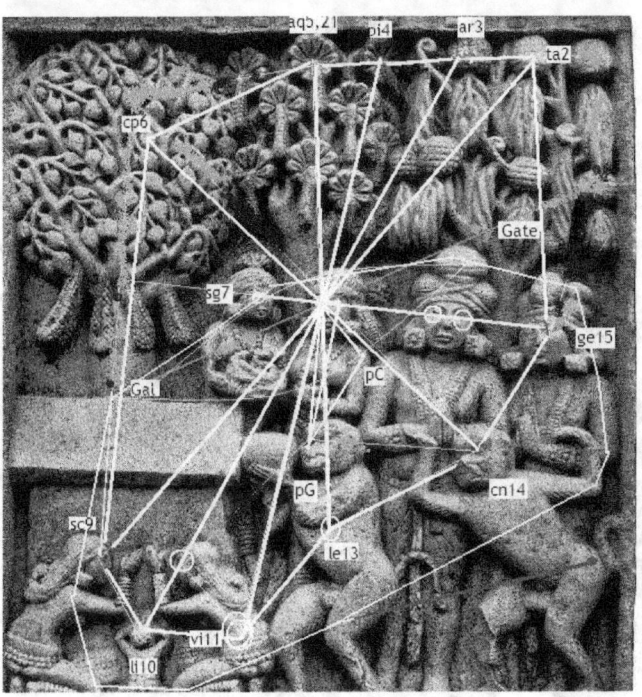

Before the Ice Age

Type Aquarius t5 t20 as a snake or eel in a migration or spring scene (Turkey, Gobekli Tepe pillar relief carving. Ineffableisland. Mindprint analysis by Edmond Furter). Pisces t4 is a crane, Aries t3 a snake or bird, Taurus t2 and t1 are large animals, Gemini t15 is a retro-facing vulture (more regular at its cardinal Virgo t11 in Turkish and Egyptian art), Cancer t14 a hippo, Leo t12 another hippo, Virgo t11 the hippo's pregnant womb (as in some Egyptian art, see type t8), Libra t10 a bird, Scorpius t9 a crane, t8 a quail, Sagittarius t7 a bag or bladder or decapitated skin (see the Egyptian Narmer palette at type t3), Capricornus t6 a quail. The geometric centre, or conceptual ecliptic pole, is unmarked, while other polar features favour limb joints as usual. The galactic pole is on Virgo t11's front hoof. The celestial pole may be on a crane shoulder, and the celestial south pole on a crane beak, both on the horizontal plane, tagging the inspirational framework to Age Cancer-Gemini, the oldest tag found in this study (see a possible Age Gemini tag among Ice Age bison at type t15). However the celestial pole may be on a quail beak, providing an Age Taurus-Aries framework. The site is dated about BC 8000, supporting the earlier tag, with the caution that polar features are much less standardised than the typological sequence, attributes and axial grid.

The curtain of time

Type Aquarius t5 t20 as a snake head, or heart-shaped body of a crane, and type Aquarius t5 t21 as a crane with a possible animal-headed tail, as in some tailcoat heads at type t5 (Turkey, Gobekli Tepe pillar relief carving. Mindprint analysis by Edmond Furter). Type Pisces t4 is a crane, Aries t3 t18 a crab (see Tarot trump 18's usual crayfish), Taurus t2 or t1 may be in a trap or keep or domestic manger, Taurus t1 or Gemini t15 is an unidentified bent figure, Cancer t14 a small bird and furthest from the pole as it often is, Leo t13 a vulture, Virgo t11 the vulture's egg-bearing womb, Libra t10 a canine, Scorpius t9 and t8 a scorpion and a large bird, Sagittarius t7 a bag or decapitated figure (see the Egyptian Narmer palette at type t4), Capricornus t6 may be t5's tailcoat head. Apparent reed-work evokes the mythic journey of Gilgamesh to Utnapishtim the Far-Away, 'behind the reed curtain'. The H-shapes flanking t4 more often appears at the cardinal Gemini t15, perhaps related to leather, rope, plant or textile. The geometric centre, or conceptual ecliptic pole, is unmarked, while other polar features favour limb joints as usual. The galactic pole is on the t11 vulture's shoulder. The celestial pole may be on the vulture wing 'elbow', and the celestial south pole on a crane tail, tagging the inspirational framework to Age Cancer-Gemini, the oldest tag found in this study. However the celestial pole may be on the moon or egg, near the horizontal plane, tagging an Age Taurus 1 -Taurus 2 framework. The two most richly decorated pillars revealed on this site seem to agree on the uniquely early tag. Both have type Gemini t15 in the topmost central position (where Taurus t1, Taurus t2 or Aries t3 habitually appear from Age Taurus onwards), tentatively supporting initial archaeological dating of the unique   site.

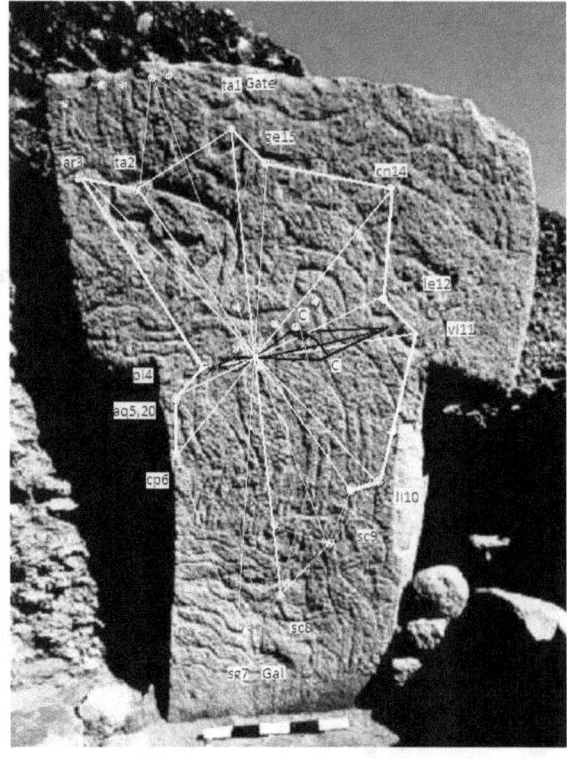

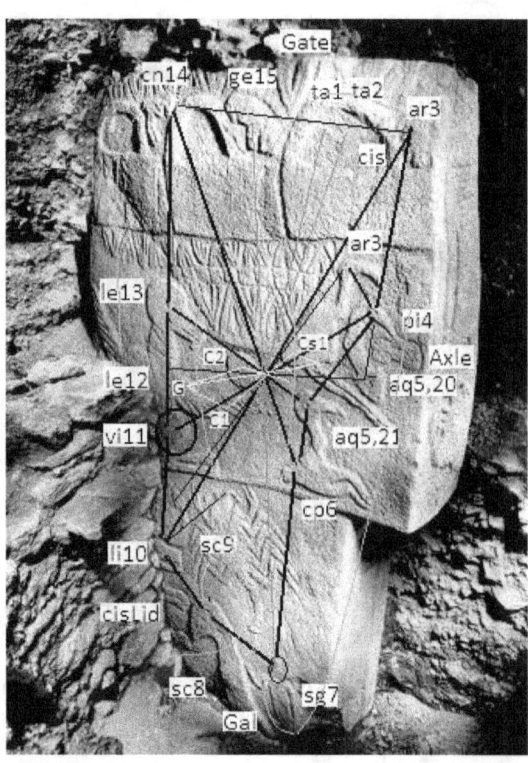

A battle on a falling bridge

Type Aquarius t5 t20 or Judgement as a right wing commander, against Pisces t4 t19 as a left wing soldier, in a civil battle on a falling bridge over a stream of workers in an underpass (South Africa, Johannesburg, Brenthurst Library commission by Leonard French of Australia; The Bridge, 1982. Oppenheimer collection. Mindprint analysis by Edmond Furter). A rift between types Pisces and Aquarius, as temporal and spiritual powers, co-incides with the current spring equinox transition from Age Pisces to Age Aquarius. Eyes and faces are camera lenses, as images contest space on news pages, dividing the silent majority and separating the archetypal Leo t13 and Virgo t11 couple below. French's media is mainly stained glass on panel, extending the concepts of lenses, pigments, cathedrals, sacrifice and alchemy. Colonial empires usually collapse under their own military weight, as the Roman empire did around the time of Christ, here recalled by crosses on both sides of the split (see another polar axis flanked by crosses and daggers in Montreal de Sos at theme t4).

Architecture and art follow economic, iconic and archetypal logic, with most of their symbolism remaining subconscious. See tower and yellow brick road motifs in a Wizard of Oz illustration at theme t11. See healers with bandoliers in rock art. See a mountain over a royal couple in a cave in a Rosicrucian emblem at theme t6. See a rope bridge as spiritual churn at theme t15.

The most famous example of expressionism is Mondrian's The Scream, also set on a bridge, expressing the claustrophobia of peer pressure and keeping up appearances. Johannesburg has no rivers, but many traffic bridges and underpasses, linking and ironically separating formerly white and black suburbs. Brenthurst library is a cruciform building with four barrel vaults, resembling a church in Aksum, Ethiopia. Its four caverns form a type of alchemical mountain and caves on one of the ridges of the modest Witwatersrand range. The previous generation of Oppenheimers and mining companies improved living conditions in the slum of Soweto by replacing stuffy tin shacks and unhealthy asbestos roofs, with low barrel roofs of mortar, also a kind of cave structure. Residents commemorated the work with the modest Oppenheimer tower on a low hillock in Oppenheimer Park in Soweto, built of coal ash clicker brick with an internal spiral staircase. It soon acquired Zimbabwe-type birds resembling the Egyptian Horus. Credo Mutwa later built a cultural village next to the tower, including murals with a rainbow.

Sections of both galactic equators are traced by the arched bridge. Celestial polar markers, the vertical plane, and the wavering horizontal plane, tag the inspiration as Age Aries-Pisces or Age Pisces, incidental with the themes of political and Age transition.

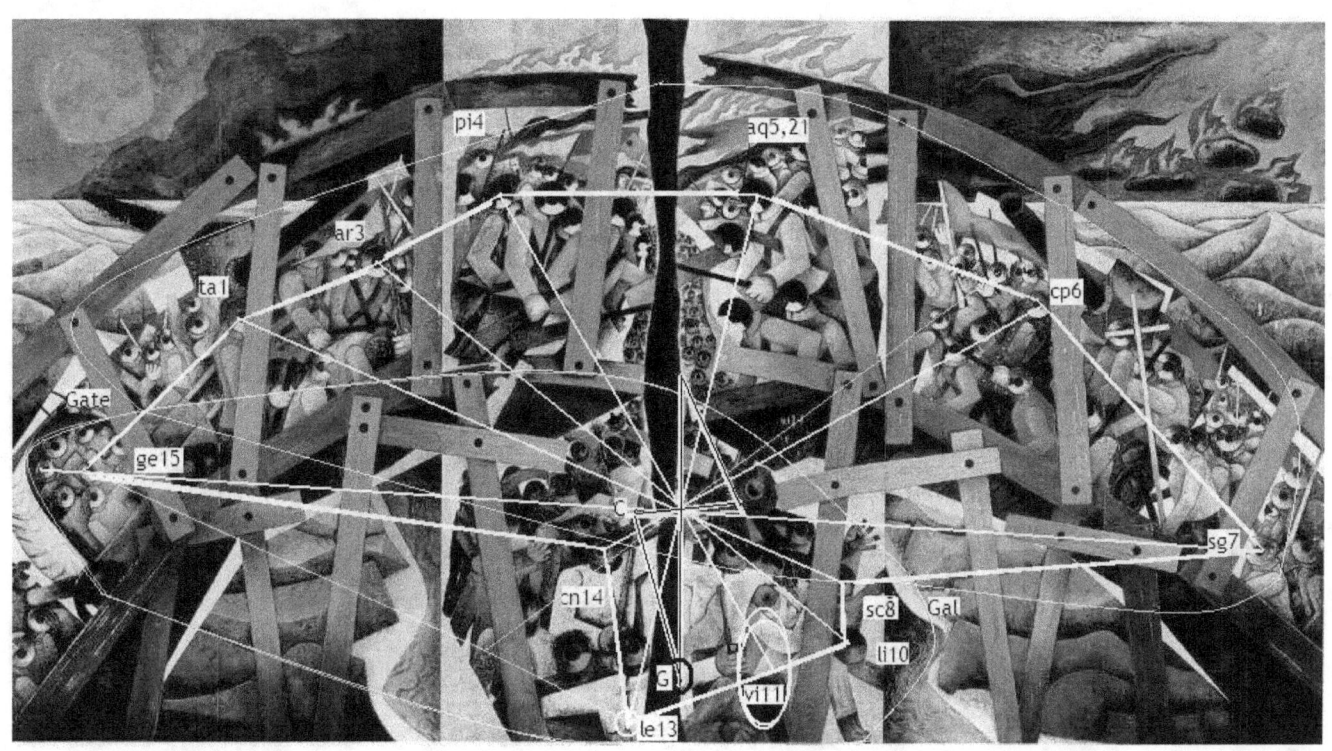

Type Aquarius t5 t21; World spirit

A painted half man and a 'white lady'

Type Aquarius t5 t20 t21 as a half-man antelope with body-painted legs, and as a white-painted man in active posture (Namibia, Brandberg White lady. Le Quellec. Mindprint analysis by Edmond Furter). The legs resemble a zedonk, zebra-donkey cross, of which one example was born in a USA park recently. Nature expresses Aquarius t5 t21 Pegasus as a range of equines capable of interbreeding, therefore of one species. Art does not require physical examples to express archetype.

The famous body-painted figure at Scorpius t8 is not a European or Eastern woman, but a Khoe or Western Bantu man, figuring Scorpius t8 Ophiuchus Giant as an initiate or healer.

See migration and ark images at theme t11. Despite the curved rock canvas forming a bulging lintel, or perhaps to counter the bulge, the usual mindprint angular equatorial distortion is regularised by equatorial line economy to a near trapezium. Celestial polar markers tag the inspiration as Age Aries-Pisces, in the last centuries BC. The work may be later.

Famous painted men

Type Aquarius t5 t21 as a body-painted man lying dreaming (South Africa, Maclear, Linton panel. Iziko Museum. Mindprint analysis by Edmond Furter). Every figure includes archetypal attributes, and the axial structure is identical to inspired art on all continents. The work could be part of a double or quadruple imprint, since it was removed from a densely painted shelter.

Libra t10 is the most famous figure in this group, expressed as painted white, implying initiation, or spiritual as opposed to physical identity. He is figured on the South African coat of arms and coins as a doubled antithetical pair, without his genitals, spears and skin shield, the latter perhaps among the features that attracted the heraldry team's attention as suitable for a national shield. The old Dutch era motto 'Unity is strength' was translated into one of the disappearing Bushman languages. See a near identical Libra t10 in the Egyptian Seti 1 tomb ceiling at theme t8.

The ecliptic pole is on a foot below the twisted and elongated leg of Taurus t2. Celestial poles are marked by a minor figure's feet, and the horizontal plane, placing midsummer between Leo t13 and Cancer t14, tagging the inspiration as Age Taurus-Aries, in the centuries before about BC 1500. The other foot of Taurus t2, tags the inspiration as Age Pisces.

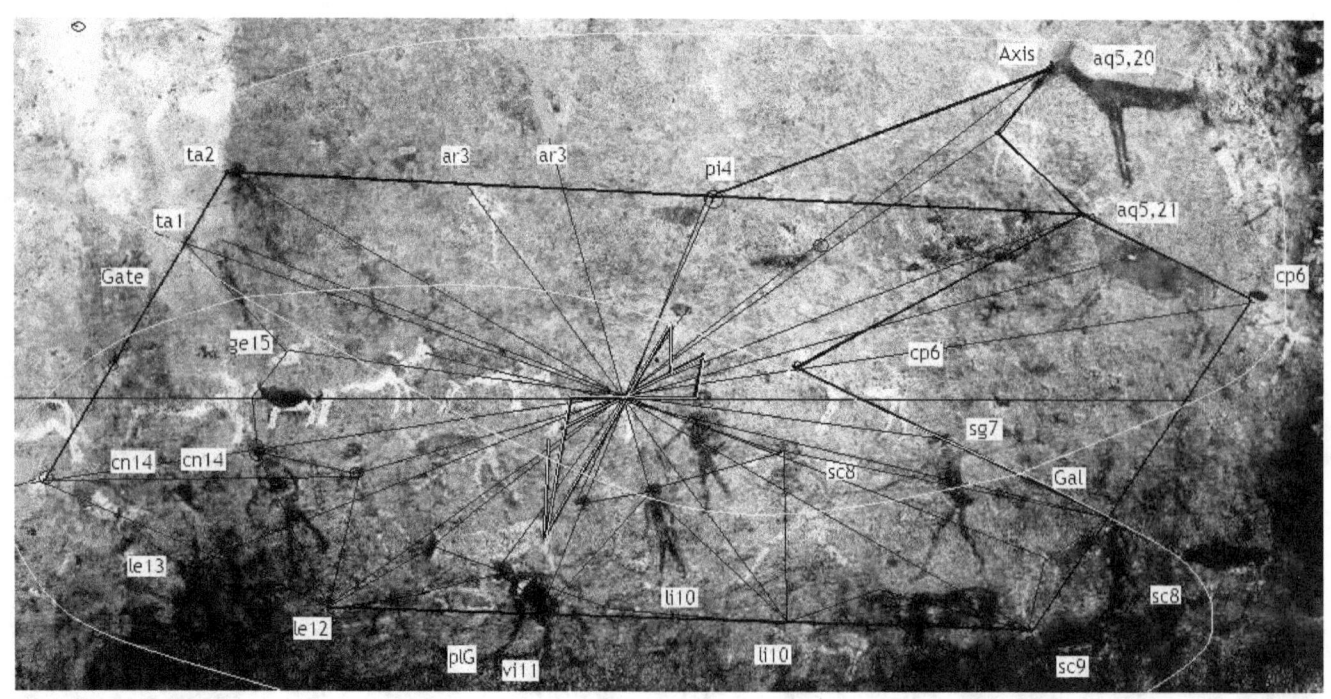

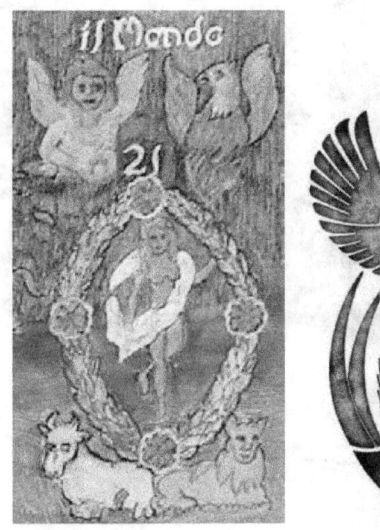

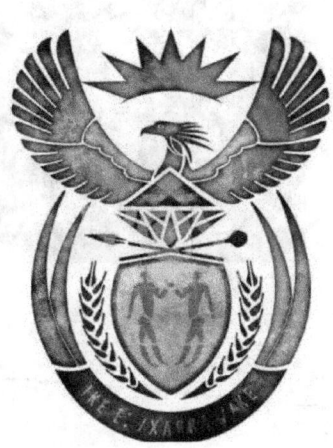

A painted half man and an error

Type Aquarius t5 t21 as a half-man antelope with painted legs, in a body-painted sub-group (Zimbabwe, Murhwa cave. Copyist CH. SA Archaeological Bulletin. Mindprint analysis by Edmond Furter).

Libra t10 contains a very rare artistic or copyist error. He is inverted (usually an attribute of Leo t12), and his eye has no counterpart at Aries t3, unless his front leg is taken as a head, and apparent water flow lines are his arms. His head does find a counterpart if the Aries antelope had turned its rearing head forward. This triple ambiguity raises the possibility that either Libra or Aries were painted by subconsciously mistaking the posture of the opposite figure, implying that artists have a built-in eye alignment skill which on rare occasions is misled by the equally built-in gestalt function of seeing mistaken wholes in parts. The problematic Libra is also marked by an axis on his hand, or a small bag in his hand. Scorpius t8 is also inverted, and marked by an axis on his hand, or a small bag in his hand, perhaps for lack of a face. This inversion may have contributed to the artist's mistake at the Libra type. The concept of a bauble, or fake head on a wand, is universal. See type Libra as a kachina doll (totem dance group icon) in a Californian Piedra Pintada rock art copy at theme t5 t20.

A celestial pole on a hand tags the inspiration to Age Aries-Pisces. The earlier Age Taurus 1 –Taurus 2 is tagged by a woman's knee and a porcine knee.

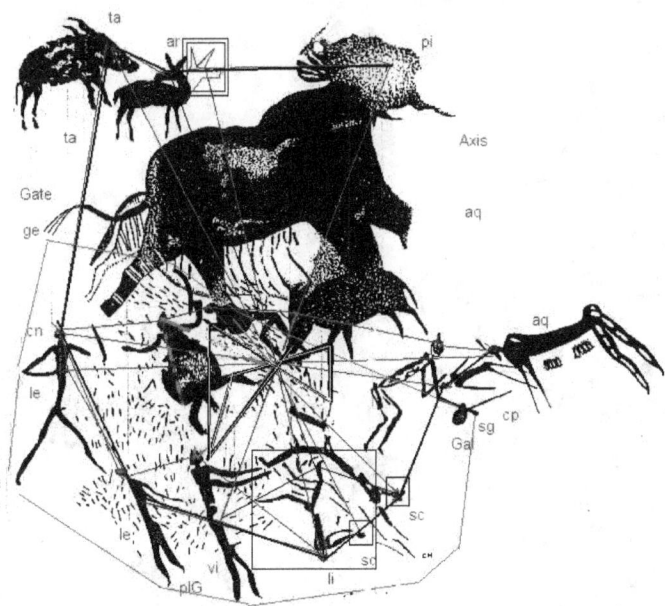

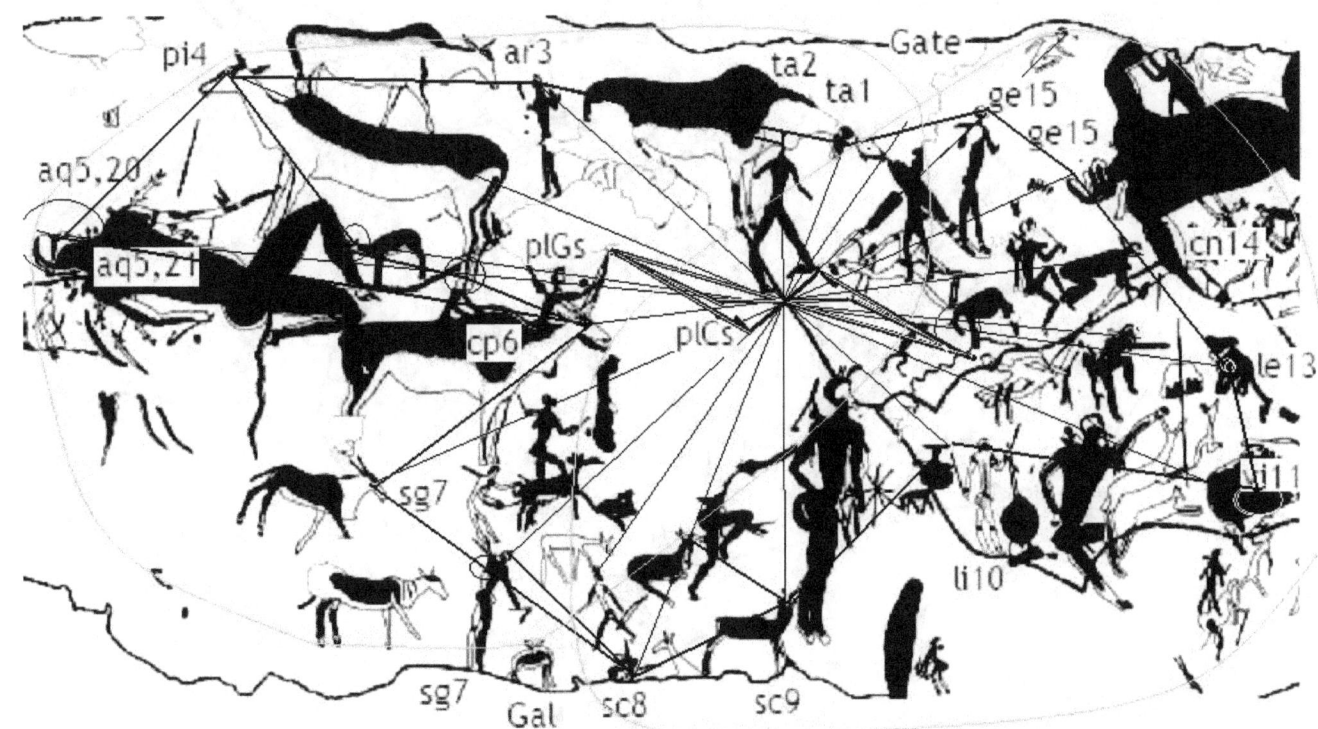

Goat with a tailcoat head

Type t5 t20 t21 Aquarius as a goat with a tailcoat head
(USA, Nine Mile Canyon Backway goats. Mindprint by
Edmond Furter). Unequal heads, or a tailcoat with a head
still attached, is one of the attributes of t5 t21, while equal
heads indicate t6 Capricornus. T15 Gemini is similar to a
Mexican churn figure (see t15). Celestial polar markers and
the horizontal plane of some of the figures and legs, tag
the inspiration to Age Taurus-Aries, probably prior to the
work.

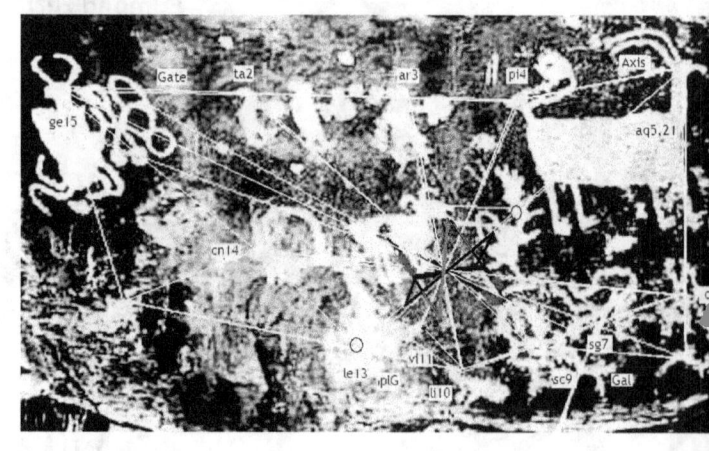

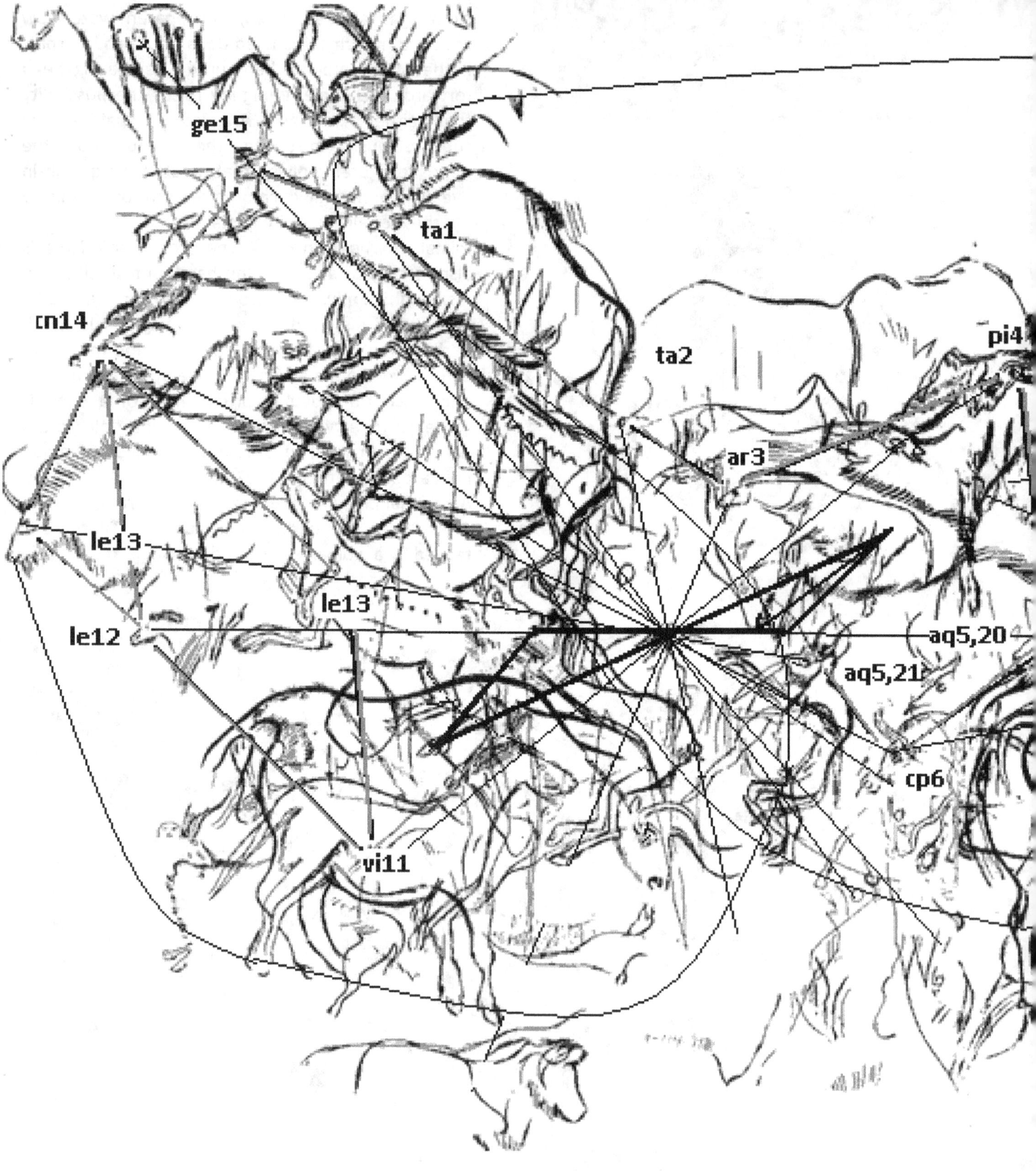

ce Age bull men

Type t5 t21 Aquarius as single bull men in a double imprint France, Trois Frere cave overworked engraving. Abbe Breuil, 1952. Georges Bataille. Mindprint by Edmond Furter). The healer on the left is one of the most celebrated figures in rock art. T5 themes include thunder bulls and ritual leaders such as the Pope. Long before patriarchs in Rome, Avignon and elsewhere, this pope had his own Cistine ceiling. The type is usually human,

sometimes bovine, here both. A near-vertical fault in the rock face prompted the double mindprint, here sharing an interlocking galactic equator. The four galactic corners are pronounced, typical of t21 Aquarius themes. Celestial polar markers, and two slightly different horizontal planes, tag the inspiration on the left to Age Taurus 1 -Taurus 2, and on the right to Age Taurus 2.

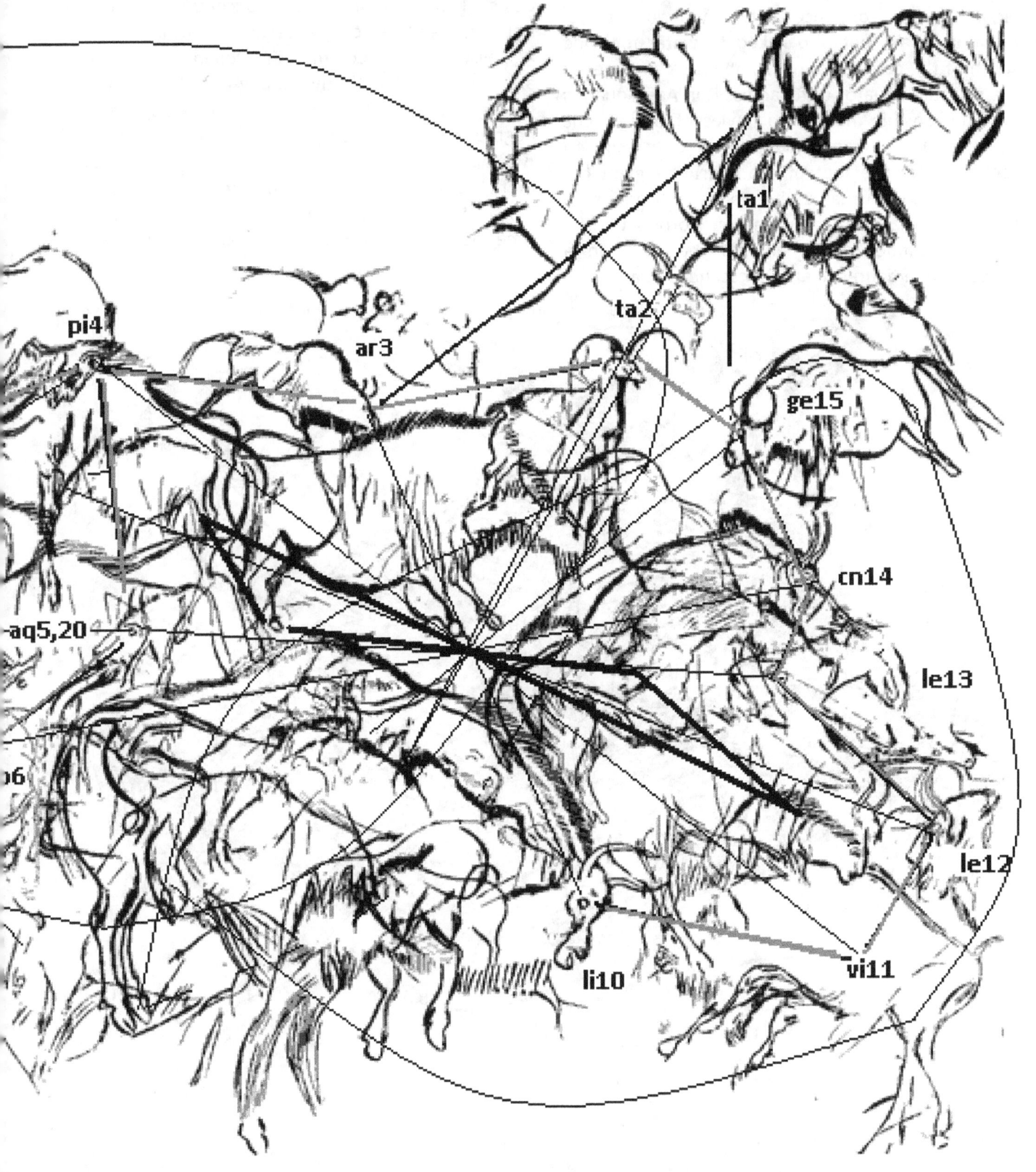

A world spirit with ropes

Type Aquarius t5 t21 as a world spirit (Zimbabwe, Matobo fish pool lower left group. Elspeth Parry, Amabooks. Mindprint analysis by Edmond Furter). The four major types or groups anchor the corners, although the Scorpius group is damaged. See typical cardinal cornice designs in Tarot trump 21 (World). The four cardinal elements of water, earth, fire and air, are usually pronounced in type Aquarius themes. Aquarius is air, but also linked to water for lying south of the celestial equator, about to 'emerge' as the celestial equator drifts across it in Age Aquarius (see the Cosmic map). Two havles of the galactic equator almost frame the pool in a fish-shaped section, from the foot of the Taurus t1 giant (an attribute more usual at its opposite Scorpius t8 Ophiuchus Giant), to the hand of Scorpius t9. The image continues above and to the right, in a procession of figures to another scene, also a

mindprint, and is thus part of a double sphere. Artists and healers experience and express most calendric, symbolic, iconic, alchemical and esoteric features at a subconscious level. These themes could take a lifetime of study to express at a conscious level and could still be in error. Artistic inspiration offers a shortcut to holographic expression. The high level of rigour in the iconic sequence and geometry of mindprint is a natural wonder of the world.

Celestial polar markers are uncertain, but the horizontal and vertical planes tag the inspiration to Age Pisces, in the Common Era. Iconographic Ages are of unequal length, the 30 degrees of Age Pisces having lasted a little more than 2000 years, the 20 degrees of Age Aries only about 1300 years, and the two Ages of Taurus together about 2600 years or more. For its early centuries, before about BC 3000, earth obliquity, precession rate, and the value of time should not be assumed from current values.

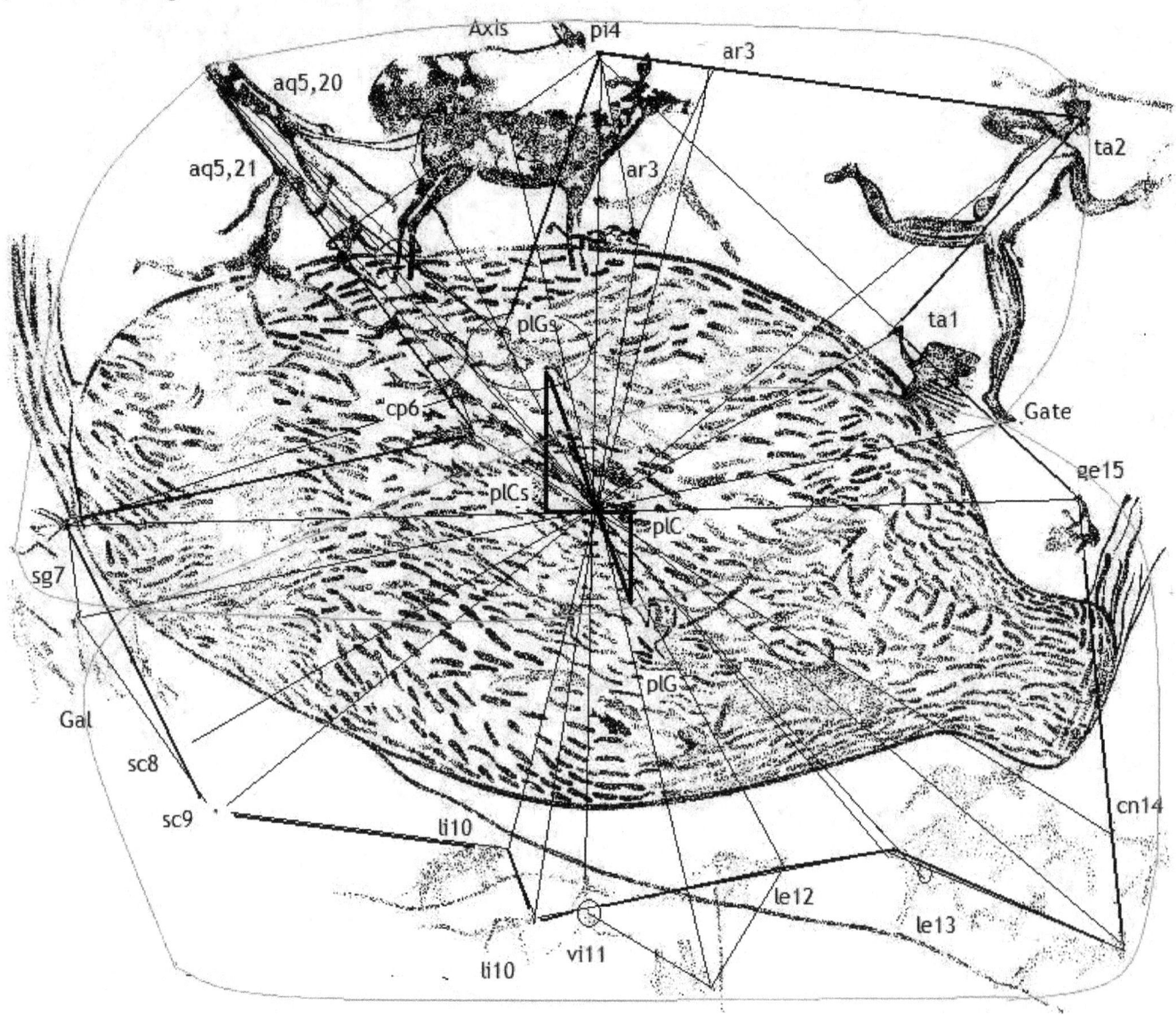

As below, so above

Type Aquarius t5 t21 as a star or galactic polar sigil, and as a Pegasus boat figurehead, in a double vertical imprint with a pictographic lintel (Babylonian Pazuzu stele, limestone altar or plaque. Mindprint analysis by Edmond Furter). The adjacent Aquarius t5 t20 takes on the t21 role of an encompassing world spirit instead. Aquarius t5 t20's face is part of the pictographic (picture alphabet) sequence in the top register, that duplicates the top half of the upper mindprint (see an Egyptian pictographic lintel in the Dendera crypt at theme t2 t17).

The larger size of Aquarius t5 t20's face on top compensates for his combination with Aquarius t5 t21 in register two, and his role as polar axis churn below, where his equatorial position is filled by a humble fish in the lowest register.

Register three holds six types, all shared in the overlap by the two contra-rotating imprints.

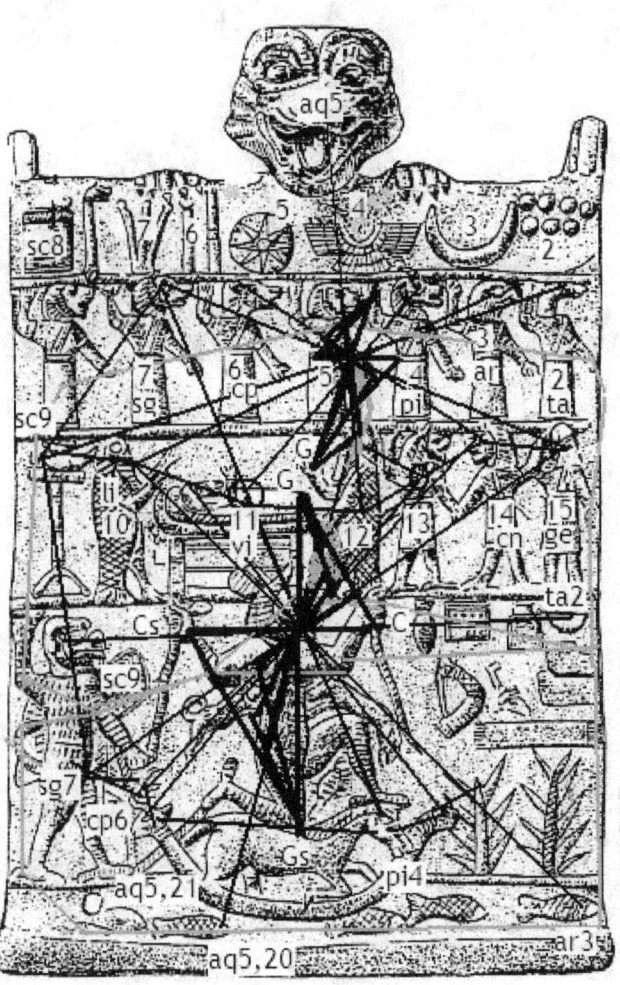

Aquarius t5 t20 below rests on Aquarius t5 t20 Pegasus and Cetus (as a horse in a boat), while he reaches up to Leo Crater (Grail), here part of the adjacent Virgo t11 bier, under the hand towards Leo t12. The kneeling posture and serpents, however, are more usual at the cardinal (crosswise) pair of Taurus t1 or t2 t17 Perseus and Scorpius t8 Ophiuchus (Serpent holder) and Hercules. Virgo t11's assistants, either midwives, healers or embalmers, sometimes slaughterers, are Leo t12 and Libra t10, as usual, here as Oannes fish men (see t11 figures, and an Amatola horse slaughter scene at theme t13). Incarnation and sacrifice are implicit in the central Virgo t11 as a birth or death figure, as well as the horned altar outline and a layered cosmos.

Celestial polar markers in the lower sphere tag a range of eras, from the vertical plane (Age Gemini-Taurus), via the Oannes front toes and Pazuzu hip (Age Taurus), Oannes front heel and Pazuzu's dog leg (Age Taurus-Aries), Oannes rear toes and Pazuzu's dog jaw (Age Aries), Oannes rear heel and Pazuzu shoulder (Age Pisces), to Pazuzu's two hands and snakes on the horizontal plane (Age Aquarius). Celestial polar markers in the top sphere are gauged by the lion-headed Aquarius t5 t20's foot and jaw, shoulder, hand and heart, and finally the adjacent Pisces t4 belt and its own belt. The work may date from an iconographic transition period, perhaps Age Taurus-Aries, about BC 1400, but its inspiration is prophetic of future Ages when the rocking boat of the sky, precession, would click into the next cardinal configuration, due about 2016.

In a study of 600 inspired subconscious imprints, this work is most remarkable for its apparently effortless double imprint, underpinning a highly stylised and formulaic cultural theme (see similar cylinder seal imprints in the Ashmolean Museum in Oxford). It also offers an additional pictographic register as a kind of Rosetta stone allowing translation between archetypes, shapes, concepts, letters, sounds, principles, gods and attributes. The equally effortless four polar gauges add to the hologram of concepts as a mirror to archetypal structure. If any work of art could lay claim to recording an eternal story, readable across millennia, in near indestructible low tech format, this is it.

A jester as nature spirit

Type Aquarius t5 t21 as a nature spirit (Jeanne Morgan-Lefay; Masks. Mindprint analysis by Edmond Furter). See Arcadian tomb scenes at theme t5 t20. In this sparse work, Aquarius t21 is just a puffed shoulder, more often the eye of a figure holding the world on his shoulder or in his hand. It is combined with Capricornus t6, which is sometimes double-headed. The motley outfit, hairstyle and active posture are Aquarian attributes. Libra t10 is a raised hand and knife instead of his usual staff. Virgo t11 is a womb as usual. Gemini t15 is the man's hand on an elongated arm, grasping the woman by a topknot of hair (see Gemini t15 as a smiter in the Narmer palette at theme t3, and Achilles smiting Trojans at theme t15 t0). Mindprint follows a rigorous sequence of attributes and geometry, but expression of necessity also breaks some rules to keep others. The artist was unaware of the sequence and pattern while expressing layers of autobiographical meaning. She may have been subconsciously influenced by the earliest of Poussin's Arcadian themes, focussed on a skull, but could not consciously recall that work (see theme t5 t21). She also paints pseudo-Egyptian scenes, but could not consciously relate the work to smiting twins, nor to Tarot trump 15 (Devil or earthly creator) or trump 0 (Jester). Galactic poles are on two jaws, as they often are (see baby Christ 'speaking' a celestial pole at theme t12). Celestial polar markers on a wrist and an elbow, and the horizontal plane, tag the inspiration to Age Pisces, incidental with the Gothic styling and the work.

Migration across a chasm

Type Aquarius t5 as a lion in the left sphere, and elephant in the right sphere of a double imprint (France, Chauvet cave migration of rhinos flanked by lions. Don's Maps. Mindprint analysis by Edmond Furter). The Aquarius t5 figures are both rampant (climbing), a typical posture. The spheres do not interlock by figures, but part of one of the galactic equators of each meet across the chasm, like two distorted bubbles merging into an elegant curve, hinting at a galactic positioning or framing function (see the Mexican Palenque lid at theme t4). Some double imprints link at other types, leaving galactic equator links distorted or impossible.

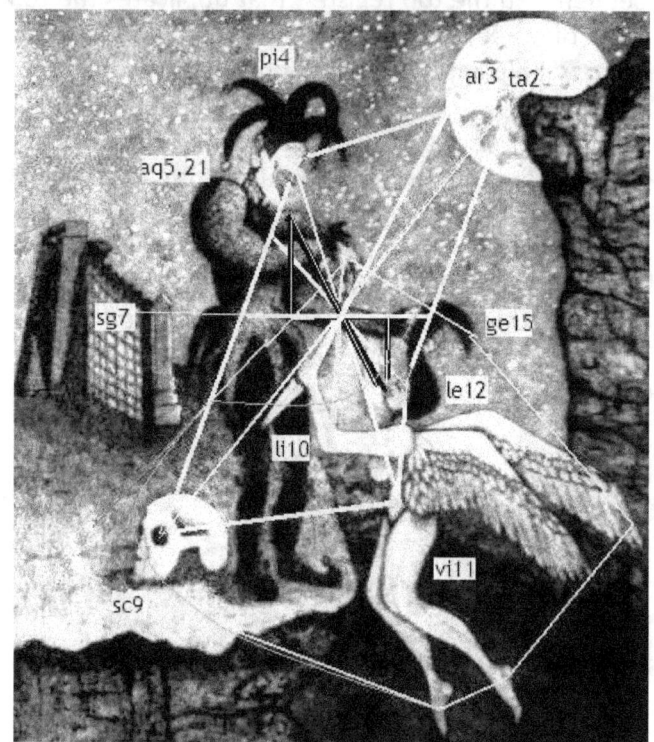

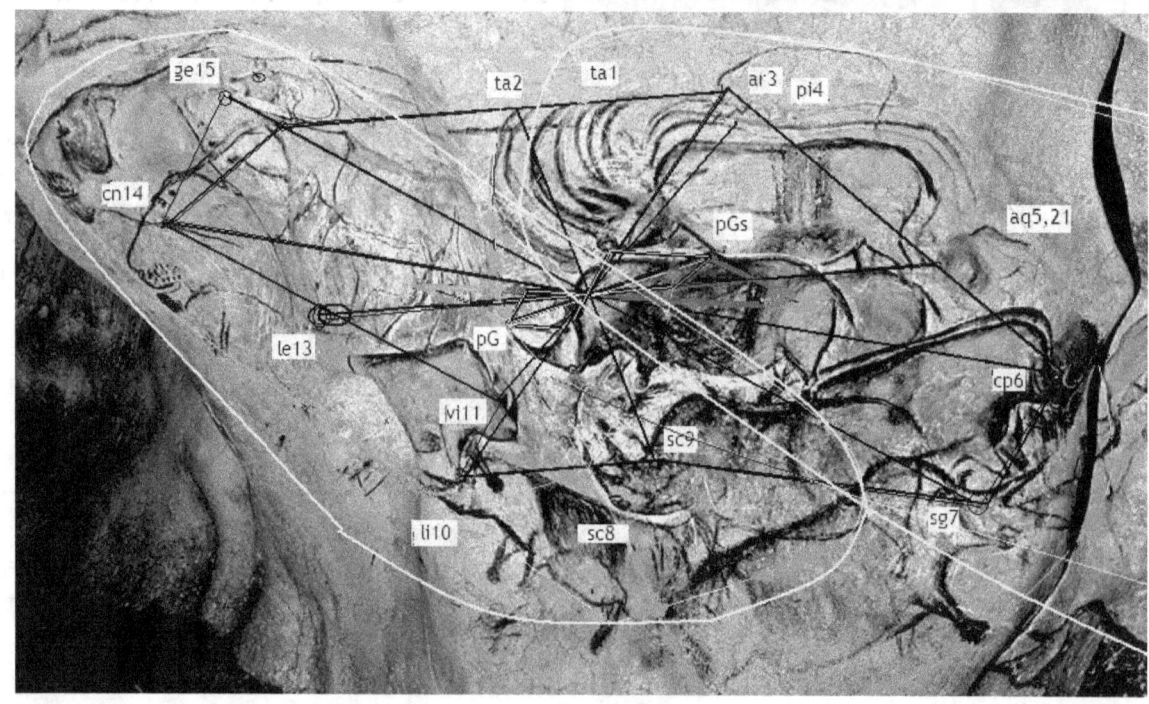

See perspective rows of heads in Egyptian art at themes t3 and t6, and in Indian art at themes t2 and t7. See lions in a migration scene in an early Egyptian mural at theme t13. See animal feet pictured as tracks in Turkey at theme t5 t21, and in Namibia at theme t12. See rows of flying or falling antelope in rock art at theme t2.

One popular version of this theme is the flying reindeer of Santa Claus, with geometric repetition in trees, horns, fences, sleighs, reigns, mushrooms, coats and bags.

Celestial polar markers are uncertain. The horizontal plane on the left (which does not always agree with one of the polar triangle planes) indicates Age Taurus-Aries, between about BC 1700 and BC 1300. Archaeology dates the work much earlier. The left half offers tags to Age Cancer, about BC 6800 as calculated by current assumptions, but the right half does not seem to confirm that, and no other work or premise in this study lead back that far. A separate study of attested Ice Age works is required.

A tree person as world spirit

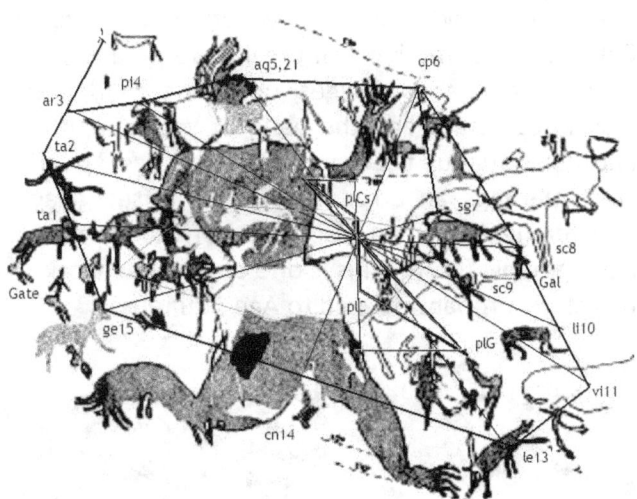

Type Aquarius t5 t21 as a world spirit (South Africa, Aliwal North master of animals. Ben1. SA National Museum. Mindprint analysis by Edmond Furter). Aquarius t20 or t21 is usually body-painted or dappled (here with figures on his body) and in active posture, sometimes with notable hairstyles (see a Russian Shiva at theme t15).

Celestial polar markers are set by a rump, a head, and the vertical plane to Age Taurus-Aries, remarkably early, although a raised hand and the horizontal plane may tag the inspiration to Age Pisces-Aquarius. Mindprint does not date art, but includes several layers of confirmation of some aspects of the inspiration or expression.

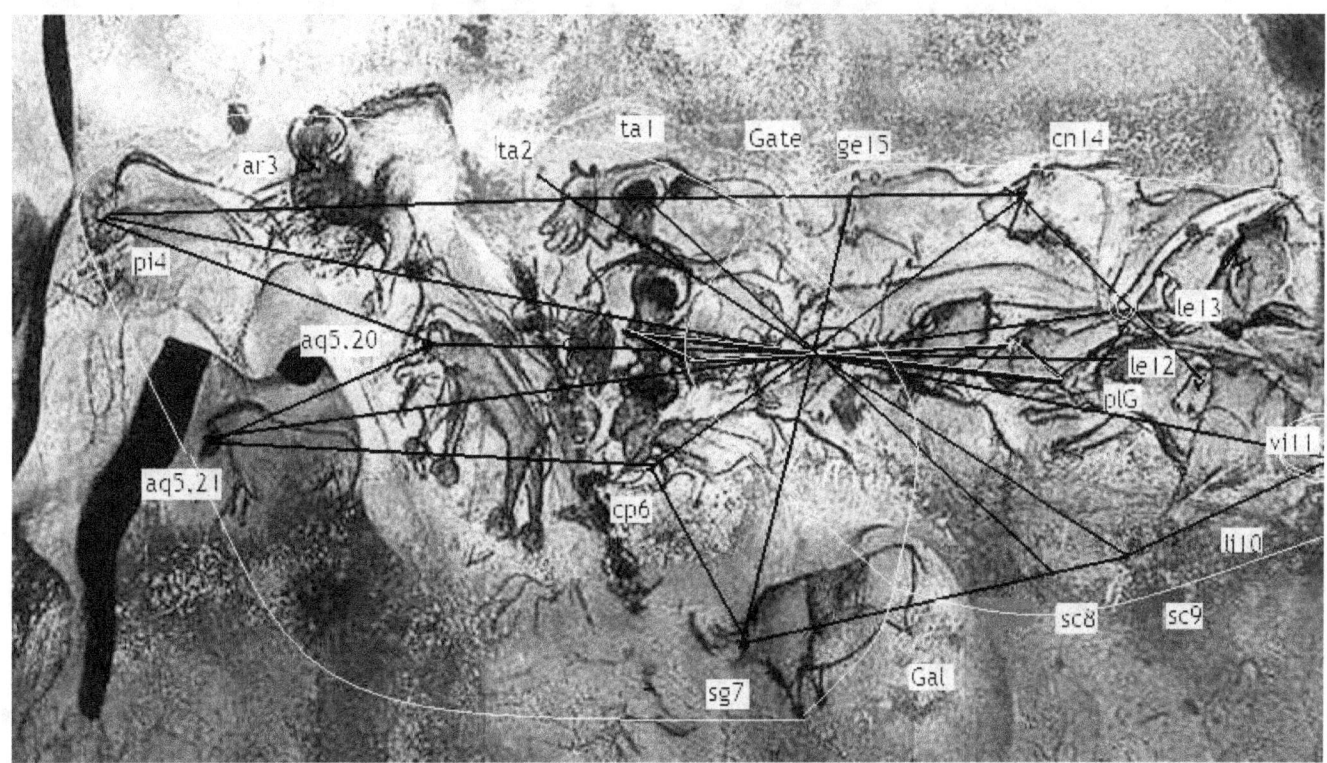

A world tree spirit

Type Aquarius t5 t21 as a world tree spirit (Mexico, Teotihuacan mural with a tree, flowers and music. Mindprint analysis by Edmond Furter). Corner guard figures confirm the Aquarius t21 theme, also found in Christian art.

A celestial polar marker on a crosier (spiral hook) and the vertical plane (here angled by the photo) tag the inspiration as Age Pisces, confirmed by the top central figure.

An Age Aquarius world tree

Type Aquarius t5 t21 as an underworld guide (Lapp drum skin drawing with ritual celebrants. Mindprint analysis by Edmond Furter). The drum cosmogram healing tradition had updated its visions with Christian elements, but the cosmic tree remains rooted between Pisces t4 and Aquarius t5. Here the flanking figures both have double staffs to calibrate the spring equinox, subconsciously in anticipation of the axial era. The ritual officials are named Juksakka, Sakarakka and Madderakka. Their fish pond or ice fishing hole has an astronomy counterpart in Aquarius t20 Pegasus, here displaced to the mystical basket position (see a Roman sarcophagus at theme t11), the only sequence error in the work.

See Nordic Amlethus myths of a 'many-coloured cover' and salt mill (De Santillana and Von Deschend; Hamlet's mill).

Libra t10 is a tree or branch, as it is in a South African Amatola work (see theme t5), but branches are more usual at its cardinals, Cancer t14 or Capricornus t6 (see Egyptian and Mexican palettes, and the Externsteine carving at theme t4).

This study adopts the principle that there is no limit to what artists, and thus all people could subconsciously know; and that language, art, music and conscious or semi-conscious symbolic codes are all inadequate to fully express human experience. Individual experience could only partly comprehend nature or archetype. Display of art supports the human need to express, create, celebrate and share inspiration, cast in terms of experience, as the ritual celebrants in the image imply. This drum and its mindprint, with its implied social ritual, are as adequate or inadequate as any myth or art could be. Celestial polar markers on a calibrated ladder, as a gauge, tag a series of Ages, up to the hand of the central celebrant and the hand of World man (yet another Aquarius t21 stand-in) at the Age Aquarius start, perhaps an error due to the offset galactic register (level), or an inspiration of our immanent iconographic future. This is one of very few works in this study probably tagged to Age Aquarius.

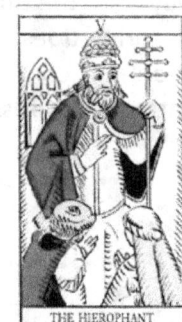

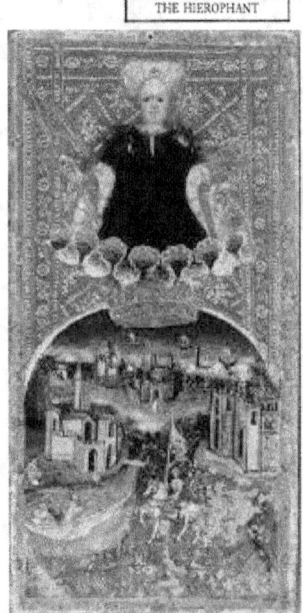

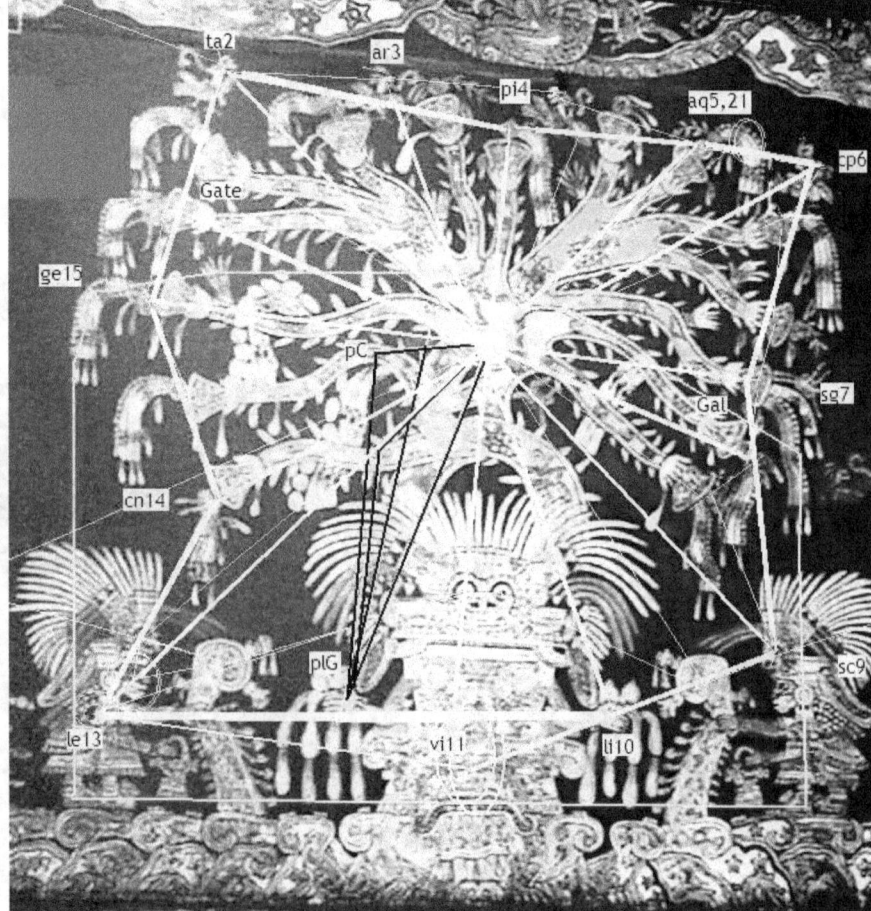

An Age Aquarius world skambha

Type Aquarius t5 t20 and t5 t21 as a spring solar couple or twins (Peru, Pablo Amaringo; spinning top. Mindprint analysis by Edmond Furter). Leo t13 is in the lotus position, an attribute more usual at its opposite, Aquarius t21. Icelandic myths of a 'many-coloured cover' and salt mill (reviewed by De Santillana and Von Deschend in Hamlet's mill), here churn in dayglow colours. The equator of eyes forms an outline of butterfly wings, incidental with the theme of transformation and flickering motion. Symmetry in the equator, named ecliptic in this study for convenience, is uncommon in art, and usually subtracts from galactic symmetry, as it does here, as if expression were projected through either one or the other. The ecliptic pole is on the hand of Capricornus or Aquarius. Celestial polar markers are absent, but the horizontal plane of some figures tags the inspiration to Age Aquarius 1, and the general plane tags for Age Aquarius 2, confirmed by the identity of the central human pair and the axial design. Toppled and upright pots below, a Leo t12 Crater theme, will soon mark autumn. Some other Amaringo works tag the Age Pisces-Aquarius transition. This work moves the familiar Pisces t4 twins into Aquarius.

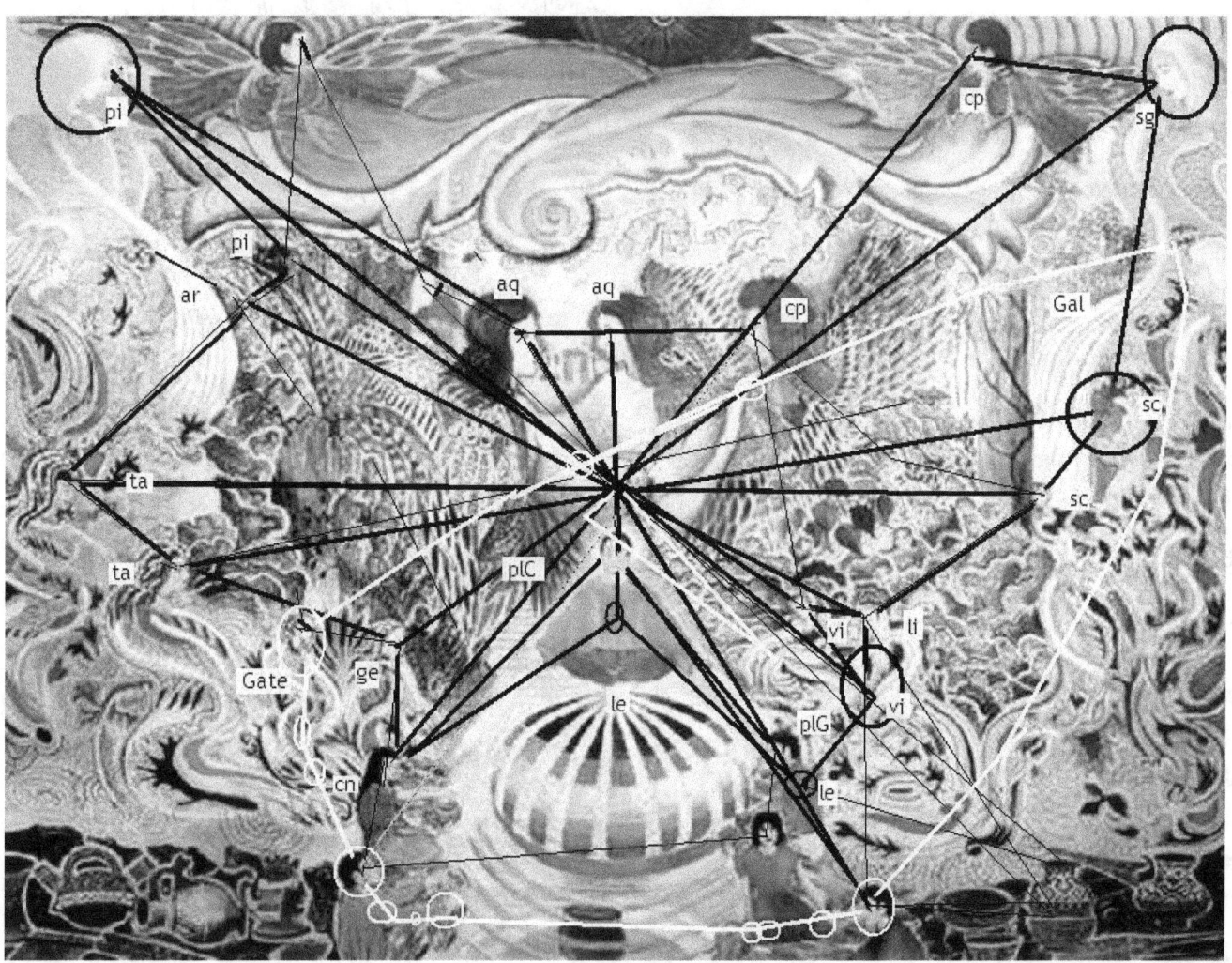

A silk baroness

Type Aquarius t21 as creator serpent goddess Nu Gua in a knotted sash, in a double imprint (Chinese silk tomb drape of Lady Dai, Han dynasty, AD 100s. Mawangdui, Changdu. Mindprint analysis by Edmond Furter). Type Aquarius t21 in her encircling sash between two corner guards, compares directly to Tarot trump 21. The work is in an afterworld, heaven and hell format, as in Babylonian, Egyptian, Grecian, Chinese, Mexican and other funerary art. A tree of life (top centre) and seven suns (circles on the right) grow towards the nature deva. As in the Mexican Palenque lid, a tree grows from the adjacent Pisces (see theme t4). Her crow of death is in the sun, her toad of rebirth in the moon. She baked clay people in an oven which is part of the central tree (see Tarot trump t4 as twins flanking a furnace. Also a Hildegard of Bingen tapestry of an oven, not illustrated). The two spheres connect at the Taurus-Gemini gate, figured as a gate. Celestial polar markers and the vertical plane in the top sphere tag the inspiration to Age Aries, but lower sphere tags may indicate Age Aries-Pisces, in the last centuries before about BC 150, about 300 years before the design or its eventual use in the tomb.

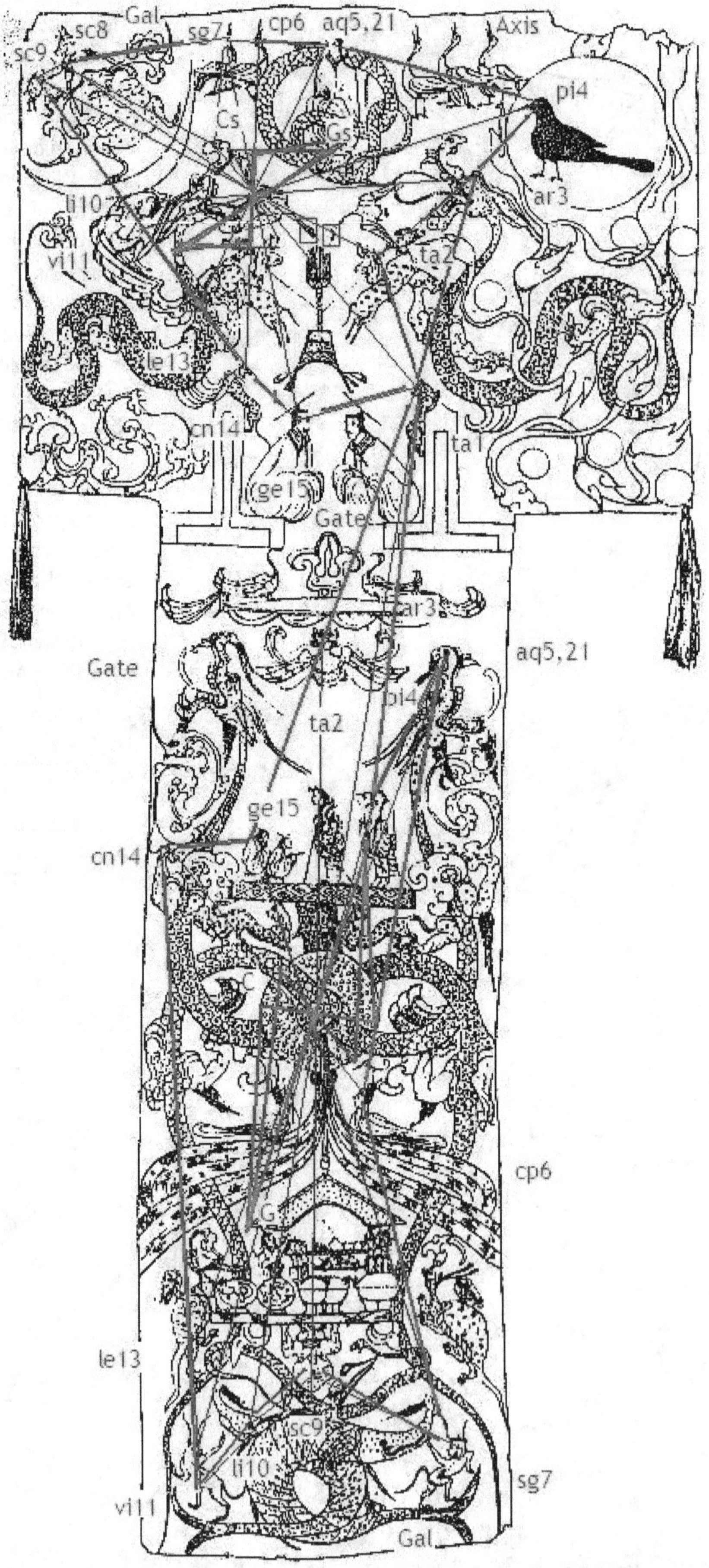

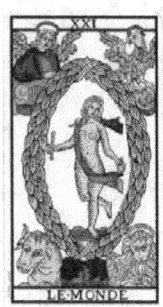

Russian Atlas holds a world

Type Aquarius t5 t21 as a man holding up a buck bag world (Russian Aimaly Tash, Ferghana engraving of ploughs. Mindprint analysis by Edmond Furter). A cross-legged deva in a halo or bag appears in Tarot trump 21 (World), as Atlas in some variants. The usual corner guards are churn groups. At bottom left is a type of galactic centre. Aries t3 is a wheel behind a reindeer team, as of Santa Claus. A lattice of horns and ropes form the Taurean t2 basket of mystery (see a Roman sarcophagus at theme t11). Celestial polar markers tag the inspiration as Age Taurus-Aries, before about BC 1300. Exaggerated horns are typical of Bronze Age Celtic sites. The work could be more recent, of retro inspiration and styling.

Bull tribe colonisers

Type Aquarius t5 t21 and Aquarius t5 t20 as a mother, child and a bull-man in rampant posture, in a double imprint with many overlaps (South Africa, Pretoria old council chamber Union mural, right cornice. Mindprint analysis by Edmond Furter). A central bridging imprint is about to form on the t4-t5 axis, the current Age transition era marker. Celestial polar markers and the vertical plane tag the inspiration in the right sphere to Age Pisces, and in the left sphere to Age Pisces-Aquarius.

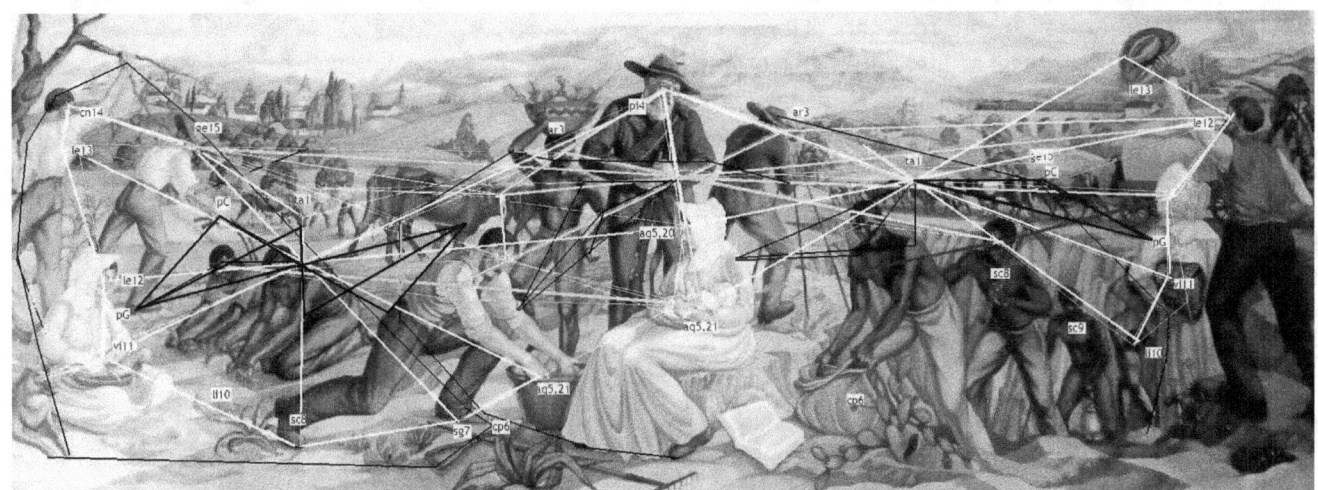

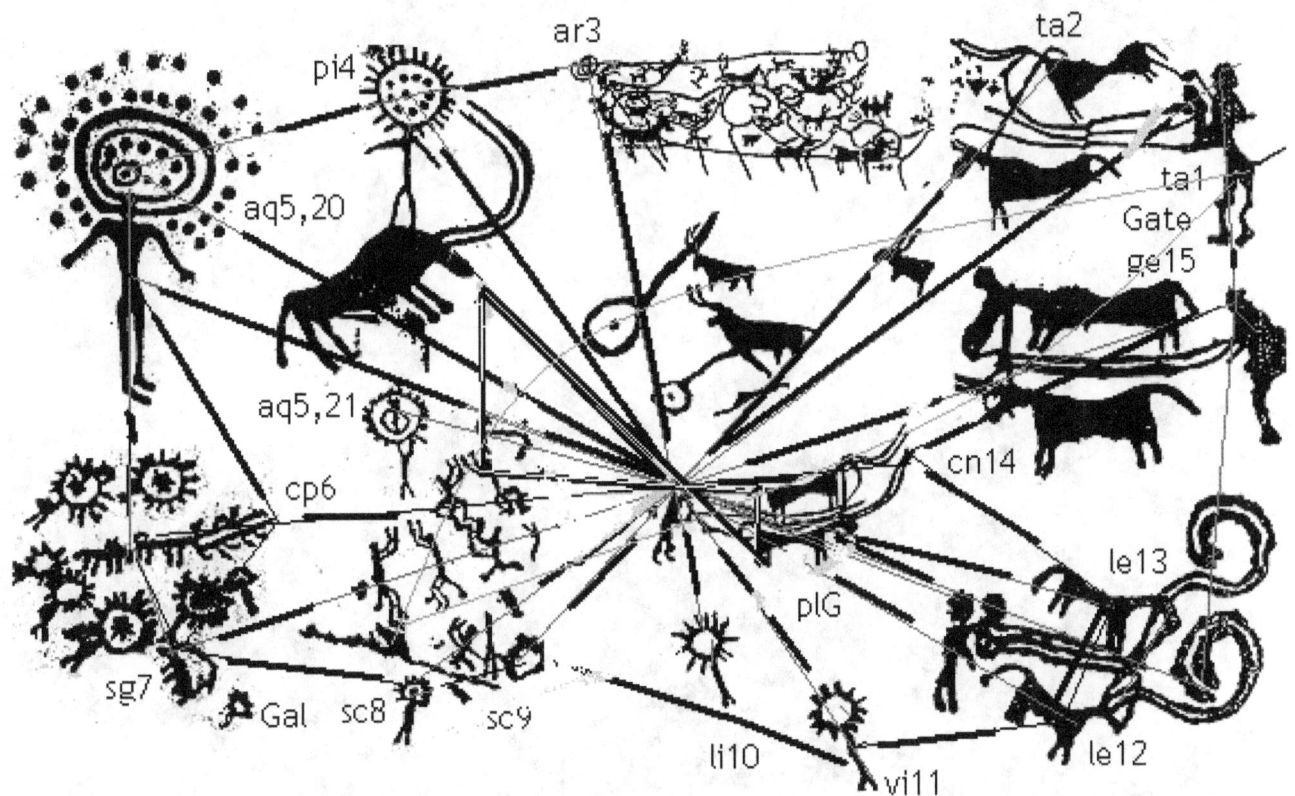

Type Capricornus t6; Pan

A double-headed Janus

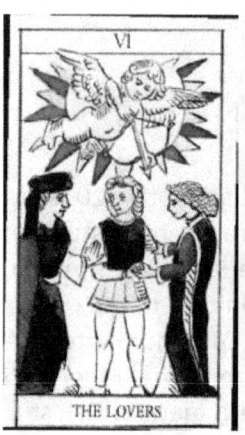
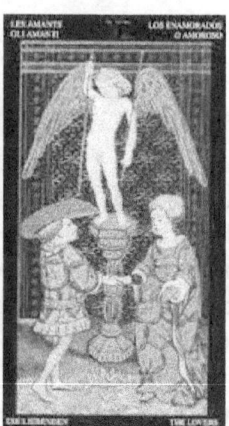

Type Capricornus t6 as a double-headed Janus, Pan or Hermes pillar (Poussin; Dance to the music of time, 1638. Mindprint analysis by Edmond Furter). Time belongs to its opposite, Cancer t14, here strumming a tune as a bookend to the herm. Capricornus t6 expresses choice (as in the Paris legend), and the present, difficult to obtain in a consciousness preoccupied with past and future, requiring meditation. Taurus t2 is a rain goddess or priestess, as she often is in rock art. Libra t10 expresses wheel or carousel of life, here figured only by a foot, as some of Poussin's figures habitually do.

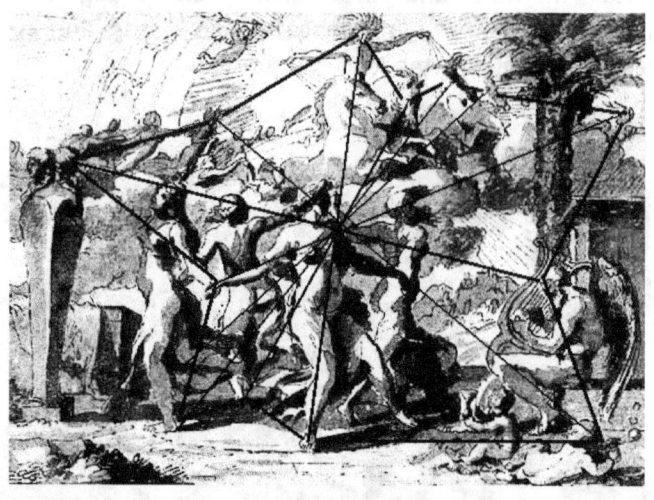

A celestial polar marker on an elbow tags the inspiration to Age Pisces or Age Pisces late, incidental with the Renaissance. Polar markers are among the best examples of synchronicity, the apparently meaningful co-incidence of events or attributes, not traceable by physical causation or conscious logic.

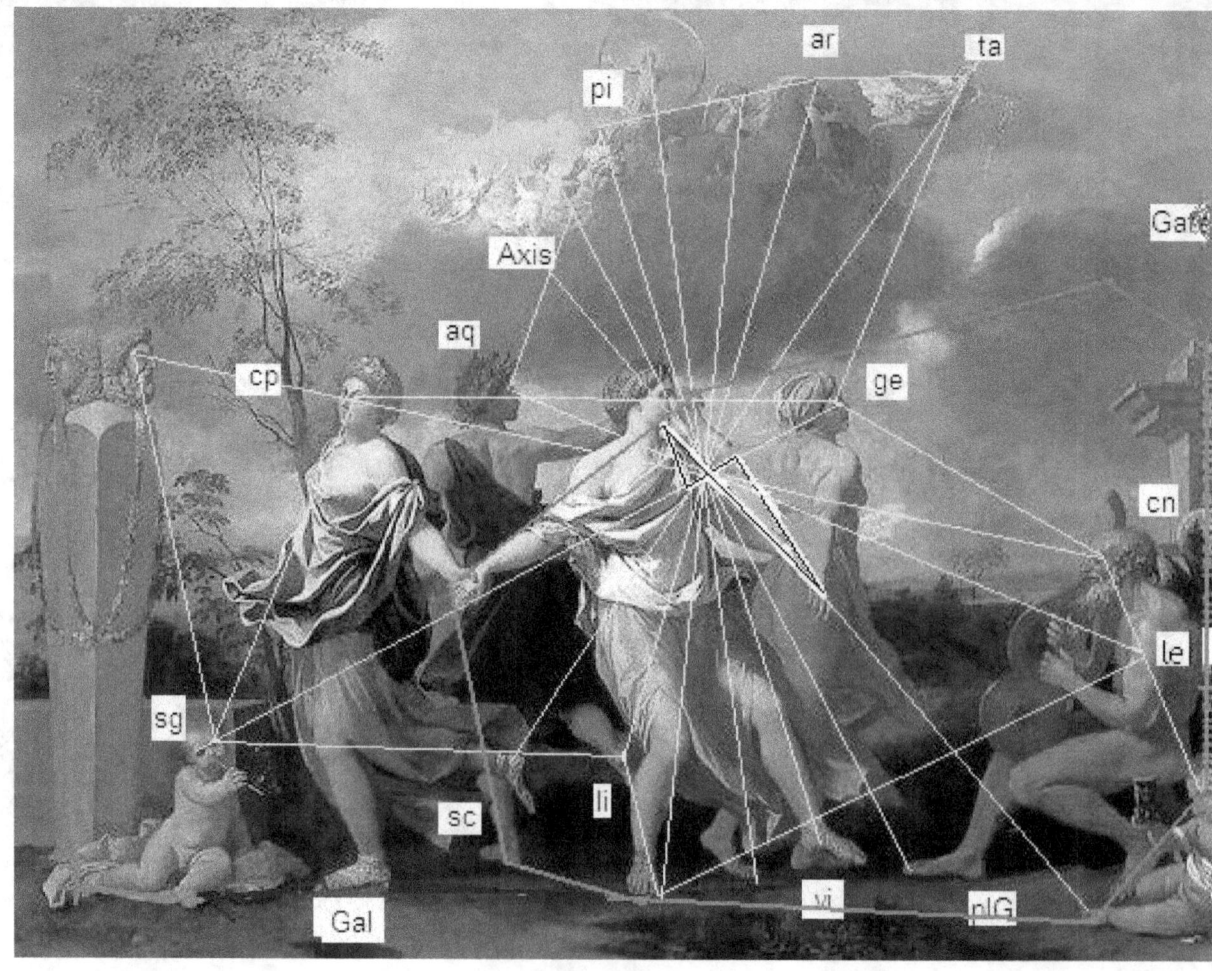

Pan, Kokopelli, Krishna, Jethro Tull

Type Capricornus t6 as a goat and a human, between a double-headed figure and a flute player (Canada, Kokopelli. Mindprint analysis by Edmond Furter). The double-header, perhaps head-butters or wrestlers, or a figure with six legs, is at Scorpius t8 or the galactic centre, and the flautist is at Aquarius t5 t21, a type prone to sharing and swopping attributes (see theme t5). Krishna, Pan, Kokopelli and other flute players as lord of animals and forest appear in rock art in the Americas, Zimbabwe and India. Ian Anderson, composer and flautist of jazz rock band Jethro Tull, is possibly an incarnation of Krishna, or at least unconsciously started expressing the repertoire; chromatic music of close-fitting notes, arpeggio slides, meditative riffs, standing on one leg, hairy, popular with goat herdesses, and campaigning for forest preservation.

Anderson discovered on a concert tour of India that "They thought I was making fun of Krishna and I had to explain that I had no idea that Krishna did this... I discovered that I was not the only one-legged flute player on earth." (Ian Anderson; Jethro Tull, Living with the past, DVD EREDV266, Eagle Vision). A bagpipe with lilting tunes over a set of drones is also a kind of Pan music.

Aquarius t5 t21 is dominant, with a Capricornian t6 trunk (see a similar figure with large genitals in the USA California Piedra Pintada copy at theme t5, also linked to t6). Some Capricornus t6 types have Pinocchio noses doubling as flutes.

Celestial polar markers on Pan's genitals and hip (damaged by flaking) tag the inspiration to Age Pisces-Aquarius. The horizontal plane tags for Age Aquarius. This poor copy of a damaged image demonstrates the order and focus that mindprint brings to apparent doodling chaos, and the window it opens on the human subconscious.

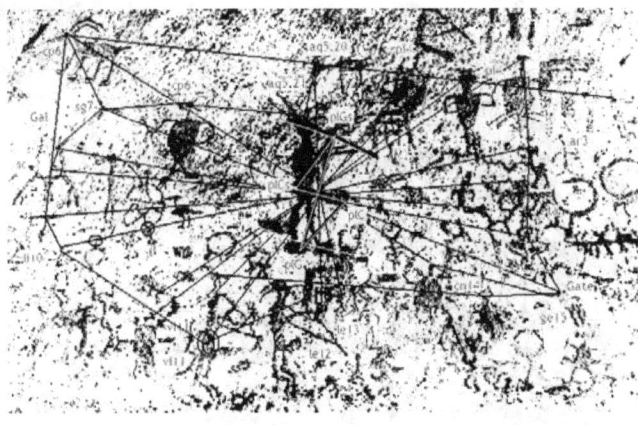

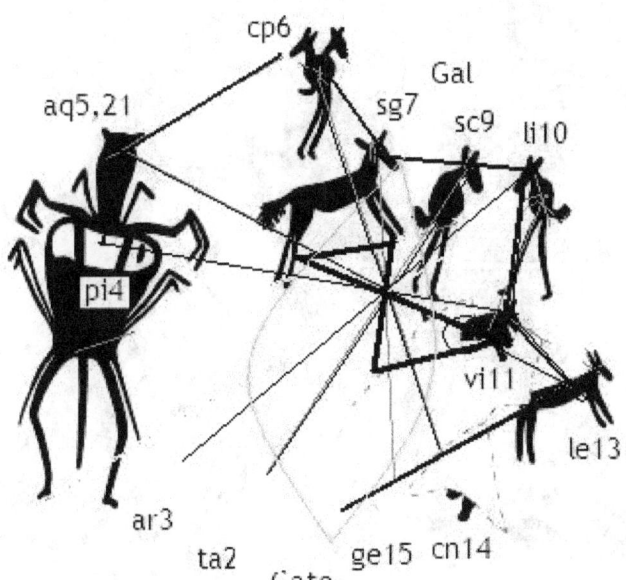

A double-headed half-man

Type Capricornus t6 as a double-headed buck bag man (South Africa, Fouriesburg, multi-armed. Bet1. SA National Museum. Mindprint analysis by Edmond Furter). See the same distinctive attribute in the Egyptian Hunters palette at theme t8, and in other Pan themes. See buck bags unfolding as a kind of bagpipe in Pan themes. The type seems to include exuberance. A chameleon with human legs is also known in rock art (South Africa, Schweizer Reneke chameleon buck bag, Ditsong Cultural History Museum, not illustrated).

Aquarius t5 t21 is multi-armed, typical of figures flanking the galactic corners. He is large, active and body-painted as usual, with some attributes of his opposite Leo t13 in a large chest and an extra axis to his heart (usually Leo t13 is the only figure 'seeing' by his heart instead of his eye). Here Leo t13 and Virgo t11 share an axis. Due to damage, noted as prior 'attempted removal' in the museum, this work has only two demonstrated axes. A celestial polar marker on a hoof, and the vertical plane of the polar figure and some other figures, tag the inspiration to Age Pisces-Aquarius.

Overworked mirror of art and nature

Type Capricornus t6 as Mercury in a fount on a planetary hill, over a cave of mystical marriage (Cabala as mirror of art and nature, Alchemia, 1615. Mindprint analysis by Edmond Furter). The mindprint axial structure is not symmetrical to the artist's conscious design structure, confirming that archetypal attributes and axes are subconscious, despite intensive conscious symbolism in the overworked scramble of alchemy. The Rosicrucian emblem reads to its intended viewers as a variation on a standard allegory of the mystical marriage of Christian Rozencreutz, with seven steps of alchemy under seven planets. Even standard astrology is scrambled here, but the subconscious structure is unaffected, as usual.

The mindprint sequence ropes in four personified planets, a phoenix, three zodiac figures from a planetary 'house' sequence, two alchemists and two rabbits. Capricornus t6 is a Mercury under Gemini, with some of its planetary attributes relevant to the type. His kicked-out leg is the Venus part of his combined sigil (see dance illustrations in the Hypnerotomachia Poliphili, discussed at type t2 t17), his feathered headdress is the Mars part of his sigil, his fount a bath for planets passing archetypal Capricornian midwinter in Age Aries.

The artist and the tradition did not consciously understand Mercury as potentially a multi-headed or horned Pan, Paris or Capricornus.

Aquarius t5 t21 is a phoenix in active posture as a dappled world spirit.

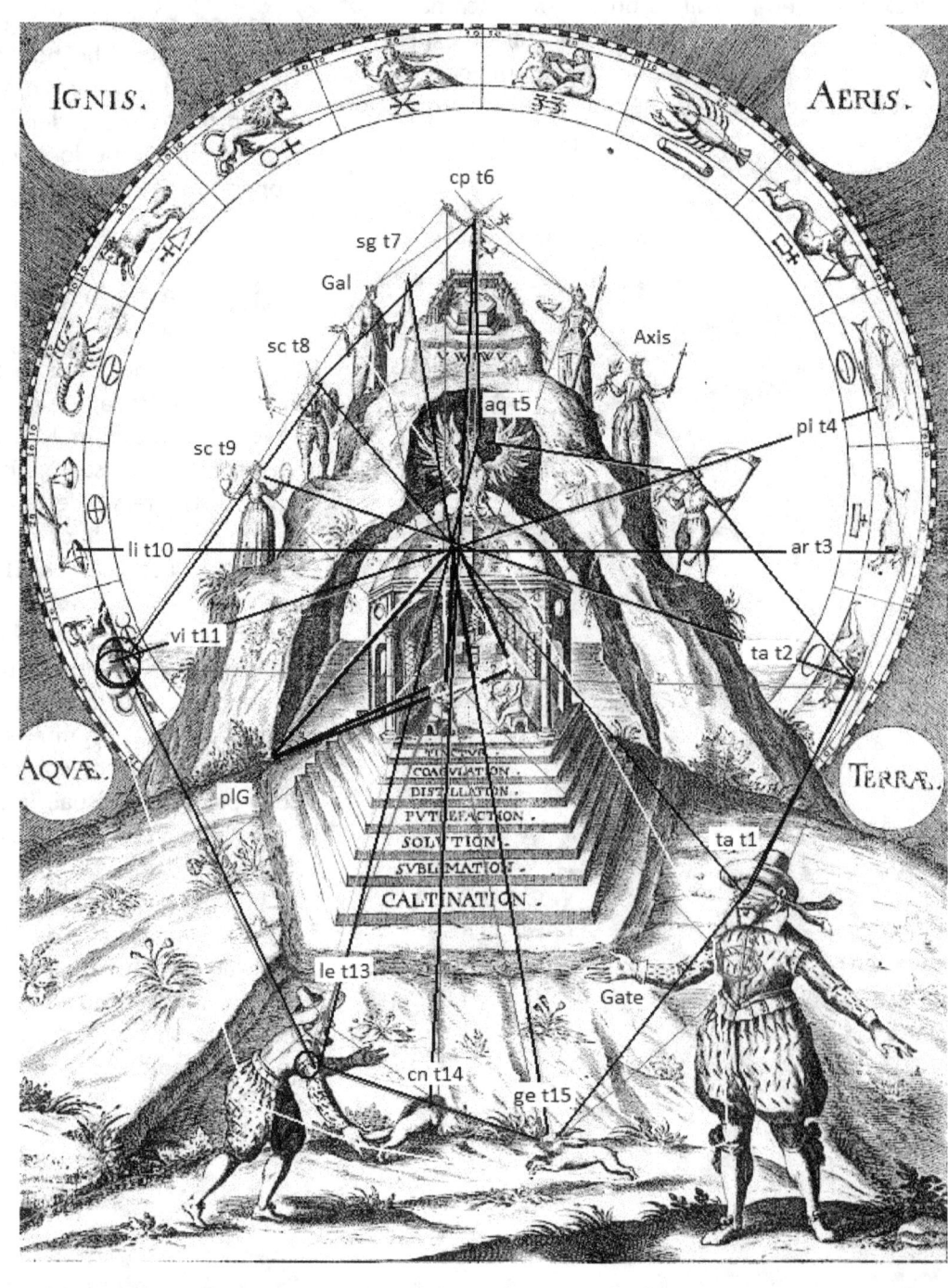

The moon and Jupiter are not figured in the mindprint sequence, yet Jupiter stands in for the cosmic tree on the Cetus-Pegasus (Whale-Horse) polar axis, supported by Aquarius as a sea horse centaur. Pisces t4 is a Saturn as temporal ruler. Aries t3 is a Capricornian goat instead of a dragons pair, a common ambiguation. Taurus t2 is a waterbearer in error, yet a kind of rainmaker. Taurus t1 is a blindfolded querent, following nature and instinct to the hidden work, thus a healer and hunter as usual. Gemini t15 Canis is a rampant rabbit instead of a dog. Cancer t14 is a rabbit entering a hole in the mount of earth, instead of a bear, lynx or bees. Leo t13 finds a route to the heart of the mount, but as difficult as for a camel to pass through the eye of a needle (see a camel eye on a 'needle' axis in Arabic rock art at theme t8, and cattle in a U gate at theme t3). Virgo t11 is a contradictory Taurus, but is pregnant as usual. Libra t10 is a pair of scales on a staff. Scorpius t9 is a Venus, but with arms up in the regular W shape of the t9-t10 combination. Scorpius t8 is a Mars. The galactic centre is at the foot of the Sun, which is also figured by two eyes on a sun face on the dome, one of which marks the ecliptic pole. Sagittarius t7 is a bauble on the sun's staff. Co-incidences between alchemy and mindprint derive from their respective holographic properties as subconscious expressions of archetypal order. Inspiration favours prepared minds, particularly of students of nature, but not necessarily of learned minds.

The supposed secret tradition of alchemy is based on chemistry, thus on glimpses of natural structure, a means to transformation and an end in itself. Manifestos, tracts, laboratories and institutions are perpetually distracted from the goals of transformation by conventions and technology, as the consciously symbolic layer of this work is distracted from natural structure.

The galactic pole is on a corner where four elements meet. Seven celestial polar markers on the king's shoulder, elbow, hand and staff, and on the queen's trefoil and jaw, form a gauge calibrating millennia through Age Taurus-Aries, Aries, Aries-Pisces, Pisces, and Pisces-Aquarius. The vertical plane tags the inspiration as Age Aries-Pisces, the most recent Age transition, but about 1700 years before the work. As in all mindprints, only the wheels of the mill of inspiration could grind this fine.

Old and young at a feast

Type Capricornus t6 as a harpist at a festival of gods (H De Clerck; Wedding of Peleus and Thetis, 1606. Louvre. Mindprint analysis by Edmond Furter). A wedding is an allegory for choice and initiation, as in the alchemical wedding of Christian Rozencreutz. Celestial polar markers on the Aquarius t5 t20 elbow and the bride's elbow, both on the horizontal plane, tag the inspiration to Age Aries-Pisces, incidental with the Capricornian t6 theme of old and young, past and future. The work is about 2000 years younger than its inspiration.

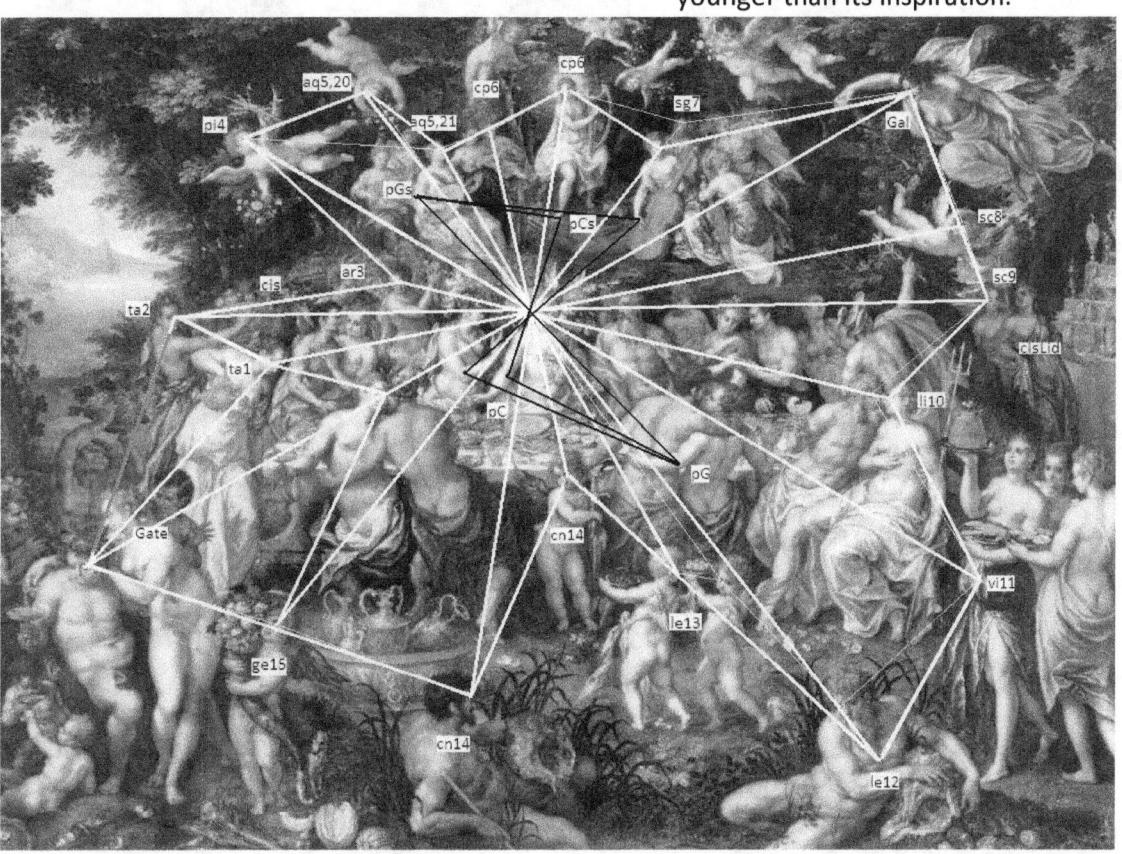

Type Sagittarius t7; Chariot

A galactic vortex

Type Sagittarius t7 Scutum (Shield) as a vortex bag (South Africa, 102hc vortex. Thornycroft. RARI. Mindprint analysis by Edmond Furter). An oblique vortex may be one of the primary stages of visual inspiration, a kind of merry-go-round from which figures emerge, fixed by their limbs to two oblique circles, and their eyes to axes, perhaps sliding and somewhat rotating individually to fit the rock or canvas. Variant horizontal planes in some works indicate some residual rotation or jostling. Nostradamus wrote of a vortex in his brass bowl of water, perhaps stirred to induce visions. Boer prophet Siener (Seer) van Rensburg said he felt a pain at the back of his head, perhaps involving the visual cortex, with churning images, "then I could do nothing but recline with my hands behind my head and wait, then figures move and act before me as clearly as if they were here." (Prof AWG Raath and N van Zyl). Vortex or churn groups often remain at Sagittarius t7 or at the adjacent Scorpius t8 tail, flanking the galactic centre, perhaps an anchor point of visual inspiration or expression. Some churn groups also remain at the four galactic, structural corners of mindprint (conventionalised in Indian art), often with ropes, particularly opposite the galactic concept at Gemini t15. One of the galactic equators is usually nearly circular, here on the right (thin oval line). Celestial polar markers are uncertain, and there are several horizontal planes. One possible vertical plane tags the inspiration as Age Aries.

A funeral cart

Type Sagittarius t7 as a widow following a funeral cart (illumination of the funeral of Charles 6, by Duke Bedford, 1422. Mindprint analysis by Edmond Furter). Some death and trance scenes evoke the Capricornian t6 Choice of Paris theme, here figured by the mourner nearest the body's head. Pisces t4 is the colour knight bearing the shield, opposite Virgo t11, her pregnancy shrouded. An unmarked and unlabelled figure with a staff below the body's head is a slightly misplaced Libra t10, raising the possibility that the expression was interfered with, perhaps by succession politics. Taurus t2 Pleiades as a falcon and branch are also slightly misplaced, and could figure the basket of mystery (see a Roman sarcophagus at theme t11). Celestial polar markers on the body's hands and head, and the horizontal plane, tag the inspiration to Age Aries-Pisces, retro to the work.

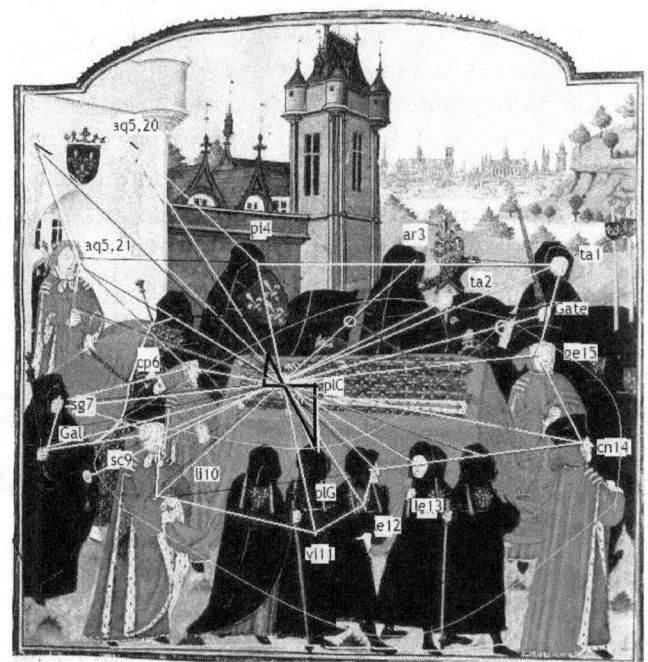

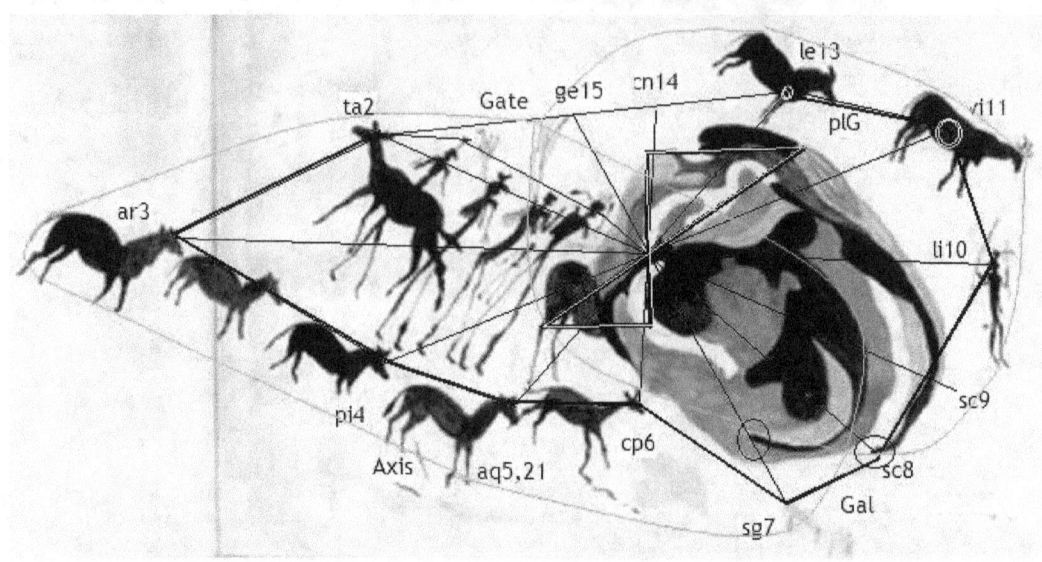

A horse griffin chariot

Type Sagittarius t7 Aquila (Eagle) as the central extended vortex (Zimbabwe, Matobo range winged horse. Elspeth Parry, Amabooks. Mindprint analysis by Edmond Furter). This work as a whole expresses Sagittarius t7 themes of vortex, chariot, griffin wings, manifestation, symmetry and distortion. Virgo t11 is a horse with ten passengers, a kind of chariot (see Tarot trump 7, Chariot). Celestial polar markers are tagged by a front hoof, or nearby rear hoof on a long leg (both flanking the vertical plane) to Age Pisces or Age Pisces-Aquarius.

A vortex with passengers

Type Sagittarius t7 Scutum (Shield), as the main figure in a vortex bag (Zimbabwe, Matobo range plant bag. Elspeth Parry, Amabooks. Mindprint analysis by Edmond Furter). The bag forms a cartouche similar to a royal name tag in Egypt (see formlings, bags and hives at theme t7 and other themes).

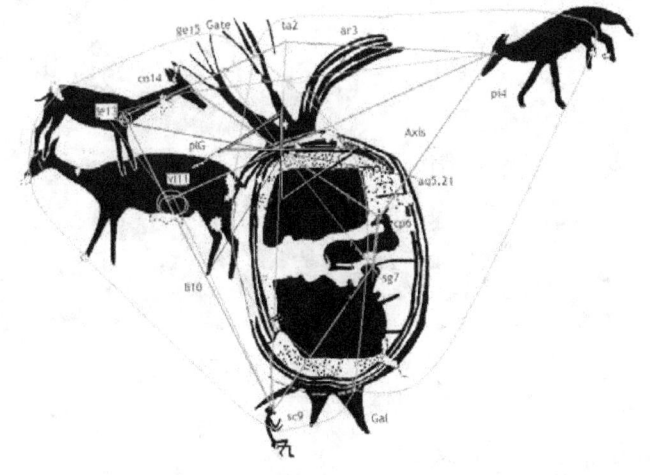

The galactic equator on the right frames the left side of the bag, but the left galactic equator, representing the sphere flipped around and viewed from the underside (here unusually the northern hemisphere) forms an ovoid crossing many limb joints, as usual. The bag is also a kind of womb of Virgo t11, a large pregnant antelope mid-left. Her belly profile may be typical of afterbirth, but damage at the critical point obscures the belly line (the dotted line marks a missing rock flake). The usual ropes at Gemini t15 here may figure afterbirth or umbilical cords, and the teats below could figure her udder, but not in the physical sense alone, as many idealised or surreal aspects in art testify. Art, like myth, expresses conceptual structure, and favours events that also express structure. The artist may have had a vision of a bag pulsating with light, known among Bushman and Khoe remnant people and their mixed race descendants as 'the eye'. An informant in a documentary about the Karoo desert said; "That is of course the eye, it is. Sometimes when I return at night across the veld I see the eye and it lowers, there is a light inside and people moving there inside. That is the eye, it is." Analogy with UFO and abduction experience is obvious, as anthologised by several authors. A vortex does not always express t7 (see an electric bulb eye at Taurus t1 or t2 in Picasso's Guernica at theme t1 t16).

Celestial polar markers are uncertain, but the vertical plane tags the inspiration as Age Pisces-Aquarius, our current era. Our midsummer sun is leaving Gemini, crossing the gate and entering Taurus, while our midwinter sun is leaving Sagittarius, crossing the galactic centre's gate and entering Scorpius (the galactic centre itself is a few degrees south of the sun's path across the galactic equator, see the Cosmology graphic).

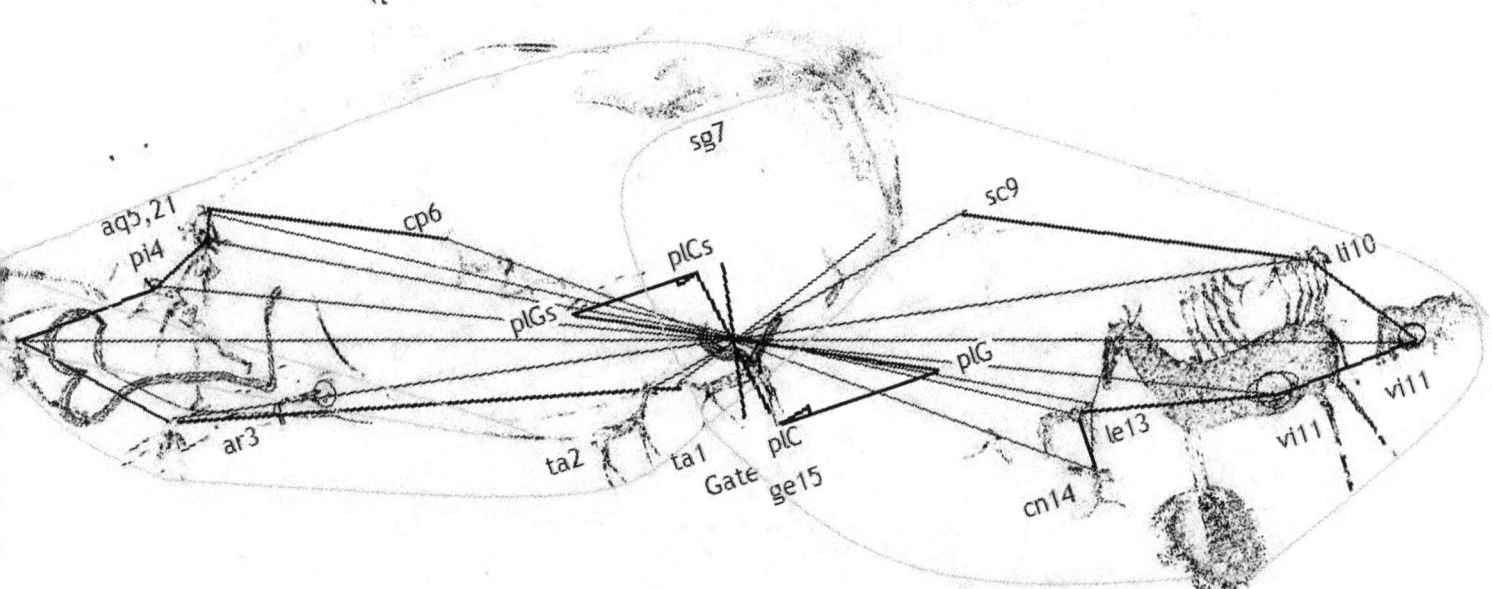

The triumph of legend

Type Sagittarius t7 as a supplicant (left sphere) and chariot horse team (right sphere) in two adjacent imprints with the same rotation, connected by jumps or 'crankshaft' lines (Egyptian engraving, battle and votive scene. Mindprint analysis by Edmond Furter). What seems like a central sphere is only a set of lines connecting four identical types, and one of the equator lines of the right sphere, that happen to cross in one point. Vocabulary for this unique arrangement is still lacking.

Ptah is not identified in the sequence, and could be a rival Thoth, as he is in one of the three Egyptian theologies. He sits between t6 and t7 of both spheres, in astronomical terms at Sagittarius Cygnus (Swan) on the galactic equator at the smaller dark rift. Capricornus t6 appears as a vulture protector, and as Seshat, who is more usual at the opposite Cancer t14 as a spiritual surveyor. She wears a starburst headdress of hemp leaves, a stock crop for making cloth and rope, only recently replaced by cotton. Seshat is marking a notched palm branch calendar with a curved top. As librarian and the official tasked with 'pulling a chord' with the king, she and her counterparts worldwide are patron saints of mindprint.

Celestial polar markers in the left sphere on two knees, and the horizontal plane, tag the inspiration to Age Aries-Pisces, confirmed in the right sphere by a throne and hip, and the horizontal plane. If the central clutch lines had developed into a sphere, it may have had a southern celestial polar marker on Ptah's knee, confirming Age Aries-Pisces.

A mantis griffin

Type Sagittarius t7 as a praying mantis female (South Africa, Vanessa Von Mollendorf; Man-eater. Mindprint analysis by Edmond Furter. See a discussion of this artwork in the text). Mantids, like some spiders, eat bees and eat their males, to be eaten by birds in turn. The species more usually express Scorpius t9 as healers in trance ritual with two sticks, or Aquarius t5 as a priest. A tripod table is the most elegant southern polar concept found in this study. The artist had no conscious knowledge of the constellations Mons Mensa (Table Mountain) and the round Magellanic Cloud. All inspired artworks include some features of both conceptual hemispheres. Celestial polar markers among the pseudo rock art figures, and the horizontal plane, tag the inspiration to Age Aries-Pisces. Other markers tag for Age Pisces-Aquarius, our current era. Both confirm the theme of transition.

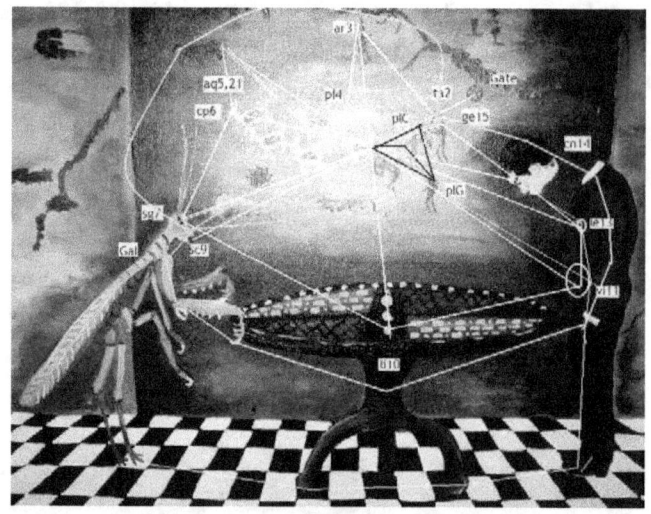

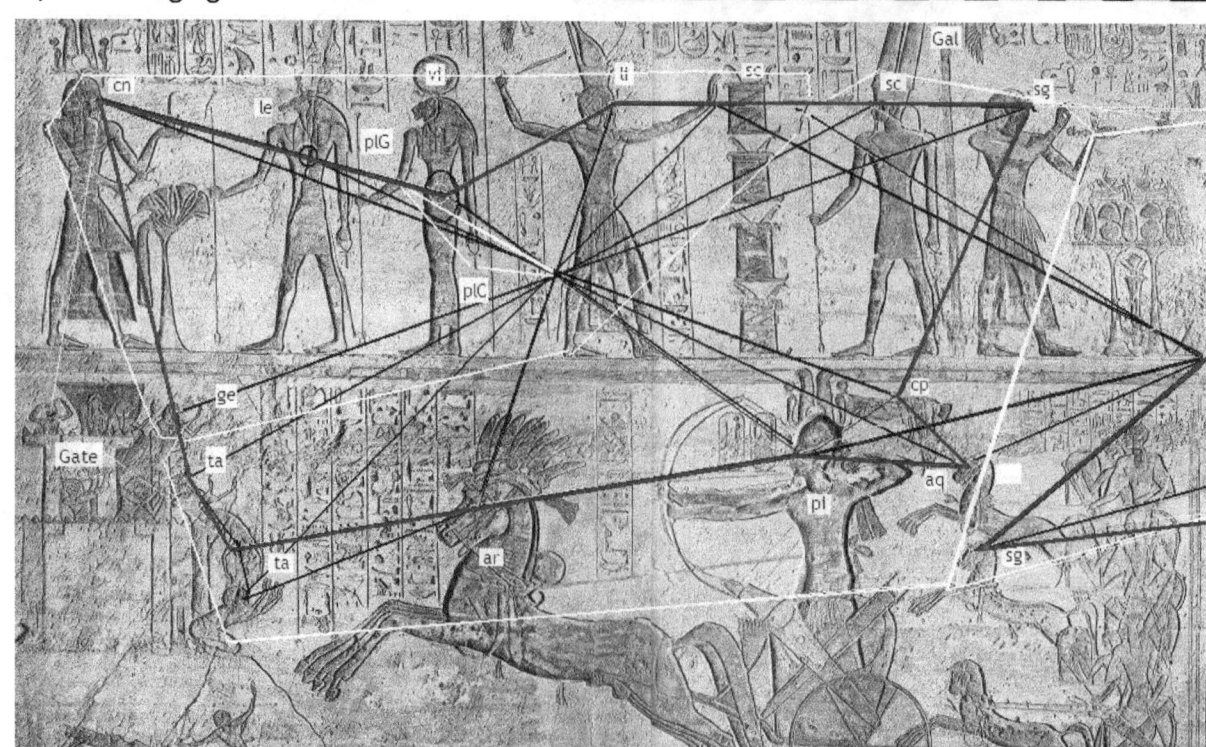

Eagle griffin chariot

Type Sagittarius t7 Aquila (Eagle) and Scutum (Shield) as a griffin drawing a vortex chariot (William Blake; Dante meets Beatrix in paradise. Mindprint analysis by Edmond Furter). Scutum expresses a vortex of manifestation directly on the galactic equator, including attributes of light, oblique symmetry, and distortion. Tarot trump 7 is a frontal image of a chariot and horse team pulling in different directions, perhaps expressing the ecliptic and galactic equators.
In the novel and movie of Percy Jackson and the Olympians, this griffin is brought to Olympus in a water bubble, perhaps from the adjacent galactic centre to the opposite galactic gate, a conceptual Olympus (see Credo Mutwa's rain tree mural with bubbles at the galactic centre, at theme t1 t16). A mixture of realistic and visionary elements, myth, history, expressionist elements and some imperfections are all typical of mindprint. Some double identifications, as if rotation had not completely stopped before expression, or continued during expression, make this one of very few generally distorted works in this study, as if the artist wanted to say more than standard subconscious logic allowed, and thus interfered with inspiration or expression. A celestial polar marker on an elbow, and the vertical plane, tag the inspiration to Age Aries-Pisces.

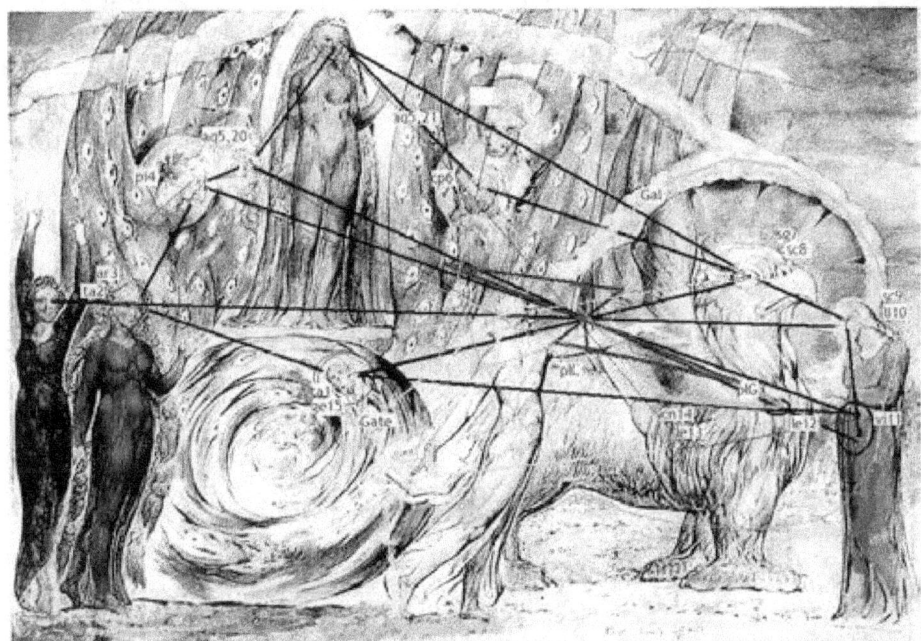

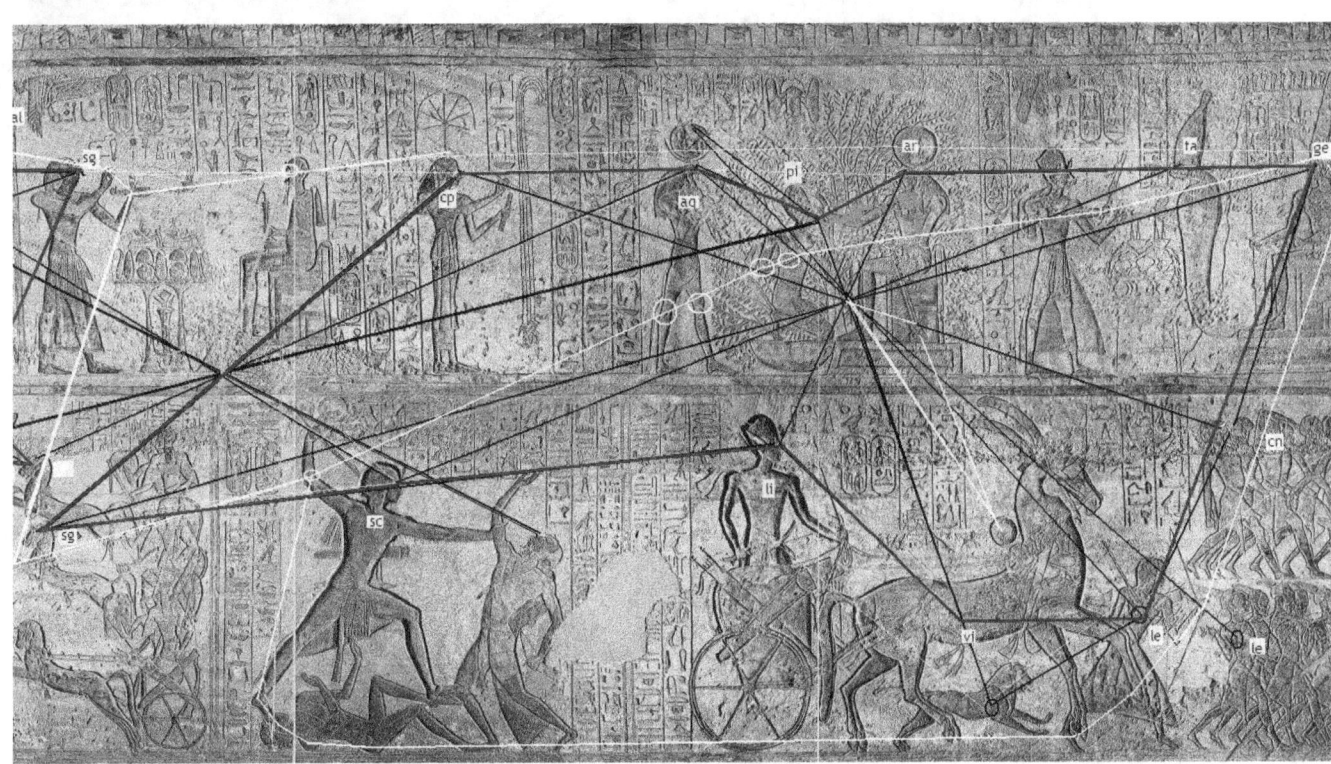

Goat people from buck bags

Type Sagittarius t7 as a goat person (Turkey, Mount Latmos goat people. Mindprint analysis by Edmond Furter). The centaur theme in myth and art is sustained by visions of buck bag therianthropes resembling goats, sometimes mistaken as ostriches in rock art. Pendant breasts could be mistaken as arms, an occasional style also found in Australia and southern Africa. The work is on a small rock shelter ceiling near Ephesus, where Artemis was celebrated as clutching two goats or antelopes, a type of Taurus t1 Auriga, Perseus, Medusa and female Hermes or Janus in one (see t1), with multiple breasts, ostrich eggs or small bags on her torso. Artemis is now identified with aspects of virgin mother Mary. Celestial polar markers are uncertain, but the vertical plane tags the inspiration as Age Aries-Pisces, in the last centuries BC.

A vortex man duplicated

Type Sagittarius t7 as a polar figure in a caravanserai battle (Algeria, Tassili caravan rock art on a postage stamp. Mindprint analysis by Edmond Furter). Horses, camels, bags, loads and chariots are stock t7 themes. Archetype favours duplication (as in seals, coins, cards and stamps) with great variety in theme, as in biology, chemistry and tools. Duplication and commemoration involves a benefactor, decree, commission, committee, mentor and our cultural impulse to popularise individual inspiration that popularises culture in turn. Movies and brand names continue the talismanic tradition of spiritual 'pills', imbued with notions of popularity and celebrity, their content often stripped down to formula and style, perhaps in subconscious recognition that only styles and signatures are unique. Celestial poles on a foot and a hand tag the inspiration to Age Aries-Pisces.

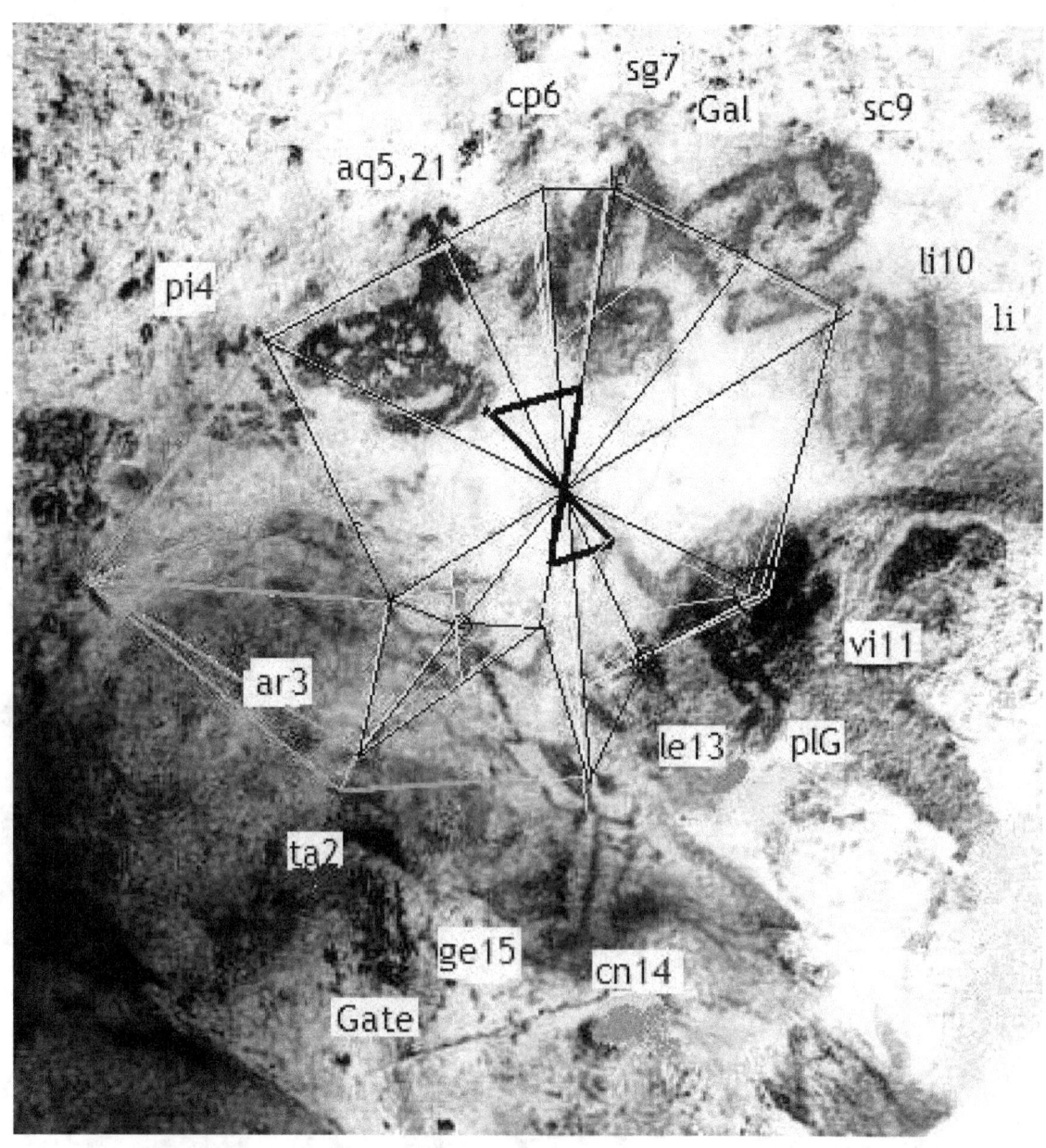

Manna and quail vortex bags

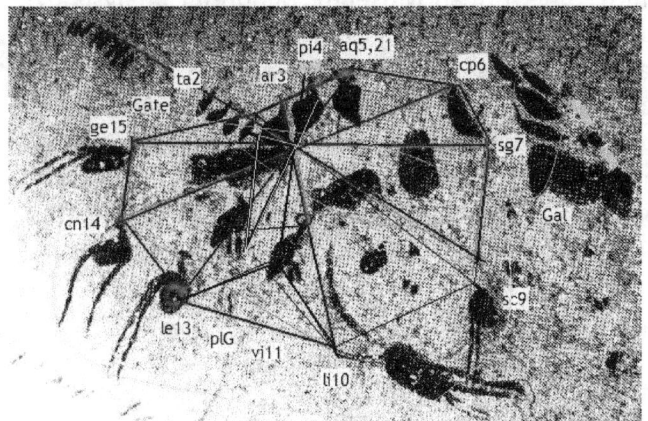

Type Sagittarius t7 Aquila (Eagle) as buck bag vortexes unfolding into P people, birds and centaurs (South Africa, nicknamed 'nightjars'. Mindprint analysis by Edmond Furter). Goat, ostrich and hatchling ambiguity seems typical of an intermediary inspirational stage. See the Biblical Exodus motif of manna and quail, linked to sustenance and vortexes such as pillars of smoke and fire, a regular spiritual vision, and occasionally physical scenes of volcanic plumes. See rows of bird carcasses in Egyptian art at theme t10. The figures equator is unusually symmetrical. Celestial polar markers are uncertain, but one of the horizontal planes may tag the inspiration to Age Pisces-Aquarius.

P people, X people, and ++ people

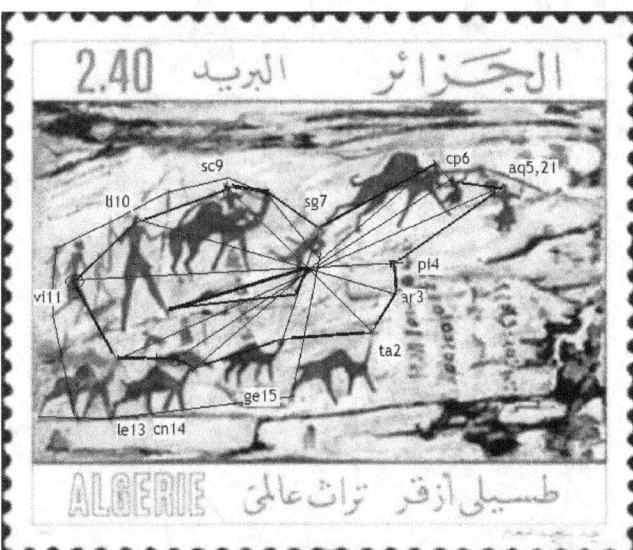

Type Sagittarius t7 as a P person, among P, X and ++ people (USA Wyoming P shapes. Mindprint analysis by Edmond Furter). P people, drawn in groups in some cave art dated to the Ice Age, are similar to goat people as a kind of centaur half-human, perhaps vortexes in various stages, from separation, to buck bags, to rows, perhaps to figures sequences, churn groups, and ultimately the mindprint sequence (see ostriches at themes t2, t12 and t13). Celestial polar markers on a ++ foot and a P hand, tag the inspiration to Age Aries-Pisces.

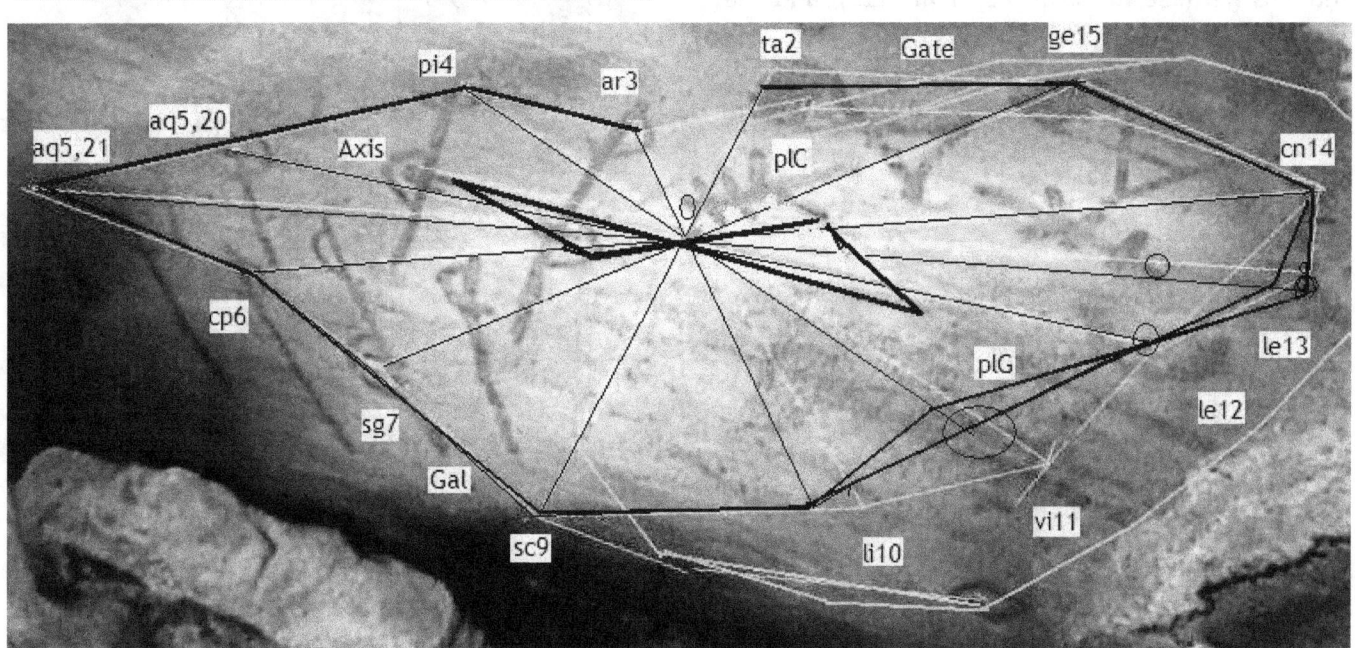

Type Scorpius t8 Ophiuchus; Giant snake holder

A giant rope controller

Type Scorpius t8 Ophiuchus Galactic rift, as a bauble head on a rope walker's staff (Egyptian Hunters palette, Hierakonpolis, Naqada 3 culture. Perdyn. Smith 1949. British Museum. Mindprint analysis by Edmond Furter). Its adjacent Scorpius t9 is bent in trance ritual as usual, holding a rope to an extra Capricornus t6 and a rear leg of Aquarius t5 t21 as a lion (the guise of its opposite). The other end of the rope passes under Libra t10 (see the Linton panel at theme t5 t21, and the Seti 1 ceiling at theme t8). Bushmen say they "climb" out

A shellfish palette

Type Scorpius t9 t8 Ophiuchus (Giant) as a shellfish harvester (South African palette, Plettenberg Bay, Robberg G bag. SAM-2828. Lewis-Williams, 1984. SAAS Goodwin series 9, 2012. Mindprint analysis by Edmond Furter). The bag is a palette shape, which is a standard stone tool shape. Practicality may not be the only design consideration of the enduring artefact standard, and diffusion may not be its only propagation. Tool development from core selection, to flaking, to a micro toolkit from one core with minimal waste, to fire-hardening, to hafting by sinews, and complex glue manufacture, may re-calibrate and sustain conscious and subconscious intelligence, as technology still does. Bored stones as digging stick weights and as maces likewise carry symbolic and practical value. Tools manipulate more than soil, just as money manipulates more than barter. A similar palette (Robberg D, see theme t15 t0) records practical and surreal elements of shellfish or honey gathering, in addition to expressing mindprint structure. Libra t10 has an arm or staff up as usual, here in a winged posture.

Celestial polar markers on the bag figure's elbow and t9's hip (see hip icons at theme t15), and the vertical plane of the leading figure, tag the inspiration as Age Aries or Aries-Pisces, typical of palette formats.

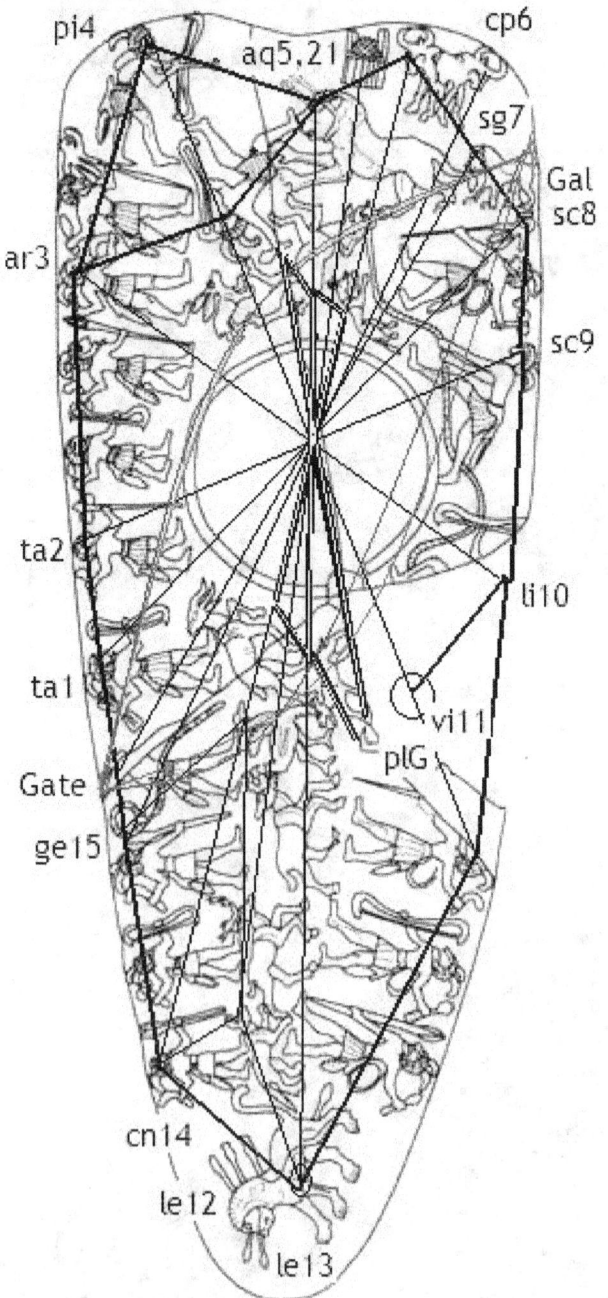

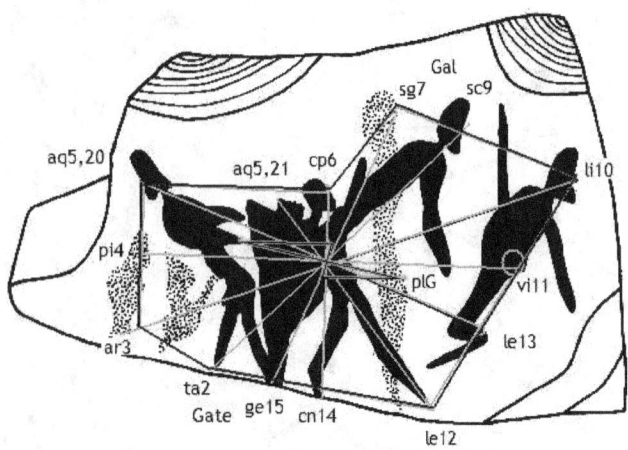

of trance by "the rope of the sky" (Biesele, cited in Lewis-Williams). Scorpius t8 Ophiuchus and Hercules are Samson types, roping torches to fox tails, adjusting pillars and paradigms (see fox tails in a Chinese tile at theme t11). To view Samson as arising from a constellation, as De Santillana and many other writers do, is to disown his archetypal pedigree, and to reduce culture to fragments of incidental and incremental hearsay.

Sagittarius t7 is often a youth, here a lion cub. Capricornus t6 is a 'double bull' with two heads, here a gnu (see a Utah image at theme t5 t20). Aquarius t5's body overlaps Capricornus, as it does among constellations, one of the holographic co-incidences that mislead many researchers into assuming that myths and icons derive from astrology, while the reverse applies.

Between t6 and t5 is a serekh (proto cartouche), perhaps a midwinter marker in Age Aries. Celestial polar markers on a hoof and a canine jaw, on the axis of the rope end, tag the inspiration to Age Aries.

A giant in a pool vortex

Type Scorpius t8 Ophiuchus as a small vortex controller at giant legs in an infinity pool (Zimbabwe, Matobo range, Nanke cave pool. Elspeth Parry, Amabooks. Mindprint analysis by Edmond Furter). The infinity wimple or Moebus ring as a hat, and the posture of controlling a vortex or monster maw, appears in Tarot trump 8 (Strength) and in trump 1 (Juggler), typological opposites. Samson, his oracular

riddles and pillar demolition are part of this type. Vortices also represent chaos theory, as a graph of a step change in two dimensions, via a third and fourth dimension, or one edge of a plane bent in an S-shape. The wimple represents a totality of responses to external pressures, named 'panarchical discourse' in history.

Nanke cave was one of a series of oracles, on par with Bronze Age and classical cultures. Africa oracles fell victim to political power struggles before and since independence from colonial rule. Roman spiritual centres such as the oracle of the dead at Baia, in a volcanic bay near Rome, likewise had graphic panels at their entrances, likewise destroyed by rulers to suppress or replace cults among servants (RF Paget; In the footsteps of Orpheus).

Taurus t1 is the shoulder and ropes of the central figure, a kind of bull foreleg (see Egyptian ceilings at themes t8 and t2). Taurus t2 is the central large figure with two rope streams up, instead of kneeling to pour two water streams down, while the pools express the jugs. Aries t3 t18 is an ostrich with a long neck. Aquarius t5 t21 has an active posture. Capricornus t6 has a companion, and an ingressed companion, instead of two heads. Libra t10 has raised arms. Virgo t11 is pregnant. Leo t13 is a lion, its heart marker confirmed by equatorial line economy on three eyes each from both sides. Cancer t14 is a Y-shape. Gemini t15 walks on a rope. Implied galactic equators across the sphere, frame the main figure and the two lower edges of the pool, a type of cartouche (royal name frame) with an eternity knot. The celestial pole is on the main figure's elbow, tagging the inspiration as Age Pisces.

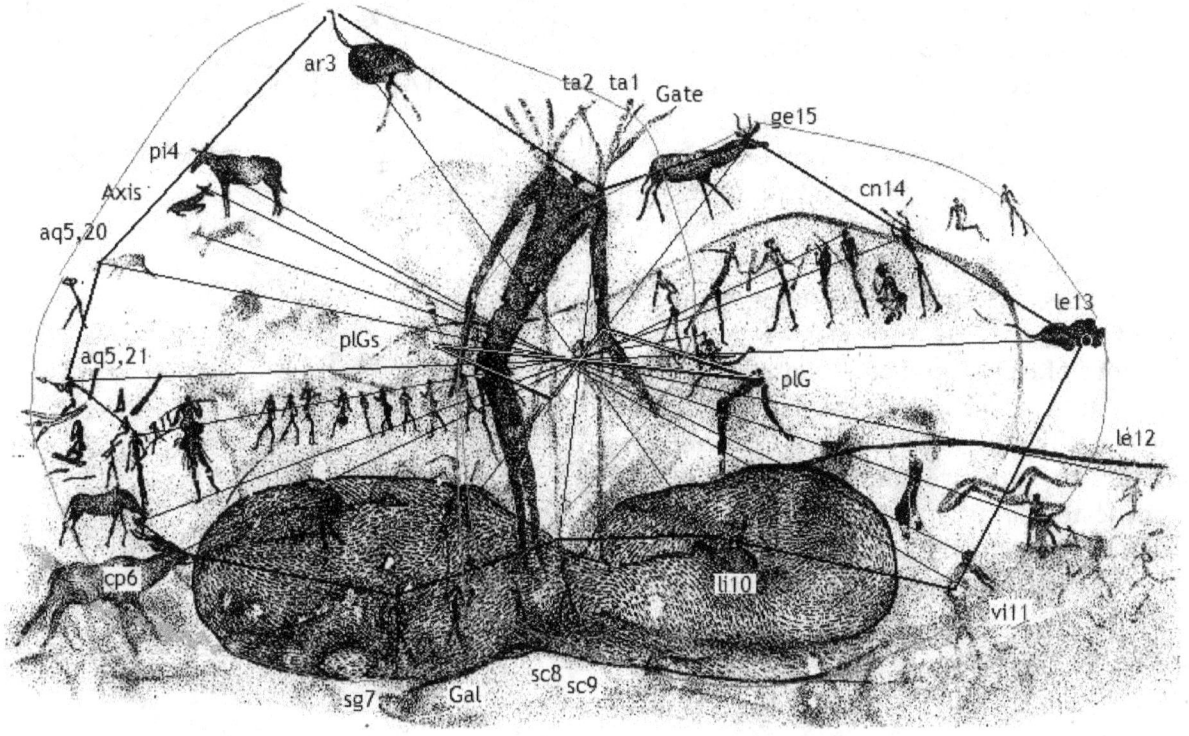

A giant with bow and thongs

Type Scorpius t9 t8 Ophiuchus Giant as a migrant (Susiana seal with a migration scene. Sitchen. Mindprint analysis by Edmond Furter). Libra t10 is flanked by palm fans, its usual Bootes staff borne by Virgo t11 as an implement. Egyptian posts (poles) could be read as El Tih, Those Raised (Andis Kaulins; Stars, stones and scholars). See Virgo t11's post in the Narmer palette at theme t3 t18. Virgo t11 is with an agricultural crop determinant (theme pictograph). Leo t13 is the ark of a covenant priest, borne by Cancer t14 and Gemini t15, the latter often linked to portable shrines in Egypt (see the Dendera crypt at theme t2 t17). Determinants flanking Capricornus t6 may be a kind of serekh (royal name) or signature. Arrows express Sagittarius t7, who is sometimes expressed as a bowman.

Some authors have identified Egyptian immigrants from Africa or Arabia at about BC 10 000, some cast the Exodus not from Egypt, but from Babylonia to Palestine, some identify Phoenicians or a post-Trojan War dispersion, and some set the Exodus in the New Kingdom as expulsion of an elite group. The event is archetypal, since every continent and region has known overpopulation, scouting, pandemics, emigrants and colonisers.

A celestial polar marker on a rear knee tags the inspiration as Age Aries. A knee and elbow of the polar figure's catapult arm, and one of the vertical planes, provide for Age Pisces-Aquarius, our current era.

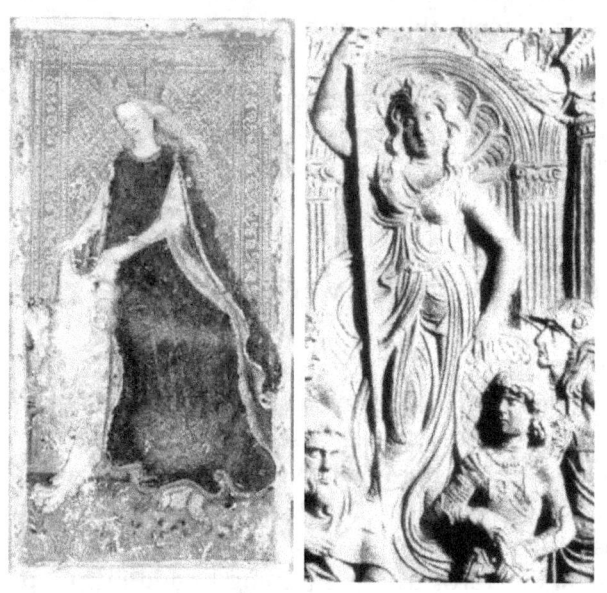

A bee person makes honey

Type Scorpius t9 t8 Ophiuchus Giant as a bee person with mouth effluent and a solar plexus sting (South Africa, Marquard Twy1 dance. SA National Museum. Mindprint analysis by Edmond Furter). See Egyptian Osiris figures with false genitals on the solar plexus at theme t4 and theme t15. Remnant Bushmen refer to effluent from dying or dreaming figures, as potency or spiritual energy, equated with fat or honey. Séance literature of the last century described and photographed supposed plasma from the mouths of mediums. Yellow bands or pollen loads on the limbs of ululating singers identify them as buzzing bees (see Arabian bee people at theme t8). The type includes Samson and his riddle, strength and health from sweetness, and oracular mottos to advocate spiritual thought. Leo t13 and Virgo t11 seem to share an axis.

Poles are often marked by jaws, and galactic corners by effluent. A celestial polar marker on a clapping hand, and the vertical plane, tag the inspiration to Age Pisces-Aquarius, our current era.

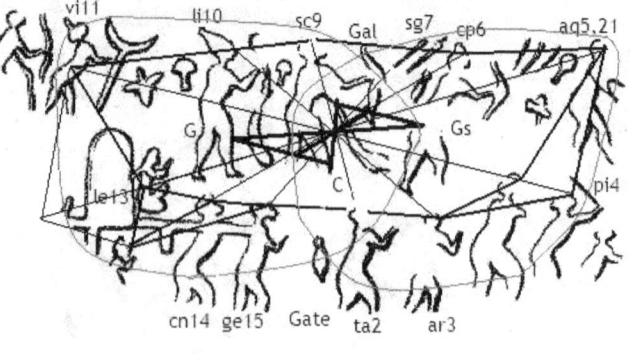

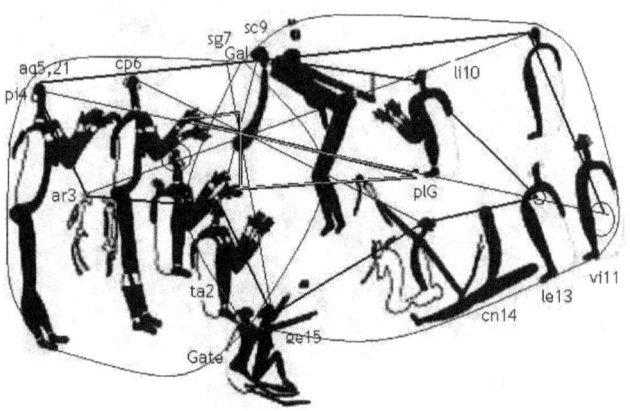

A giant bee pirate

Type Scorpius t8 Ophiuchus (Serpent holder) and the galactic centre, as intestinal sky ropes between an ophiotaurus and a bee person's hand (Saudi Arabia, Bir Hima camels. Lars Bjurstom /SAWDIA. Mindprint analysis by Edmond Furter). The ophiotaurus (cow-snake, in Ovid; Fasti, 3.793) emerges from Chaos (Void or Prior state, not disorder) with Gaia and Ouranos as a trio. Its entrails, if burnt, grant power against gods. Artemis tries to kill it, but a Titan ally does instead, and an eagle from Zeus saves the entrails (see eagles with snakes in Mexican and other heraldry).

Taurus t2 t1 and their opposites, Scorpius t9 t8 Ophiuchus (Serpent holder) are both trios, as in some geometric works (see a Scottish palette at theme t12 t13). The mace shape could derive partly from pollen; more than a digging, hunting and war tool (see Narmer holding his mace at theme t3). Maces, antennae or feathers, domesticated transport, bags and exposed genitals are typical of raiders (see pirates in Naqada, Amatola and American art).

Bees are raiders, and every bee tribe, though of the same species, breed soldiers and buzz a different dialect. The Babylonian and Biblical Tower of Babel myth express this theme, identified in this study as Taurus t1 t16 Auriga Orion, opposite Scorpius t8 Ara (Altar). Swifts, swallows and bees build hanging clay nests, a type of tower. External threat is a core theme at Taurus t1 t16, while the language confusion theme may apply more directly to Scorpius t8 Ophiuchus. Their axis also connects the two galactic gates. The camel is newly engraved, but it does not violate mindprint, so it was either re-carved or elaborated, or a second artist subconsciously continued the initial pattern. Collaboration and overwork is not the norm in rock art, as if mindprints repel elaboration or contradiction. Virgo t11 is pregnant, here a kind of beehive shape, one of the stock images of fertility, dream experience and secret societies (see Trophonios). Mindprint typology allows art to illuminate myths and characters, and vice versa.

A celestial polar mark on a giant bee's genitals or sting, and the vertical plane, tag the inspiration to Age Pisces-Aquarius, our current era.

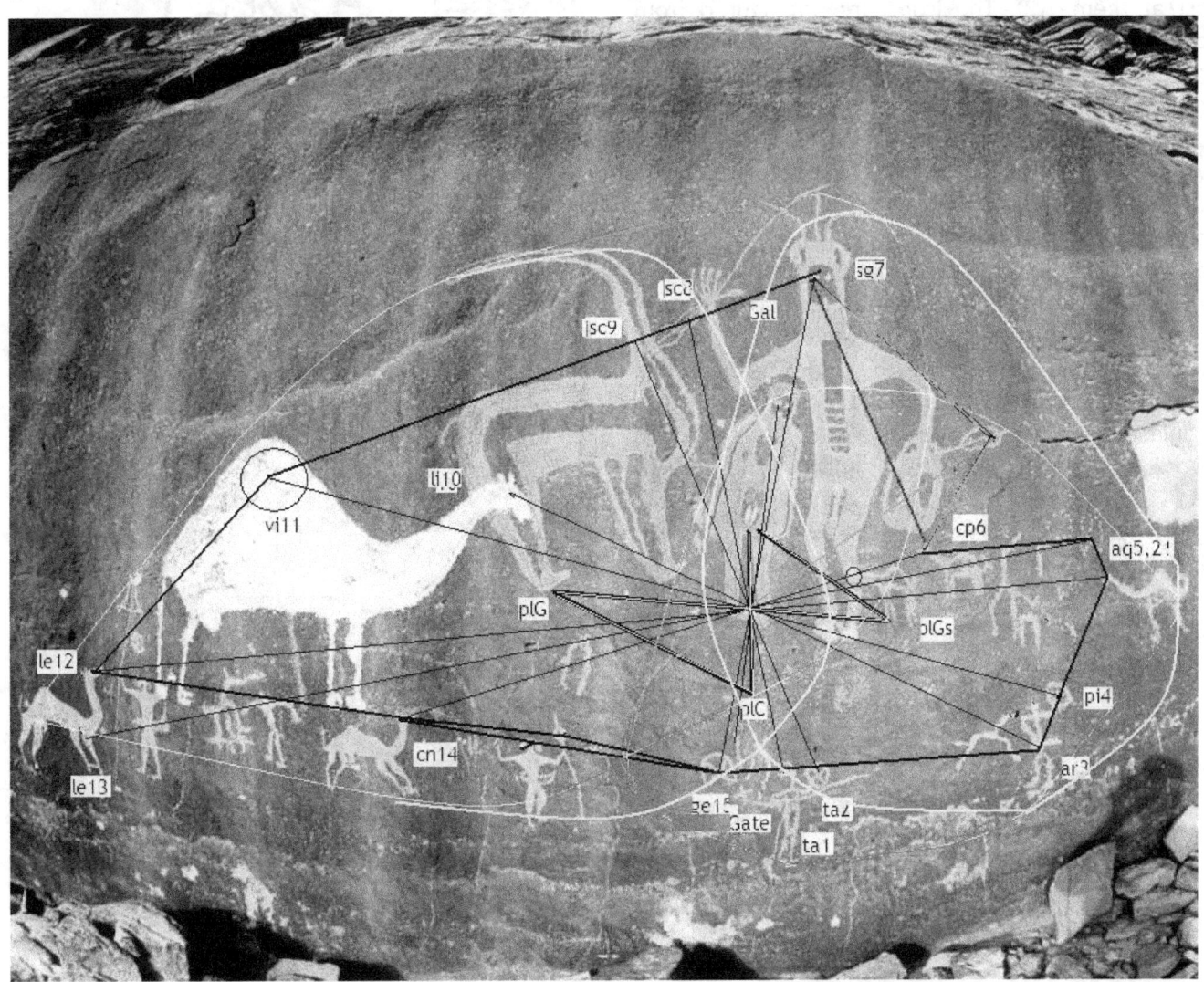

A tree dragon and a hero

Type Scorpius t8 Galactic centre as a large half-eye in the plumage of a bird in a galactic tree, which is rooted in the opposite galactic gate (Mexican palette with a dragon tree. Mindprint analysis by Edmond Furter). Pisces t4 is the face of Xipe Totec carved on a stone belt buckle, worn over the solar plexus in a spring ritual. Xipe priests also wore the skin of a flayed victim as a kind of Greensleeves symbol. The iconography was well developed in a tradition of some centuries, spanning three relatively brief civilisations, yet it remains firmly rooted in archetypal inspiration, with the sequence, structure and internal logic overriding conscious traditional, theological and political conventions, as in inspired art worldwide. The style is instantly recognisable as Mexican, developed in south and Central America, yet none of the icons, when stripped of style, belongs to any particular culture (see galactic trees and birds with a Swedish Fafnir dragon at theme t3 t18. See galactic birds on a Chinese silk tomb drape at theme t5 t21. See Taweret and a crocodile composite in Egyptian Seti 1 art at theme t8). The icons are not figured from constellations, but form a string of emblems, like a rhapsody of jazz melodies, each introducing more motifs than those shown on the canvas, each shedding or activating attributes to form a new whole. Thus aspects of Atlas, Hercules, Samson, Oannes, Osiris and St George are present. The distinct melody of every artwork is played over the backing of what jazz musicians name 'expensive chords', unfolding combinations beyond any rule-book. A certain level of technical skill allows communicable inspiration to come through the artist. While their technical skill is developing, artists could resort to stock themes and styles, as in this work, and allow the already implicit inspiration to activate renewed access to archetype. A celestial polar marker on a hand tags the inspiration to Age Pisces, incidental with the cultural date and the Xipe Totec spring theme.

Galactic spiral mountains

Type Scorpius t8 tail and the galactic centre as a spiral mountain range (USA Arizona engraving with mountain peaks in the border. Mindprint analysis by Edmond Furter). Mountain peak horizons bordering paradise or Eden scenes, as a lost or future earthly heaven, appear in many cultures (see a Naqada pot at theme t3). Spirals are a type of labyrinth, as a gate to the spirit world, expressed by all cultures in arts and crafts (see Chinese feng sui nested curved ranges, and supposed Atlantis maps). Virgo t11 is marked by her eye, not womb, a rare exception to the standard exception.

Celestial poles are uncertain. The vertical plane of the Libra t10 pyramid tags the inspiration as Age Aries, probably retro to the work, but incidental with the theme of a former paradise.

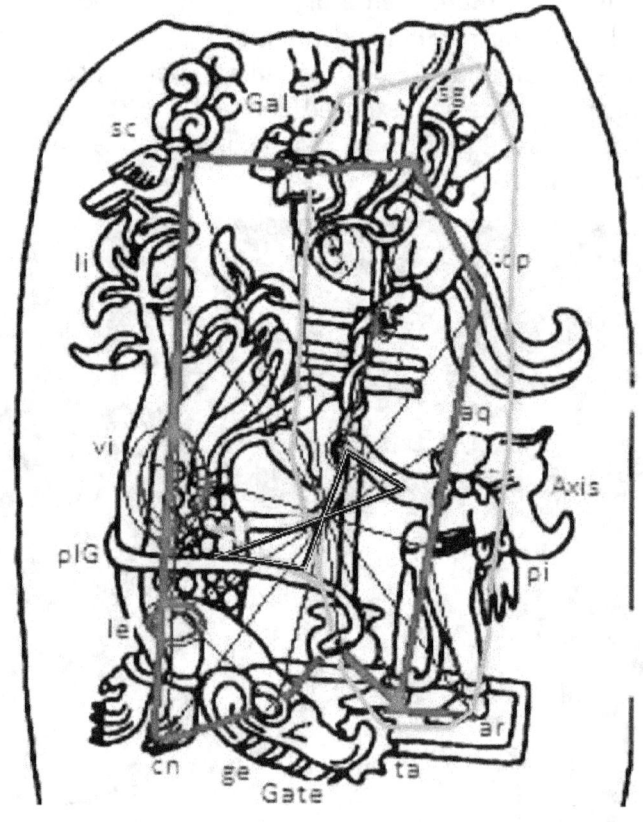

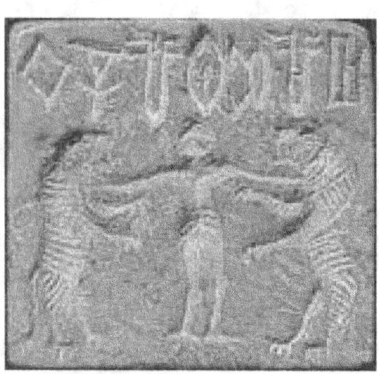

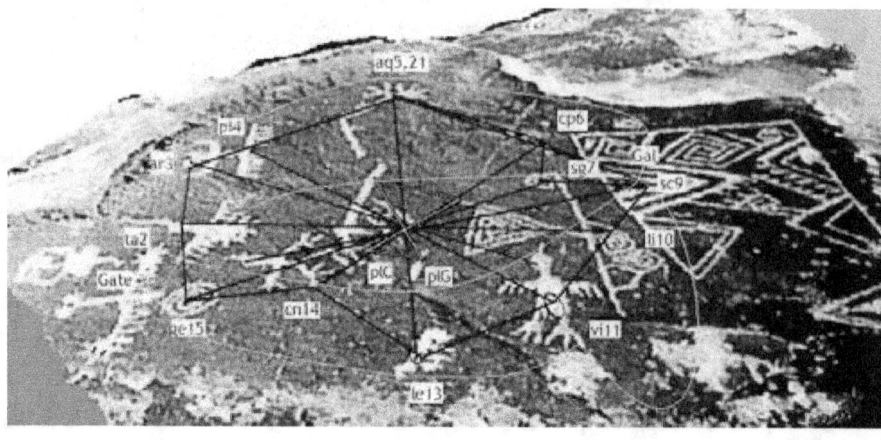

Polar mechanics on a vault

Type Scorpius t9 t8 Ophiuchus (Serpent holder) as Horus with a notched palm branch bent towards the galactic pole (Egyptian decans in the Seti 1 tomb. Mindprint analysis by Edmond Furter). As a raptor, Horus is also a serpent holder, as he is in the Mexican coat of arms. Scorpius t9 is often combined with Libra t10, as here, with t9 assuming the W-shaped arms and staff. He often leans on two staffs in trance ritual. Libra t10 is marked by his feet on a small bull foreleg, roped via the galactic pole and Gemini t15's hands (see rope controllers at theme t15) to the galactic gate (see a near identical Libra t10 in the South African coat of arms, taken from the Maclear Linton panel at theme t5 t21). The galaxy and the gate are each marked, as they are in complex scenes with doubled major types. Aquarius t5 t21 is a lion, standing in for his opposite Leo t13, which is a Taweret hippo maw (Leo t12 and t13 are swopped, as they often are). Aquarius t5 is its usual painted or dappled self, expressed by the string of stars along its back.

Leo t13 Ursa was often a bear or horse with a string of former polar positions along its back, before the celestial pole moved to Cancer t14 Ursa Minor. The rope is in the hands of Gemini t15, but still on the t14 axis. Virgo t11 as a pregnant Taweret is often figured as Draco encircling the ecliptic pole in a U-shape which is sometimes expressed as Draco's sword, or Draco's short rope to a foreleg with a jackal on it (see the Dendera round zodiac in the Decans section). Here the jackal is absent, but the foreleg is in place relative to the alter ego of Taweret.

Other versions of this polar scene are each recast with their own mindprint and therefore own inspiration, like musicians re-interpreting a classic song with a new arrangement, a new verse, and the same chorus (see the Ramses 6 ceiling at Luxor, inset). Variety and mutation are as necessary in art as in genetics.

Celestial polar markers on Gemini t15's hands and Sagittarius t7's wrist, tag the inspiration to Age Taurus-Aries, in the final centuries before about BC 1500.

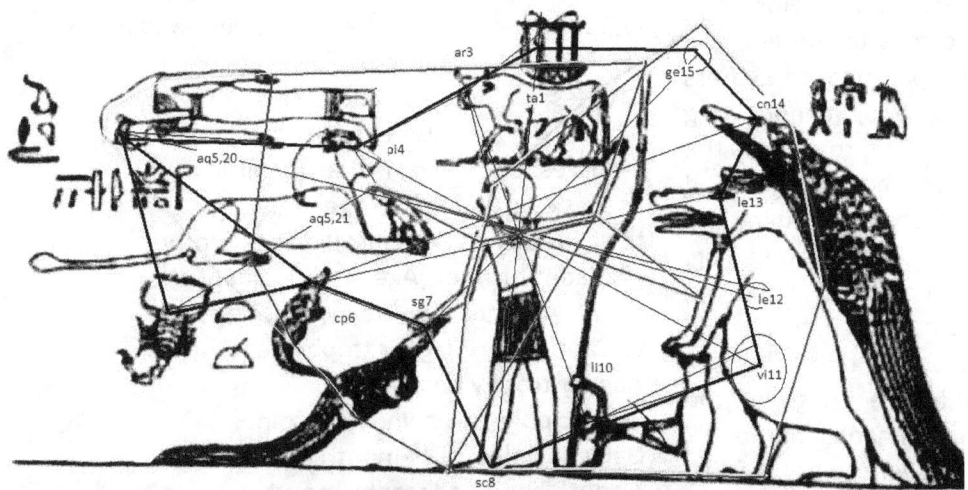

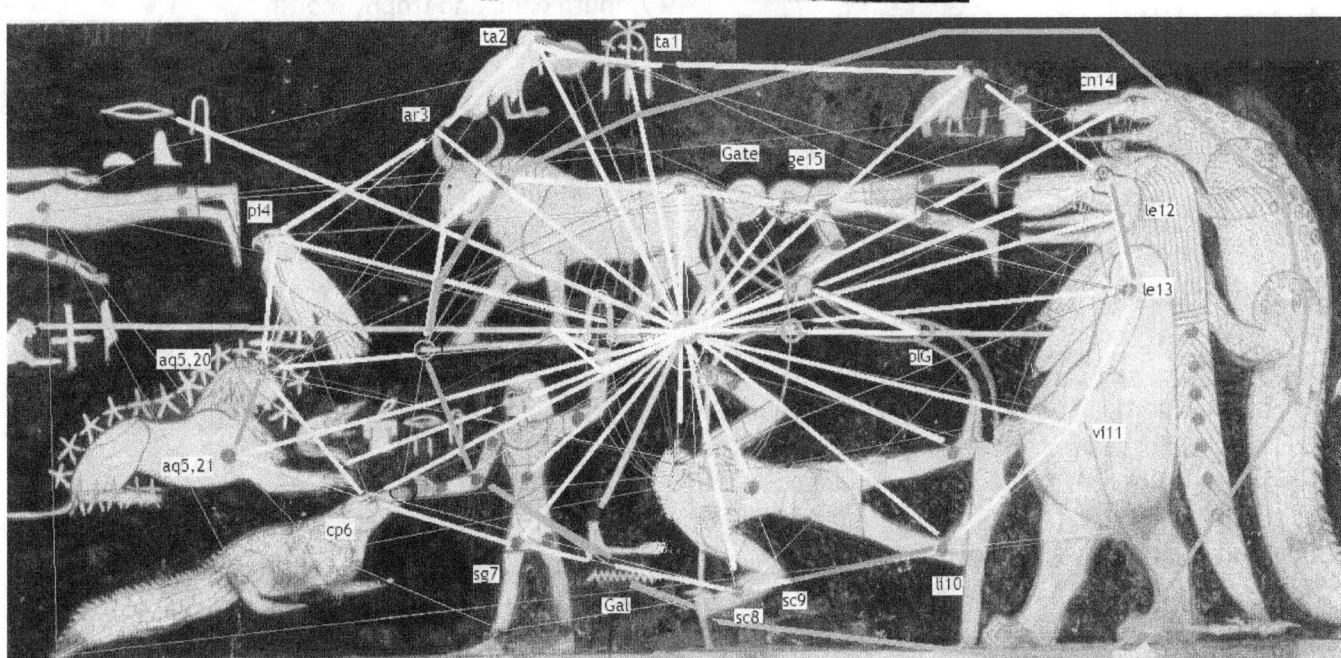

Solomon's pillar in Notre Dame

Type Scorpius t8 Galactic centre as a candelabrum post (Paris, engraving of a Notre Dame service. Anonymous, 1865. Mindprint analysis by Edmond Furter). Cathedrals replicate forest canopies and the sky in stone. Scorpius T8 expresses the concept and image of the galactic centre as a large pool of light, at one of the four major structural points, as a post (a truncated or broken pillar) often carried by the Scorpius Ophiuchus Giant (see Tarot trump 8, Strength, as a strong man opening a lion maw or bearing a post). Paris of posts at Aquarius t5 and Leo t12 are the cardinal counterparts (forming a cross) to this post, and so is Taurus t1 t16 Auriga and Orion as a tower; all are kinds of 'pillars of Hercules' (see posts in Tarot trump 5, Pope, and 2, Priestess). The 'Solomon pillar' that explorer Charles Warren found while burrowing into the Jerusalem temple mount is archaeological fancy, but archetypally correct.

Some worshippers are in bent posture, incidental with communal trance experience in rock art. Libra t10 holds a staff as usual, and Scorpius t9 has an arm in a V posture, as when combined with Libra t10. Inspiration works with what comes to the eye and hand, framing scenes with the potential to express mindprint, shuffling, shunting and manoeuvring figures into the best possible position to express the sequence of attributes, as a dialogue of compromises between archetypal inspiration, subconscious expression and conscious meaning. This conversation continues unabated since we became human and re-created nature and experience, giving new meaning to the stock spiritual mottoes of "made in the image of the creator" and "not made by human hands (mirifact)". Finding mindprint in nearly every work of art featuring Notre Dame Cathedral is no more remarkable than finding mindprint in nearly every complex artwork. It is more difficult to find acclaimed or earnest works that do not contain mindprint, except portraits, landscapes, still lifes and commercial decorative art.

A pillar of eyes and Ages

Type Scorpius t8 t9 as a cayman neck eye on the female side (left), and a cayman forehead eye on the male side (right), of a carved cayman dragon pillar (Peruvian Tello obelisk, Chavin de Huantar, Olmec culture. Peter G Roe, 2007. Mindprint analysis by Edmond Furter). The subconscious sequence of types of the known characters, by their mindprint

identification (according to the present study), compared to their cultural names (according to Dr Peter G Roe), on female and /male sides of the obelisk are;

t7 Sagittarius; vampire bat /vampire bat
t8 Scorpius; neck mouth eye /neck mouth eye
t9 Scorpius; lower forehead eye /lower forehead eye
t10 Libra Bootes; forehead eyes' tongues' eye /forehead eye top
t11 Virgo; gourd [womb] full of peanuts /forehead tongues' eyes [uraeus], oyster [womb]
t12 Leo; profile eye of Taurus [error, not on grid] /jaguar escaping cayman
t13 Leo; coiled snake bracelet [heart] /cactus slice [heart], and elbow eye and heart
t14 Cancer; black eats spectacled cayman [poleC] /manioc semen tree eye [poleC]
t15 Gemini; jaguar in belly /cat snake penis eye [Lynx, and rope]
Gate; SS-shaped peanut /snake anklet [Apophis]
t1 Taurus; knee eye and Pleiades hand on rope /Pleiades hand on tope [without opposite]
t2 Taurus; snake anklet and Pleiades hand /Pleiades eye and cactus flower inner eye
t3 Aries; Pleiades eye and cactus flower eyes /cactus flower outer eye [U shape]
t4 Pisces; pelvis eye, fishtail [genitals] /pelvis eye, and fishtail [genitals]
t5 t20 Aquarius Pegasus; Pleiades brother /Pleiades brother [Age Pisces-Aquarius]
t5 t21 Aquarius; vulva eye /tuber eye
t6 Capricornus; jaguar trophy head /jaguar trophy head alive
Ecliptic pole; jaw spine /jaw spine.
Galactic poles; neck mouth and vulva /mouth band and trophy mouth.

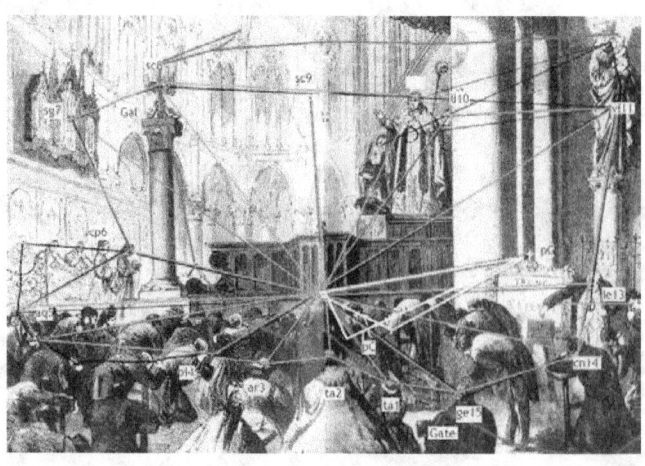

Celestial poles; t15 jaguar's dead eye and t7 bat's foot, tagging Age Pisces late, the work date.

/t14 manioc semen branches [Cancer Ursa Minor] and t6 jaguar trophy skull, and horizontal plane, tagging Age Aries-Pisces, the Olmec traditional date. Taurus t2 t17 Pleiades is twisted as usual, only his hand remaining to grip a rope or the Medusa head bag at the old spring point while he vaults over the Pisces t4 base and Aries t3 U-shape. He stands squarely (literally) at the current spring point at Pisces Pegasus as a rectangular frontal face, and at Pisces Cetus (Whale) as a fish tail tongue. This precessed brother's eye figures Aquarius t5 t20 Pegasus, anticipating the immanent Age. He is identified as the star Taurus Pleiades Alcyone (brightest among seven siblings) in anthropology, confirming his vacated mindprint point (and contradicting the stray archaeological 'Taurus' label near the missing Leo t12). See Taurean rope handlers in the Narmer palette at theme t3 t18.

This subconscious conceptual brilliance, with some seasonal structure peeking out into the conscious elements of Olmec myth and calendar, validates the finding of spring attributes being precessed (see a spring dog on a Babylonian cone at theme t11, and a spring monkey in an African tree mural at theme t1 t16). Most faces in Olmec style are rendered in halves, as in some mask traditions, and in Picasso's works based on African masks.

Some artists and viewers can visualise doubled overlays of inspired works, thus making picture generators and animation (Maurice Cotterell; The amazing lid of Palenque). The effect may also have been discovered by mechanical means, such as semi-transparent textiles, ticker tape-styled panels, mirror or water projection, or by learning to see in stereo. The rarity of visual prodigies, such as the master of this pillar, Picasso, Imhotep, the Duke of Chou or Dawid Kruiper, imply that few Mayan, Spanish, Egyptian, Chinese or Bushmen could express or perceive dynamic overlays. Most artists and viewers consciously appreciate only the legendary story.

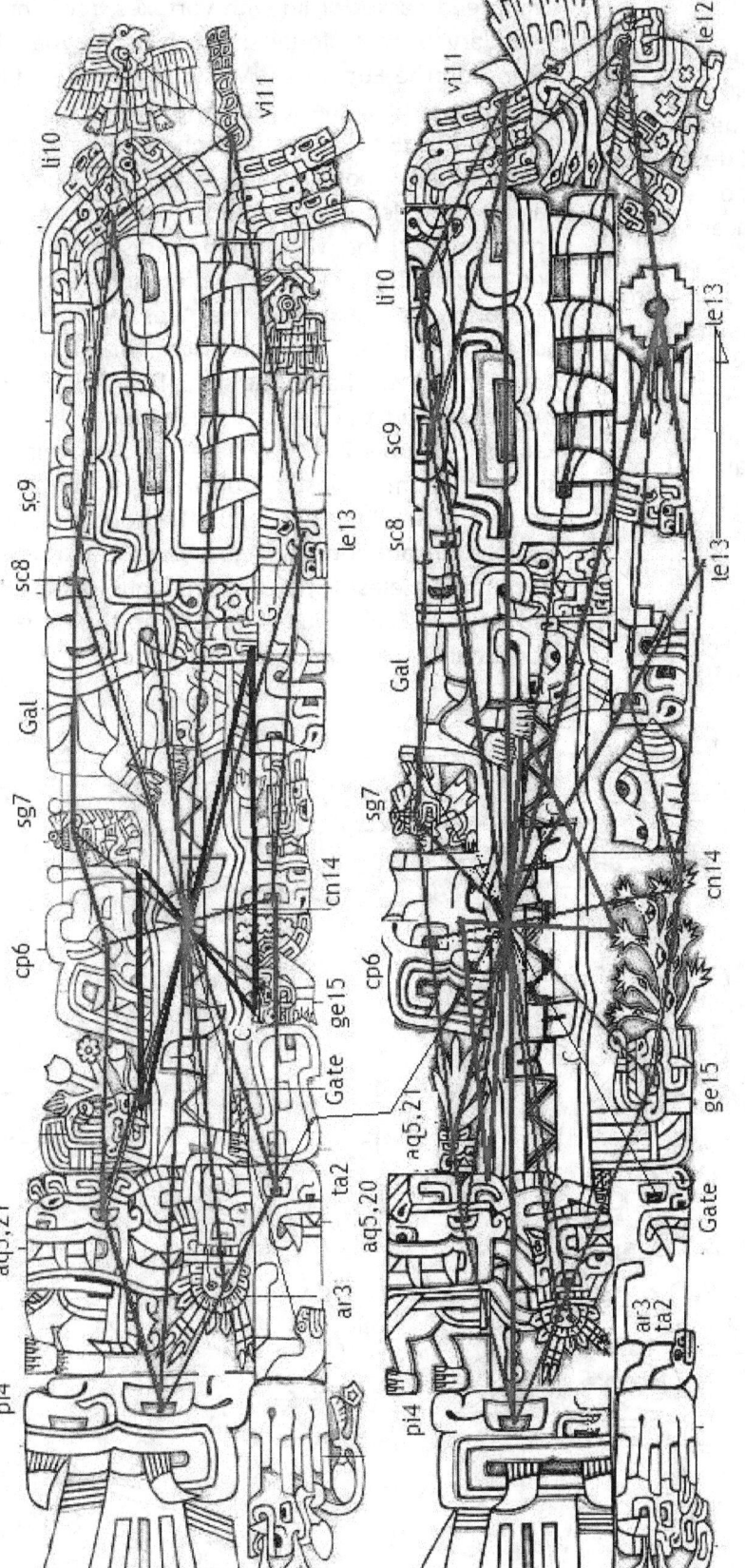

A tower struck by time

Type Scorpius t8 Galactic centre as a moon, and as a heaven with a falling tower, in an emergent (half separated) double imprint (India, Buddha's death with Mount Meru. De Santillana and Von Deschend; Hamlet's mill. Mindprint analysis by Edmond Furter). Five types are co-incident, using the same figures in both spheres. Gemini t15 and Cancer t14 are two different eyes of the Leo t13 (heart) figure at left. Inspiration or expression may start with the four large types (Leo and his cardinals) as if sheared off a vortex (see the Layers section in the text), then proceed to the medium types (Virgo and her cardinals), then the small types (Cancer and its cardinals). Some expressions of mindprint seem to be a snapshot or interruption of progression from one to two spheres. Implied galactic equators (thin curves, here as a horizontal fish shape, growing into a larger shape to the right) may initiate shapes that turn into limbs, and retain many limb joints, while eyes move to the figures equator, typically in profile views, perhaps maturing to frontal views (see one-eyed figures as alive, and double-eyed figures as half dead or ancestors, in Olmec art at theme t8). Dual identification of the same figure (see decans variants at theme t12) is a step in an apparent process of identity dissolution (see theme t13, and a rending

veil in the Externsteine deposition carving at theme t4), incidental with the theme of a guru's death and a masked womb perhaps holding the next guru (on the right). The intermediary stage may be incidental with the theme of a falling world post, skambha or many-coloured cover implying radial sections (pizza slices), often expressed at the galactic centre between t8 and t7. Libra t10 of the right sphere is a flying reed basket or lid with vortexes, recalling the legendary birth of founders such as Assyrian king Sargon on the Euphrates, Moses on the Nile, Christ in a manger near the Jordan and the mystic basket lid. Aquarius t5 t21 of the left sphere is the hand of a figure in active posture, and in the right sphere he has painted legs in the sense of standing in a decorated pot, and wearing a head disc as the future Age marker. Top figures in the left sphere spell out (subconsciously, as usual) the Ages by their spring houses as Taurus, Aries and Pisces, with future Age Aquarius as just a hand. The same figures in the right sphere expand the precession sequence from Age Taurus 1, Taurus 2, Aries, Pisces, to Aquarius in an adjacent room. Celestial poles on the left, on an elbow and Buddha's wrist, and the horizontal plane, tag the inspiration to Age Pisces-Aquarius, our current era. Celestial poles on the right, on an elbow and wrist of Sagittarius t7 A, also on the horizontal plane, confirm the prophetic inspiration.

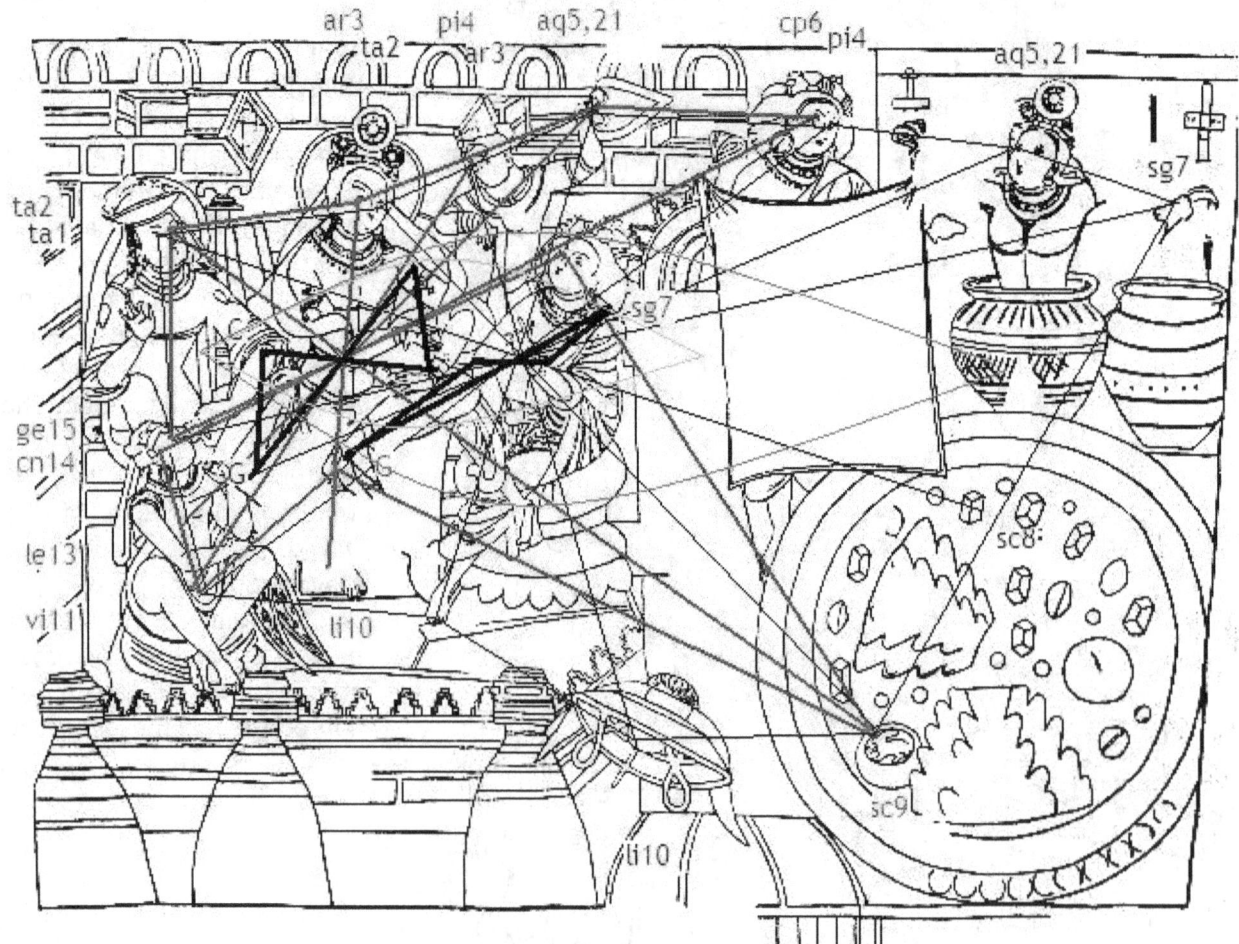

Angels pull spring into Aquarius

Type Scorpius t9 t8 Galactic centre as globes and a tutelary spirit (Peru, Pablo Amaringo; snake in a field. Mindprint analysis by Edmond Furter). Parts of the conceptual galactic equators across the sphere (forming a fish shape) are marked by a string of angels in a horizontal S shape, as if figuring half of the one half, then half of the other half in turn. Their central S-shaped flip section also mark summer and thus celestial polar positions in a gauge from the Leo axis on the vertical plane (Age Taurus), through Cancer (Age Aries), Gemini (Age Pisces), to the first Taurus axis on the horizontal plane (Age Aquarius). Aquarius t5 t20 is a focal group in the ayahuasca brewing hut, as a spring marker.

Leo t12 is a lion (top centre), taking the place of the usual Taurus t1 bull of most mindprints and alchemy of the last 6000 years. Taurus t1 with its gate and churn is now a grail (mid right) dragged from Leo t12 Crater (Grail). The summer sun and celestial poles are also dragged from Leo t12 to Taurus t1. Scorpius t8, formerly an eagle, now acquires the Aquarian angel. Pisces t4 is a snake with reared head, formerly of Aries t3 t18, adding the smaller cog change of about 30 degrees as the spring equinox is about to move from Pisces into Aquarius. Aries t3 t18 becomes devoid of cosmic drama, here just six children in a pool (the seventh invisible), a former Taurus t2 t17 Pleiades icon. The two Amaringo snake paintings in this study express sweeping forthcoming Age Aquarius iconographic adjustments, each artwork using different figures and orientations to do so.

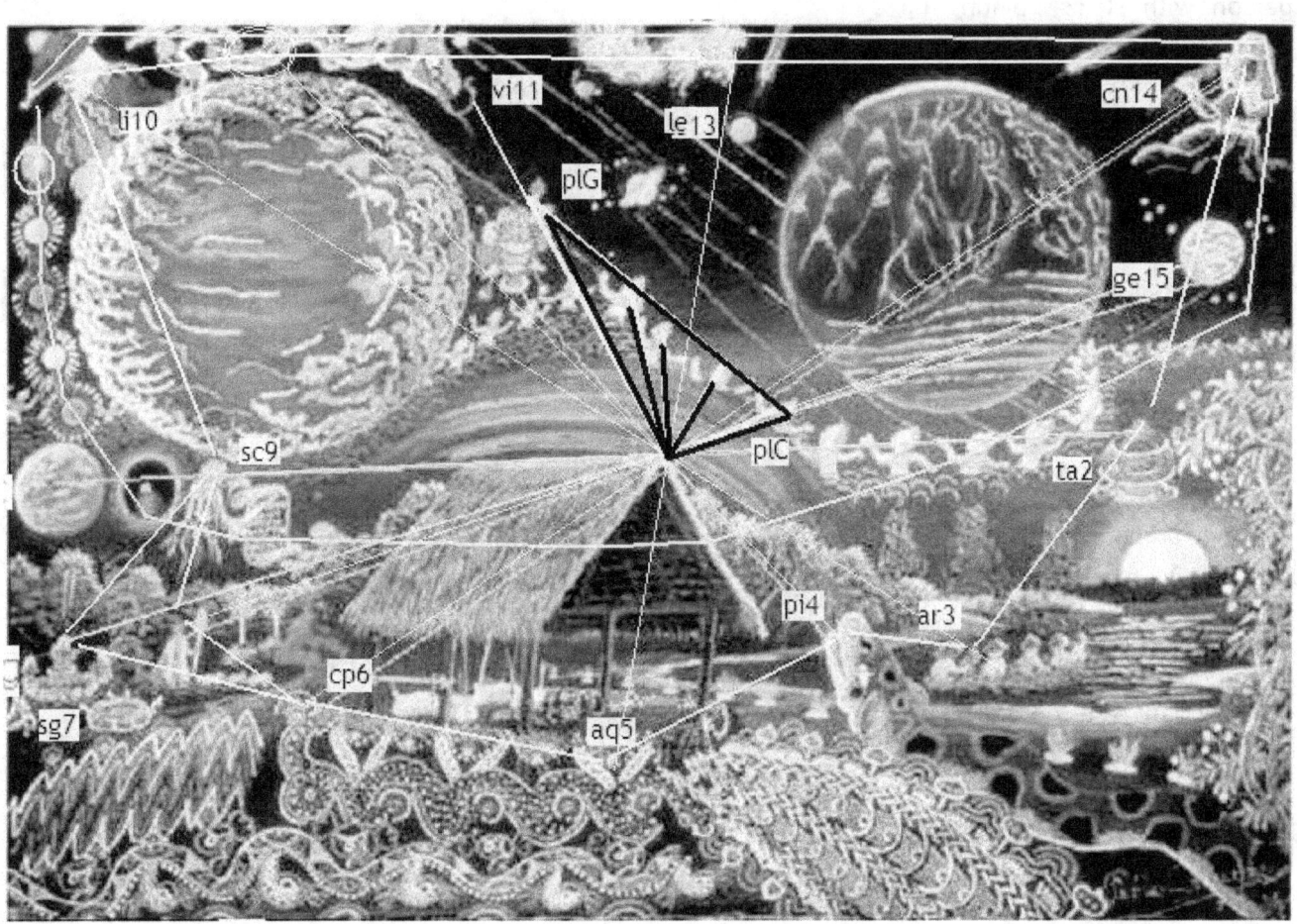

Type Scorpius t9; Giant in trance

microcosmic visions in a light-burst. Antlered antelope such as elk have a distinctive gait, much like mantis insects, and like healers entering trance. There are no species with antlers in Africa, so other attributes express the type.

Celestial poles on a knee and a shoulder, and the vertical plane, tag the inspiration as Age Pisces.

Praying mantis healers

Type Scorpius t9 as a praying mantis person in a homogenous (single kind) artwork (Zimbabwean mantis dance. Elspeth Parry, Amabooks. Mindprint analysis by Edmond Furter). Some postures and attributes are sufficiently different to anchor the identification sequence. The posture and multiple legs of these insects could be an analogy of the sensation of far-striding, jumping, or semi-airborne motion of dreams, as on elastic stilts or sapling branches. The insects also figure antelopes, as some moth species do (Jeremy Hollmann). See a mantis woman in schooled amateur art at theme t7. Celestial poles on a horn and a hip tag the inspiration as Age Pisces-Aquarius, our current era.

Coat people dancing

Type Scorpius t9 as an antelope coat person with a staff in a healing dance (South Africa, KZN healers, staffs and karos coats. Orpen. Mindprint analysis by Edmond Furter). See coat people at theme t12 and elsewhere. The galactic polar 'puller' is not uncommon in inspired art.

Most artists cite practical and symbolic reasons for postures now revealed to also function as subconscious concepts.

Celestial poles on a knee and a muzzle tag the inspiration to Age Pisces-Aquarius, our current era.

Mantis people dancing

Type Scorpius t9 as a mantis person with sticks pointing up like horns (South African Drakensberg, healers dancing on staffs. Lewis-Williams; Images of mystery. SAAS, Digging Stick newsletter. Mindprint analysis by Edmond Furter). Sticks are used by healers to prevent falling over and to mimic prancing antelope (Francis Thackeray). See Tarot

trump 9 (Hermit) and the Hermit icon in medieval and Renaissance emblematic art, usually with two staffs, a coat, stag horns or a stag companion, sometimes with a lamp, perhaps to express the sensation of seeing by spiritual light. This entoptic effect is described by some healers and students of kabbalah and other esoteric traditions. Alchemists saw

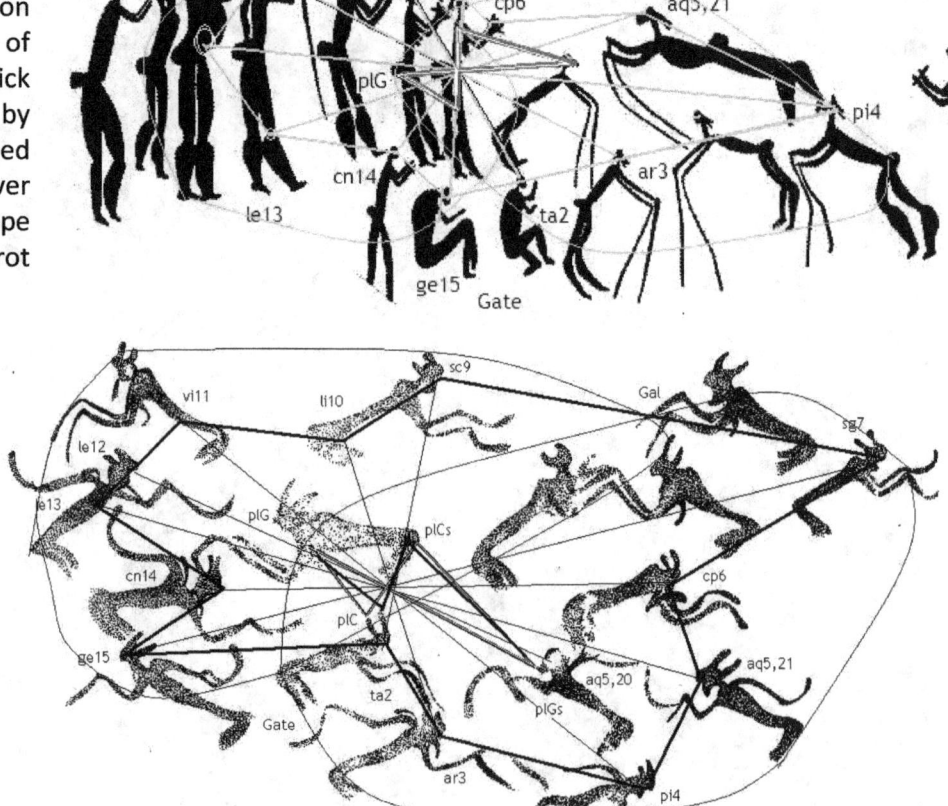

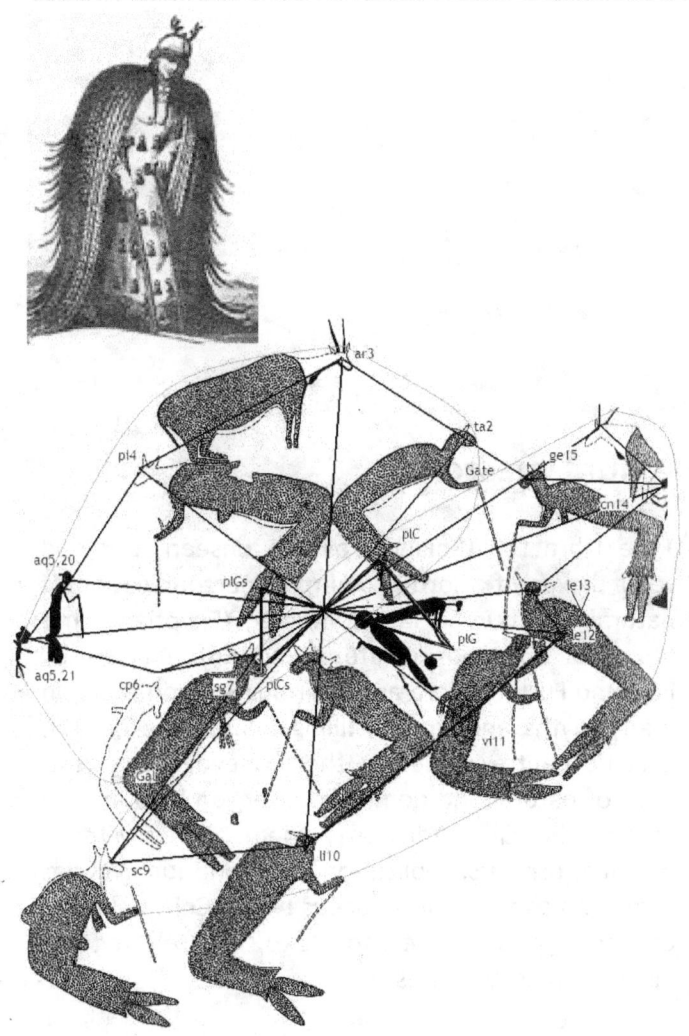

Eternal order in the eternal battle

Type Scorpius t9 as a woman warrior in a cosmic battle (Tamil Nadu, Mahabalipuram cave, Mahisamardini or Mahishasura frieze. Archaeological Survey of India. Mindprint analysis by Edmond Furter). The equator of eyes is unusually regular. Aquarius t5 t21 Pegasus is a bull, as in the Narmer palette (see theme t3 t18). Taurus t2 t17 Perseus, in the usual posture, is an Amazon, as she is named in Greek myth referring to their preceding colonists, identified with Artemis (Taurus t1 t16 Auriga, sharing some Taurus t2 Perseus attributes). The type is also expressed in suras and asuras (angelic spirits), perhaps as the galactic or 'formative limbs' version of Perseus. The eternal cosmic battle is cast here as lion versus bull, in economical symbolism as bear versus bull. Leo and Ursa (Bear) are interchangeable as summer icons.

Celestial poles on the heroine's shoulder and a lion eye, tag the inspiration to Age Pisces.

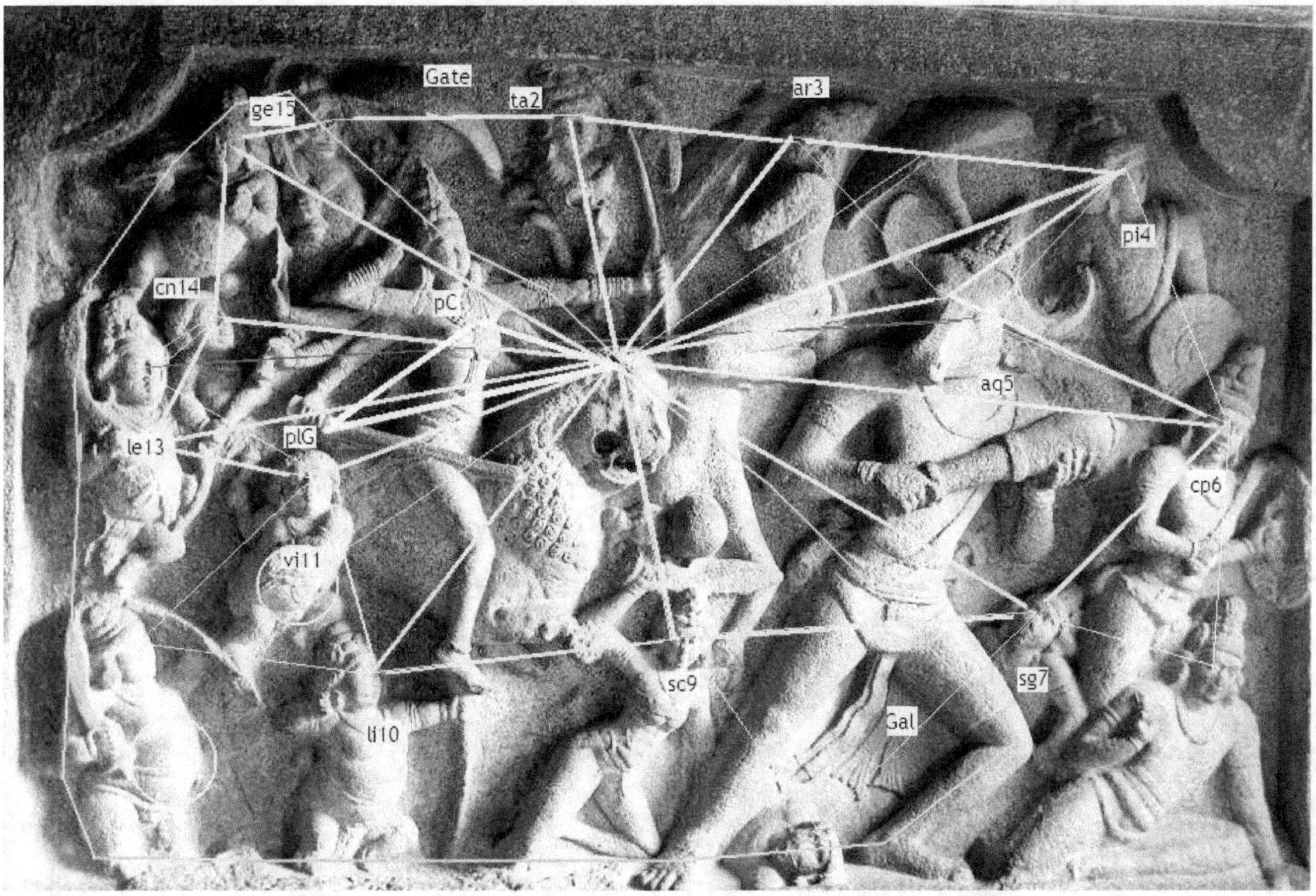

Type Libra t10;
Lord of nature

Fat of the land

Type Libra t10 as biers carrying poles and a large bundle, echoed at its opposite Aries t3 (Indian story cloth. Mindprint analysis by Edmond Furter). Libra t10 usually has a staff and one or both arms in V posture, here doubled by two figures and poles, with its usual wheel shape added. Baskets or bundles between t3 and t2, and lids between t10 and t9, also express the mystic basket (see a marble sarcophagus at theme t11). Bier groups are stock exploration images. Celestial polar markers on bovine legs, and the horizontal plane, tag the inspiration as Age Aries-Pisces or Age Pisces.

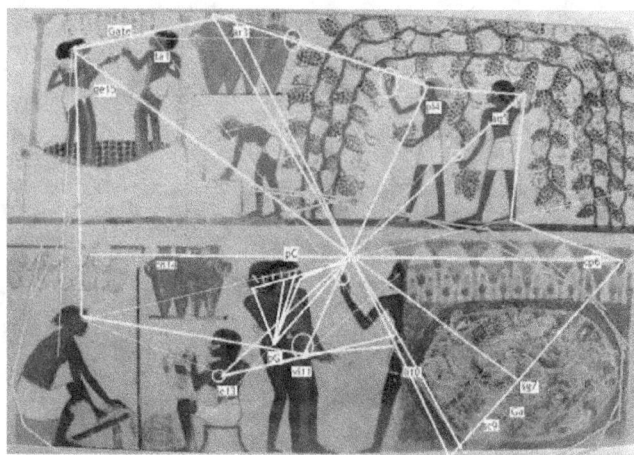

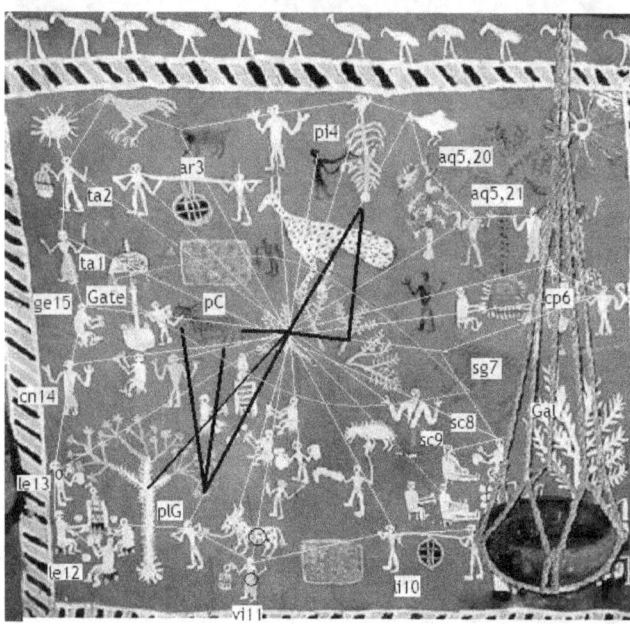

A hunt master

Type Libra t10 (Balance) as the unseen foot and solar plexus of a lord of animals, personification of natural and human law combined (Egyptian tomb mural of a manor estate. Mindprint analysis by Edmond Furter). Libra and Scorpius are combined in many myths and icons. Milling figures express the galactic centre. Funerary themes evoke registers, here of natural and domestic order, on land and on water. The Libra-Aries axis themes are systemic balance, osmosis, replication, DNA and lunar cycles forming a conceptual caduceus twine. Celestial poles on three jaws on the same axis, securely tag the inspiration as Age Aries.

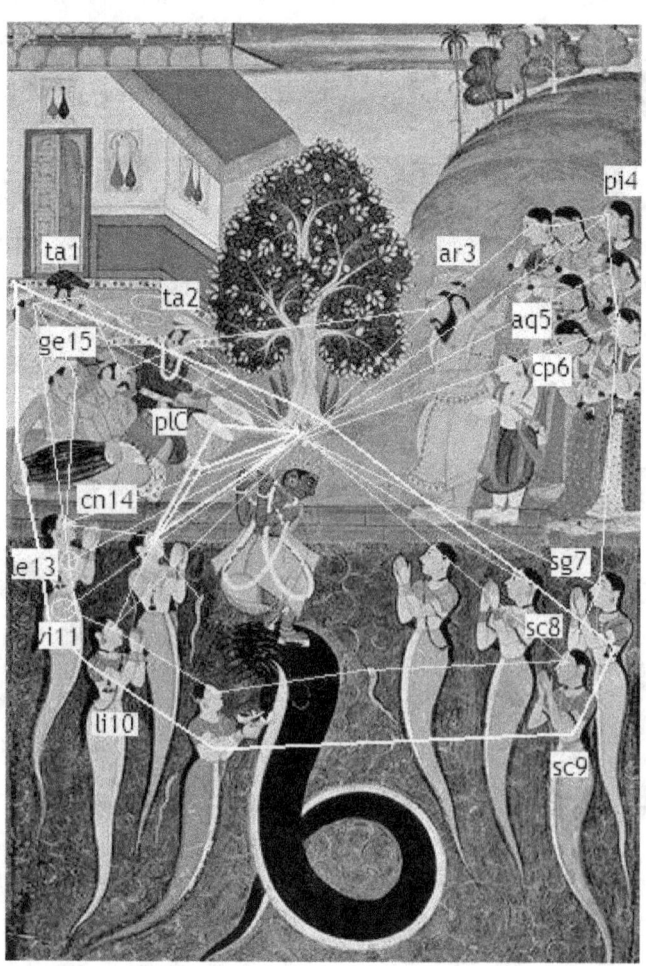

A cosmic balancing act

Type Libra t10 and Scorpius t9 combined as lord of natural and cultural law, in conscious and subconscious symbols (Illumination of Krishna on a snake. Historic India, Time Life. Mindprint analysis by Edmond Furter). The two main figures are not part of the mindprint sequence, but repeat and combine their adjacent figures, perhaps the start of a split into a concentric double imprint, or a remnant of a heraldic icon portrait elaborated into a scene. Libra t10 has arms up in a W posture as usual, together with the snake figuring the outline of a scorpion.

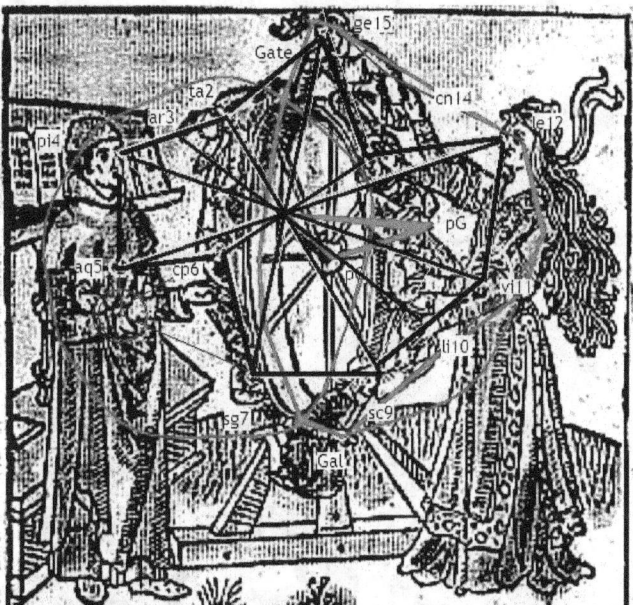

Myth and astrology often picture Libra as Scorpius' claws. Libra t10 often appears as Serapis, an oracular snake with several heads in a shrine. A celestial pole on a drum, as a kind of mouth, tags the inspiration to Age Aries-Pisces.

Fortune at work

Type Libra t10 (Balance) as the lower hand of Fortune, multi-armed natural and human law, with a printing press (Renaissance emblem of the Wheel of Fortune. Mindprint analysis by Edmond Furter). Print blocks of necessity invert the design, but do not change the sequence or the polar triangles. Duplication is part of the theme of Libra t10. Celestial poles on a spoke end and on a crank handle, tag the inspiration to Age Aries.

Seasonal balance

Type Libra t10 as autumn (Botticelli's Primavera. Mindprint analysis by Edmond Furter). See Poussin's Dance to the music of time at theme t6, where the upper part of the sequence, here reduced to fruit, is figured by gods and angels. Design elements such as framing limbs, considered in art studies as guides to keep the viewer's eyes circulating inside the frame, are now revealed to mark galactic equators. Celestial poles are not marked, but the horizontal plane tags the inspiration as Age Aries-Pisces.

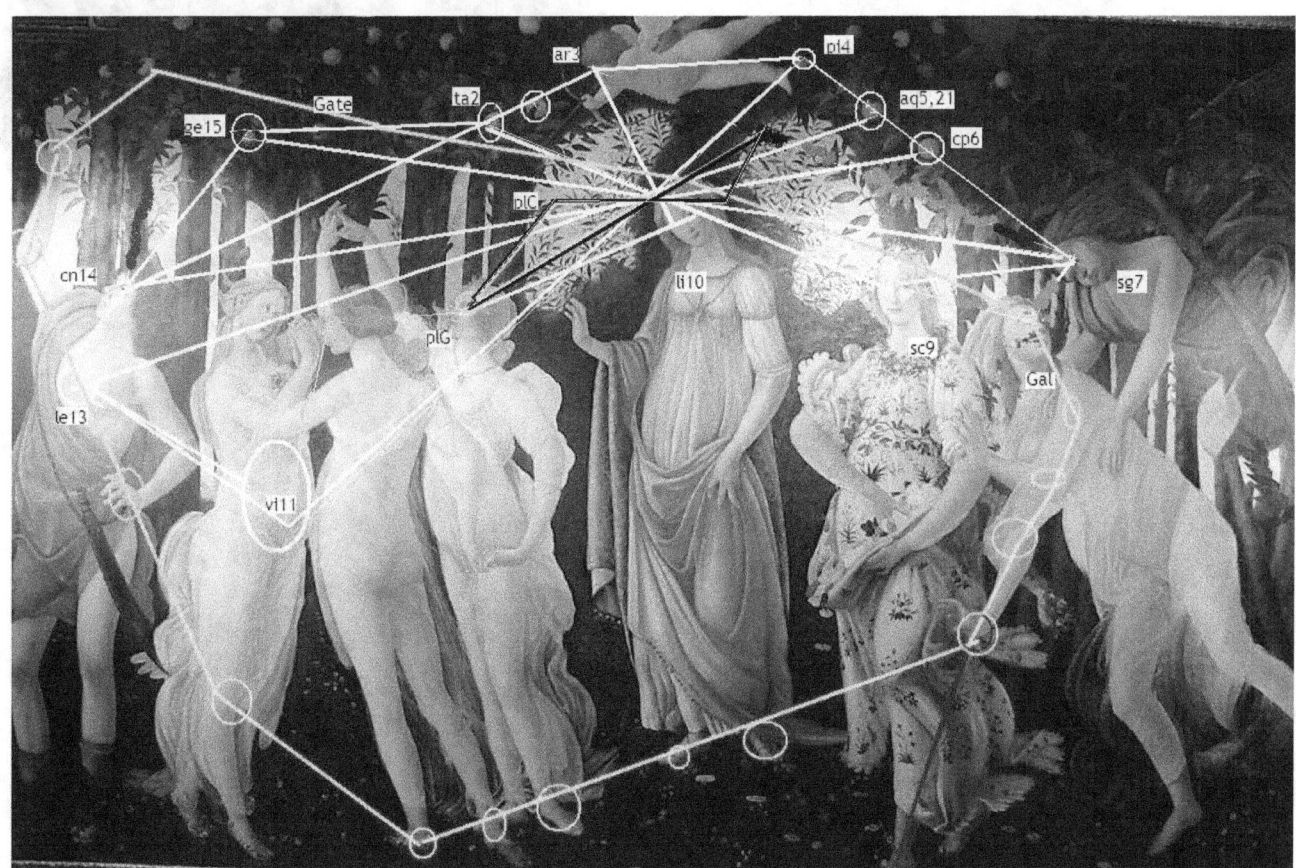

Dogs of a river paradise

Type Libra t10 Lupus (Wolf) as a canine, its body extended under the celestial south pole (Egyptian palette, Two Dogs. Oxford University Press. Mindprint analysis by Edmond Furter). The celestial south pole is at the centre of the cosmetics bowl, implying this side of the palette as south, and as the reverse. The t6-t14 axis and the vertical plane tag the inspiration as Age Aries.

Palette bowls function as small mirrors for applying eye cosmetics, when filled with a few drops of oil or water. Canines are also solstice markers (see a spring dog marker in a Babylonian cone at theme t2 t17). Capricornus t6 as an ostrich continues the necks theme of the four small types on the t3 t18 to t10 axis. Palette outlines are incidental with the four small zodiac constellations; the U of Aries t3, V of Capricornus t6, Y of Cancer t14 and W of Libra t10 Bootes (see the cosmic map in the text). A neat mark on the Virgo t11 womb, repeated damage at Pisces t19, and a slight mark on Leo t13's heart, raise suspicion of conscious understanding of mindprint, probably not by the artist.

The celestial north pole in Cancer t14 Ursa Minor is often a polar canine. The celestial south pole host was Tucana (Bird of paradise) in Age Aries, was Octans in Age Pisces, and will be Chameleon in future, but these 'southern' characters vary in myth, while Libra t10 Lupus is more universal.

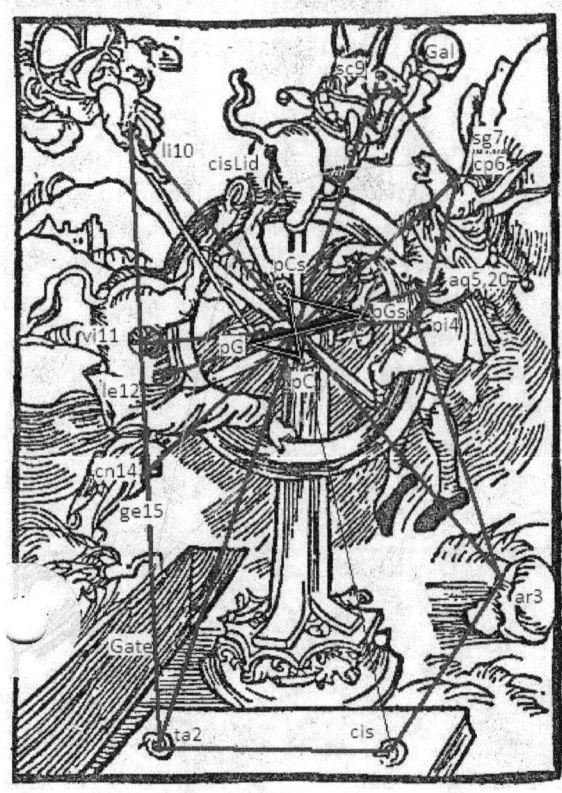

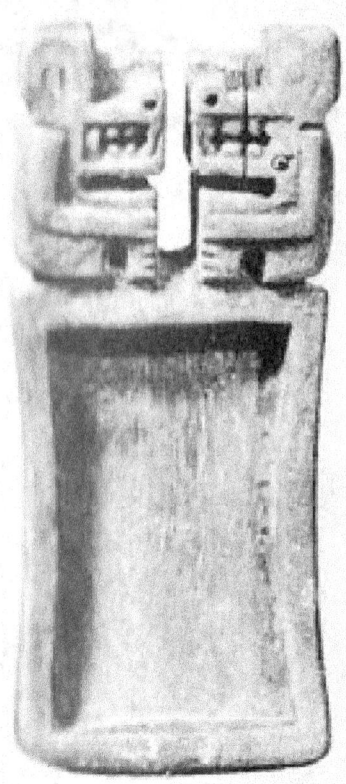

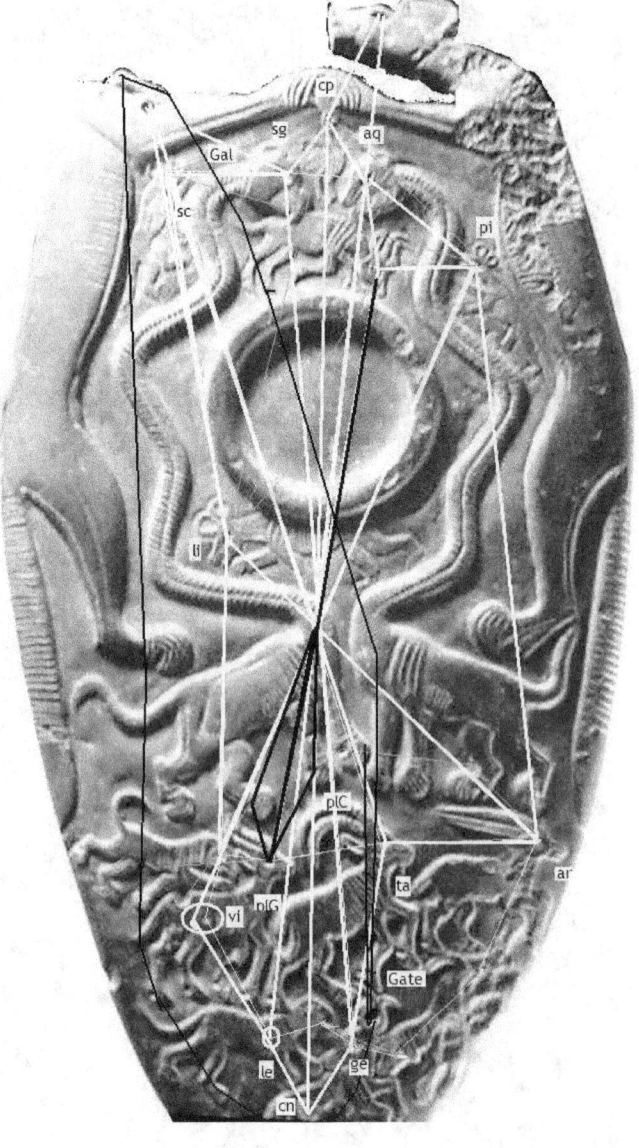

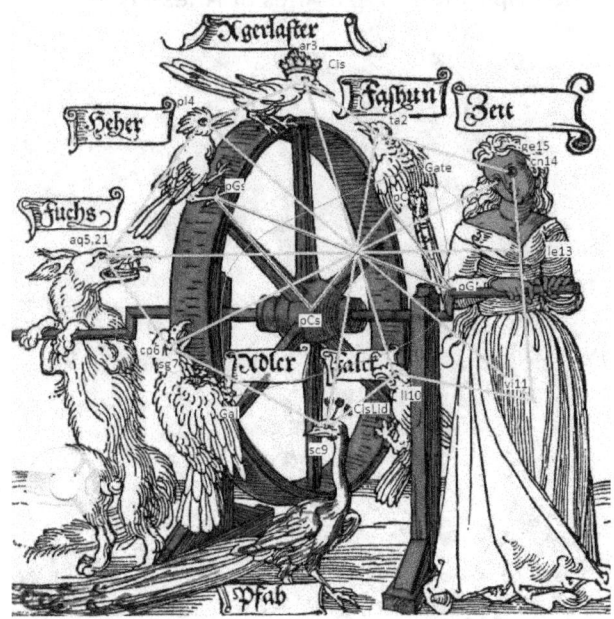

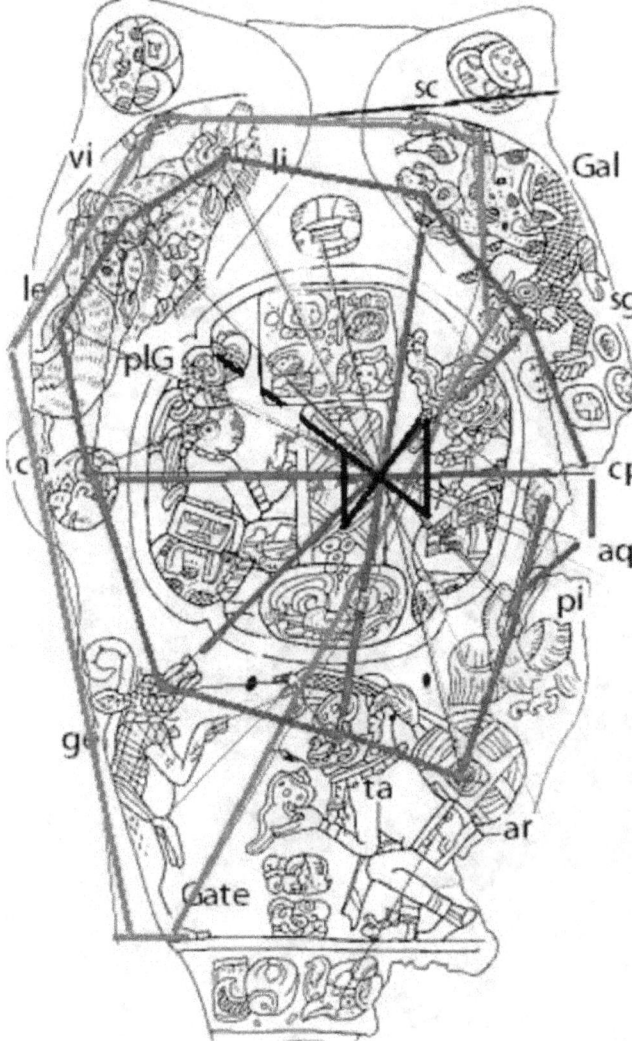

Dogs of a jungle paradise

Type Libra t10 as a canine and wheel (Mexican dogs palette. Mayan culture. Mindprint analysis by Edmond Furter). Libra t10's position here is unusually ambiguous, and so is its opposite Aries t3 t18 as a coiled bag. The Libra t10 wheel lies between itself and Scorpius t9 (see a basket lid with Buddha's death at theme t8).

Wheels or mechanisms tend to appear opposite the mystic basket that emerged as an occasional t2-t3 border feature in this study (see a marble sarcophagus at theme t11). The basket is expressed here as a coil or pack on Taurus t2' back. Opposite, and antipodal (spherical opposite) to the basket or rope of the Medusa head, which is 23 degrees north of the ecliptic, are the Lupus tail and Hydra tail, 23 degrees south of Libra. Thus the lid is lifted on part of the mystery of the Serapis, which had temples in Greek, Roman and Egyptian classical cities such as Ephesus. UFO theorists may well study these icons for clues on unidentified vortexes, lids, snakes, wolves, black dogs, centaurs, healers or scaly teachers leaning on two sticks, that tend to appear in art in this particular conceptual position. Telescopes are less useful in reading the human subtext. Spring and autumn have long since left Taurus Pleiades and Scorpius, yet the eyes of Taurus Perseus Algol Medusa mystic basket remain fixed. Its holographic opposite at the Scorpius t9 Lupus tail and Hydra tail, or cysta revelata to coin an iconographic label, also seems fixed. In Hindu and Buddhist theology, turning of a pearl or marble initiates the dharma wheel, or layers of law. The pearl of conceptual motivation also applies to Scorpius t9 and the adjacent Libra t10, lawgiver and wheel turner, who share Lupus as a decan. Some mythical doors are also identified with Libra t10 (see wheel-shaped Mexican caves at theme t15). The central disc may also figure an eclipse (see theme t3 t18), caused by a spectacular natural pair of marbles or eyes. Central woven vines or bark ropes may indicate an ayahuasca brew as trance inducer.

Celestial poles on a knot and a jaw, and the vertical plane, tag the inspiration as Age Pisces late.

Crowning balance

Type Libra t10 as a ball-headed person with a head disk, leading a procession (Algeria, Tassili ball-heads. Explorer website. Mindprint analysis by Edmond Furter). Libra t10's crown expresses the Scorpius t8 Galactic centre. A smaller crown on Gemini t15 marks the opposite gate (see a roundhead in the Afro-Mexican Nelson Mandela mural at theme t5 t20). It is tempting to interpret mindprint art as induced by supposed 'racial memory', culture or astrology. Popular imagination also easily jumps from assumptions of astronomy to supposed ancient astronauts or alien visitors, yet the standard imprint, its features, and its prevalence are evidence that art, artists, cultures, inspiration and spirit are human, terrestrial, subconscious, and beyond the faculties of memory or conscious culture. Where spirit may reside in the afterlife is unknown, perhaps in an undivided pool, conceptually in our earth or our sun, but probably not in an utterly distant, utterly different mixture of gases and vibrations, such as Sirius, Orion, the Pleiades, Vega or Achernar. These places sound familiar only due to the mythic characters and names that we gave them. Even science is not immune from popular notions of super races and space colonisation, and some scientists do not care to better inform public perception as long as public funding maintains 'programmes' such as the Search for Extra-Terrestrial Intelligence (SETI).

This study offers a simpler explanation. Culture is our expression of our holographic corner of nature. A celestial pole on a shoulder and the vertical plane tag the inspiration as Age Aries or Aries-Pisces.

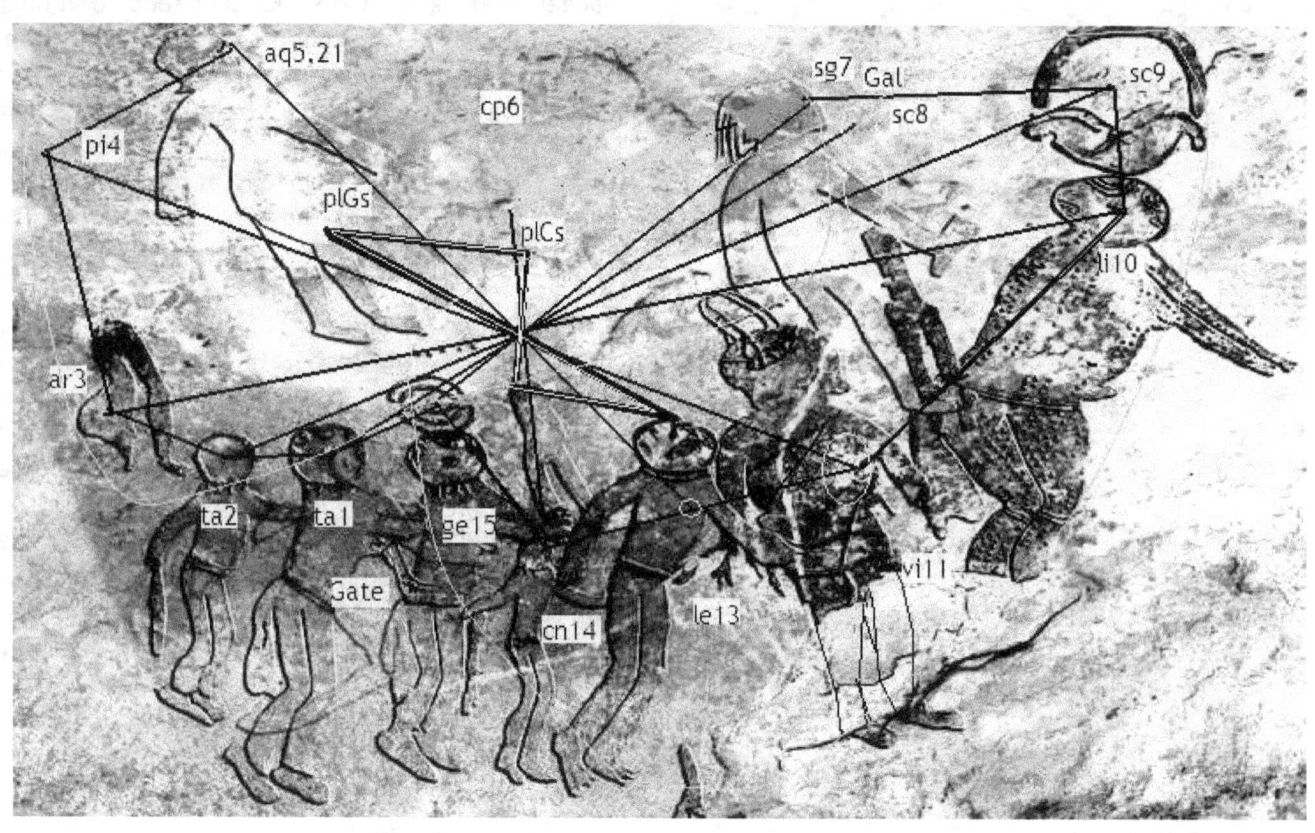

The law of paradise

Type Libra t10 Bootes as a lord of animals, half human, half spirit, judged by two laws (Blake; Pale figure, initially titled 'pyle figure'. Mindprint analysis by Edmond Furter). Galactic features separate physical and spiritual realms. T1 and t15 are missing above, as are their opposites t8 and t7 below. The vertical plane indicates an inspiration keyed to Age Pisces.

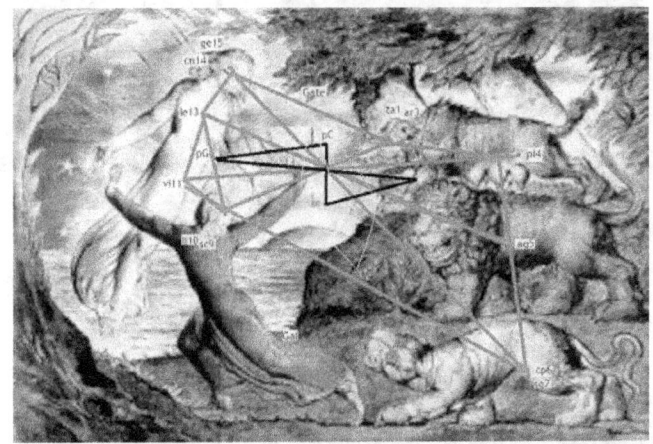

Legal balance and cosmic blessing

Type Libra t10 as a divine law-giver under a crown (Roman frieze named Gemma Augustus. Mindprint analysis by Edmond Furter). Coronation is by Scorpius t9, linked to Libra in some myths and constellation allocations as chelae, claws (see t9-t10 as a ring, wheel or basket lid in a Mayan palette at theme t10). The galactic south pole is on a vulture's tail, expressing the general concept of birds populating the less explored hemisphere. The south celestial pole was in Tucana (Bird of Paradise) in Age Aries, but this bird and other southern birds and reptiles such as Vultur Volans (Flying Gripe) and salamanders are highly variant characters in myth and in the sky. Astrology is an imperfect mirror of archetype, partly since scientific re-naming of constellations by La Lande, Herschel and others, was more extensive and haphazard in the south.

The artist's conscious faculties were engaged in political and aesthetic considerations, while inspiration filled in the usual gaps, in the usual sequence, accepting a wide variety of guises while retaining the typological sequence.

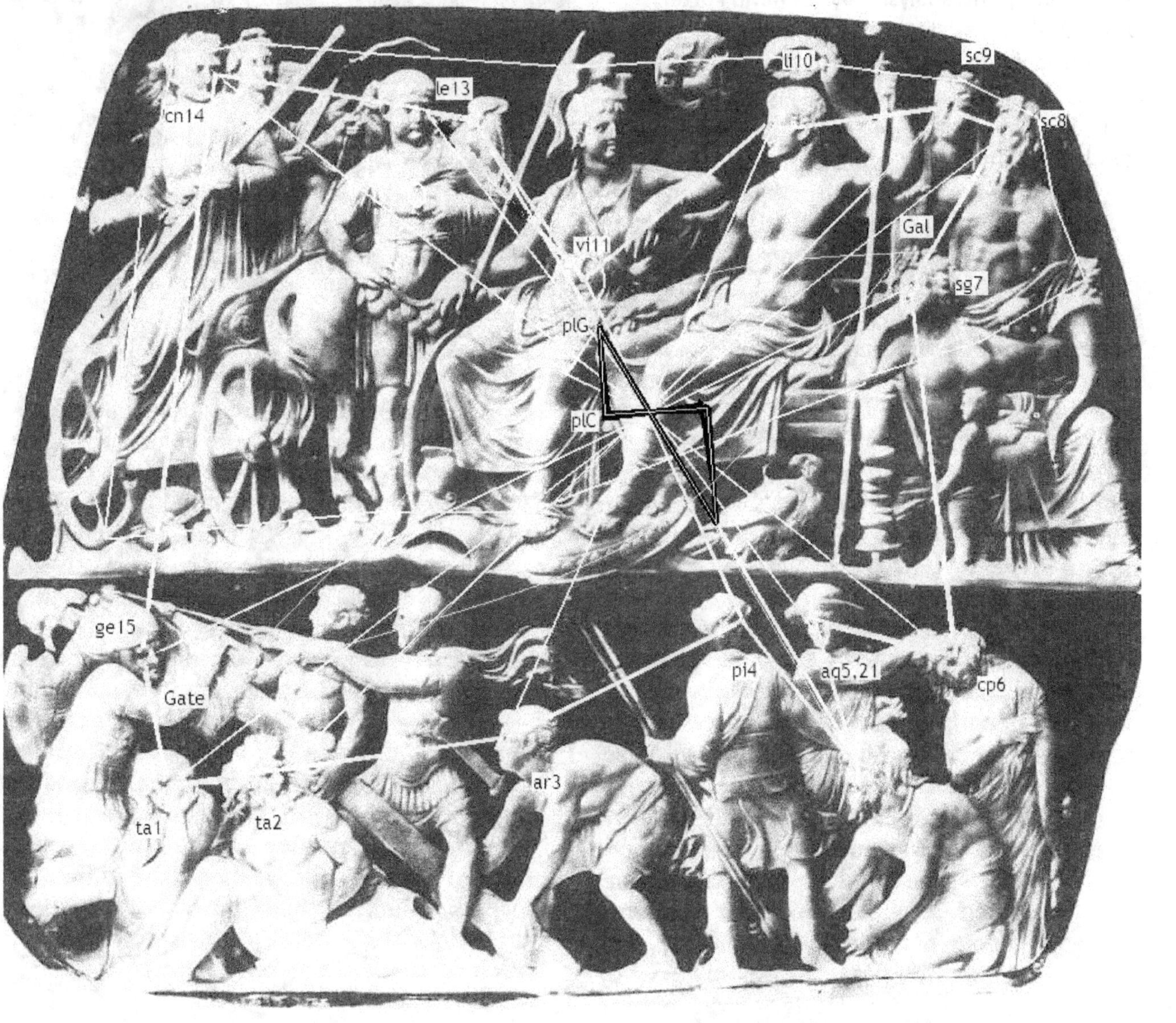

A midwife in India

Type Libra t10 as a midwife (Illumination of a princely birth. Historic India; Time Life. Mindprint analysis by Edmond Furter). The ecliptic pole (centre right, with darker axes) is on the elbow of a drummer. The celestial poles on the hand of a trumpeter (centre left, with lighter axes), and the mouth of a trumpeter (centre right), as well as the horizontal plane, tag the inspiration to Age Aries, as usual in works where Libra t10 is prominent or central. The celestial pole anchors an alternative axial grid, but with a questionable sequence of attributes. Stages in separation of double imprints may involve one of the celestial poles, in concert with some galactic features.

A midwife and surrogate mother

Type Libra t10 as Mary's mother (Ghirlandaio; Birth of the Virgin, among her life episodes. Tornabouni chapel. Mindprint analysis by Edmond Furter).
Libra t10 often assists either Virgo t11 or Scorpius t9. Celestial poles on the horizontal motto in the cornice tag the inspiration as Age Aries -Pisces, about BC 150, incidental with the retrospective legendary theme.

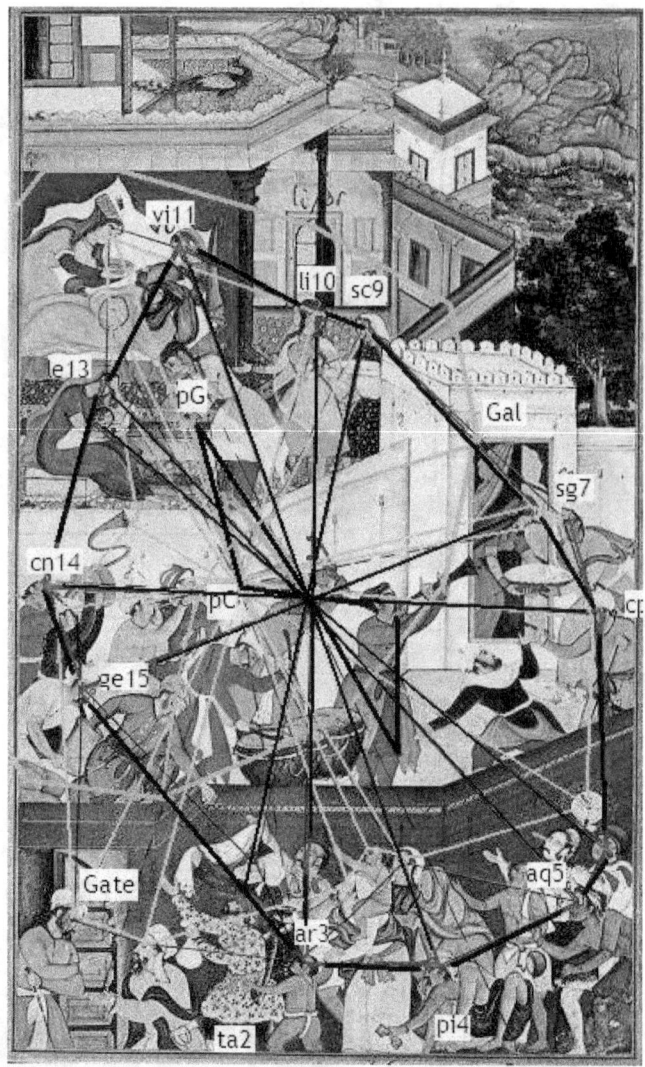

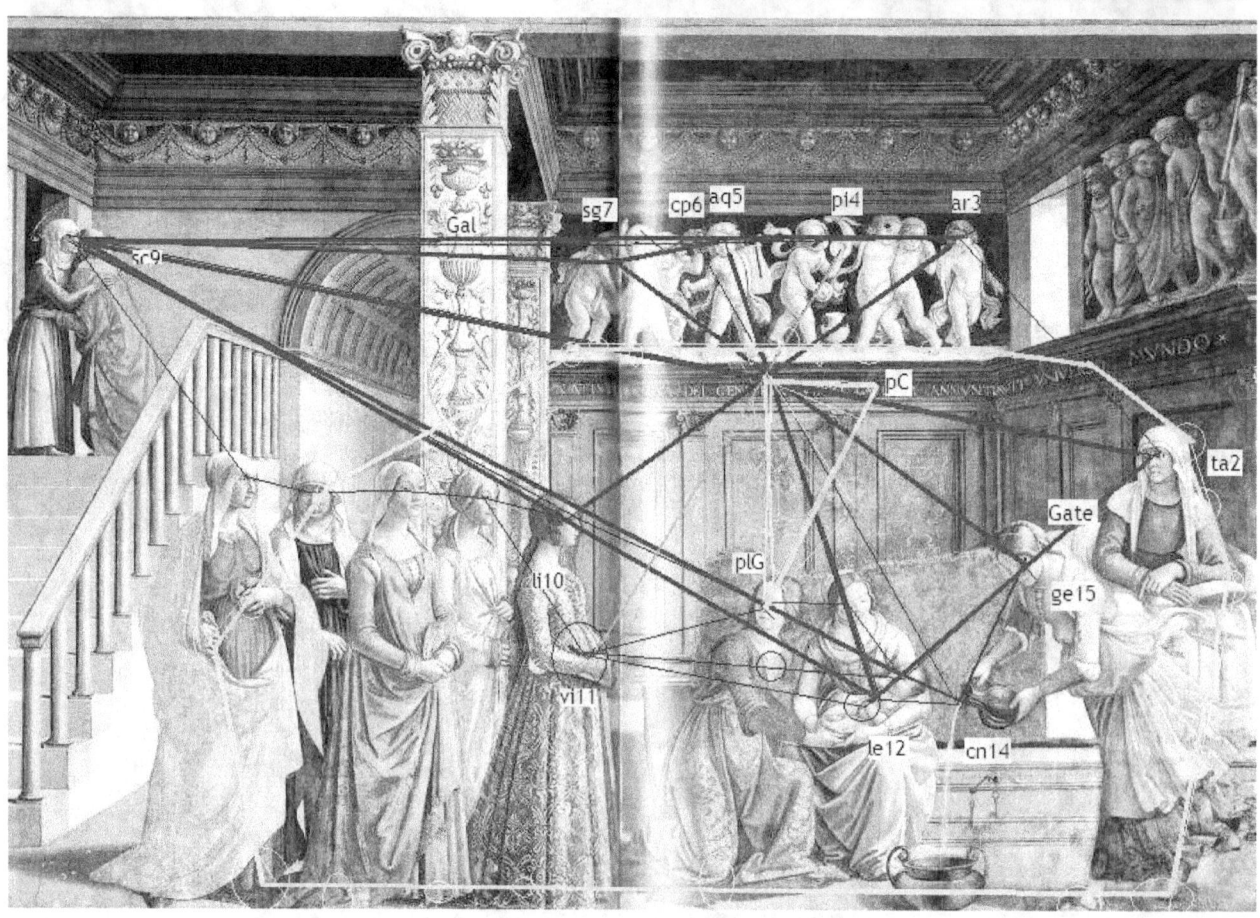

Axis
pi
aq
aq
cp
sg
ar
ta
Gal
pIC
sc
Gate
ta
sc
ge
li
cn
le
le
pIG
vi
le

Self-portrait of balance

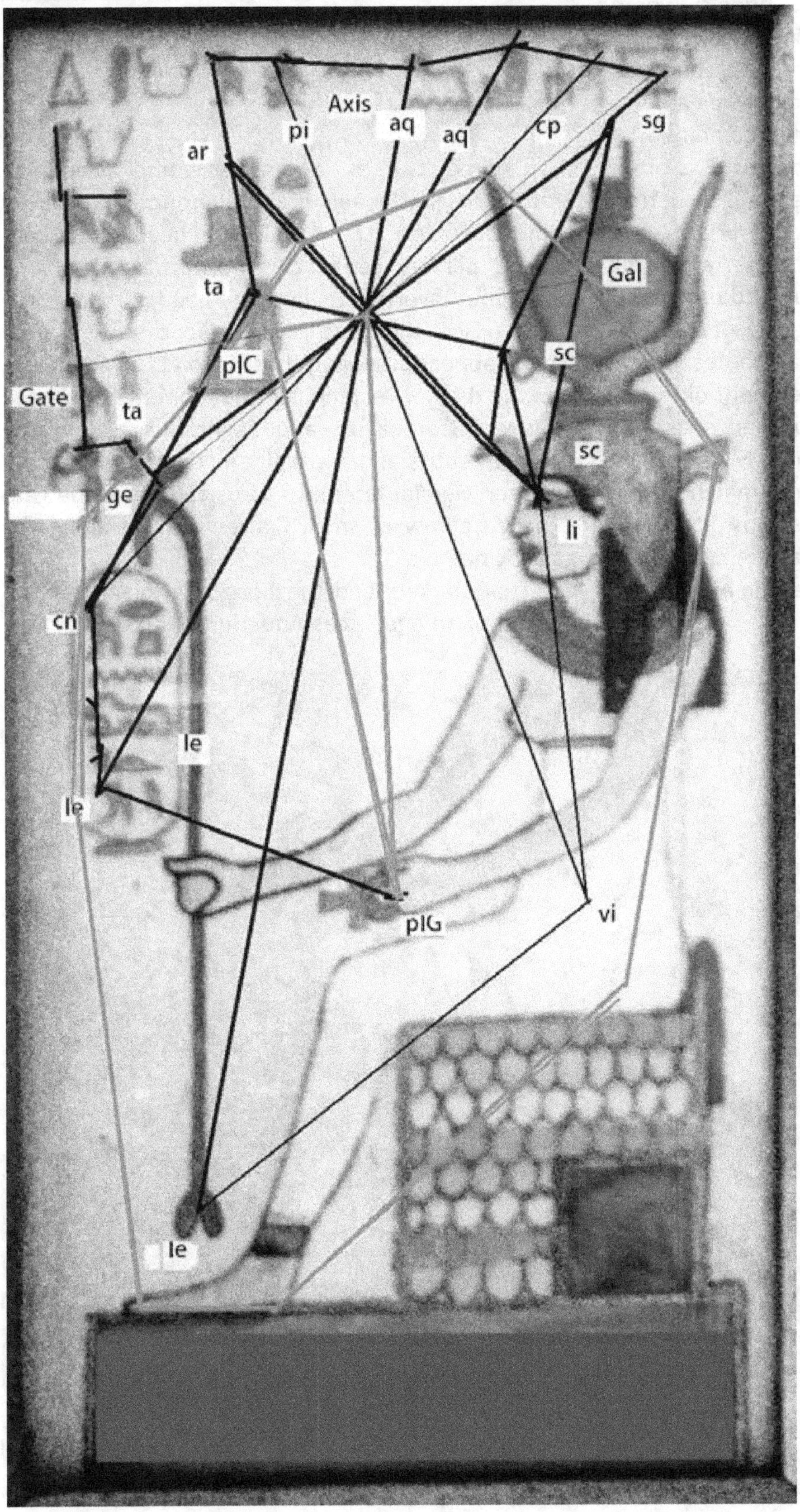

Type Libra t10 as a crowned Isis, a lawgiver, combined with Virgo t11 as Justice (Jeanne Morgan-Lefay; Isis. Pseudo-Egyptian style. Mindprint analysis by Edmond Furter). Hieroglyphs (sacred words) spell out divine and human laws, and play most of the parts in this imprint, as in some Babylonian, Egyptian, Mexican and other political and religious murals, papyri and jewels. The artist considers her work a type of prayer and devotion. She reads and writes hieroglyphics on a post-graduate level, but had no conscious knowledge of the mindprint sequence or structure in her art, or in any art.

A celestial pole on the shoulder or jaw of a scribe, perhaps Thoth, and the horizontal plane, tags the inspiration to Age Pisces-Aquarius, our current era.

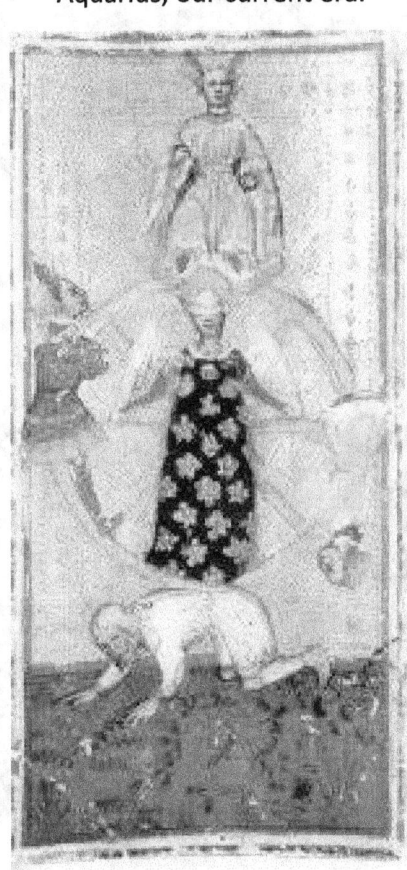

Type Virgo t11; Womb

Oracular wedding

Type Virgo t11 as a woodland bride's womb (Mantegna's Parnassus. Mindprint analysis by Edmond Furter). Taurus t2 and Gemini t15 share the figure of the hermit, opposite Scorpius t9 as a hero, and Sagittarius t7 as a winged horse, combined by their joint axis into a centaur. Sagittarius t7 is often figured as reining a chariot team. The hermit combines Gemini t15 as a benedicting priest, with the twisted posture of Taurus t2 t17 as rainmaker and Taurus t1 as healer, one arm up and one down over his ritual utensils on a table (see Tarot trump 1, Juggler). He also takes in some attributes of his opposite, Scorpius t8 Ophiuchus (Serpent holder) as a cloaked Loacoon, holding an unseen snake or galactic rope, an attribute of this axis. Mythological figures come ready-made to mix and match in art, with optional attributes and positions attached. Cancer t14 as Eros points a spear at the composite hermit, or at the implied Medusa head in his

downward hand. Capricornus t6 is figured as two dancers in unison, a kind of double-headed Hermes (see Poussin's Dance to the music of time, and double-headed Capricorni at theme t6). Libra t10 is just a staff, the caduceus of its opposite Aries t3 t18, which here is a lute player, the instrument forming its customary shield outline. Celestial polar markers are absent, but the vertical and horizontal planes tag the inspiration to Age Pisces-Aquarius.

A giraffe womb

Type Virgo t11 as a giraffe womb (Namibian Brandberg giraffe and grid. Mindprint analysis by Edmond Furter). Leo t13 is the heart of a lion-headed person. Leo t12 is horizontal, elsewhere sometimes inverted. Its hunter's bag figures Leo t12 Coma (Hair), the conceptual galactic pole. Several figures appear pregnant, thus Virgo t11 near the top sets the theme. Rectangular grids sometimes appear between Scorpius t8 and Sagittarius t7, on the galactic centre, more usually in the opposite gate between Gemini t15 and Taurus t16. Here the gate is a dense row of small figures walking along the galactic path.

Celestial markers and the horizontal plane tag the inspiration to Age Pisces-Aquarius, our current era.

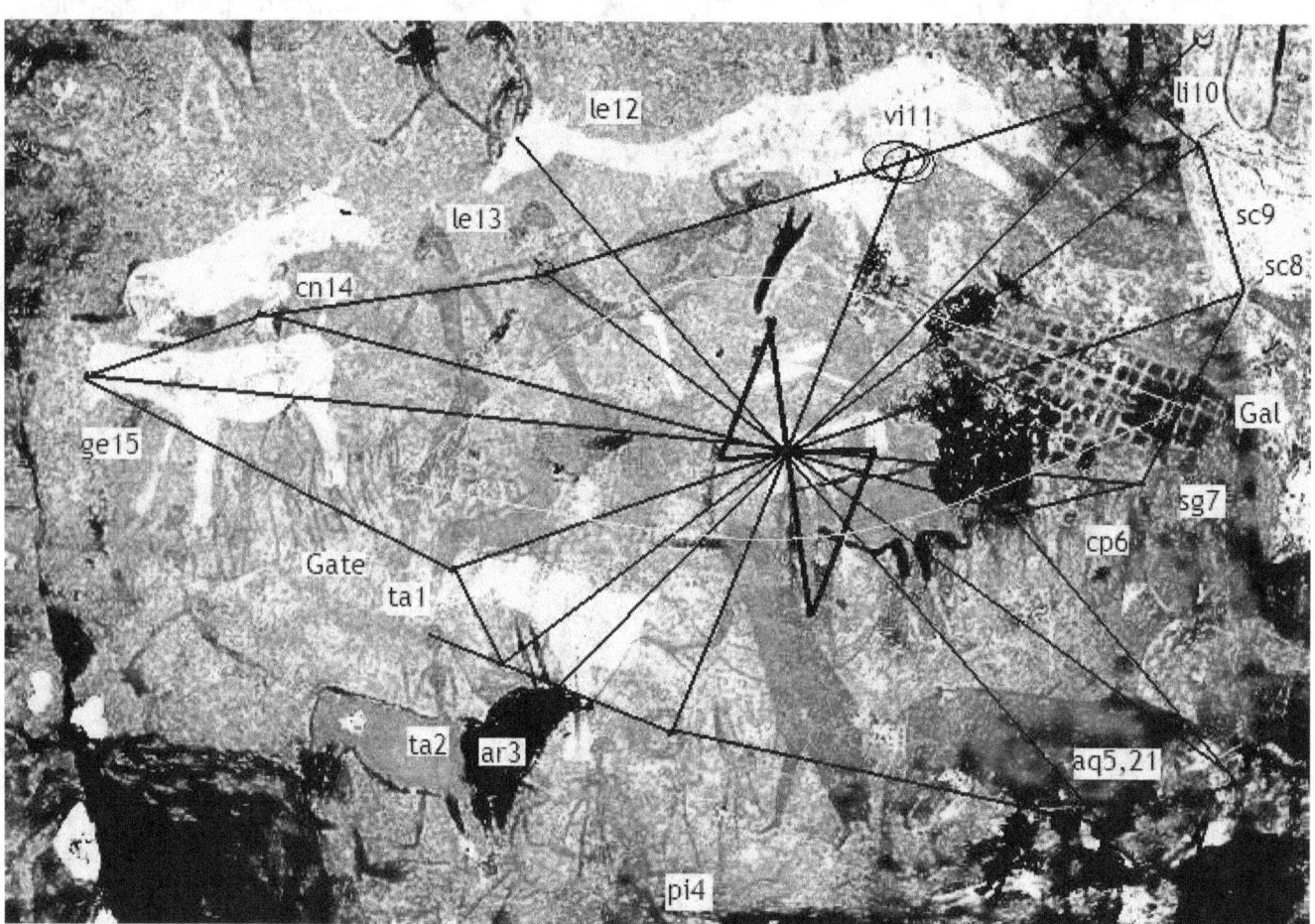

Two mothers, one house

Type Virgo t11 as a bride's womb, and a bridesmaid or mother (USA, Oz the Great movie promo 3D triptych. Disney. Mindprint analysis by Edmond Furter). Cinema animation is an excellent medium for expressing archetype, more versatile than opera. Some rock art evoke scenes as lively and dynamic as cinema.

The Wizard of Oz story is already archetypal, including the Taurus t16 Orion tower as a city (here doubled as rival cities flanking a natural cliff tower), and a yellow brick road (here between the polar axis to the galactic gate). Characterisation is sparse and the landscape is overly detailed, but mindprint is fully and compulsively expressed. The horizontal plane tags the inspiration as Age Pisces-Aquarius, our current era.

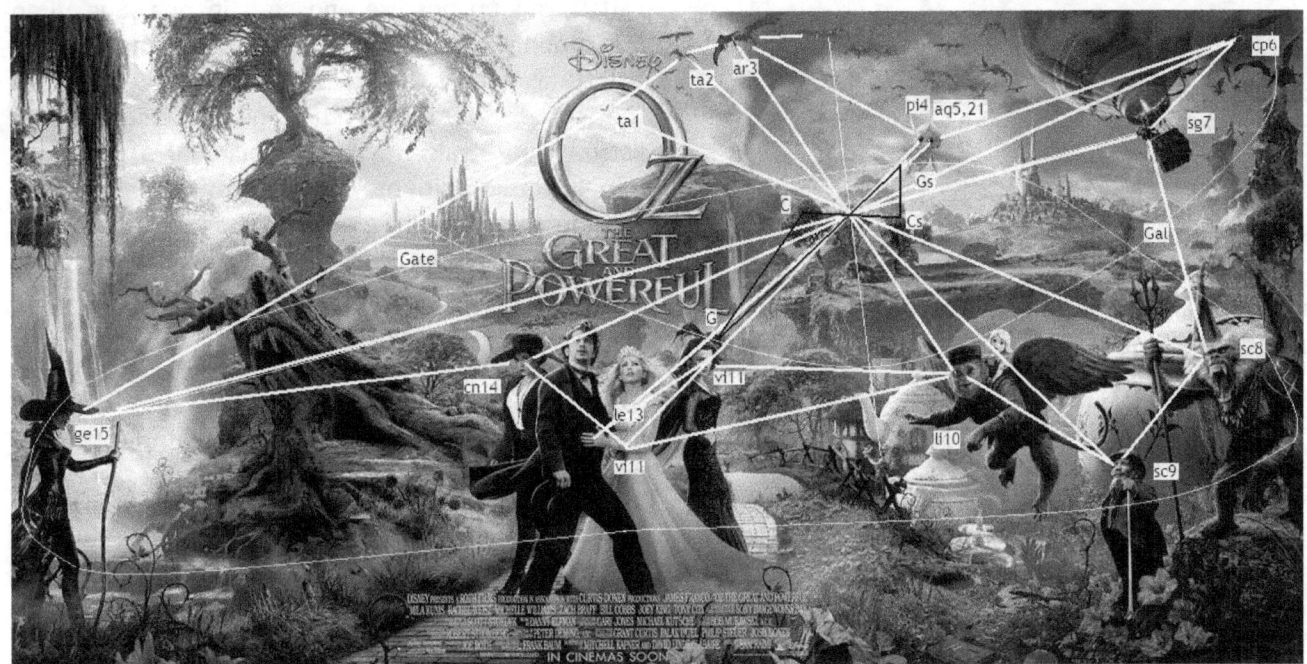

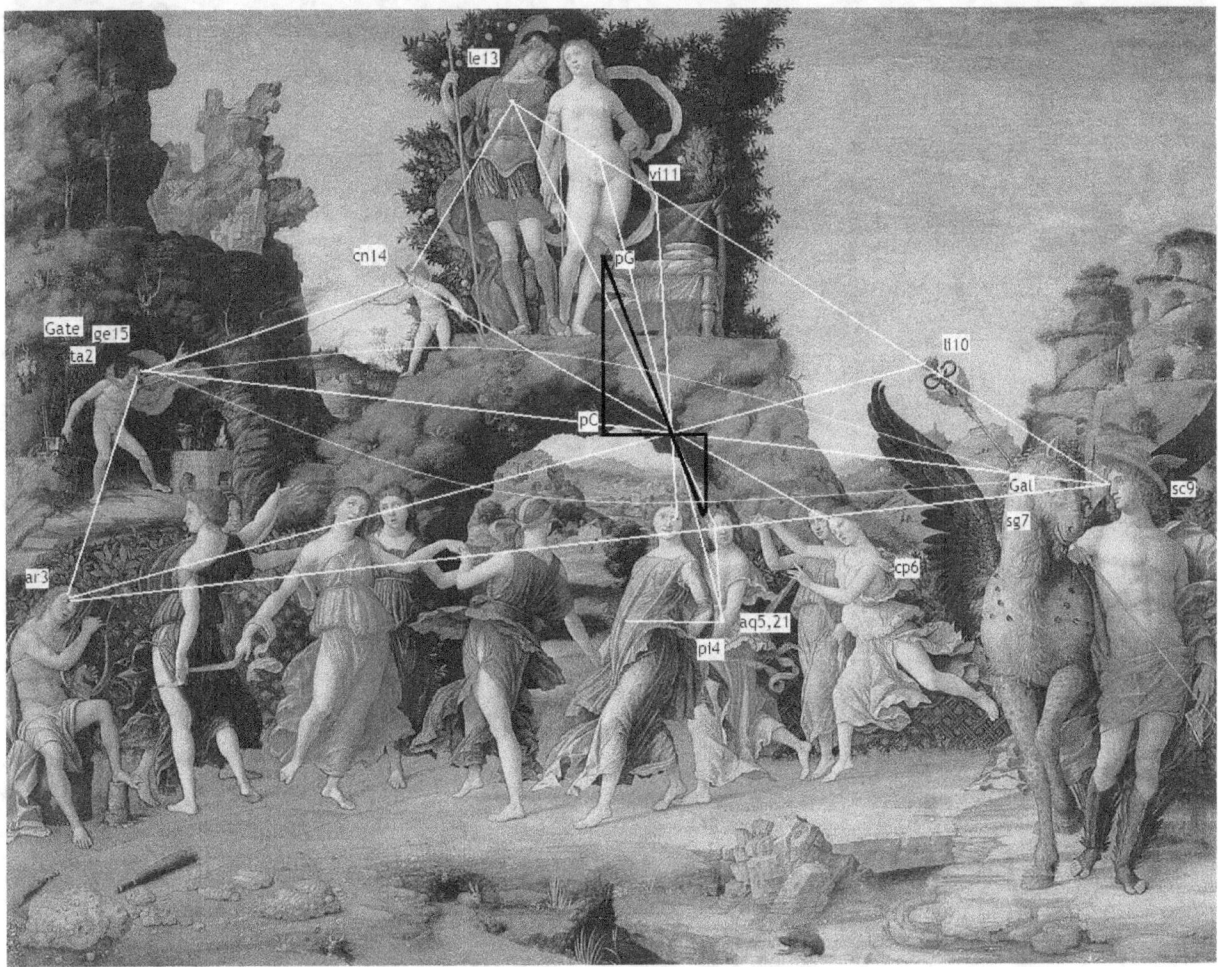

An ark and covenant mother

Type Virgo t11 Crater (Grail) as the womb of a polar woman (Salvador Dali; Spain. Mindprint analysis by Edmond Furter). Figures seem to emerge from a chest of drawers, inverting the ark theme (where figures enter a box). Her rectangular chest echoes the opposite buildings on a dusty street, above Aquarius t5 and Pisces t4 Pegasus (which is often a horse, pond or field grid). Here Spain's Ampurdan plain is gridded by field lines (top left). Plains are always more alive than meet the eye. Libra t10 is a see-saw rider, the concept of balance as the turner of the wheel of life, doubling as nipples on the transparent breasts that overlay the landscape as the body of the beloved. A celestial pole on a rider's hand tag the inspiration as Age Taurus-Aries, one of the most retrospective inspirations in this study, incidental with the theme of passing events and evaporated time.

A mother's altar

Type Virgo t11 retro as the 'womb' of a podium topped by a corn ear or plough, and Virgo t11 Bootes as a U-shaped staff with two necks (Babylonian kudurru boundary stone in profile. Rawlinson. Mindprint analysis by Edmond Furter).

Other podiums in the work are topped by omphali (navels or wombs) that also figure large bread cones, while the profile of the stone itself sets a womb theme. The galactic pole is on the jaw of the rear head of Hydra (which also figures the heart of Leo t13), via Leo t12 Crater (Grail) in a southern spherical (transparent) concept view, super-imposed on northern hemisphere concepts. Libra t10 Bootes is the other face on the U-shaped staff, forming its usual arms-up posture and staff in one. See Virgo t11 among tall staffs or standards in the Narmer palette at theme t3 t18. See some rollout detail of this cone at theme t2 t17. The artefact is partly astronomical, raising the possibility of a conscious mindprint tradition, but formulaic symbolic elements like the three orbs on top (poles as well as planets), a unique design, and asymmetrical poles on a symmetrical surface, indicate the usual subconscious artistic inspiration at work in a politico-religious monument. The work could result from a programme (a conventionalised set of images), which is prone to error and attribute exchange (see the Decans section in the text, and decanal variants at themes t2 t17, t8 and t12). The archetypal sequence and structure remain unfaulted, in their usual integrated, hardy, all-or-nothing format.

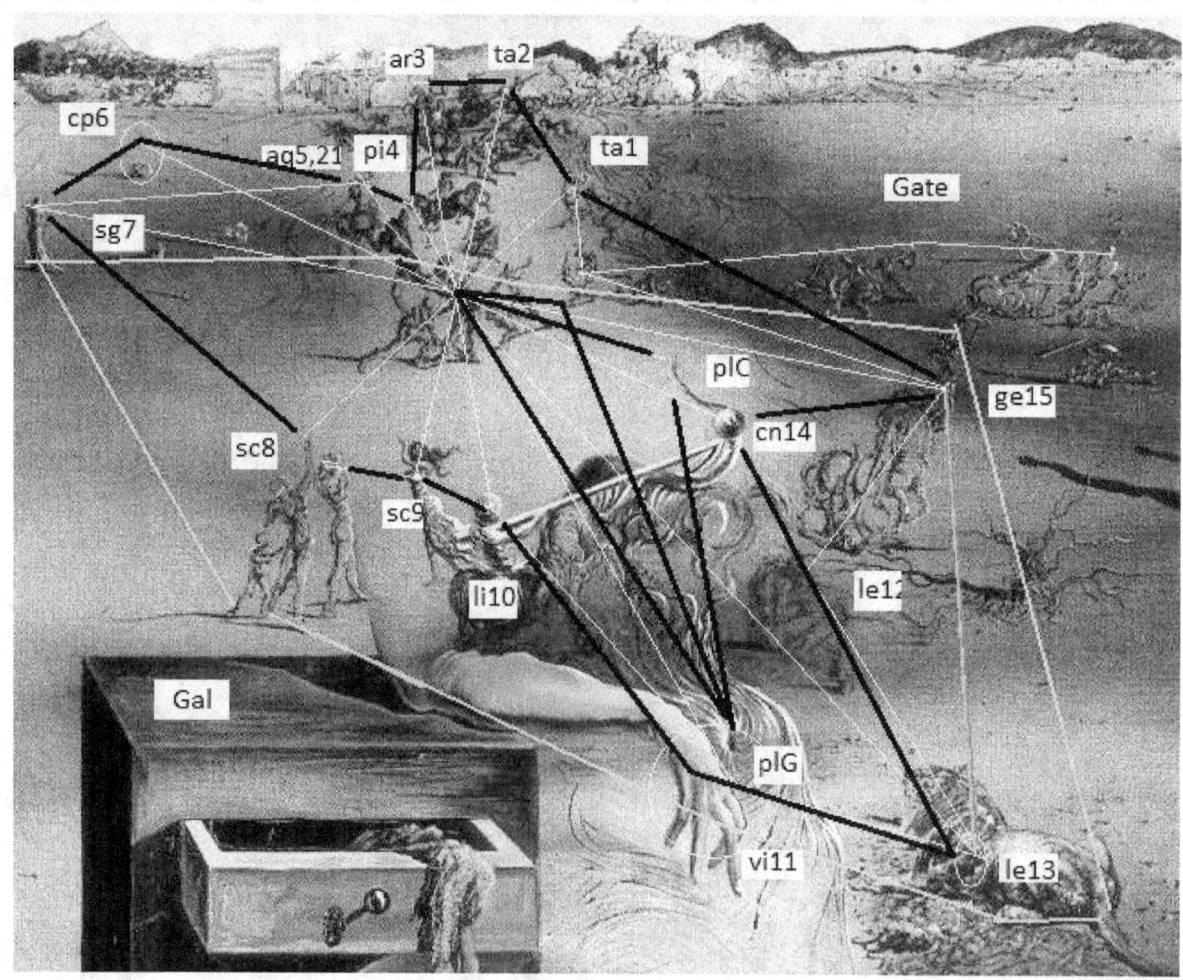

Ark mother

Type Virgo t11 Crater (Grail) as a womb and as the entrance to Noah's ark (Kaspar Memberger; Animals entering the ark, 1588. Vienna Art Museum. Mindprint analysis by Edmond Furter). The ark theme remains popular in art, partly for its close analogy to the full round of types in nature, life and culture, and a large structure as a visual anchor point and analogy to the concept of structure itself. The stranded box is a type of cosmic and cultural pole on the galactic axle between t11 and t12, opposite the large rectangle of Pisces t4 Pegasus floating in celestial 'water'. The portable Exodus ark, a model of a boat in Babylonian, Egyptian, Ethiopian and other traditions, with angel wings on its boathouse box, also expresses Pisces t4 Pegasus and its cardinals (Gemini t15 boat shrine, Virgo t11 and the galactic pole, Virgo t11 Corvus Crow and Sagittarius t7 chariot coach).

A celestial pole on the hip of one of the sons, and the horizontal plane, tag the inspiration as Age Pisces-Aquarius, our current era.

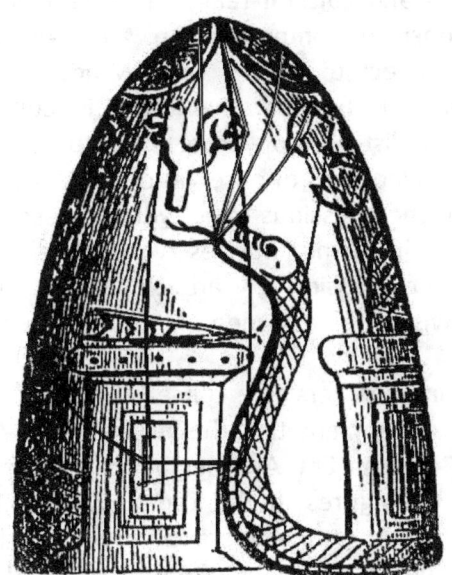

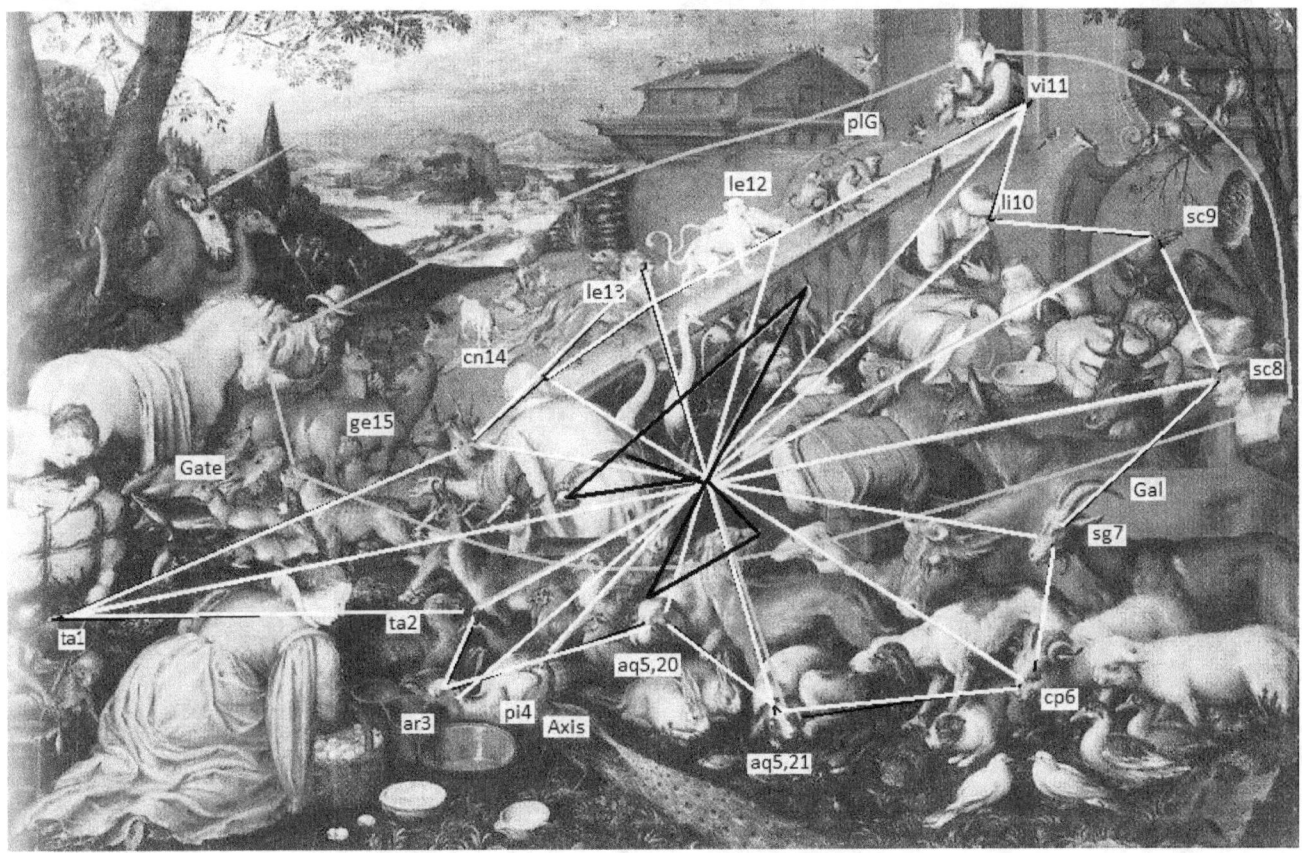

A giraffe mother

Type Virgo t11 as a giraffe womb (Zimbabwe, Matobo range, Nanke cave formlings. Elspeth Parry, Amabooks. Mindprint analysis by Edmond Furter). Repeated ovoid shapes, named formlings in archaeology, derive from archetype, entoptics and inspiration. They are incidental with a range of natural shapes such as termite eggs, termite nest interiors, caves, beehive cakes, people wearing skin coats, bags (see theme t15), clouds, fungi, intestines and cultural shapes such as bundles, hut doors, windows, domes, tympanums (covers in stress-relieving domes above door lintels) and niches, all magnets for inspired art. See domic outlines and registers (levels) in religious tympanums at theme t11, in esoteric emblems such as Rosicrucian caves at theme t6, and Mexican caves at theme t15. The bases and dark portions of formlings framed by the implied galactic equators in the usual fish-shaped section, hint that formlings may originate in the structural, galactic components of inspiration, and that the equator of eyes may be a secondary function of the geometric elements of perception, incidental with the bright galactic equator in the sky.

The galactic concept is never featured as a single band, or Milky Way, but as two intersecting bands, their flipped or mirrored crossing points on the figures equator at two constant points in the sequence of eyes. The result is a four-dimensional structural frame obscured in two-dimensional images of mythic episodes. A hologram or clockwork seems scrambled when squashed.

Unrealistic figures such as forms, ropes, flight and half humans, are reminders that art is not realism, and that realism is not the function or measure of art. Individual and cultural reality extends beyond literal and conscious comprehension. Art, crafts and culture are subject to natural laws. Mindprint art exposes some of the pervasive order in culture. Cosmic and holistic vision involve features that require several lifetimes of observation and study to appreciate in the conscious mind, yet expressed by most artists, including novices worldwide. Our subconscious expression of archetypal structure should likewise be assumed in other human domains.

Celestial polar markers are uncertain, but one possible horizontal plane tags the inspiration to Age Pisces, the Common Era. Another horizontal plane, of most of the figures in the top half, tags Age Pisces-Aquarius, our current era of about the last 200 years, when some inspirations or expressions ticked over in expectation of the forthcoming Age.

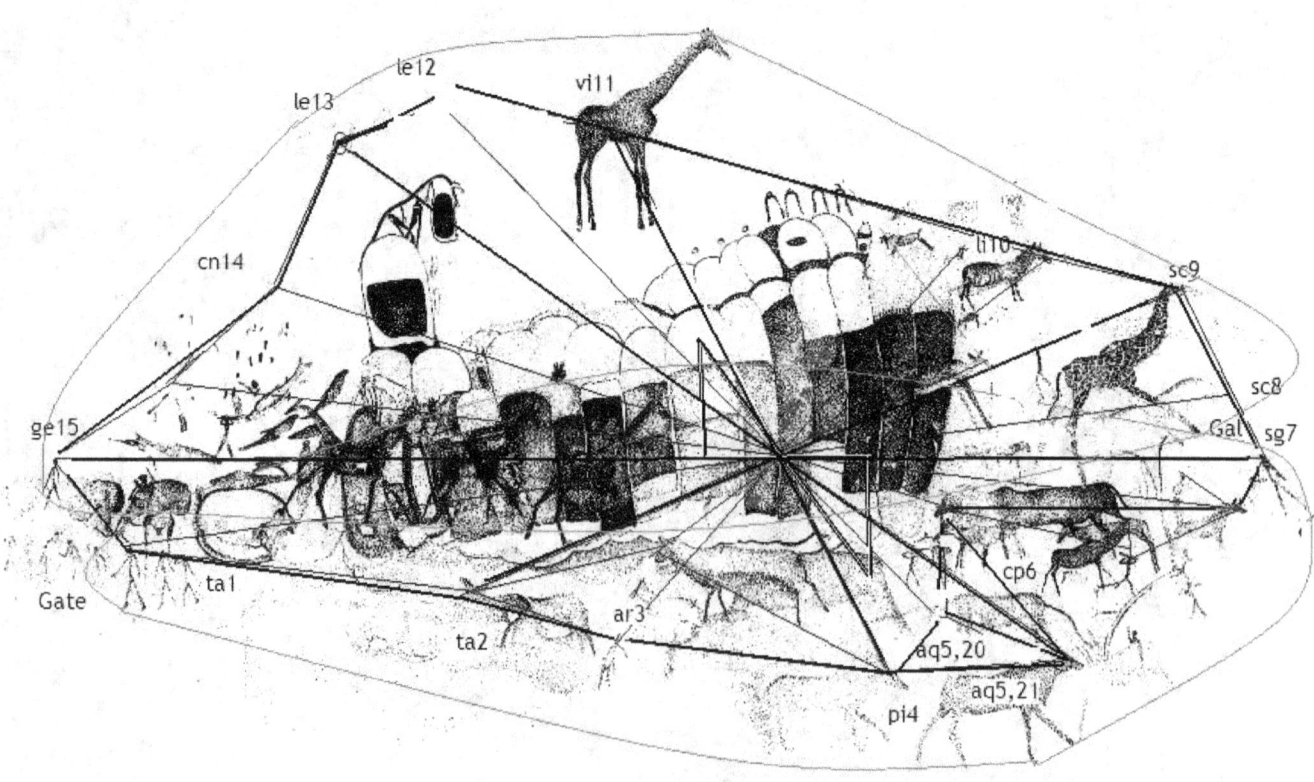

Mother Mary

Type Virgo t11 as Mary with the Christ child (Paris, Notre Dame west tympanum. Newsweek. Mindprint analysis by Edmond Furter). See domic formlings and registers (levels) in some rock art at theme t11

and elsewhere, esoteric emblems such as Rosicrucian caves at theme t6, Mexican caves at theme t15, and Stargate movies.

Celestial poles on two jaws, and the horizontal plane, tag the inspiration as Age Pisces, incidental with the work.

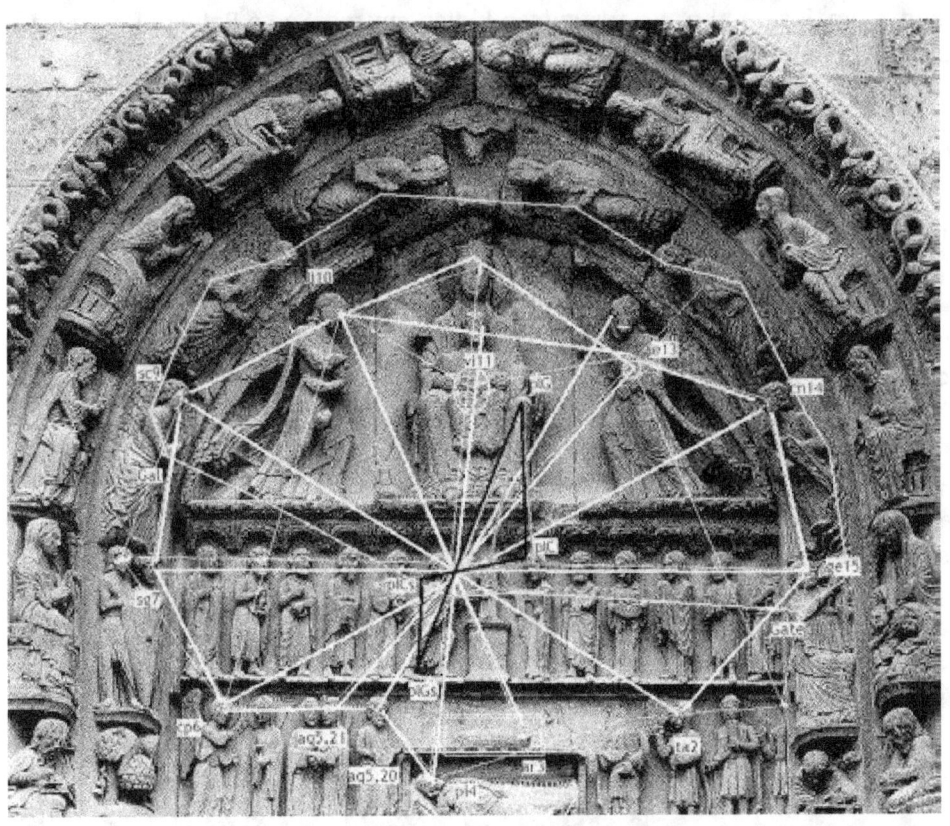

Our Lady of the harbour

Type Virgo t11 as the womb of Justice or the queen of heaven with a fleet (Spain, Seville, Alcazar triptych named Discovery of the Americas, or Virgin of navigators, by Fernandez. Mindprint analysis by Edmond Furter). The usual scales of Justice (a concept shared by Virgo t11 and Libra t10) are figured as nobles and ships, subject to trade balance, politics and weather. The scales are also figured as the shutters with images of donors. See a harbour scene in the Santorini 'Atlantis' harbour mural at theme t4. Leonard Cohen's song Suzanne also expresses this type.

Leo t13 has a companion with colourful leggings, more usual at its opposite Aquarius t5, which in turn is a mounted decapitator, more typical at the opposite Leo t13. Libra t10 has a staff as usual. Celestial poles on a knee and a foot, and the horizontal plane, tag the inspiration to Age Aries-Pisces, retro to the event and the work.

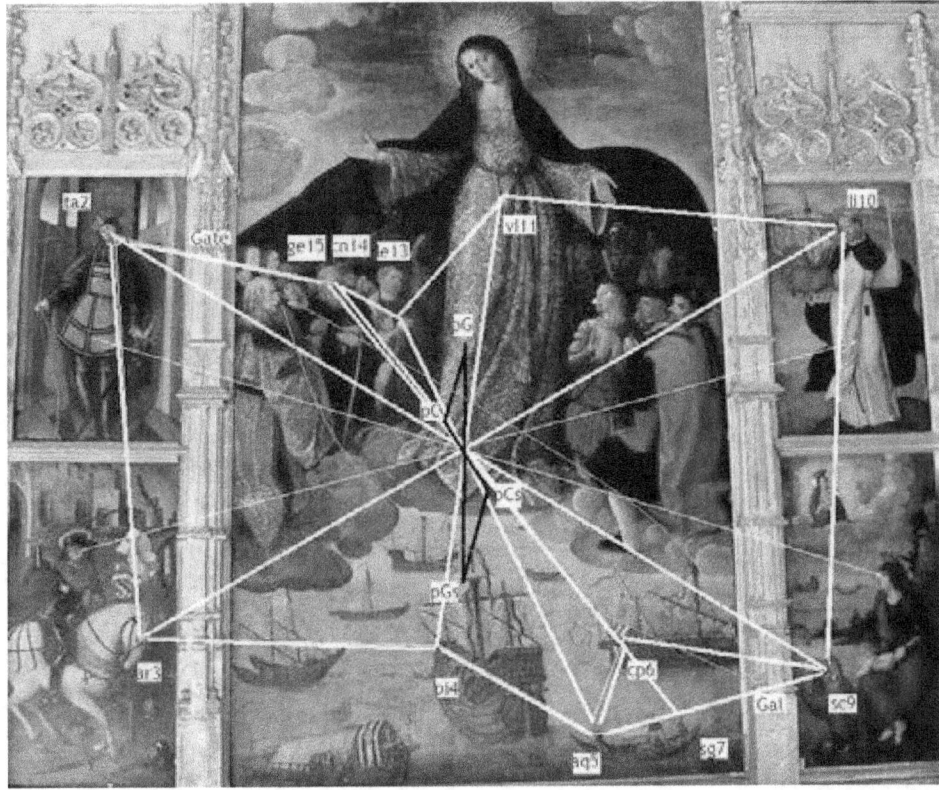

Allotted time

Type Virgo t11 Crater (Grail) as autumn riding a beast (Italy, Bacchus and four seasons marble sarcophagus, AD 220. New York Metropolitan Museum of Art. Mindprint analysis by Edmond Furter). Some unusual attributes and axial interchange (swopping of opposites) suggest that the artist may have consciously used an axial grid, or re-worked an existing work, or that the inspiration includes a spherical flip, as seen from inside the coffin. The ecliptic pole is on autumn's elbow. She is marked by her eye, not womb as usual, which here figures a future celestial pole instead. Gemini t15 is a pair of duck victims. Aries t3 t18 is a ram with its neck crossed by a staff as a Lamb of God. The staff top marks the transition of autumn from Libra t10 (with Aries' bent neck) to Virgo t11 in Age Aries-Pisces. Cancer t14 is Pan, more usual at the opposite Capricornus t6, who here holds his occasional tree. Leo t13 is Pan's crown instead of the usual heart. Between Aries t3 and Taurus t2 is a cista mystica (basket of mystery) with a snake. The exposed rump just above the basket expresses Taurus t2 t17 Perseus standing on the Pleiades (his twisted foot on the basket), holding the contained Medusa head which he had cut off by aiming a blow backward in a shield mirror. The perilous head concept, assigned to the star Algol, is about 23 degrees north of the ecliptic, equal to earth's current obliquity, and antipodal (spherical opposite) to Scorpius t9 Lupus tail and Hydra tail (see a basket lid with Buddha's death at theme t8, and a vortex lid in a Mexican palette at theme t10). Astrology is a holographic myth map. Celestial poles on the season's breast and the beast's jaw, tag the inspiration to Age Aries-Pisces. Her womb tags Age Pisces-Aquarius, our current era, prophetic for the work. Both datings and the position of the basket support the theme of transition.

A chariot seat

Type Virgo t11 Crater (Grail) as the womb of a goddess in a quadriga or four-horse chariot (Persian Sabazius plaque. Ghirshman; Iran, 1962, Thames and Hudson. Mindprint analysis by Edmond Furter). Scorpius t8 Galactic centre is a snake around a post (see Tarot trump 8 with a post). Gemini t15 and Taurus t1 t16 share a thunderbolt as a galactic gate churn group. Capricornus t6 is a tree. Aquarius t5 is a turtle (see Indian churns. See a Babylonian Pazuzu plaque at theme t5 t21). The galactic pole is on the central figure's jaw. Celestial polar markers tag the inspiration to Age Taurus, Aries-Pisces or Pisces.

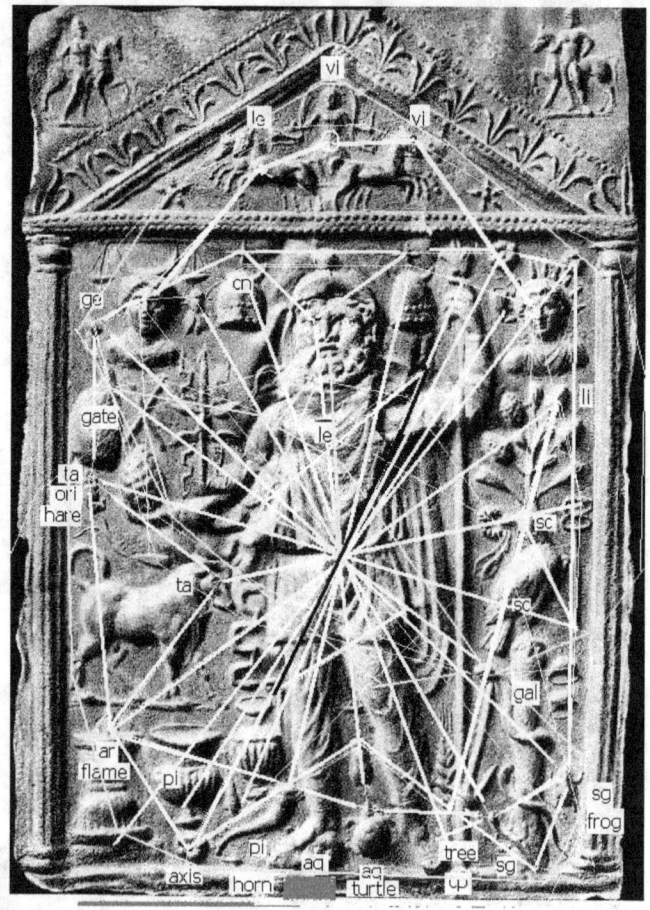

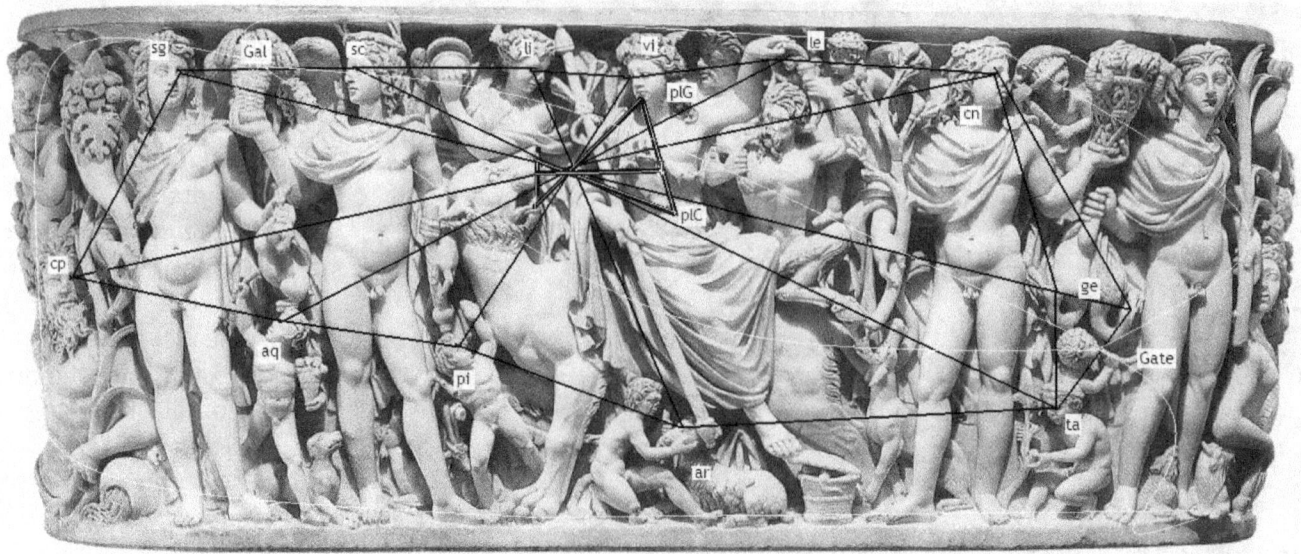

A dragon seat

Type Virgo t11 Crater (Grail) as the eye and womb of a queen on a lion-dragon monster (Chinese funeral tile, Queen of the west. El Shaughnessy; Ancient China. Duncan Baird. Mindprint analysis by Edmond Furter). Tiles, seals, palettes, printing blocks and cards invite mindprint due to their inherent duplication and perpetuation. The t11 theme extends to her opposite, Pisces t4 as a frog on a bridge (see Virgo t11 as a frog in some Egyptian embalming scenes).

Leo t13 has its axis on its eye, but its opposite Aquarius t5 is the heart of a human-faced dragon (manticora or mandragora. Human-faced water dragons also appear in American rock art).

Cancer t14 Ursa Minor (Small Bear) is a fox of nine tails, signalling a series of celestial polar markers just as Leo t13 Ursa Major did earlier with its nine stars. Both bears or forelegs are rectangles with a curved tail or foot. Their bulks are 90 degrees from Taurus, where the spring equinox hovered for millennia (see the Cosmic map). Both feature in the Biblical episode of Samson setting foxes with torches tied to their tails into the corn fields of his enemies. Samson is a type of Hercules, but both are better placed at Libra t10 Bootes, while Hercules constellation is Hercules as a strong baby. Gemini t15 as a rabbit holds ropes linked to the nine polar tails (see an Egyptian t15 rope handler in the Seti 1 ceiling at theme t8). He also holds three poles by the three mushroom stems in his hands. The wobbly stems elegantly express polar precession.

A celestial pole on a knee, and the horizontal plane, tag the inspiration to Age Aries-Pisces.

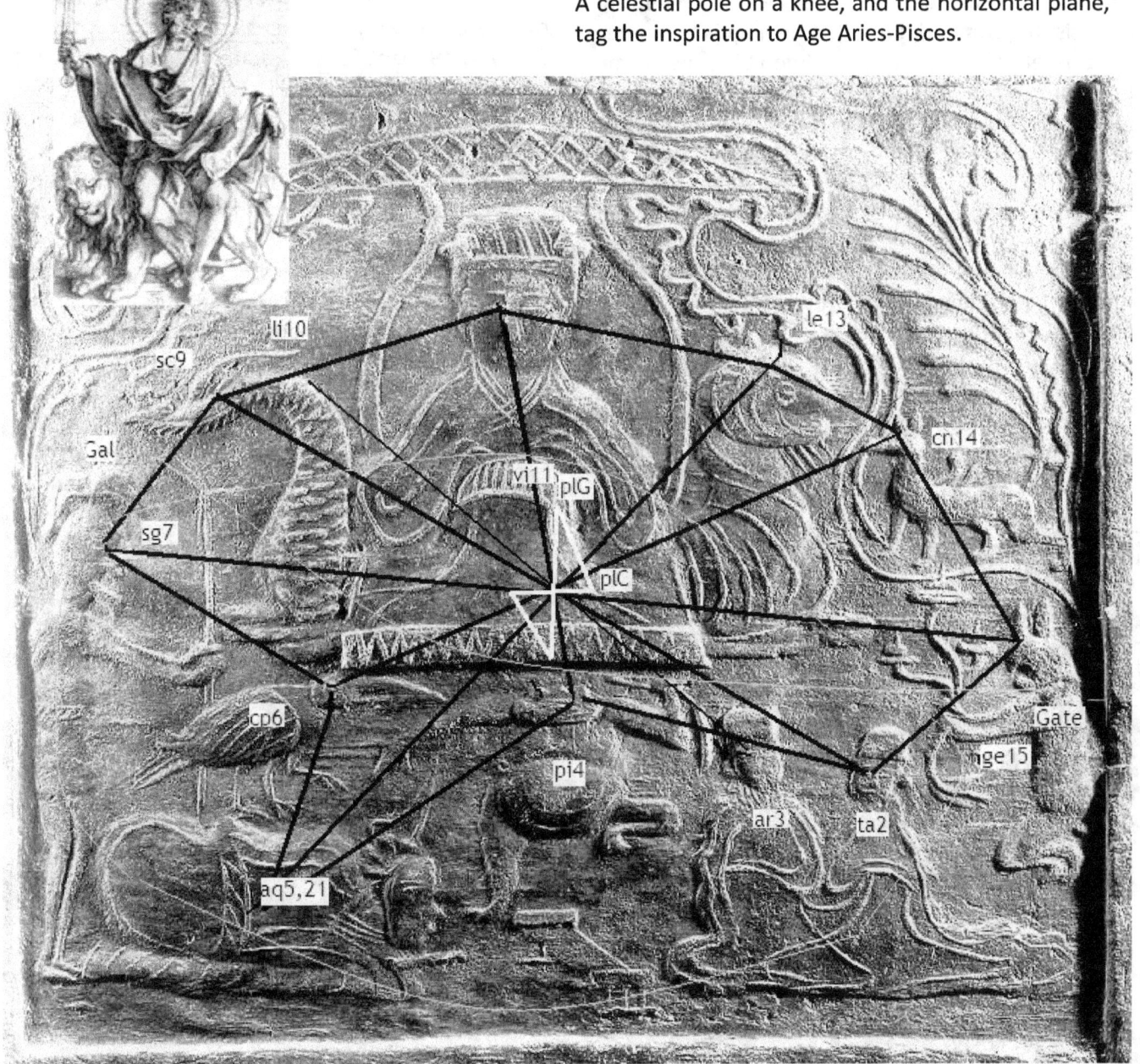

Type Leo t12;
King inverted

Betrayed by a disciple

Type Leo t12 and t13 as the heart of Christ (Leonardo Da Vinci; Last supper and prediction of betrayal. St Mary of the Graces, Milan. Mindprint analysis by Edmond Furter). The Inquisition once tried heretics in the building. Virgo t11 is the womb of John, often equated with Mary Magdalene (Baigent, Leigh and Lincoln; Holy blood, holy grail), which is below the hand of Judas. Libra t10 is the money bag of Judas, whose eye is not on the grid. Scorpius t9 and t8 is Bartholomew's hand. He is bent forward as t9 often is. Scorpius t8 may be James the Younger, who is not on the grid. Sagittarius t7 is Andrew's right hand. Capricornus t6 is Andrew's left hand, and nearing the poles as usual. Aquarius t5 t21 and t5 t20 are Peter and Mary. Pisces t4 is Christ's eye, in the centre of a rectangle of light. Aries t3 is Thomas and Philip. Taurus t2 and t1 is James. Gemini t15 is Thaddeus, doubled by Matthew. Cancer t14 is Simon, and far from the poles as usual.

The horizontal design enforces three compromises; the t15-t7 and t14-t6 axes are nearly combined, and end on two hands, and t9 is on a hand, instead of the usual eyes. Disciples and apostles form similar groups in art and esoterica, but identifications of the disciples diverge.

The galactic pole is on Christ's elbow and the vertical plane. The celestial pole is on Christ's shoulder and the horizontal plane, tagging the inspiration to Age Aries, as in most religious art of the last 2000 years.

Four perspectives

Type Leo t12 Galactic pole as tree-climbing bears (USA Colorado, bears, trees and ropes. Greer. Mindprint analysis by Edmond Furter). Leo t12 attributes include a polar axis tree or frame and bodily suspension, as of Odin or Indian gods in trials of perspective. T12's suspension is distinct from the Scorpius t9 bent-forward state, or Aquarius t5 t21 on one leg (adjacent to Capricornus t6. Also see Kokopellli). It is also distinct from Taurus t2 t17 Perseus twisting to look forward in a mirror. The four large cardinals thus include four distinct postures and sensations linked to dreams or surreal, subjective experience. Gymnosophy (bodily wisdom) such as yoga and animal mimic, is known for its spiritual rewards. Tree climbers in rock art may find practical explanations, but mindprint explains the identities and context of recurring postures in myth and art (see a Greek Minoan jewel with a tree and multi-legged squirrel at theme t12). Hanging upside down, or imagining doing so, is an inherent part of cosmology, geography, mythology and iconography,

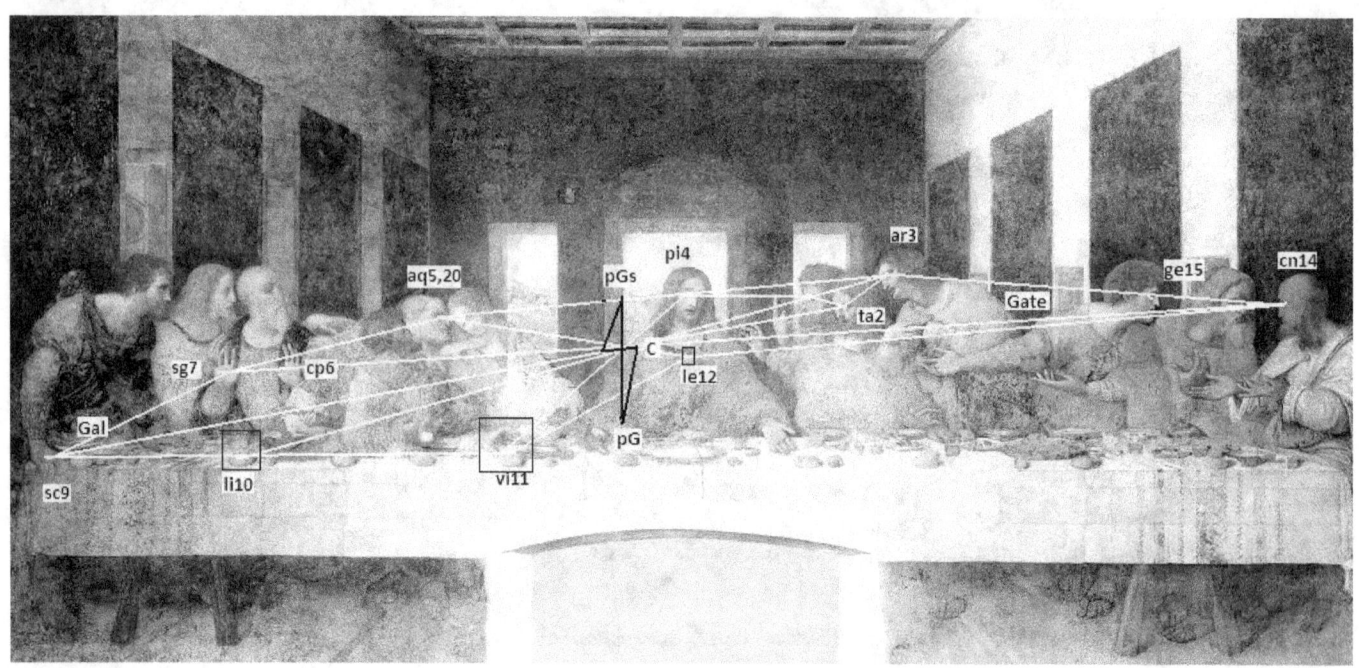

incidental with the Leo t12 theme of inversion. The world cross tree, defined by galactic features, flanked by eight particular types, is ambiguous only with occasional tree icons at Cancer t14 and its opposite, Capricornus t6, here both figured as trees. Ambiguity of galactic stargates and the t14-t6 soul gates is on record back to Greek philosophers, supposed by archaeo-astronomers (Gary A David; Orion zone) to derive from Cancer t14 as midsummer in Age Aries. The tropics, where the sun reaches its extreme north and south positions, place all of latitude 23.4 degrees north directly under the sun on one day in the year, and the same for about 23.4 degrees south. These latitudes are still named tropics (actually solstices) of Cancer and Capricornus, although the sun now shines on its northernmost parallel from the background of the Gemini-Taurus gate, and on the southern midsummer from the Sagittarius-Scorpius Galactic centre gate. Transformation is part of the theme of Leo t12. Celestial polar markers are uncertain, but the vertical plane tags the inspiration as Age Pisces-Aquarius, our current era, confirming the axial tree theme.

The spring equinox is now on the axis defined by the two static poles, a concept expressed as a cosmic tree rooted between the concepts of Pisces and Aquarius in all cultures.

Lords of surf and turf

Type Leo t12 and its opposite Aquarius t5 as predators and hunters, linking a double imprint (Korean Daegok Ri sea cliff engraving with whales. Sang Mong Lee. Mindprint analysis by Edmond Furter). As usual in double imprints, there is some 'slippage' between the two spheres. Only one axis could cross the divide to connect with a counterpart. Here the two Virgo t11s link in oblique gearing.

The constant horizontal plane is probably due to the position of this work on a cliff face. The artist may have worked on a boat or on ropes, or during low tides. Archaeologists assume separate phases, perhaps separate artists, due to stylistic differences.

Mindprint reveals the work as a single inspiration, though it could be months of work, or a team expressing one member's vision, with a few uninspired additions (see a collaborative Afro-Mexican Mandela mural at theme t5 t20). Here Aquarius t5 t21 figures express their decan Piscis Austrinus (Southern Fish) as a large penguin (far right), deriving from the same attributes that gave the constellation its name. Astronomers borrow from myth and art to map the sky, not vice versa. See a set of four whaling spheres in Russia's Murmansk glacial pavement engraving at theme t12. Celestial poles in the left sphere on a fish gill (jaw) and the vertical plane, tag the inspiration to Age Pisces, and in the right sphere on a fish gill, rob fin and the vertical plane, as Age Pisces-Aquarius, our current era.

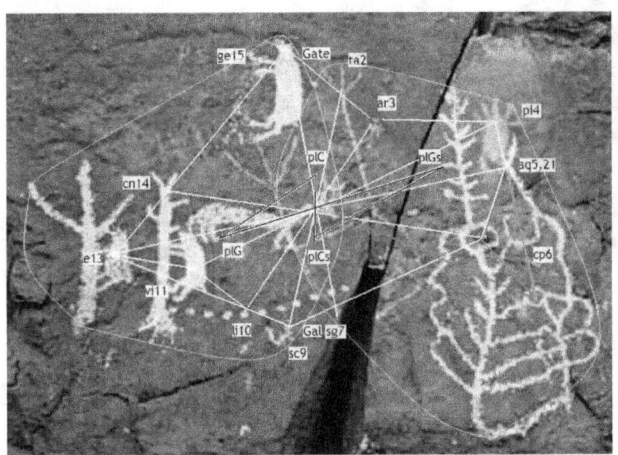

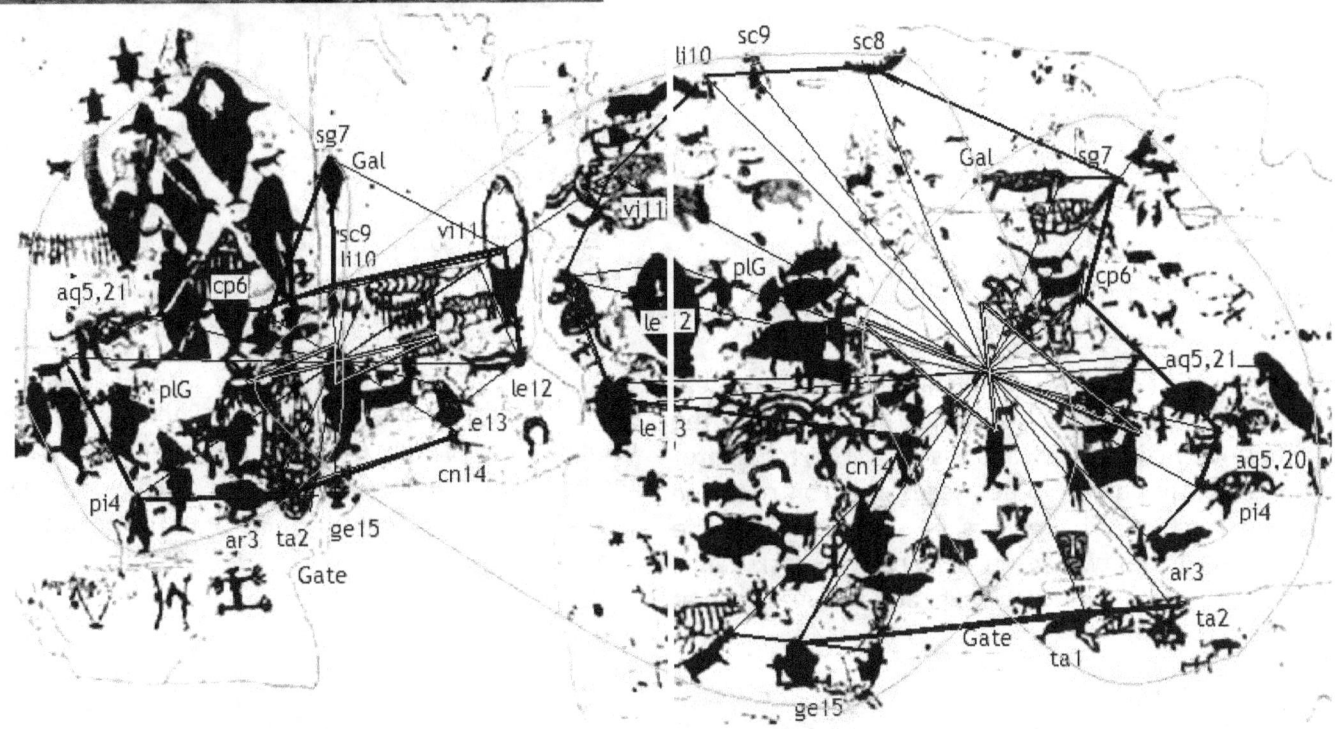

Four spheres on one pavement

Type Leo t12 as predators and corner guards in a quadruple imprint (Russian Murmansk Oblast, Kanozero, Kamenniy 7 glacial pavement engraving. Mindprint analysis by Edmond Furter). Leo t12 themes include axial inversion, frames, doors, gravity, rotation, pendulums and precession (see Tarot trump 12, Hanged Man). Variant groundlines hint that inspiration may be free of planes, that artists decide groundlines in expression, and that figures expressing types rotate on their axes to remain upright. Energy ropes connect many figures, as in Eskimo images of spiritual connections and Bushman images of sky ropes (see theme t15). The glacial straight line, a common geological feature in this kind of rock pavement (as at South Africa's Driekops Eiland, Nootgedacht and Redan), seems to

The 'chasm' is bridged by Gemini t15 and its galactic gate, incidental with the rope theme (see ropes added as spherical division lines in USA Rochester Creek, at theme t5 t20, and Australian rock art at theme t15).

Galactic equators link adjacent spheres two by two, not across their common centre, hinting that the artist used the pavement in peripheral format to place four spheres, just as each mindprint uses the periphery of its canvas to place the sequence of types. Hemispheric pairing also hint that double imprints are a norm, and that the few instances of triple imprints found in this study could be incomplete or transforming (see a similar whaling theme in a Korean engraving at theme t12).

Celestial poles in the larger sphere tag the inspiration to Age Aries-Pisces. Its companion, the second largest sphere, lack celestial polar markers.

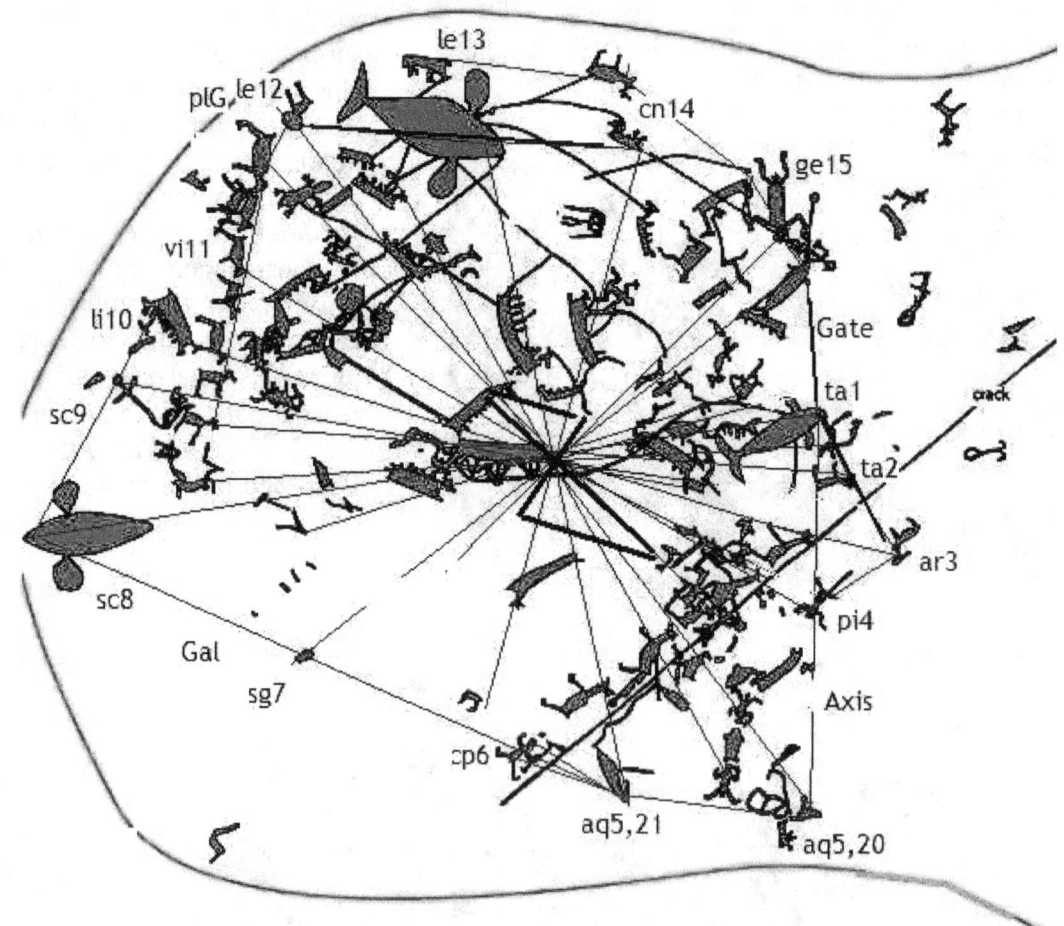

slightly distract the artist and to attract a linear cluster of images, but does not distort any of the imprints. Artistic inspiration is robust. Extra figures in elaborate panels do not necessarily contribute to the structure of imprints. A deep glacial line separates the two lower spheres, as rock faults often do (see Trois Frere cave, and Chauvet cave at theme t5 t21).

Polar markers in the two smaller spheres tag the inspiration to Age Pisces. These features do not date the work, but are noted in this study mainly as a seal of subconscious authenticity, and a basis for further study.

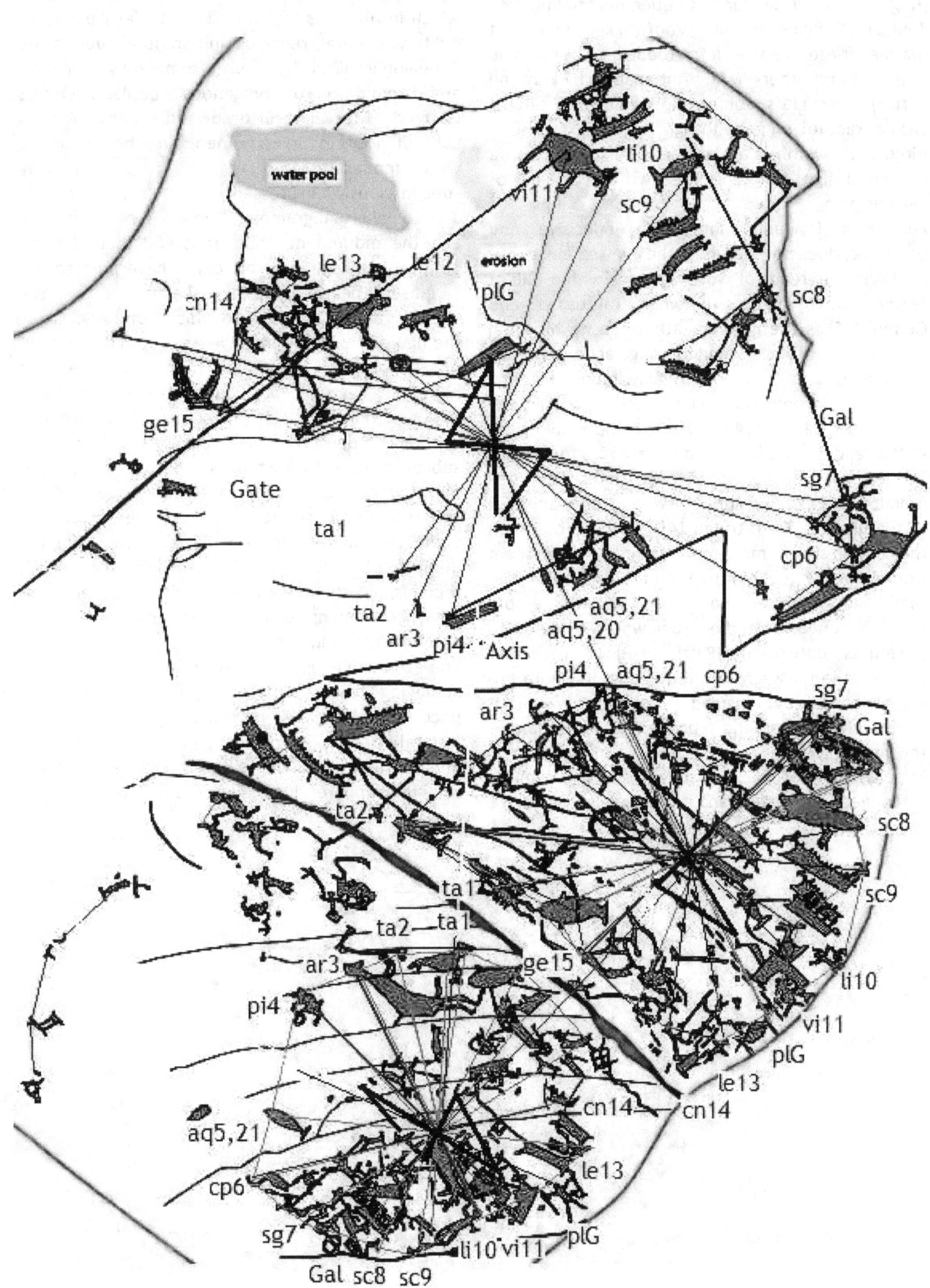

A coloniser and martyr

Type Leo t12 t13 as the heart of the Trekboer (Migrant Farmer) leader Piet Retief, negotiating with Zulu king Dingane (Pretoria, Voortrekker monument marble frieze, centre left. Modelled by Hennie Potgieter and others. Mindprint analysis by Edmond Furter). Virgo t11's womb is Retief's leather satchel with a tract for Dingane to sign. In the next episode Virgo t11's womb is a Masonic water bottle with a cosmic design including the two t12 pillars or galactic pole.

Zulu king Dingane, notoriously indecisive and psychotic, does not feature in the eye sequence, but his inkatha (wreath of woven grasses with a ball of feather down) figures between Taurus t1 and Gemini t15 as the galactic gate, opposite his kraal (hut city) in the background as the galactic centre, all subconscious to the artists. His jaw, about to utter the reputed command 'kill the conjurers', figures Gemini t15. Cancer t14 is a servant whose hands are at the ready at the king's hip to catch his royal solar spittle, based on a kind of taboo that all cultures practice, here a version of Cancer t14's spiritual water jugs (see Tarot trump 14). Solar symbolism in the Gothic-styled monument includes a sunbeam from an oculus (eye) in the top of the spherical void that lights up a motto on Retief's empty cenotaph on a lower floor below this frieze on 16 December, date of the Battle of Blood River that avenged the massacre of the negotiators. Libra t10 has his hands down instead of up, and is without a staff or rifle, part of the subconscious expression of the inversion theme.

Hyper-realism of the epic frieze panels, combined with legendised history and movies instigated by nationalist author and journalist Gustav Preller, used stock mythical themes, just as colonisers had used the Biblical Exodus to legitimise their rebellion against British exploitation in the Eastern Cape, which in turn was legitimised by similar illusions of military, cultural, religious and spiritual superiority. Rebellion ironically legitimised complete subjugation and exploitation of indigenous people. Architect Gerhard Moerdijk incorporated many African cultural motifs in the monument, and the four artists who modelled the marble frieze in clay subconsciously expressed their commission in archetypal visual grammar. The value of the friezes, and the monument, thus transcend their defunct political impulse. Some art critics have pointed out supposedly heathen, pre-Biblical elements, such as a fire altar and pagan gods, to which iconic analysis of the figures could add many more, but in the context of subconscious, universal human culture, not imitation. The two central panels are not linked as a double sphere, and both rotate anticlox, indicating separate design and inspiration, perhaps subconsciously to distinguish between the four narrative episodes, two back-to-back in each of the spheres. Commissioned art involves a captive audience, the very domain of archetype. After the demise of colonial and Apartheid (separatist) regimes, Freedom Park was built on an adjacent hillock, continuing solar symbolism in an eye-shaped amphitheatre and pool.

The ecliptic pole is on the eye of a Boer with a land surveying rope. Celestial polar markers are uncertain, but the horizontal plane tags the inspiration to Age Aquarius, about half a century ahead of the work. This is one of very few works in this study apparently keyed to the forthcoming Age.

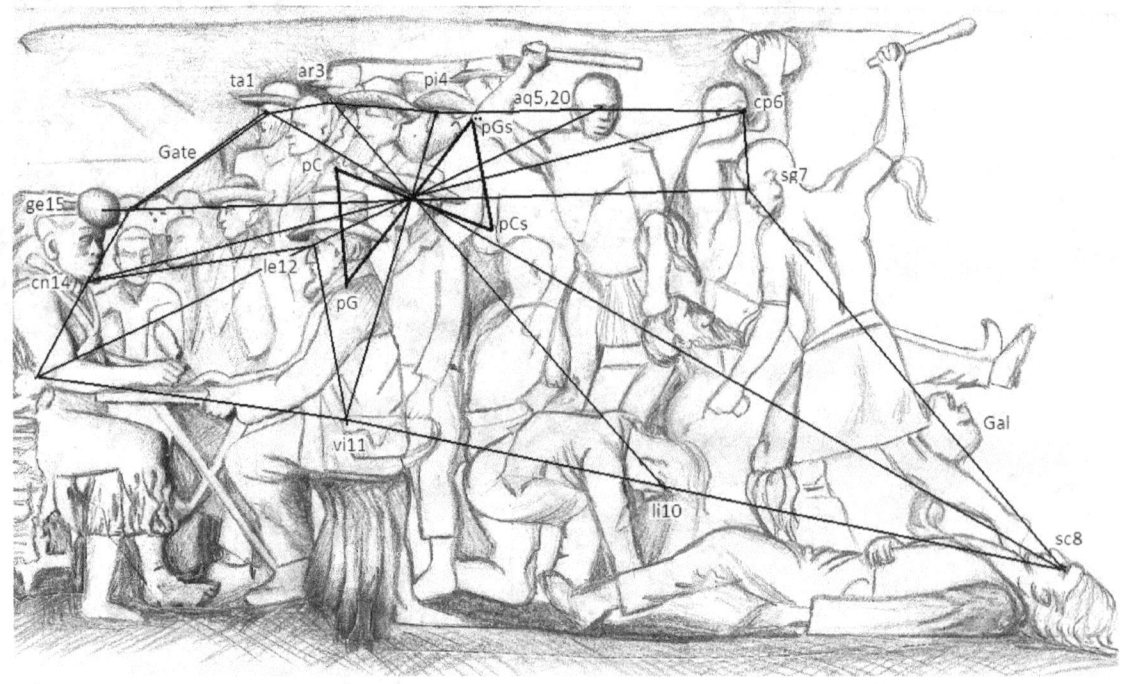

Negotiation and ambush

Type Leo t12 t13 as the jaw and heart of Trekboer (Migrant Farmer) leader Piet Retief, witnessing the slaughter of his men. Virgo t11 is a Masonic bottle on his hip. The bottle itself is in a museum in Pietermaritzburg. Masonic bottles were common in pioneer days. Retief was briefly a pub owner and may have acquired the bottle from a British soldier in the Eastern Cape. The monument is no more or no less 'Masonic' than it is 'Boer' or 'Persian', despite an altar and an eternal flame niche in the basement.

Nor is it 'pagan' on account of a mother and child group incidental with Artemis or Helen on the central front exterior (backing the fire niche), or 'Egyptian' on account of sloping fluted corners, or 'Aryan' on account of its gothic windows copied from the Battle of the Nations monument in Germany, commemorating the 1813 Battle of Leipzig. It is just a commission that allowed a privileged architect and hand-picked artists to practice their craft, to serve what they saw as an ancestral common cause, and incidentally, subconsciously, to speak archetypal language. Leo t12 themes continue at the end of the next wall to the right, where Boer architects build Pretoria using scaffolds and plumb lines resembling Leo t12 gantry gallows (see Tarot trump 12, Hanged man).

Rock art, perceived as a mixture of spiritual and mundane inspiration, is no less cultural, political and spiritual than schooled art. Recent analyses of some contact period (colonisation) rock art in southern Africa, as 'protest art' or 'rituals seeking protection against superior forces' are moving towards equating rock art with art. Some analysts still seek literal explanations for every figure, attire, posture and action, while iconic logic does not require conscious explanation. Inspiration, testable by mindprint and many other qualities, accommodates conscious reality within the wider human subtext.

Celestial polar markers on a Zulu heart and genitals, and the vertical plane, confirm the Age Aquarius tag, although a hand and shoulder tag two eras in Age Pisces-Aquarius, that should be read as 'some time before the forthcoming axial era', incidental with the work.

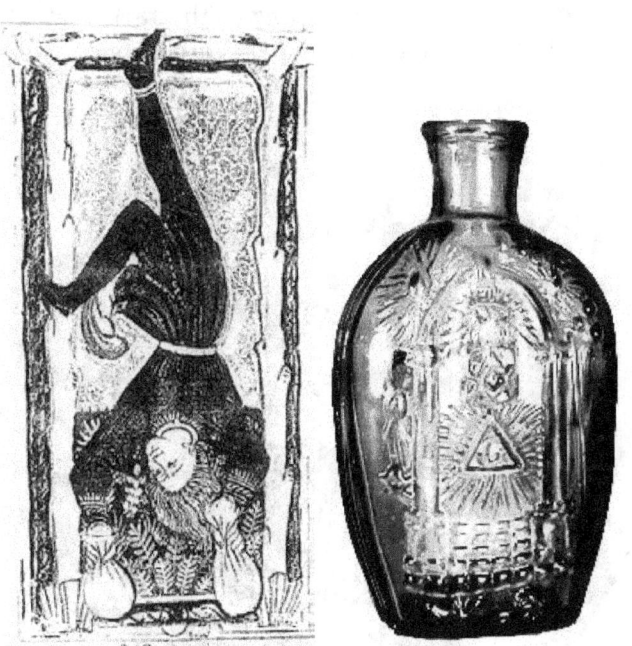

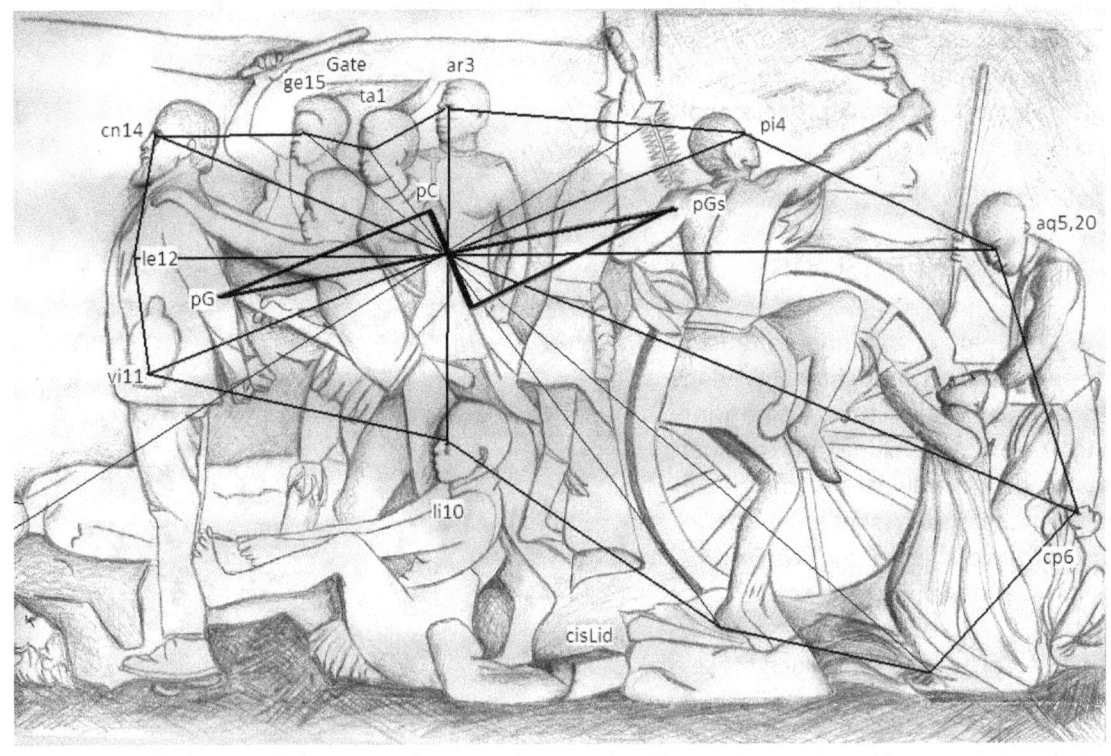

A disc of many dimensions

Type Leo t12 t13 as the heart of a fish-goat griffin (Egyptian Hierakonpolis disc. Antropologie, 1849, IX, plate 131, 2. Mindprint analysis by Edmond Furter). Its eye is on Cancer t14, opposite Capricornus t6 which is sometimes a goat-fish, a fish-goat inversion. The disc may have a flip side image or a companion, or the sequence may be read in two directions, even from some different starting points, as a kind of spherical double, quadruple, or picture generator. The dragon is similar to some of its opposites at Aquarius t5, such as Oannes of Babylonia, Nommo of Mali, Shamir of Palestine and other scaly teachers (see a USA sketch copy of a charismatic swimmer at theme t5 t21).

Comparison to near identical dragons in the Guinea calabash carving tradition is irresistible, yet this Egyptian artefact is not public art, and Hierakonpolis was a sand-covered ruin for centuries, until well after Napoleon's ambitions sparked a European craze for Egyptian treasures and styles.

A celestial polar marker on the monster's jaw tags the inspiration as Age Aries-Pisces, but earlier markers on the scorpion's sting and elbow tag Age Taurus, prior to many Age Aries artefacts from the Hierakonpolis main deposit. No exact date could or should be derived from these tertiary features in inspired art, and all dates in early Age Taurus, about BC 3000 and earlier, should be suspect on astronomical grounds, the very basis of supposed precise dating. Archaeo astronomer Andis Kaulins is on record for withdrawing his proposed precise dates for early artefacts and sites (Andis Kaulins; Star stones and scholars blog). Several discrepancies have emerged between astronomy automation software (see the Cosmic map) and archaeological data, linked to the uncertainty of precessional history and the value of time itself in early Ages of higher obliquity.

Turn over for more dimensions

Type Leo t12 t13 as the heart of a hunting dog in a doubly antithetical and inverted sequence (Egyptian palette with four dogs, Hierakonpolis. Mindprint analysis by Edmond Furter). The facing and cardinal dogs prompt flips, jumps, inversions and rotations. See an archetypal sequence with similar jumps in the Seti 1 tomb murals layout at theme t8. On the rear (with the bowl), axes may figure their opposites or cardinals (types that should be 90 degrees apart), unless some front figures are taken to replace these, a kind of stitching sequence with axes woven in and

out like a cloth or basket, incidental with digital codes. On the front (right) the vertical axis is a tree from Capricornus t6 to Cancer t14, perhaps the only un-diverted axis here. Some figure sequence jumps are diagonally across the palette, thus bending their axes by 90 degrees, since this figure sequence is partial. One of the general themes is of Scorpius-Libra t9-t10 Lupus (Wolf) as a galactic wheel impeller (see a Mexican dogs palette at theme t10). Geometric logic is not sustained, but the concept of flipping and mirroring is typical of Leo t12 themes. Orientation play and dual direction sequences form a maze of spokes and rims, to adapt Ezekiel's expression of near inchoate wonderment at his vision of wheels on legs (Ezek 1:16, 10:10). Virgo t11 as a giraffe womb is a frequent expression in rock art (see a Namibian engraving with track feet at theme t12). Celestial polar markers are inconclusive.

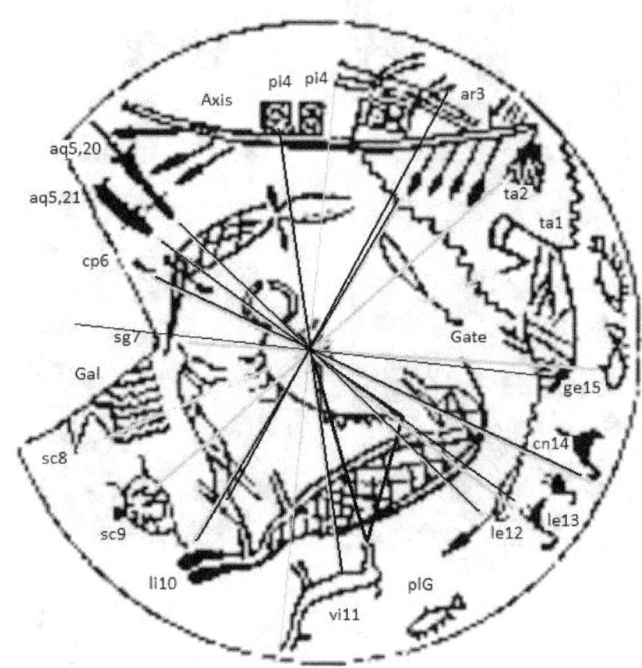

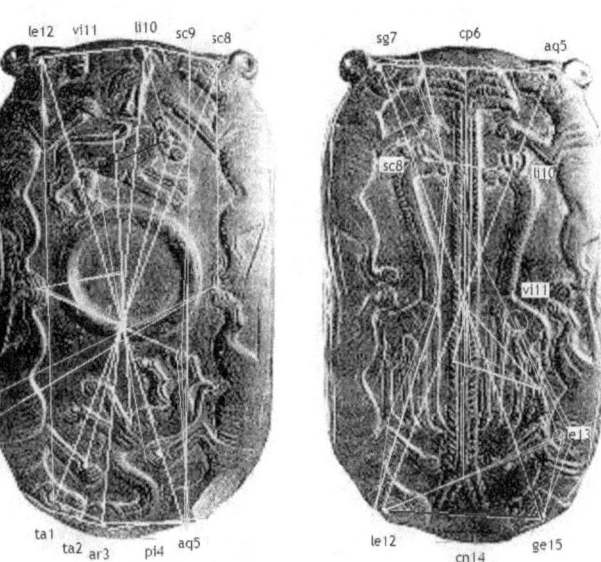

The calabash that started a school

Types Leo t12 as a snake, and Leo t13 as a lizard (Guinea calabash rollout with saureans. Cardin. De Santillana and Von Deschend. Mindprint analysis by Edmond Furter). The snake is a kind of external heart of the lizard, like an ophiotaurus (cow-snake. See an intestinal animal with bee pirates at theme t8). Free-hand rollout copying of the hemispheric calabash necessitated some breaks in the projection, so the exact position of Gemini t15 is uncertain, and Cancer t14 is misplaced. Virgo t11 is a lizard womb. Scorpius t9 is a goose with a long neck. Sagittarius t7 Galactic centre is a starburst. Capricornus t6 is a horned animal. Aquarius t5 t21 is a propeller cross. Aquarius t5 t20 Cetus is an armillary cross (two equatorial bands) appropriate to the galactic south pole. Pisces t4 Pegasus is a lizard intersecting another to form a rectangular body. Aries t3 Andromeda is a hero, as sometimes figured instead of a princess, repeating Taurus t2 Perseus, which here is a seated hero. Cancer t14 is a Y-shaped rabbit head. Libra t10 Lupus tail or Hydra tail is one of three tail-ends (see a basket lid in a Mexican palette at theme t3 t18). Capricornus t6 is adjacent to seven stars, the consciously misplaced hallmark of Taurus t2 t17 Pleiades. The carver understood the Pleiades as stellar, and placed them next to horns assumed to be Taurus. Mindprint errors are always linked to conscious interference.

The central fish-shaped dragons are also semi-conscious, since the galactic equators intersection never completely frames any single, large interior feature, as if some residual rotation remained at work. Celestial polar markers on a head and a lizard intersection, tag the inspiration as Age Pisces.

The work is probably a version of a conventional craft set supported by a myth cycle. Complex myth and legend cycles such as Homer's epics, may have been composed as much in art as in dramatic poetry. Shakespeare likewise may have relied as much on his access to the royal gallery as to the royal library. Alchemical writers rely on emblems as a kind of visual opera.

The 'ethnography as astronomy' school was initiated by Prof Giorgio de Santillana and Prof Hertha von Deschend's Hamlet's mill, a review of Icelandic myth applied to precession. Their conclusion (although not clearly formulated) that myth is proto astronomy, sustained by oral tradition, is not supported in the present study. They included some images at the back of their book, briefly captioned, and not directly explained in the text. This study examined several other calabashes in the carving tradition of West Africa said to be astronomical, but with little proof or motivation. Even late Islamic scientific writing, preserved in Mali at Timbuktu (Thebu Medupe; Cosmic Africa project), contain very little astronomy (great circle directions to Mecca, and measuring time by the sun to determine noon) and no astrology. A vesica piscis (fish section) as in the outline of the lizards, appears in a Mali treatise, derived from shadow pattern geometry, but devoid of symbolism. Astronomy and symbolism do not readily mix.

De Santillana and Von Deschend implied this calabash and other folk art images to be directly astronomical, or symbolic oral history. The present study takes Hamlet's Mill to its more logical conclusion; Epic poetry expresses mythical structure, and only tips its hat at astrology and history. Symbolic art likewise expresses visual structure and tips its hat at other structural sets.

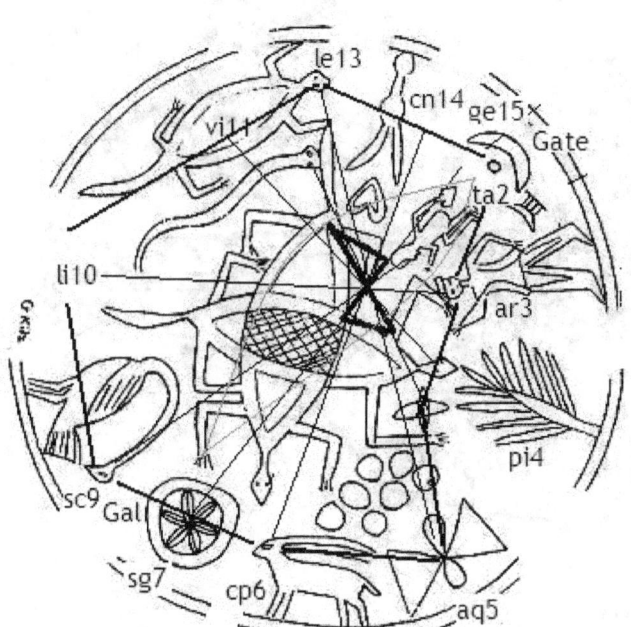

Between figures and shapes

Type Leo t12 t13 as heart-shaped concentric circles, in a geometric set on a palette-shaped stone (Scotland, Knowth engravings. Mindprint analysis by Edmond Furter). Each figure contains some attributes of its opposite, allowing two sequences; t1 to t15, or t8 to t9. Sagittarius t7 holds the galactic centre, sometimes held by Scorpius t8 tail. Gemini t15 as a quartered rectangle <+> of alternating black and white, expresses its more usual rectangular grid [+] in rotated form, maintaining the circular style of the figures. Taurus t1 t16 Orion is three concentric circles, one slightly out of line, each one opposite one of three circles at Scorpius t8 Ophiuchus. Taurus t1 Orion's belt is currently notable for marking the celestial equator 24 degrees south of the current summer solstice (to northern hemisphere residents), and Scorpius Ophiuchus holds on his shoulder the celestial equator 14 degrees above the current winter solstice (to northern hemisphere residents). These asterisms are equatorial opposites in ecliptic ascension (east-west angles) and also spherical opposites in declination (north-south angles). Both are currently on the celestial equator on the ecliptic meridian of the two eternal galactic gates.

The sky remains an analogy of structure, just as this calabash, calendars, myth and art are analogies of structure, neither being archetype or origin itself.

Nothing on earth or in heaven, however well sequenced and complex in its correspondence to nature, characters or events, is an original or complete artefact. Visions of akashic halls of records, golden books, law codes, angels and tablets are all expressions of archetype (see crop circle-styled geometric figures at theme t14).

Celestial polar markers are uncertain, but the long axis of the stone tags the inspiration to Age Pisces-Aquarius, our current era, confirmed by the doubled emphasis on Taurus t1 Orion's belt, temporary host of the celestial equator.

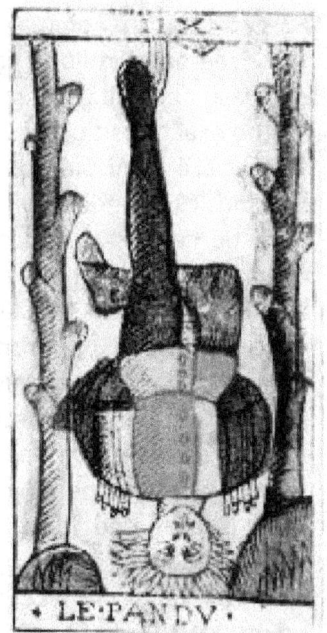

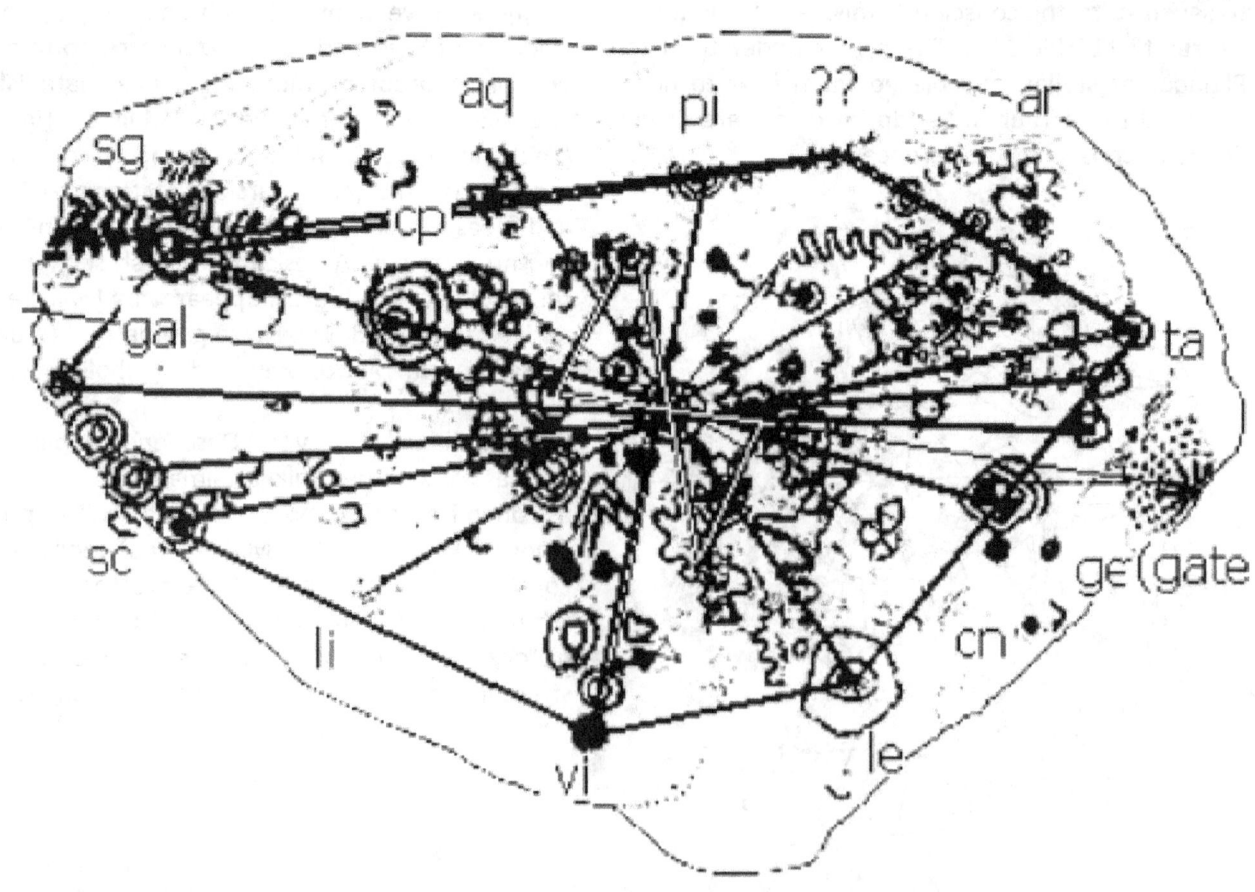

Dynamic microcosms

Types Leo t12 and Leo t13 as the bowl-shaped hearts of spermiform figures, in a double concentric and dual-rotating mindprint (Bolivian disc 3. Klaus Dona. Mindprint analysis by Edmond Furter). See Egyptian cosmetic palettes with bowls, as in the Hunters palette at theme t8.

Leo t13's opposite at Aquarius t5 t21 is a flamboyant figure in active posture as usual, and Aquarius t5 t20 is a stylised waterbearer. Leonine and Aquarian types are doubled, as they are in mindprint art, but Taurus and Scorpius types are not doubled, hinting at jumps between concentric registers.

Aries t3 t18 is an antithetical dragon or snake, as usual, but its opposite Libra t10 is a man under a horizontal angel, more relevant to the concept of Aries t3 Andromeda and Perseus than Libran t10 attributes. In turn, Taurus t2 is a dragon with a long tail, more relevant to its opposite Scorpius t9, which figures a hero with one arm in and one out, a timid Taurus t2 Perseus.

Thus some opposites are swopped, and parts of the sequence jump by 180 degrees, or parts of the sequence are flipped around.

Celestial polar markers on a hand and feet, and the likely horizontal plane, tag the inspiration to Age Pisces.

Kinds of types

Classes of distinctively shaped or hybrid people (see a People list in the text), are named 'kinds' in this study. They could express any type, depending on their attributes, but 'kinds' seem to favour the types flanking the four galactic, structural corners;

T15 t0 Gate; X, Y, coat, bag, face, rope, footprint, H or house people

T1 t16 Gate; X people, swift people

T7 Galaxy; centaur people

T8 Galaxy; goat or P people

T4 t19 Axis; fish people

T5 t20 Axis; mantis people

T11 Pole Galactic; cone, raptor, snake people

T12 Pole Galactic; pot people.

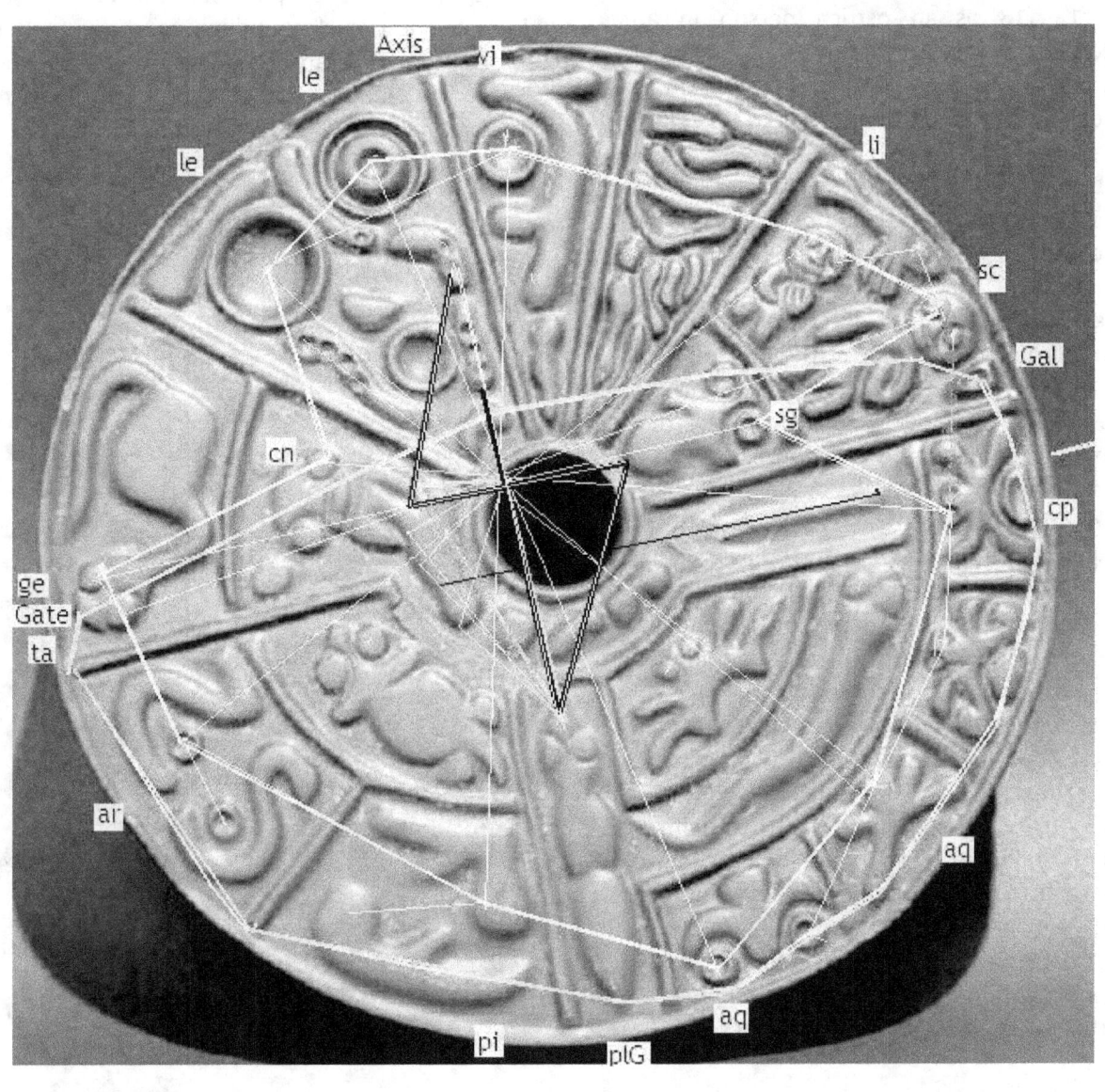

A humble steed for a new Age

Type Leo t12 Galactic pole as a donkey bearing Mary and the Christ child (Stock theme of the flight into Egypt in tourism market art. Mindprint analysis by Edmond Furter). The work has only eight mindprint eyes, thus only four mindprint axes, while three trees and a rump potentially complete the usual sequence. The galactic equator is strongly marked. The ecliptic pole is on Virgo t11's shoulder, the galactic pole is on her hand, and the celestial pole is on the child's jaw on the horizontal plane, tagging the inspiration to Age Pisces. Libra t10 is on the donkey's rump, arguable and even ridiculous, except for rumps and hips marked by wounds or symbolic wounds, emerging as a recurrent theme in this study, supporting research by Prof Francis Thackeray. See Virgo t11 on a double-headed dragon seat in a Chinese tile at theme t11.

Artefacts and fictions

Type Leo t12 t13 as an ostrich person in an embellished copy of rock art (South Africa, Herschel district Witteberg range, ostrich disguise in a contested copy. Stow, cited in Bleek. Iziko Museum. Mindprint analysis by Edmond Furter).
Adjacent; Leo t12 t13 as an ostrich person in art (South Africa, Robert Moffat; hunter in an ostrich skin, contested as fancy. Mindprint analysis by Edmond Furter).
Both images are disputed, not detracting from their structure and function as artworks. The implied rock art image, said to be reported by an informant and accessed by ropes, was seen only by Stow. Ostrich decoy hunting is not attested elsewhere, except in an 1880 novel by SW Fenn, Off to the wilds. The linguist and ethnographer Bleek notes reports of hunting disguises of hartebeest (attested as a dance ritual), blesbok, vulture, zebra and ostrich, but these may be anecdotal, legendary or ritualistic. Missionary artist Robert Moffat may have followed Stow, but mirrored the orientation, shown here reversed for comparison (Lewis-Williams; Ostrich controversy, SA Archaeological Society, Digging stick, 2012). Most current scholars see these kinds of images as subjective therianthropic (half-animal) sensations of healers in trance ritual. Some cling to the idea of realism and a method of decoy hunting, and some reconcile the opposing views as occasional dancing masks, or trance visions instigating decoy hunting by taking advantage of ostriches' curiosity behaviour, and decoy guises or

'sympathetic magic' in turn as instigating trance (F Thackeray). The images are studied here as curiously poised between rock art and art, yet carrying mindprint on par with both, with the greatest economy (fewest possible figures). Whether Stow embellished a rock art copy, or faked a copy to support an assumption or a pet theory, whether Moffat copied Stow, or pictured a dance, a hunt, or anecdotes, is irrelevant to this study. Both artists, or all three artists if there was a rock art source, imprinted the gist of the archetypal sequence, geometric structure and polar markers. Stow's inspiration is tagged to Age Pisces-Aquarius (hinting that he had a free hand), and Moffat's to Age Pisces, confirmed by his vertical plane. The bowman, or supposed bowman in both panels figures an extra ostrich face, heart and womb (a body inside a body). Even near identical artworks (see decans at theme t12) and even by the same artist, always express mindprints of different angular shape (degrees between axes), different equatorial outline, rotation direction, orientation (groundline, and figure on top), polar markers and galactic features. See ostriches on a Naqada pot at theme t3. See an Egyptian ostrich palette in Manchester Museum.

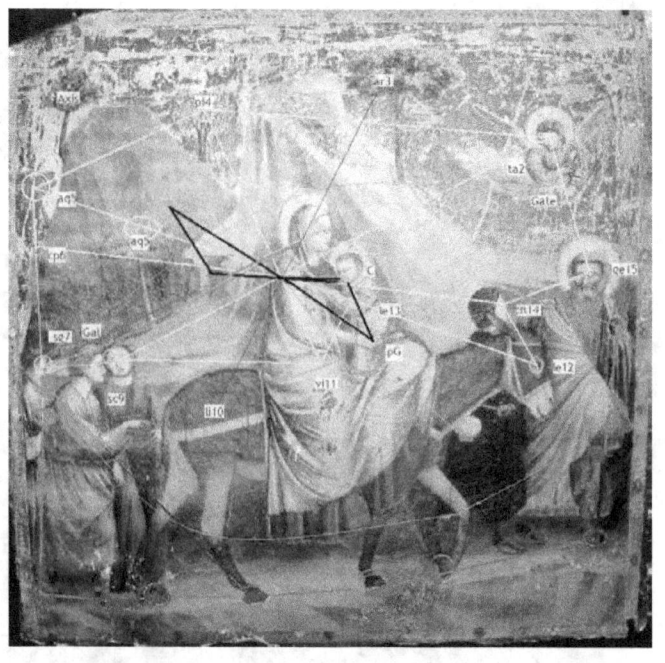

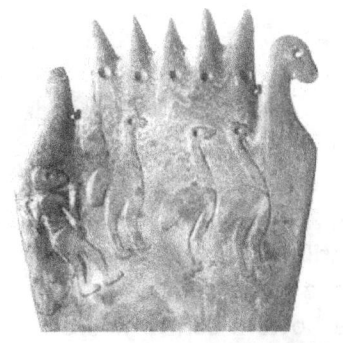

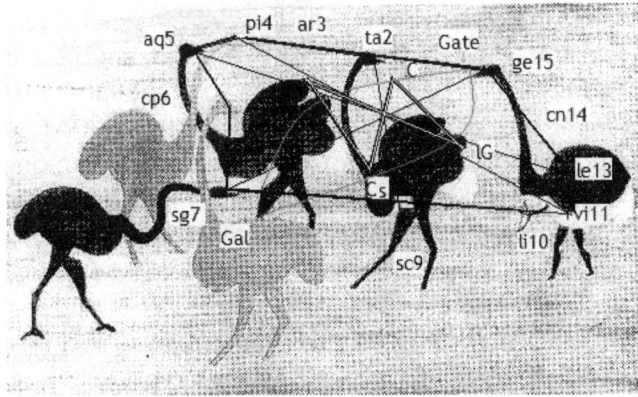

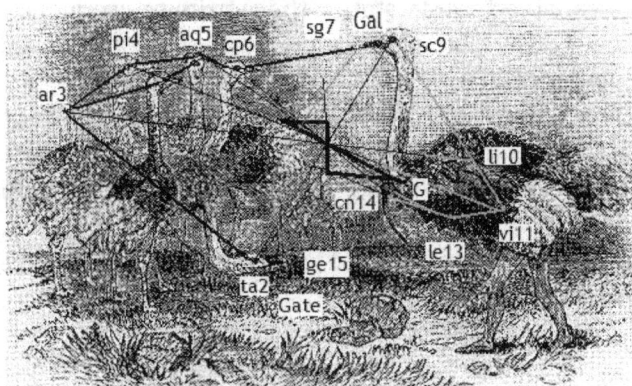

Alchemy in domestic tedium

Type Leo t12 as a donkey (South Africa, Pippa Skotnes; Down here a starless sky, 1985. Sanlam collection. Mindprint analysis by Edmond Furter). Leo t12's wooden frame sets a general theme, expressed in incidental detail such as a window frame and shelf frames. Mindprint is fully expressed, resorting to eyes on masks, a clock face, a portrait face and an absent face under a hat. The galactic equator includes a chequered field, as it often does in alchemical and kitchen scenes. Libra t10 is on the donkey's rump, unremarkable and even ridiculous, except for rumps and hips marked by wounds or symbolic wounds (F Thackeray) confirmed as a stock icon in this study. Iconic logic and geometry lives a subconscious life of its own underneath the conscious visual language, here of domestic tedium at twenty minutes past eight in the morning (if the frame is a window), or in the evening (if the frame is a painting). The donkey's jaw speaks the galactic pole. Celestial poles on a bird in flight, and on the rear position of the rocking bird figurine of Capricornus t6 (see its opposite Cancer t14 as a polar bird in a South American dragon rock art pavement at theme t14), tag the inspiration to Age Aries-Pisces, confirming pre-Christian themes such as prophecies of a Saviour on a donkey.

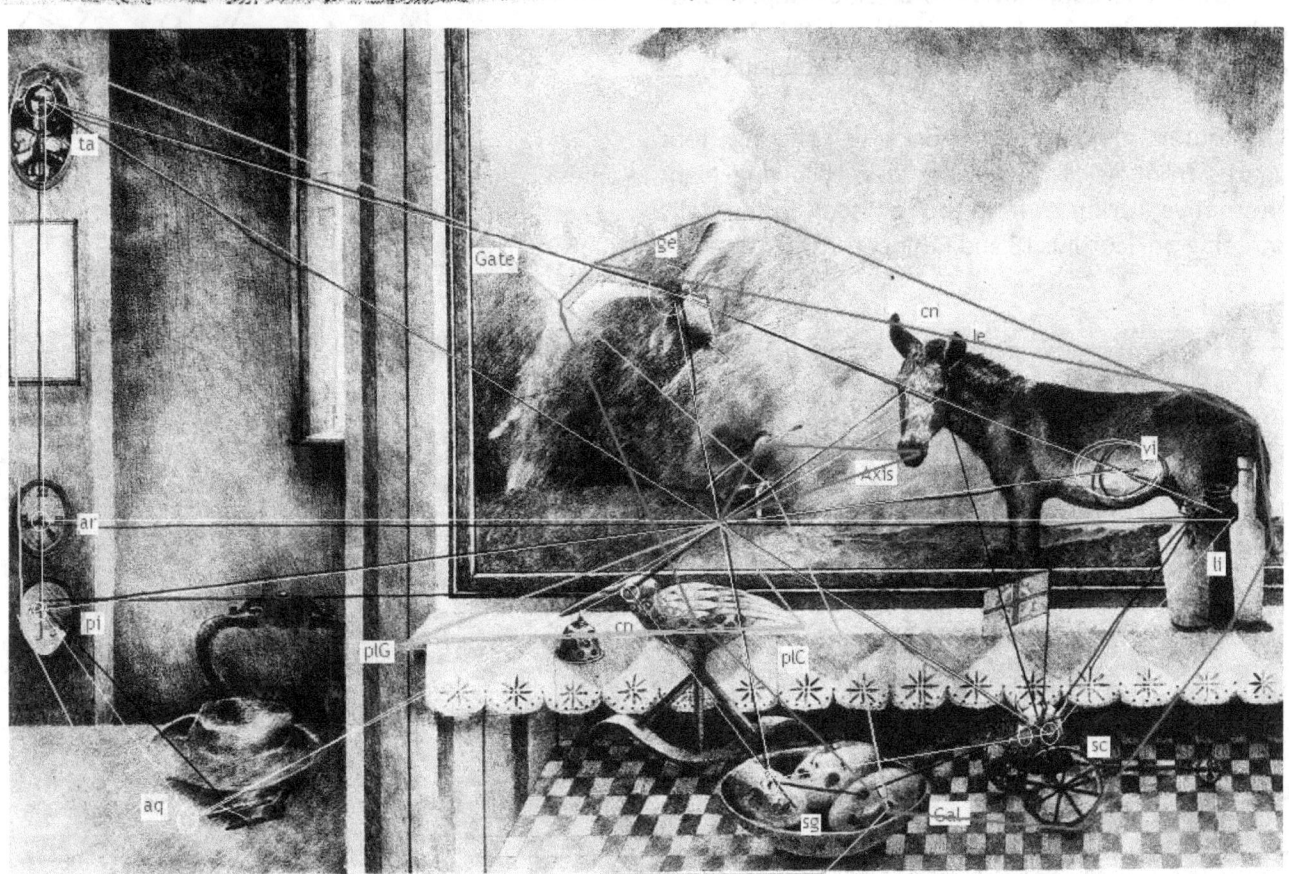

Doubled duats

Type Leo t12 as the heart of the outer of four inverted figures, and the outer of four figures before the retro face of a double-headed leonine sphinx, in a partially concentric, contra-rotating double imprint of decans on three registers (Egyptian Book of Caverns section 3, BC 1426. AG Shedid cited in Wim van den Dungen. Sofiatopia. Mindprint analysis by Edmond Furter). Decans are fairly simple and probably consciously recognised as hours, or reduced to twelve that could also signify months. Here the sequence is boustrophedon (as the ox ploughs, in alternating directions), with a few quirks. Top register left to right; Aries t3 t18 Agnus between two serpents, with the sun as a spring marker. Taurus t2 t17 Pleiades as seven bull men, with a former spring marker. Taurus t1 t16 Hyades and Auriga-Orion as mummies under mounds. Galactic gate as three shrines. Gemini t15 in a shrine with strings of ten mummies.

Middle register right to left; Cancer t14 Hydra group. Leo t13 Ursa group as a burial. Leo t12 retro Crater group. Virgo t11 as the sphinx womb. Libra t10 as Amun with a staff.

Lower register oscillating; Central, Scorpius t9 as a shrine snake, Scorpius t8 Ophiuchus and Galactic centre as a snake shrine. Right is Sagittarius t7 as decapitated Ages (see the Narmer palette at theme t3 t18), left is Capricornus t6 as small supplicants, right is Aquarius t5 as large prisoners, left is Pisces t4 as large supplicants, centre is a Pisces-Aquarius t4-t5 Pegasus square.

The outer mindprint is clockwise, sharing four figures from Aries to Cancer, then following eight alternative attributes from Leo to Pisces, incidentally agreeing on Scorpius t8 and Capricornus t6.

The inner mindprint among figures in the lower two registers, on the right, forms an independent anticlox sequence, agreeing with decans on t14, t13, t12, t11, t10, then below on t9, t8, (not t7 or t6), t5, (not t4, t3, t2, t1, t15). Some groups have extra figures with relevant attributes at the ready. Outer and inner mindprints agree on t14 and t9.

Dual identifications (the bottom centre figure here carries triple labels) appear in several decanal sets (see Seti 1's ceiling at theme t8, and another at theme t2 t17). Decans are prone to great variety (O Neugebauer and RA Parker. See also Aldred). Double imprints may account for confusing variety among decanal sets. Some conscious genius may be added to inspiration here, as also practiced by legendising and historicising mythology and theology. Decanal sets are examples of schooled inspiration, yet conscious and subconscious sequences live separate lives. No standard set of decans ever emerged. Decanal art understates the attribute, sequence, structure, polar and orientation features of mindprint.

Celestial polar markers of the outer mindprint, on burial feet and a Sphinx elbow, tag the inspiration to Age Aries, incidental with the spring sun over decanal Aries. Celestial polar markers in the inner mindprint on an inverted foot and knee, confirm Age Aries.

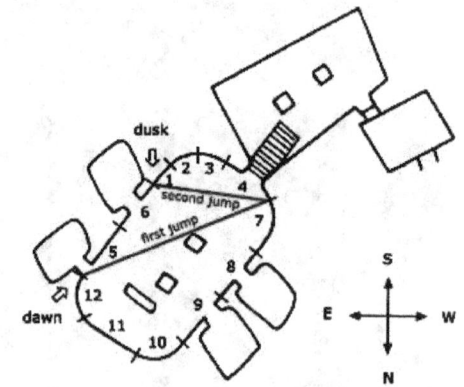

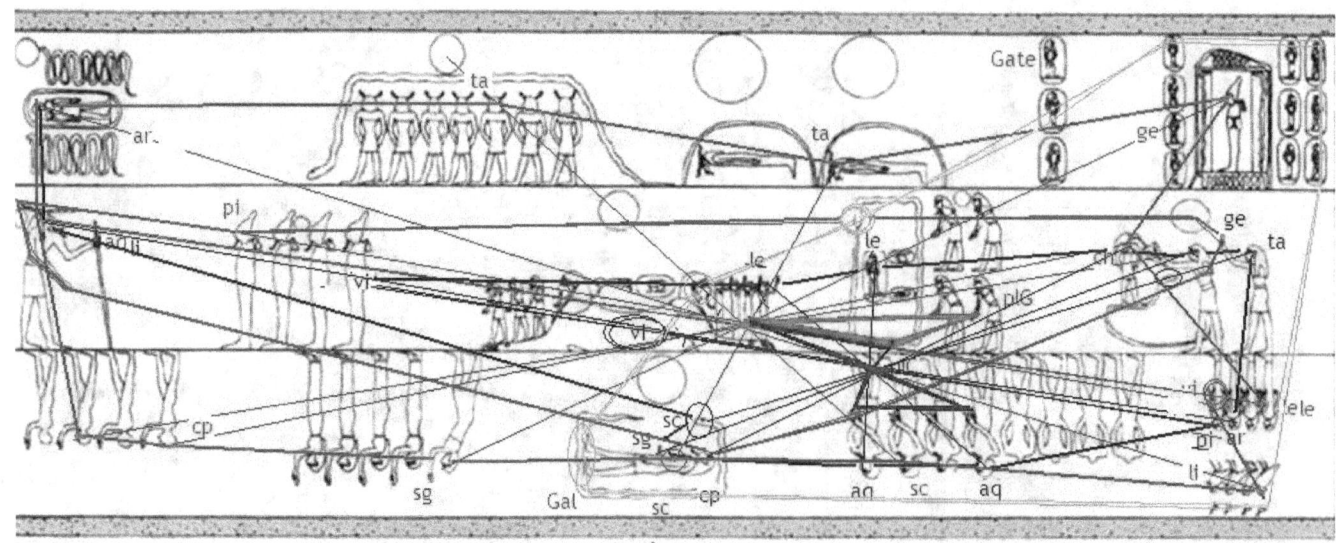

Shortcuts among hours

A sequence of hours and directions in a decorated tomb (Tuthmose 3 tomb plan. Wim van den Dugen; Book of hours. Sofiatopia). The murals follow a diagonal 'jump' scheme as in Sed festival courts; hours 1-4 west, 5-6 south, 7-8 north, 9-12 east. The viewer follows diagonal jumps tracing triangles, with two night-time adjustments. The Sed festival circuit race is similar to healing dances worldwide. Van den Dugen explains; "In the Amduat, in New Kingdom theology, Re takes the place of the king. His ordeal is to reverse depletion of his power at the end of the day, as a pharaoh seeking rejuvenation. Re moves from west, where he sets and is swallowed by Nut, to east where he reappears out of her thighs. This half-circle of night is defined as a rectangle with two transversal jumps. The first jump between hours 4 and 5 (placing the latter adjacent to hour 12), is from the deepest, darkest point, before rejuvenation. The second jump is between hour 6 and hour 7; the regenerated solar Ba jumps the first four hours (western wall), as if reversing them. Re confronts his enemy in hour 7, to appear in new clothes, vision, and rejuvenation by time reversal… some passages are in cryptographic script, the registers partially cross, and the solar bark, of serpentine form, is towed. In hour 7, Apophis tries to destroy what was gained, but Isis and the Eldest Magician Seth fail." Thus academic Egyptology is often pure esoterica. Regarding Nut's thigh, see thigh wounds in several artworks that may also signify a tally of days or seasons. See towing ropes and high-prowed boats in some Babylonian, Naqada, Egyptian and Nordic works. Apophis and Seth are probably at Gemini t15, and Isis at Taurus t1 Auriga.

Four quarters under a tree

Type Leo t12 as a retro-facing lion statue (Greece, Minoan jewel of tree quadrants. Mindprint analysis by Edmond Furter). See cosmic tree crosses spanning the four galactic corners in Mexican and other art at themes t1, t5, t8 and t12. Leo t13 often figures Death, here on a bier or monument, with twisted neck and uniquely not marked on his heart. Aquarius t5 t20 leads a dance in his usual active posture. Taurus t1 conducts a ritual with one arm up and one down at bottom right. Equatorial line economy in the equator causes an unusual emphasis on hips in the compact, almost microscopic design, as if the ecliptic equator had not yet separated from the galactic equators of limb joints. The upper galactic equator follows shoulders on both registers, and the lower galactic equator follows knees and feet on both registers, leaving most hips off the galactic ovals. Eyes may separate from hips and genitals in initial visual inspiration. Since the theme involves death and life, the consistent theme of rump and hip wounds in art may be relevant. The celestial polar marker on a heel tags the inspiration as Age Pisces-Aquarius, confirmed by the horizontal plane, unusually far ahead of the Minoan era. With our without ancient provenance, the jewel remains an exquisite work and a revealing mindprint.

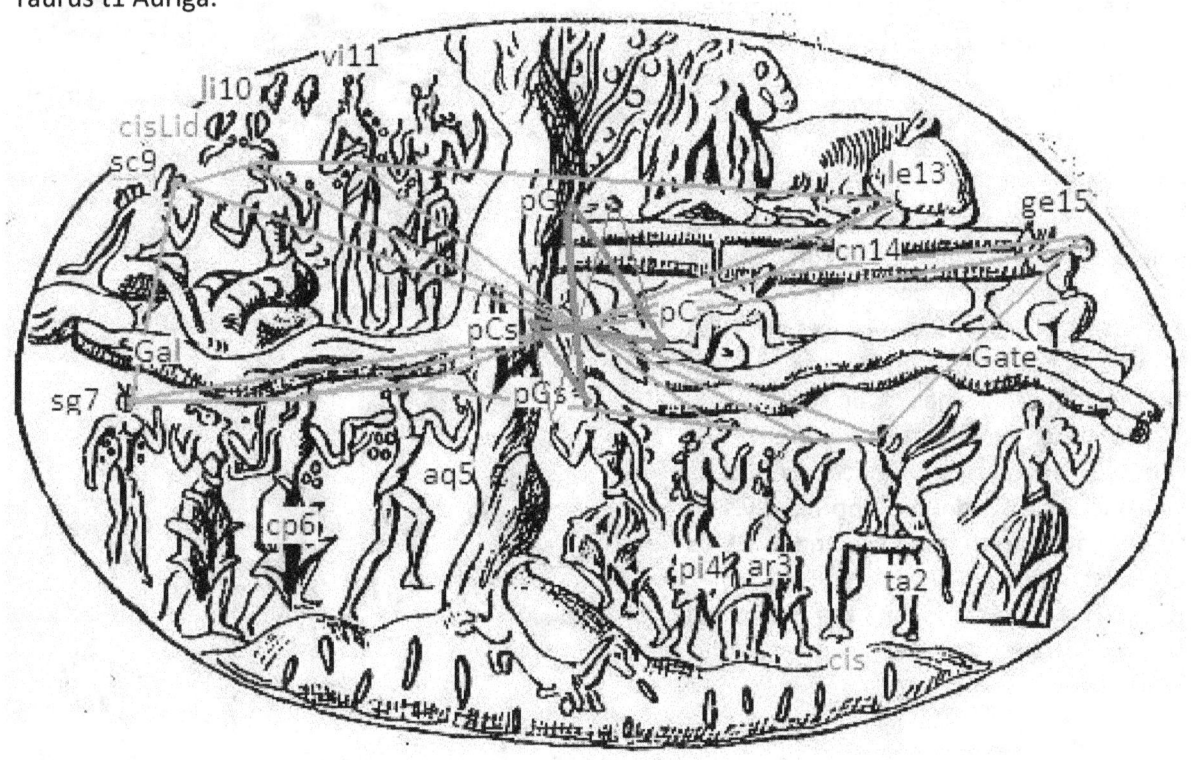

Type Leo t13; King's heart

A horse of many legs

Type Leo t13 Ursa as the heart of the multi-legged horse Sleipnir (Gotland boundary stone with a horse and a ship. Mindprint analysis by Edmond Furter). See Shiva and other multi-legged leonine heroes in rock art and art. The palette shape raises the expectation of a double imprint. Border markers were placed in 'cartoon' series, each with a sub-cycle of an epic event, treaty or legend, as a kind of movie. Serial images may be related to picture generators (see the Palenque lid at theme t4). Artists, ancient and modern, do what comes naturally to the eye, mind and hand, including serial images.

Celestial polar markers are absent, but the horizontal plane tags the inspiration to Age Pisces or Age Pisces-Aquarius, depending on the uncertain position of Gemini t15 and Sagittarius t7. The work is in an Age Pisces style.

An African Shiva in a cosmic battle

Type Leo t13 Ursa as the heart of a multi-headed hero or army (South Africa, Albany Alb03 1r multi-bodied figure. Mindprint analysis by Edmond Furter). See multi-headed healers and horses in Indian art. Leo retro makes a better horse than a lion, and Ursa retro makes a better horse than a bear. Visual expression is a function of an integrated set of concepts, and some are incidental with some of the variant stick figures that we animate among incidental dots in the moving sky. Ursa offered a string of 'heads' along its back as polar markers during Age Taurus (see a lion with stars along its back in the Seti 1 ceiling at theme t8). Ursa was a torn-off foreleg, as summer to the former spring point at Taurus t1 Hyades (Bull face), then at Taurus t2 Pleiades, a cluster of seven stars. Cancer t14 Ursa Minor took over the summer foreleg role in Age Aries, and by coincidence also has seven stars.

Aquarius t5 t21 here mirrors the posture of its opposite, Leo t13. Scorpius t8 Galactic centre is marked by a rope, as in a double imprint division rope in Australian art (see theme t15), and in USA's Rochester Creek (see theme t5).

A celestial polar marker on a hip, and the horizontal plane, tag the inspiration to Age Pisces-Aquarius, our current era.

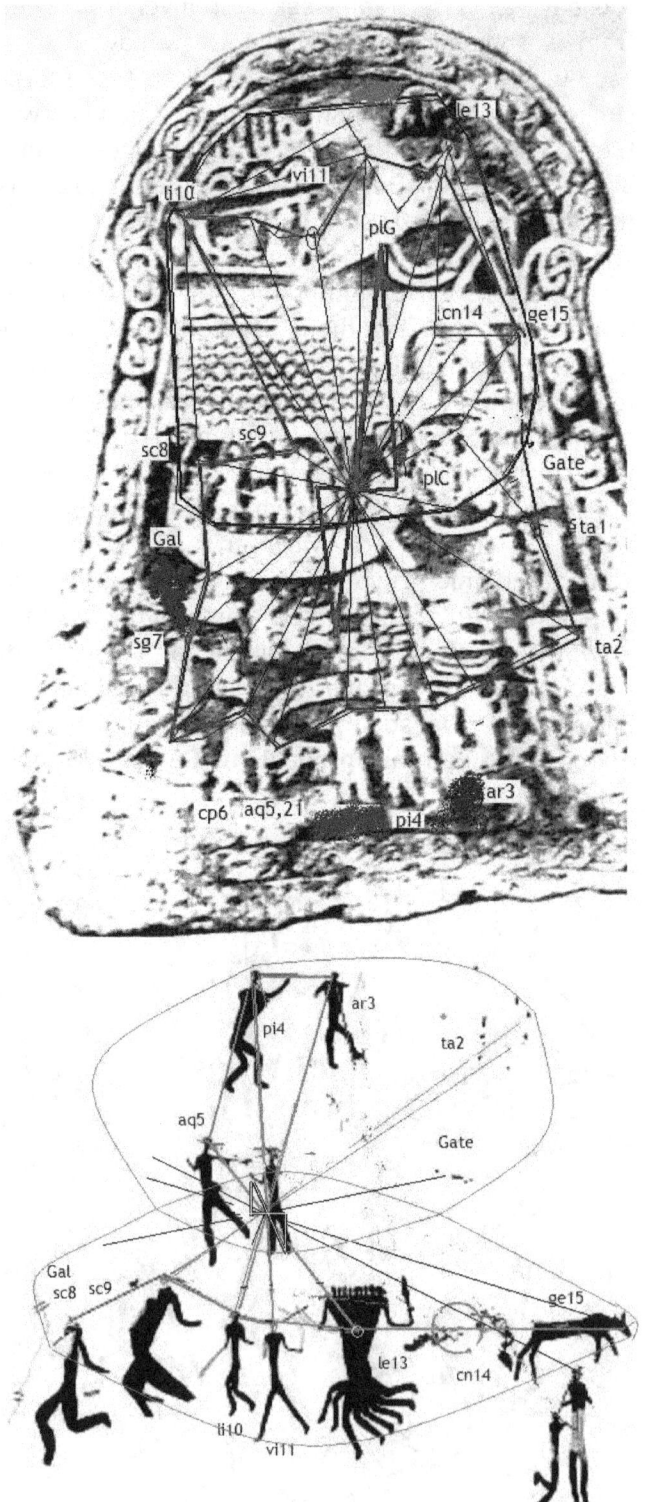

The horse of many legs rides again

Type Leo t13 Ursa as the heart of a multi-legged horse, Sleipnir (Gotland boundary stone with a horse and a boat. Mindprint analysis by Edmond Furter). Rope knot borders and large sails introduce weaving, textile and digital (warp and woof) styles and themes into the engraving. Nordic boundary stones and the much earlier Babylonian conical boundary stones (see themes t2 t17 and t11) may be picture generators as well. Equatorial outline economy among these eyes is similar to textile formats. The style may have been developed in weaving, or in felt, where curved or entwined stitching lines are the norm to prevent tearing. See funeral boat scenes on Pacific cloths and folk crafts using a digital matrix and stylised outlines).

Celestial polar markers and the horizontal plane tag the inspiration to Age Pisces-Aquarius, somewhat prophetic for the apparently Age Pisces work.

Hearts and minds in a cosmic battle

Type Leo t13 Ursa as the heart of a multi-legged horse or army of a hero (Indian Asuras and Daityas seeking elixir. R Storm; Legends and myths of India, Egypt, China and Japan. Hermes House. Mindprint analysis by Edmond Furter). See flying antelope and flying horses in rock art. See Tarot trump 13 as death militant on a horse.

A celestial pole on a covered foot tags the inspiration to Age Aries-Pisces.

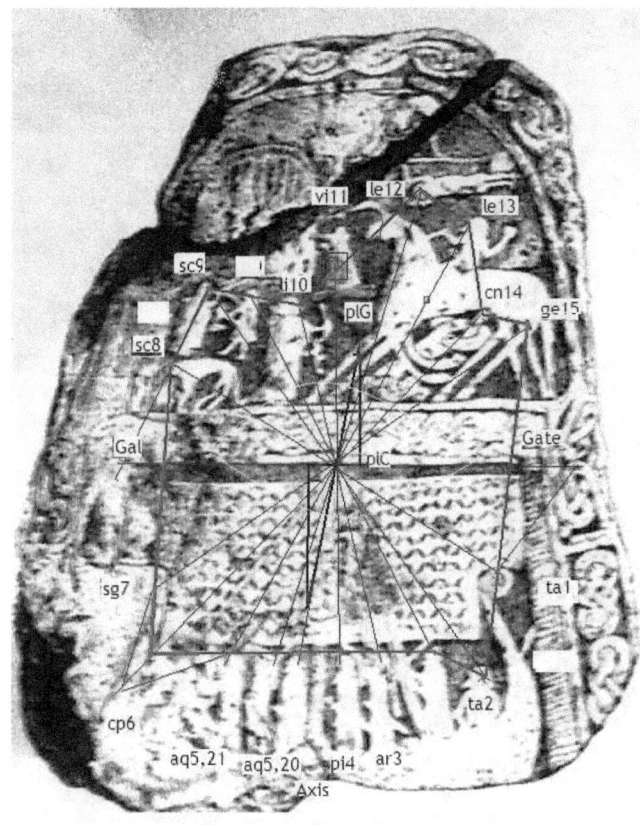

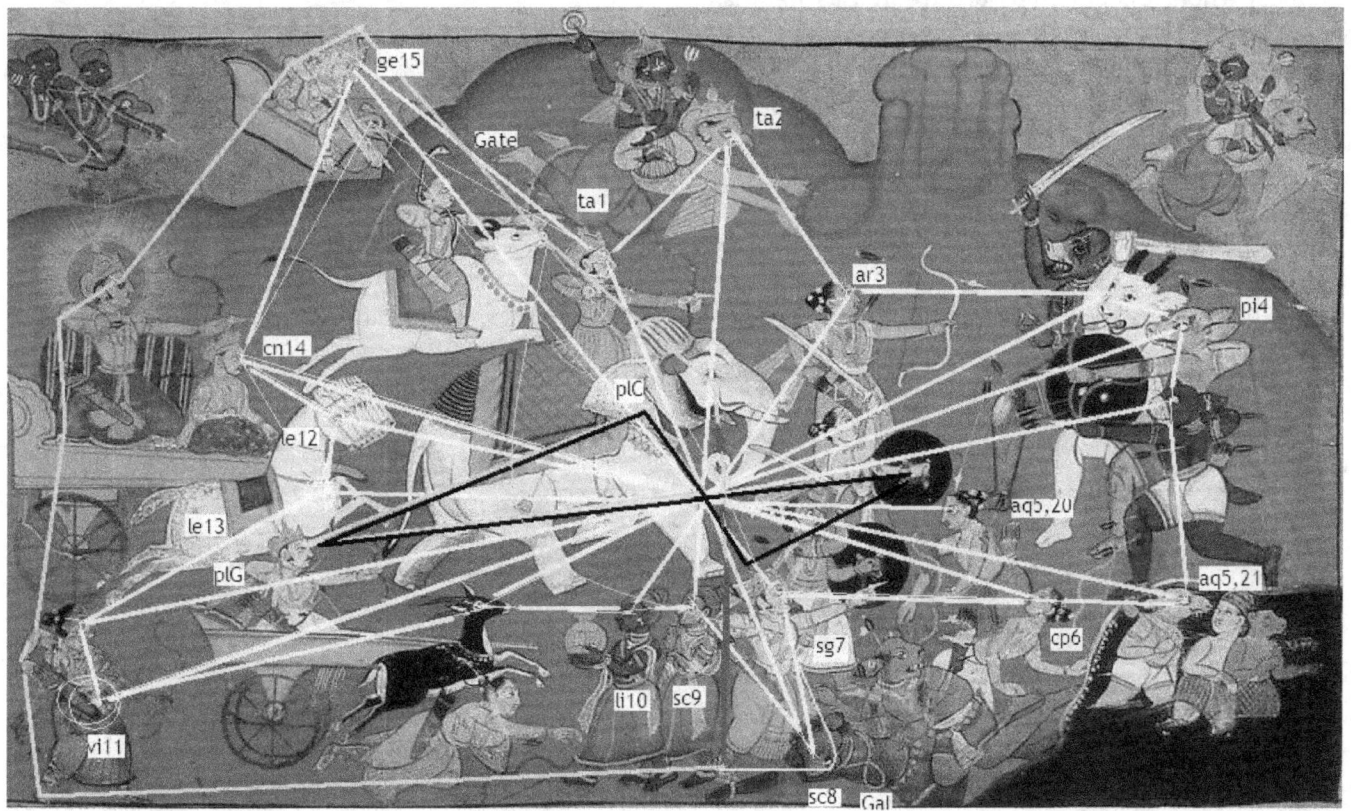

A giant holds life and death strings

Type Leo t13 t12 Ursa as the heart of a runner
(South Africa, HB 01 549hc. Henri Breuil. RARI.
Mindprint analysis by Edmond Furter). His streamers
could be sky ropes. Watercolour copies of rock art
by a handful of early researchers are remarkably
consistent in their accurate spacing, enabling the
geometric component of this study to extend to
some works that were damaged or vandalised in the
last decades. Some, like Pager, applied tint to his
own large black and white photographs on site.
Celestial polar markers on a lion knee and a hand,
and one of the horizontal planes, tag the inspiration
to Age Aries, while two other hands (later in
seasonal terms and earlier in precessional terms)
recall Age Taurus.

A nature deva and a good catch

Type Leo t13 as the heart of a boat (South African
Underberg, 02 28r. SA National Museum. Mindprint
analysis by Edmond Furter). See similar Nordic ship
themes, where distant ships are treated as figures.
Aquarius t5 is in typical active posture. Virgo t11 is
the womb of a guiding or tutelary (teaching) water
deva (Geoffrey Hodgson; Land of the gods). Some
swimmers among the fish prompt the theme of
limbless fish as limbs, supporting the Leo t12 t13
theme of dissolution (see Tarot trump 13 as Death
among strewn limbs). Harpoons here figure the
more usual scythe of Leo t13.
A celestial polar marker on Leo t13's harpoon impact
point tags the inspiration as Age Aries.
 Taurus.

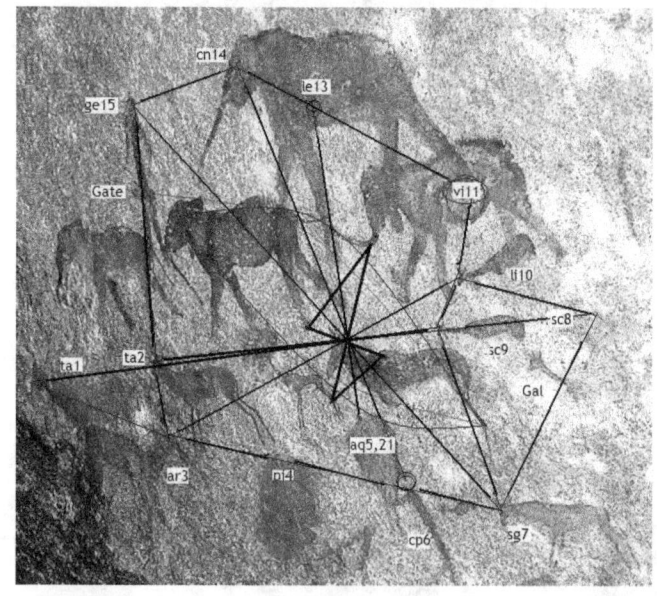

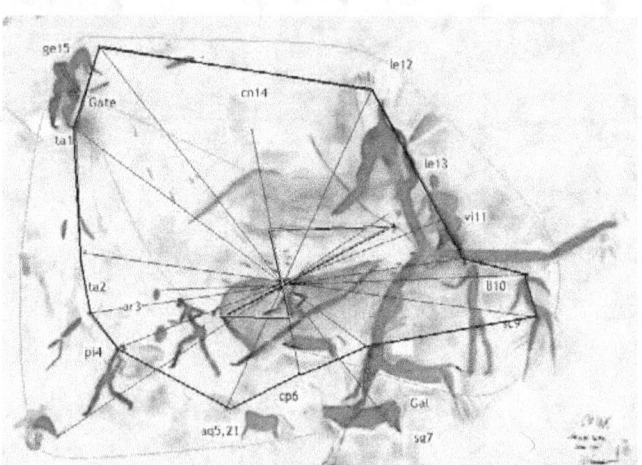

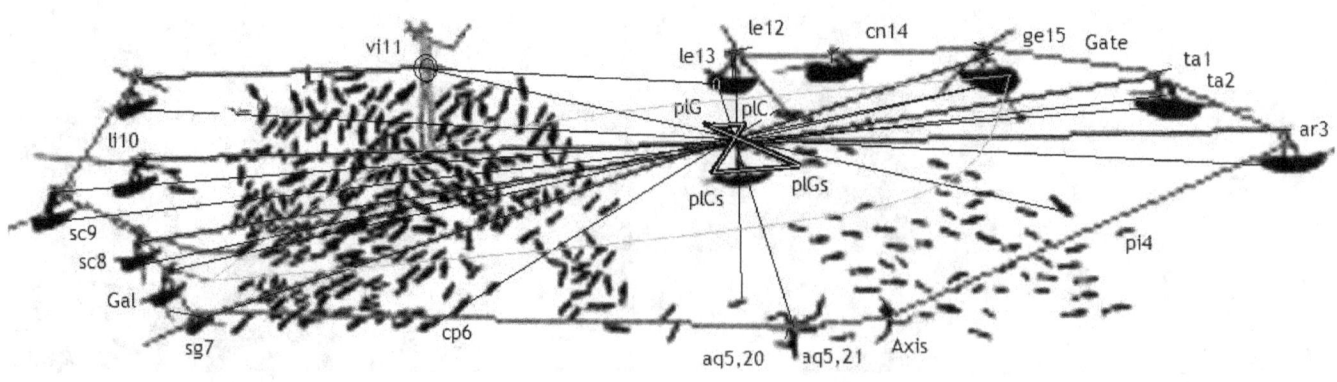

Strident elephants

Type Leo t13 Ursa as the heart of an elephant patriarch (South Africa, Mbombela Nelspruit, Rocky Drift Sun Rock. Mindprint analysis by Edmond Furter). Elephants often express tall, spindly legs (see tall polar axis elephants in Dali's Temptation of St Anthony). The work is on a natural stack of massive granite boulders, suggesting elephant backs. A Y-shaped figure below is a rear apron thong linked to female initiation sites (Ed Eastwood; Preliminary report on females' aprons, 2008. See also Jeremy Hollmann). Celestial polar markers on one of the extended elephant legs, or a track, and the hump of the polar animal, tag the inspiration as Age Pisces-Aquarius, our current era.

A rope factory marks time

Type Leo t13 Ursa as the heart of a rope factory worker (Egyptian mural of flax rope production. Mindprint analysis by Edmond Furter). Leo t13's inner figure's heart is marked by a rope from a twine ball via a dye cup (here highlighted by boxing the axis instead of adding a line over it). The dyed rope was painted as a dashed line. Multicolour is more usual at the opposite Aquarius t5, which often shares its attributes with Leo t13. Leo t12 has an extra figure as a polar controller, his limb joints offering a range of celestial polar markers; his elbow tags Age Pisces, his far elbow and the vertical plane provides for Age Pisces-Aquarius and his far hand for Age Aquarius 1 -Aquarius 2. Implements rarely appear as polar markers; but here a rope twine roller stick marks the ecliptic pole.

Between Aquarius t5 and Pisces t4, on the polar axis, is an ox-goad rope in a sharp triangular shape, a good analogy for three poles, and for steering of the straining celestial pole. Its apex marks the galactic south pole. Between Taurus t1 and t2 is another large ox-goad in triangular shape, incidental with the shape of Taurus Hyades (Bull face), perhaps the secondary origin or 'feedback' sustenance of the ox-goad hieroglyph. The two goad-ropes express different meanings in the context, but both add to the subconscious polar theme. Cancer t14 and Gemini t15 are twining ropes from a bank of twelve smaller strands (see Tarot trump 14, Temperance, Angel of Time, with twined water between two jugs, and Tarot trump 15, Demiurge or earthly creator, with ropes or chains). A rope grid (below centre) figures the galactic gate, where grids often appear. This is one of very few works in this study that may have been designed on an axial grid, yet only one rope marks out half of one axis. Lack of any hint at axes in the artworks studied, force the conclusion that the sequence and structure is always subconscious.

Sufism, an Islamic ecstatic tradition grafted onto the craft of wool and weaving, extends craft symbolism to spiritual symbolism, as Masonry and some other crafts do. Islam turned iconoclast early in its religious development, prohibiting representations of living creatures, and resorted to calligraphy and arabesque (twines of plants, vines, leaves and flowers) to express the eternal feature named 'rope of the sky' in rock art. Thus geometry, curves and some archetypal attributes persist even in iconoclast art. Myth, legend, wisdom literature (such as Hadith, sayings of the Prophet) maintain expression of the full round of archetypes in all religions.

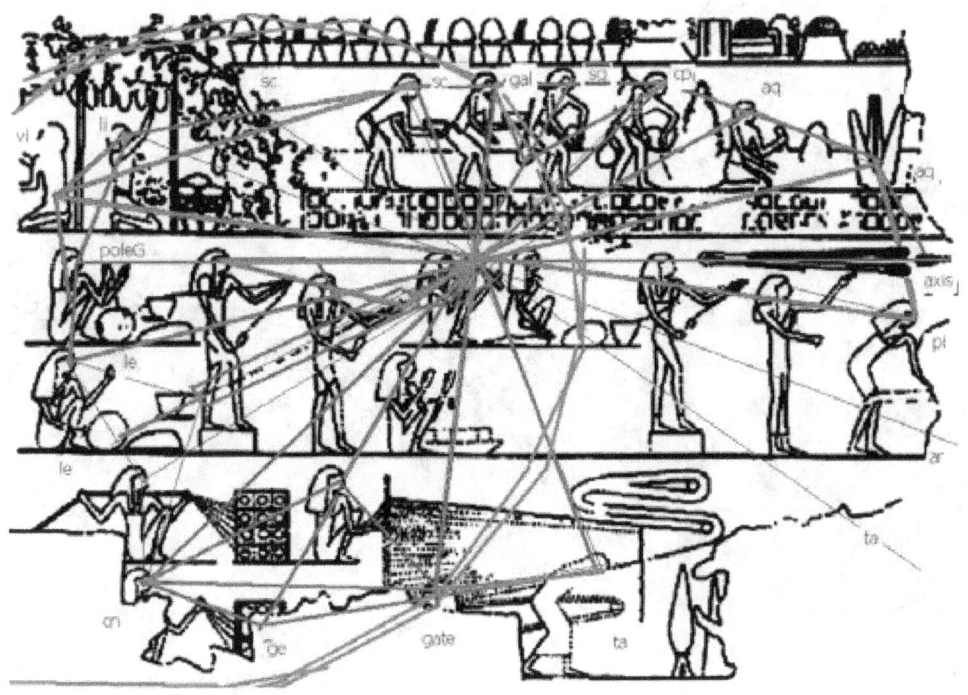

Stations for planets

Type Leo t13 Ursa as the heart of an antelope (Zimbabwe, formlings and a buck snake. Elspeth Parry, Amabooks. Mindprint analysis by Edmond Furter). See an ophiotaurus (cow-snake) with bees and a camel at theme t8. See classical, medieval and Renaissance processional triumphs of Death, Bacchus, Cybele, Mars or other planets. Optional attributes of types may be activated by planetary types in turn. The raft of dating clues in the alchemical verses of Nostradamus' Centuries may provide the key. These patterns do not arise from random events or prophecy, but from time signatures incidental with episodes that occasionally co-incide with real events, sometimes in minute detail. The iconographic mill grinds slowly, but could grind exceedingly fine. The enigma of eschatological (end-time) battles would dissolve if prophetic books were understood as dramatised, localised and historicised archetypes, knowable from recurrent manifestation in nature, culture and history. See formlings at theme t11. See a Rosicrucian emblematic cave at theme t6, and a Mexican emblematic cave at theme t15.

Celestial polar markers on a wolf and an elephant knee, and the vertical plane, tag the inspiration to Age Pisces-Aquarius, our current era.

The other Sphinx

Type Leo t13 t12 Ursa as the heart of Amun on a leonine Sphinx funeral boat (Egyptian decans with Amun. Mindprint analysis by Edmond Furter). In Age Aries, from about BC 1500 to BC 150, the Amun ram absorbed and expressed many roles in his turn, as epoch overlords do. Here he figures the former summer in Leo, and his Uas (Was) sceptre figures the galactic pole as a Horus falcon, cradled by Virgo t11. Amun's home address is Aries t3, here occupied by his adjacent Pisces t4 as two Min (phallic Fish) or underworld lords as spring markers, while Amun himself is off on polar duty. His front foot is on the ecliptic pole, his front hand or staff on the galactic pole, his rear hand on the celestial pole on the Cancer t14 Scarab axis (with a scarab determinant of precession), tagging Age Aries. The Sphinx and the boat express Cancer t14 Hydra, a long snake extending below Leo and Virgo. Taurus t1 and Gemini t15 flank the rudder oars as a churn group (see Horus and Set churning the pneuma (lung) drill by reed ropes, at theme t15). Astronomy is only an analogy for archetype, as some Egyptians understood. An extra celestial polar marker on Amun's rear knee provide for Age Pisces, confirmed by the extra Min at Pisces t4. Spring in Aries and Pisces, summer in Cancer and Gemini, autumn in Libra and Virgo (here nearly the same axis), and winter in Capricornus and Sagittarius, express the start of Age Pisces.

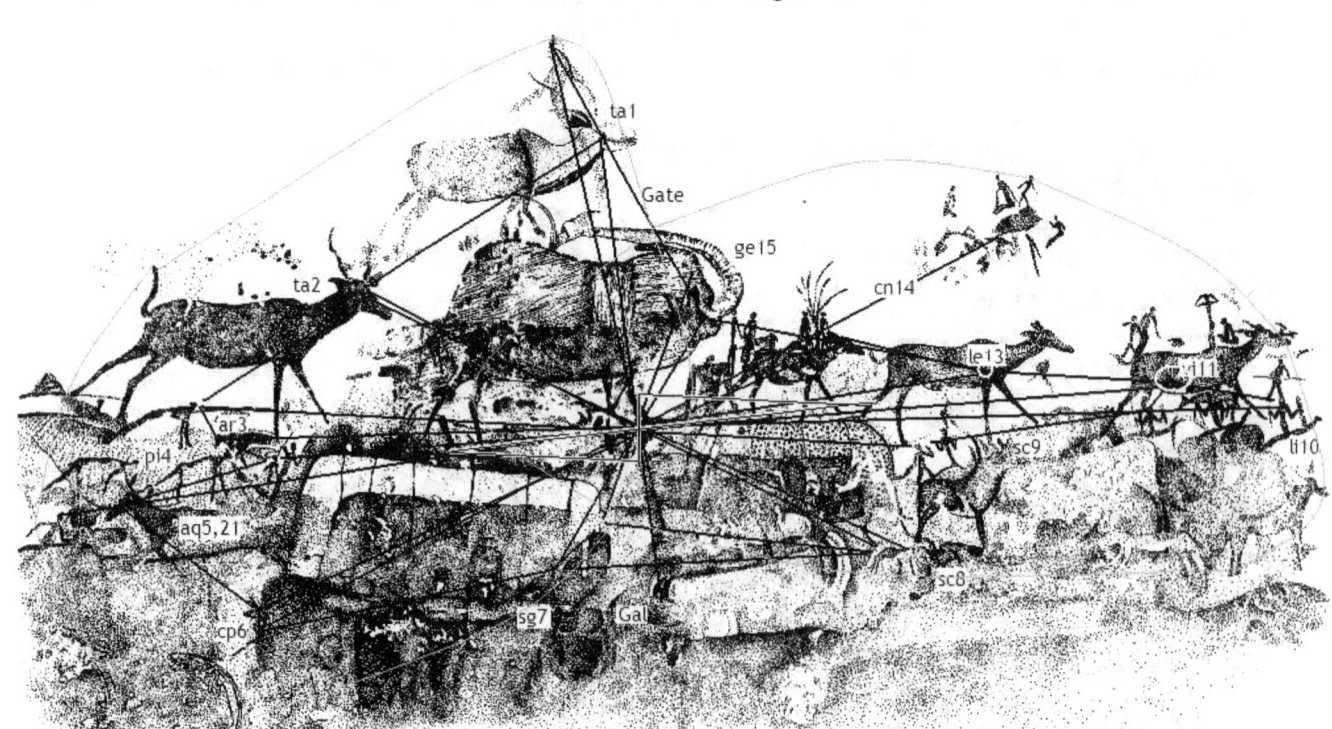

The other hall of records

Co-incidence of the three main Giza pyramids with the three Orion belt stars has become an axiom and anchor point for archaeo-astronomical 'correspondence theory', derived from a panoramic (horizontal) 'implosion' projection as seen from Heliopolis. In a simpler star map view, either the pyramid site plan or Orion has to be inverted and flipped to correspond with one another. The Sphinx then lies behind the small of the back of Orion, facing rearward (east), its causeway angled towards Gemini t15 Canis Minor as Anubis.

Another correspondence that archaeo astronomy has overlooked, is the three Giza pyramids as the three poles; ecliptic, celestial and galactic. This analogy is even elaborated by the Menkaure pyramid causeway and harbour temple as the Leo t13 Ursa rectangle (and thus the erstwhile forthcoming Age Taurus 2 midsummer), and by the Sphinx water pit as the shared Cancer t14 and Gemini t15 Ursa Minor rectangle (the Sphinx causeway thus forms a radial to the position of the then still distant Age Pisces Pegasus celestial pole). All these correspondences are probably as subconscious as mindprint art is, excepting the canine and Anubis elements of the Sphinx as guardian of the dead (see Robert Temple's book on the Sphinx). Anubis may relate to Gemini t0 Lynx or Canis Minor (both on the same ecliptic and celestial meridian as Ursa Minor), which marked spring in the mythic Age Gemini or tep zepi, long preceding Egyptian history.

A double-headed sphinx icon is named Akhet, Horizon. It could be pictured as a macro-constellation extending from Cancer t14 to Libra t10.

The core of this figure is Leo t13 Hydra as a long Sphinx, dragon or Nut, inverted (upside down south to north), its paws just below Cancer (sometimes figured as a head, extending the Nut figure between the two galactic gates), its inverted head under Leo Regulus (Royal heart), its chest as Sextans under Leo, its body or womb at Leo Crater under the galactic pole, its rump at Virgo Corvus (Crow), or pecked by the Crow (see rump wounds at theme t13), and its rear legs below Libra (see a mystic basket lid in a death of Buddha image at theme t8, and in a Mexican dogs palette at theme t10). Its treasure is structure and time, hinged on the celestial pole in Cancer Ursa Minor. Cancer t14 Hydra macro-Sphinx spans a quarter of the sky, as some Chinese macro-constellations do, each containing animal figures within them, some with lintels and borders different from western constellation figures, yet also sustained by archetype, myth, art and culture. Chinese astrology accommodated Western iconographic imports without difficulty, just as Egyptian cosmology incorporated the Greek and formerly Babylonian zodiac versions, due to archetypal overlap. A canvas of irregular dots, or of pure numbers, is most accommodating of myth (compare African geomancy divination, the I Ching, Tao te Ching and T'ung shu). Astronomy and numerology (like symbolic monuments) are holographic jukeboxes, or records of popular fragments of structure.

Art of necessity and by compulsion express aspects of the entire round of attributes and structural outline in each work (see another Sphinx riddle at theme t12). Architects, like artists, do not consciously consider archetypal structure when they plan monuments with a host of geological, elevation, engineering and esthetical aims in mind.

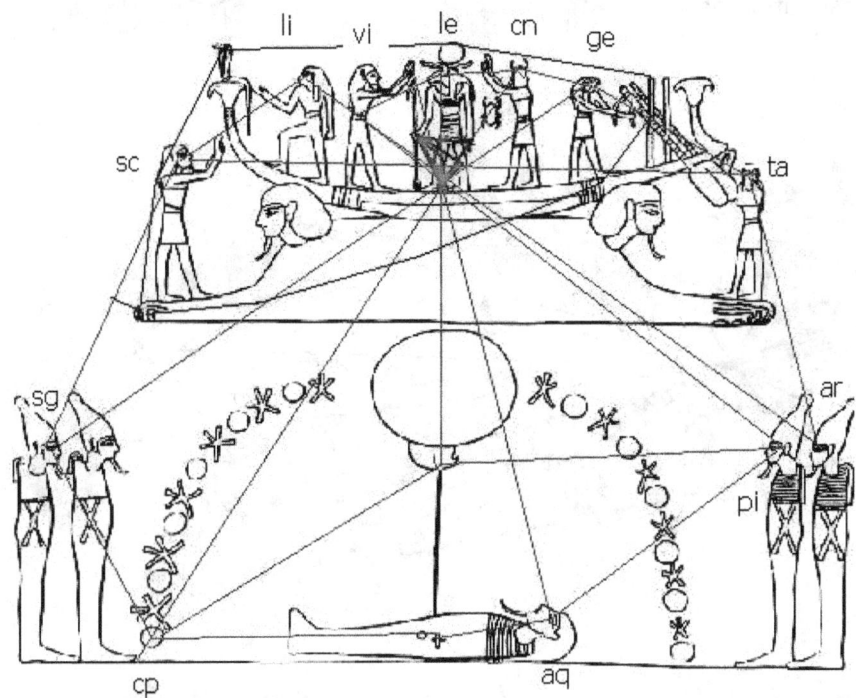

Antelope bags and rain lions

Type Leo t13 as the blood of a dying lion, and Leo t12 as the heart of hunter (South Africa, Clarens, Coerland farm dying lions. Townley Johnson. RARI. SA Archaeological Society, Digging Stick, 2011. Mindprint analysis by Edmond Furter). Zimbabwean Shona myth speaks of a lion heart being brought up and swallowed again, thus the effluent could signify a heart. The two halves of the leonine type are interchanged, as they sometimes are. Their opposites at Aquarius t5 t21 and Aquarius t5 t20 are near identical, in typical horizontal spread-eagled action. Lions in death or trance, instead of bovines, are a common feature in art and legend. The Swiss Guard chose a mortally wounded lion for a relief carving at Lucerne to commemorate guards killed in the French Revolution of 1792. Leo t13's scythe is figured as a number of bows and arrows, potential energy and spent energy, or inversion. The polar figure amid the dying lions recalls Samson's riddles. The restraining figure grabbing the knees of the polar controller recalls Samson being roped to two pillar posts as a type of Leo t12 and Scorpius t8 Ophiuchus (90 degrees apart), which he pulled inwards to end an old Age and start a new Age. Earth obliquity is still righting itself from a bump of unknown magnitude in an unknown era. Prehistoric righting may have been substantial but unrecorded due to cultural disruption (Gary Els; Astronomical Society SA Johannesburg presentation, 2009). Mindprint probably precedes and incorporates such cosmic changes in the diameter of the celestial polar axle.

A celestial polar marker on the staff of Cancer t14, and the horizontal plane, tag the inspiration as Age Aries.

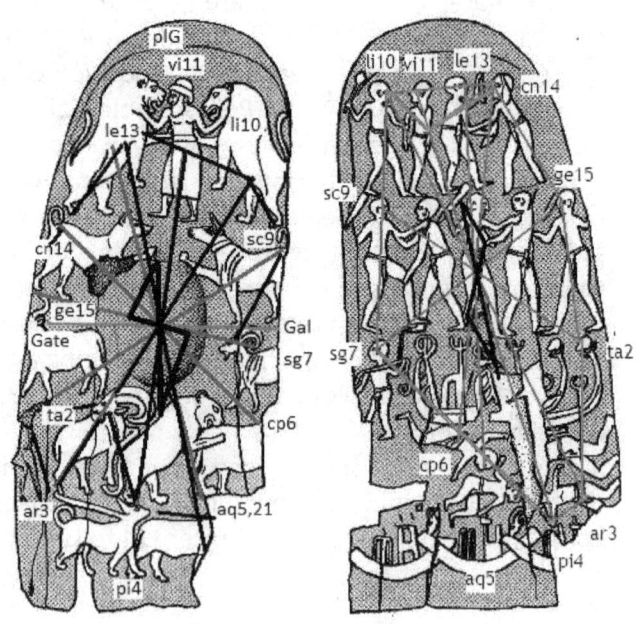

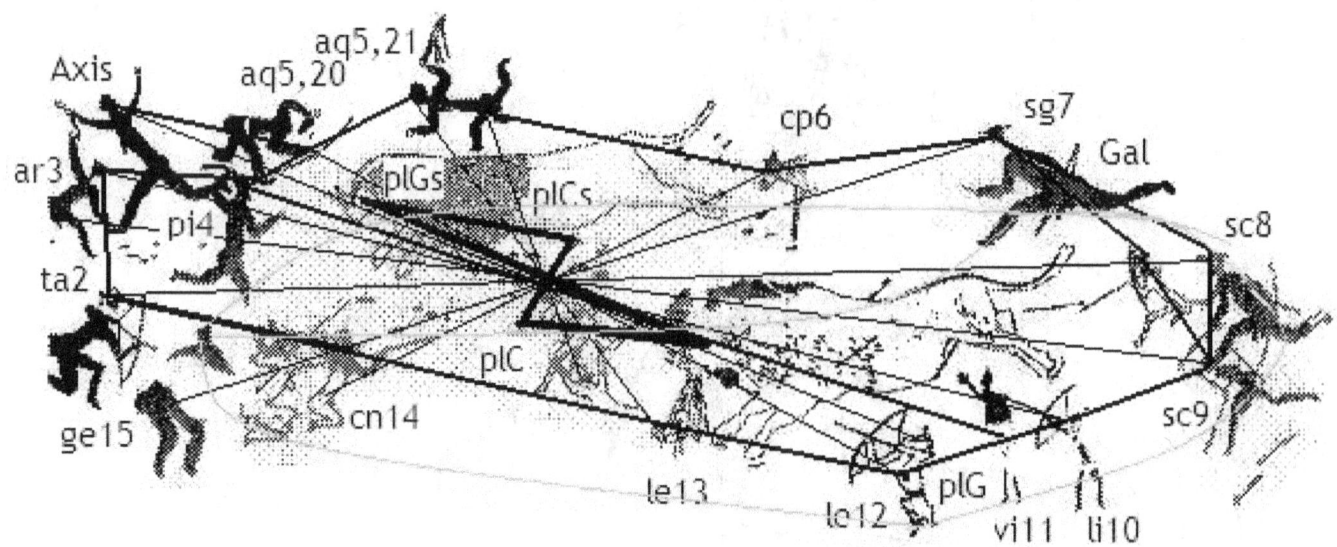

Both sides of the story

Type Leo t13 t12 as the heart of a lion in a double-sided imprint (Egyptian Naqada culture knife handle, Gebel al Arak from Abydos. Mindprint analysis by Edmond Furter). Lion-taming churn groups are usually 90 degrees away at Scorpius t8 Ophiuchus (see the Nekhen mural at theme t13). Galactic corner groups confirm that our conceptual structure is cruciform, and that shapes, angles, positions and sequences carry or enable meaning, some incidental with, and some independent of figurative and conscious meaning. Libra t10 Lupus (Wolf) is on the eye of a wolf as wheel animator (see an Egyptian dogs palette and a Mayan dogs palette at theme t10), its tail as Scorpius t9 (which shares the Lupus decan). Double-sided artefacts usually involve registers, here dividing a land and sea battle, and domestic versus wild order. Several flip side or 'stitching' sequences are allowed by front-to-back correspondences, oppositions or continuations. Archetypal order is obscured by the superficial structure of design, themes, species, rank, value, characters, names or legend. Mindprint crosses artificial conscious boundaries of classes, disciplines and schools. Celestial poles on a canine knee and a goat jaw tag the inspiration to Age Aries-Pisces.

Liberty sacrifices people

Type Leo t13 t12 Ursa as the heart of Liberty in the French revolution (Delacroix; Liberty leading the people. Mindprint analysis by Edmond Furter). The usual scythe is figured by her rifle bayonet and flag, and by the sword of the adjacent Cancer t14. Liberty, as in many Leo t13 t12 combinations, figures courage, military massing, trial, sacrifice, inversion and dissolution.

A celestial pole on Cancer t14's shoulder, horizontal to Liberty's hip, tags the inspiration as Age Aries-Pisces, harking back to anti-empire, puritanical and nationalist revolutionary impulses in several cultures at the start of the Christian era. Gemini t15's far shoulder anticipates Age Aquarius, incidental with the yearning for a new order, new measures of length (metre), time (calendar reform) and values (equality), that nevertheless still include all the standard measures of human culture (posturing, power politics, factions, exploitation and corruption), as it does in the supposed clean slate of the Americas. Mindprint, a timeless norm, ironically also appears in art celebrating new norms and standards, as it does in nationalist and revolutionary art.

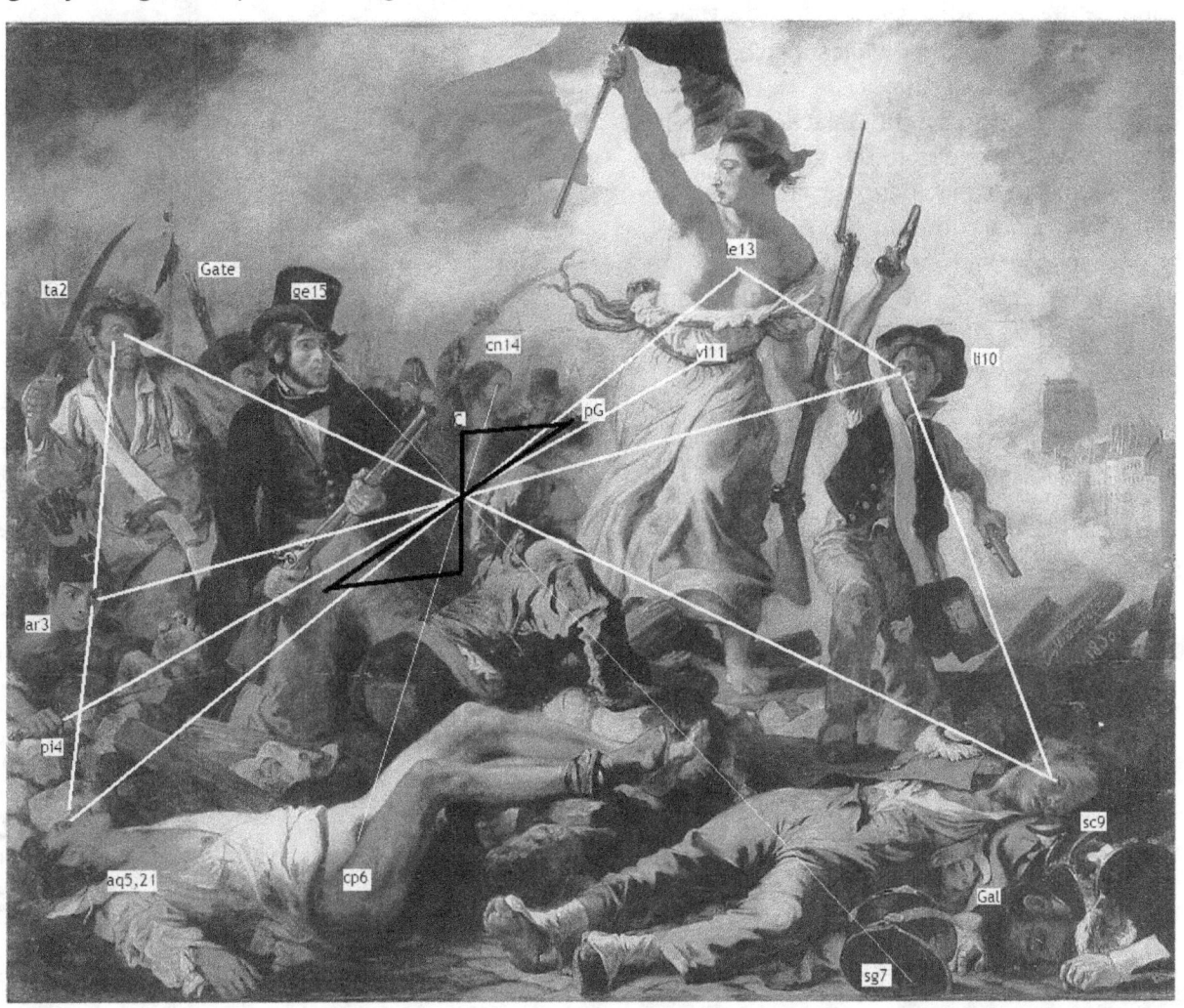

Three chapters in an Exodus

Type Leo t13 and its opposite Aquarius t5 t21 as lions, linking a triple imprint (Egyptian Nekhen mural, Hierakonpolis tomb 100. Cairo Museum. Mindprint analysis by Edmond Furter). Shared galactic equators also link the three spheres in a semi-symmetrical chain.

In the left sphere, Scorpius t8 Ophiuchus and Serpens cauda (Snake holder and Snake tail) are expressed as a lion tamer or feat of Strength, a stock churn group icon that sometimes appears at one of the three other galactic corners (see the Gebel al Arak knife at theme t13). Libra t10 as an antelope has a rearing neck, more typical of its opposite Aries t3 t18. Libra t10 is also under an antelope carousel, figuring a wheel of fortune emblem, labelled a heraldic group in archaeology. Aries t3 t18 is merely a palm branch and boat house, lending its attributes to its opposite at t10. Virgo t11 is a slaughter victim's womb (see slaughter scenes at theme t13). Polar features tag the inspiration as Age Taurus, incidental with archaeological dating of about BC 3500.

In the central sphere, Scorpius t8 Galactic centre is a boathouse palm, although boathouse shrines are usually allocated to Gemini t15, as here in the left sphere, and at its opposite Sagittarius t7. These types all flank galactic features, indicating that boat shrines are a type of churn group.

In the right sphere, Scorpius t8 Galactic centre is again a boathouse, analogous to the galactic centre bulge. Astronomical co-incidences are due to holographic effect, since coherent sets of archetypes resemble one another, and appear to derive from one another, while each derive independently from inspired expression of the structure of perception and nature.

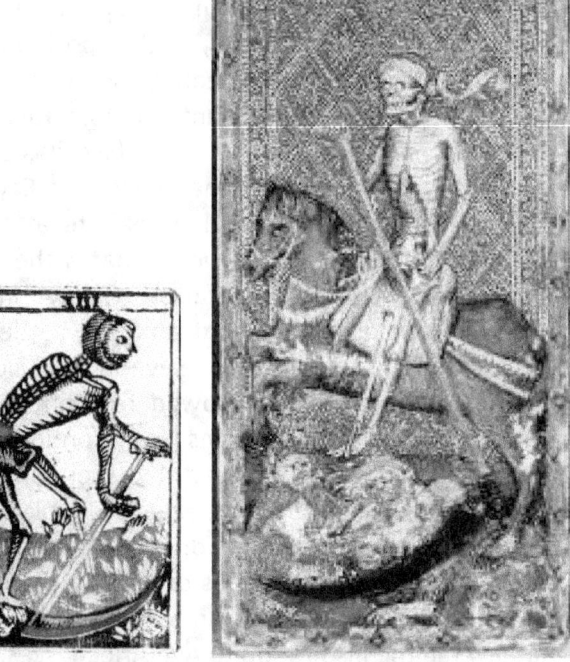

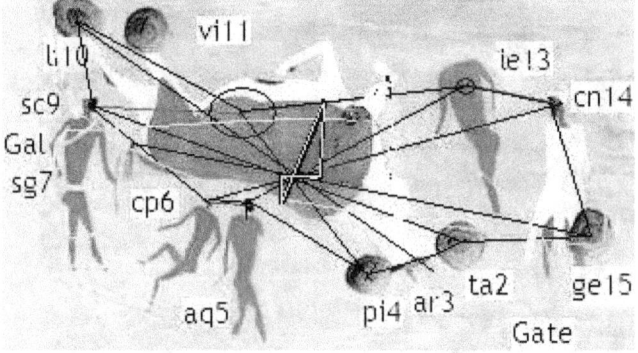

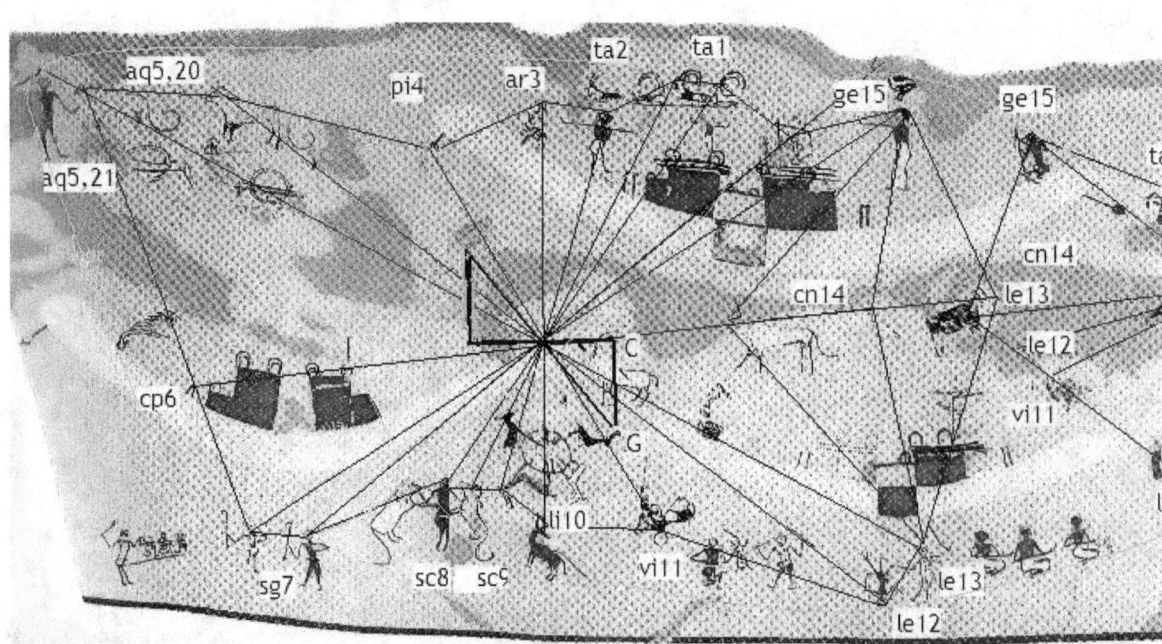

A pregnant quarry

Type Leo t13 t12 Ursa as a hunter's heart (South Africa, 144d. George Stow. RARI. Mindprint analysis by Edmond Furter). Slaughter scenes usually invert Leo t12 and Virgo t11 (see alchemical emblems, such as De Bry's Renaissance discovery books). The bull also figures Taurus t2 t1 and Aries t3, all three sometimes figured with a bent foreleg as former spring hosts, sometimes flanked by healers or hunters.

Bags and tracks are equated here, shedding some light on both themes (see track people in USA art at theme t15 and elsewhere). Gemini t15 is a bag held by a figure in white, but the type is more often figured as a large white face. Sagittarius t7 is the eye of a newborn emerging.

Polar markers are uncertain, but two of the possible horizontal planes indicate an Age Aries-Pisces or Age Pisces inspiration.

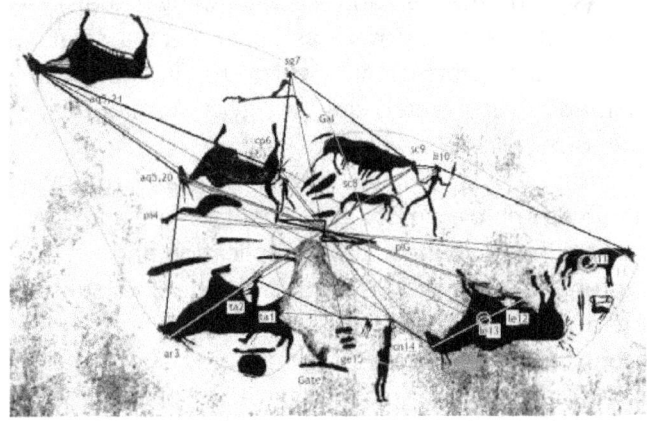

Death and dismemberment

Type Leo t13 Ursa (Bear or horse) as the heart of a battle victim horse, and Leo t12 as the heart of a slaughterer (South African Underberg, Amatola battle slaughter. Sam Challis, RARI. Mindprint analysis by Edmond Furter). Aries t3 t18, also inverted, has Taurus t2 and t1 for riders or slaughterers. Strewn limbs are a stock theme in alchemy as the stage of dissolution, and in iconography as the triumph of death (see medieval and Renaissance icons such as Tarot trump 13). Some limbs are in scythe shapes, confirming attributes of Leo t13 Ursa and Cancer t14 Ursa Minor, larger and smaller severed bull forelegs. The latter sometimes figures the sword of the hippo Taweret (see the Seti 1 ceiling at theme t8). The work could record or legendise a raid, battle or defeat, and the limbs could even be euphemisms for fallen comrades or enemies. The strong Leo t12 theme invokes its sub-themes by holographic or halo effect. Horses were introduced in South Africa in the late 1700s, and in the 1800s assumed the iconographic functions of eland, the most prized large antelope for their excellent fat. The scene was as harrowing to the mixed pirate band of Amatola as to colonisers. Aquarius t5 t20 appears dappled as usual. Thigh wounds are emphasised.

A celestial polar marker on a small horse, and the vertical plane, tag the inspiration as Age Pisces-Aquarius, our current era.

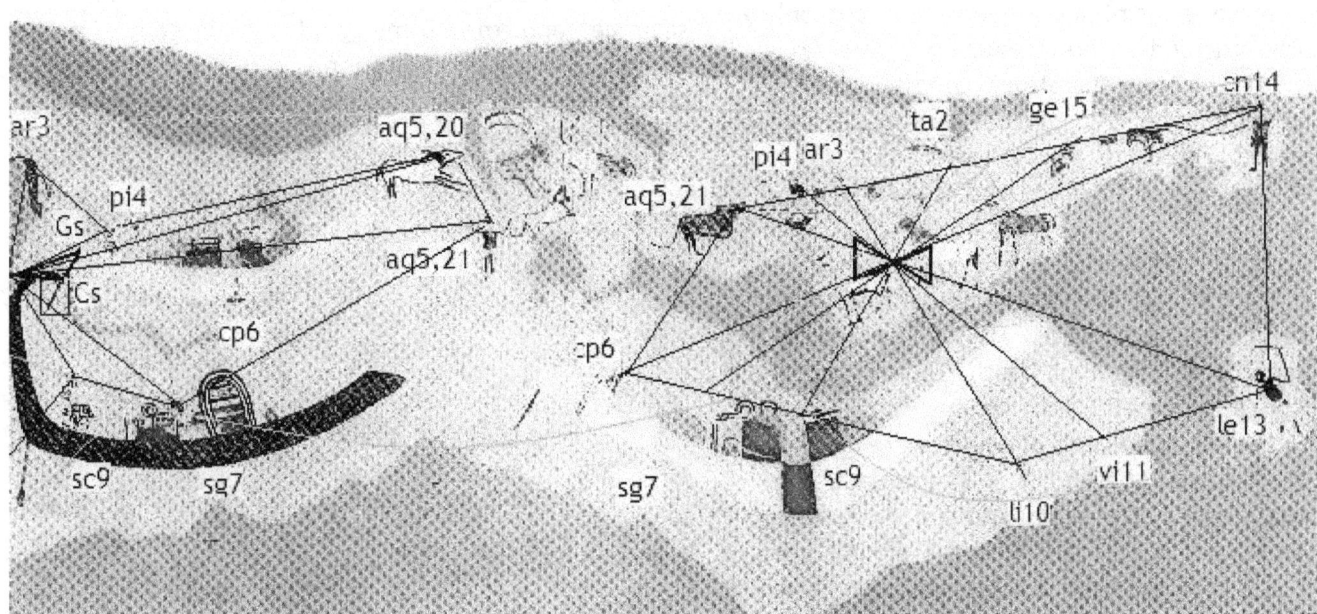

A dying eland and buck bag people

Type Leo t13 as the heart of a dying eland, among moth antelopes (South Africa, dying eland and therianthropes morphing into flying buck. Origins centre display. Mindprint analysis by Edmond Furter). The near identical figures have distinctive attributes in their postures, but share in the style and theme of bags. They are also moth people, perhaps in various stages of their life cycle (several species of moths figuring antelope species are described by Jeremy Hollmann). This work is displayed next to the preserved body of an eland bull in the same posture, one of the central themes in South African rock art. Here it figures Leo t13, although it usually figures Taurus t1 (but see dying lions at theme t13).

Death of the quarry, marked by the bent knee posture, is typical of spring and sometimes of summer icons (see themes t1, t2, and Aries Agnus lambs at theme t3 t18). Some attributes of spring sacrifice icons were dragged along as the equinox precessed. There is iconic logic even in this ambiguation. Dying bulls do not appear at Age Aries cardinals (t3 t18, t14, t10, t6), nor in Age Pisces cardinals (t4 t19, t15 t0, t11, t7). Future studies may explore Mithras killing bulls as t2, St George killing dragons as t3, Xipe Totec dressed in the skin of a flayed victim as t4, and their midsummer companions; dying lions as t13, water monsters as t14, and hero twins as t15. Retro dragging of seasonal attributes appear to occur only after the end of the following era, thus Aries t3 t18 still holds the slayed lamb and dragon icons, due for transfer to Pisces t4 t19 as a slayed horse or whale after the spring equinox moves into Aquarius (see the Cosmic map).

Gods, or rather principle concepts of a preceding era, are often demonised. Thus Taurus t1 t16 Orion as Osiris, once a spring god, became god of death. Taurus t1 t16 Auriga, equated with Artemis and Taurus t2 t17 Perseus as god of death, were dragged in turn to Aries t3 t18 Andromeda and Triangulum after the end of Age Aries. A celestial polar marker on the eland's jaw, and an unidentified counterpart over Capricornus t6, tag the inspiration as Age Aries.

Three magi and an antelope holding a staff

Type Leo t13 Ursa as the heart of a herder (South Africa, Kwa-Zulu Natal Ndedema Gorge herder trio. SA Tourism. Mindprint analysis by Edmond Furter). Wild animals kneel before the nature lords, types of Apollo, Orpheus or three magi, as tall people, a kind of figure expressed worldwide.

Libra t10 has a craned neck (more usual at its opposite Aries t3), and one arm in a V posture, clutching a staff, noteworthy since it is an antelope with no other human components. The effect resembles its opposite Aries t3 t18 as Lamb of God clutching a staff or standard post. Scorpius t9 is figured only by the Libra t10 elbow. This type is often part of Libra t10, and often holds two staffs, typical of a healer transformed into an antelope in trance (see theme t9, and buck-jumping rituals). Aries t3 t18 has a long neck as usual, here a solar plexus phallic protrusion, similar to images of embalmed or resurrected kings in Egypt. Gemini t15 has a white face.

The southern polar triangle frames an eland rump, in a panel with nine or more prominent rumps and hips that could imply abundance, multiplication and slaughter, as do bags, arrows and bows, a sub-theme of Leo t13 t12.

Celestial polar markers are absent, but the horizontal and vertical planes tag the inspiration as Age Aries-Pisces, incidental with the theme of birth, sacrifice, and the former early spring (now late spring). The polar orientation is incidental with the last few centuries before about BC 150, although the work could be later.

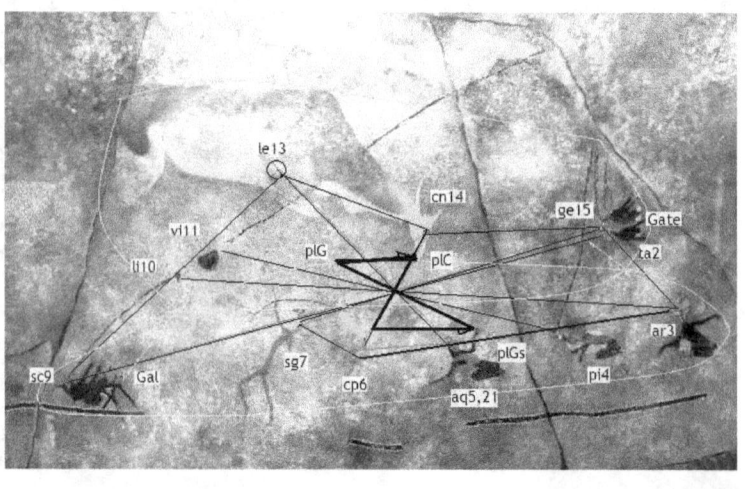

An overpainting warp

Overpainting in this work is insufficient to resolve the painting layers, and problematic due to ambiguous overlays between Aquarius t5 and Capricornus t6. Parts of both overlay parts of the other, indicating that the artist may have followed a haphazard sequence of painting. One possible order could be a bottom layer consisting of;

t15ge =ta2 =ar3, le13 =cn14, vi11; then a middle layer of sg7, sc9 =li10 [?], pi4; then a top layer of aq5 cp6, apparently by cardinal steps of 90 degrees, not by a combination of opposites and cardinals (see the Layers section in the text).

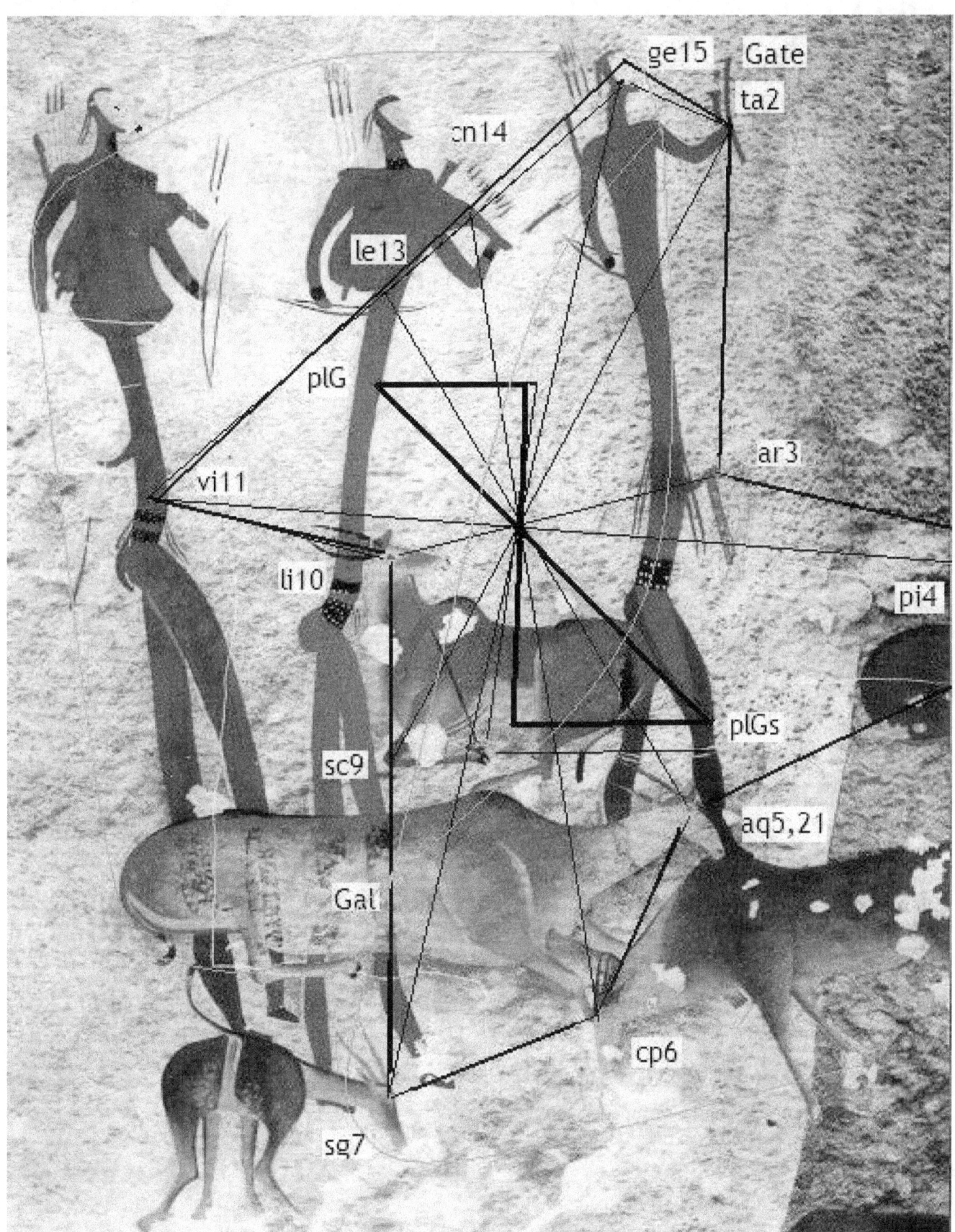

Type Cancer t14;
Time scarab

A crop circle galaxy

Type Cancer t14 Ursa Minor as a large spiral over a large circle in sephirothic, crop circle-styled art (Shutterstock 68647132. Mindprint analysis by Edmond Furter). See Tarot trump 14, Temperance, as a Time angel with spiralling water. Aquarius t5 t21 is a large flamboyant figure as usual, with a halo mirroring its own shape (see Tarot trump 21, World, as a figure in a halo, and haloes at theme t5 t21). Five figurative types below break from the oval to cross the interior, following the approximate galactic equator instead, hinting that the two types of equators are not fully differentiated here, just as the figures were also still being formed when expressed (see a turtle giant with semi-geometric figures in a USA engraving at theme t2 t17). Several features recall crop circle elements, such as insects, wings, spirals and grapeshot dots, supporting reports of similarities between localised artistic inspiration of semi-geometric shape, and subsequent local crop circle themes. Crop circles may express galactic or lunar types (see the text).

Celestial polar markers on an elbow and a spiral, tag the inspiration to Age Pisces-Aquarius, our current era.

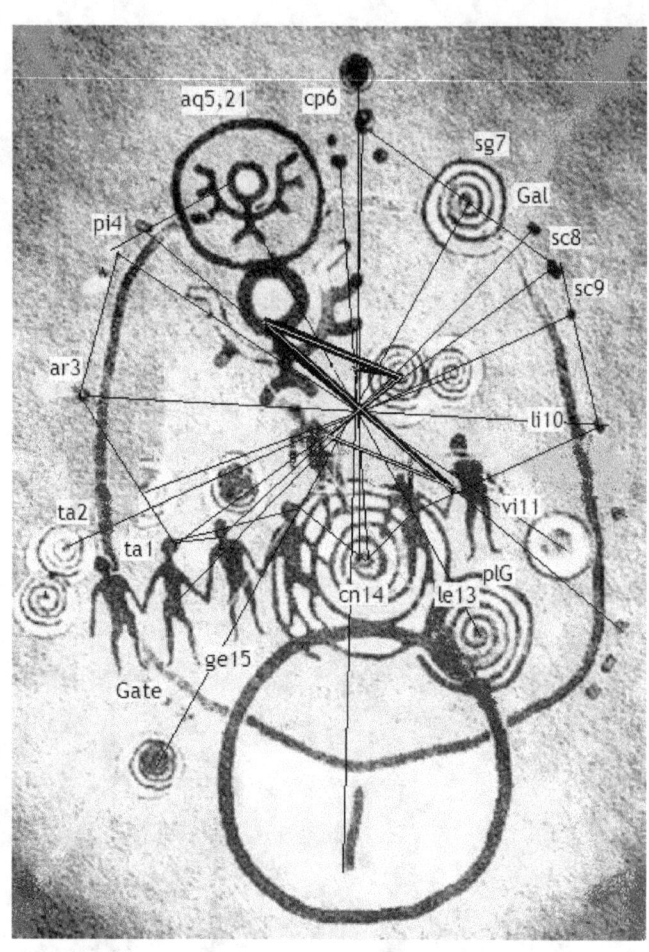

A scarab rolls a time ball

Type Cancer t14 as a dung beetle (Egyptian scarab jewel of Amenophthis. Mindprint analysis by Edmond Furter). Some hieroglyphs express archetypes (see artworks by jeweller Jeanne Morgan-Lefay at themes t10 and t11). Even hieroglyphic captions carry some mindprint attributes, in addition to spelling out myth. Libra t10 is a pair of Maat feathers, conscious symbol of cosmic balance. Sagittarius t7 is a large eye over a bowl, figuring the galactic centre in addition to its conscious conventional and formulaic meanings. Celestial polar markers on two beetle knees tag the inspiration to Age Aries.

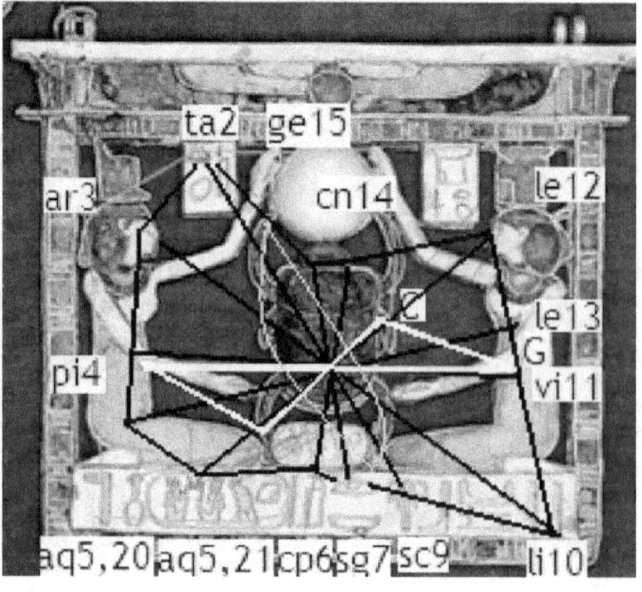

Nature expresses structure

Type Cancer t14 as a winged scarab (England, Wiltshire, Alton Barnes east 2005 August crop circle in a wheat field). Nature routinely makes shapes and creatures, and occasionally images of shapes and creatures. Crop circles may express galactic or lunar types rather than ecliptic (zodiac) types. See a list of galactic types in the text, such as Cancer tg14 Argo Vela (Ship Sail). This crop circle speaks broken Egyptian, but fluent archetype.

Geosymmetry

Type Cancer t14 Ursa Minor as concentric circles with geometrics and V people (USA, Ferron Box, San Rafael Swell rainbow. Mindprint analysis by Edmond Furter). Semi-geometric figures tend to express near-symmetrical mindprints, while figurative art usually includes only one symmetrical galactic equator. Celestial polar markers on a shoulder and an ear tag the inspiration as Age Pisces-Aquarius, our current era.

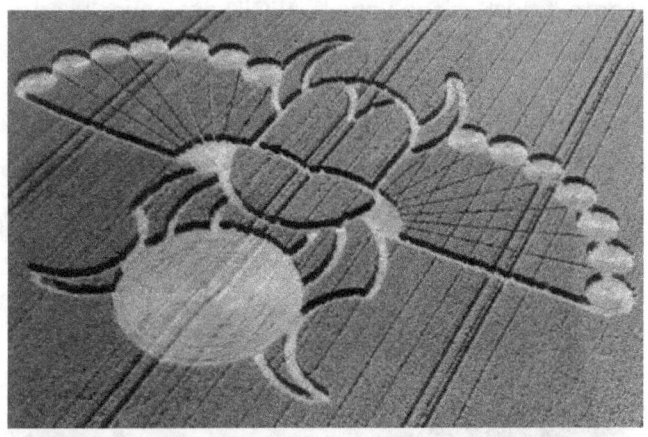

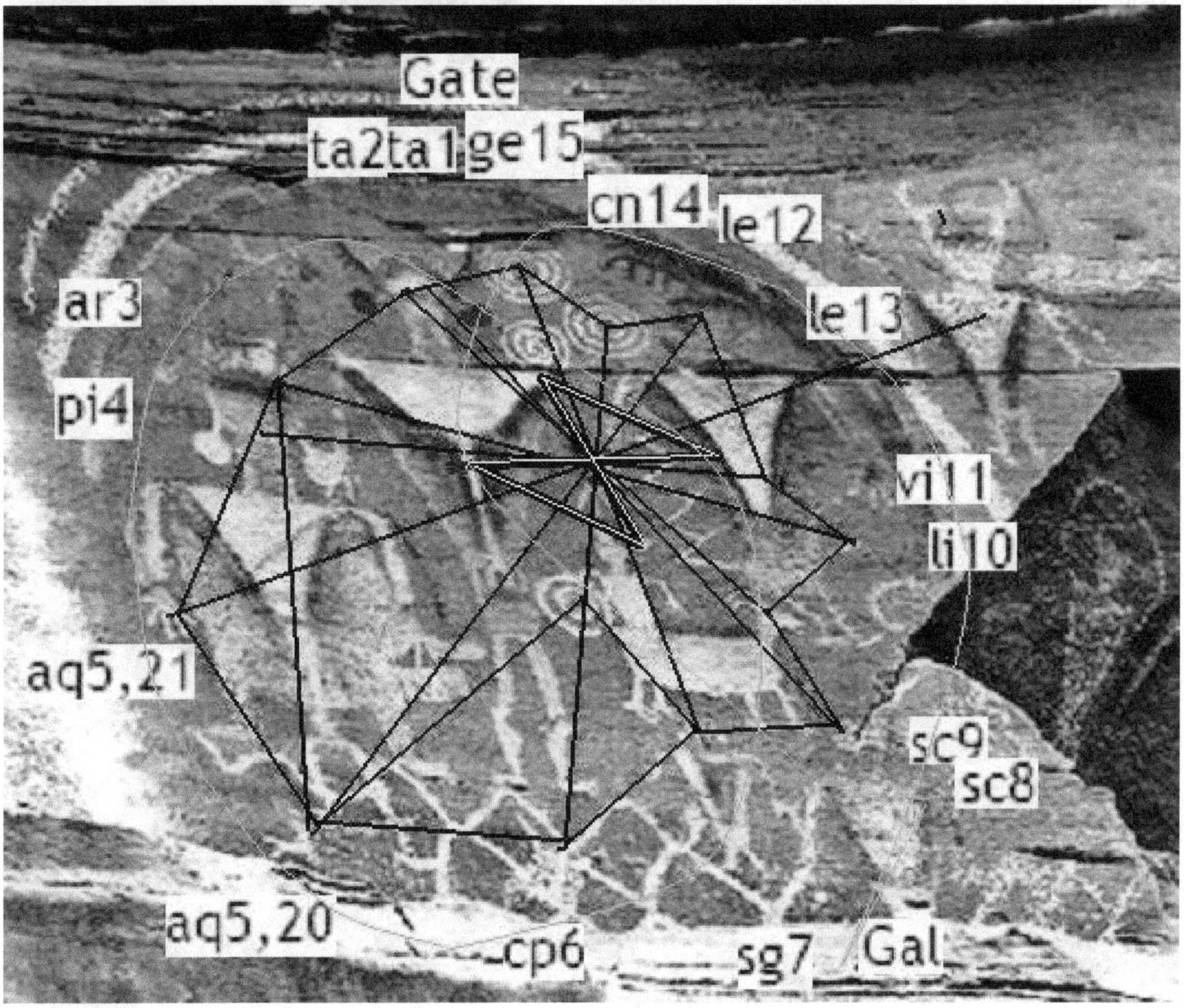

The craft of ages

Type Cancer t14 as a cartwheel on a building site (French illumination of Notre Dame building with a horse cart. Newsweek. Mindprint analysis by Edmond Furter). Celestial polar markers on a hip and a mason's shoulder tag the inspiration as either Age Aries-Pisces, or Age Pisces, the former as the Christian inspiration, the latter as the Christian Age.

A wheel cart

Type Cancer t14 as a wheel or cart in a semi-geometric engraving. Its opposite, Capricornus t6, is the only other wheel in the large work. (USA Utah, San Juan County, Monticello Newspaper rock. James Q Jacobs. Mindprint analysis by Edmond Furter). See a buck bag vortex carousel wheel at their mutual cardinal of Libra t10, in an Egyptian mural at theme t13, and in an Algerian cattle wheel or bowl at themet3. Some parts of this complex American work contain smaller mindprints, due to holographic effect.

Giant footprints have a legendary life as supposed evidence of survival of hominid or humanoid races, or spirits made manifest. The nearest physical evidence for yeti is of a hairy and timid species of bear in the Himalayas. Tracking and estimating time are universal human and animal skills. Some archetypal shapes are co-incident with footprints and tracks (see a track as a fish pond frame, among the initial illustrations in the text).

Celestial polar markers on a head and genitals, and the vertical plane, tag the inspiration as Age Pisces-Aquarius, our current era.

The Horus eye of Ages

The Horus eye in isolation expresses three poles; the iris as the eternal ecliptic (annual) pole, the cheek spiral as Draco's tail towards the eternal galactic pole, and the eye's foreleg's jaw as the slowly moving celestial pole (formerly Leo t13 Ursa as a large foreleg, then Cancer t14 Ursa Minor as small foreleg, recently the foreleg hoof over Gemini t15). The Horus eye is never consciously used in this context, just as the vowels AEOIU are never used as a word.

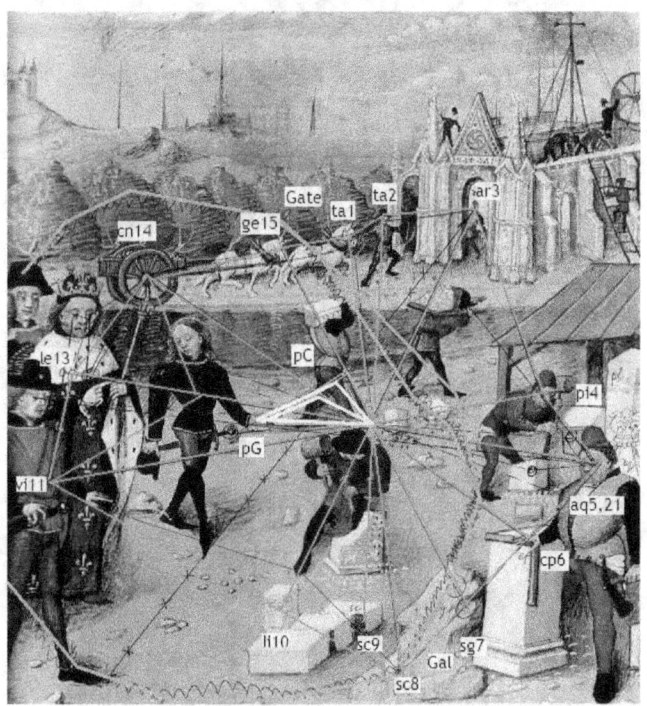

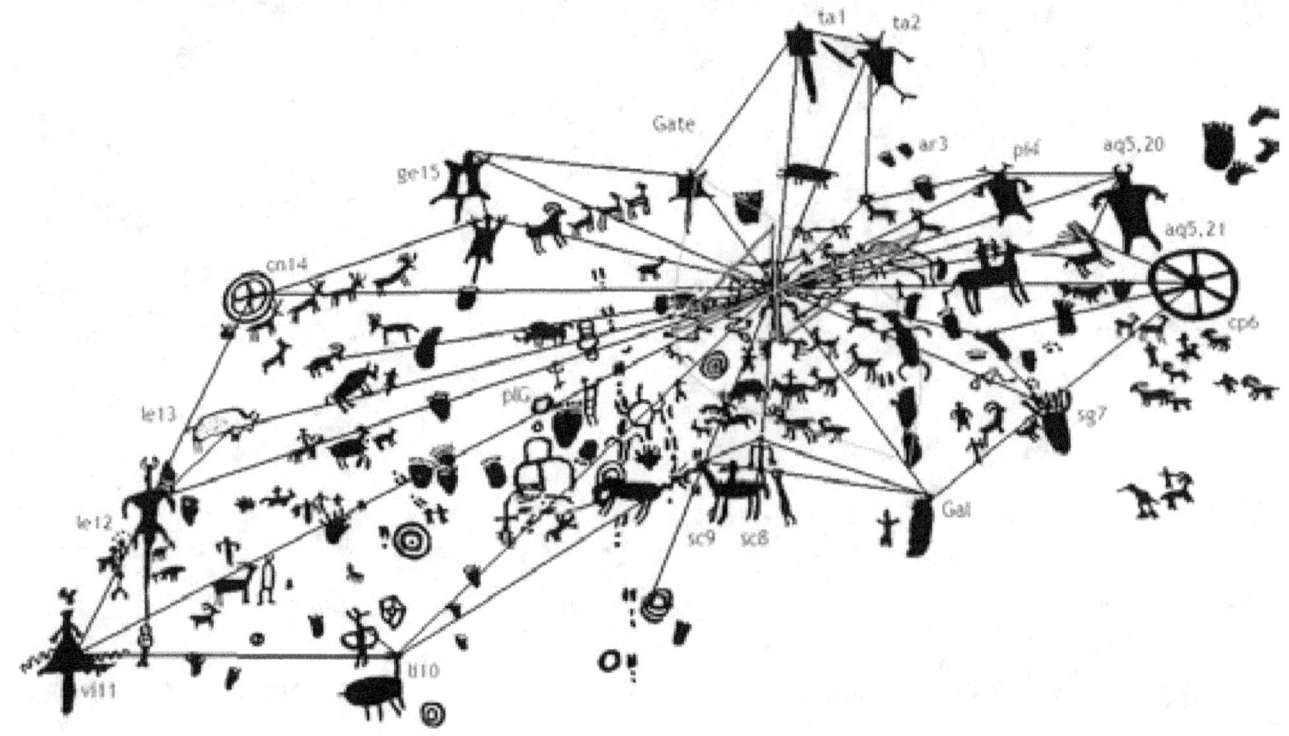

Mindprint in an eye jewel

Type Cancer t14 as a supplicant in a solar disc, and its opposite Capricornus t6 as a scarab (Egyptian scarab jewel for Tutankhamun. Mindprint analysis by Edmond Furter). Galactic poles on the Horus eye cheek stem, and Horus eye tear gland along the widest diagonal of the sigil, and celestial poles on the vertical plane, tag the inspiration as Age Aries-Pisces, in the last centuries BC, incidental with the work and the theme. Precession is due to the rearward rolling celestial pole.

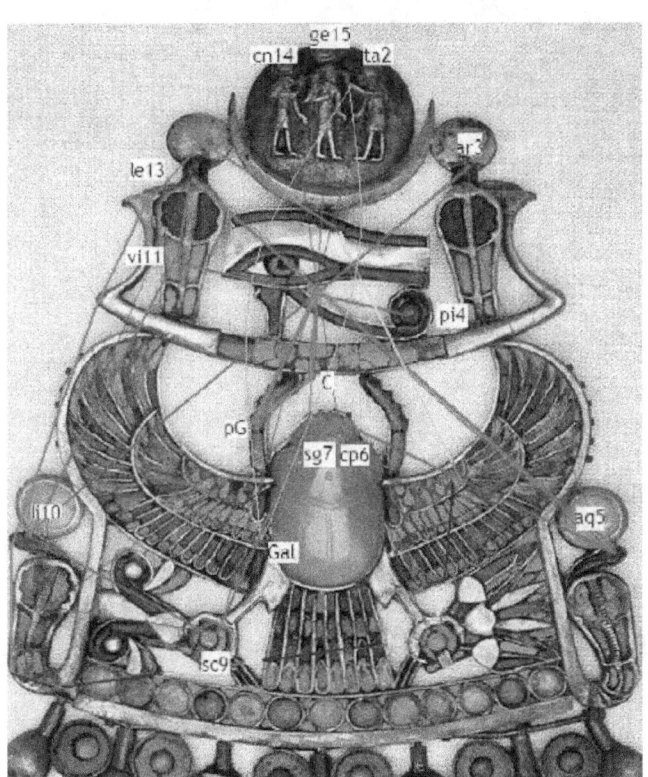

Asian pirates with scarabs

Type Cancer t14 as Y people with scarabs (Asian Tien Shan range, Kangjiashimaji heads. Scen.org. Mindprint analysis by Edmond Furter). Cancer t14 is often a Y-shaped tree, here a Y person flanked by the only two scarabs in the work as determinants of time and regeneration. The scarabs mimic dancers with both arms up and hands bent inward, as of Naqada dancers. Feathers, maces, genitals, belt tails and horses appear in all pirate art (see theme t13). H people, house people or footprint people seem to favour Cancer t14 and Gemini t15, former and current midsummer and celestial polar hosts. Heads or faces all over the work, probably understood as ancestral souls, express the Gemini t15 theme.

Virgo t11 wears a face on her body, incidental with her pregnancy. Pisces t4 and Aquarius t5 are near horizontal, typical of t5. Some galactic equator sections are marked by tight rows of small figures in a kind of snake dance. A distorted periphery, as usual, conceals the figures equator, as well as one near symmetrical and one distorted galactic equator (the galactic circles and their gates are here marked in error, they should cross the main equator between ge15 and ta2, and between sg7 and sc9).

A celestial polar marker on a head and the vertical plane, tag the inspiration as Age Aries-Pisces, in the last few centuries before about BC 150, perhaps incidental with the work.

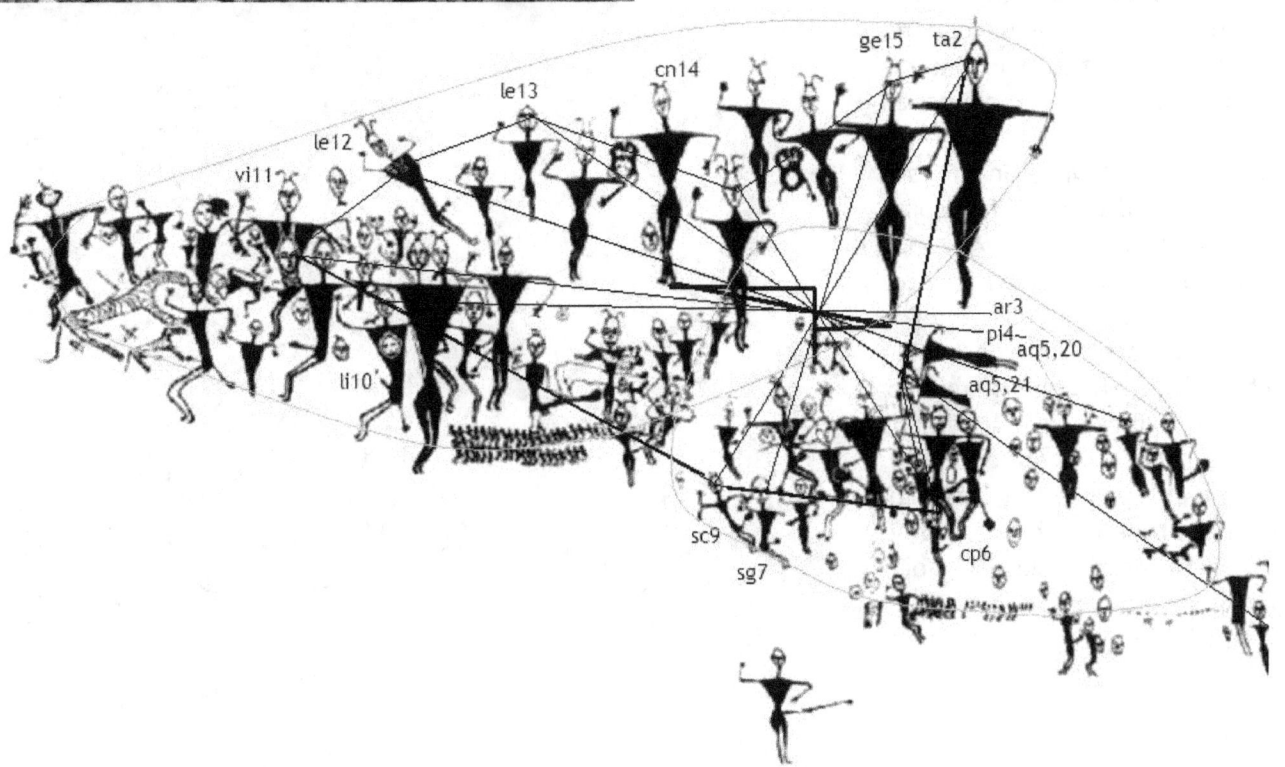

A spirit mirror on a pavement

Type Cancer t14 Ursa Minor as a polar bird (Peruvian dragon pavement. National Geographic. Mindprint analysis by Edmond Furter). Cancer t14 is ingressed towards the pole as usual, partly due to its polar decan hosting the celestial pole. Ursa Minor lends itself to a bird shape, although it is rarely pictured as a bird. Its southern counterpart was formerly Tucana (Bird of Paradise). Pavements and geoglyphs (landscape figures) tend to invite semi-geometric styles, although some apparent entoptic geometrics may instead represent real craft items such as headbands, baskets, aprons and thongs (Ed Eastwood. Also Jeremy Hollmann). Here some figures are house people or H people, related to track people. Sparse figuration and an armillary (crossed armbands) design at Pisces t4 raise the possibility that this design could be consciously astronomical, but lack of symmetry, inconsistent style, and spirals at unrelated types, confirm that the sequence and structure of this work is as subconscious as it is in almost all art. Libra t10 Bootes stands over Serpens, while in the sky they are adjacent. The spiral figuring Pisces t4 and Aquarius t5 could outline a noon shadow marker during the course of a year. The artist was occupied with the usual range of mythic, ritual, political and perhaps astronomical considerations. The ecliptic pole (axial crossing), is on the base of a house, shrine or pillar post. Celestial polar markers are uncertain, but one of the possible vertical planes tags the

inspiration to Age Aries, confirming the dragon theme and the position of the large spiral. To illustrate Ages by a hypothetical example, if the Cancer t14 bird took two

steps backward, or the Taurus dragon took two leaps forward, either with equal and opposing movement of their opposite numbers, the imprint would mark the start of Age Aquarius. This kind of iconographic hologram does not appear in celestial zodiacs of twelve stereotypical figures of 30 degrees each. Subconscious structure is beyond the conscious capability of most artists, and beyond the ability of this study to fully explain.

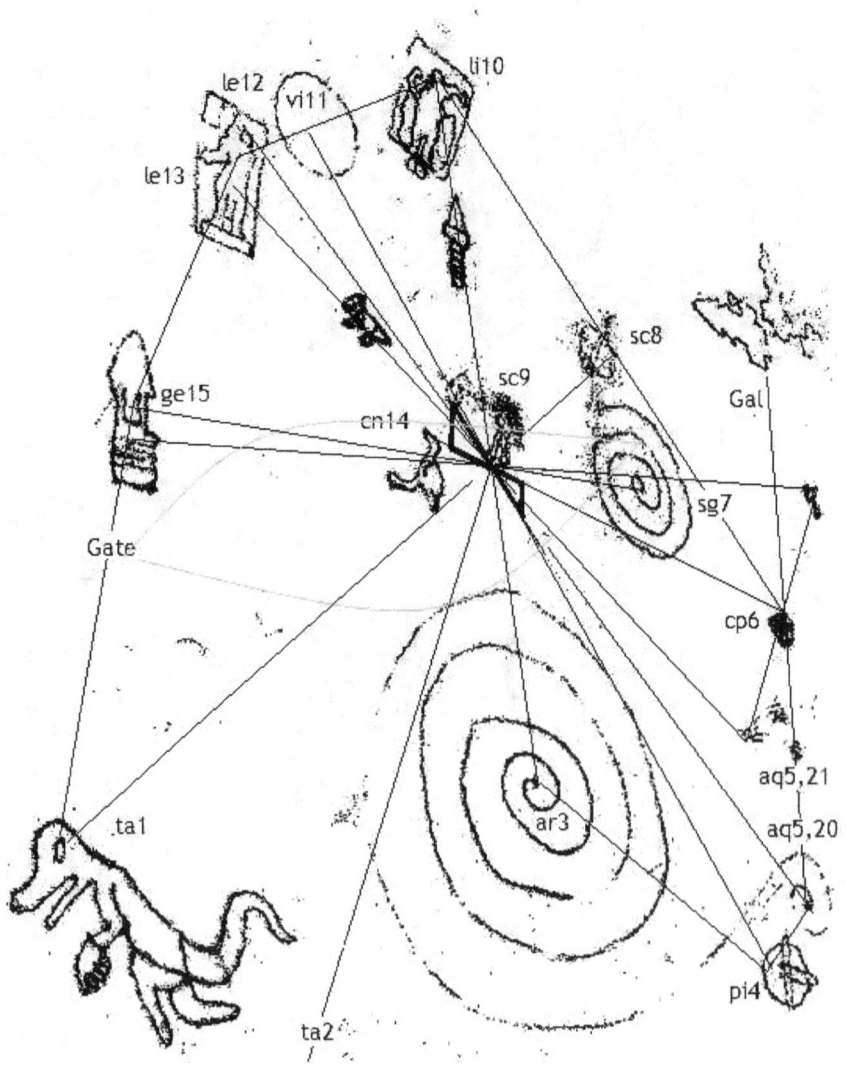

A bag of the bones of time

Type Cancer t14 as a preserved blowfish among a collection of paintings and shapely items (Francken the Younger; Collections. Louvre. Mindprint analysis by Edmond Furter). A blowfish is a type of skin bag with part of its skeleton on the outside, as of dragons (see buck bags and dragons at themes t3 t18, t10, and t6). A picture of a gallery of pictures is an occasional artistic device (see a donkey in a frame at theme t12) invoking juxtaposition (Umberto Eco; Infinity of lists). Images of galleries also allow anachronistic (apparently unrelated) figures in subconscious service of archetype, which is a function of synchronicity (co-incidence of apparently unrelated items or events). A little sea horse as the Aries t3 dragon, expressing a long neck and partly external skeleton, is among the marks of subconscious genius.

Opposite a little marble womb as Virgo t11, stands the artist or investor as 'father' of the growing collection, a discovery more delicious for knowing that the investor and the artist were unaware that archetype is the collector, and collectors are at its service. An axis to the heart of a man in one of the smaller paintings on the painted wall, as Leo t13's heart, is one of the marvels of mindprint, since it involves the positioning of a rendering of an entire painting and gallery, not juggling of individual figures to complete the sequence and the axial grid.

Celestial polar markers are uncertain, but the vertical plane tags the inspiration to Age Aries, and an ear tags for Age Pisces. Many works themed on Cancer t14 are tagged between these two, to Age Aries-Pisces.

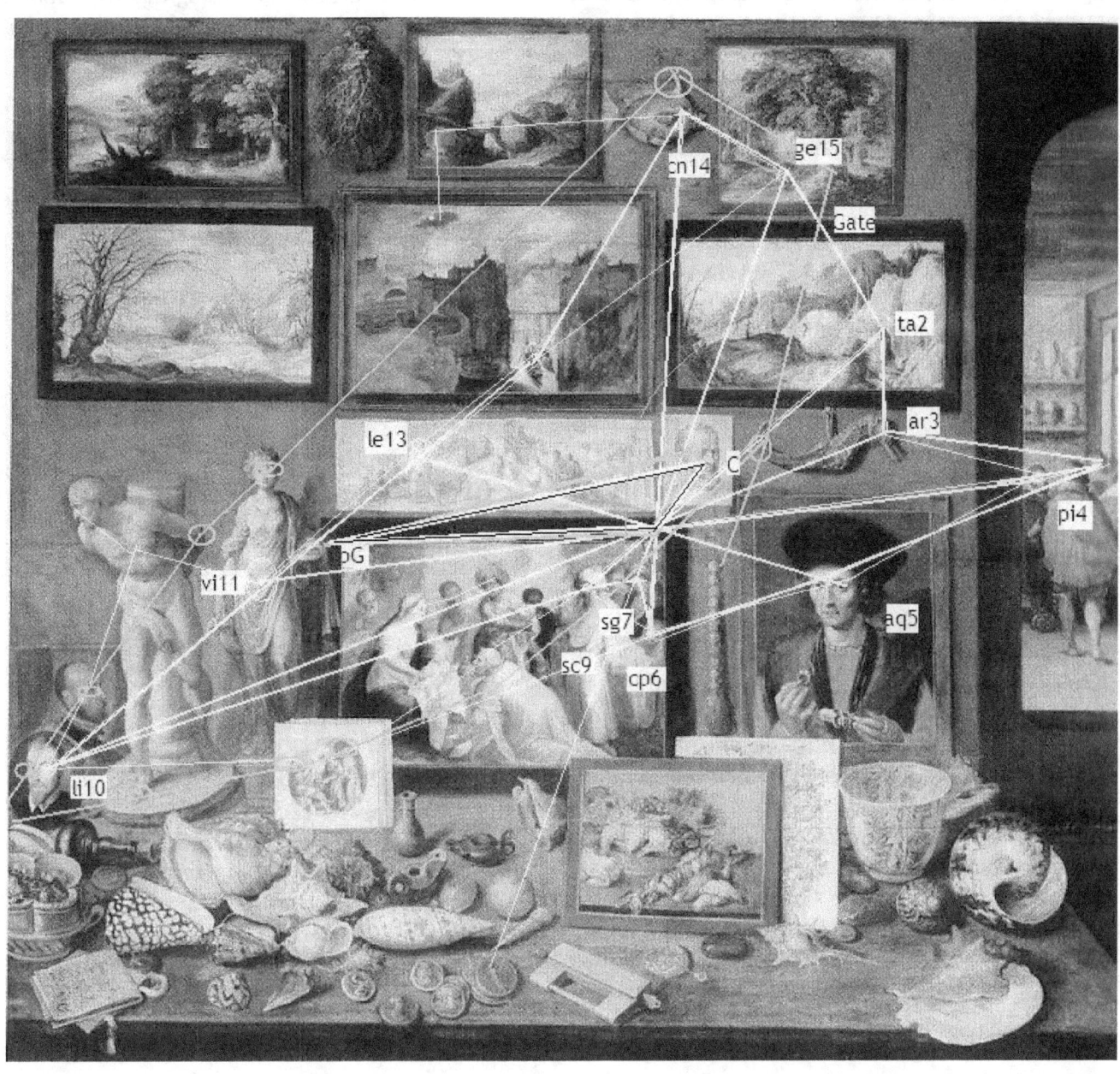

The phoenix flies again

Type Cancer t14 Ursa Minor and its antipode (spherical opposite) Capricornus t6 Tucana (Bird of Paradise) as a Phoenix nest (England, 2009 June 12 Phoenix crop circle). Ursa Major held the moving celestial pole, and thus summer, over Leo in Age Taurus, then transferred its attributes of bull foreleg, summer fire, Age marker, bag, horn of plenty, seven stars and raptor, to Ursa Minor over Cancer in Age Aries, and over Gemini in Age Pisces. Similar iconic transfer is noted at the spring equinox (see Clothes of spring at theme t1 t16). The same precession (anti-seasonal movement) passed the celestial south pole from the bright star Achernar, figured as a Phoenix nest or egg, to Tucana, then to Octans. Attributes of the southern summer remain linked to Phoenix, including nest of fire, Age marker, resurrection and obelisk. The crop circle expresses the concept of three poles or eggs, forming an equilateral triangle or obelisk, incidental with the current polar arrangement at the Age Pisces-Aquarius transition. Northern poles form an L or |\ shape, with an added short leg in the opposite direction forming a mirrored JL or /|\ shape, if the celestial south pole is made visible as if on a transparent sphere (see the Cosmic map). The resulting polar 'obelisk' frames Ursa Major's retro head in the northern hemisphere, and frames Phoenix with its nest and egg in the southern hemisphere. The crop circle expresses a part of a concept map, not a constellation map.

Mountain pirates marking time

Type Cancer t14 as two healers and a polar figure (South African Underberg, Amatola camp. Sam Challis, RARI. Mindprint analysis by Edmond Furter). The inner member of the Cancer group marks two alternative celestial polar positions, its hand for Age Aries, its foot for Age Aries-Pisces, both inspirations being more than 2000 years retro to the work. See another camp with demarcated areas in Amatola art at theme t15. See pirate raiders with maces, spears, feathers, belts, bags, dance postures and trees in Naqada culture at theme t3, thousands of miles and 5000 years distant. Both cultures favoured mountain ranges as a kind of paradise. Drakensberg foothills, named Underberg, offer a maze of nooks and crannies for hiding raided stock.

A winged scarab in disguise

Type Cancer t14 as a falcon and polar controller (Egyptian jewel of Horus on a vulture and snake, for Ramses at Saqqara. Mindprint analysis by Edmond Furter). Hieroglyphs as characters are common in jewels and murals in Babylonia, Egypt and Mexico. Pisces t4 is a Wippet mouth opener tool or jaw, subconsciously identified with concepts that also appear in the sky as Ursa Major and later Ursa Minor, thus near the celestial pole in all of the last three Ages. Aries t3 is a priest or queen. Taurus t2 is a cross. Gemini t15 Canis is an Anubis dog-headed sceptre. The galactic pole is on the falcon's tail feathers (the galactic south pole is sometimes a phoenix, incidental with the constellation Phoenix that held the celestial south pole in Age Taurus, now moved through Tucana into Octans).

A celestial polar marker on Horus' shoulder, and the horizontal and vertical planes, tag the inspiration as Age Taurus-Aries, in the last centuries before about BC 1500. The artefact could be later.

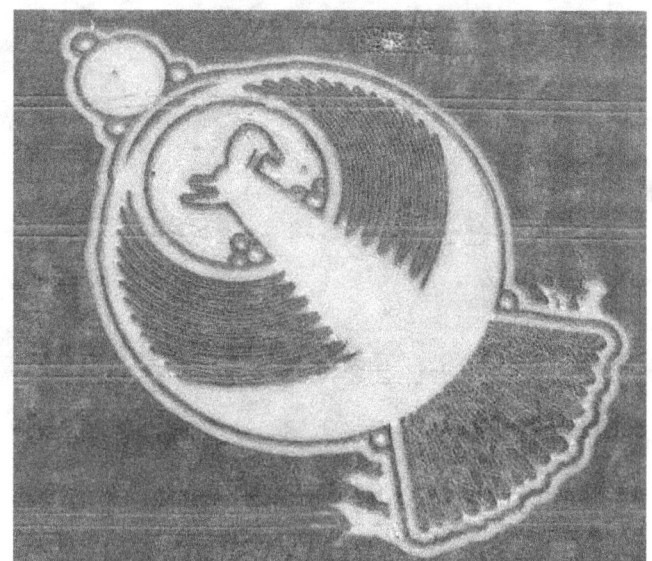

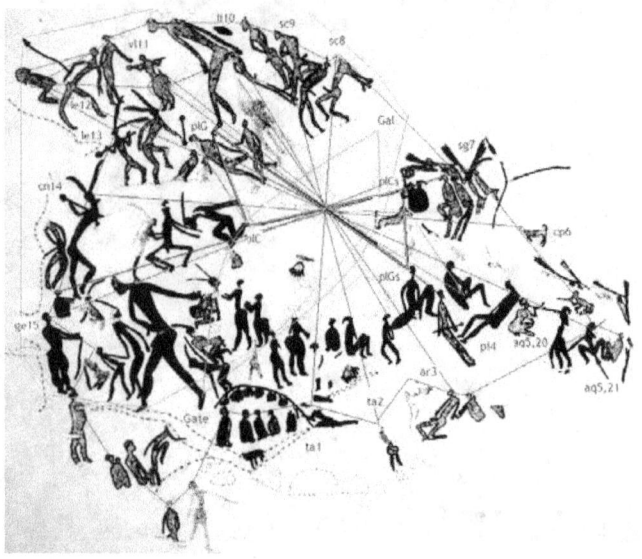

A pavement legend

Type Cancer t14 Ursa Minor as a male canine (Swedish pavement engraving with boats and a starburst. Art Media Photography. Mindprint analysis by Edmond Furter). Ursa is sometimes expressed as a fox (see a fox of nine tails in a Chinese tile at theme t11). The prominent ecliptic polar marker is unique among 600 works in this study of art of all ages and cultures. Suns and sunbursts are common in semi-geometric art, but seldom central. Its position could be coincidence, or subconscious expression. The large cardinals, Taurus t2, Leo t13, Scorpius t9 and Aquarius t5 t21, define a nearly regular square, unaffected by glacial marks on the rock, hinting that major cardinals are often carved first, as in the stratigraphy analysis of overpainted rock art (see the Layers section in the text). Gemini t15 and the galactic gate are in a cup depression near a rectangular grid. Pisces t4 t19 as a crossed circle may be a spring sun marker. Dots could mark warriors. Tracks and footprints compare directly with some USA rock art, whether by re-invention or guided by diffusion is irrelevant to this study.

Celestial polar markers on a boat prow and a hook person, tag the inspiration to Age Pisces. The earlier Age Aries-Pisces is also indicated.

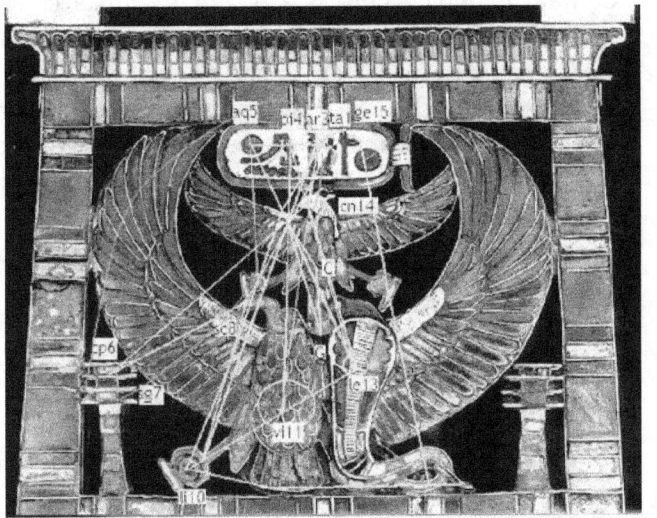

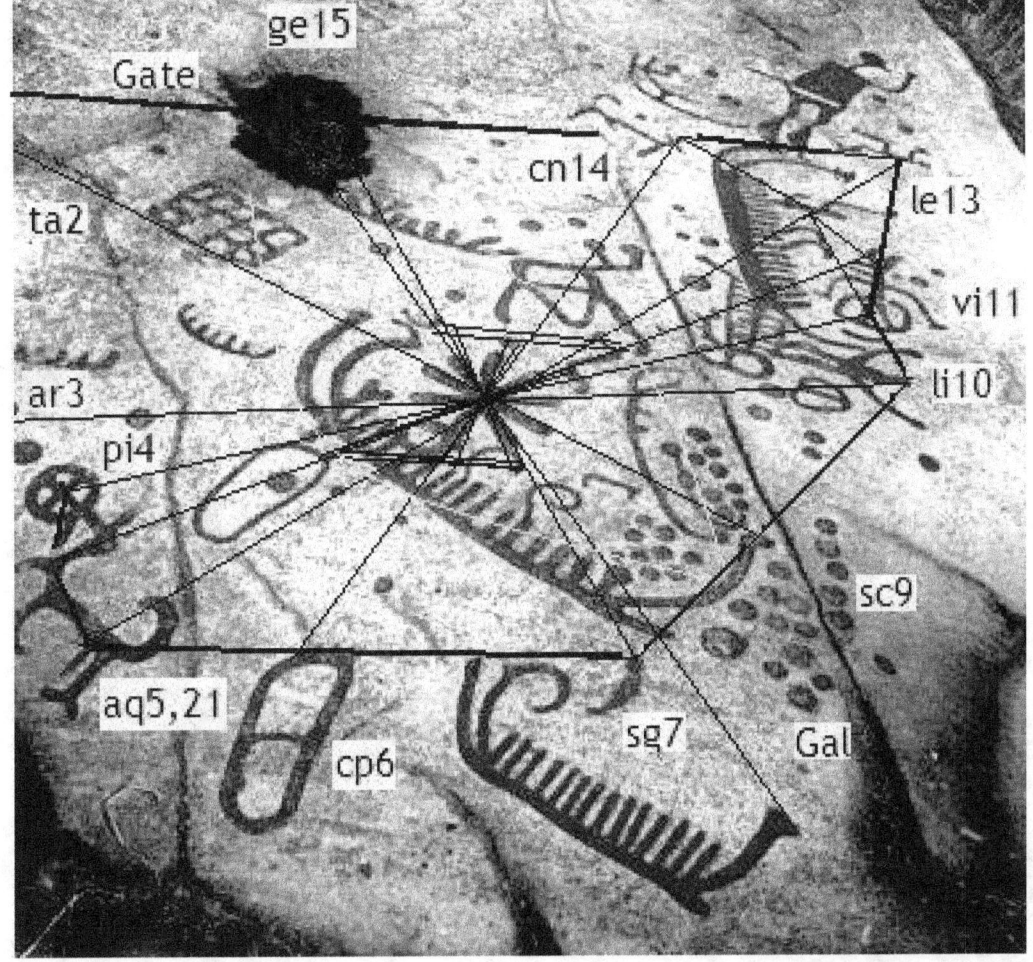

Type Gemini t15;
Creator and rope churner

Vishnu in Russian rock art

Type Gemini t15 as a rope churn man among horned V-people (Russian Sayan Zaba, Lake Baikal Rupestre pavement. Mindprint analysis by Edmond Furter). The unique figure resembles a mantis, more common at Scorpius t9 or Aquarius t5 t20, but is a double-bodied man, combined vertically (see two Niaux bison combined horizontally, and a Peche Merle rope man at theme t15. See also Indian churn groups). Migration and multitude is a stock theme in art and inherent in the 'full circle' of the mindprint structure. Celestial polar markers may tag the inspiration as Age Pisces-Aquarius, our current era.

A different type of healer

Type Gemini t15 as a rope churn man (France, Peche Merle cave. Mindprint analysis by Edmond Furter). The figure is linked to two Trois Frere cave 'sorcerers' in academic and popular literature, but he has a different posture, attributes, function, and mindprint identity as rope controller, creator, double-bodied, cosmic churn, and wounded on his thigh (see Niaux bison at theme t15). He is not riddled with arrows as St Sebastian was, but is directly comparable to multi-armed eastern gods (see theme t15, and the Seti 1 tomb ceiling at theme t8).

Polar markers are uncertain, but the vertical plane tags the inspiration to Age Taurus, among the few very old works in this study.

Goat people in bat dung

Type Gemini t15 as a large dancer or tamer among goat people (Bulgarian Magura cave. Mindprint analysis by Edmond Furter). Pisces t4 is damaged but large. The image was made in guano, bat dung leaving vivid purple traces until damaged by bacteria. The warped rock canvas is no obstacle to mindprint. See goat people at theme t7, and P-people at theme t7). Virgo t11 as a woman has a goat companion, perhaps expressing the concept of a hybrid. Goat people are a kind of centaur, ambiguous with Sagittarius t7, or with Libra t10 Centaurus, which here is a bowman with a cloven goat footprint.

Goat people here cluster around t7-t8 at the galactic centre, core of the Milky Way, figured as a milk goat and recalling myths of Hercules' goat mother Amalthea. Scorpius t8 Ophiuchus is a type of Hercules.

A celestial polar marker on large genitals tag the inspiration as Age Taurus, but a knee and the horizontal plane tag Age Aries-Pisces, in the last few centuries before about BC 150, perhaps incidental with the work.

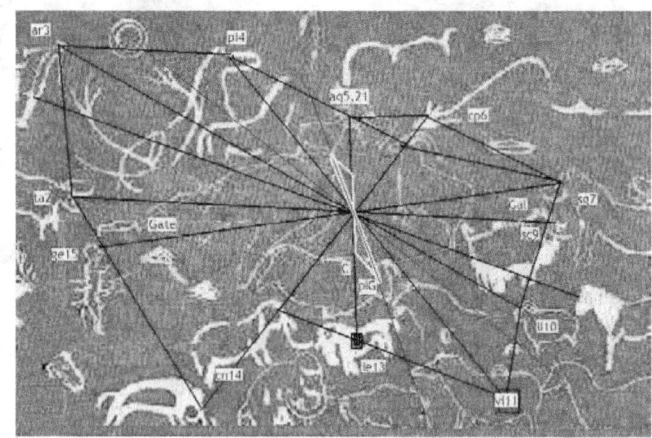

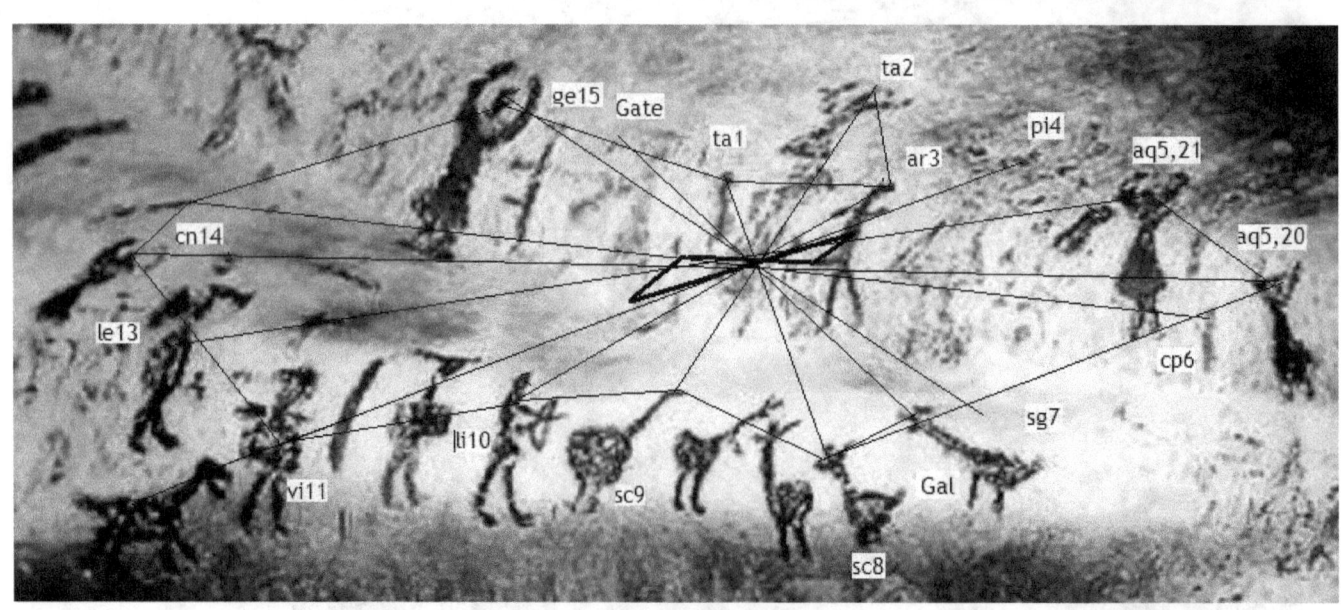

Artists posed as philosophers

Type Gemini t15 as a philosopher with Alexander (Raphaello Sanzio; The school of Athens. Vatican. Mindprint analysis by Edmond Furter). There is general agreement on the identity of most of the philosophers represented, and the features of the artists used to model them (named in brackets). Some attributes reside in their ideas and writing styles, the ultimate concept art, however subconscious positioning, postures and attributes form the usual inspired college;

Taurus t2 Plato (Leonardo Da Vinci) with a book, arm up, arm down.

Taurus t1 Aeschines or Xenophon, twisted, with Socrates.

Gemini t15 ? with Alchibiades or the smiter Alexander, and Aristhenes or Xenophon or Timon.

Cancer t14 Federico 2 of Mantua, or Epicurus, and ingressed Parmenides (Leonardo?) or Heraclitus.

Leo t13 heart of Averroes.

Leo t12 Boethius or Anaximander or Empedocles; a pupil of Pythagoras.

Virgo t11 womb of Hypathia or Fornarina, also Pythagoras as initial Libra t10 in the sketch.

Libra t10 Heraclitus (Michelangelo) with a chisel, inserted.

Scorpius t9 Diogenes of Sinope.

Scorpius t8 ? bent forward, with Euclid or Archimedes (Bramante).

Galactic centre as the astronomy group, Zoroaster (Bembo), Ptolemy, Apelles, Perugino (Raphael).

Sagittarius t7 ?

Capricornus t6 ? ingressed.

Aquarius t5 t21 Plotinus (Donatello).

Aquarius t5 t20 ?

Pisces t4 Creto?

Cista Mystica as Aristotle with a book. Cista Lid at his feet.

Aries t3 an empiricist?

The perspective and design centres are between the two central figures, independent of the mindprint geometry as usual. Rafael's initial cartoon has Pythagoras as Libra t10, on the t11 axis. Heraclitus (Michelangelo) is a late addition. The ecliptic pole is on the sacrum and book of Aristotle. The galactic pole is on the elbow of Parmenides (Leonardo?). The galactic south pole is on t3's or t4's jaw. The celestial pole is on a hip of Plato (Leonardo?), the celestial south pole on a hip, dating the inspiration to Age Aries-Pisces, incidental with the end of the classical era.

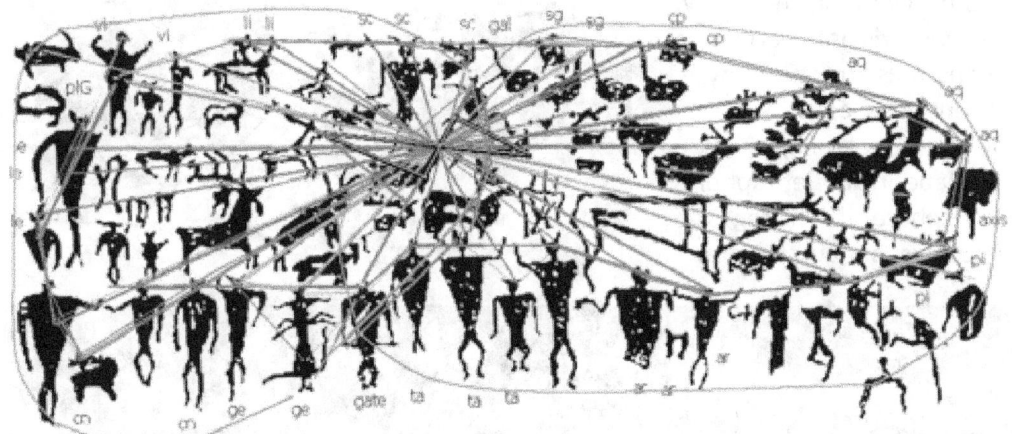

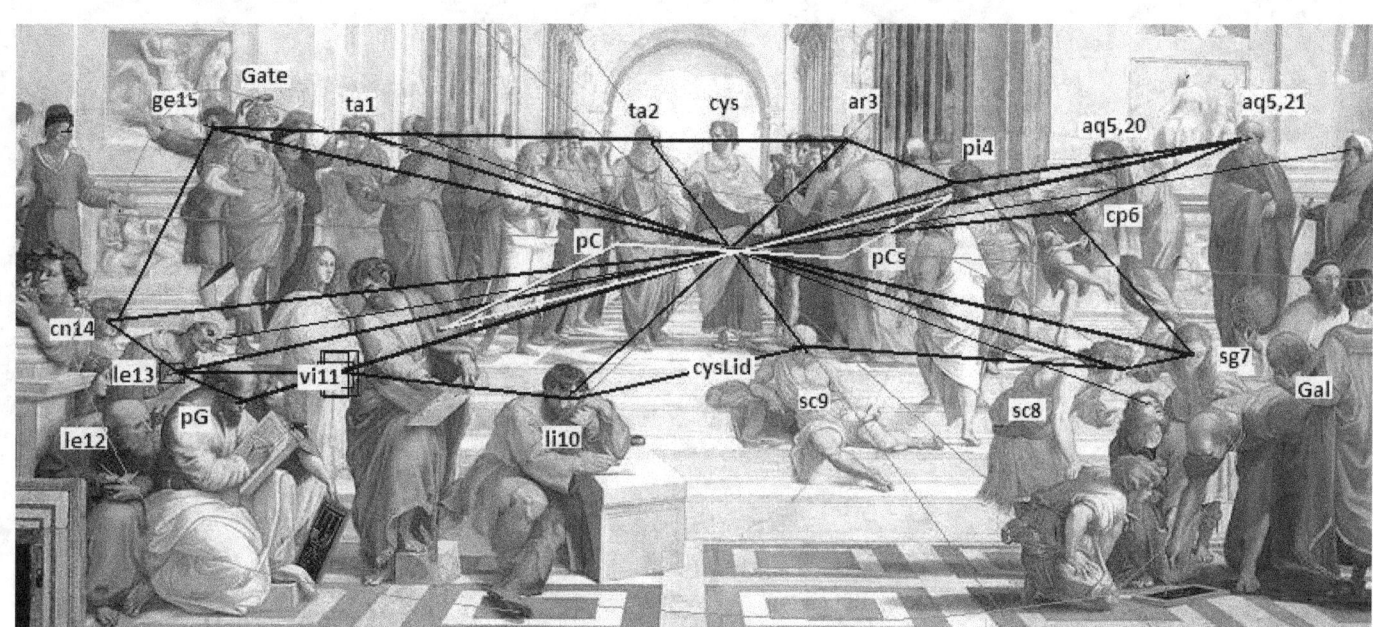

Two spheres, three paths

Type Gemini t15 as a white figure in a tight churn group, in a double imprint (Australia, Djuliri emu at a tree. Mindprint analysis by Edmond Furter). The figure is damaged and indistinct, but the position of its head is clear. Capricornus t6 is a giant emu with rearing neck, egressed away from, instead of ingressed to the centre as usual. Elongated or split canvases seem to induce double imprints, usually separated by a tree or rope (see a USA Utah image at theme t5) or cleft (see Chauvet cave, and Trois Frere cave at theme t5 t21). One of the galactic equators in each sphere is shared, as usual in double spheres touching near the Pisces-Aquarius t4-t5 polar axis, or the opposite Virgo-Leo t11-t12 polar axis. To visualise the double sphere, focus on the two irregular primary equators, which are drawn in angular, point-to-point style for clarity in this study. The language of dreams and inspired art is a compromise between subconscious structure, myth, images ready to hand, and conscious logic.

Celestial polar markers are uncertain, but a headdress and the vertical plane in the left sphere, and a hand in the right sphere, both tag the inspiration as Age Pisces-Aquarius, our current era.

A footprint person

Type Gemini t15 t0 as a footprint (USA, Nine Mile Canyon owl. Mindprint analysis by Edmond Furter). Footprints resemble multi-headed figures (see an African multi-headed hero in rock art at theme t13). The low resolution image illustrates one of the uses of mindprint to rock art research, allowing visual recognition and conceptual study of overworked, damaged or unclear images. Celestial polar markers tag the inspiration to Age Pisces late.

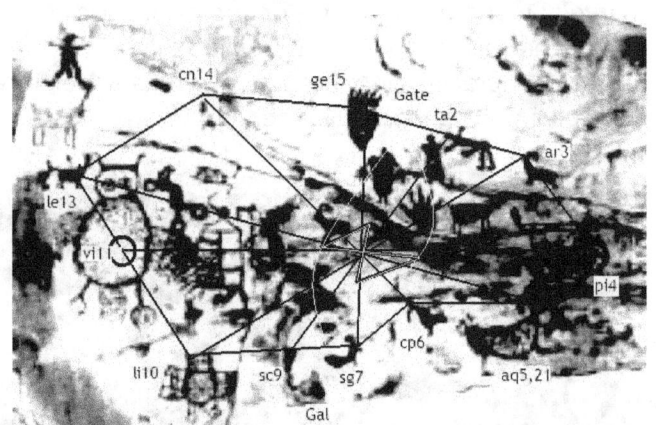

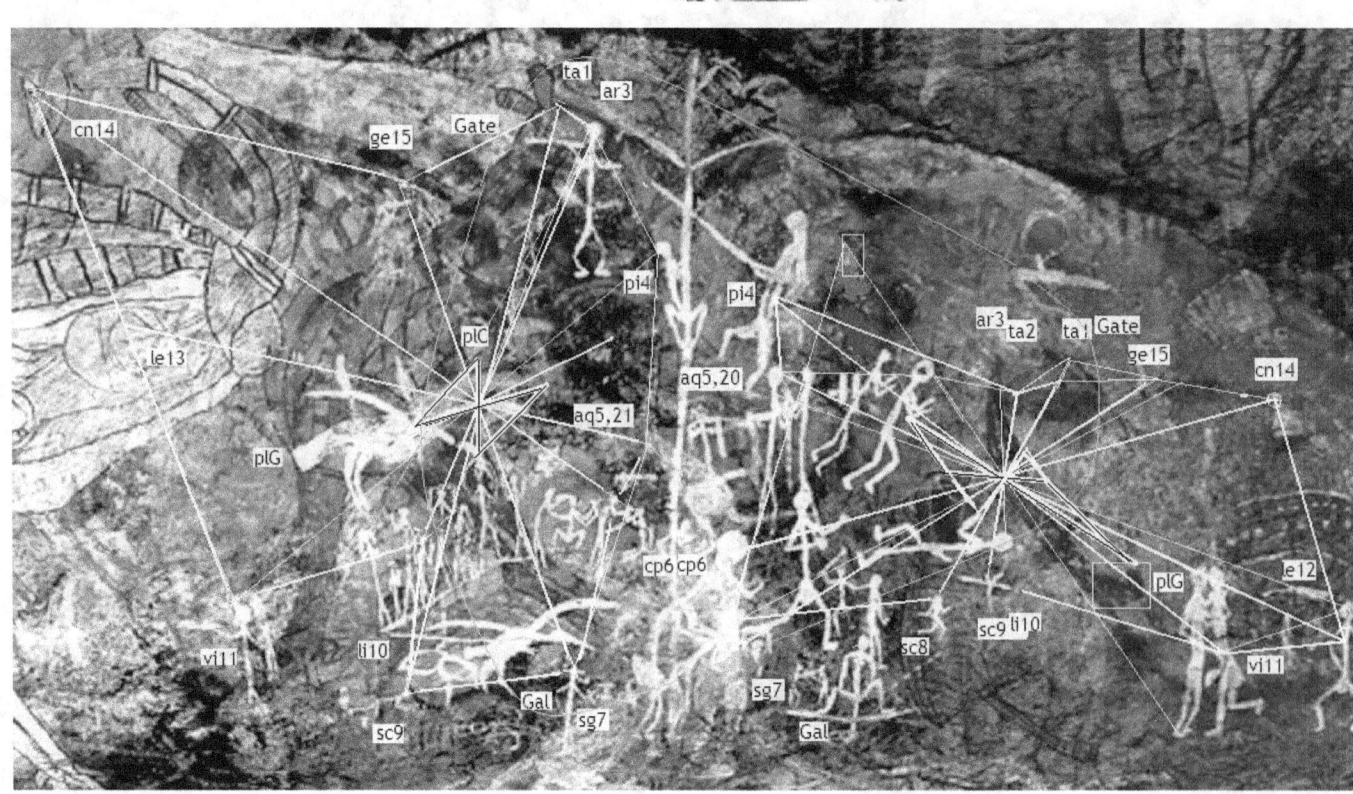

A galactic rope

Type Gemini t15 as the leader of a row of heifers tethered by a rope (Algerian Tassili milking herd. Ankhonline.com. Mindprint analysis by Edmond Furter). Gemini t15's attributes include a rope and a gate, here figured by a tether line and a U-shape used in cattle rituals (see a Saharan U-shaped gate at theme t3). The southern galactic equator (large, thin, oblique circle in the right half) follows the shoulders and rumps (hips) of most of the aligned cattle, and many limb joints in the periphery outside the figures equator. The northern galactic equator (large, thin, oblique circle on the left) follows some human limb joints below and a string of oval corrals on the left. Aries t3 t18 has a craned neck, as only two other cattle in this panel have.

Celestial poles on a rump and a rear hand, tag the inspiration to Age Pisces.

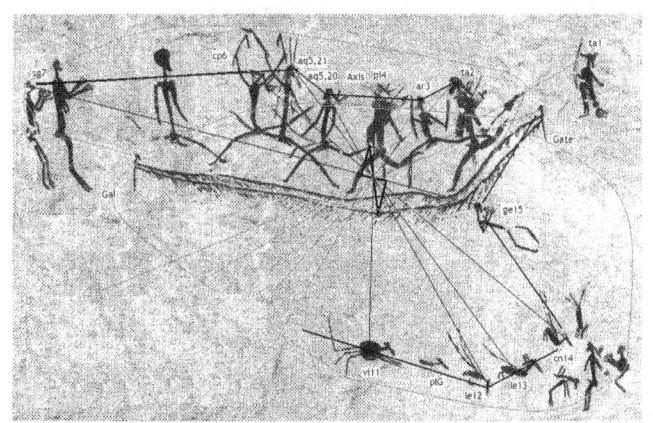

A rope bridge churn

Type Gemini t15 as a rope bridge churn holder (South Africa, Didima Gorge rope bridge. SA Archaeological Society. Mindprint analysis by Edmond Furter). Ropes express links to the supernatural and spirit world, as in Inuit Eskimo art, maintained during dream or trance. The rope bridge is a subconscious analogy to an oblique equator crossing the spherical imprint, perhaps initiating and unfolding into the imprint. Both ends are churns, operated by two rope-armed people resembling Seshat. Classical Greeks would probably identify this as a bridge to the afterlife. Spiritual power lines expressed as ropes of the sky is a stock theme in rock art around the world. The concept of a rope path is analogous to our particular view of our galaxy, and this bridge incidentally lies on one of the galactic equators. Ships, paths or other markers could express the same concept. The rope runner at left on the left, with a large head, is an example of many sickle-shaped or saddle-shaped heads in rock art, perhaps of the kind that mythologises canines and dog-headed (cynocephalus) baboons (see a saddle-shaped head in Mondrian's The Scream, set on a bridge). Capricornus t6 has two heads, as the type often does. Trance is ritualised in dance involving dehydration, hyperventilation, clapping, humming and ululating, in clan-based groups of about twenty (P Myburgh).

Celestial polar markers on a whisk (a standard item among healing equipment) and a knee, tag the inspiration as framed by the Age Pisces polar arrangement.

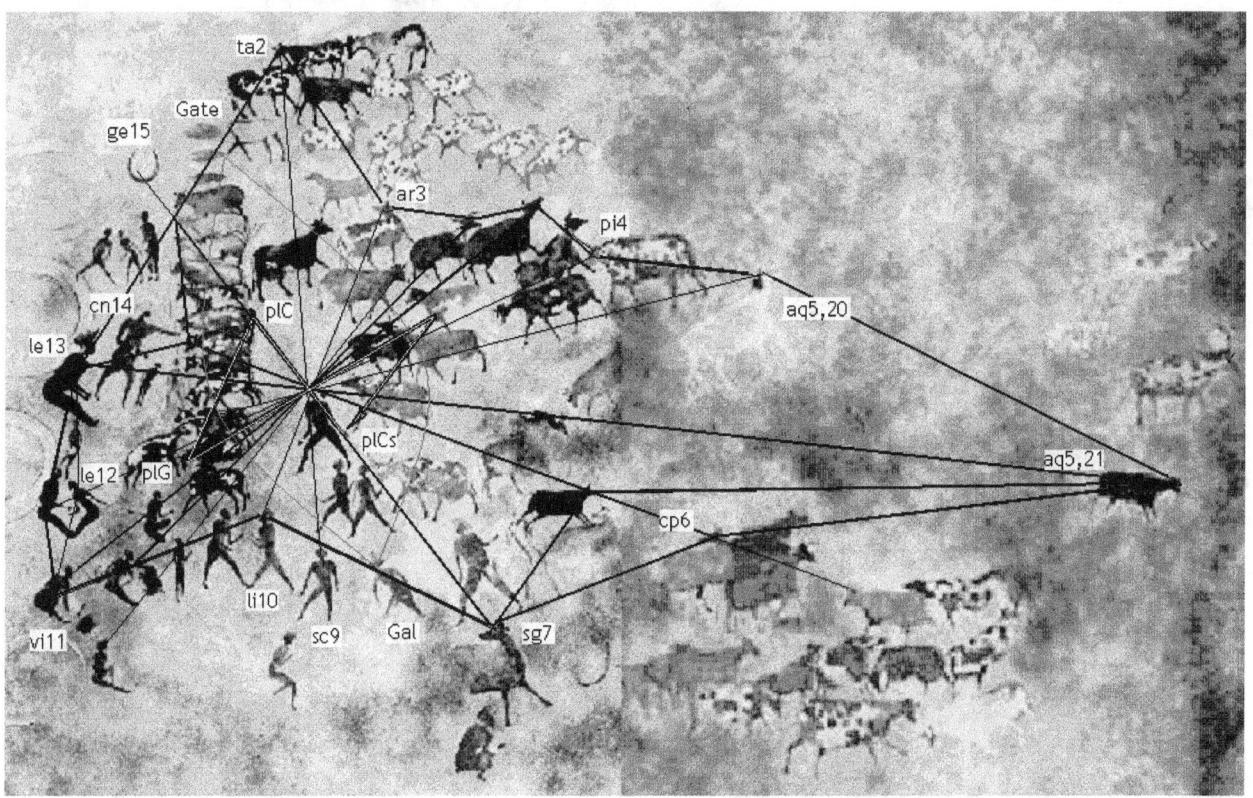

An afterlife churn

Type Gemini t15 as a rope or canal controller in afterlife fields (Egyptian duat, coffin lid inner of Dynasty 1 at Gua. Mindprint analysis by Edmond Furter). The long and winding route may be a river in the upper register, and canals in the lower. Cancer t14 Ursa Minor is a Wippet jackal on a ramp (see the Dendera round zodiac in the Decans sections). Leo t13 is a dragon boat, not marked on its heart as usual, but on eyes at both ends. Virgo t11 is the womb of a Set animal, perhaps an antbear (aardvark wild porcine) living and raising young underground. Libra t10 Lupus (Wolf) as a healer on a staff, and Scorpius t9 Lupus as a bent half man with a knife, share an axis as they share the Lupus decanal concept. Sagittarius t7 Corona has a prominent crown and tail, among its southern attributes rarely expressed, but typical of late period zodiacs. Some of these figures may have been influenced by a Hellenic zodiac, in turn influenced by Babylonia, yet only the dragon boats seem Babylonian, and the others are stock early Egyptian-styled icons. Capricornus t6 is horned and egressed, but misplaced by intrusion of the central band. Aquarius t5 is a dragon boat and animal cargo (see the Babylonian Pazuzu plaque at theme t5 t21). Pisces t4 is a kind of far-striding Pegasus. Aries t3 t18 may be a long-necked dragon, sharing an axis with Taurus t2 Auriga or Perseus as a twisted rainmaker, or canal control system. Remarkably few iconographic ambiguities or structural errors appear in duat underworld images, despite multiple versions over thousands of years, implying that artists, individually or in collaboration (as in specialised craft villages or large commissions) maintain living artistic inspiration and expression to rectify traditional and religious errors. There are no entirely identical copies, therefore each work is open to inspiration. Celestial poles on the horizontal plane tag the inspiration to Age Aries-Pisces.

Seven caves

Type Gemini t15 as four ancestors with a skull and an arm (Mexican seven caves in Mt Mashu of Hopi myth. Mindprint analysis by Edmond Furter). The skull is a kind of white face, typical of t15. The arm totem may express the concept of double-bodied, as multi-armed principles in Indian art do.

The churner on the hill in a canine skin is in the gate, between the caves of Gemini t15 and Taurus t1, thus a type of Gemini t15 Monoceros and Canis (Dog), where a churn group is often figured. The curved mountain sigil or glyph on top expresses a secure homestead with a blind entrance, as in the Egyptian hieroglyph for house. Chinese feng sui pictures a similar shape as an ideal home site. See a hill cave and gate in a Rosicrucian emblem at theme t6, and in movies such as Stargate. Cultures and scientists   perceive archetypal vision as tribal legend or history. Celestial polar markers on an elbow and a staff tag the inspiration to Age Pisces.

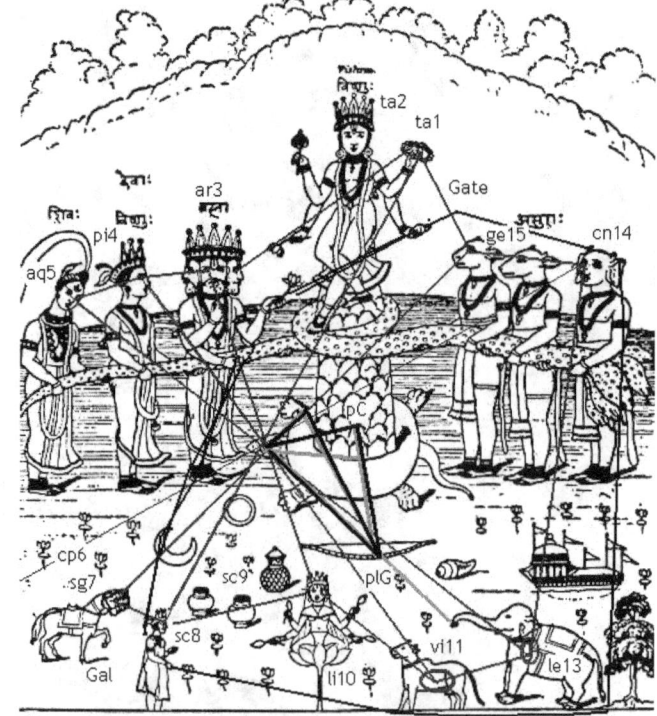

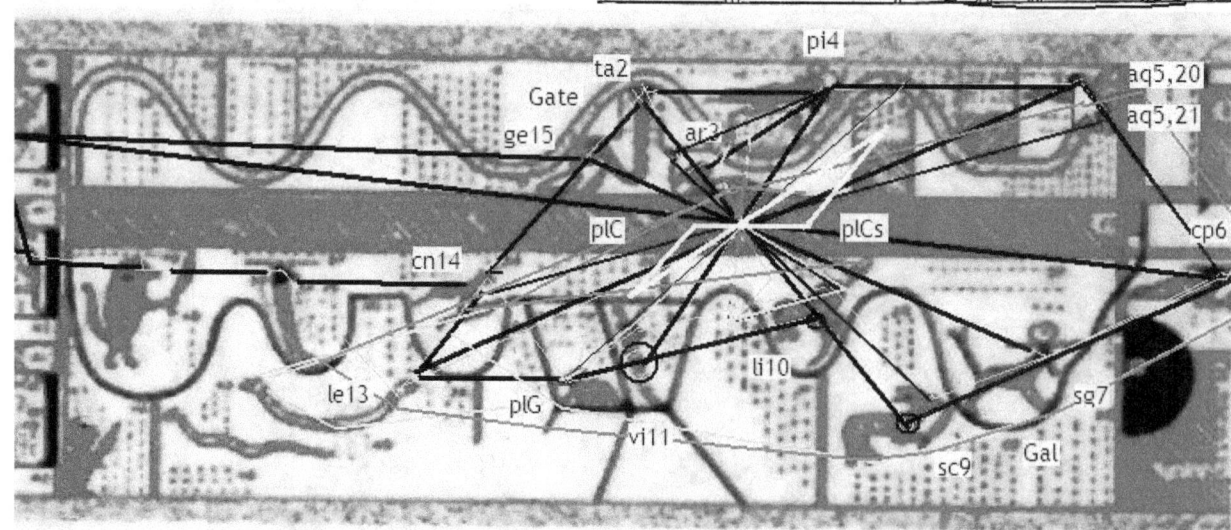

Astrology included

Type Gemini t15 as a rope churn on a turtle (Indian Vishnu pillar in the Mahabharata. De Santillana. Mindprint analysis by Edmond Furter). Gemini t15 is multi-armed and double-bodied as usual. This is one of the few illustrations cryptically included in De Santillana and Von Deschend's Hamlet's Mill, the book that launched ethnographic archaeo astronomy. They mistook myth as coded astronomy, a kind of club secret, and did not investigate the role of archetype in myth, art, artefacts, astronomy and science. De Santillana roped in this image to imply that astrology was fragile proto-science converted to folk tales. These scientific assumptions are misleading. The image demonstrates several levels and structures of spiritual inspiration, including the attribute sequence and geometric grid of mindprint as a carrier wave or matrix for human experience, perception and expression, incidental with natural structure (including astronomy). Despite many myth-astronomy correspondences, astronomers consider mythic labels as arbitrary, animistic, fanciful, primitive, or deriving from the sky and seasons. Artists have a more realistic view of astrology as spiritual expression, but many artists underestimate the extent of subconscious structure. Mindprint art is a mechanism to raise subconscious and spiritual values into the conscious realm, not to illustrate science.

Which gates

Souls switch from the ecliptic or solar path to the galactic path at its narrowest point, in the galactic gate between Taurus t2 and Gemini t15, and re-enter the round of figures in the opposite gate at the galactic centre between Scorpius t8 and Sagittarius t7. Here Greek mythographers and esotericists like Plato also placed entry points to a path to the afterlife, yet confuse it with adjacent Cancer t14, perhaps for its access to the celestial north pole (in Age Aries and perpetually in the astronomical framework), just as its opposite Capricornus t6 is ambiguous with its adjacent t7 regarding ascension. Iconographic and mythic ambiguity between the four static galactic structural points and the four moving seasonal points, persists in cosmology and archaeo astronomy. Gary A David (in Orion Zone) ascribes the confusion to copy errors, but this study finds an archetypal ambiguity. Another layer of 'street name' ambiguity awaits as the former major seasonal points exchange places at the start of Age Aquarius, with the spring point (and the celestial south pole) taking over traditional late winter, and the summer point (with its celestial north pole) taking over traditional late spring. Resolution may come from a 'new heaven and new earth' as foreseen in Revelations and other prophetic books.

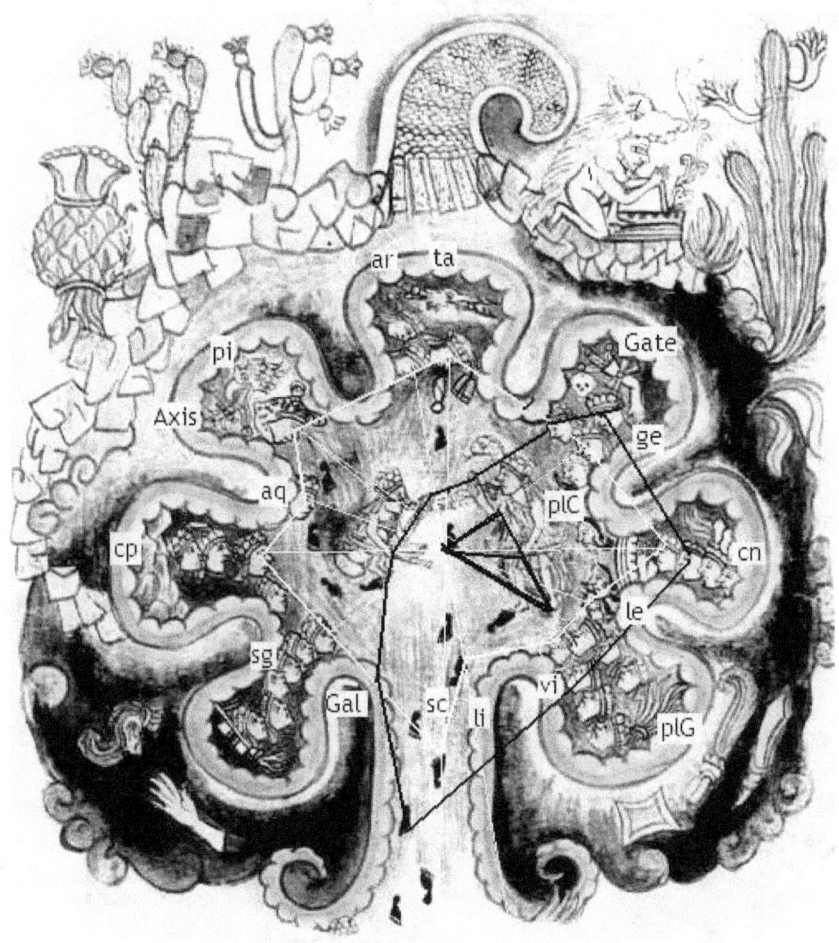

A baboon in churning

Type Gemini t15 as a baboon on the implied galactic rope (Zimbabwe, Matobo range tree pond. Elspeth Parry, Amabooks. Mindprint analysis by Edmond Furter). See Gemini t15 as a rope handler in the Seti 1 ceiling at theme t8. Artists experience inspiration primarily in a galactic framework, which also in the sky is the largest, most instantly visible and most constant feature. The galaxy is also a seasonal marker, changing its direction across the visible hemisphere by almost 90 degrees and back during the year, from (-) to (\) to (|) and back, an effect of our orbit around the sun and stellar rising times slipping by about four minutes per day. The rotation forms what some authors label a midwinter 'dying sun chariot wheel'. The baboon's thigh is prominent, touched and perhaps ripped by the Cancer t14 Lynx feline (see an Achilles shield with two heel and thigh wounds at theme t15 t0). This study presents evidence of a subconscious, non-figurative, conceptual level of expression, beyond the scope and terminology of symbolism. This overwhelming evidence refutes the popular archaeological premise of 'lost science corrupted by oral tradition'. Anthropology also suffers from an assumption of diffused, memorised and corrupted 'knowledge', while there is no evidence that oracles hinge on knowledge or on extensive teaching. Few oral traditions last longer than four generations, while oracle operations could last centuries. Even sacred books do not deal in knowledge, but in structure, cast as myth cycles and theologies, constantly renovated by visions, not by research or knowledge. Celestial polar markers on a pair of hands, and the vertical plane, tag the inspiration as Age Pisces-Aquarius, our current era.

Ropes, paths and herbs

Type Gemini t15 as ropes and herbs (South African Underberg, Amatola camp. Ditsong Agricultural Museum Willem Prinsloo. Mindprint analysis by Edmond Furter). Gemini t15 and Cancer t14 are figured only by herbs, stems, vines or ropes. Vine ropes mark some sections of both galactic equators, continuing the theme of spiritual paths. The figures are a mixed race raider band, with the usual pirate ensemble and prominent genitals (see t2 and t3, and Asian Y-people at theme t14, and USA Box Canyon raiders at theme t15). Celestial polar markers on a coat and horns, and the vertical plane, tag the inspiration as Age Pisces-Aquarius.

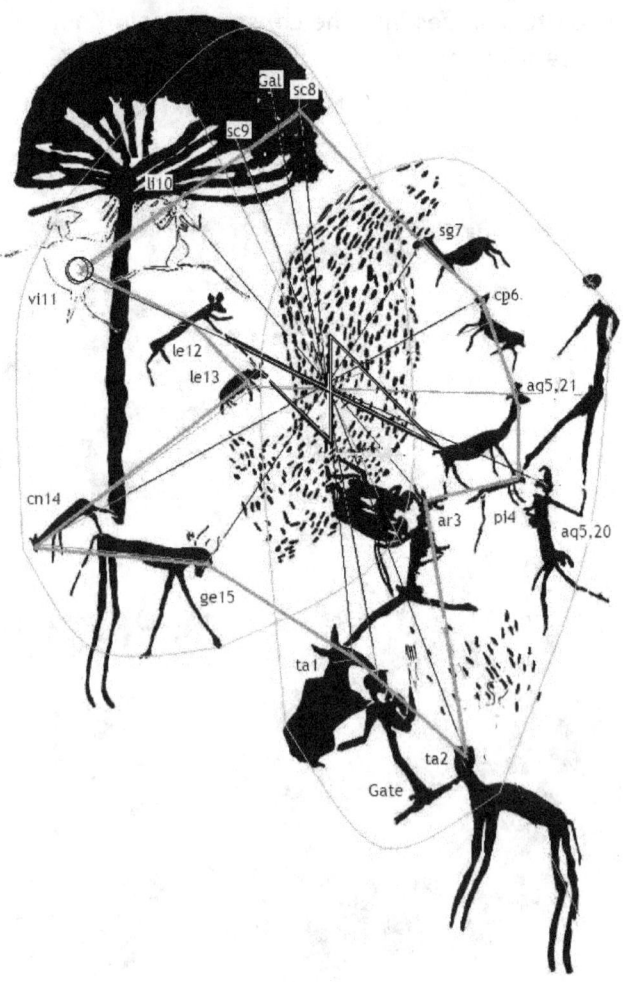

Same figures, different churn

Type Gemini t15 as a double-bodied rope churn in the sea, over crossed whales (Mandra, Kangara churn. R Storm; Legends and myths of India, Egypt, China and Japan. Hermes House. Mindprint analysis by Edmond Furter). The pillar and whales express the concept of the galactic equator. The four galactic corners often host churn groups, slightly ambiguous with Libra t10's Wheel of Fortune, which is more relevant to physical aspects of life.

Archetype does not strangle its own expression by detail, yet every inspired myth and image (and possibly melody) contains sufficient figures, characterisation and motion to express mindprint. If attributes were lacking or the sequence scrambled, or some axes unaligned, as in a bad movie, viewers would instantly know, without bothering to analyse or explain why.

A celestial polar marker on the main figure's feet tags the inspiration to Age Aries-Pisces, although the vertical plane and his hip may tag Age Pisces-Aquarius, our current era.

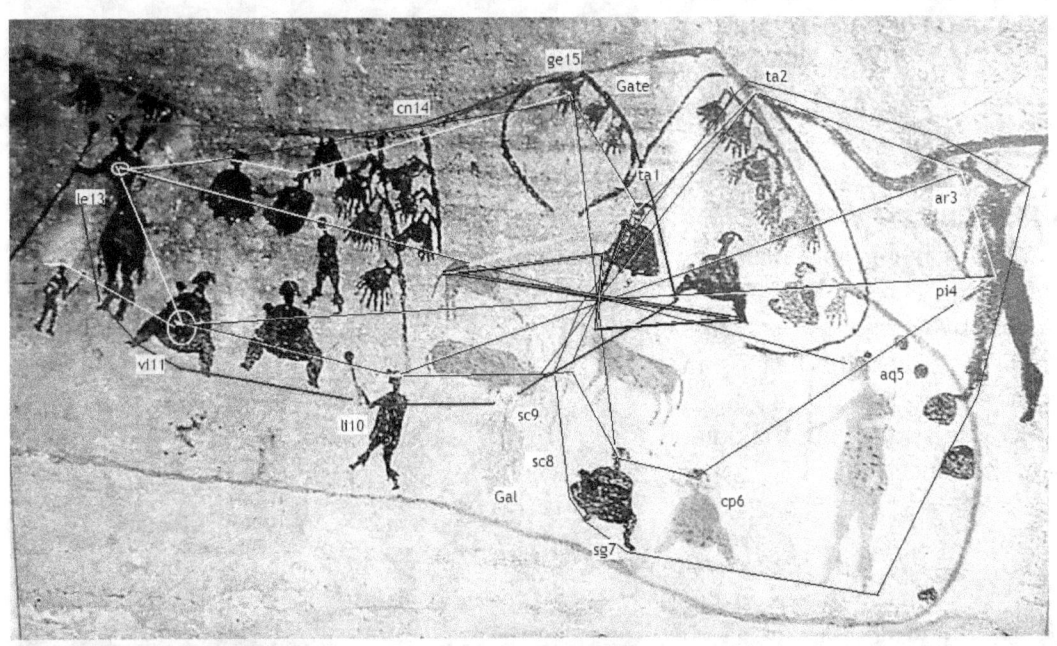

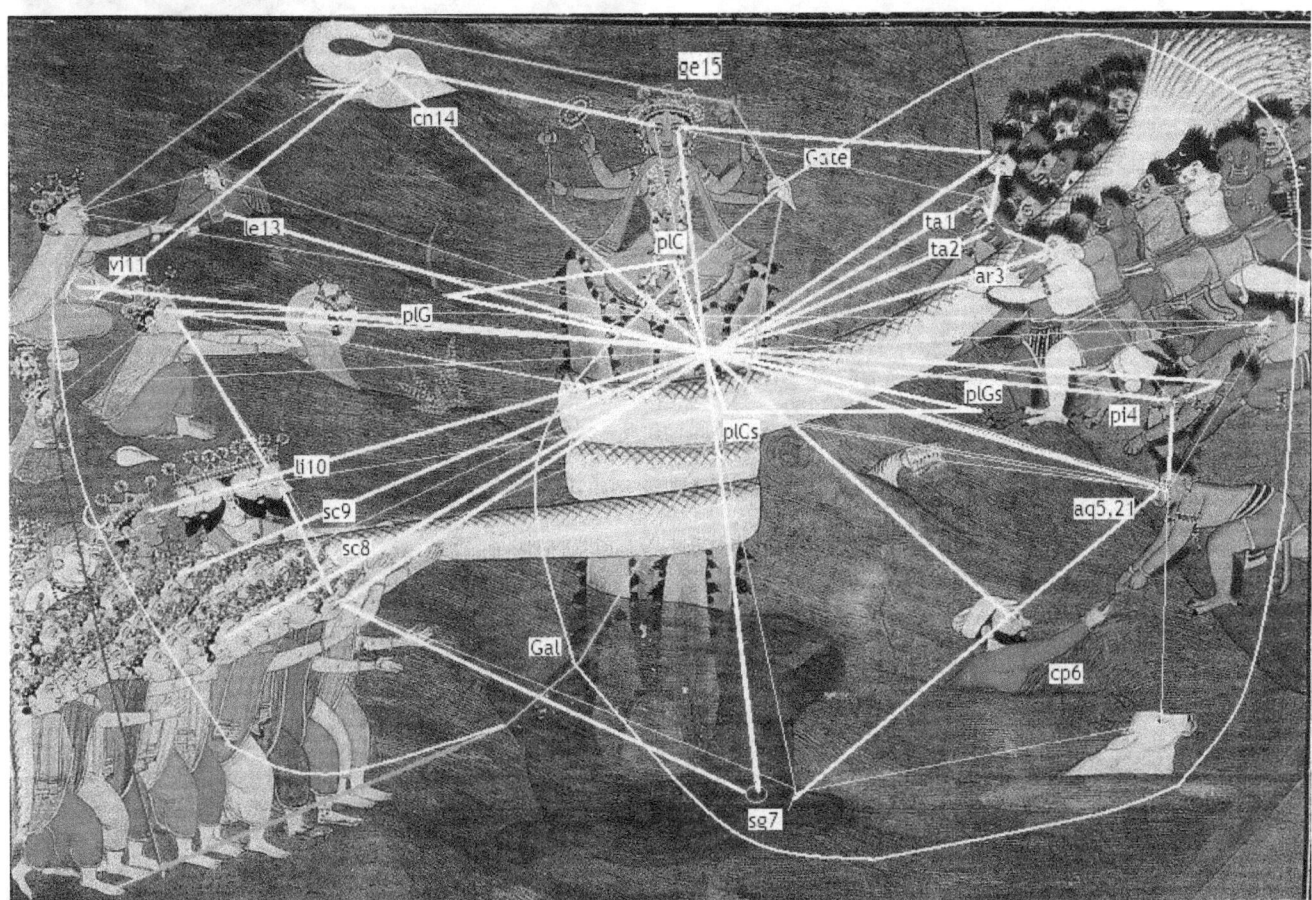

Line and texture practice

Type Gemini t15 t0 as a polar dancer (Jeanne Morgan-Lefay; Dancers. Mindprint analysis by Edmond Furter). Energy lines forming ropes express a regular Gemini t15 attribute. The style is typical of artists in training, and shows some affinity with expressionism. Similar Ice Age works were unknown to the artist. Celestial polar markers tag Age Pisces-Aquarius, our current era. Historical context and inspirational dating separate the last conventional Ice Age dating and the modern work by 5000 years, yet the sequence and geometry in both conform to the mindprint standard.

Outline practice

Type Gemini t15 t0 as a dancer and a polar tumble dancer (Sicily, Addaura line carving with dancers. Mindprint analysis by Edmond Furter). The style is typical of figure studies by artists in training. Celestial polar markers on hair, and the hair of an incomplete figure, tag the inspiration to Age Taurus 1, among the earliest tags in this study, but the polar markers are unusual and thus uncertain.

Happy legs

Type Gemini t15 as a peripheral figure, and as an extra polar figure (South Africa, Battle Cave. Origins Centre display. Mindprint analysis by Edmond Furter). The central figure carries the galactic pole in his lower hand, and celestial pole on his jaw or head on the t15 axis, thus tagging Age Pisces. His other hand recalls the earlier Age Taurus 2.

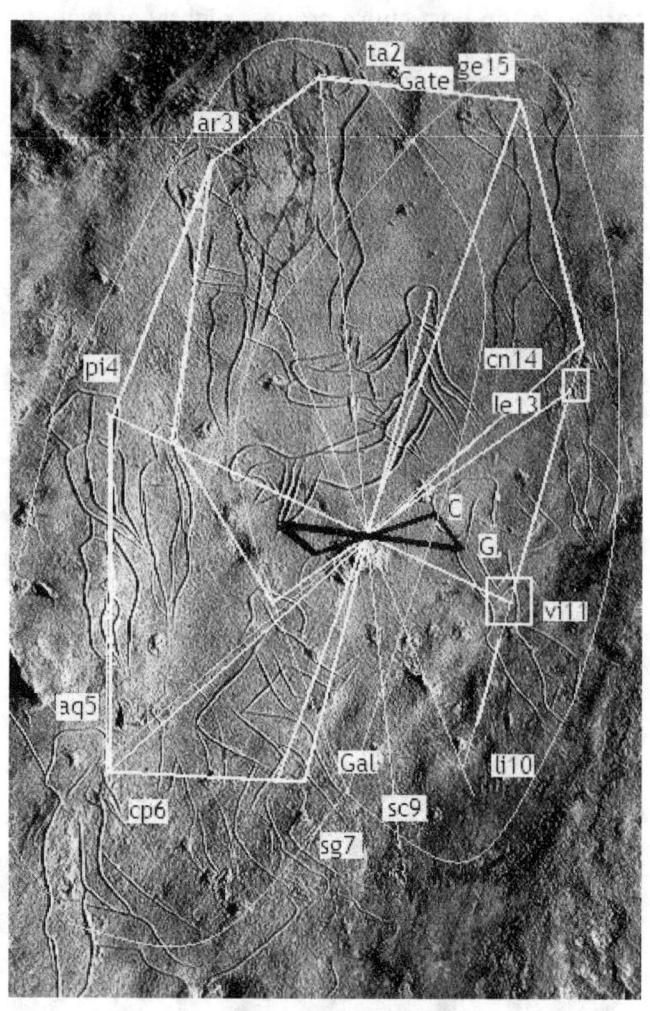

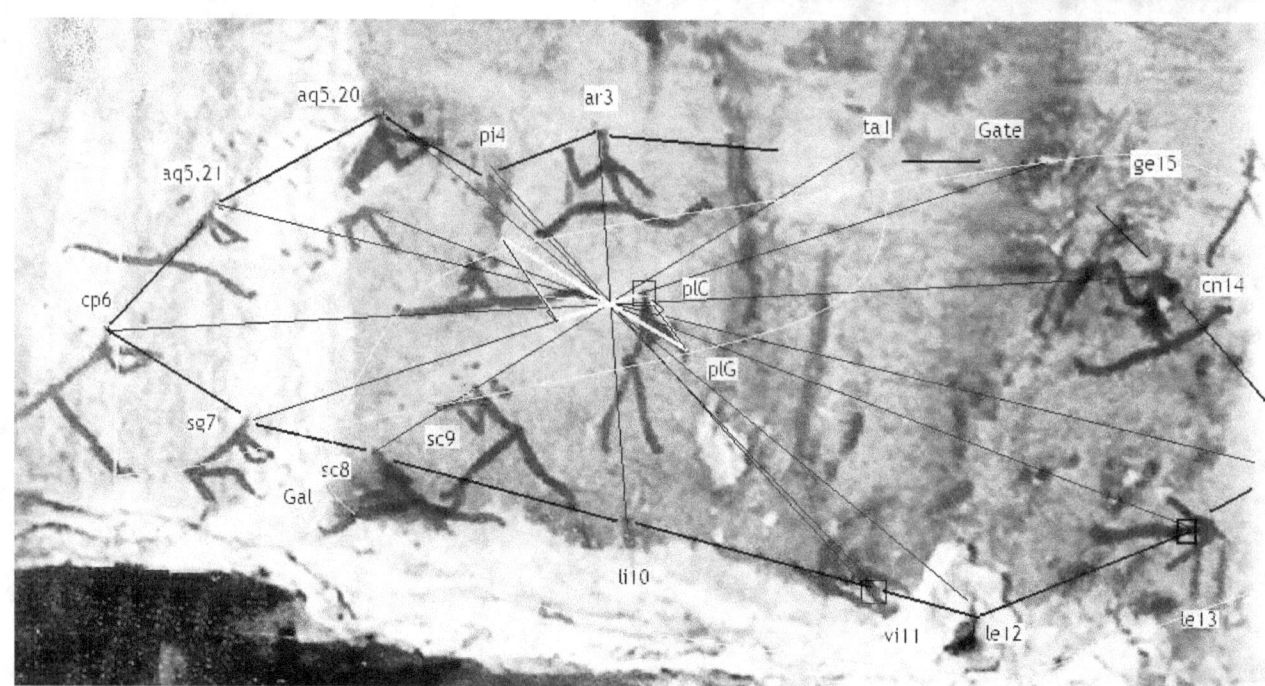

An axial Ice Age bison

Type Gemini t15 as a double-bodied bison (France, Niaux cave bison herd. Bradshaw Foundation. Unknown Europe. Mindprint analysis by Edmond Furter). The facing bison appears only as a back line, its intended head behind Taurus t2. Both heads find axial counterparts, better visible in the museum reconstruction (inset) as it probably looked before calcination (flow rock) of millennia. Alchemical emblems occasionally include two flanking bodies with one head, unrelated to t6 as one body with two heads.

Virgo t11 is pregnant and wounded, against hunting practice, hinting that the arrows may be markers of potency, or some yet unstudied concept, but not hunting rehearsal magic.

The galactic pole is on the hoof or knee of an extra Leo t12 t13 figure, and the celestial pole on its dewlap or jaw. Polar markers form one line, as the three poles formed one line in Age Gemini-Taurus. This is the only example of that axial era, '90 degrees ago', found in this study, perhaps confirming early archaeological dating of this work. The museum copy (see inset) is quite exact, except for polar features, where the delicate alignment is lost.

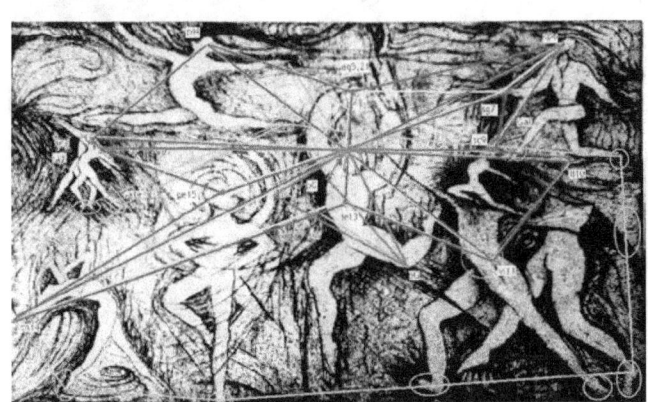

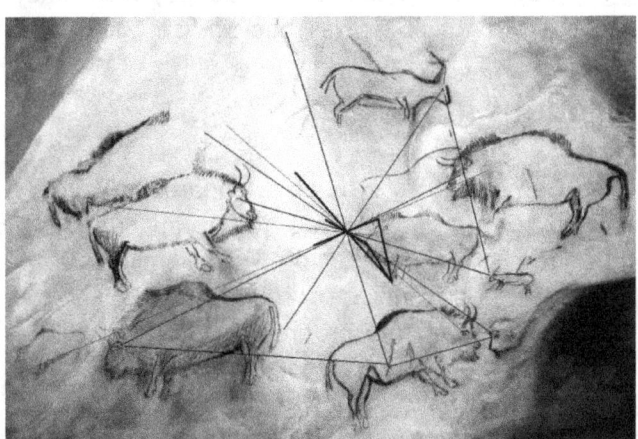

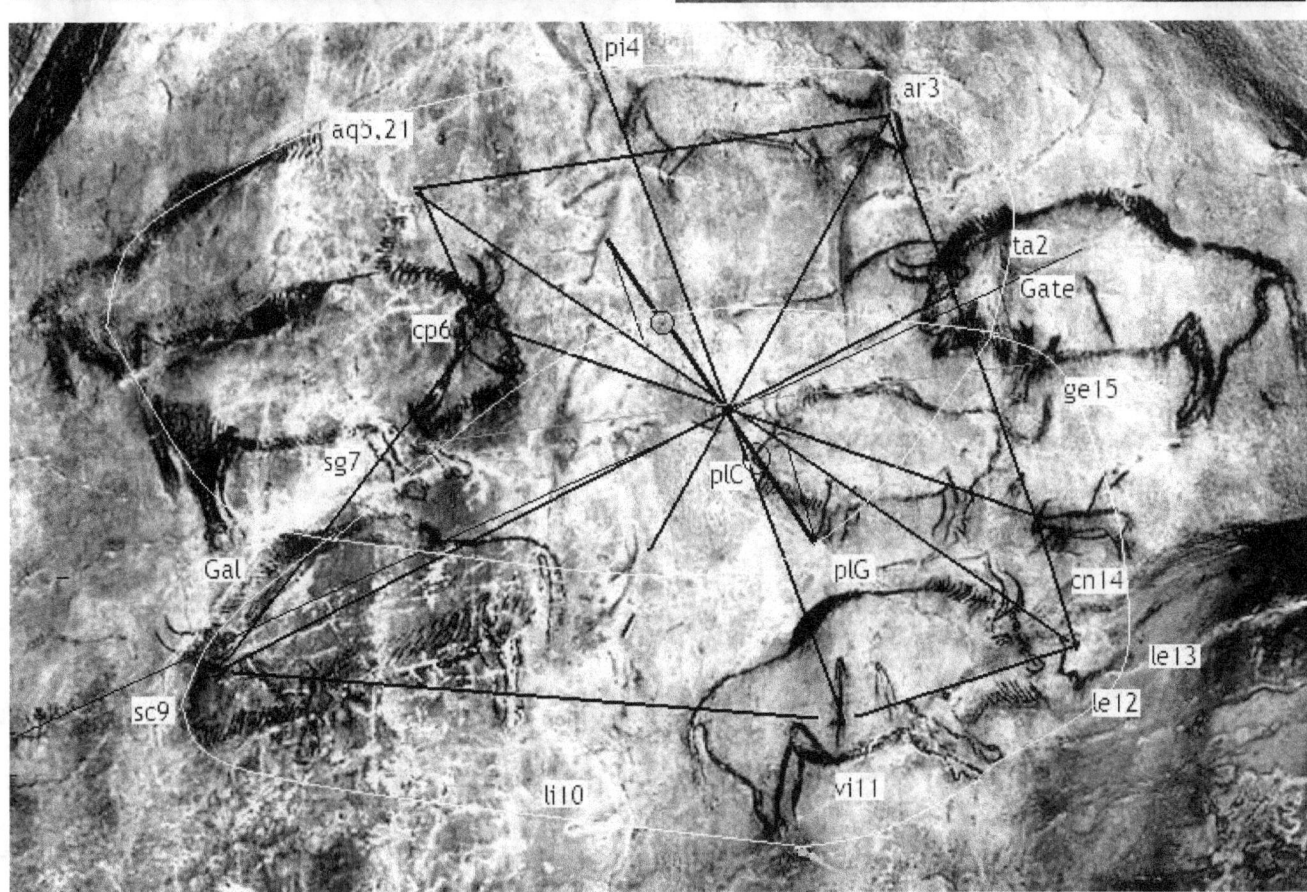

Type Gemini t15 t0;
Creator wounded

Orpheus leads an animal orchestra

Type Gemini t15 t0 as a polar donkey (Turkey, Tell Halaf relief engraving of an animal concert. Berlin Museum. Mindprint analysis by Edmond Furter). Libra t10 Lupus is a wolf. Aries t3 Andromeda or Cassiopeia is a queen enthroned, as in Tarot trump 3, Empress.
Celestial polar markers on a hand and a rump, and the vertical plane, tag the inspiration as Age Pisces-Aquarius, our current era, although other markers on a foot, or another foot and donkey front knee, provide for two earlier eras, back to Age Aries.

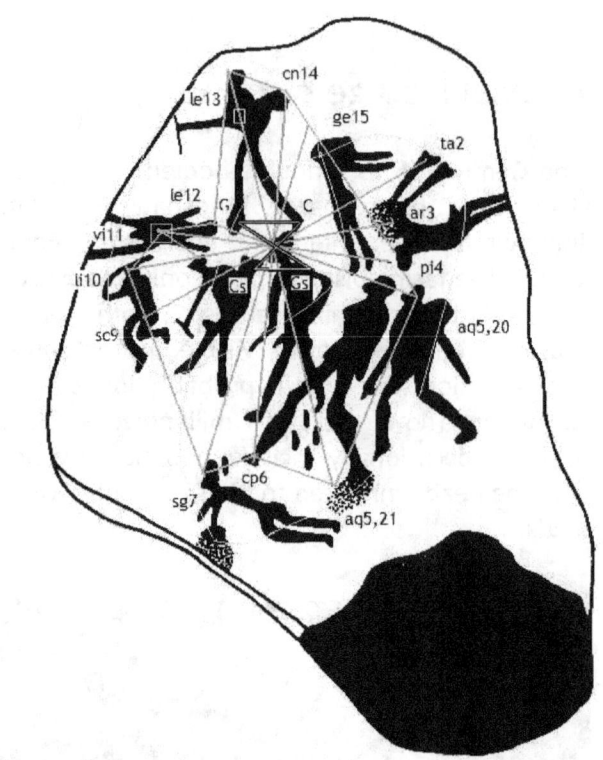

Orpheus in rock art

Type Gemini t15 t0 Lynx as a leopard (SA rock art copy by George Stow, RARI. Mindprint analysis by Edmond Furter). Some of the Gemini t15 t0 attributes are transferred to Taurus t1 (see the posture and staff of Tarot trump 0, Jester with a staff and bag, and a canine jumping to his thigh). Aries t3 t18 is a buck bag with a long neck. Aquarius t5 t20 is a duck bag. Many prominent rumps in the image extend the Gemini t15 t0 hip wound theme. Most of these figures express some of the attributes of their opposite numbers.
Celestial poles on the solar plexus and genitals of the central figure, and the vertical plane of t5 and t6, tag the inspiration to Age Pisces-Aquarius, our current era.

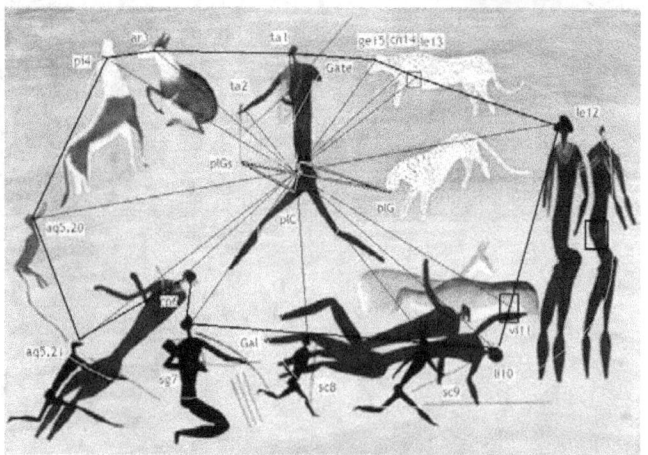

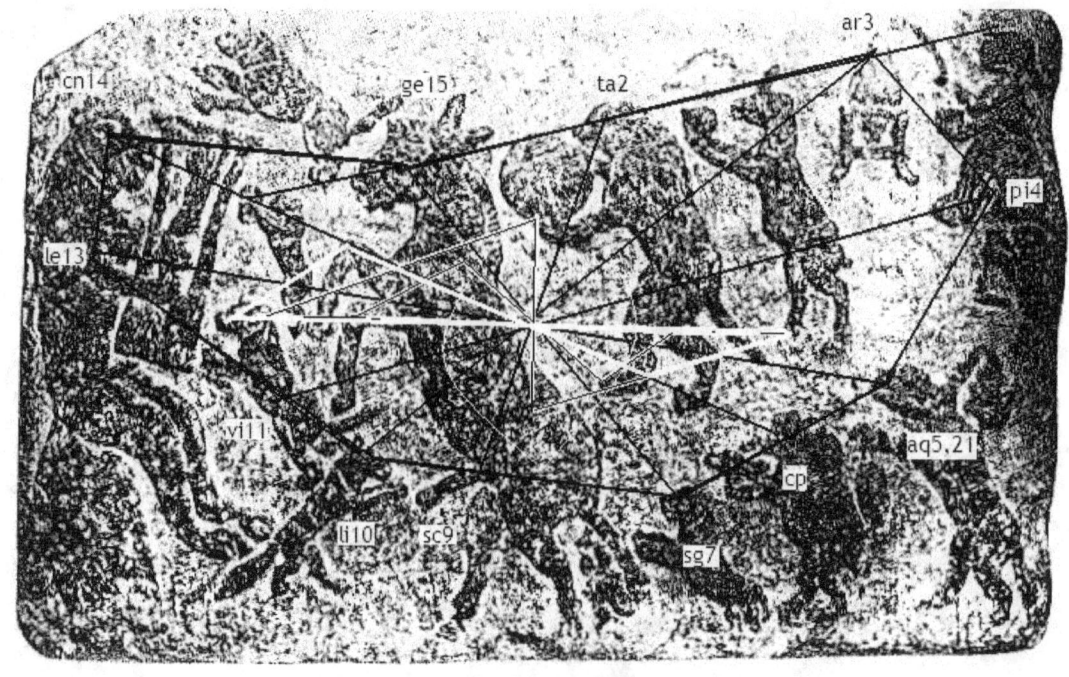

Trance ritual at a shellfish harvest

Type Gemini t15 t0 as a double-bodied figure with a backpack and rearward arms (South African palette Robberg D with flying people. SAM-2616, Lewis-Williams, 1984. SAAS Goodwin series 9, 2012. Mindprint analysis by Edmond Furter). Backpacks could be realistic artefacts of shellfish gatherers, but are also incidental with the Geminian t15 t0 bag attribute. Aries t3 t18 has long ears instead of necks. This beach palette shows a watery trance scene, a localised art tradition on the South African south coast, but also in the interior and worldwide. Celestial polar markers on a jaw and one of the vertical planes tag the inspiration as Age Aries, any time after about BC 1500, although a foot and a backpack provide tags for Age Pisces-Aquarius.

Travel bag people and rope people

Type Gemini t15 t0 as a multi-bodied bag of ropes, over a hartebeest gnu (Southern African rock art of a half-man boat copied to handmade paper by Wornell and Hallavainio. Mindprint analysis by Edmond Furter). See the boat of Ra in Egypt, and flying chariots in Indian and other art (some at theme t7).

The surreal style is a reminder that inspired art expresses dreams or healing experience. Some classical art contains comparable images, but sanitised by euphemism and realism, as all emblems are. An extra rope or snake marks the gate. The boat or soil expresses the galactic centre (see spherical and hemispherical images at theme t12 and t13). Water pools induce trance and attract legends of giant snakes and tutelary, guiding or baptising spirits such as Oannes. Such appearances are also described by Soshanguve healers at Tswaing meteorite crater near Pretoria (personal communication). Pools are anchor points for what healers experience as astral travel, and lairs from where they lure rain animals, resembling various large mammals, cows for gentle rain, or storm bulls, all containing snakes at their core (Bleek, cited in G Spiller; Origins, the films, DVD. Wits University. See an ophiotaurus with bee pirates at theme t8, and Dendera lotus bulbs at theme t2 t17). Egyptian hippopotamus Taweret and her composites are also rain animal types. Ophiotauri are revealed in this study to derive from ropes and bags, keyed to Gemini t15 t0 and the adjacent Taurus t1 t2.

A celestial polar marker on a frog, and the vertical plane, tag the inspiration as Age Aries-Pisces.

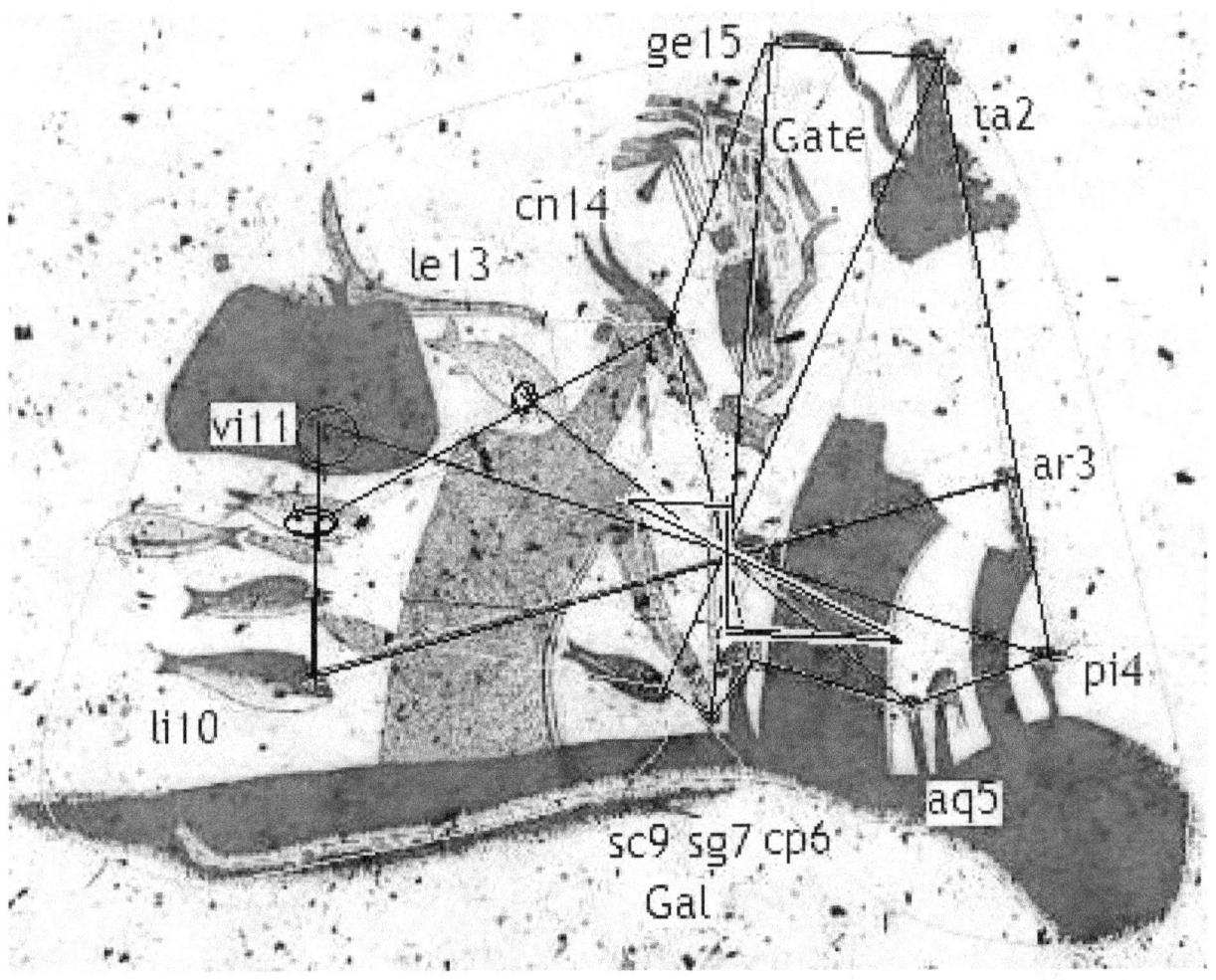

A new smiter takes over

Type Gemini t15 t0 as the scarab cartouche (roped bag) of a conquered ruler (Egyptian jewel of a Sudanese king smiting an Asiatic. Mindprint analysis by Edmond Furter). Ursa Minor scarabs and Lynx jackals are typical Cancer t14 Ursa Minor and celestial pole markers, but these two decans also lie within the concept, attributes, and ecliptic meridians of Gemini t15, which hosted the celestial pole since about BC 150. Celestial polar markers on the left cartouche infinity knot, and on an arrow flight, tag the inspiration as Age Aries-Pisces, in the last centuries BC, incidental with historic dating of the jewel. The right cartouche figures an animal and triple reed knot as Taurus t1, and a fold as Taurus t2. Aries t3 t18 is a uraeus snake. Pisces t4 is a big snake on a reed on the right, sharing an axis with Aquarius t5 as the smiting Sudanese king with his swamp (sud) and reedy home behind his heel. Aquarius t5 includes the attribute of a ruling theocracy, as in the Papacy. Pisces t4 includes the attribute of royalty, as in Tarot trump 4, Emperor. The smiter for once is not Gemini t15, but the smitten ruler is its opposite Sagittarius t7, carrying a Gemini t15 badge in a cartouche, which is a kind of roped bag. The attribute of double-bodied is expressed by the two cartouches and two rulers (see Gemini t15 as a king smiting an identical but unequal twin in the Narmer palette at theme t3 t18 and elsewhere). Stock figures do not always express the same types, and dominant figures do not always determine the major theme of the work. Cancer t14 as a Horus priest is a type of Seshat, 'drawing a chord' and marking a notched palm branch calendar, perhaps a polar and equatorial measure of eras. The king usually holds the other survey staff, here just arrow flights over a conquered ruler. Cosmic order, political order and the expression of subconscious structure is maintained by a new incumbent and his court.

Smiting horses

Type Gemini t15 t0 smiting horses and controlling poles by his hip, shoulders and hand (USA, Box Canyon horses and giant. M Mitchell. Mindprint analysis by Edmond Furter). Hip marks or wounds are common at Gemini t15 t0, expressing the concept that also appears as Canis Minor below the hip of Gemini (see Tarot trump 0, Jester). Some horses are dying or in trance, judging by nosebleed or effluent. A horseman far left, and a contra-facing horse far right, hold the polar axis from Leo t12 Ursa to Pisces-Aquarius t4-t5 Pegasus, which is a rectangular horse also in astrology. An expectation raised in the mythical iconography in this study that Age Pisces may end in horse or whale sacrifice, is borne out here. The artist had more mundane themes in mind, such as horse steak, or horses as enemy troops (Egyptians figured some enemy tribes as hippopotami and other destructive game).

The polar triangle offers a series of celestial polar markers, from the left shoulder to the right shoulder and hand, the latter tagging Age Pisces-Aquarius, confirmed in the southern polar triangle by a knee and finally a hip. The smiting hand figures Taurus t1 galactic gate as a midsummer marker.

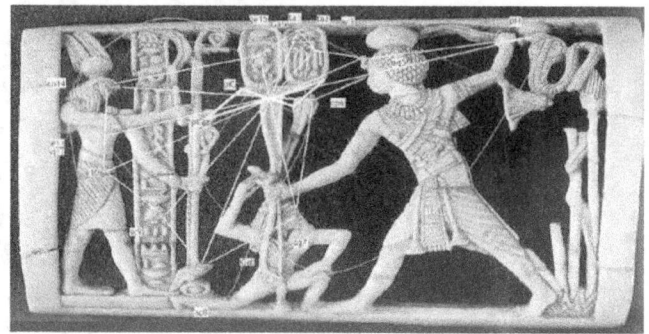

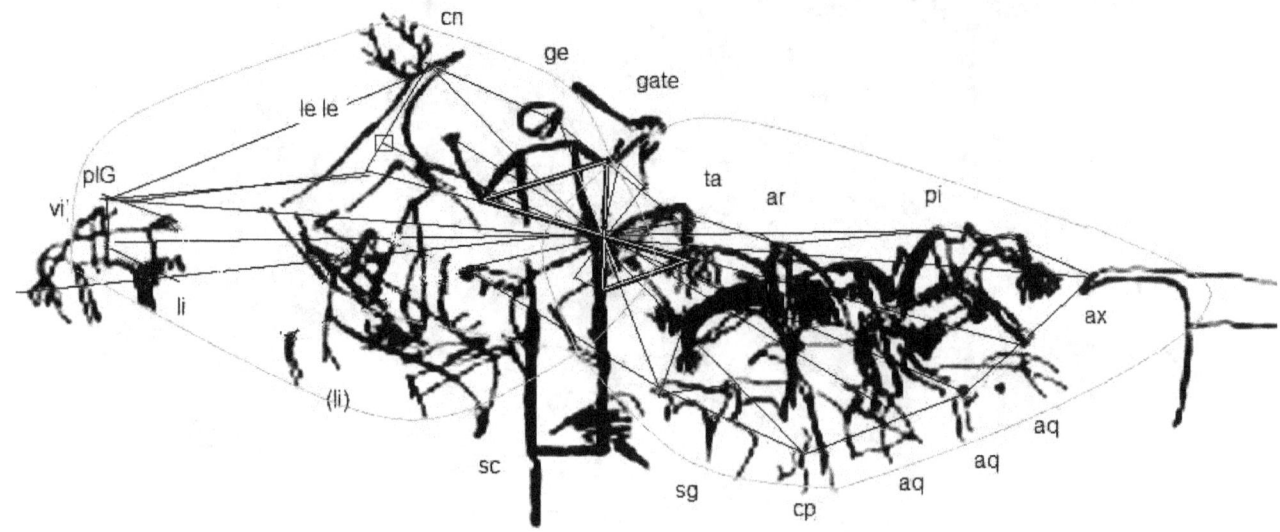

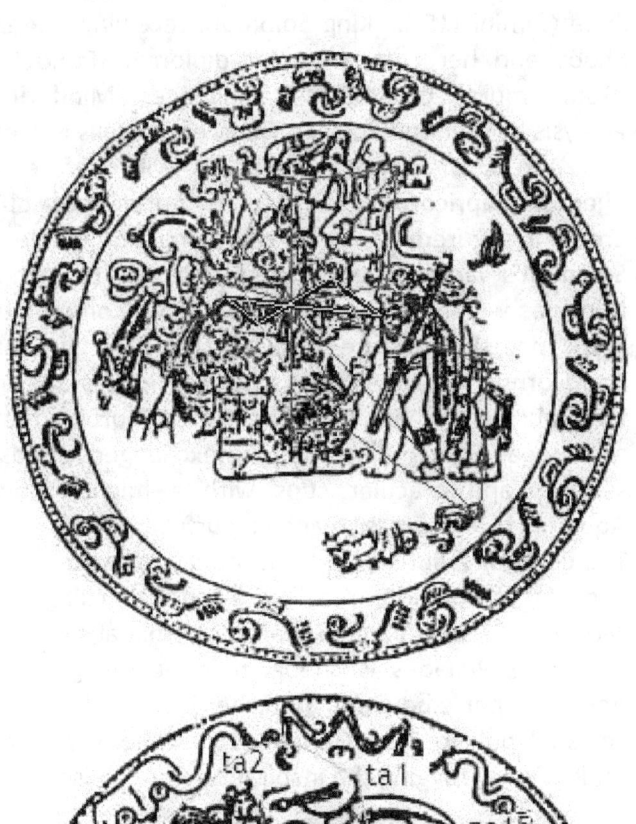

A silk road raid

Type Gemini t15 as a ruler or raider smiting from horseback (Indian Bhimbetka cave with a silk route scene. Mindprint analysis by Edmond Furter). The gestures could be a show of force, or a pirate raid on traders, who resist with bows and arrows. Gemini t15's horse is on a carpet or in a trap, its subconscious meaning linked to the attributes of ropes and a bag. Celestial polar markers and the horizontal plane tag the inspiration as Age Pisces.

An antelope mask and a smiter

Type Gemini t15 t0 as an antelope-masked warrior, and as a descending smiter, in two related mindprints (Mexico, Mayan shields. Sitchen; Lost realms. Mindprint analysis by Edmond Furter). On the left, Gemini t15 wears an antelope head, incidental with one of its attributes as a large face or head (see Tarot trump 0, Jester, with large ears). Blood from the nose is more usual at the adjacent Taurus t1 t2, and here extends over those axes. Both Gemini t15 figures are also marked near their knees, perhaps expressing the hip wound attribute. Cancer t14 and Capricornus t6 are ingressed as usual. Libra t10 is a bovine with horns in the V position, instead of its usual arms. Aquarius t5 in both spheres is marked on the heart, as their opposites at Leo t13 usually are. Aries t3 t18 is a dragon controller instead of the usual dragon. Taurus t1 is a bull with large horns. Celestial polar markers on a jaw and a hip tag the inspiration as Age Aries.

The right sphere contains several variations on an apparently legendary episode (see Narmer at theme t3 t18, and Achilles smiting Trojans in a near identical legendary shield tradition at theme t15). Ropes or plants in the margin confirm the general Geminian theme. Uncertain celestial polar markers may tag Age Aries.

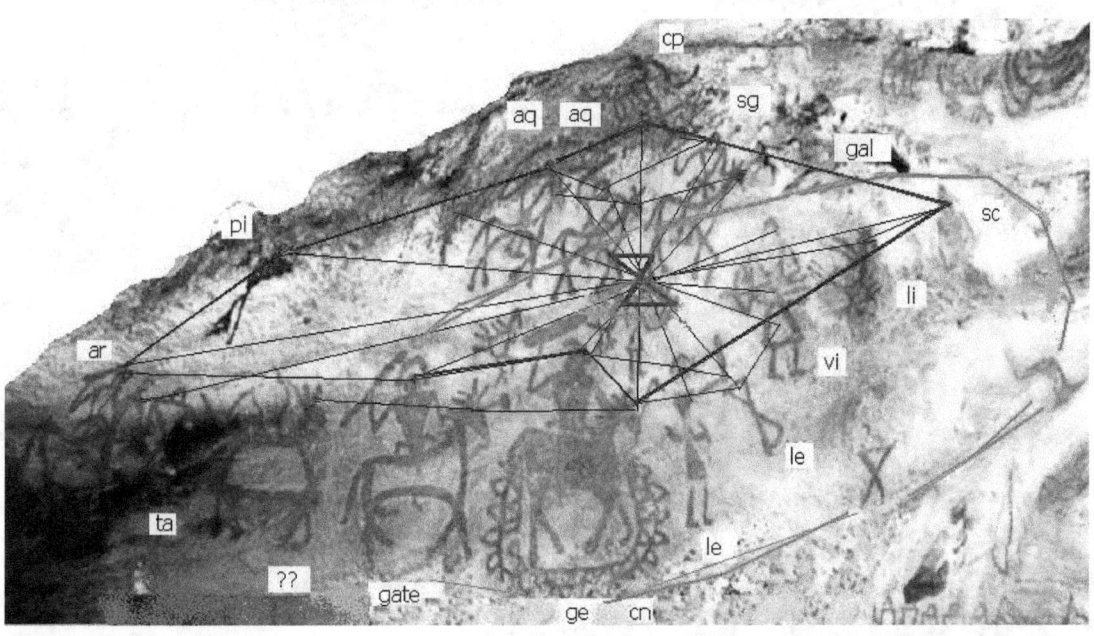

Rump wound

Type Gemini t15 t0 as genitals or a rump wound (Lesotho hunting palette. Origins Centre display. Mindprint analysis by Edmond Furter). Rump shots by poisoned arrows slow down the quarry during the chase, and do not spoil or contaminate the intestines. Myth and art seek out practical considerations that also mirror archetypal themes, but hunting finesse does not account for the prevalence of thigh wounds in Gemini t15 t0 icons in art. An academic discussion of the theme (see F Thackeray) has not broached archetypal territory, exploring the usual paradigm of cultural transmission. This study offers evidence of inspiration and nature as reliable repositories of detailed structural expression in culture. The New Testament motif of a Roman soldier spearing Christ in the thigh is not necessarily acquired from earlier cultures.

Feet, hoofs and paws complete mindprint in sparse scenes (see Poussin's Dance to the music of time at theme t6). Hunting and rainmaking is often interchangeable in art. Aquarius t5 t20 has a dappled shield and headdress, perhaps of grasses, expressing its usual painted and adorned attribute.

Celestial polar markers on a knee and a rump (marked by ritual wounding), and the vertical plane of most of the images, tag the inspiration to Age Pisces-Aquarius, our current era.

Healer Sheba and king Solomon talk

Type Gemini t15 as King Solomon, receiving queen Sheba and her companion or diplomat (Ethiopia, Aksum mural of Sheba. Travelimages. Mindprint analysis by Edmond Furter). The scene recalls Moses and Aaron, or Abraham and his wife before a Pharaoh. Capricornus t6 and its opposite Cancer t14 are not figured, a very rare omission, unless Solomon's famed mouth speaks Cancer t14 Ursa Minor as well as the celestial pole (jaws sometimes mark poles), opposite one of the rich gifts as Capricornus t6. Three hands bearing gifts stand in for figures, perhaps in subconscious proof that archetypal Sheba, like Joseph, exchanged goods, services and oracular cups with a mighty king. Aquarius t5 is expressive and colourful as usual.

The central, ecliptic pole is on the jaw of Aries t3 as Sheba's companion, recalling Aaron speaking for Moses, as Greek priests speak for pythia at oracles. Taurus t2 Pleiades is Sheba, marking the galactic pole with her elbow and staff, her jaw speaking the celestial pole on the Gemini t15 axis, our current midsummer, tagging the inspiration as Age Pisces.

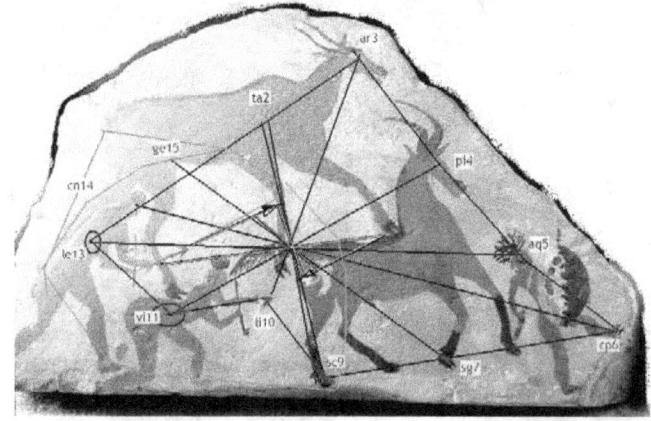

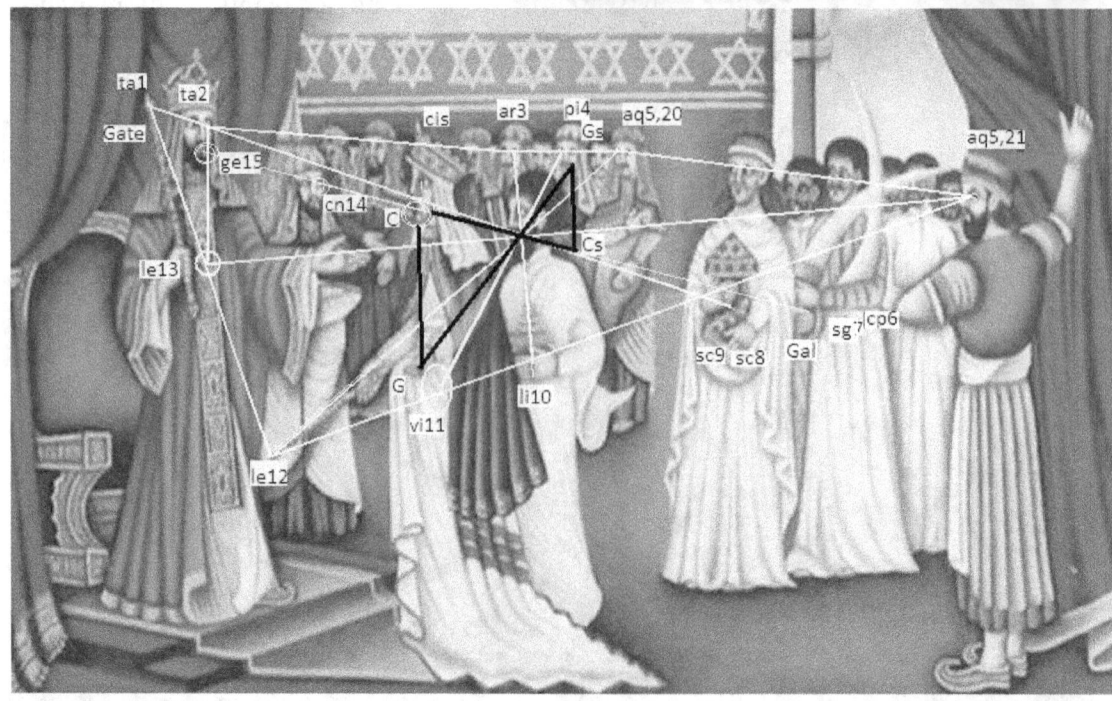

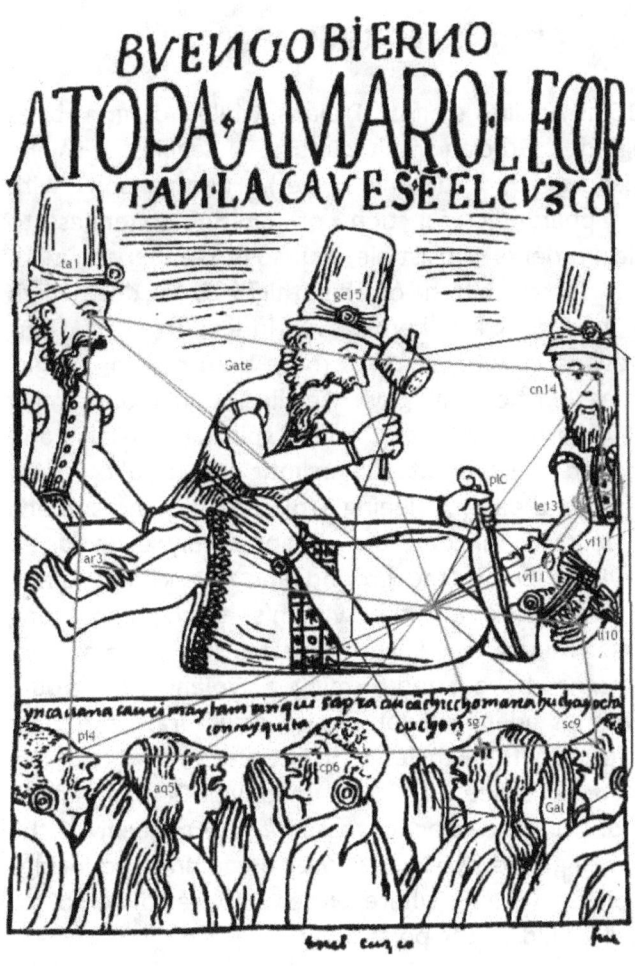

Regicide in Mexico

Type Gemini t15 smiting the captive supreme Inca (king) after his ransom, to forestall revolt (Mexican codex, conqueror Loyola executes Inca Tupac Amaro. Mindprint analysis by Edmond Furter). Virgo t11 is on a Spaniard's body, but that axis also runs through the Inca's eye. The ecliptic pole is on the king's heart, the galactic poles on his jaw and elbow, thus he remains a central icon even in the memory of his infamous defeat, as subconsciously expressed by the Inca artist. A celestial polar marker on Loyola's knife hand tags the inspiration as Age Aries-Pisces, incidental with the theme of a passing era marked by sacrifice.

Christian smiters

Type Gemini t15 as a crusader smiting and binding prisoners for beheading (French illumination of English King Richard's massacre of Acre. Mindprint analysis by Edmond Furter). Richard the Lion Heart is not at Leo t13, but his dappled opposite at Aquarius t5 t21, incidental with his flamboyant character. Sagittarius t7 as a row of victims recalls the Egyptian Narmer palette (see theme t3 t18), perhaps a semi-conscious allegory for a tally of seasons, campaigns, enemies or fallen comrades. Celestial polar markers on a knee and a foot, tag the inspiration as Age Aries-Pisces or Age Pisces, incidental with the themes of regime change, revenge and battle sacrifice.

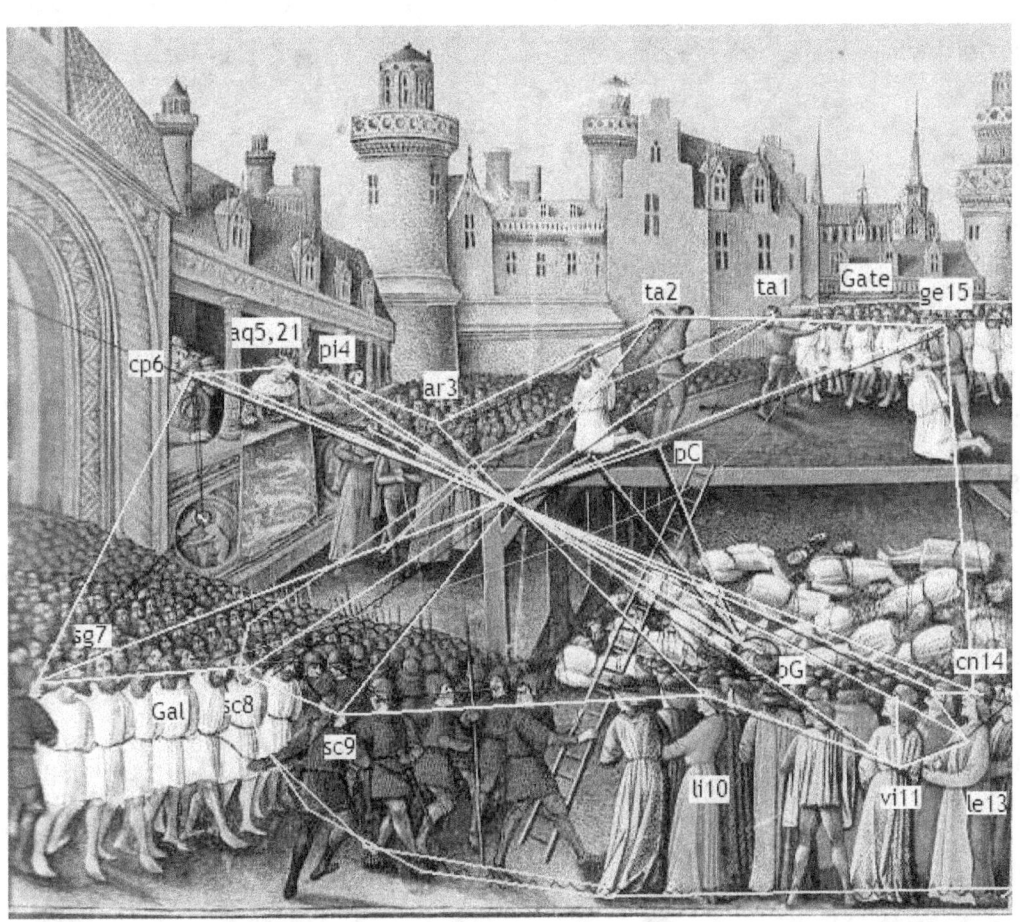

A bag face flagstone

Type Gemini t15 t0 as a vacant space in the equator, displaced to the centre as a frontal face (Persian Sassanian bowl, theatric tragedy after Sileus, 600s. Hermitage Museum. Mindprint analysis by Edmond Furter). A white face, as a kind of human bag, is one of the attributes of t15. Most artistic styles show faces in profile, with one eye visible, thus a frontal face may express the attribute of double-bodied. Gemini hosts the celestial pole in the current era (for the last 2160 years). Its face on the bowl base makes it a southern celestial pole in the concept of Octans (Octagon), or a flagstone below the feet of equatorial figures who are oriented north by archetypal expression and by convention. Northern circumpolar types such as Ursae (Bears, of foreleg shapes), Draco (Dragon or S-shape), and Cepheus (Sea monster or a king of pentagonal shape), are more regular capstones, likewise monstrous and semi-geometric. Roman drain covers often featured faces of Neptune or Ocean, expressing the unknown parts of the conceptual universe, incidental with the part of the sky invisible to northern cultures. The same mythical landscape applies to southern hemisphere cultures, since both polar areas are represented in the subconscious, mythical and artistic realm.

Cancer t14 is also not figured, raising the possibility that it is also represented on the base. T14 and t15 share the attributes and decan of Ursa Minor and the celestial pole. Celestial polar markers on two feet, and the vertical plane of the large legs of Leo t12, tag the inspiration to Age Aries, assuming the triangular shape as Capricornus t6.

Achilles the smiter is wounded

Type Gemini t15 as Achilles smiting Trojans, while a dragon bites his heel (Megiddo, Grecian multi-culture, Achilles' shield. Mindprint analysis by Edmond Furter). Comparison with the Egyptian pharaonic function of smiting enemies to maintain political order is irresistible, but so is comparison with Tarot trump 0, Jester, bitten on his thigh by a dog. Thigh wounding is a stock rock art theme, even in Ice Age art. This archetype in every culture involves more than hunting magic, war magic, or a slapstick 'fall guy'. Achilles, Christ and many other heroes share physical and spiritual trial and wounding. A bound prisoner at the ecliptic pole (axial crossing) adds the usual rope theme. A fleeing Trojan figures the smiter's twin. Given political history, the escapee may even be a brother of the victor. Below the ground line is a canine biting a prisoner, its rear paw on the victim's thigh, expressing a type of Ursa Minor, Lynx and celestial pole combined, doubling the theme above it and forming a Trojan churn group. The shield's themes adapt subconscious structural elements of the Achilles myth. Achilles' front foot is on the unmarked galactic axis (see the Cosmic map with Gemini's front foot, Tejat Prior, on the galactic crossing). The concept of the infant Achilles being held by his heel over a cauldron, co-incides with Leo t12 Crater (Grail), where either Leo retro, Virgo, or both dip the Horus child on the polar axis.

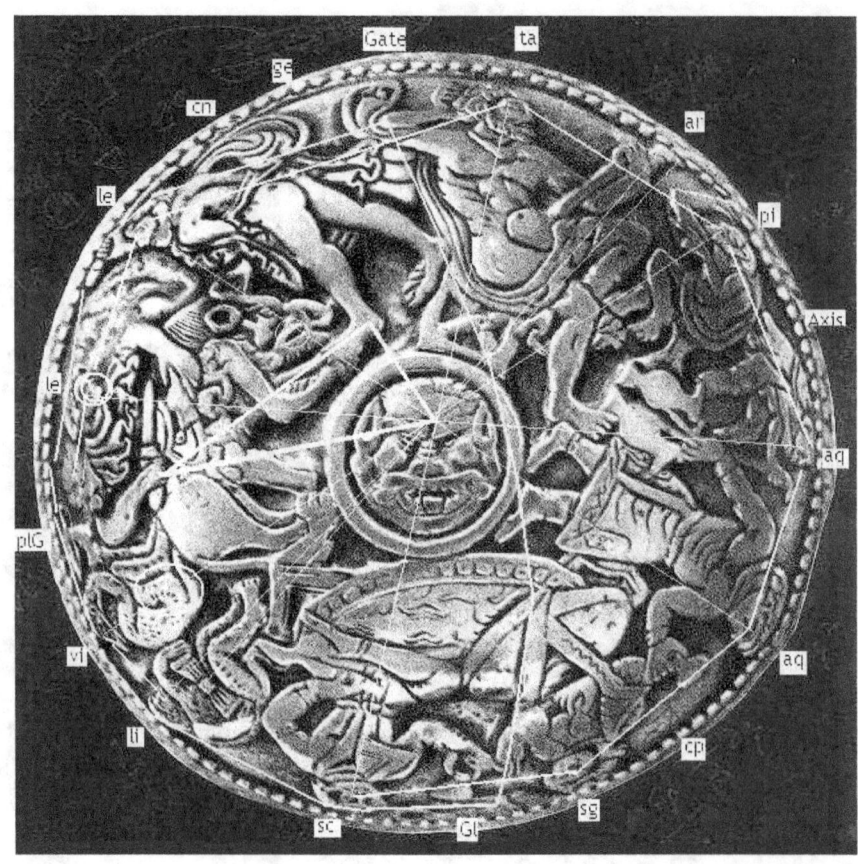

Hills at Sagittarius t7 and Capricornus t6 are similar to Babylonian creation myth hills, a Rosicrucian caved hill at theme t6, a Mexican caved hill at theme t15. The baseline at Aries t3 or Taurus t2 is a turtle, hut or basket (see a cysta mystica in a Roman sarcophagus at theme t11).

Celestial polar markers on Achilles' hip and a horse rump, on the first of two t15-t7 axes (last in precessional terms), tag the inspiration to Age Pisces late, incidental with the work.

Concept and myth remain prior to legend, art and astronomy, and unknowable archetype is prior to all. These figures and episodes would not be on any star map, nor in legend or art, if there were no archetype, collective subconscious, or natural expressions of universal structure.

Homer had good material in the works of lesser poets, but he may as well have worked form hearsay alone. Cultures apply selective memory and stock archetypal structure to legendise already archetypal events. Attributes originate from, and are maintained by archetype, despite obvious Egyptian influence in some stylistic elements (but see similar shields in Mexico at theme t15 t0).

Art is a hologram of infinitely varied faces, on par with the heroes, gates, caves and halls of popular myth, hidden in plain sight, locked behind the self-imposed human paradigms of what history, myth, astronomy, archetypes and art should be. Art does not play by the rules imposed on it by art history or popular imagination.

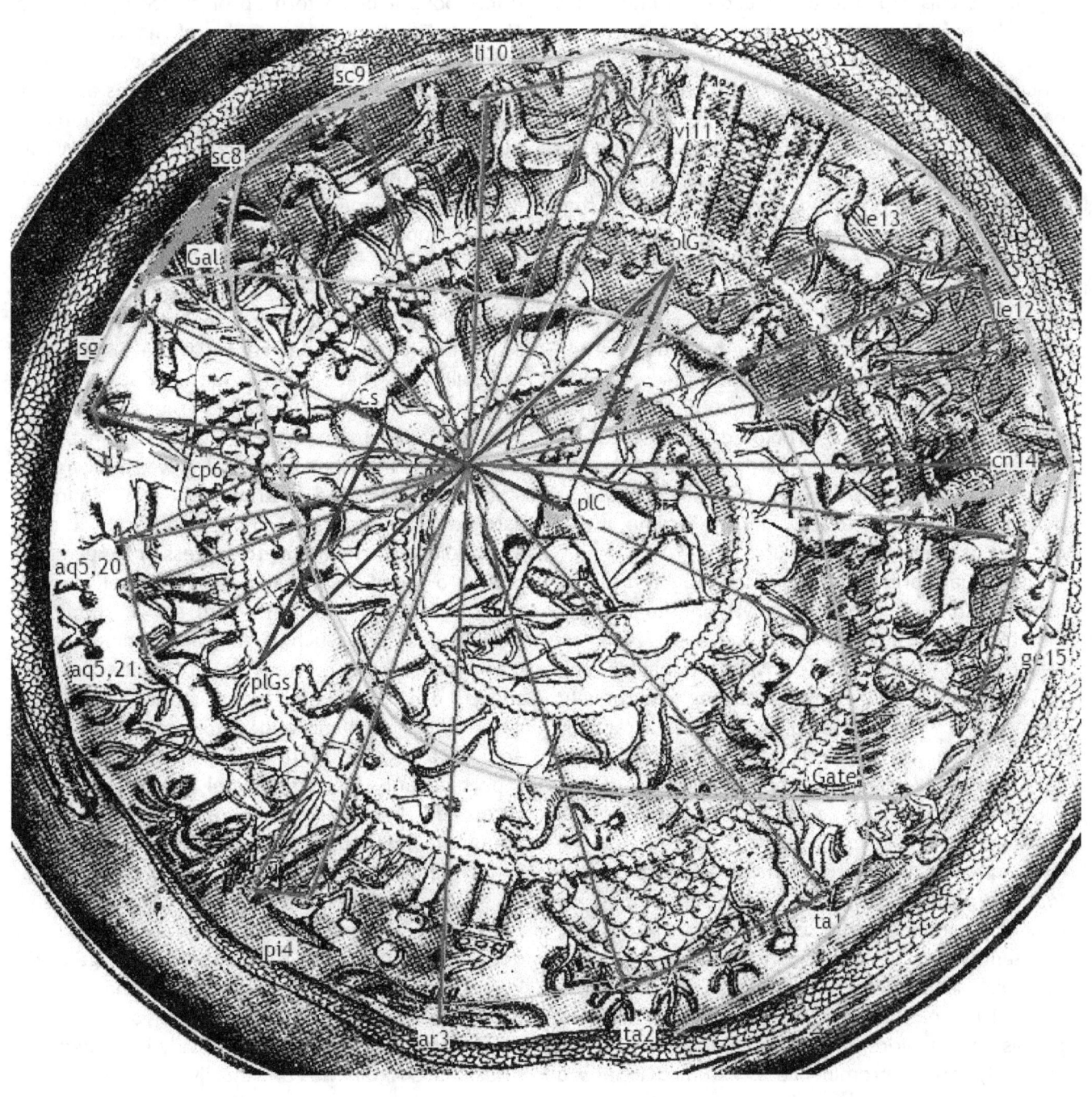

How mindprint was discovered

Postscript

Themes, moods, rhythms, styles and fads in poetry and lyrics could each be reduced to a distinctive format among a limited range of modes or 'grooves', and compared across a gulf of millennia to identify the character of the inspiration. So it seemed to a literature student raised on Homer and Jethro Tull.

"We should study poem cycles for their mythic structures, and study writing techniques only for how they support thematic structure," I announced to a poetry lecturer, who suggested that I should study philosophy or psychology instead.

My next thesis explored the structure of phonemes (speech sounds) and the limits of meaning as revealed by their artistic use in what I took to be lyrical 'modes', bent to similar structural rules as parts of speech. Each phoneme's pronunciation and perception is influenced by the succession it occurs within. We perceive the distribution and succession as a whole, a kind of auditory speed-reading that support some meanings and obscure others. The grammar lecturer replied that I should consider studying anthropology instead.

From a combination of Freudian psychology and myth, including Fraser's apparently fragmented Golden Bough, emerged vague but persistent impressions that some elements of the human psyche and culture were structured, compulsive and somewhat mechanistic, but partly subconscious and expressing spiritual logic beyond conscious definition. Jung I had to read in my own time, it was not part of the psychology course.

An eventual career in journalism taught me that living myth and legend, or myth in the making, dictates which news, history and even technical magazine content would sell. No story is as difficult to write and to read as one containing new thought patterns or new assumptions. News gradually revealed itself as the sceptic's definition of history; a set of fictions we agree to tell one another.

Archaeology Society field trips and aerial photography flips over extensive kraal (cattle corral) cities in South Africa offered me a visual framework for interpreting cultural artefacts as shaped by individual and collective economy (paths of least resistance), using ready physical material and symbolic spacing. Culture seemed also to 'write itself'. The idea that visual art express stock themes, just as poems, lyrics, phonemes, huts and music do, gradually rose to prominence as I studied supposed astronomical artefacts, to find archetypes instead. Zulu healer and artist Credo Mutwa's plaques (wooden palettes), panels and murals often include swallow nests and high-rise buildings, swifts in half-human shape, bridges over water and a vortex in the sky, such as a falling tower or falling street lamp-post. The half-human birds are what archaeologists label 'swift people' (see theme t1 t16), but archaeological literature fails to address the rest of the ensemble, or visual 'mode', resembling predictions of the 9/11 2001 New York terror attack. An alchemical emblem by Basil Valentine of the 1300s (see t1 t16) contains the same elements that I had linked to swift people in rock art, in Mutwa's art, and in Tarot trump 16 (Tower struck by lightning), several years before the iconic event of November 2001. Valentine's alchemical emblem shows a high-rise city, on an island across a bridge, on fire, with a tract above it being torn up or struck by lightning. The medieval caption speaks of national pride, meddling in foreign affairs and mixed messages coming home to roost, in the same terms and tone used by critics of former USA president George W Bush. Illustrations to the modern tale of the Wizard of Oz, with the related theme of a towering city and a yellow brick road, and the synonymous song by Bernie Tauplin and Elton John, closely fit the type or mode. Lyrics to Yellow brick road ("When are you gonna come down, when are you going to land... I bet that'll shoot down your plane") below an image of the fallen World Trade centre, came as a shock of recognition to Theosophists and the informal class of aspirant archaeo astronomers that I taught. I gradually came to understand that the subject of my short course in archaeo astronomy was a misnomer, since it revealed structures in supposed astronomical artefacts that do not require archaeology or astronomy to express or to read.

If the Tower of Babel had a type number (such as t16), and came with a standard set of supporting icons and themes, such as language, diplomacy and trade tracts, then other icons in art, rock art, poetry, supposed prophecy and even historic events could carry similar heraldic and emblematic markers. If archetypal events tend to be well recorded and reported, and less archetypal events selectively recorded, then visual art could reveal a visual grammar, and in turn crack the archetypal code.

While following this approach in research, I chanced on an image of the Lamb of God (Agnus Dei) in a Papal seal imprint in ash-laden wax, posed as a query in an archaeological magazine (Voyage of the Planet, now defunct). I recognised the image from a Babylonian cylinder seal and the Egyptian Narmer palette that I had already tentatively identified with Aries. Since Agnus was universally known in Judaeo-

Christian iconography as well as astrology, it offered an anchor point for the underlying structure of myth. The Lamb of God also appears in alchemical emblems and Tarot trump 18 (Moon), anchoring a camouflaged sequence of correspondences, affinities, or 'tacking' between several esoteric sets. Conventional logic that tagged the Tarot's crayfish to Cancer had to be wrong. The creature had to be Cetus or its tail, expressing the concept of a Kraken-type sea monster, the scaly component of a dragon, by definition a composite beast. Conventional astrology that cast Aries as a ram and ram only, had to be wrong.

Yet another clue to the sequence of types emerged from my own archaeo astronomy course material; a music DVD interview with rock icon Ian Anderson, genius of the band Jethro Tull, explaining how he eventually discovered that his chromatic, lilting, riffed music and one-legged stance resembled Krishna and Kokopelli (Jethro Tull, Living with the past, Eagle Vision DVD). Anderson does not mention Pan, but I already had his number from mythology, since Capricornus 'tacked' to Trump 6 (Lovers) in the Tarot deck.

Combining these and other anchor points and filling in the gaps, I cracked the sequence of attributes that populate myth, alchemy, art, astrology and Tarot trumps. The little list (actually a semi-spiral with four expandable parts) soon became a lens with which to read rock art, which emerged as identical to myth and schooled art in inspiration, compulsion and structure, across the gulf of millennia and continents.

Art history and archaeology are prone to exaggerating diffusion and conventions, despite examples of independent development of similar pantheons, rituals, pyramids, temples, monuments and the entire repertoire of culture in the Americas and elsewhere.

All have characters near identical to Perseus, Hercules and the rest, and modes similar to the ode, the sonnet, the gloria, the blues and the epic. The concept of cultural elements as idiosyncratic developments, prompted and 'framed' by learning, had to be wrong.

Comparing ancient Egyptian rock art and Egyptian formal (dynastic) art with Zimbabwean rock art, allowed a series of breakthroughs beyond the broadest thesis or imagination of my earlier research in lyrics, speech sounds and emblems. Many figures include standard attributes in implicit elements such as a staff, a long or craned neck, certain postures, relatively larger or smaller size, pregnancy, position relative to the approximate centre, species, attire, skin paint, status or apparent social function. The frequent distinctive attributes appear in the periphery, in a standard sequence, and as axial opposites, which in turn reveal the standard geometric structure. The more I tested, the simpler the sequence and structure became to identify. If academia was right, archetypes should be scattered at random in art, and every region or culture should have a unique set of figures, and display different stages of development in different eras. Yet artists all sing the same hymn to an archetypal tune, over the same set of polar 'chords'.

If art history was right, there should be no axial structure in art. Iconographic analysis of large political art panels at Wits University (see T'Kama Adamastor at theme t3 t18), Brenthurst Library (see Leonard French's Bridge at theme t1 t16), and the Voortrekker Monument (see Hennie Potgieter's marble friezes at theme t12) confirmed the same 'rock art sequence' in schooled art. Only some stylistic elements differ. Learned artists, and supposedly primitive rock artists whose visionary figurative and geometric engravings I had puzzled over on field trips, share subconscious recourse to archetypal structure.

The universal structure also appears in myth and wisdom literature.

A deceptively simple little list of seasonal evening stars in the Mishnah confirmed astrology as just another layer or medium, and not the origin of structure (see the Literature section).

From years of searching for a 'unified field theory' in esoteric literature, I knew that lists appeared in hundreds of guises, but were nowhere reduced to a universal set, except in the stereotype of astrology, but without the 'rounded' haloes of meanings that I had found in emblems and art.

When I had casually asked sculptor Danie de Jager about geometric ratios in art, he explained that artists had "geometry built in". To find these 'built-in' structures on a larger scale, I developed a template from what I had thought at first to be a re-construction of a 'Babylonian' division of the cosmos and constellations, keyed to galactic features, mythic figures of various relative sizes and extent, as well as star lore. Once I understood this structure as archetypal, not an 'oral tradition', legacy or secret source, but re-invented by every culture, and innately understood by artists, viewers, healers and patients, it became obvious that the sequence and geometric structure were part and parcel of perception. Most artists do not study astronomy, and would have to invest some months of conscious effort to become familiar with the sky. Yet the innate structure of perception, as revealed in artistic expression, could be super-imposed on a cosmogram or star map, or on any sufficiently complex natural or cultural set. I systematically super-imposed astrological, alchemical, emblematic, mythic and conceptual elements on the sequence revealed by my affinitive 'tacking', then on a multi-cultural armillary projection of the sky developed for an educational installation in a theme park (not yet built). I tested the sequence and its structure on rock art, then on famous artworks, then on amateur art.

The structure hinges on the eyes of each figure (or in frontal faces on the eyes nearest to the geometric focal point), and on axes to the eyes of each opposite but complementary pair of types (with two constant exceptions; a heart and a womb, corresponding to type Leo t13 and type Virgo t11). These axes always cross in one point.

One of the first rock art works to confirm the test in all its complexity was a group of goat people (half human figures) in Turkey, in a small shelter at Mount Latmos near Ephesus. Perhaps it was an informal oracle site, or just the haunt of an inspired goatherd that may have been a candidate for a temporary appointment at one of the earlier 'Amazonian' oracles, or the later formal temples. Perhaps by an aristocrat ordained for religious service as a Vestal virgin or priest, or a poet such as Aesop. As I compared the 'primitive' figures to sophisticated, ritualised, formulaic, programmatic art depicting Artemis and her goats, it became clear that the elaborate oracular rock art of the Matobo range in Zimbabwe was no different in impulse, core content, structure, impact or style. Panel after panel of rock art reproductions (particularly in the book by Elspeth Parry), as well as a range of works by classical and modern masters, chosen for their apparent differences, cracked under the lens of what I eventually named mindprint.

Another strand in the braid of archetypal expression came from the order of painting. Archaeologists carefully label strata, often paper thin, as they dig down, leaving portions they name 'witness sections' stuck with an array of flagged pins to re-check their dig reports and subsequent seasons or other sites against.

This method, named the Harris matrix, they also apply to rock painting, useful where many figures partially overlay one another (assuming that each figure is completed in a separate episode). The method reveals likely episodes of painting, typically grouping three, four, five or six figures into three, four or five episodes. Comparison of a meticulous academic paper on stratigraphy in a Drakensberg rock art work, to mindprint analysis of the same work, revealed that the artist had painted pairs of opposite figures together. This may not apply to all artists (see stratigraphy problems in the 'Three Magi' rock art scene at theme t13), but the cloth of evidence was woven to demonstrate the collective subconscious inspiration, or at least expression in practice. The evidence awaited only a statistical test, which added the final strand to the art code. Despite my habitual reluctance for quantitative grammar, the test and results 'wrote themselves', and revealed some visual and structural qualities that the new conceptual sequential and geometrical lenses did not initially detect visually.

This study traces the structure in visual expression back to the invisible structure of inspiration and perception, and thus to the structure of nature, as far as we could know her, ultimately to archetype which existed before creation and time. Breaking through the layers of disguise and distraction that protect our conscious logic from subconscious logic, required following thousands of trails in a forest of scientific and esoteric mazes, locking out dead ends, and returning to unexplored turns.

The reputed skill of artists in translating inspiration into visual form, as a tool of individual spiritual transformation, is confirmed. Our conscious and scientific views of art, perception and ultimately identity, have to recognise that we are essentially re-creators of archetypal structure.

Since the sequence and structure of visual types were sufficiently demonstrated, as repeated and repeatable, it stood as an artefact requiring a theory, no longer a theory supported by artefacts. Relevant sciences, arts and crafts will probably find their own explanations for mindprint.

This book was written twice, first as 200 captions to art and rock art images, to demonstrate how artists express eternal archetypes in a mixture of consciously understood and subconscious, universal esoteric terms, then as a research report. Together, the images and text place mindprint, our involuntary art code, in context with archaeology, anthropology, mythology, philosophy, psychology, art history and popular culture.

The two spheres of this book, theoretical and practical, hopefully enable conscious access to the vast array of subconscious meanings in art, in acclaimed individual works and seemingly different cultures.

The three sides of the artistic, esoteric and scientific divide meet here on their own terms. Mindprint leads several crafts, arts and sciences through their commonalities to the subtext in cultural and natural expressions of archetype. Science and esoterica both operate on the principle of predictability and isolation (distinction), although science proceeds from measurables in theoretical context, and esoterica from intrinsic correspondences. This study describes and tests archetype in both contexts.

- Edmond Furter, Johannesburg, May 2014

Acknowledgements

Ditsong Museums allowed access to healers using the Twaing crater reserve.
Johannesburg Heritage allowed access to the Soweto Cultural Village.
Guest lectures at Origins Centre, SA Astronomical Society Johannesburg, Ancient Egyptian Society Johannesburg, Ancient Egyptian and Near Eastern Society Pretoria, Theosophical Society Pretoria and Theosophical Society Johannesburg, offered forums to test scientific and esoteric responses to this interdisciplinary approach.
Delegates to archaeo-astronomy short courses acted as a sounding board.
Artists Vanessa Von Mollendorf, Jeanne Morgan-Lefay, Eljana van der Merwe, Pippa Skotnes and Cyril Coetzee allowed analysis of their work.
Four academic reviewers made helpful suggestions.

About the author

Edmond Furter wrote Mindprint after extensive research in iconography, archaeology, history and astronomy, spanning 26 years.

He says of his subject; "At first I studied psychology about what we feel, then archaeology about what we make, astronomy about what we observe, record and deduct, then cognitive archaeology about what we think. Ironically, this book is not based on the premises or findings of any of these disciplines. Mindprint is about what we do not consciously feel, make, see, record, read or think. It is about the archetypal attributes, sequence and structure that we subconsciously express. I am therefore not an archaeologist, psychologist, astronomer or art historian by definition, but a structural archaeologist."

He works as a freelance researcher and editor in Johannesburg and Pretoria.

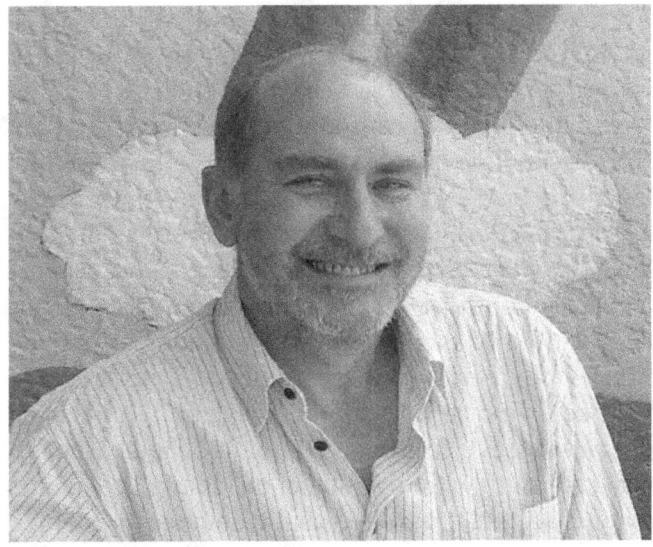

Terminology

[] Ages mean a series of epochs during which the four seasons occupy a set of four constellations (not signs, since signs move with Ages). Ages are named after the spring position. The four markers, 90 degrees apart, move in concert, retrograde (rearward against the seasonal direction) over the backdrop of stars, due to precession (a slow wobble of earth's rotation against its orbit). Age Gemini is not attested in mindprint art, with one possible exception found in Ice Age art. Age Gemini-Taurus with summer over Virgo-Leo, when the three poles were aligned in a row, is possibly attested by one Ice Age mindprint artwork. Age Taurus 1 (spring under Auriga, over Orion, later over the Taurus head, named Hyades) with summer in Leo retro (celestial pole over Ursa Major) is rare in art, perhaps due to the ravages of time or low population numbers. Age Taurus 2 (spring at the Pleiades) with summer over Leo's heart, is common in classical art worldwide, commemorated by Perseus and other twisted heroes killing rain bulls. Age Aries with summer over Cancer (celestial pole near Ursa Minor) is common in the art of many cultures, commemorated by sacrificed lambs or slayed dragons. Age Pisces with summer in Gemini (since about BC 150), will give way to Age Aquarius with its summer over Taurus, in about AD 2016. The event will be marked as usual by gradual and subtle changes in iconography, esoteric crafts, heraldry and popular culture.

[] Archetype means a component of the pre-existent structure which is imprinted on the cosmos, nature, perception and culture. It is unknowable, except in variant, optional and incomplete expressions.

[] Axis means a straight line connecting the eyes of an opposing and complementary typological pair, across the geometric centre of the conceptual ecliptic (earth orbit) plane.

[] Axle means a line connecting the northern and southern projected ends of a pole, either ecliptic, galactic or celestial.

[] Celestial; see Equator, Ages, Pole

[] Constellation means a group of stars habitually used to form an imaginary stick figure by gestalt, which is a function of their relative proximity, brightness (magnitude), position relative to the ecliptic, galactic and celestial equators, the context of other constellations, and seasons (see Precession). The arrangement is of unequal angular extent (uneven width or 'slices'), but generally universal and constant. Not to be confused with astrological, virtual, equalised signs.

[] Court scenes are a stock theme in art, but the format of presiding entities apply equally to cultures without royalty, such as Bushman rock art, implying that court scenes are concerned with cosmic balance, order and social functions, and that politics merely appropriate this ceremonial and ritual impulse. Culture seems to need 'good weddings', sports, games and occasionally war.

[] Dance has many functions, including a natural impulse to mimic nature (as some primates and birds also do), dramatising order and thought patterns, or sorting a finite number of elements such as relationships. The Egyptian royal Sed festival race route, labyrinthine floors and geoglyphs are kinds of dance.

[] Dream and trance are states or levels of consciousness extending into the subconscious, linked to distinct brain frequency patterns. The states relevant to artistic inspiration and expression are probably distinct from possession, which is recorded in studies on wilful invocation in New Orleans, Haiti and West Africa, often involving alcohol or other depressants. These practices prompt and invoke a limited set of stereotypical characters that seem to derive from the collective shadow, anima and animus, apparently of lesser variety and of a smaller attribute range than archetypes such as Perseus, Pegasus, Pan and the rest, and a smaller range than pantheons. Bushman, Hopi and South American rituals aimed at inducing trance for communal and individual healing likewise seems distinct from possession, and perhaps from artistic inspiration.

[] Ecliptic; see Equator, Pole

[] Equator means a plane of rotation or orbit, or widest extent, 90 degrees from either pole. The celestial equator is caused by earth's daily rotation. The ecliptic equator is earth's annual orbital equator, made visible by the apparent path of the sun that we orbit around, and by other planets that orbit in more or less the same plane. Most planets deviate about one degree from this equator, Venus deviates up to three degrees, the moon deviates up to five degrees, and Mercury deviates up to seven degrees. Apparent planetary deviation is labelled apparent (seen from earth) orbital obliquity, not to be confused with rotational obliquity. The points where planets cross the ecliptic equator are named nodes, notably lunar nodes. When a planet is on the ecliptic where the sun also happens to be, an eclipse occurs, labelled eclipse for the moon, and solar transit (of inner planets, Mercury and Venus) or occlusion for other planets.

[] Galaxy means a massively large group of stars spread out in a flat S-shaped disc. Most stars are in pairs or small groups orbiting one another. Some stars have planets, while some planets have satellites (moons). The galactic disc or vortex shape is visible from a planet as the galactic equator, also named Milky Way. Other stars in the galaxy, at different distances from a viewer, appear to form a shell. Their relative apparent proximities and sizes offer a canvas to the cosmos and the imagination. The galactic equator appears to cross our orbital plane (ecliptic equator) between the constellations (not signs) of Gemini and Taurus, and on the opposite side between Sagittarius and Scorpius. The galactic centre appears to lie just south of the Scorpius-Sagittarius border.

[] Holographic means an image on a flat surface that appears to be three-dimensional.

[] Kind means humanoid figures with identifiable stylistic attributes that are not archetypal attributes. X people are kinds of figures, but they could express almost any types. See People and Type. Kinds include goat people, P people, fish people, X people, Y people, coat people, bag people, rope people, footprint people, H people, house people, cone people, snake people, swift people, ball people, ship people, and more.

[] Mindprint is sixteen sets of conceptually related optional archetypal attributes, each set consisting of one or two frequent attributes, and three, four, five or six decanal (related) and less frequent attributes, arranged in a standard sequence near the edge of an artwork, with their eyes (replaced by one heart and one womb in constant and adjacent positions, at type Leo t13 t12 and type Virgo t11) in an approximate oval, at varied radii, each on an axis with its opposite type.

These axes cross in one point, analogous to the ecliptic (orbital) pole. The structure is analogous to a flattened cosmic sphere, with some features of the underside visible, and 'galactic' features doubled and antithetical (mirrored). Galactic poles are usually marked by limb joints near and between the heart and womb figure, and on the opposite side (conceptual 'underside') between the eyes of type Aquarius t5 and Pisces t4.

Each conceptual galactic pole centres one of the oblique galactic equators, traceable along prominent limb joints, partly inside and partly outside the equator of eyes. One of the 'celestial' poles is usually marked by a limb joint, such as a jaw, shoulder, hand or ankle, near the axial pole, incidental with the position of the midsummer and midwinter solstices in one of the last three astrological Ages (or four mindprint Ages, since Taurus is doubled). Celestial poles move in an arc around the ecliptic pole due to precession. The general Age of artworks, specifically the inspirational Age, is incidental with the position of the 'celestial' markers.

Four 'large' types are optionally doubled as one or two expressions; type Taurus t1 and t2, opposite type Scorpius t8 and t9; and/or type Aquarius t5 t20 and t5 t21, opposite type Leo t12 and t13. When type Aquarius t5 is doubled it retains the same lower number, therefore the highest type number (the sixteenth) is type Gemini t15, while type Taurus t16 overlaps Taurus t1 as a kind of decan.

Seven types are thus overlapped by their own decans (Gemini t15 t0, Taurus t1 t16, t2 t17, Aries t3 t18, Pisces t4 t19, Aquarius t5 t20, t5 t21).

The entire arrangement is subconscious and compulsive to artists, and independent of conscious and conventional attributes, design grids, perspective lines and meanings.

Conscious symbolism and style is determined by the culture and experience of the artist, but mindprint in all its detail is standard in all cultures, areas and ages.

Mindprint was discovered in 2010, and its types, attributes, geometry, polar structure and correspondence with myth, emblems, the Tarot deck and astronomy were assigned, numbered and tabulated by Edmond Furter and published in the book Mindprint, the archetypal art code, in 2014 (Lulu.com). Mindprint identified in artworks is marked by axial lines between eyes crossing in one point, each labelled by zodiac equivalents and the lower range of type numbers, from ta1, ta2, ar3, pi4 and so on, to ge15.

[] Obliquity means deviation of a planet's rotational plane (equator) and polar axis, from its orbital plane (equator) and axis. Earth's current obliquity is about 23.4 degrees, but was larger in the past, righted itself at an unknown and diminishing rate, and is still righting itself at a minute rate. The Newcombe curve assumes that obliquity slowly oscillates by about two degrees around the current value, but it is unproven.

[] Pole means either end of the conceptual axle of a rotation, orbit, or plane. A tri-polar system such as earth within its solar system and galaxy, could be projected from either of the three poles, with the southern counterpart of the chosen projection point directly below it, while the other two polar axles would then appear as oblique. The cosmic map in this study is centred on the ecliptic (yearly orbital) poles, as dictated by artistic expression. Most star maps used in astronomy are centred on the celestial (daily rotation) poles, and do not co-incide with artistic expression. Some software programmes could show the sky in celestial or ecliptic or galactic polar projection.

[] Sign means an imaginary 30 degree slice of time and space, keyed to the current position of the spring equinox, named in the sequence of ecliptic constellations. It is currently almost 30 degrees precessed (moved backward against the seasonal direction). Thus the sign of Aries now lies over the constellation of Pisces. People born with a 'sun in Aries' are born while the sun is in Pisces constellation. The disjunction has several quirks, since constellations are of uneven extent. Thus the sign Taurus lies partly over constellation Aries, and partly over constellation Taurus at the Pleiades. Sign Gemini lies over the rest of constellation Taurus. Astronomers list positions of planets according to signs. Astrologers calculate horoscopes on signs, implying that some natural structures such as tendencies, traits and events, are mirrored by the relative orientation of the earth and the sun, while the stars are merely a formula.
Correspondences between signs and constellations were never entirely aligned, although partially aligned about BC 150, when the first point of Aries sign corresponded with the first point of Aries constellation, and the first point of Taurus sign was in Taurus constellation at the Pleiades cluster.

[] Subconscious means involuntary, embedded human perception keyed to universal structure and content. It is larger than our individual or collective conscious mind, which is limited by conventions, communication media, prejudice, expectations and psychological defence mechanisms that camouflage the structure of nature, culture and perception itself.

[] Therianthropes are half-human and half-animal figures. Attributes from specific cultural expressions, such as the Minotaur in a labyrinth in Crete, do not imply that there once was such a creature and building in Crete, although a multi-level palace with a maze of rooms was built there, as Arthur Evans had reconstructed. Extensive ruins of an earlier labyrinth were found at Hawara near Lake Moeris in the Fayyum in Egypt, again not implying that the Greek version derived from Egypt. Also see Kind.

[] Trance; see Dream

[] Types, in mindprint typology, are identified by analogous astronomical constellations, with type numbers, such as type Cancer t14. The sixteen types are derived from typical artistic figures. Types are also identified by frequent optional attributes, as well as the sequence of adjacent types, and their geometrically opposite type, as parts of a standard set and structure (see Attributes and Tables of types in the text). Single attributes may be stereotypical, but all the optional attributes of each type from a holographic conceptual unit. Types are verified by corresponding attributes of figures in art, rock art, concepts, emblems, cards, gods, mythic figures, star lore and legend. Art of all Ages contain the entire sequence of types and the standard geometric structure, usually with some general emphasis on any one or pair among the sixteen types. Types are further defined by their decanal constellation or asterisms, such as type Scorpius t8 Ophiuchus. Constellations map out myth cycles to some extent. Types with multiple numbers, such as type Aquarius t5 t20 t21 Pegasus, indicate doubled and split aspects, with a choice of two, three or four decans each expressing additional attributes.

Errata

Cysta mystica (Basket of mysteries), and the

abbreviation cys in labels, should be spelled

cista mystia (cis).

_____

Kindly post errata or comments on
www.edmondfurter.wordpress.com

Index of rock art geometrically tested

Division between rock art and schooled art, as well as divisions between continents and regions, are artificial. These divisions are useful to the aim of representing all major art regions and eras. All the works contain the mindprint typological sequence and geometry. Some works are illustrated and cited in more detail. Some are included in the statistical test. Citations after 'id' indicate the author and year of identification of the mindprint types and geometry in the artwork, in anticipation of citing collaborators in an expanded list.

== Egyptian rock art
af Egypt Abu Wasil wadi engr rams, id Furter 2012
af Egypt El Hosh engr, mushrooms (Kaulins, A), id Furter 2012
af Egypt , hemisphere, id Furter 2012
af Egypt west engr (Franceso Raffaele, xoomer.virgilio.it. Kaulins, A 2005), id Furter 2008

== African rock art, excluding Egypt and South Africa
af , Teshuinat 2 shelter, id Furter 2012
af Algeria Tassili black herders U gate, id Furter 2012
af Algeria Tassili camels (stamp 2.40), id Furter 2013
af Algeria Tassili cattle and hoops, id Furter 2012
af Algeria Tassili cattle parade, id Furter 2012
af Algeria Tassili cattle ritual, U-gate, id Furter 2012
af Algeria Tassili 'helmets' (Explorer), id Furter 2013
af Algeria Tassili herders, id Furter 2012
af Algeria Tassili ox via U-palm gate, giraffe snake, id Furter 2012
af Algeria Tassili disc or basin on bovine heads, id Furter 2012
af Algeria Tassili Tissoukai cattle kraal as sun disc, Id Furter 2012
af Ethiopia Oromia animals (gds1 4r), id Furter 2012
af Ethiopia Oromia cattle ? (RARI), id Furter 2011
af Ethiopia Oromia distr cattle (RARI), id Furter 2012
af Ethiopia,, lion mauling man, id Furter 2011
af Libya ,, id Furter 2012
af Libya , storm god chariot, id Furter 2011
af Libya Akaku Mountain red men, id Furter 2012
af Sahara cattle pregnant or birth, id Furter 2012
af Somalia Dhambalin , chromatic, id Furter 2012
af Tanzania , (Seppo, Wornell), id Furter 2012

== Canadian rock art
am Canada , Kokopelli touched, id Furter 2012
am Canada , vertical, ropes, id Furter 2012
am Canada plaque Chukchee fish, id Furter 2011

== South American and Mexican rock art

am Mexico Guanajuato figures, id Furter 2012
am s Argentina Patagonia hand prints id Furter 2012
am s Brazil or California Pedra Pintada engr oval, id Furter 2012
am s Brazil or California Pedra Pintada engr pentagon, id Furter 2010
am s Peru dynosaur therianth engraving (Nat Geog), id Furter 2011
am s Peru dynosaurs, id Furter 2012

== American USA rock art
am usa , ritual, id Furter 2013
am usa , Barrier Canyon , (David Lee), id Furter 2012
am usa , Box Canyon , (Mitchell, M), id Furter 2012
am usa , Capital Reef ropes, id Furter 2012
am usa , Cienega Mesa world man engr bipolar, id Furter 2012 test
am usa , Clear Creek Canyon ropes, id Furter 2012
am usa , Coso sheep, id Furter 2012
am usa , Cottonwood or Nine Mile Canyon hunt, id Furter 2012
am usa , Del Muerto canyon central, id Furter 2012
am usa , dots, id Furter 2012
am usa , Ferron Box San Rafael swell, like sand art (Fremont?), id Furter 2012
am usa , grids , (Jacobs, JQ), id Furter 2012 test
am usa , Kohta Circus (Sandcarveddesigns), id Furter 2012
am usa , Nine Mile Canyon backway, , id Furter 2012
am usa , Nine Mile Canyon owls, id Furter 2012
am usa , np Canyonlands maze district harvest, id Furter 2013
am usa , Rio Grande, id Furter 2012
am usa , slab, id Furter 2012
am usa , slide engraving, id Furter 2012
am usa , Slot Canyons ,, id Furter 2012
am usa , Three Rivers , engraving, id Furter 2012 test
am usa , VBarV Ranch squares intest, id Furter 2012
am usa Arizona (101 river), id Furter 2012
am usa Arizona , angled boulder, id Furter 2012
am usa Arizona north circles (David, Gary A), id Furter 2012 test
am usa California , id Furter 2012
am usa California Piedra Pintada, id Furter 2012
am usa California,, or Mecico Baja Sur Cave desert (San Igancio Mus), id Furter 2011
am usa Cienega Mesa engr world-man, id Furter 2012
am usa Colorado rope (Greer), id Furter 2012
am usa New Mexico Galisteo , engraving (Petroglyph Hill1), id Furter 2012 incomplete
am usa Utah Emery Rochester Creek rainbow, double, id Furter 2011
am usa Utah San Juan, Monticello, Newspaper Rock doluble. Jacobs, JQ. Id Furter 2012

am usa Utah mammoth bison. Columbian. Id Furter 2012

am usa Wyoming P-shaped people, id Furter 2012

== Asian rock art

as Arabia , camels, intestinal antelope, bee people (Fremont), id Furter 2011

as Arabia Oman Daika Wadi, id Furter 2012

as China , tigers, id Furter 2012

as China Geeraoboo Gou, id Furter 2012

as China Hua shan 1, id test

as China Hua shan 2, id Furter 2012

as China Tien Shan bee people, id Furter 2011

as China Tien Shan heraldic fertility, id Furter 2012

as India , rock art panel, id Furter 2012

as India , verticals horned, id Furter 2012

as India Bhimbetka Cave caravan, id Furter 2012

as India c , cattle and bovines white, id Furter 2012

as India Pakistan Budha engraving, id Furter 2012

as Kazak Tamgaly ww, id Furter test

as Korea Daegok ri whales, double (Lee, Sang Mong), id Furter 2011

as Mongolia dots, id Furter 2012

as Pacific Easter Island seals, fish engr, id Furter 2011

as Rrussia Kanozero lake cycle 4, id Furter 2012

as Russia Baikal Lake Sayan Zaba, id Furter 2012

as Russia Elangash elks, stags, id Furter 2012

as Russia Elangash mounted hunters, id Furter 2012

as Russia Kanozero lake cycles four, id Furter 2012

as Russia Kanozero Lake Mumansk Olbast Kamenniy 7, quadruple, id Furter 2012

as Russia Kolenga upper Lena River, village raid, id Furter 2012

as Russia Saimaly Tash, Ferghana ploughs, id Furter 2012

as Russia Sayan Zaba Baikal (Rupestre), id Furter 2012

as Russia Tom, , id Furter 2012

== Australian rock art

au Djulirri emu double, id Furter 2012

au Djulirri large, id Furter 2012

au Grenfil Mountain, id Furter 2012

au Kimberley? Long-necked masks, id Furter 2014

== European rock art, excluding France

eu , Bogdanoff U spirals, circles, id Furter 2012

eu , Evenstorp engraving, sun and moon suite, id Furter 2012

eu , Karkur Talh, oryx ostr dog giraffe auroch man, id Furter 2012

eu Bulgaria Magura Cave birds, bat guano paint, id Furter 2012

eu Denmark Ekenberg 1 ships engr, id Furter 2012

eu Norway Alta , engr pavement, id Furter 2012

eu Scandinavia , boats bovines, id Furter 2012

eu Scandinavia , rock art whale, id Furter 2012

eu Scandinavia boats, id Furter 2012

eu Scandinavia boats cliff detail, id Furter 2012

eu Scandinavia boats red, id Furter 2012

eu Sweden ships rows, spring A, id Furter 2012

eu Sweden ships rows, spring B, id Furter 2012

eu Turkey , (Rock Art Mus), id Furter 2012

eu Turkey Catal Huyuk mural 5 hunting shrine west, stag v leopard men, id Furter 2012

eu Turkey Catal Huyuk mural FV1 rain animal

eu Turkey Latmos Moutain overhang, dance, birds, id Furter 2012

eu uk Scotland , Badger engraving, id Furter 2012

eu uk Scotland Knowth engr geom, id Furter 2012

eu uk Scotland Knowth engr Site 14, id Furter 2012

== European Ice Age and French rock art

eu France , Bison panel, id Furter 2013

eu France , cave markings or, id Furter 2012 test

eu France Chauvet cave left half, id Furter 2012

eu France Chauvet cave right half, id Furter 2012

eu France Lascaux deer funnel hunt, id Furter 2012

eu France Peche Merle cave Cabreres, id Furter 2012

eu France Trios Frère cave double, id Furter 2012

eu Italy Sicily cave, dance, seal therianthropes, engr, id Furter 2013

eu Spain, Aragon, Los Caballos, antelope drive hunt, bows. id Furter 2013

== South African rock art, excluding Free State and Kwa-Zulu Natal

sa , 102hc, Thornycroft, RARI, id Furter 2012

sa , Amatola herbal group (Willem Prinsloo Agric Mus, Pretoria), id Furter 2013

sa , Amatola mounted raider (George Stow, RARI), id Furter 2012

sa , Amatola, ox wagon group, cultural contact, id Furter 2013

sa , Boer war graffiti, Lambrechts, 02 31t Ouzman, id Furter 2012

sa , eland , (Smith, B; Working with rock art, cover), id Furter 2012

sa , eland (Wits, book cover), id Furter 2012

sa , flats (Stow, George copy), id Furter 2012

sa , herbal aloe ferox laxative, rope or track (Ben-Erik van Wyk), id Furter 2013

sa , horses circles (Stow, G), id Furter 2012

sa , hunt ritual 3, (SA Arch Bul), id Furter 2013

sa , Khoe healing dance, ,, (Origins), id Furter 2012

sa , large red (Anderson, G), id Furter 2012

sa , lions chasing or dying, group dance with ropes (Smit, B, RARI), id Furter 2012

sa , monkey, 126d, Stow, Iziko Mus, id Furter 2012

sa , rain animal (Albany mus rest, or alb 02 24r), id Furter 2012 sa , rain bull, bees from shoulder (RARI 22b /p6 Andrson, G), id Furter 2012

sa , rt, faded (Lewis Willilams), id Furter 2012 test,,

sa , sun over group, cul1 1r (Smit, B), id Furter 2012

sa , therianthropes, monstrous (Smit, B), id Furter 2012

sa , trance figures, agric, arrows, , id Furter 2013

sa , trance, (Anderson G), id Furter 2012

sa , trance, birds nightjars (Vinnicombe, P), id Furter 2013

sa , vortex, figure large (102hc, Thornycrft), id Furter 2012

sa , w (Stow, G), id Furter 2012

sa ec Albert white cattle (Dowson), id Furter 2012

sa ec Elliot, cul1, ammonia print (RARI), id Furter 2012

sa ec Maclear bee people (Smit, B?) id Furter 2012

sa ec Maclear Linton, from which the SA coat of arms is taken (Iziko Mus), id Furter 2012

sa ec Maclear bee people dance (mel6, Lewis Willams, RARI) id Furter 2012

sa ec Nomandsland, dance, ghosts, id Furter 2013

sa lim , shelter (Smit, B), id Furter 2012 test

sa lim Makgabeng train (Origins), id Furter 2012

sa mp Nelspruit Rocky Drift Sun Rock, animals large, id Furter 2013

sa nc Carnarvon, elephant hunt engr, spn1 1t (Deacon. RARI), id Furter 2012

sa nc Kruiper, Vetkat Regopstaan, modern San art, id Furter 2013

sa wc , wagons, great trek. Id Furter

sa wc Barkley Wodehouse 2, giraffe neck, lion man

sa wc George, swifts, ropes

sa wc Mossel Bay site 5, river rope. Hollmann, J. SA Goodwin Series. Id Furter 2013

sa wc Oudtshoorn, falling buck, Van Riet, 1940 pl 15, SA Arch Bul, also 67 p78, id Furter 2013

sa wc palet Khoe or , (Iziko Mus), id Furter 2012

sa wc palet Plettenberg Bay, Robberg, bag, D or G. Lewis-Williams. Id Furter 2013

sa wc palet Plettenberg Bay, Robberg fliers D or G. Lewis-Williams. Id Furter 2013

sa wc palet St Fancis, Klasies River, (Lewis-Williams; Southern land), id Furter 2012

sa wc palet St Francis, Klasies River, fish. Id Furter

sa wc palet, tk1, id Furter 2012

== South African rock art, Free State

sa fs forms or geom, Khoe over San (Smit, B), id Furter 2013

sa fs Bethlehem spread, bnl1, id Furter 2012

sa fs Clarens Coerland rain lions, (Townley Johnson. RARI. Digging Stick), id Furter 2011

sa fs Clocolan , left, id Furter 2012

sa fs Clocolan overlay larger (pry1), id Furter 2012

sa fs east, dance, eland bags on periphery. Vinnicombe 1976, fig 107? SA Arch Bul 67, id Furter 2012

sa fs Excelsior snakes dogs ropes (ner1), id Furter 2012

sa fs Fouriesburg bug arms, double headed (SA Nat Mus), id Furter 2012

sa fs Fouriesburg dance, nr11 (RARI), ild Furter 2012

sa fs Fouriesburg texture, tep1, id Furter 2012

sa fs Gariep lions, horses, Korana, id Furter 2012

sa fs Harrismith Blacks attack Khoe, goe1 (Origins Centre), id Furter 2012

sa fs Ladybrand , larger distorted (org1), id Furter 2012

sa fs Ladybrand Bella Vista, wig or buccranium (Nat Mus), id Furter 2013

sa fs Ladybrand cattle large (Sarada?), id Furter 2012

sa fs Ladybrand group many, 32hc (Breul. RARI), id Furter 2012

sa fs Ladybrand rain animals, moe1, id Furter 2012

sa fs Marquard dance (twy1), id Furter 2012

sa fs Marquard, wide, spa1, id Furter 2012

sa fs Motheo [moltheno?], horses, id Furter 2012

sa fs Rouxville grazing, mrr1, id Furter 2012

sa fs Wepener rain animal, kne1, id Furter 2012

sa fs Zastron group, gna1, id Furter 2012

== South African rock art; KwaZulu Natal and Drakensberg

sa kzn , San, Thomas, River, id Furter 2012

sa kzn mt currie, horses, guns, rsa beh1 Dowson, nat mus pjv01 245hc, id Furter 2012

sa kzn , Battle Cave, happy legs (Origins Centre), id Furter 2012

sa kzn , cattle (Anderson), id Furter 2012

sa kzn Khoe cattle, horses (Anderson), id Furter 2012

sa kzn Giants Castle Main Caves North (Russel, SA Arch Bul), id Furter 2013

sa kzn , shaman (SA Arch Bul), id Furter 2013

sa kzn , spirit whites (Blundell), id Furter 2013

sa kzn Bergville , (Pager. RARI), id Furter 2012

sa kzn Drakensbeg, group images (Lewis-Williams), id Furter 2012

sa kzn Drakensberg snake (SA Arch Bul), id 2012 test

sa kzn Estcourt elephant rope (RARI, bar1 7r), id Furter 2011

sa kzn Ndedema magi (SA Tourism, Moultrie, N), id Furter 2013

sa kzn Ndedema rope bridge (SAAS), galaxy profile, id Furter 2011

sa kzn Underberg , (RARI), id Furter 2012

sa kzn Underberg Amatola , large, id Furter 2013

sa kzn Underberg Amatola eland slaughter, id Furter 2013

sa kzn Underberg Amatola raid, id Furter 2013

sa kzn Underberg baboon rope of sky, id Furter 2013

Index of art geometrically tested

af Egypt jewel pectoral scarab Rebus, Tutankamun (Aldred), id Furter 2013 test

af Egypt jewel pectoral Tanis [1] (Aldred), id Furter 2013

af Egypt jewel pectoral winged, Tutankamun (Aldred), id Furter 2013

af Egypt jewel pectoral, Mereret uraeus Sesostris 2, Dashur (Aldred), id Furter 2013

af Egypt jewel pectorals Amenophthis, Tanis (Aldred), id test

af Egypt jewel pendant Osorkon 2 (Aldred), id Furter 2013 test

af Egypt Judgement hall (Aldred), id Furter 2013

af Egypt label Heb Sed, Hierakonpolis Narmer (Ashmolean Mus Oxford), id Furter 2012

af Egypt label irovy, King Den, id Furter 2011

af Egypt label King Djet ivoy Dyn 1, Saqqara, id Furter 2012

af Egypt mace Narmer or Den, id Furter 2013

af Egypt mural epic, Hierakonpolis tomb 100, cycle 1, 2, 3 (Cairo Mus), id Furter 2011

af Egypt mural Estate workers, id Furter 2012

af Egypt mural Ramses 3 ceiling, id Furter 2013

af Egypt mural Rope factory, id Furter 2012

af Egypt mural Seti 1 ceiling, Abydos, Valley of Kings, ropes, id Furter 2010

af Egypt palet Dogs Hierakonpolis, id Furter 2012

af Egypt palet Dogs smaller, Hierakonpolis, Mesopotamian style, id Furter 2012

af Egypt palet Dogs, reverse (Oxford), id Furter 2012

af Egypt palet Dragons [Dogs?] other, hare, antelope, tree, id Furter 2012

af Egypt palet Hunters, Hierakonpolis, (Brit Mus), id Furter 2012

af Egypt palet knife Gebel el Arak, id Furter 2012

af Egypt palet Narmer front, Hierakonpolis (Egy Mus Cairo), id Furter 2010

af Egypt palet Narmer rear, Hierakonpolis (Egy Mus Cairo), id Furter 2010

af Egypt papyrus tree of life emblem, id Furter 2012

af Egypt papyrus Tree of life, birds, id Furter 2011

af Egypt papyrus Tree of life with birds, tourism copy, id Furter 2012

af Egypt papyrus, Elysian fields, id Furter 2013

af Egypt papyrus, Horus Shmesu boat, id Furter 2012

af Egypt pot Naqada funeral boats, grave 454 (Petrie), id Furter 2012

af Egypt zodiac coffin lid, oriental, frog, Polemaic, id Furter 2012

af Egypt zodiac Dendera rectangular, decans rows, id Furter 2011

af Egypt zodiac Dendera round, Ptolemaic (Trevisan C, www.iuav.unive.it), id Furter 2011

af Egypt,, Palestine,, zodiac Warat Mizaw,, ceiling, id Furter 2013

== African art excluding Egypt and South Africa

af Ethiopia mural Aksum, or illum, id Furter 2012

af Guinea calabash carving (De Santillana; Hamlet's mill), id Furter 2011

af Guinea calabash carving 2 (De Santillana; Hamlet's Mill), Id Furter 2010

af Namibia Muafangelo, John; Adam, id Furter 2013

af Namibia Muafangelo, John; Ark, id Furter 2013

af Namibia Muafangelo, John; Battle of Rorke's drift, id Furter 2013

af Namibia Muafangelo, John; Muafangelo's kraal, id Furter 2013

== American art

am Bolivia? disc metal relief (Dona), id Furter 2013

am Brazil engraving, Pedra Pintada, id Furter 2010

am Canada plaquette wood, Chukchee net fishing, id Furter 2012

am Guatemala frieze , , id Furter 2012

am Inca jewel earring, id Furter 2013

am Mexico , print red margins, id Furter 2012

am Mexico Aztec cross, id Furter 2010

am Mexico Aztec day signs, gods (Codex Hamburgensis; Denzel), id Furter 2011

am Mexico Chavin de Huantar, Olmec pillar (Peter G Roe), id Furter 2012

am Mexico Codex , Popul Vuh, Mayan, crocodile, tree, tube, id Furter 2012

am Mexico codex, Mayan,, Mt Mashu caves (Wikipedia), id Furter 2011

am Mexico engraving, Mayan disc, id Furter 2013

am Mexico frieze Palenque lid, Lord Pacal, id Furter 2011, 2012

am Mexico frieze Winds lintel, id Furter 2012

am Mexico mural Cuzco Coricancha, and rendition (Herschel), id Furter 2012

am Mexico palet Dogs, Mayan, id Furter 2012

am Mexico vase, Mayan, 14 monsters, id Furter 2010

am Mexico,, weaving,, world tree, honeysuckers, ceiba, id Furter 2013

am Peru jewel Sican, gold, id Furter 2013

am USA Mormon, Christ Last supper, sparse

am USA skin painting, bison, Dakota Mandan Indian war scene, id Furter 2012

am usa Walter Quirt; Tranquility of previous experience, 1940s (NY Met Mus), id Furter 2013

am, Amaringo, Pablo [trance city 2?], id Furter 2011

am, Amaringo, Pablo; ,, id Furter 2011

am, Amaringo, Pablo; [trance city], id Furter 2011

am, Amaringo, Pablo; dome, ayahuasca, id Furter 2013 Age Aquarius

== Asian and Mideast art

as , Christian, Ajanta cave medallion, id Furter 2012

as , Kyrgyz[istan] Chopon Ata boulder, id Furter 2013

as , Sidon zodiac with Perseus 'Mithras', temple frieze, AD 400, id Furter 2011

as , Susiana seal, procession, id Furter 2013

as Arabia papyrus amuletic, id Furter 2011

as Babylonia kudurru carving (Rawlinson), id Furter 2009

as Babylonia plaque bronze Pazuzu v Lamashu, id Furter 2013

as Babylonia seal, Etana on eagle, two ages (Sitchen), id Furter 2010

as Babylonia seal, Enkidu v lions (Sitchen), id Furter 2010

as Borneo carving, Tree of life triad, id Furter 2013

as Cambodia , Shiva seduces wife, praises Devi, id Furter 2013

as China tile from tomb, duck hunt, rice harvest, id Furter 2013

as China tile Queen of the west (Shaugnessy I), id Furter 2010

as China women miners at bath, sparse

as India , Buddha's death, Mount Meru collapse, id Furter 2011

as India , Krishna dances on snake Kaliyq, wives pray, id Furter 2012

as India , Visnhu churn Mount Mandra, Kangara, id Furter 2013

as India brass Hindu, sun, Suryq, id Furter 2012

as India Buddha enlightened, id Furter 2013

as India Buddhist engr, Pakistan, id Furter 2012

as India cloth panel, domestic scenes, id Furter test

as India frieze Buddha under tree impels wheel (Schulberg), id Furter 2011

as India frieze Buddha walks on water (Schulberg), id Furter 2011

as India frieze Buddhist Sanchi stupa gate by Ashoka BC 230 c, id Furter 2011

as India frieze Buddhist, monkey offers honey (Schbulberg), id Furter 2011

as India frieze Vishnu on bier (Arch Surv India), id Furter 2013

as India frieze Shiva seduces Devi, id Furter 2013

as India Hindu,, , cosmogram, id Furter 2011

as India Hindu,, Churn, Mahabarata (De Santillana), id Furter 2010

as India illum , Akbar in drunken revelry, Islamic (Schulberg), id Furter 2011

as India illum , Akbar moves to Fathpur Sikri 1569, double (Schulberg), id Furter 2011

as India illum , Akbar sieges Ranthambor, Islamic (Schulberg), id Furter 2011

as India illumination , Akbar trains war elephants, Islamic (Schulberg), id Furter 2011

as India illumination , diplomats at court (Schulberg), id Furter 2011

as India illumination , Krishna bathes with women, Hindu (Schulberg), id Furter 2011

as India illumination , Krishna eats Agni's fire, Hindu (Schulberg), id Furter 2011

as India illumination , Krishna escapes giant bird, Hindu (Schulberg), id Furter 2011

as India illumination , Krishna saluted by Brahma, Hindu (Schulberg), id Furter 2011

as India illumination , monkeys at play in fables (Lights of Canopus), id Furter 2011

as India illumination , prince born to Akbar, feast, Islamic (Schulberg), id Furter 2011

as India illumination , prince Salim born at Sikri, Islamic (Schulberg), id Furter 2011

as India illumination, Hindu,, Kali dances on Shiva, id Furter 2013

as India Tamil Nadu Mahishasura frieze (Arch Surv India), id Furter 2013

as Iran , Kurdistan Hasanlu, rollout (Teheran Arch Mus), id Furter 2012

as Palestine mosaic zodiac, Seopphoris, id Furter 2012

as Persia bowl, tragedy scenes, Sileus, Sassanian, id Furter 2013

as Persia engraving, lion woman, Yasilikaya, Hurri, id Furter 2011

as Persia frieze Nergal, id Furter 2012

as Persia miniature, garden pool (Gray), id Furter 2013

as Persia miniature, polo (Gray), id Furter 2013

as Persia miniature, tree, village, Muraqqa Gulshan, id Furter 2013

as Russia bowl, Kustanai, Euripides scenes (Sassanian art, Hermitage), id Furter 2013

as Russia bowl, Maikop, silver, id Furter 2012

as Russia drums Minusinski variants 4, id Furter 2013

as Sumatra cloth, Boat of dead, soul ship, tampan cloth, id Furter 2013

as Syria Megiddo Greek multiculture roundel, silver plate, id Furter 2011

au 3D, Oz the great, movie 2012 c, id Furter 2013

au Papua carving bamboo, brothers Wain, Kambot, id Furter 2013

au Papua carving bamboo, spirit brothers, Kambot village, id Furter 2013

== European art

eu , Artemis, Cassandra, Trojan horse, id Furter 2012

eu , fresco Isis ritual, id Furter 2012

eu , mural St , and St Jerome, id Furter 2011

eu alchemy Germany, Cabala mirror of art and nature (Alchemia, 1615), id Furter 2013

eu England carving, Hell purgatory ladder, Chaldon Church, Surrey, id Furter 2012

eu England plaque, after Poussin, Et in Arcadia, Shugbourough, id Furter 2012

eu France , cave markings or, axes Furter 2012

eu,   Poussin;   John   Baptist   preaches
(www.nicholaspoussin.com), id Furter 2013
eu, Poussin; Midas and Bacchus, id Furter 2012
eu, Poussin; Moses strikes the rock, id Furter 2013
eu, Poussin; Nature of Jupiter, id Furter 2012
eu, Poussin; Pan and Siringa, id Furter 2012
eu, Poussin; Parnassus, planets personified, after
Mantegna, id Furter 2012
eu, Poussin; Triumph of Pan, id Furter 2012
eu, Roos; Menagerie of count Acart, 1728 (Louvre),
id Furter 2013
eu, Savery; Paradise 1626, double, id Furter 2013
eu, Signorelli; John Baptist preaches, id Furter 2013
eu, Van Ecks, triptych Ghent, Lamb, id Furter 2013
eu, Zuccaro; Cupid and Pan, id Furter 2013

== South African art
sa frieze Voortrekker monument central panels 2, id
Furter 2012
sa Pretoria town hall council mural, Bible donation,
double, id Furter 2012
sa Pretoria town hall mural, Liberty /Victory ?
sa Pretoria town hall mural, savanna, Id Furter 2012
sa, Coetzee, Cyril; T'Kama Adamastor Wits Cullen
Library commission 1960s, id Furter 2011
sa, La Grange, Marthinus; He walks on water, 1950c,
id Furter 2013
sa, Morgan-Lefay, Jeanne; Dancers, id Furter 2013
sa, Morgan-Lefay, Jeanne; Masquerade [Arcadian],
id Furter 2013
sa, Morgan-Lefay, Jeanne; pseudo-Egyptian Isis
enthroned, id Furter 2013
sa, Morgan-Lefay, Jeanne; pseudo-Egyptian prayer,
id Furter 2013
sa, Mutwa, Credo; Soweto Culture Village Rain Hut
murals 2 and 3, 1975 c, id Furter 2011
sa, Pinker, Stanley; Our country, farm yard 1967, id
Furter 2013
sa, Skotnes, Pippa; Down here a starless sky, 1985,
donkey (Sanlam coll), id Furter 2013
sa, Von Mollendorf, Vanessa; Man eater mantis. Id
Furter 2008, 2011

== Listing late additions
sa Lesotho Sehonghong rain shake (Challis. Digging Stick), id
Furter 2014
eu, , Burial of the virgin, id Furter 2014
eu, Collinson; Renunciation of queen Elizabeth of Hungary
(JAG), id Furter 2014
eu, El Greco; Dormition, id Furter 2014
eu, Leonardo Da Vinci; Last supper (St Mary of the Graces,
Milan), id Furter 2014
eu, Raphael; School of Athens (Vatican), id Furter 2014
eu, Rosetti, DG; How Sir Galahad, id Furter 2014
eu, Rosetti, DG; King Arthur and the maidens, id Furter 2014
sa, , Blind Justice (JAG), id Furter 2014
sa, , Boys in blue (JAG), id Furter 2014
sa, Daborn, Erica; Seeking higher ground, id Furter 2013

Graphics sources

Aldred, C; Jewels of the Pharaohs: Egyptian jewellery
of the dynastic period. 1971. Thames and Hudson
Ankhonline.com
Bleek, Wilhelm; Rock paintings in SA
Bradshaw Foundation
Brenthurst   Library,   Oppenheimer   collection,
Johannesburg
Breuil, Abbe, 1952
Briscoe, Gilbert; Johannesburg and Soweto Parks
photographs
Coetzee, Cyril; T'Kama Adamastor, Wits University,
1997. I Vladislavic, Wits Press, 2000
Colonna,   Franciscus   (attrib);   Hypnerotomachia
Polipili, 1499
The Columbian
De Montault, Barbier; Un Agnus Dei de Gregoire II,
Poiters, 1886
De Santillana G, Von Deschend H; Hamlet's Mill: An
essay on myth and the frame of time, 1969; Boston:
Gambit Inc
Digging stick; South African Archaeological Society
Fremont Foundation
Ghirshman, R; Iran, Parthians and Sassanians, 1962,
Thames and Hudson
Goodwin   Series,   South   African   Archaeological
Society
Gray, Basil; Persian miniatures, 1962, Collins
/Unesco
James, TGH; Great Pharaos, 2011, White Star
Jensen, Bernard, Escondido, California; homeopathic
eye nodes, 1977
Johannesburg Heritage
Mitchell, M
Morgan-Lefay, Jeanne; exhibition
Mutwa, Credo; cultural village murals, Soweto,
Johannesburg, 1975, destroyed 1976
Mutwa, Credo; New York plaque. By permission of
Credo Mutwa, and Sylvia Pouroulis
Numiswiki
Origins Centre, Wits University, Johannesburg
Parry, Elspeth; Rock art of the Matobo range,
Zimbabwe. Amabooks, Bulawayo, Zimbabwe
RARI, Rock Art Research Foundation, Wits University,
Johannesburg
SARADA, SA Rock Art Data Archive (see RARI)
Schulberg, Lucille; Historic India, 1968, Time-Life
Shaughnessy, E I; Ancient China, life, myth and art,
Duncan Baird
South   African   Archaeological   Bulletin,   SA
Archaeological Society
South   African   Archaeological   Society   (SAAS);
Goodwin series. Digging stick.

Storm, R; Legends and myths of India, Egypt, China, Japan. Hermes House

Tirion, Will, and Roger W Sinnot; Sky Atlas 2000.0, second edition, 1998, Sky Publishing and Cambridge Univ Press, ISBN 0-93346-87-5

Von Mollendorf, Vanessa; exhibition 2007

Wikimedia

Winston R, and Clara Winston; Notre-Dame de Paris, 1971, Newsweek

Wornell, Gary, and Seppo Hallavainio; rock art prints

Images citing RARI are curated by the Rock Art Research Institute at the University of the Witwatersrand in Johannesburg. Contributing institutes to SARADA project are Iziko Museums of Cape Town, Natal Museum, National Museum Bloemfontein, University of Cape Town, University of South Africa, Analysis of Rock Art of Lesotho (ARAL), Janette Deacon private collection, Cornelia Kleinitz private collection, Lucas Smits private collection, Alex Willcox, David Lewis-Williams, Benjamin Smith, Ukhahlamba Rock Art Mapping Project, University of Cologne, and Bradshaw Foundation.

Sources

Adams, LS. 2002; Art across time. McGraw Hill

Allen, RH. 1899; Star names and their meanings. Lost Library

Anderson, Ian; Jethro Tull, Living with the past, DVD EREDV266, Eagle Vision

Anderson, Ian; Jethro Tull, Nothing is easy, Isle of Wight 1970; DVD interview, 2004; Eagle Vision, EREDV405

Bible; NIV Study Bible. 1995, Zondervan

Bullfinche's Mythology; Ingersoll, Ernest; 1928, IN Sacred-Texts.com

Catholic Encyclopaedia, Vol 1, 1907, Robert Appleton Co, online 2003, K Knight Nihil Obstat, March 1, 1907

Cotterell, Maurice; The amazing lid of Palenque

Cozza Luzzi. 1893; Sopra un antico stampo di Agnus Dei in the Romanische Quartalschrift

De Santillana G, Von Deschend H. 1969; Hamlet's Mill: An essay on myth and the frame of time. Boston: Gambit

Duffey, Alex. 2001c. Dreaming with open eyes, the mind as sixth organ of perception in San rock art

Furter, ED; SA Department of Trade and Industry corporate culture, presentation 2011

Furter, ED; SA Gold Coin Exchange corporate culture, presentation 2013

Furter, ED; SA Mint corporate culture, pres 2010

Gibson, S. 2005; Cave of John the Baptist. Arrow

Gilbert, Adrian. 2000; Signs in the sky, Bantam

Gombrich, Ernst. 1960. Art and illusion

Gombrich, Ernst. 1981. Image and the Eye

Gombrich, Ernst. 1979. The Sense of Order

Grof, S, and Richard Tarnas; Cosmos and Psyche

Hancock, Graham. 2005; Supernatural. Century

Higgins. Anaclypsis, Vol1 bk5 ch10

Jung, CG. 1959; Flying Saucers. Bollingen Foundation

Jung, CG; Man and his symbols

Jung, CG; Readings in the History of Æsthetics, Ch 26; Art as Archetypal Form. Open source

Jung, CG. 1950; Synchronicity; an acausal connecting principle, treatise

Kasser R, M Meyer, G Wurst. 2006; Gospel of Judas from Codex Tchacos. National Geographic

Kaulins, Andis; Stars, stones and scholars, www.megaliths.co.uk

Keil and Delitzsch; Commentary on the Old Testament; Johann CF Keil 1807-1888, Franz Delitzsch 1813-1890

Knight C, and Butler A. 2010; Civilisation one. Watkins

Le Grice, Keiron. 2009; Birth of a New Discipline, Archetypal Cosmology in Historical Perspective, IN Archai: Journal of Archetypal Cosmology, vol1 nu1

Lewis-Williams D, and David Pearce. 2012; Framed Idiosyncrasy, method and evidence in the interpretation of San rock art, SA Archaeological Bulletin 67, 75-87

MacNeice, Louis. 1964; Astrology. Aldus

Neugebauer O and Parker R. 1969; Egyptian astronomical texts 3; Decans, planets, constellations and zodiacs. Brown Univ

Raath, AWG, Prof, and N van Zyl; Die Vierkleur wapper weer, visioene van Siener van Rensburg

Russell, Thembi. 2012; No one said it would be easy, Ordering San paintings using the Harris matrix, reply to David Pearce. SA Archaeological Bulletin 67 (196)

Spiller, G; Origins, the films, DVD. Wits University

Tarnas, Richard; see Grof

Thackeray, F. 2013; The principle of sympathetic magic in the context of hunting, trance and southern African rock art, Digging stick, April. Institute for Human Evolution

Thurston. 1900; Holy Year of Jubilee. London

Tresidder, Jack. 1997, 1999; Watkins dictionary of symbols. Watkins

Van Eeden, GW, 1993; A phenomenological analysis of archetypes. MA treatise, Univ Pretoria; supervisor Prof Dr AP Du Toit

Williams JG, TP Krisher, DH Boggs, JT Ratcliff, JO Dickey. 1997; Jet Propulsion Laboratory, California Institute of Technology, Pasadena; Lunar dissipation; rotational and orbital consequences. Abstracts of lunar and Planetary Science Conference XXVIII

Williams, DM, in; Nature 1998 Dec 3, 396, p453 -455, doi 10.1038 /24845; Low-latitude glaciation and rapid changes in the Earth's obliquity explained by obliquity-oblateness feedback; by Darren M Williams, James F Kasting, Lawrence A Frakes

References

Birenbaum, H. 1988. Myth and mind. Lanham: Univ Press of America

Blackmore, S. 1989; Consciousness: science tackles the self. New Scientist, 122 (1658) 38-41

Burkert, W. 1979; Structure and History in Greek Mythology and Ritual; Univ of Calif

Casey, ES. 1974. Toward an archetypal imagination

David, Gary A. 2008; Eye of the phoenix. Adventures Unlimited

David, Gary A; Orion zone, Adventures Unlimited

Dawkins, R; Beyond Stonehenge

Devettere, RJ. 1976; Human body as philosophical paradigm... Phil Today, 20

Eastwood, E. Preliminary report on females' aprons, SA Arch Bul 63, 2008

Eliade, M. 1957a. Myths, Dreams and Mysteries. Transl P Mairet; Harper & Row

Eliade, M. 1957b. Sacred and the Profane. Transl R Trask; Harcourt, Brace & World

Freud; Interpretation of Dreams

Freud; New Introductory Lectures on Psychoanalysis, transl James Strachey (1933; repr, Norton, 1965

Freud; Three Essays

Goldenberg, NR. 1975. Archetypal theory after Jung

Gunderson, LH, Hollling CS; Panarchy, transformation in human and natural systems

Haas and Saunders. 2005; Cydonia codex. Frog

Heidegger, M. 1962; Being and Time; Transl J Macquarrie, E Robinson; Basil Blackwell

Hollmann, JC. Cutting edge of rock art: motifs... on Driekuil Hill, North West Province, SA, 2007. Southern African Humanities Vol 19 p123 -151

Jones, Ernest. 1961; Life and Work of Sigmund Freud, ed Lionel Trilling and Steven Marcus, Basic Books

Jung, CG. 1912 /1952. Symbols of Transformation; IN Collected Works Vol 5, transl R Hull, Ed; Herbert Reed, M Fordham, G Adler; ed, McGuire. Bollinger Series XX, 20 volumes; Routledge & Kegan Paul; 1953-1979

Jung, CG. 1934/54; Archetypes of the collective unconscious; CW

Jung, CG. 1936-37/59; concept of the collective unconscious

Jung, CG. 1963; Mysterium Coniunctionis. CW

King, N. 1990; Myth, metaphor, memory: Archeology of the self. Journal of Humanistic Psychology, 30(2)

Kirk, GS. 1970; Myth: Its meaning and functions in ancient-other cultures. London: Cambridge Univ

Kockelmans, JJ. 1985; Heidegger and Science; Univ Press of America

Kuhn, Thomas. 1966; Structure of Scientific Revolutions, 3rd ed, Univ Chicago Press

Levi-Strauss, Claude; Raw and the cooked 1969. From honey to ashes 1973. Naked man 1981

Lewis-Williams and Dowson; Through the veil: San rock paintings and the rock face. South African Archaeological Bulletin 45: 5-16

Mitroff, II. 1983; Archetypal social systems analysis on the deeper structure of human systems; Academy of management review, 8(3):387-397

Ovason, D. 1999. Book of the eclipse. Arrow

Paget, RF. 1967. In the footsteps of Orpheus, finding and identification of the lost entrance to Hades, Oracle of the dead, River Styx [Baia Italy]

Rasula, J. 1979; Charles Olson and Robert Duncan: Muthologistical grounding. Spring

Rauhala, L. 1973. Basic views of CG Jung in the Hermeneutic metascience. Human Context, 5

Rogerson, JW. 1984; Slippery Words: Myth. In A Dundes (Ed), Sacred Narrative: Readings in the Theory of Myth; Univ Calif 62-71

Shapiro, KJ. 1985. Bodily Reflective Modes. Durham: Duke Univ Press

Steele, RS. 1982; Freud and Jung: Conflicts of interpretation. Routledge & Kegan Paul

Strenski, I. 1987. Four Theories of Myth in Twentieth-Century History. Macmillan

Von Ehrenfels, Christian. 1890; On Gestalt Qualities

Witztum, Rips, Rosenberbg; Equidistant letter sequences in the book of Genesis. IN Drosnin, M; Bible Code, 1997. Orion

Edmond Furter
Mindprint
The subconscious art code

2014
Four Equators Media [<(^)>] Johannesburg
Lulu.com

Black and white edition
ISBN 978-0-620-59685-5

ISBN 978-0-620-59685-5

Font type Calibri 11.4 point
Design by Four Equators Media [<(^)>]

Cover image from a mural by Raffaello Sanzio (Raphael); The school of Athens, Vatican.
The philosophers are modelled on Italian artists.

Back cover from an Arabian rock engraving of bee people at Bir Hima
(Lars Bjursom /Saudi Aramco World /SAWDIA) and from Gobekli Tepe.

Website: www.edmondfurter.wordpress.com

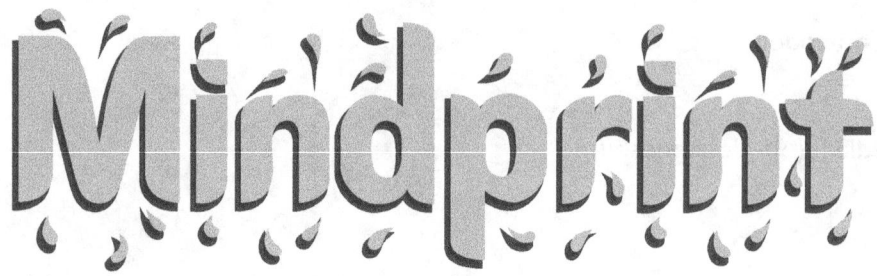

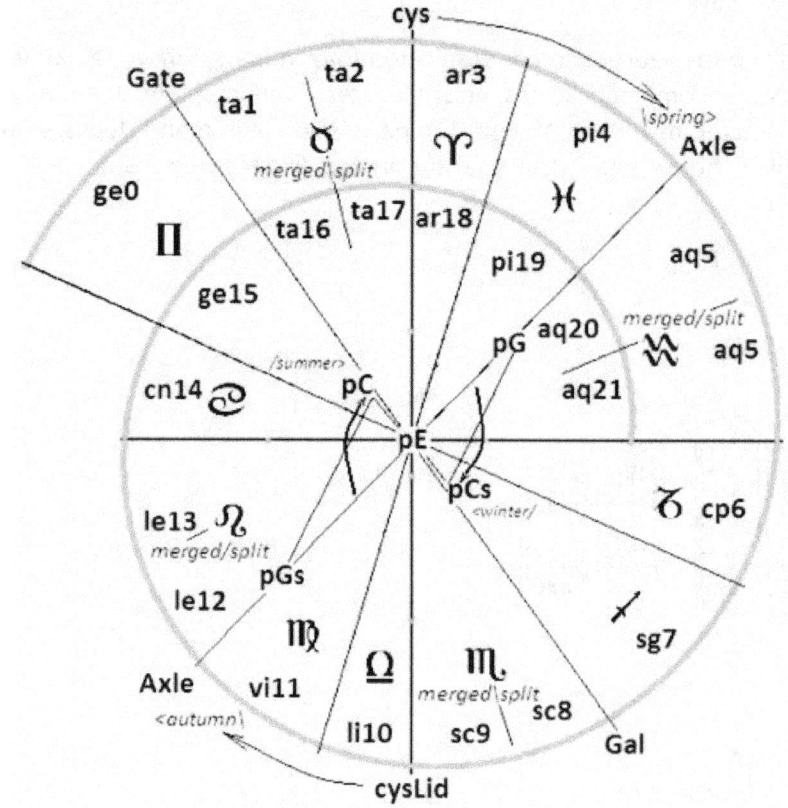

The subconscious art code
Edmond Furter

www.ingramcontent.com/pod-product-compliance
Lightning Source LLC
Chambersburg PA
CBHW081045170526
45158CB00006B/1860